Designing Solutions–Based Ubiquitous and Pervasive Computing:
New Issues and Trends

Francisco Milton Mendes Neto
Rural Federal University of Semi-Arid, Brazil

Pedro Fernandes Ribeiro Neto
State University of Rio Grande do Norte, Brazil

INFORMATION SCIENCE REFERENCE

Hershey · New York

Director of Editorial Content:	Kristin Klinger
Director of Book Publications:	Julia Mosemann
Acquisitions Editor:	Lindsay Johnston
Development Editor:	Joel Gamon
Publishing Assistant:	Keith Glazewski
Typesetter:	Keith Glazewski, Michael Brehm
Production Editor:	Jamie Snavely
Cover Design:	Lisa Tosheff
Printed at:	Yurchak Printing Inc.

Published in the United States of America by
Information Science Reference (an imprint of IGI Global)
701 E. Chocolate Avenue
Hershey PA 17033
Tel: 717-533-8845
Fax: 717-533-8661
E-mail: cust@igi-global.com
Web site: http://www.igi-global.com/reference

Library of Congress Cataloging-in-Publication Data

Designing solutions-based ubiquitous and pervasive computing : new issues and
trends / Francisco Milton Mendes Neto and Pedro Fernandes Ribeiro Neto,
editors.
     p. cm.
 Includes bibliographical references and index.
 Summary: "This book provides a general overview about research on ubiquitous and pervasive computing and its applications, discussing the recent progress in this area and pointing out to scholars what they should do (best practices) and should not do (bad practices)"--Provided by publisher.   ISBN 978-1-61520-843-2 (hardcover) -- ISBN 978-1-61520-844-9 (ebook) 1. Ubiquitous computing. 2. Ubiquitous computing--Research. I. Mendes Neto, Francisco Milton, 1973- II. Ribeiro Neto, Pedro Fernandes.   QA76.5915.D47 2010
 004--dc22
                         2009039731

British Cataloguing in Publication Data
A Cataloguing in Publication record for this book is available from the British Library.

Editorial Advisory Board

Table of Contents

Detailed Table of Contents

Chapter 1

Nirmalya Roy, University of Texas at Austin, USA
Sajal K. Das, University of Texas at Arlington, USA

This chapter discusses managing context uncertainty in smart pervasive environments. The authors specifically discuss a novel game theoretic learning and prediction framework that attempts to minimize the joint location uncertainty of inhabitants in multi-inhabitant smart homes. This results in more accurate prediction of contexts and more adaptive control of automated devices, thus leading to a mobility-aware resource management scheme in multi-inhabitant smart homes.

Chapter 2

Leili Lind, Linköping University & Santa Anna IT Research Institute, Sweden
Aseel Berglund, Saab Aerosystems, Sweden
Erik Berglund, Linköping University & Santa Anna IT Research Institute, Sweden
Magnus Bång, Linköping University & Santa Anna IT Research Institute, Sweden
Sture Hägglund, Linköping University & Santa Anna IT Research Institute, Sweden

This chapter describes technologies for using digital pen and paper as data input media for e-services and computing applications, refer a number of applications together with studies and evaluations of their usability, and finally comment upon future prospects for integrating digital pen and paper as an effortless technique for data capture, especially in order to counteract and diminish the digital divide. The use of digital pen and paper technologies is exemplified with applications demonstrating its appropriateness in home care for elderly, for free-form recording of data on paper such as maps, and as a remote control for a TV set or other electronic appliances with rich functionality in the home.

Chapter 3

Valéria Farinazzo Martins Salvador, Universidade Presbiteriana Mackenzie, Brasil
João Soares de Oliveira Neto, Universidade Presbiteriana Mackenzie, Brasil
Marcelo de Paiva Guimarães, Centro Universitário Adventista de São Paulo, Brasil

The chapter describes a study on the evaluation of Voice User Interface (VUI) in Ubiquitous Applications and discusses some of issues which may impact the evaluation process when using the voice as a natural way of interacting with computers. We present a set of guidelines and usability principles that should be considered when developing VUIs for Ubiquitous Applications and a case study in order to test and exemplify the concepts presented in this chapter.

Chapter 4

Ricardo Augusto Rabelo Oliveira, Universidade Federal de Minas Gerais, Brasil
Antonio Alfredo F. Loureiro, Universidade Federal de Minas Gerais, Brasil

In this chapter is presented a framework to a service that acts as a middleware to the applications, providing the information about the wireless network context. The increasing use of wireless communications in mobile devices calls for a new level of resource management. Users with mobile devices accessing wireless hot spots are a commonplace, and, thus, their management is becoming more important.

Chapter 5

José Cano, Universidad Politécnica de Valencia, Spain
Juan-Carlos Cano, Universidad Politécnica de Valencia, Spain
Carlos T. Calafate, Universidad Politécnica de Valencia, Spain
Pietro Manzoni, Universidad Politécnica de Valencia, Spain

This chapter describes a set of prototype applications developed in the field of ubiquitous and pervasive computing. The aim is, firstly improve several real environments from the point of view of the user and the environment itself, and secondly to extend the use of such applications to the greatest number of environments and potential users, since the benefits obtained are quite remarkable. The developed prototypes are based on personal area networks (PANs) and mobile ad hoc networks (MANETs) and make use of wireless technologies like Wi-Fi and Bluetooth.

Chapter 6

Mitun Bhattacharyya, R.V. College of Engineering, India
Ashok Kumar, University of Louisiana at Lafayette, USA
Magdy Bayoumi, University of Louisiana at Lafayette, USA

In this chapter is proposed methodologies for improving the efficiency of a control system in an industrial environment, specifically an oil production platform. They propose a data fusion model that consists of four steps – preprocessing, classification and association, data association and correlation association, and composite decision. The first two steps are executed at the sensor network level and the last two steps are done at the network manager or controller level. The second proposal is a distributed hierarchical control system and network management system. Here the central idea is that the network manager and controller coordinate in order to make delays in feedback loops as well as for increasing the lifetime of the sensor network. They finally conclude the control system proposal by giving a controlling model using sensor networks to control the flow of hydrocarbons in an oil production platform.

Chapter 7

Mitun Bhattacharyya, R.V. College of Engineering, India
Ashok Kumar, University of Louisiana at Lafayette, USA
Magdy Bayoumi, University of Louisiana at Lafayette, USA

This chapter proposes a system based on the WirelessHART standard for monitoring and controlling oil platforms using sensor networks. It propose a hierarchical distributed system where sensor nodes and process components are grouped both functionally and in terms of proximity (i.e., spatially). The authors harness the existing electrical powering supplies to some of the process components to enhance our network routing protocol. They also propose a component based addressing scheme. Then propose a hybrid routing protocol having proactive paths for high priority data and reactive paths for low priority that can help in load balancing and thus improving the lifetime of the sensor network. Finally, they discuss about methodologies for assessing the health (residual energy) of the sensor network system. Related research is discussed at appropriate points.

Chapter 8

Robert Tesch, University of Louisiana at Lafayette, USA
Ashok Kumar, University of Louisiana at Lafayette, USA
Jamie Mason, University of Louisiana at Lafayette, USA
Dania Alvarez, University of Louisiana at Lafayette, USA
Mario Di'Mattia, University of Louisiana at Lafayette, USA
Shawn Luce, University of Louisiana at Lafayette, USA

This chapter introduces the motivation for low power design considerations by discussing the power limitations of ubiquitous computing devices. Then these authors discuss the research directions that are being pursued in literature for reducing power consumption and increasing efficiency of ubiquitous computing systems.

This chapter discusses how the advances of the Wireless Sensor Networks may be useful to assist in the development and creation of smart environments, essential to the ubiquitous computing can become real and present in our everyday life.

Chapter 10

This chapter discusses a novel approach to manage the human environment interaction in case of disability. It provides accessible services to the user in smart environment. This approach is based on the user limitation capabilities ("handicap situations") in smart environment. It is built upon formalisms based on Description logic (DL) named Semantic Matching Framework (SMF). The architecture of SMF is designed in a way that Human-Environment Interaction (HEI) is generated online to identify and compensate the handicap situation occurring in the course of daily life activities. The SMF architecture is based on modules and implemented using semantic web technologies and integrated into a demonstrator, which has been used to validate the concept in laboratory conditions. The chapter includes the time response and the scalability analysis of SMF.

This chapter shows research issues related to open wireless sensor network (WSN) from the viewpoints of task description language, runtime task management, self-adaptability, and security, and introduce XAC project which is a research project to develop a middleware for open WSN.

Chapter 12

Thienne Johnson, University of Sao Paulo, Brazil
Eleri Cardozo, State University of Campinas, Brazil
Eliane Gomes Guimarães, Information Technology Center Renato Archer, Brazil

This chapter provides an overview of pervasive computing environments for eHealth applications. The most common applications and some technologies to provide pervasive computing environment to collect information for the eHealth applications are described. Some challenge issues such as security, use of context, user acceptance and performance requirements are presented.

Chapter 13

Carlos M. S. Figueiredo, FUCAPI – Research and Innovation Foundation, Brazil
Antonio Alfredo F. Loureiro, Univerdade Federal de Minas Gerais, Brazil

This chapter presents an overview of self-organizing networks, introduces important functions and techniques applied to Ad Hoc Networks, and focuses on important design aspects that can be useful to new designs.

Chapter 14

Andrey V. Gavrilov, Novosibirsk State Technical University, Russia

This chapter applies an hybrid approach to development of intelligent systems to ubiquitous computing systems, in particular, to smart environment. Different classifications of Hybrid Intelligent Systems (HIS) are looking and two examples of hybrid approach for smart environment are suggested: framework based on expert system and neural network for programming of behavior of smart objects and paradigm of context-based programming-learning of behavior of intelligent agent. Besides this chapter offers an attempt to systematize concepts for development of HIS as any introduction to methodology for development of HIS is suggested. Author hopes that this chapter will be useful for researchers and developers to better understand challenges in development of ambient intelligence and possible ways to overcome them.

Chapter 15

Cristiano André da Costa, Universidade do Vale do Rio dos Sinos, Brazil
Jorge Luis Victoria Barbosa, Universidade do Vale do Rio dos Sinos, Brazil
Luciano Cavalheiro da Silva, Universidade Federal do Rio Grande do Sul, Brazil
Adenauer Corrêa Yamin, Universidade Católica de Pelotas, Brazil
Cláudio Fernando Resin Geyer, Universidade Federal do Rio Grande do Sul, Brazil

This chapter review essential concepts of the ubiquitous computing area, its evolution, and challenges that must be managed. To deal with these issues, the authors describe the main requirements for the development of ubiquitous software. This analysis starts with the discussion of limitations in the use of traditional programming models, and then goes on to the proposition of techniques to address these limitations.

Foreword

Provide computing and communication services anytime and everywhere. Some decades ago, it would be only a weak possibility. Due to the intensive work of researchers, professionals, academy and industry on such a challenge, we can say that it is a reality. A great example is the relevant contribution materialized in this book. If you are just beginning to think about the ubiquitous and pervasive computing, or if you are researching or applying it, this book will provide you important elements.

Relevant topics concerning wireless sensor network advances, experiences, challenges and trends provide a wide and rich context of the area. Subjects on self-organizing networks, hybrid intelligent systems, smart pervasive environments and uncertainty brings the state of the art. Some chapters deal with motivating technologies, such as data capture, monitoring, data fusion, oil production and eHealth. Challenging topics include voice interface, disability, low power, middleware, interference and mobility.

Significant and decisive advances come from from hard work. *Designing Solutions-Based Ubiquitous and Pervasive Computing: New Issues and Trends* is an academic effort that will certainly provide a solid reference for researchers and professionals engaged in ubiquitous and pervasive computing. My pleasure and honor to write a foreword for the work delivered with competence and commitment of many colleagues, specially the editors, that have been dedicated to publish a relevant and qualified document. In a few words, thank you all for the precious work.

Marcelino Pereira dos Santos Silva
Professor
State University of Rio Grande do Norte, Brazil

Marcelino Pereira dos Santos Silva *is professor of computer science at Rio Grande do Norte State University (UERN) since 1996, where was the Director of the Post Graduate Department and Coordinator of the Master Program in Computer Science. Born January 16, 1970 in São Paulo, Brazil, he earned his bachelor's degree in computer science from the Federal University of Campina Grande in 1992 and his Ph.D. from the National Institute for Space Research in 2006. Member of Association for Computing Machinery and Brazilian Computer Society, his research interests, projects and publication include data mining, geoinformatics, image processing, artificial intelligence, and computer technologies for oil industry.*

Preface

The book "Ubiquitous and Pervasive Computing: New Issues and Trends" has as overall objective to clarify the new technologies, applications and researches in the ubiquitous and pervasive computing area. It intends to help students, teachers and researchers to obtaining a larger understanding of both the potential of the related technologies and the trends that are being followed to make ubiquitous and pervasive computing more effective.

The implementation of ubiquitous and pervasive computing is not a trivial task. The accumulated experience and know-how of the researchers in this area, which have invested time and effort in study in the attempt of solving problems in this area, are, therefore, important success factors. This book shares this know-how with other researchers, students and interested professionals in this area. It shows the current trends, practices and challenges faced by designers of ubiquitous and pervasive computing projects. These includes from theoretical assumptions and empirical researches to practical implementations and case studies. In the end, the readers have a clear notion about which is the actual stage and which are the future tendencies in this area.

The book "Ubiquitous and Pervasive Computing: New Issues and Trends" is very valuable to researchers and teachers working in both areas ubiquitous computing and pervasive computing. ubiquitous and pervasive computing is a genuinely interdisciplinary area that strives for creating a better comprehension of the requirements of mobile architectures that is mediated by a diverse set of computer technologies. Therefore, this book is addressed to a wide audience, including researchers and students, educators and industrial trainers interested in various disciplines, such as network sensors, embedded systems, distributed systems, computer networks and, mainly, computer science. Given its depth and breadth of coverage, this book is also of interest to a wide audience of researchers in the fields of electrical engineering, as well as computer science. It is helpful for scholars and business professionals entrusted for implementation of mobile devices and ubiquitous and pervasive applications. The major scholarly value of this book is to provide a general overview about researches on ubiquitous and pervasive computing and its applications, as well as a notion about the recent progress in works in this area. This overview support future academic researches with the background provided by the experts in this book. Also, it points out to scholars what they should do (best practices) and should not do (bad practices).

In relation to the contribution to information science, technology and management literature, one important improvement, which can be provided by this book, is the discussion about new methodologies, technologies and approaches that are being used in ubiquitous and pervasive computing and their advantages and challenges. The topics covered in this book, which include the current best practices in ubiquitous and pervasive computing, can also stimulate the implementation and the use of the related technologies in academic and industrial context. In addition, this book serves to highlight some of the most important gaps in the development of ubiquitous and pervasive computing support tools, patterns of development, and so forth.

The book is organized in fifteen chapters. In the following we give a brief description of each of the chapters that comprise this book.

Chapter 1, by Nirmalya Roy and Sajal K. Das, discusses managing context uncertainty in smart pervasive environments. The authors specifically discuss a novel game theoretic learning and prediction framework that attempts to minimize the joint location uncertainty of inhabitants in multi-inhabitant smart homes. This results in more accurate prediction of contexts and more adaptive control of automated devices, thus leading to a mobility-aware resource management scheme in multi-inhabitant smart homes.

Chapter 2, by Leili Lind, Aseel Berglund, Erik Berglund, Magnus Bång and Sture Hägglund, reviews existing technologies and refer a number of exemplifying applications together with studies and evaluations of their usability, which show a promising degree of user acceptance and convenience. The practical use of digital pen and paper technology is discussed with applications demonstrating its appropriateness in home care for elderly, for free-form recording of data on paper such as maps and sketches, and as a remote control for a TV set or other electronic appliances with rich functionality in the home.

Chapter 3, by Valéria Farinazzo Martins Salvador, João Soares de Oliveira Neto and Marcelo de Paiva Guimarães, describes a study on the evaluation of Voice User Interface (VUI) in Ubiquitous Applications and discusses some of issues which may impact the evaluation process when using the voice as a natural way of interacting with computers. We present a set of guidelines and usability principles that should be considered when developing VUIs for Ubiquitous Applications and a case study in order to test and exemplify the concepts presented in this chapter.

In Chapter 4, Ricardo A. Rabelo Oliveira and Antônio Alfredo Ferreira Loureiro present a framework to a service that acts as a middleware to the applications, providing the information about the wireless network context. The increasing use of wireless communications in mobile devices calls for a new level of resource management. Users with mobile devices accessing wireless hot spots are a commonplace, and, thus, their management is becoming more important.

Chapter 5, by José Cano, Juan-Carlos Cano, Carlos T. Calafate and Pietro Manzoni, describes a set of prototype applications developed in the field of ubiquitous and pervasive computing. The aim is, firstly improve several real environments from the point of view of the user and the environment itself, and secondly to extend the use of such applications to the greatest number of environments and potential users, since the benefits obtained are quite remarkable. The developed prototypes are based on personal area networks (PANs) and mobile ad hoc networks (MANETs) and make use of wireless technologies like Wi-Fi and Bluetooth.

In Chapter 6, Mitun Bhattacharyya, Ashok Kumar and Magdy Bayoumi propose methodologies for improving the efficiency of a control system in an industrial environment, specifically an oil production platform. They propose a data fusion model that consists of four steps – preprocessing, classification and association, data association and correlation association, and composite decision. The first two steps are executed at the sensor network level and the last two steps are done at the network manager or controller level. The second proposal is a distributed hierarchical control system and network management system. Here the central idea is that the network manager and controller coordinate in order to make delays in feedback loops as well as for increasing the lifetime of the sensor network. They finally conclude the control system proposal by giving a controlling model using sensor networks to control the flow of hydrocarbons in an oil production platform.

Chapter 7, by Mitun Bhattacharyya, Ashok Kumar and Magdy Bayoumi, proposes a system based on the WirelessHART standard for monitoring and controlling oil platforms using sensor networks. It propose a hierarchical distributed system where sensor nodes and process components are grouped both functionally and in terms of proximity (i.e., spatially). The authors harness the existing electrical powering supplies to some of the process components to enhance our network routing protocol. They also propose a component based addressing scheme. Then propose a hybrid routing protocol having proactive paths for high priority data and reactive paths for low priority that can help in load balancing and thus improving the lifetime of the sensor network. Finally, they discuss about methodologies for assessing the health (residual energy) of the sensor network system. Related research is discussed at appropriate points.

In Chapter 8, Robert Tesch, Ashok Kumar, Jamie Mason, Dania Alvarez, Mario Di'Mattia and Shawn Luce introduce the motivation for low power design considerations by discussing the power limitations of ubiquitous computing devices. Then these authors discuss the research directions that are being pursued in literature for reducing power consumption and increasing efficiency of ubiquitous computing systems.

Chapter 9, by João B. Borges Neto, Rossana M. C. Andrade and Pedro Fernandes Ribeiro Neto, discusses how the advances of the Wireless Sensor Networks may be useful to assist in the development and creation of smart environments, essential to the ubiquitous computing can become real and present in our everyday life.

In Chapter 10, Rachid Kadouche and Bessam Abdulrazak discuss an approach to manage the human environment interaction in case of disability. It provides accessible services to the user in smart environment. This approach is based on the user limitation capabilities ("handicap situations") in smart environment presenting a technical model, which could be handled by any technological system, based on clinical, sociological, and usage analysis studies in the field of assistive technologies and quantified the users and environment characteristics and formalized the relationship between the user's physical parameters and the technical parameters of the environment under a semantic framework which brings out the handicap situation for each user in a given environment which allow him to identify the accessible services in this environment.

In Chapter 11, Kenji Tei, Shunichiro Suenaga, Yoshiyuki Nakamura, Yuichi Sei, Hikotoshi Nakazato, Yoichi Kaneki, Nobukazu Yoshioka, Yoshiaki Fukazawa and Shinichi Honiden show research issues related to open wireless sensor network (WSN) from the viewpoints of task description language, runtime task management, self-adaptability, and security, and introduce XAC project which is a research project to develop a middleware for open WSN.

Chapter 12, by Thienne Johnson, Eleri Cardozo and Eliane Gomes Guimarães, provides an overview of pervasive computing environments for eHealth applications. The most common applications and some technologies to provide pervasive computing environment to collect information for the eHealth applications are described. Some challenge issues such as security, use of context, user acceptance and performance requirements are presented.

Chapter 13, by Carlos Maurício Seródio Figueiredo and Antonio Alfredo Ferreira Loureiro, presents an overview of self-organizing networks, introduces important functions and techniques applied to Ad Hoc Networks, and focuses on important design aspects that can be useful to new designs.

In Chapter 14, Andrey V. Gavrilov applies an hybrid approach to development of intelligent systems to ubiquitous computing systems, in particular, to smart environment. Different classifications of Hybrid Intelligent Systems (HIS) are looking and two examples of hybrid approach for smart environment are suggested: framework based on expert system and neural network for programming of behavior of smart objects and paradigm of context-based programming-learning of behavior of intelligent agent. Besides this chapter offers an attempt to systematize concepts for development of HIS as any introduction to methodology for development of HIS is suggested. Author hopes that this chapter will be useful for researchers and developers to better understand challenges in development of ambient intelligence and possible ways to overcome them.

In Chapter 15, Cristiano André da Costa, Jorge Luis Victoria Barbosa, Luciano Cavalheiro da Silva, Adenauer Corrêa Yamin and Cláudio Fernando Resin Geyer review essential concepts of the ubiquitous computing area, its evolution, and challenges that must be managed. To deal with these issues, the authors describe the main requirements for the development of ubiquitous software. This analysis starts with the discussion of limitations in the use of traditional programming models, and then goes on to the proposition of techniques to address these limitations.

Francisco Milton Mendes Neto
Rural Federal University of Semi-Arid, Brazil

Pedro Fernandes Ribeiro Neto
State University of Rio Grande do Norte, Brazil

Acknowledgment

We would like to thank our family for the support they provided us and, in particular, we must acknowledge Luana (Milton's wife) and Yaskara (Pedro's wife) and our children João Pedro, Maria Eduarda and João Guilherme (Milton's children) and Yasmin, Yngrid and Pedro Filho (Pedro's children). We would like to thank too our parents Benedito and Maria José (Milton's parents) and Paulo and Meyre Ester (Pedro's parents) by their love and dedication.

We would also like to thank our colaborators of the Technological Nucleus in Software Engineering, who have supported us with their comments for this book.

Francisco Milton Mendes Neto
Rural Federal University of Semi-Arid, Brazil

Pedro Fernandes Ribeiro Neto
State University of Rio Grande do Norte, Brazil

Chapter 1
Managing Context Uncertainty in Smart Pervasive Environments

Nirmalya Roy
University of Texas at Austin, USA

Sajal K. Das
University of Texas at Arlington, USA

ABSTRACT

The essence of pervasive computing lies in the creation of smart environments saturated with computing and communication capabilities, yet gracefully integrated with human users (inhabitants). Context Awareness is perhaps the most salient feature of such an intelligent computing environment. An inhabitant's mobility and activities play a significant role in defining his contexts in and around the home. Although there exists optimal algorithm for location and activity tracking of a single inhabitant, the correlation and dependence between multiple inhabitants' contexts within the same environment make the location and activity tracking more challenging. In this chapter, we discuss a cooperative reinforcement learning and a non-cooperative Nash H-learning approach for location-aware resource management in multi-inhabitant smart homes that attempts to minimize the joint location uncertainty of inhabitants. Experimental results demonstrate that the proposed framework is capable of adaptively controlling a smart environment, significantly reduces energy consumption and enhances the comfort of the inhabitants. We also present open problems in this area.

INTRODCUTION

Advances in smart devices, mobile wireless communications, sensor networks, pervasive computing, machine learning, middleware and agent technologies, and human computer interfaces have made the dream of smart pervasive environments a

DOI: 10.4018/978-1-61520-843-2.ch001

reality. According to Cook and Das (Cook & Das, 2004), a "smart environment" is one that is able to autonomously acquire and apply knowledge about its users (or inhabitants) and their surroundings, and adapt to the users' behavior or preferences with the ultimate goal to improve their experience in that environment. The type of experience that individuals expect from an environment varies with the individual and the type of environment considered. This may include the safety of users, reduction of cost of maintaining the environment, optimization of resources (e.g., energy bills or communication bandwidth), task automation or the promotion of an intelligent independent living environment for health care services and wellness management. An important characteristic of such an intelligent, pervasive computing and communication paradigm lies in the autonomous and pro-active interaction of smart devices used for determining users' important contexts such as current and near-future locations, activities, or vital signs. In this sense, *context awareness* is a key issue for enhancing users' living experience during their daily interaction with smart devices including sensors and computer systems, as only a dynamic adaptation to the task at hand will make the computing environments just user friendly and supportive.

Context awareness is concerned with the situation a *device* or *user* is in, and with adapting applications to the current situation. But knowing the current context an application or system is used to and dynamically adapting to it only allows to construct *reactive* systems, which run after changes in their environment. To maximize usefulness and user support, systems should rather adapt in advance to a new situation and be prepared before they are actually used. This demands the development of *proactive* systems, i.e., systems which predict changes in their environment and act in advance.

To this end, we strive to develop methods to learn and predict future contexts, thus enabling systems to become proactive. Our goal is to provide applications not only with information about the current user contexts, but also with predictions of future contexts. When equipped with various sensors, a system should classify current situations and, based on those classes, learn the user behaviors and habits by deriving knowledge from historical data. The focus of our work is to forecast future user contexts lucidly by extrapolating the past and derive techniques that

enable context prediction in pervasive systems. An instance of such an intelligent indoor environment is a *smart home* (Das, Cook, Bhattacharya, Heierman & Lin, 2002) that perceives the surroundings through sensors and acts on it with the help of actuators. In this environment, the most important contexts like user mobility and activity create an uncertainty of their locations and hence subsequent activities. In order to be cognizant of such contexts, the smart environment needs to minimize this uncertainty.

Contributions

In this chapter we summarize an information-theoretic learning and prediction framework that minimizes context uncertainty in multi-inhabitant smart homes. This framework is based on Reinforcement Learning (Cooperative) (Roy, N., Roy, A., Basu & Das, ICOST 2005; Roy, N., Roy, A., Basu & Das, MobiQuitous 2005) and Nash Q-learning (Non-cooperative) (Roy, N., Roy, A., & Das, PerCom 2006) algorithms. The novelty of our work lies in the development of learning algorithms that exploit the correlation of mobility patterns across multiple inhabitants and attempts to minimize their joint uncertainty. This is achieved with the help of a *joint utility function* of entropy. Optimization of this utility function asymptotically converges to *Nash Equilibrium* (Hu & Wellman, 2003). Minimizing this utility function of uncertainty helps in accurate learning and estimation of inhabitants' contexts (locations and associated activities). Thus, the system can control the operation of automated devices in an adaptive manner, thereby developing an amicable environment inside the home and providing sufficient comfort to the inhabitants. This also aids in context-aware resource management, for example, minimizing the energy usage and hence reduction of overall maintenance cost of the house. We conclude this book chapter with open directions for research. (Details of our approaches are presented in (Roy, 2008)).

RELATED WORK

The vision of ubiquitous computing was first conceived by M. Weiser at Xerox PARC as the future model for computing (Weiser, 1991). The most significant characteristic of this computing paradigm lies in smart, pro-active interaction of the hand-held computing devices with their peers and surrounding networks, often without explicit operator control. Hence, the computing devices need to be imbued with an inherent sentience (Hopper, 1999) about their important contexts. This *context-awareness* is perhaps the key characteristic of the next generation intelligent networks and associated applications. The advent of smart homes is germinated from the concept of ubiquitous computing in an indoor environment with a goal to provide the inhabitants with sufficient comfort at minimum possible operational. Obviously, the technology needs to be weaved into the inhabitants' everyday life such that it becomes "technology that disappears" (Weiser, 1991). A careful insight into the features of a smart home reveals that the ability to capture the current and near-future locations and activities (hence 'contexts') of different inhabitants often becomes the key to the environment's associated "smartness". Intelligent prediction of inhabitants' locations and routes aids in efficient triggering of active databases or guaranteeing a precise time frame of service, thereby supporting location-aware interactive, multimedia applications. This also helps in pro-active management of resources such as energy consumption.

Given the wide variety of smart, indoor location-tracking paradigms, let us summarize below some of the important ones. The Active Badge (Harter & Hopper, 1994) and Active Bat (Harter, Hopper, Steggles, Ward & Webster, 1999) use infrared and ultrasonic time-of-fight techniques for indoor location tracking. On the other hand, the Cricket Location Support System (Priyantha, Chakraborty & Balakrishnan 2000) delegates the responsibility of location reporting to the mobile object itself. RADAR (Bahl & Padmanabhan, 2000) another RF-based indoor location support system, uses signal strength and signal-to-noise ratio to compute 2-D positioning. The Easy-living and the Home projects (Krumm, Harris, Meyers, Brumitt, Hale & Shafer, 2000) use real-time 3D cameras to provide stereo-vision positioning capability in an indoor environment. In the Aware Home (Orr & Abowd, 2000), the embedded pressure sensors capture inhabitant's footfalls, and the system uses this data for position tracking and pedestrian recognition. The Neural Network House (Mozer, 1998), Intelligent Home (Lesser et al., 1999) and Intelligent House_n ("House n Living") projects focus on the development of adaptive control of home environments to anticipate the needs of the inhabitants.

In (Roy, Das & Basu, 2007), the authors proposed location-aware resource management considering a single-inhabitant smart home. However, the presence of multiple inhabitants with varying preferences and requirements makes the problem more challenging. A suitable balance of preferences arising from multiple inhabitants (Shelton, 2000) needs to be considered. Thus, the environment (or system) needs to be more smart to extract the best performance while satisfying the requirements of the inhabitants as much as possible.

MULTIPLE INHABITANT LOCATION TRACKING

From information theoretic view point, an inhabitant's mobility and activity create an uncertainty of their locations and hence subsequent activities. In order to be cognizant of such contexts, a smart pervasive environment needs to minimize this uncertainty as captured by Shannon's entropy measure (Cover & Thomas, 1991). An analysis of the inhabitant's daily routine and life style reveals that there exist some well defined patterns. Although these patterns may change over time, they are not too frequent or random, and can thus be learnt. This simple observation leads us to assume that the inhabitant's mobility or activity follows a *piece-wise stationary, ergodic stochastic process* with an associated uncertainty (entropy), as originally formulated in (Bhattacharya & Das, 2002) for optimally tracking (estimating and predicting) location of mobile users in wireless cellular networks. In (Roy, Das & Basu, 2007), the authors adopted the framework from (Bhattacharya & Das, 2002) to design an optimal algorithm for location (activity) tracking in a smart environment, based on compressed dictionary management and online learning of the inhabitant's mobility profile, followed by a predictive resource management (energy consumption) scheme for a single inhabitant smart space. However, the presence of multiple inhabitants with dynamically varying profiles and preferences (selfish or non-selfish) make such tracking much more challenging. This is due mainly to the fact that the relevant contexts of multiple inhabitants in the same environment are often inherently correlated and thus interdependent on each other. Therefore, the learning and prediction (decision making) paradigm needs to consider the joint (simultaneous) location tracking of multiple inhabitants (Roy, N., Roy, A., & Das, PerCom 2006). As mentioned earlier, the multiple inhabitant case is more challenging. Mathematically, this can be observed from the fact that conditioning reduces the entropy (Cover & Thomas, 1991). In (Roy, N., Roy, A., & Das, PerCom 2006) we proved that optimal (i.e., attaining a lower bound on the joint entropy) location tracking of multiple inhabitants is an NP-hard problem. In the following, we present two different algorithms (cooperative and non-cooperative) for multiple inhabitant cases.

Cooperative Reinforcement Learning Algorithm

Assuming a cooperative environment, a game theory based reinforcement learning policy was proposed in (Roy, N., Roy, A., Basu & Das, MobiQuitous 2005) for location-aware resource management in multi-inhabitant smart homes. This approach describes an algorithm for a rational and convergent cooperative action learner.

Inhabitant's Utility Function Based on Cooperative Learning

In a smart home environment, an inhabitant's goal is to optimize the total utility it receives. To address these requirements of optimization, the decision making component of smart home uses reinforcement learning to acquire a policy that optimizes overall uncertainty of the inhabitants which in turn helps in accurate prediction of inhabitants' locations and activities. In this section we present an algorithm from an information-theoretic perspective for learning a value function that maps state-action pairs to future discounted reward using Shannon's entropy measure.

Entropy Learning Based on Individual Policy

Most reinforcement-learning (RL) algorithms use evaluation or value functions to cache the results of experience for solving discrete optimal control problems. This is useful in our case because close approximations to optimal entropy value function lead the inhabitant directly towards its goal by possessing some good control policies. Here we closely follow the Q-learning (associate values with state-action pairs, called Q values as in Watkins' Q-learning) (Watkins, 1989) for our Entropy learning (*H*-learning) algorithm that combines new experience with old value functions to produce new and statistically improved value functions in different ways. First, we discuss how the algorithm uses its own system beliefs to change its estimate to optimal value functions called *update rule*. Then we discuss a *learning policy* that maps histories of states visited, probability of action chosen $\pi(a_j)_i$ current hamming distance d_h and the utility received $H_t(s_t, a_t)$; into a current choice of action. Finally, we claim that this learning policy results in convergence when combined with the H-learning update rule.

To achieve the desired performance of smart homes, a reward function, r, is defined that takes into account the success rate of achieving the goal using system beliefs. Here r is the instantaneous reward received which we have considered as success rate of the predicted state. One measure of this prediction accuracy can be estimated from per-symbol Hamming distance d_h which provides the normalized symbol-wise mismatch between the predicted and the actual routes followed by the inhabitants. Intuitively, this measure should have correspondence with the relative entropy between the two sequences. A direct consequence of information theory helps in estimating this relationship (Roy, Das & Basu, 2007).

Using the state space and reward function, the H-learning is used similar to Q-learning algorithm to approximate an optimal action strategy by incrementally estimating the entropy value, $H_t(s_t, a_t)$, for state/action pairs. This value is the predicted future utility that will be achieved if the inhabitant executes action a_t in state s_t. After each action, the utility is updated as

$$H_{t+1}(s_t, a_t) = (1-\alpha)H_t(s_t, a_t) + \alpha[r_t + \gamma \min_{a \in A} H_t(s_t, a_t)]$$

where H_t is the estimated entropy value at the beginning of the t-th time step, and s_t, a_t, r_t are the state, action and reward at time step t. Update of $H_{t+1}(s_t, a_t)$ depends on $\min_{a \in A} H_t(s_{t+1}, a_{t+1})$ which relies on comparing various predicted actions (Singh, Jaakkola, Littman & Szepesvari, 2000). The parameters α and γ are both in the range 0 to 1. When the learning rate parameter α is close to 1, the H-table changes rapidly in response to new experience. When the discount rate γ is close to 1, future interactions play a substantial role in

defining the total utility values. After learning the optimal entropy value, a_t can be determined as

$$a_t = \min_{a \in A} H_t(s_t, a_t)$$

Here we propose a learning policy that selects an action based on the function of the history of the states, actions and utility. This learning policy makes decision based on a summary of history consisting of the current state s, current estimate of the entropy value function as a utility, number of times inhabitant j has used its action a_j in the past and Hamming distance d_h. Such a learning policy can be expressed as the probability $\Pr\left(a \mid s, H_t(s_t, a_t), \pi(a_j)_i, d_h\right)$, that the action a is selected given the history. An example of such a learning policy is a form of Boltzmann exploration (Singh, Jaakkola, Littman & Szepesvari, 2000):

$$\Pr\left(a \mid s, H_t(s_t, a_t), \pi(a_j)_i, d_h\right) = \frac{e^{\pi(a_j)_i} H_t(s_t, a_t) / d_h}{\sum e^{\pi(a_j)_i} H_t(s_t, a_t) / d_h}$$

The differential distance parameter, d_h, will be decreased over time as the inhabitant reaches its goal. Consequently, the exploration probability is increased ensuring the convergence.

Entropy Learning based on Joint Policy

For cooperative action learners (CAL), the selection of the actions should be done carefully. To determine the relative values of their individual actions, each inhabitant in a CAL algorithm maintains beliefs about the strategy of other inhabitants. From this perspective, inhabitant i predicts the Expected Entropy Value EEV of its individual action a_i at t-th time step as follows

$$EEV_t(a_i) = \sum_{a_{-i} \in A} H_t\{(s_t, a_{-i_{(t)}}) \bigcup (s_t, a_{i_{(t)}})\} \prod_{j \neq i} \pi(a_{-i})_j$$

A New Algorithm for Optimizing Joint Uncertainty

In this section we describe an algorithm (see Table 1) for a rational and convergent cooperative action learner. The basic idea is to vary the learning rate used by the algorithm so as to accelerate the convergence, without sacrificing rationality. In this algorithm we have a simple intuition like "learn quickly while predicting the next state incorrectly", and "learn slowly while predicting the next state correctly". The method used here for determining the prediction accuracy is by comparing the current policy's entropy with that of the expected entropy value earned by the cooperative action over time. This principle aids in convergence by giving more time for the other inhabitants to adapt to changes in the inhabitant's strategy that at first appear beneficial, while allowing the inhabitant to adapt more quickly to the other inhabitants' strategy changes when they are harmful (Bowling & Velso 2001). We use two learning rate parameters, namely "succeeding" δ_s and "failing" δ_f, where $\delta_s < \delta_f$. The term $|A_i|$ denotes the number of available joint actions of *i*-th inhabitant. The policy is improved by increasing the probability so that it selects the highest valued action according to the learning rate. The learning rate used to update the probability depends on whether the inhabitant is currently succeeding δ_s or failing δ_f. This is determined by comparing the current estimation of the entropy value following the current policy, π, in the current state with that of following the joint policy. If the individual entropy value of the current policy is smaller than the joint expected entropy value, then the larger learning rate δ_f is used in the sense that the inhabitant is currently "failing".

Proposition 1: Our CAL algorithm converges to a Nash Equilibrium if the following two conditions hold:

i) Optimization towards Believing in Rationality:

$$EEV_t\left(a_i\right) \in \arg\min_{a_t}\left(H_{t+1}\left(s_t, a_t\right)\right)\forall t$$

The joint expected entropy value tends to be one of the candidates of the set of all optimal entropy values followed by our H-learning process defined previously.

ii) Convergence towards Playing in Believing:

$$\lim_{t\to\infty}\mid H_{t+1}\left(s_t, a_t\right) - EEV_t\left(a_t\right)\mid = 0$$

The difference between the current entropy value following the current policy π in the current state with that of the joint entropy value tends to 0.

These two properties guarantee that the inhabitant will converge to a stationary strategy that is optimal given the actions of the other inhabitants. As is standard in the game theory literature, it is thus reasonable to assume that the opponent is fully rational and chooses actions that are in its best interest. When all inhabitants are rational, if they converge, then they must have converged to a Nash equilibrium. Since all inhabitants converge to a stationary policy, each rational inhabitant must converge to the best response to the opponent choice of actions. After all, if all inhabitants are rational and convergent with respect to other inhabitant strategies, then convergence to a Nash equilibrium is guaranteed (Bowling & Velso, 2001).

Proposition 2: The learning rate $\alpha(0 \leq \alpha \leq 1)$ decrease over time such that it satisfies

$$\sum_{t=0}^{\infty}\alpha = \infty \, and \sum_{t=0}^{\infty}\alpha^2 = \infty$$

Proposition 3: Each inhabitant samples each of its actions infinitely often. Thus probability of inhabitant *i* choosing action a_t is nonzero. Hence $\Pr_i(a_t) \neq 0$

Proposition 4: The probability of choosing some non optimal action in the long

Table 1. Procedure of a cooperative action learner (CAL)

Procedure CAL
Input: Individual and joint expected entropy values
Output: Decision on the learning rate
1. Let α and δ_f, δ_s be the learning rates. Initialize

$$H_t(s_t, a_t) \leftarrow 0, \; \Pr\left(a \mid s, H_t(s_t, a_t), \pi(a_j)_i, d_h\right) \leftarrow \frac{1}{|A_i|}$$

2. Repeat

a) From state s select action select action a with probability $\Pr\left(a \mid s, H_t(s_t, a_t), \pi(a_j)_i, d_h\right)$

b) Observing reward H_t and next state s_t, update

$$H_{t+1}(s_t, a_t) \leftarrow (1-\alpha)H_t(s_t, a_t) + \alpha[r_t + \gamma \min_{a \in A} H_t(s_{t+1}, a_{t+1})]$$

c) Calculate Joint Entropy value as

$$EEV_t(a_i) = \sum_{a_{-i} \in A} H_t\{(s_t, a_{-i_{(t)}}) \cup (s_t, a_{i_{(t)}})\} \prod_{j \neq i} \pi(a_{-i})_j$$

d) Update $\Pr\left(a \mid s, H_t(s_t, a_t), \pi(a_j)_i, d_h\right)$ as

$$\Pr\left(a \mid s, H_t(s_t, a_t), \pi(a_j)_i, d_h\right) \leftarrow \Pr\left(a \mid s, H_t(s_t, a_t), \pi(a_j)_i, d_h\right) +$$

$$\begin{cases} \delta & \textit{if } a = \arg\min_{a_t} H_t(s_t, a_t) \\ \dfrac{-\delta}{|A_i| - 1} & \textit{otherwise} \end{cases} \qquad \textit{where, } \prime = \begin{cases} \prime_s & \textit{if } H_{t+1}(s_t, a_t) > EEV_t(a_i) \\ \prime_f & \textit{otherwise} \end{cases}$$

---

run tends to zero since each inhabitant's exploration strategy is exploitive. Hence,

$$\lim_{t \to \infty} \Pr\left(a \mid s, H_t(s_t, a_t), \pi(a_j)_i, d_h\right) = 0$$

Proposition 2 and 3 are required conditions for our Entropy learning algorithm. They ensure that inhabitants could not adopt deterministic exploration strategies and become strictly correlated. The last proposition states that the inhabitants always explore their knowledge. This is necessary to ensure that an equilibrium will be reached.

Classification and Estimation of the Uncertainty Level

Mahalanobis distance (Schneps-Schneppe & Iverson, 2003) is a very useful way of determining the "similarity" of a set of values from an unknown sample to a set of values measured from a collection of "known" samples. In our scenario, the entropy values calculated by the inhabitants once in an individual mode and on the other hand in a cooperative mode in the smart home environment are correlated to each other. From this perspective we have used Mahalanobis distance as the basis for our analysis which takes distribution of the entropy correlations into account compared to the traditional Euclidean distance. The advantage of using this approach lies in extending the inhabitants to choose the most efficient route with the minimum entropy value.

To provide the most efficient route to the inhabitants of smart home, we consider an N-dimensional space of individual Entropy Value Level (EVL) $q = [q_1, q_2, q_3, \ldots, q_N]$ evolved by N different actions at different time instant. In our model, due to cooperative learning among the inhabitants, another set of EVL such as $e = [e_1, e_2, e_3, \ldots, e_N]$ could be evolved due to the joint actions of the inhabitants. Thus we have two different estimation of the entropy values. One estimation has been done due to individual action and the other estimation is due to joint actions in a cooperative environment. Therefore we have two points, q and e in the N dimensional space representing two different EVL "states".

Let us have two groups, g_1 and g_2 consisting of different inhabitants distinguished by their EVL measures. For example, group g_1 may contain inhabitants who provide route in accordance with EVL, q and group g_2 in accordance with e. If we now have one new entropy value h, the problem is to classify it as either belonging to g_1 or g_2. We reduce this problem to the classification of two Gaussian groups by means of multi-dimensional statistical analysis. For characterizing these two groups, we choose two N-dimensional Normal (Gaussian) distributions $\mathbb{N}_n(\mu_1, V)$ for group g_1 and $\mathbb{N}_n(\mu_2, V)$ for group g_2, respectively. Therefore for these two cases, we have the following characteristic functions:

$\mu_1 = (\mu_{11}\mu_{12}.....\mu_{1N})^T$ for g_1 assuming as "succeeding" cases, and $\mu_1 = (\mu_{21}\mu_{22}.....\mu_{2N})^T$ for g_2 assuming "failing" cases, where T denotes transposition. Here μ_1 and μ_2 represent the means for all the entropy in the multivariate space defined by the EVL in the model. These points can be called as group *Entropy Centroid*. For each new entropy values, we can then compute the Mahalanobis distances from each of the group *Entropy Centroid*. We would classify the EVL as belonging to the group to which it is the closest, that is, where the Mahalanobis distance is the smallest.

The Covariance matrix $V = [\sigma_{ij}]$ is the same for both the distributions.

Our N-dimensional EVL measures are given by $h = [h_1, h_2,....., h_N]$. For the two-group case, we use a linear discriminant function that can also be thought of as multiple regression. In general, we fit a linear equation of the type: $z = x_1h_1 + x_2h_2 +..... + x_Nh_N$ which is a scalar product of vectors x and h, where the vector $x = [x_1, x_2,....., x_N]$ represents unknown regression coefficients. We have defined the following deci-

sion rule depending upon some threshold value y, such that $h \in g_1$ if $z \leq y$, otherwise $h \in g_2$.

Thus we reduce the classification issue into two problems: a) to determine the N unknown coefficients $x_1, x_2,.....x_N$ so that the distance between the projections of mean vectors μ_1 and μ_2 on vector x is maximal, and b) to choose point y between these projections on vector x, minimizing the probability of wrong classification which in turn provides the optimal EVL to the inhabitants.

The overall classification process is shown in Figure 1 for two naturally occurring EVL groups g_1 and g_2, which can be divided by the line $x_1h_2 + x_1h_2 = y$.

Mahalanobis distance: Mahalanobis distance (Schneps-Schneppe & Iverson, 2003), $\mathbb{D}_m^2$, is a generalized measure of the distance between two correlated groups as it adequately accounts for the correlations. If our point h belongs to group g_1, then variable x defined previously has one-dimensional normal distribution with mean and variance as follows.

$$z_1 = \sum_{i=1}^{N} x_i\mu_{1i} = x^T\mu_1 \quad z_1 = \sum_{i=1}^{N} x_i\mu_{1i} = x^T\mu_1$$

$$\sigma_z^2 = \sum_{i=1}^{N}\sum_{j=1}^{N} x_i x_j \sigma_{ij} = x^T V x$$

$$\sigma_z^2 = \sum_{i=1}^{N}\sum_{j=1}^{N} x_i x_j \sigma_{ij} = x^T V x$$

In a similar way if h belongs to group g_2, then z has a normal distribution with mean z_2 and the same variance.

$$z_2 = \sum_{i=1}^{N} x_i\mu_{2i} = x^T\mu_2 \quad z_2 = \sum_{i=1}^{N} x_i\mu_{2i} = x^T\mu_2$$

$$\sigma_z^2 = \sum_{i=1}^{N}\sum_{j=1}^{N} x_i x_j \sigma_{ij} = x^T V x$$

$$\sigma_z^2 = \sum_{i=1}^{N}\sum_{j=1}^{N} x_i x_j \sigma_{ij} = x^T V x$$

Figure 1. Geometric interpretation of entropy value level classification

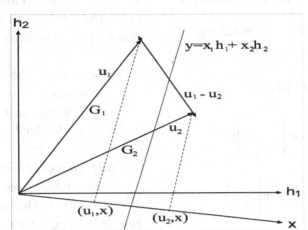

The distance between groups g_1 and g_2 can be expressed as

$$\mathbb{D}_m^2 = (\mu_2 - \mu_1)^T V^{-1}(\mu_2 - \mu_1)$$

using mean and variance equations. Now we need to find out the constants $x_1, x_2, \ldots x_N$ maximizing the so called Mahalanobis distance $\mathbb{D}_m^2 = \dfrac{(z_2 - z_1)^2}{\sigma_z^2}$. The solution of x as obtained from (Schneps-Schneppe & Iverson, 2003) is $x = V^{-1}(\mu_2 - \mu_1)$. Thus, the guaranteed best entropy value level can be determined as $z = x_1 h_1 + x_2 h_2 + \ldots + x_N h_N$.

Next we need to minimize the misclassification probability. Classification is the process by which a decision is made whether a particular inhabitant belongs to a particular group. Let N_1 denote the number of inhabitants that truly belong to group g_1, and let N_2 denote the number of inhabitants that truly belong to group g_2. Let N_{11} be the number of inhabitants that actually belong to group g_1 and assigned to group g_1 (i.e., correctly classified). Let N_{12} be the number of inhabitants that belong to group g_1 but are assigned to group g_2 (i.e., incorrectly classified). Similarly, N_{21} denote the number of inhabitants that belong to group g_2 but

are incorrectly classified into g_1, and N_{22} denote the number of inhabitants that belong to group g_2 and are correctly classified into g_2. Then the total number of incorrectly classified inhabitants is $N_{12} + N_{21}$ and hence the probability of incorrectly classified inhabitants is $\Psi = \dfrac{N_{12} + N_{21}}{N}$ where N is the total number of inhabitants. Thus Ψ denotes the probability of choosing group g_1 when the correct group is g_2 or vice versa. The probability (Ψ_1) of choosing group g_2 when the true one is g_1 can be expressed as (Roy, Das, Basu & Kumar, IPDPS 2005).

$$\Psi_1 = \Pr[g_2 | g_1] = \Pr[z > y | g_1] = 1 - \Phi$$
$$\left(\frac{y - z_1}{\sigma_z}\right) = \frac{N_{12}}{N}$$

where Φ denotes the normal distribution function. Similarly, the probability (Ψ_2) of choosing group g_1 when the true one is g_2 can be expressed as

$$\Psi_2 = \Pr[g_1 | g_2] = \Pr[z \leq y | g_2] = 1 - \Phi$$
$$\left(\frac{z_2 - y}{\sigma_z}\right) = \frac{N_{21}}{N}$$

Assuming the threshold value of the entropy value level y as $\dfrac{z_1 + z_2}{2}$, the total probability of misclassification can be expressed as

$$\Psi = \Psi_1 + \Psi_2 = \Pr[g_2|\,g_1] + \Pr[g_1|\,g_2]$$

$$= \left\{1 - \Phi\left(\frac{y - z_1}{\sigma_z}\right)\right\} + \left\{1 - \Phi\left(\frac{z_2 - y}{\sigma_z}\right)\right\}$$

$$= 2\left\{1 - \Phi\left(\frac{z_2 - z_1}{2\sigma_z}\right)\right\} = 2\left\{1 - \Phi\left(\frac{\mathbb{D}_m}{2}\right)\right\}$$

$$= 2\Phi\left(-\frac{\mathbb{D}_m}{2}\right) = \frac{N_{12} + N_{21}}{N}$$

Predictive Nash H-Learning Framework

Hypothesizing that every inhabitant wants to satisfy his own preferences about activities, we assume he behaves like a selfish (non-cooperative) agent to fulfill his own goals. Under this circumstance, the objective of the system is to achieve a suitable balance among the preferences of all inhabitants residing in the smart home. This motivates us to look into the problem from the perspective of non-cooperative game theory where the inhabitants are the players and their activities are the strategies of the game. Moreover, there can be conflicts among the activity preferences. Our proposed game theoretic framework (Roy, N., Roy, A., & Das, PerCom 2006) aims at resolving these conflicts among inhabitants, while predicting their activities (and hence locations) with as much accuracy as possible.

NP-Hard Problem

The multi-inhabitant location prediction problem is defined as follows: *For a group of η location predictions, one for each of η inhabitants residing in the smart home consisting of L different loca-* *tions, the objective is to maximize the number of successful predictions.* The following theorem characterizes the complexity of this problem.

Theorem 1: The problem of maximizing the number of successful predictions of multiple inhabitants' locations in a smart home is NP-hard.

Proof: We reduce this problem to the *Set Packing* problem, which is known to be NP-hard (Garey & Johnson, 1979). The Set Packing problem arises in partitioning elements under strong constraints on what are allowable partitions. The key feature is that no element is permitted to be covered by more than one set. As shown in Figure 2, the input to the Set Packing problem is a set $S = \{S_1, S_2, \ldots, S_\xi\}$ of ξ subsets of the universal set $U = \{1, 2, \ldots, \eta\}$, where η is the number of prediction requests as defined above. The goal is to maximize the number of mutually disjoint subsets from **S**. In other words, given the condition that each element from the universal set U can be covered by *at most one subset* from **S**, the objective is to maximize the number of mutually disjoint subsets from **S**. In order to prove the theorem, we assume that each location as identified by the sensor is occupied by at most one inhabitant. The sensor deployment and coverage in a smart home is assumed to be dense enough to make this distinction.

The maximum successful prediction process in a smart home having L locations and η prediction requests, is equivalent to the Set Packing problem with η subsets and a universal set **U** of L elements. At any instance of time, an inhabitant i can actually reside under the coverage of one or more sensors (locations), say li. Then the prediction process, pr*edicti,* for inhabitant i *is* a collection of its possible locations, i.e., pr*edicti=* {li}. Every such prediction is mapped to a particular subset Si. Each single location (sensor coverage-area) of the smart home is mapped to an element of the subset Si. The strategy that maximizes the number of successful predictions is basically the one that

Figure 2. Analogy of set-packing problem

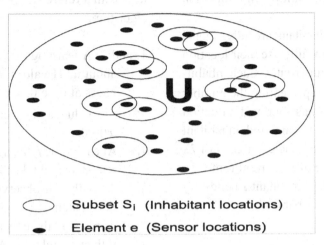

maximizes the number of disjoint subsets from **S**. Thus, we conclude that the multi-inhabitant optimal location prediction is NP-hard.

Therefore, it is computationally infeasible to find an optimal strategy for maximizing the number of successful location predictions across multiple inhabitants. In the following, we devise a suboptimal solution based on game theory. It attempts to reach an equilibrium and maximizes the number of successful predictions across all inhabitants.

Non-Cooperative Nash H-Learning Algorithm

The concept for general-sum games builds from the Nash equilibrium (Nash, 1951), in which each player effectively holds a correct expectation (generally expressed in terms of payoff, reward or utility value) about the other players' behaviors, and acts rationally with respect to this expectation. Acting rationally means the agent follows the strategy which corresponds to a best response to the others' strategies. Any deviation would make that agent worse off from achieving that equilibrium point. In extending the Q-learning (Hu & Wellman, 2003) to our multi-inhabitant smart home context aware resource manage-

ment problem we adopt the basic framework of general sum stochastic games. In single-agent systems, the concept of optimal Q-value can be defined in terms of an agent maximizing its own expected payoffs with respect to a stochastic environment. In multi-agent systems, Q-values are contingent on other agents' strategies. In the framework of general-sum stochastic games, the optimal Q-values are the subset of the Q-values received in a Nash equilibrium, and referred as Nash Q-values. The goal of learning is to find Nash Q-values through repeated game. Based on learned Q-values, the agent can then derive the Nash equilibrium and choose its actions accordingly. In Nash Q learning (Hu & Wellman, 2003) algorithm, the agent attempts to learn its equilibrium Q-values, starting from an arbitrary guess. Thus here the Nash Q-learning agent maintains a model of other agents' Q-values and uses that information to update its own Q-values based on the payoff value and takes their equilibrium actions in each state.

Our proposed Nash H-learning algorithm in this section enhanced the Nash Q-learning algorithm in that it captures the location uncertainty in terms of entropy at each and every step of the inhabitants' path. Thus, in our case, Nash H-value is determined which satisfies both Nash condition as well as our imposed entropy minimization constraint.

We assume that the inhabitants are fully rational in the sense that they can fully use their location histories to construct future routes. Each inhabitant i keeps a count C_a^j representing the number of times an inhabitant j has followed an action $a \in A$. When the game is encountered, inhabitant i believes the relative frequencies of each of j's movements as indicative of j's current route. So for each inhabitant j, the inhabitant i believes j plays action $a \in A$ with probability:

$$p(a)^i = \frac{C_a^j}{\sum_{b \in A} C_b^j}$$

This set of route strategies forms a reduced profile of strategies for which inhabitant i adopts a best response. After the game, inhabitant i updates its possible belief of its neighbor appropriately, given the actions used by other inhabitants. We consider these counts as reflecting the observations an inhabitant has regarding the route strategy of the other inhabitants. As a result, the decision making component should not directly repeat the actions of the inhabitants but rather learn to perform actions that optimize a given reward (or utility) function.

Indeed, the decision making component of a smart home applies learning to acquire a policy that optimizes joint uncertainty of the inhabitants' activities which in turn helps in accurate prediction of their activities and thus locations. For this optimization, our proposed entropy learning algorithm, called Nash H-learning (NHL), learns a value function that maps the state-action pairs to future reward using the entropy measure, H. It combines new experience with old value functions to produce new and statistically improved value functions. The proposed multi-agent Nash H-learning algorithm updates with future Nash equilibrium payoffs.

Table 2 describes the pseudo-code of the Nash H-learning algorithm which has been explained

next with a reference to each line number of the algorithm.

1. and 2. A learning agent, indexed by i, learns about its H-values by forming an arbitrary guess at time 0. We have assumed this initial value to be zero, i.e., $H_0^i(s, a^1, \ldots, a^n) = 0$.

4. At each time t, the agent i observes the current state and takes its action.

5. After that, it observes its own reward, actions taken by all other agents and their rewards, and the new state s'.

7. It then calculates a *Nash Equilibrium* $\pi^1(s'), \pi^2(s'), \ldots, \pi^n(s')$ at that stage and updates its own H-values as follows.

$$H_{t+1}^j(s, a^1, \ldots, a^n) = (1 - \alpha_t)H_t^j(s, a^1$$
$$\ldots, H_{t+1}^j(s, a^1 \, a^n) = (1 - \alpha_t)H_t^j(s, a^1$$
$$a^n) + \alpha_t\left[r_t^j + \beta Nash H_t^j(s')\right],$$
$$\ldots, a^n) = (1 - \alpha_t)H_t^j(s, a^1, \ldots,$$
$$a^n) + \alpha_t\left[r_t^j + \beta Nash H_t^j(s')\right],$$

where $Nash H_t^i(s') = \prod_{j=1}^{n}\pi^j(s')H_t^i(s')$

where the learning rate parameters α_t and β_t are in the range 0 to 1. For every agent, information about other agents' H-values is not given, so agent i must learn about those values too. Agent i forms conjectures about those H-functions at the beginning of the game. We have assumed $H_0^j(s, a^1, \ldots, a^n) = 0$, for all j and all s, $a^1, \ldots, a^n$. As the game proceeds, agent i observes other agents' immediate rewards and previous actions. That information can then be used to update agent i's conjectures on other agents' H-functions. Agent i updates its beliefs about agent j's H-function, i.e., $H_{t+1}^j(s, a^1, \ldots, a^n)$ according to the same updating rule it applies to its own. Thus, we have

Table 2. Nash H-learning algorithm (NHL)

Procedure NHL

Input: Individual entropy values

Output: Joint entropy values

1. Let the learning agent be indexed by *i*;

2. $t := 0$, $H_t^j(s, a^1, \ldots, a^n) := 0$, $\forall s \in S$ and $a^j \in A^j$, $j = 1, \ldots, n$;

3. Repeat

4. Choose action a_t^i;

5. Compute $r_t^1, \ldots, r_t^n$, $a_t^1, \ldots, a_t^n$ and $s_{t+1} = s'$

6. for $(j = 1, \ldots, n)$

7. $H_{t+1}^j(s, a^1, \ldots, a^n) = (1 - \alpha_t) H_t^j(s, a^1, \ldots, a^n) + \alpha_t [r_t^j + \beta Nash\, H_t^j(s')]$

   where $\alpha_t \in (0,1)$ is the learning rate

   and $Nash\, H_t^j(s') = \prod_{k=1}^{n} \pi^k(s') H_t^j(s')$

8. $t := t+1$

9. until(true)

$$H_{t+1}^j(s, a^1, \ldots, a^n) = (1 - \alpha_t) H_t^j(s, a^1$$
$$, \ldots, H_{t+1}^j(s, a^1\, a^n) = (1 - \alpha_t) H_t^j(s, a^1$$
$$a^n) + \alpha_t \left[r_t^j + \beta Nash\, H_t^j(s') \right].$$
$$, \ldots, a^n) = (1 - \alpha_t) H_t^j(s, a^1, \ldots,$$
$$a^n) + \alpha_t \left[r_t^j + \beta Nash\, H_t^j(s') \right].$$

The proposed Nash H-learning (NHL) algorithm (Roy, N., Roy, A., & Das, PerCom 2006) significantly enhanced the Nash Q-learning algorithm (Hu & Wellman, 2003) in that it captures the location uncertainty in terms of entropy at each and every step of the inhabitants' mobility path. Thus, in our case, Nash H-value is determined to satisfy both Nash condition as well as our imposed entropy (uncertainty) minimization constraint. We assume that the inhabitants are fully rational in the sense that they can fully use their location histories to construct future routes. As a result, the decision making component should not directly repeat the actions of the inhabitants but rather learn to perform actions that optimize a given reward (or utility) function. For this optimization, our proposed entropy learning algorithm (NHL) learns a value function that maps the state-action pairs to future reward using the entropy measure, H. It combines new experience with old value func-

tions to produce new and statistically improved value functions. The proposed multi-agent Nash H-learning algorithm updates with future Nash equilibrium payoffs and achieves a Nash equilibrium such that no inhabitant is given preference over others. This results in more accurate prediction of contexts and better adaptive control of automated devices, thus leading to a mobility-aware resource (say, energy) management scheme in multi-inhabitant smart homes. Experimental results demonstrate that the proposed framework adaptively controls a smart environment, significantly reduces energy consumption and enhances the comfort of the inhabitants.

Resource and Comfort Management

The objectives of a smart home include how to efficiently automate device control, provide the inhabitants with maximum possible comfort, minimize operational cost and consumption of resources, say energy. By managing the uncertainty related to the inhabitant's location, the house can facilitate accurate predictions of inhabitants' activities that help smart control of automated devices and appliances, leading to better resource utilization. Minimizing energy consumption reduces the maintenance cost, furthermore, reduction in explicit manual operations and control, in turn, increases the inhabitants' comfort. In the following, we develop a mobility-aware resource management scheme for multiple inhabitant smart homes.

Mobility-Aware Energy Conservation

Let us first consider two simple but extremely useful energy management schemes. In the worst-case scenario, a house may use a static scheme where a certain number of devices (electric lights, fans, etc.) are switched on for a fixed amount of time during a day. Intuitively, this results in unnecessary energy consumption. On the other hand, in the best-case scenario, devices are manually controlled every time while leaving or entering particular locations inside the house. However, such manual operations are against the smart home's goals of intelligent building automation and support of calm computing. We believe a smart energy management scheme ought to use the predicted routes and activities from the NHL algorithm for smart control of devices, thus minimizing unnecessary consumption of valuable resources. This will allow devices like lights, fans or air-conditioner operate in a *pro-active* manner to conserve energy during the inhabitant's absence in specific locations (zones) in the home. These devices also attempts to bring the indoor environment, such as temperature and light control, to amicable conditions before the inhabitant actually enters into those locations.

Let Q_{ij} denote the power of *i*-th device in *j*-th zone, ψ denote the maximum number of electrical devices which remained turned on in a particular zone, η denote the number of zones, $t_1 \leq t \leq t_2$ denote the time during which the device remains turned on, and let $p(t)$ denote the probability density function of uniform time distribution. Then the expected average electric energy (ε) consumed due to these devices will be:

$$\varepsilon = \frac{t_2 - t_1 + \Delta_t}{2} \sum_{j=1}^{\eta} \sum_{i=1}^{\psi} Q_{ij}$$

where Δ_t is the interval between the time for predictive device operation and the entry time of the first inhabitant in the zone.

We have developed a distributed temperature control system with a goal to conserve energy. This control system is intelligent enough to bring the temperature of specific locations (inside the home) to an amicable level before an inhabitant enters those locations. The operation of temperature control is termed as *pre-conditioning*, the time required is called *pre-conditioning period*, and the *rate of energy* required during this period is known as *pre-conditioning load* (Estop, 1978). Our predictive location management scheme estimates the most probable jointly-typical-set of routes and near future locations. For a specific pre-conditioning period, the constant rate of energy at full capacity is supplied to bring down the temperature to the appropriate comfort level. The shorter the duration of pre-conditioning period, the larger is the pre-conditioning load.

Estimation of Inhabitants' Comfort

The comfort is a subjective measure experienced by the inhabitants, and hence quite difficult to derive analytically. In-building climate, specifically temperature, plays the most important role in defining this comfort. Moreover, the amount of manual operations and the time spent by the inhabitants in performing the house hold activities also have significant influence on the inhabitants' comfort. We define the comfort as a joint function of temperature deviation, $\Delta\theta$, number of manual device operations (M) and time spent τ for those activities by the inhabitants. Thus,

$$Comfort = f\left(\frac{1}{\Delta(\theta)}, \frac{1}{M}, \frac{1}{\tau}\right).$$

Our mobility-aware resource management framework attempts to reduce empirical values of these controlling parameters, thereby increasing the inhabitants' comfort. Note that the reduction of joint entropy by using our proposed NHL algorithm described in Table 2, endows the house with sufficient knowledge for accurate estimate of current and future contexts (locations, routes and activities) of multiple inhabitants in the house. Successful estimate of these contexts results in adaptive control of environmental conditions and automated operation of devices.

Experimental Study

In this section, the proposed Nash H-learning framework is implemented and we conduct a series of experiments in MavHome (Youngblood, Cook & Holder, 2005) smart home environment to study its performance on a group of three inhabitants in a smart home equipped with smart devices and wireless sensors. The inhabitants wear radio frequency identification (RFID) tags and are tracked by RFID-readers. The house is equipped with explicit monitoring of inhabitants' activities and locations for performing a trace-driven simulation of the inhabitant's mobility followed by the resource management scheme.

Simulation Environment

We have developed an object-oriented discrete-event simulation platform for generating and learning inhabitants' mobility profiles, and predict the likely routes that aid in the resource and comfort management scheme. In order to collect the test data associated with the inhabitants' life-style, the appliances in the MavHome are equipped with X10 ActiveHome kit and HomeSeer ("X10 web"), thus allowing the inhabitants to automatically control the appliances. The identity of the inhabitants, their locations and activities are captured by wireless sensors placed inside the home. The inhabitants wear the RF-tags, which are sensed by the RF-readers to gather their identities. The raw data (Youngblood, 2005) as shown in Table 3 is first parsed using parsing tools like Perl and Tcl to remove unnecessary information. The different

Table 3. A snapshot of the collected RAW data

Mark	Zone	Number	State	Level	Source
2005-01-03 09: 47:30	i	5	1	100	X10
2005-01-03 09: 56:17	i	5	0	0	X10
2005-01-03 13: 04:45	a	1	1	100	X10
2005-01-03 13: 05:37	i	3	1	100	X10
2005-01-03 13: 06:11	c	4	1	100	X10
2005-01-03 13: 06:22	c	4	0	0	X10
2005-01-03 13: 16:32	S	1	1	10	ArgusMS
2005-01-03 13: 16:33	S	2	1	152	ArgusMS
2005-01-03 13: 16:33	S	3	1	13	ArgusMS
2005-01-05 23: 59: 00	V	23	1	100	ArgusD
2005-01-05 23: 59: 01	V	23	0	0	ArgusD
2005-01-05 23: 59:04	V	21	0	0	ArgusD
2005-01-05 23: 59: 12	V	21	1	100	ArgusD
2005-01-05 23: 59: 12	V	21	0	0	ArgusD

column headings in Table 2 have the following meanings: Mark as the data and time stamp, Zone and Number as unique sensor zone identifier and sensor number within it, State as binary 'on' or 'of' of the sensor, Level as specific value if on, Source as the network mode. Subsequently, we use these data to validate the mobility-aware resource management scheme. The energy and comfort management framework is compared with two reference platforms: (i) energy management without any predictive scheme, and (ii) energy management associated with per-inhabitant location prediction. The results are presented by sampling every sensor at a time and performing simulation experiments for a period of 12 weeks over 3 inhabitants and 2 visitors.

Performance Results

We have divided the entire set of simulation results into three categories. First, we demonstrate the accuracy of our proposed predictive scheme in multi-inhabitant smart homes and compare the results with our previous H-learning algorithm (Roy, N., Roy, A., Basu & Das, MobiQuitous 2005) with current modified Nash H-learning approach. Then

we show the storage and computational overhead associated with it. Finally, we discuss the effect of this predictive framework in terms of energy conservation and inhabitants' comfort.

Predictive Location Estimation

Recall that the Nash H-learning framework aims at reducing the location uncertainty (entropy) associated with individual and multiple inhabitants. Figure 3 shows the variation of the individual and joint entropy over the entire time period of the simulation using H-learning approach. Note that our existing H-learning framework (Roy, N., Roy, A., Basu & Das, MobiQuitous 2005) reduces the joint entropy quickly to a low value. While the entropy of every inhabitant lies in the range ~1-3, the visitor's entropy is typically higher~4. This is quite logical as the house finds the location contexts of the visitors more uncertain than the residents (inhabitants). In comparison, Figure 4 shows that initially the entropy associated with three individual inhabitants is around 4 using Nash H-learning approach. As the predictive framework becomes knowledgeable of the inhabitants' lifestyle, the individual entropy values reduce to

Figure 3. Variation of entropy (uncertainty)

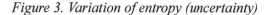

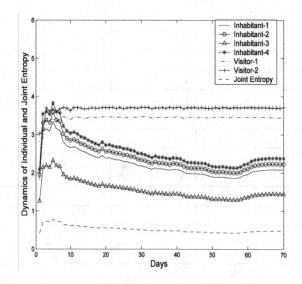

Figure 4. Variation of entropy (uncertainty) using H-learning using Nash H-learning

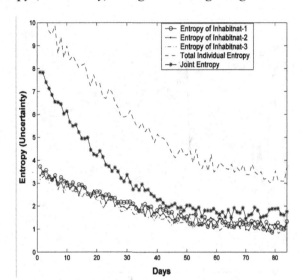

1.0. Therefore, the joint entropy is quite less than the total entropy of all the inhabitants. Initially the joint entropy is close to 8.0, but gradually it reduces to almost 1.0. The total entropy, on the other hand, lies in the range 4.0-10.0. In this way, the entropy minimization procedure formulated by Nash H-learning helps increase the efficiency of the location estimation technique.

The goal of our first experiment is to investigate into the dynamics of this entropy. The Nash H-learning framework also leads to higher success rate than simple H-learning. Figure 5 demonstrates that our co-operative H-learning strategy is capable of estimating the location of all the resident inhabitants with almost 90% accuracy within 3 weeks span. The house takes this time to learn the joint movement patterns of all inhabitants. The success rate of location estimation for visitors is however 50%-60%, as the house finds it difficult to get the knowledge of the random visitors. In comparison, Figure 6 shows the variation of prediction success for individual inhabitants and joint prediction success using Nash H-learning framework. Initially, the success-rate is pretty low as the system proceeds through the learning stage. Once the system becomes cognizant of inhabitants' profiles, the success rate increases and saturates

at a particular value. The individual prediction process does not consider the correlation among different inhabitants. Thus, it fails to capture some important contexts and results in comparatively lower prediction success up to 80%. The joint prediction, however, takes the correlation among different inhabitants into account and results in higher success rate (close to 95%) than the simple H-learning framework.

The collection of the inhabitants' joint typical-set is the key behind the development of efficient energy and temperature control system in the smart home. As discussed earlier, the joint-typical set is relatively a small subset of all routes (of all inhabitants) containing most of the probability mass (i.e., set of most probable routes). Figure 7 provides the percentage of total routes categorized as individual and joint typical routes. It is clear that the size of the individual and joint typical set is initially less than 50% of total routes. This size then gradually shrinks to as low as about 10% as the system captures the relevant contexts of inhabitants' movement-profiles.

Figure 5. Dynamics of prediction success

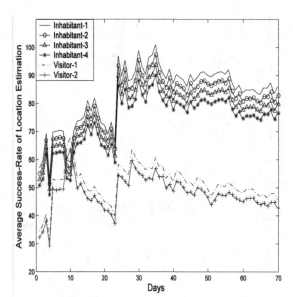

Figure 6. Dynamics of prediction success using H-learning using Nash H-learning

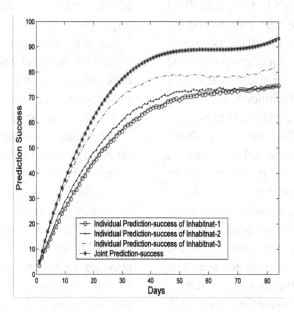

Storage and Computational Overhead

Another important criteria of our predictive framework is its low storage (memory) requirements. Figure 8 shows that the storage requirement of the joint prediction scheme is sufficiently less than the total storage requirement of the individual prediction schemes. The storage requirement of joint prediction initially starts increasing and then saturates at a reasonable value of 10 Kbytes, whereas the storage overhead for individual prediction is around 40 Kbytes.

Figure 7. Dynamics of typical routes

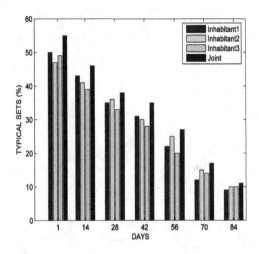

For practical use, it is important to ensure that the savings in storage is not negated entirely by the additional computational cost of the proposed algorithm. For this purpose, we computed the average time complexity per day in the smart home for our multi-inhabitant predictive framework, as well as for the existing per-inhabitant location-prediction algorithm (Roy, Das & Basu, 2007) applied over all inhabitants. We observe that the average number of operations for the proposed multi-inhabitant prediction is around 13413

where as the same for per-inhabitant prediction is 22357. Thus, the multi-inhabitant predictive framework reduces the time complexity by 40% in comparison to the per-inhabitant location tracking framework.

Energy Savings and Inhabitants' Comfort

With a goal to maximize the inhabitants' comfort with minimum energy consumption, the predictive

Figure 8. Storage overhead

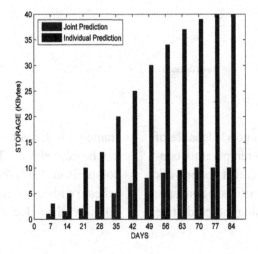

Figure 9. Energy consumption

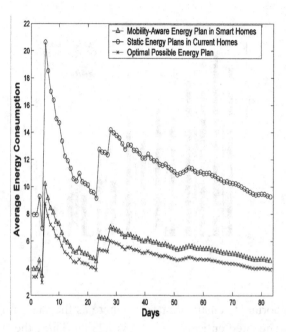

Figure 10. Manual operations and time spent

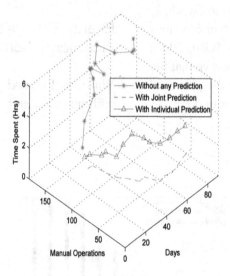

framework makes the system knowledgeable of inhabitants' profiles. The smart temperature control system and energy management framework makes intelligent use of these profiles to conserve energy. Figure 9 shows that using the predictive framework, the daily average energy consumption can be kept about 5 KiloWatt-hour (KW-Hr), in comparison to 9 KW-Hr for energy management scheme without the predictive framework. Figure 10 shows the reduction of manual operations and time spent for all the inhabitants. The predictive Nash H-learning scheme aids the system with sufficient automation, by reducing the overall manual operations performed by the inhabitants and the time spent behind all such operations which in turn increases the overall comfort.

FUTURE RESEARCH DIRECTIONS

There are many ongoing challenges that researchers in this area continue to face. The first is the ability to handle multiple inhabitants in a single environment. While this problem is addressed from a limited perspective (Roy, N., Roy, A., & Das, PerCom 2006), modeling not only multiple independent inhabitants but also accounting for inhabitant interactions and conflicting goals is a very difficult task, and one that must be further addressed in order to make smart environment technologies viable for the general population. Similarly, we would like to see the notion of "environment" extend from a single setting to encompass all of an inhabitant's spheres of influence. Many projects target a single environment such as smart home, smart office, smart mall, smart airport. However, by merging evidence and features from multiple settings, these environments should be able to work together in order to customize all of an individual's interactions with the outside world. As an example, how can we generalize intelligent automation and decision-making capabilities to encompass heterogeneous smart spaces such as smart homes, vehicles, roads, offices, airports, shopping malls, or hospitals, through which an inhabitant may pass in daily life. An interesting direction that researchers in the future may consider is not only the ability to adjust an environment to fit an individual's preferences, but to use the environment as a mechanism for influencing change in the individual's behavior or life style. For example, environmental influences can affect an individual's activity patterns, his mood, and ultimately his state of health and mind. Finally,

a useful goal for the research community is to define figure of merits, performance metric, and benchmarks to evaluate and compare different smart environments. While performance measures can be defined for each technology, those for an entire smart environment still need to be established. This can form the basis of comparative assessments and identify areas that need further investigation.

CONCLUSION

In this chapter, we have discussed a novel mobility-aware resource management framework in a multi-inhabitant smart home. Characterizing the mobility of inhabitants as a stationary, ergodic, stochastic process, the framework uses the information theoretic measure to estimate the uncertainty associated with all the inhabitants in the house. It has also been shown that the direct use of per-inhabitant location tracking fails to capture the correlation among multiple inhabitants' locations or activities. We have proved that the multi-inhabitant location tracking is an NP-hard problem. We also formulated a cooperative and non-cooperative learning paradigm based on stochastic game theory, which learns and estimates the inhabitants' most likely location (route) profiles by minimizing the overall entropy associated with them. Automated activation of devices along the predicted locations/routes provide the inhabitants with necessary comfort while minimizing energy consumption and cost.

REFERENCES

X10 web resources. (n.d.). Retrieved from http://www.x10.com

Bahl, P., & Padmanabhan, V. (2000). RADAR: An In-Building RF-based User Location and Tracking System. In *Proc. of IEEE Infocom,* (pp. 775-784). Los Alamitos, CA: IEEE CS Press.

Bhattacharya, A., & Das, S. K. (2002). LeZi-update: An information theoretic approach for personal mobility tracking in PCS networks. [WI-NET]. *ACM Wireless Networks, 8*(2/3), 121–137. doi:10.1023/A:1013759724438

Bowling, M., & Velso, M. (2001). Rational and Convergent Learning in Stochastic Games, In *Proceedings of the Seventeenth International Joint Conference on Artificial Intelligence*, Seattle, WA.

Cook, D. J., & Das, S. K. (2004). Smart Environments: Technology, Protocols and Applications. Chichester, UK: John Wiley & Sons.

Cover, T. M., & Thomas, J. A. (1991). Elements of Information Theory. Chichester, UK: John Wiley.

Das, S. K., Cook, D. J., Bhattacharya, A., Heierman, E., & Lin, T. Y. (2002). The Role of Prediction Algorithms in the MAVHome Smart Home Architecture. [Special Issue on Smart Homes]. *IEEE Wireless Communications, 9*(6), 77–84. doi:10.1109/MWC.2002.1160085

Estop, T. D. (1978). Applied Thermodynamics for Engineering Technologists: S.I. Units. London: Longman Publishers.

Garey, M. R., & Johnson, D. S. (1979). Computers and Intractability: A Guide to the Theory of NP-Completeness. New York: W. H. Freeman Publishers.

Harter, A., & Hopper, A. (1994). A distributed location system for the active office. *IEEE Network, 8*(1), 62–70. doi:10.1109/65.260080

Harter, A., Hopper, A., Steggles, P., Ward, A., & Webster, P. (1999). The anatomy of a context-aware application. In *Proc. 5th Annual Int'l Conference on Mobile Computing and Networking*, (pp. 59-68).

Hopper, A. (1999). *Sentient computing*. The Royal Society Clifford Patterson Lecture. House n Living Laboratory (n.d.). *Introduction*. Web resource available at http://architecture.mit.edu/house n/web/publications

Hu, J., & Wellman, M. P. (2003). Nash Q-Learning for General-Sum Stochastic Games. *Journal of Machine Learning, 4*, 1039–1069. doi:10.1162/jmlr.2003.4.6.1039

Krumm, J., Harris, S., Meyers, B., Brumitt, B., Hale, M., & Shafer, S. (2000). Multi-Camera Multi-Person Tracking for Easy Living. In *Proceedings of 3rd IEEE International Workshop on Visual Surveillance*, (pp. 3-10). Piscataway, NJ: IEEE Press.

Lesser., et al. (1999). The Intelligent Home Testbed. In Proc. of Autonomy Control Software Workshop.

Mozer, M. C. (1998). The Neural Network House: An Environment that Adapts to its Inhabitants. In *Proc. of the American Association for Artificial Intelligence Spring Symposium on Intelligent Environments*, (pp. 110-114).

Nash, J. F. (1951). Non-cooperative games. *The Annals of Mathematics, 54*, 286–295. doi:10.2307/1969529

Orr, R. J., & Abowd, G. D. (2000). The Smart Floor: A Mechanism for Natural User Identification and Tracking. In *Proceedings of Conference on Human Factors in Computing Systems (CHI 2000)*. New York: ACM Press.

Priyantha, N., Chakraborty, A., & Balakrishnan, H. (2000). The Cricket location support system. In *Proc. 6th Ann. Int'l Conference on Mobile Computing and Networking*, (pp. 32-43).

Roy, A., Das, S. K., & Basu, K. (2007). A Predictive Framework for Location Aware Resource Management in Smart Homes. *IEEE Transactions on Mobile Computing, 6*(11), 1270–1283. doi:10.1109/TMC.2007.1058

Roy, N. (2008) *A Context-aware Learning, Prediction and Mediation Framework for Resource Management in Smart Pervasive Environments.* Ph.D Thesis, University of Texas at Arlington, TX.

Roy, N., Das, S. K., Basu, K., & Kumar, M. (2005). Enhancing Availability of Grid Computational Services to Ubiquitous Computing Application. In *IEEE International Conference on Parallel and Distributed Processing Symposium*, Denver, CO.

Roy, N., Roy, A., Basu, K., & Das, S. K. (2005). A Cooperative Learning Framework for Mobility-Aware Resource Management in Multi-Inhabitant Smart Homes. In *Proc. of IEEE International Conference on Mobile and Ubiquitous Systems: Networking and Services (MobiQuitous)*, (pp. 393–403).

Roy, N., Roy, A., & Das, S. K. (2006). Context-Aware Resource Management in Multi-Inhabitant Smart Homes: A Nash H-learning based Approach. In *Proc. of IEEE Int'l Conf. on Pervasive Computing and Communications (PerCom)*, (pp. 148–158).

Roy, N., Roy, A., Das, S. K., & Basu, K. (2005). A Reinforcement Learning Framework for Location-Aware Resource Management in Multi-Inhabitant Smart Homes. In *Proc. of 3rd International Conference on Smart Homes and Health Telematic(ICOST)*, (pp. 180–187).

Schneps-Schneppe, M., & Iverson, V. B. (2003). Service Level Agreement as an issue of Teletraffic. In *Proceedings of the ITC*, Berlin.

Shelton, C. R. (2000). Balancing Multiple Sources of Reward in Reinforcement Learning. *Advances in Neural Information Processing Systems*, 1082–1088.

Singh, S., Jaakkola, T., Littman, M. L., & Szepesvari, C. (2000). Convergence Results for Single-Step On-Policy Reinforcement-Learning Algorithms. *Machine Learning, 38*(3), 287–290. doi:10.1023/A:1007678930559

Watkins, C. J. C. H. (1989). *Learning from delayed rewards.* PhD thesis, King's College, Cambridge, UK.

Weiser, M. (1991). The computer for the 21st century. *Scientific American, 265*(3), 94–104. doi:10.1038/scientificamerican0991-94

Youngblood, M. (2005). *MavPad Inhabitant 2 Trial 2 Data Set, The MavHome Project.* Computer Science and Engineering Department, The University of Texas at Arlington, http://mavhome.uta.edu

Youngblood, M., Cook, D. J., & Holder, L. B. (2005). Managing Adaptive Versatile Environments. In *Proc. of IEEE Int'l Conf. on Pervasive Computing and Communications (PerCom)*, (pp. 351-360).

Chapter 2
Effortless Data Capture for Ambient E–Services with Digital Pen and Paper Technology

Leili Lind
Linköping University & Santa Anna IT Research Institute, Sweden

Aseel Berglund
Saab Aerosystems, Sweden

Erik Berglund
Linköping University & Santa Anna IT Research Institute, Sweden

Magnus Bång
Linköping University & Santa Anna IT Research Institute, Sweden

Sture Hägglund
Linköping University & Santa Anna IT Research Institute, Sweden

ABSTRACT

In order to counteract the digital divide and to enable the society to reach all its citizens with various kinds of e-services, there is a need to develop access methods and terminal technologies suited also for groups with weak access to the Internet, not the least elderly and people needing care in their homes. In this chapter, the authors will describe technologies for using digital pen and paper as data input media for e-services and computing applications, refer a number of applications together with studies and evaluations of their usability, and finally comment upon future prospects for integrating digital pen and paper as an effortless technique for data capture, especially in order to counteract and diminish the digital divide. The use of digital pen and paper technologies is exemplified with applications demonstrating its appropriateness in home care for elderly, for free-form recording of data on paper such as maps, and as a remote control for a TV set or other electronic appliances with rich functionality in the home.

DOI: 10.4018/978-1-61520-843-2.ch002

INTRODUCTION

The modern information society assumes to an ever increasing degree that the citizens can utilize the Internet and computing appliances for getting information, paying bills, buying things and to communicate with healthcare and public sector service suppliers. However, quite a number of people find it difficult to access and manage e-services and standard computers, due to the general complexity and lack of convenient terminal designs and user-friendly interfaces for the inexperienced user. In order to promote convenient access to e-services for all citizens, not the least for the elderly, there is a need for consumer-oriented solutions for everyday e-services enabling access to IT-based services also for individuals with a low propensity to use computers and Internet.

Standard computers are becoming more and more affordable and are available for a large part of the population. Mobile phones and handheld computers offer alternative modes of access to Internet-based e-services. But in order to effectively deal with the digital divide, and also to offer convenient access to e-services in special situations, still other terminal devices may be required. For elderly and infrequent users of computers, neither standard PC systems with complex operating systems – subject to recurring changes not the least for security threats – nor mobile phones offer convenient interfaces with a low access threshold.

Thus, there is a quest for new types of access terminals suited for users and situations, where ease-of-use with respect to requested services is a prime requirement. Not the least is there a need to improve availability to public e-services for the elderly and groups of users with some kind of functional handicaps.

A core activity in getting convenient access to everyday e-services is support for effortless data capture, i.e. easy ways to enter information into a digital system, be it for recording of data or for controlling some kind of service (or device). For public places examples of such services can be buying a fare ticket, self-scanning in a food store, registration in connection with a hospital visit or reserving a parking space. In these cases some kind of touch-screen terminals are becoming more and more usual. For home-based applications, this technology has a more limited applicability, even if more advanced mobile phones may offer this kind of interaction mode.

In this chapter, we will focus on semi-mobile applications in the home and describe technologies for using digital pen and paper technology as data input media for e-services and some computing applications. We will exemplify opportunities with a number of innovative applications together with documented studies and evaluations of their usability. In particular, we will comment upon future prospects for integrated use of digital pen and paper as part of combined solutions for easy access and maneuvering of various kinds of e-services, especially in order to counteract and diminish the digital divide in the society.

Thus digital pen and paper technology offers an interesting opportunity for data entry, with a low access threshold and easy-to-use qualities. By employing artifacts such as pen and paper, which are well known to most people, the threshold for acceptance of new technology may be comparatively low. It is also important to offer solutions with a smooth learning process, encouraging the user to start directly to use the system and then gradually acquiring enhanced skills in utilizing the full functionality of offered services.

BACKGROUND

Throughout the history of computing, there has been an interest in using some kind of pen or stylus for convenient input of data, relying on skills and habits familiar to the ordinary user. Several technologies for recording and transmitting what is written have been tried, also for home applications (Venkatesh, 1996). We will in this chapter shortly review and assess the main solutions available and in particular discuss experience of using a "digital" pen for writing on ordinary paper as a means for effortless data capture in everyday applications. This area bears the promise of uniting the paper-based and digital worlds (Schreiner, 2008).

In general, many researchers have noticed the significant merits of paper. It is ubiquitous, highly portable, easy to use in a wide range of environments, inexpensive, can be annotated easily, and provides excellent readability properties (Hansen & Haas, 1988). So far, paper as an interface has mainly been studied in the work environment (Johnson, Jellinek, Leigh Klotz, Rao, & Card, 1993; Sellen & Harper, 1997; Sellen & Harper, 2001) and compared with computer interfaces (Hornbæk & Frokjer, 2003). Recent work with a similar approach as the one presented below has been made in joint European projects (Luff, Heath, Norrie, Signer, & Herdman, 2004; Signer, 2008).

Previous research has shown that the use of paper in the modern world is persistent because of paper's physical properties, not just despite these properties (Johnson et al., 1993). Johnson et al. claim that paper has utility that will not disappear with the increase in the electronic world, therefore the main goal should be to integrate, and not remove paper from the electronic world. Furthermore, Koike, Sato and Kobayashi (2001) show that the integration of paper and digital information is effective. Sellen and Harper (1997) predict that paper in support of reading tasks will be one of the hardest paper-based tasks to shift to the digital world. They also identified four affordances of paper supporting the flexible interweaving of reading and writing; the paper's tangibility, its spatial flexibility, its tailorability, and the manipulability of paper (Sellen & Harper, 2001).

DIGITAL PEN TECHNOLOGIES

We may distinguish between digital pen technologies which make use of some kind of active pad or screen for writing and those where the pen is the active component. One particular interest concerns when the writing can be done on ordinary paper, with the text recorded at the same time digitally and in ink on the paper. There are basically two modes of entering data into the background system. One is by transmitting the written text and figures for later character and pattern recognition in the computer. The other input mode uses selection rather than interpretation, by choosing alternatives from menus. An intermediate variant is when the user is filling in a form, where the fields define the semantic context for entered information, be it a check in a box or a free text.

An important breakthrough for digital-pen technology took place some ten years ago, when the C-pen used for text scanning was introduced. Later the Anoto technology with an active pen and a specially prepared paper (Fåhraeus, Hugosson, & Ericson, 2006) has been made commercially available for different applications. Anoto provides an ink pen with a digital camera that records everything the pen writes on any paper imprinted with a non-repeating dot pattern. The nearly invisible Anoto pattern consists of numerous black dots, all with a specific displacement relative a coordinate system, which the digital pen reads to establish its exact position. Each paper can have a unique pattern, which means that the technology can recognise, for instance, which specific copy of a form is used for data entry by reserving a page with a unique pattern. Anoto has become a de-facto digital pen and paper standard, and applications to support data capture exist in several areas, including healthcare, government, finance, education, transportation, and banking (Schreiner, 2008). Various digital pens for the consumer market using Anoto technology have been introduced over the years; For example, the

Sony Ericsson Chatpen™ and the Nokia Digital Pen SU-1B which could transfer handwritten text to computers directly or via mobile devices using Bluetooth and GPRS (General Packet Radio Service) mobile phone communication. Polyvisions Eno is a digital whiteboard using the Anoto digital pen and paper technology. The Pulse™ Smartpen from Livescribe adds audio with microphones and a built-in speaker to a digital pen and synchronizes written text with sound recordings.

Several manufacturers deliver products and applications built on the Anoto digital pen. Logitech provides the io2 Digital Pen, which is combined with a digital notebook and coded Post-it notepad. LeapFrog has introduced "the world's first pentop computer", which offers games and educational software applications that let users, for example, draw their own drums, piano keyboards, and calculators, and use them to make music or do math. Users can, for instance, create an application interface on any piece of its custom paper by simply writing specific letters or symbols and then circling them to create "buttons."

DRAWING PADS AND TOUCH SCREENS

For tasks such as to edit photos, to create special hand drawn effects, or to create digital artwork and graphics with programs like Adobe Photoshop, drawing pads using electromagnetic techniques for tracing a pen, can be useful. The tablets may have special keys and touch strips, allowing the user to access menus and scroll and zoom easily. The digital drawing tablets are sometimes built around an LCD screen, so it is easy to see where the pen is and obtain a high precision.

A drawing pad has an embedded grid of conductive wires, running in the x and y coordinate directions. Electrical current is pulsed into each parallel pair of adjacent wires. The resulting magnetic field is picked up by a coil in the pen. The pen then sends a delayed magnetic pulse back into the wire grid, where it is picked up and converted into a position defined by x and y coordinates.

This technique has a number of virtues. The pen can be fed energy from the pad, meaning that it will not need a cable connector or a battery. The accuracy of the pen tracing is high. Pen tilt can be measured in higher-end systems. A limited range of pen identities can be identified. On the other hand, the drawing pad is bulky and its cost quickly increases when size is increased. The accuracy decreases near the ends of the wires, so a frame of a couple of "dead" centimetres typically surrounds it. The system cannot detect what paper is being written on. Nor does it support multiple simultaneous pens on one surface. For the purpose of supporting effortless data capture in everyday applications, this technique has its limitations.

A technique with resistive touch screen is used for some smartphones, GPS navigators, etc. It uses two thin resistive films, which are placed on a surface. An electric voltage is applied between the sheets on each respective corner. The electrical resistance is measured, and the further away from that corner that the sheets are in contact, the greater the resistance. Distances from four corners yield an over-determined touch position.

An advantage with this technique is that it works with any passive pointing device, including plastic tips and fingers. It is relatively cheap and can be applied on top of displays. There are no problems with pen tip parallax and the power consumption is low. On the other hand, only limited accuracy can be obtained. The sensitive surface can be destroyed by sharp objects. The resistive sheet decreases contrast for displays and it does not work well for large areas. Neither does it work with multiple pens, nor can pens be uniquely identified. Pen tilt and pressure cannot be measured. The screen needs calibration.

Figure 1. The ATOMIK keyboard, optimized for speed, and example word patterns for Shape Writing defined by this keyboard layout (a dot indicates the starting end)

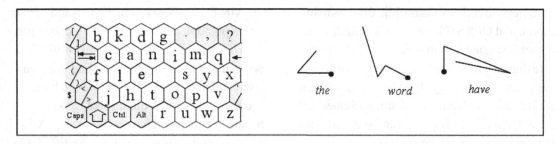

SHAPE WRITING

Natural handwriting with character recognition as a method for text input to computing devices can be slow and inaccurate. Stylus keyboards (e.g., Zhai, Smith, & Hunter, 2002), on the other hand, are more fast but tedious to use and require constant visual attention since every key tap must be exactly within the key boundaries. However, by combining handwriting with a stylus keyboard or a touch screen, a novel method – Shape Writing – of efficient text entry that allows the user to draw patterns has been developed as a mode of entering "shorthand" words (Zhai & Kristensson, 2003; Kristensson & Zhai, 2004). Each pattern of a word is formed by the trajectory through all of the letters of the word on the stylus keyboards, from the first to the last in order (see Figure 1).

Rather than tapping individual keys, one simply draws a continuous line from letter to letter on a graphical keyboard. The resulting pattern is recognized by ShapeWriter as a "shorthand" pattern figure, rather than having the user to articulate one letter at a time (longhand). A Shape Writing system displays a graphical keyboard to the user, usually with a QWERTY layout or with a customized layout made for special purposes or different languages. For high performance, an optimized graphical layout on screen keyboard, Atomik, has been designed. Word patterns defined on this layout are efficient to produce, tolerant to error, and easy to remember.

Shape Writing capitalizes on the extraordinary human ability to recognize, memorize and draw patterns. It is also "intelligent", in the sense that the number of legitimate words (ranging from thousands to tens of thousands in a lexicon) is only a fraction of the number of all letter permutations (tens of millions). This technique takes advantage of the regularities of words formation and recognizes user's ink trace on keyboard with maximum flexibility and error tolerance. An intended word can still be recognized although irrelevant letters between intended letters are crossed or even if some of the letters in a word are missed in the stylus trace.

Shape Writing bridges initial ease of use with eventual high performance by embedding learning in use. For initial ease of use, the user interface needs to be recognition-based and supporting action by visual guidance. To reach high performance, however, the user interface should support recall-based skills. In shape writing, these two modes are gradually connected. One shifts from recognition to recall over time. The graphical keyboard serves as a visual map and a training wheel from careful visual tracing towards a fluid form of shorthand writing. Error correction is supported in several ways. Underneath each word in ShapeWriter's text stream editor is a list of probable alternative words that can be selected with one additional pen stroke. One can also delete or insert words anywhere in the text stream editor.

However, for infrequent users such as elderly people, the usefulness of this kind of stylus or touch screen methods has a limited attraction. After all, it takes some time to understand the principles and even if a smooth learning curve is expected for Shape Writing, the main benefit of the method comes after some training. Experiment shows that a small vocabulary of patterns for frequently used words can be learnt and effectively used within a few hours of training, and that for a skilled user it can be the most rapid method available for text entry (Kristensson, 2007).

DIGITAL WRITING ON ORDINARY PAPER WITH AN ACTIVE PEN

Ultrasonic/Infrared techniques are used in some systems (for instance, Pegasus Tech, EPOS pen, MIMIO whiteboard pen system). Such systems consist of two parts; an active pen and a base station. The base station has two ultrasonic microphones and a photodiode sensitive in the infrared region. When the pen tip touches a surface, it simultaneously flashes an IR LED, and emits a short ultrasonic click. The base station picks up the IR flash and starts to listen for the ultrasonic click using the two microphones. An exact time for the arrival of the click in each microphone is measured. Using time-of-flight of the ultrasound, the pen tip position can be calculated using simple triangle geometry.

This is a relatively inexpensive solution and easy to use in everyday environments. The pad itself is not active, only the base station and the pen which need batteries. This technique can be made to work on larger areas (up to a couple of square meters). However, the accuracy is low and decreases as the pen is distanced from the base station.

The system cannot detect what paper is being written on. Nor can the system compensate for pen tilt parallax, and tilt cannot be measured. Multiple simultaneous pens may not be supported.

Occlusion by hands or other objects can disrupt the system.

DIGITAL PEN AND PAPER: THE ANOTO SOLUTION

To exemplify in more detail the use of digital pen and paper technology, we will explain how the most widespread technology, the Anoto Digital Pen and Paper technology, works and how it has been used for various everyday applications, including studies of usability and effectiveness. This technology is based on a combination of an ordinary ink pen and a digital IR camera (as well as supporting hardware) designed to digitally record everything written with the pen on a specially prepared paper. The pen works by recognizing a special non-repeating dot pattern that is printed on the paper but is almost invisible to the eye (see Figure 2). The non-repeating nature of the pattern means that the pen is able to determine which page is being written upon, and where on the page the pen is writing. The size of the total pattern space exceeds 60.000,000 square kilometers which is more than the combined area of Europe and Asia. The dots are slightly displaced from an orthogonal grid with a nominal spacing of 0.3 mm. The digital pen needs to register a matrix of at least 6 x 6 dots to determine its exact location in the full pattern.

The strokes made by the pen are recorded and can be transferred via a docking cradle or wireless access to a PC or a server-connected mobile phone. The dot pattern needed on the paper can be printed on a professional offset printing press, or on a laser printer. The pattern must be printed with an ink containing carbon which can be registered by the pen and because of that, the other graphics and text on the page cannot be printed with this type of ink.

Be it hand-written text, a sketch, or a check in a box the digital pen automatically captures all handwritten information as you write. Digital

Figure 2. The Anoto digital pen with the dot pattern which identifies an exact position on the paper, and also the specific paper or form which is used (copyright Anoto AB)

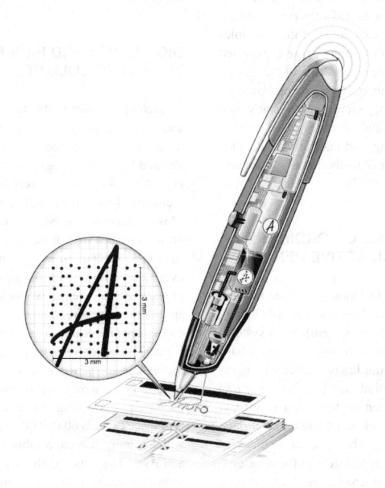

snapshots of the pattern on the paper are automatically taken at a rate of 75 pictures per second. Every snapshot contains enough data to determine the exact position of the pen and what it writes or draws. This data is then recorded in the pen's memory as a series of coordinates.

The Anoto pattern can be used to uniquely identify a specific page cut out of a huge area. Thus a particular customer or service vendor can obtain a license to use certain pages and, for instance, define a particular form associated with that page. This form is then used to interpret the meaning of what is written in a specific position on the paper. For instance, a special check box can

be defined to trigger the sending of a completed page as a transaction to a receiving server.

The pen data includes all information about the pen strokes written on the page, including:

- The location (coordinates for each pen camera picture taken by the pen).
- Exact time of when they were written.
- The identity of the pen which was used.
- The identity of the specific page licensed from Anoto and any associated paper form.
- Data documenting writing speed and pressure.

The digital pen user can transfer data wirelessly with Bluetooth either by ticking a box on the paper, interpreted by the pen as a "send" command or streaming directly to a receiving unit. Only the written information is transmitted, thereby keeping the data files to a minimum. Data may be then exported in any preferred format to suit the recipient application system. Typically, data may be exported as a picture but most often it needs to be translated into letters and digits by character recognition software.

At the receiving point, completed forms are identified by a form-id and can be routed to the corresponding application for processing. Handwritten text can be automatically converted into a digital representation. If any uncertainty remains or if data doesn't comply with stated business rules an operator corrects any error or sends the information back to the user in real time for validation.

Several development kits are available for defining forms for data entry and for building software applications on top of forms and data streams delivered from the digital pen. For instance, an existing pdf document can be extended with definitions of areas to be treated as specific fields for data entry, areas to check for starting or ending an input transaction, etc.

Though the digital pen and paper technology emphasize data entry, there may be some feedback mechanisms provided by the pen, for instance vibration to signal a successful completion of a transaction. In addition to tactile feedback, other modalities to be considered for direct feedback from the pen include auditory feedback and visual feedback (Liao, Guimbretiere, & Loeckenhoff, 2006).

A very interesting aspect of the digital pen and paper technology is the possibility to support simple and well-known techniques for verifying a transaction through a written signature. For all applications, where a written signature today is sufficient, the Anoto digital pen and paper technol-ogy enhances the verification possibilities by also recording characteristics writing dynamics.

In some cases, it is preferable to be able to write on a paper without leaving marks, for instance when a specific form is used repeatedly for controlling some external device or for recording the current time. There may also be a need to write confidential information, which should not be available for other to read on the paper, but only recorded in the receiving system. In this case, the paper can be prepared with a transparent "plastic" surface, where no trace of the pen's ink is left behind. An even better solution from a confidentiality point of view may be to use an inkless stylus.

USING DIGITAL PEN AND PAPER FOR EFFORTLESS DATA CAPTURE

The digital pen and paper technology, in particular when using the Anoto technology, offers new opportunities for providing easy-to-use access to e-services of various kinds for everyday applications (Boldt & Raasch, 2008). In a number of projects, we have studied conditions for user acceptance and effectiveness of everyday applications of digital pen and paper technology. For the purpose of this paper, we will in particular identify and discuss three types of application scenarios where interesting lessons can be learnt from prototype implementations and usability studies in these domains:

1. *Forms-based reporting of data to be electronically transferred.* Traditionally, many types of transactions with banks, government offices, healthcare, etc., are handled by submitting paper forms using ordinary mail. For people who are not regularly using computers, the current trends towards substituting personal visits or papers sent by mail with Internet-based transactions are not always conveniently accessible. Digital

pen and paper technology may offer a way to fill in a form printed on paper as before, but submitting the transaction electronically with no delay via, for instance, a phone with a wireless connection. The Anoto digital pen and paper technology can automatically detect which special form or document the user is writing on and thus immediately interpret the intended meaning when the user, for instance, checks a box or symbol on the paper. When the user enters free text, there is reasonably well-functioning software available for character recognition and text understanding, even if final manual post-processing is usually assumed.

2. *Free-form recording on paper.* For messaging tasks where a predefined form is appropriate, the digital pen and paper technology offers the possibility of transmitting a facsimile of what is written on paper without any specific support for interpretation of its meaning. In order to allow automatic processing of the input some kind of content recognition and interpretation is required. In addition to the obvious application with character and text recognition, for some applications, communication via special markings on a 2-dimensional picture might be useful. For instance by making annotations on maps, blueprints, drawings or for documentation of medical symptoms. Simple map applications may involve, for instance, entering a position by making marks on a paper map, while a more complex application can require support for recognition of a more versatile set of symbols available for the user to enter with a digital pen.

3. *Controlling and maneuvering technical equipment in the home.* Another type of situation is when additional functionality is introduced for everyday devices in the home, such as the telephone and the TV receiver. As more and more functions are added to formerly simple artifacts, the controls become increasingly complicated to use even for normal tasks, such as making a phone call or watching a preferred standard TV channel. We envisage a scenario where a fairly simple physical control with few, easy-to-understand controls and buttons for default tasks, can be complemented by a digital pen and paper interface for special tasks such as sending a message by the phone or initiate a recording of a TV program. At the same time, digital pen and paper can also be offered as an alternative way of accessing some of the standard controls, for instance selecting a channel to view on the TV or initiate recording of a specific program.

We will illustrate these scenarios with three concrete applications, where systems have been implemented and where their usability and effectiveness has been subject to research studies.

The first usage domain focuses on effortless forms-based messaging over the Internet, for instance for elderly or diseased people who find it difficult or inconvenient to log on to a standard PC even for accessing a simple reporting service. The second exemplifying domain deals with more mobile applications, where paper-based artifacts, such as maps or drawings, together with handwritten annotations are very useful, and where a digital communication connection can provide significant added values. The last application, the Paper Remote, deals with the task of using digital pen and paper as a control unit for maneuvering of everyday electronic devices, such as a TV set. The main virtue in this context is to offer a solution with a simple remote control, designed to support routine use with few control buttons, complemented with the digital pen and paper for more complex or seldom used functions.

SYMPTOM REPORTING WITH A DIGITAL PEN IN HOME HEALTHCARE

Today more patients are cared for by different home healthcare organizations, rather than receiving hospital care, which leads to the possibility of staying at home even during grave illness, and when caring for home care patients in a palliative state an adequate symptom control is one of the most important components (Dudgeon, Harlos, & Clinch, 1999). Therefore, a systematic assessment of pain and other symptoms are decisive for cancer patients in a palliative state. However, symptom control presents a challenge for home healthcare because patients are geographically separated from their caregivers, and when using information and communication technology, the patients' need for easy-to-use solutions is paramount. Although electronic, handheld pain diaries have been found useful and to provide a high degree of patient satisfaction in studies with patients suffering from chronic pain (Stone, Shiffman, Schwartz, Broderick, & Hufford, 2003), pain assessment can be complicated by sensory and cognitive impairment, and motor loss for an older patient group. Older users of handheld computers, such as PDAs and mobile phones, often find the screen brightness insufficient and the screen fonts too small to read clearly (Lee & Kuo, 2007). Digital pen technology can offer an alternative.

In a study of how to offer unobtrusive on-line communication with the hospital for cancer patients in a late or terminal state receiving care in the home, the patients were given the opportunity to assess their pain by using paper pain diaries together with digital pen and mobile-phone Internet connection. Necessary infrastructure in the patient's home included one wall socket and sufficient coverage for GSM/GPRS. The patients assessed their pain and intake of pain medication three times per day by using a visual-analogue scale. Diary data could be completed in less than a couple of minutes including the sending of

data to the hospital-based home care clinic. The writing was automatically transmitted wirelessly to the caregiver, who monitored their patients' assessments in real-time and made adjustments in pain treatment accordingly. To safeguard the privacy of patient data the most secure level of the technology was used, which comprised both encryption and authentication of devices. Furthermore, no identification data (social security number or name) were sent over the Bluetooth or GSM/GPRS links by the digital pen. The system mapped the pen requests to the current patient by using the information in the database and the unique serial number of the pen. The system was developed and implemented by the Department of Biomedical Engineering, Linköping University, Sweden (Lind, 2006).

Twelve palliative cancer patients participated in the first study which was evaluated through qualitative content analysis. The caregivers' outlook was initially cautious due to low expectations concerning the patients' abilities and due to uncertainty about how to use the system. In particular, elderly women were excluded and never asked to participate. Although there was an initial reluctance to use the system and change their way-of-working the caregivers experienced positive outcomes and took an interest in improvements for future use (Lind, Karlsson, & Fridlund, 2007).

Interviews with the patients and spouses revealed that the pain assessment method was regarded as being effortless in spite of the patients' state of health. The understanding of the technology and pain assessment system was limited but the digital pen was looked upon and used as an ordinary pen. Further, the patients made it clear that they could handle the digital pen and they did not need help from their next-of-kin in writing with the digital pen. The motivation to use the method was not decreased by technology problems. If they experienced any technical problems, both patients and spouses participated to try and to solve the problems (charging the pen, checking the sending of data) or notified the caregivers about them. The minor technical problems seen during the first study concerned the digital pen, a Sony Ericsson Chatpen, which was new on the market. There were never any problems with data transfer via the mobile phone during the first study (Lind, Karlsson, & Fridlund, 2008a).

The patients experienced an increased and improved contact with their caregivers during the pain assessment period. Using the digital pen and pain diary was described as superior to using the phone for reporting the pain, since the former was seen as a less intrusive way. The patients also took a greater part in their own care. By keeping the original pain diaries the patients could go back and see for themselves how the pain had varied over time and this led to a wish to continue with the pain assessment after the period with the digital pen. Above all, the patients appreciated that the pain assessment method resulted in a sense of increased security. The caregivers also saw that the patients had benefited from the pain assessment method by means of increased participation in their own care, increased security and by improved responses to pain fluctuations in terms of changes in treatment (Lind, 2006; Lind et al, 2008a; Lind, 2008b).

In summary, the technology allowed patients to combine the comfort of being cared for in their own homes with real-time monitoring and control of their pain levels. Benefits are:

- More prompt and accurate treatment.
- Patients get an increased sense of security and participation in their own care.
- The contact between patients and caregivers is improved.
- Digital pen and paper is familiar, light and easy to use, even for terminally ill patients with a limited capacity to manage technical equipment.

A second study, randomized and controlled, comprising palliative patients living in two coun-

ties in Sweden is being conducted during 2008-2009 with terminally ill cancer patients using the Anoto digital pen technology. However, mobile telephony for digital pen data transfer has proved to be an instable solution. For example, the mobile phone has lost its Bluetooth connection with the digital pen, and sometimes the mobile phone has not been able to send the data. The problem is supposed to have its origin in the increasing complexity due to more and more functions in the mobile phones resulting in less stability. Therefore, dedicated communication devices are to be preferred for robust and reliable remote connections. In the second study the patients report on various symptoms and intake of pain relieving medicine using a Symptom Diary, and in addition they can write messages about other important things to the caregivers (see Figure 3).

DIGITALLY ENHANCED PAPER MAPS AND SKETCHES

Forms-based data entry simplifies sending complex information with limited input of written data from the user. In some situations the text-oriented structure of forms is not enough for efficient reporting. A good example is the use of annotation on maps, which is very common, for instance, in military operations. Here a special language of symbols, written by the user on a map to document location of resources and various live observations, is used. Similar needs can occur in reporting of medical symptoms, where sketches or annotations on a picture over the human body can be made to illustrate a complaint.

In rescue missions and military operations, paper maps thus provide an important means for reporting positions, observations, etc. Typically special symbols are written on the map, conveying information defined by symbol and position. For soldiers in the field, conventional computers are not always easy to use. By using digital pen and paper technology, a more robust and flexible

Figure 3. A patient in home care reporting on assessments of various symptoms with a digital pen, connected to the care center by Bluetooth and mobile broadband (copyright Leili Lind)

solution may be obtained. Such a system must be able to recognize customized symbol languages, since there is no single standardized set of symbols agreed upon.

The Kartago project (Sylverberg, Kristensson, Leifler & Berglund 2007) demonstrates the use of a digital pen, a mobile phone and paper maps as the basis for creating such digital paper map information systems for command and control applications. The basic idea is to digitize map-related tasks, by augmenting the traditional paper map as means of combining the virtues of traditional map-related work practice with the availability of electronic services. The goal was to achieve a printable leg-pocket sized system with a map-sized interface (folded and carried in hand or in a leg-pocket) with symbol-based interaction, and information/communication task management. A special feature of the Kartago Platform is symbol management and symbol recognition for the use of hand-written symbols in interactive systems for effortless data capture. In order to support different military symbol languages a special symbol format was developed, which permits

the symbol recognition engine to be loaded with different symbol languages.

The Kartago system uses paper maps together with a mobile phone, and an Anoto pen (see Figure 4). The pen deduces where the user is drawing by the special dot pattern which is printed on the paper map to be used. The user draws symbols with a digital pen on the map. The pen is connected wirelessly to a cell phone, which in turn is connected to a server over the mobile network (e.g. GSM, EDGE, 3G, etc.). The mobile phone used in experiments was a standard phone with Bluetooth. This technology allows the soldier to have a full-size paper map which can be folded and put in a pocket. Altogether, this hardware configuration assures that the system is easily wearable.

Within the framework of the Kartago System the symbol recognition module is one important component. This service allows the soldier to draw a symbol, and get it recognized. When the symbol is recognized the soldier is allowed to position the symbol and can, optionally, add information which can be used by a background information system.

Figure 4. Annotating a map with the digital pen connected on-line via a mobile phone

The information collected by annotations in the field is attached to an XML-representation of the map which can be sent through SMS/MMS, or web services to other soldiers or to headquarters.

The system provides support to load symbols expressed in XML format. A symbol is represented by various attributes, such as an image file, a sound file, and an ordered set of points defining the symbol. The symbol recognizer only requires the ordered set of points, together with information regarding whether the symbol could be rotated, and how far it should be between each rotation of the symbol. Since a common pen-gesture recognizer, such as the Rubine (1991) recognizer based on a "classic" statistical linear machine that extracts a feature vector and attempts to find the most similar class by statistical inference, has some limitations for the dynamic "alphabets" in the map application, a special recognizer was developed for Kartago.

The recognition engine is based on similar principles as Shape Writing, described above, and uses the concept of proportional matching presented by Kristensson and Zhai (2004). The symbol recognition is template-based and the symbol templates are used by the recognizer to identify the user's intended symbol. User input is saved as ordered strokes and is equidistantly sampled and normalized in scale and translation to permit comparison with the reference pattern.

In this way, information can be captured in the field and communicated to a command and control center, presuming a map printed on a pen-readable paper, a digital pen and a mobile phone. Since only the position and symbol for each recording has to be transmitted a low band-width communication channel, such as a GSM phone, is enough for the transmission. The symbols can either be interpreted by a human operator, or as in the Kartago project, automatically recognized by special software. In an experiment where fifteen participants were trained to use twenty distinct symbols (NATO primitive field symbols) to be written on a map, only a short period of training was required before 100% correct recognition of the registered data was obtained (Sylverberg et al., 2007).

THE PAPER REMOTE

The television set is notably the central device for entertainment and is also a source for information in most homes. However, as the number of available channels increase and overall functions for controlling the TV become more and more complex, interaction through a limited set of specialized buttons on a remote control becomes difficult. Searching and finding TV programs is an increasingly time-consuming task and the remote control combined with menus on the TV screen has its limitations as an interaction device. Combining the remote control with a traditional keyboard for entering text or for more complex control commands is usually not an attractive solution.

The main ways of changing channels on interactive digital TVs are:

- Scrolling by using the remote control, which can be time consuming (Ehrmantraut, Härder, Wittig, & Steinmetz, 1996).
- Entering channel numbers from the remote control which may result in memory overload for managing more than 50+ channels.
- Using an on-screen TV guide, usually called Electronic Program Guide or EPG for short (Daly-Jones & Carey, 2000; Ehrmantraut et al., 1996; Taylor & Harper, 2003). EPGs are operated by point-and-click maneuvers from the remote control or wireless keyboards.

The problems with complex viewer interaction can cause frustration and irritation. In general, research has also shown that entertainment is relatively important with regard to technology adoption in the home environment (Venkatesh & Brown, 2001) and that TV is actually one of the most important entertainment devices in the home (Herigstad & Wichansky, 1998). Enhanced remote controls, speech control and also digital

pen and paper technology have been tried together with improved dialogue design as alternatives to a traditional keyboard to alleviate the problems (Berglund, 2004). Even for households with Internet access through a set-top box connected to the TV, the same problem of easy everyday interaction occurs.

Given that the interaction technology is improved, there is also a potential to provide a TV-based solution for home information systems. Integrating familiar physical artifacts, such as paper and pen with TV technology may provide easy access to information services usually provided by PCs and the Internet. In usability studies of various ways to enhance user interaction with a TV offering many channels and additional information services, it was found that using a TV Program Guide printed on paper readable by a digital pen is a feasible way of achieving this (Berglund, Berglund, Larsson, & Bang, 2006).

Three studies were performed where a remote control was implemented by using a TV Guide printed on paper (see Figure 5) together with a TV set. Viewers tick designated areas on the paper-based guide to perform actions such as channel switching and setting up program reminders. The project studied the user's attitude toward and anticipated interest in a future digital program guide. The results document the value of using paper-based TV guides and also identify some deficiencies. Indications were found that the advantages and disadvantages of paper-based TV guides are related to the physical properties of paper. These user studies on linking digital paper to the TV for everyday information navigation illuminate the possibilities of providing innovative solutions also for home information systems.

In these studies, Anoto digital pen and paper technology was used as an alternative way of remotely controlling the TV. The system implemented for the experiments, the Paper Remote, was designed to handle six types of requests:

Figure 5. Example page from the printed Program Guide used in the experiment with the Paper Remote (copyright Aseel Berglund)

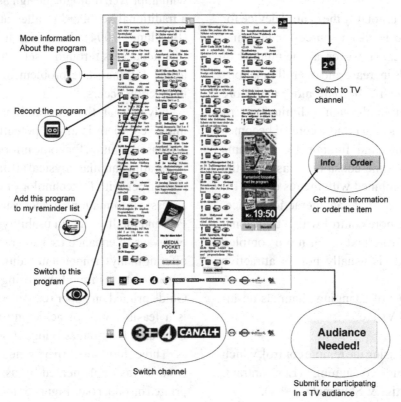

- Viewing detailed information on specific TV programs, such as description of the programs, reviews, and trailers: A beneficial consequence for TV guide design is that the amount of information printed on the paper can be reduced.
- Switching directly to a selected program. This may eliminate the number of steps necessary to access the program.
- Adding programs to favorite program lists. These lists can also remind viewers of upcoming programs.
- Program the recordings of TV programs. By ticking an icon in the printed TV guide, all the necessary information is sent to the recorder (e.g., start and end time, date, television channel, and program).
- Interacting with TV program providers directly during ongoing TV programs, for instance to apply to a TV program audience.
- Interaction with services through advertisements, for instance to learn more about or to order a product.

The first user study examined the audience's TV habits and TV guide usage, and indicated the advantages and deficiencies of TV guides printed on papers. The study also provided design implications for the Paper Remote concept, with its combined character of an interactive paper-based guide as well as a remote control for the TV. The second study involved usability evaluation of the Paper Remote prototype with concrete use cases, while the third study was focused on the users' attitudes towards the future TV guide. For more reliable data, however, continued investigations including a wider range of viewers of different ages, experiences, abilities, and interests need to be conducted.

The results of the studies show a definite potential for using digital pen and augmented paper-based TV guides as an interface to the TV set. This was particularly apparent for tasks like channel switching, planning of TV watching, time reminding, and programming of VCR recordings. The familiar way of interacting by using a pen contributed to the initial acceptance and ease of introduction of the Paper Remote concept.

One interesting experience was that it turned out to be convenient to have a comparatively complete printed TV Guide, rather than a brief program list to choose from. This was important in order to avoid switching attention between the paper and the screen, when requested information was displayed on the screen, rather than being available in the printed TV Guide. This solution also contributes to the possibility of performing some TV tasks without the need to be in front of the TV device. In the third study, for example, it emerged that planning of TV viewing using paper-based TV guides usually occurs in another place than in front of the TV, for example in the kitchen while eating breakfast. Thus, augmenting the mobility property of paper-based guides with increased functionality may add extra values that can ease the interaction. For example, viewers will be able to order recording with ticks without the need to be in front of the TV set and without the need to enter special codes through the remote control unit.

An advantage is also that it may be easier to use Paper Remote than on-screen guides because it is easier to shift focus between the printed guide and TV shows since they do not occupy the same screen. This conclusion is also supported by previous research (Taylor & Harper, 2003). The traditional remote control device is still needed, as some functions, such as channel zapping, are more appropriately conducted by means of the remote control. A notable experience that was observed in the third study is that despite the fact

that speech input was not in focus in the context of the study, participants asked for speech interaction and showed positive attitudes towards it.

The regular commercial paper-based TV guides provide many possibilities for computer augmentation. The layout with pictures, icons, and menus is well tuned to be used in a design of interactive surfaces. For instance, channel logos serve as naturally occurring icons which viewers can tick with the digital pen to change TV channel. Compared to Electronic Program Guides and web guides, printed Guides provide superior overview and mobility. In addition, the participants in the studies reported that they trusted the paper-based TV guide more than EPGs and web guides, even if they have a potential of being more up to date. Ease of browsing, robustness and fast startup-time for the application were considered as positive aspects. The studies of TV habits show that many people use paper-based TV guides for planning of their TV viewing, for instance by marking the interesting TV programs that they want to see with a pen. By using the digital pen and paper technology, the cognitive overload for the user can be diminished.

Thus, the possibility of linking paper and pen with TV technology holds the promise of providing easy access to information services for users who need an alternative to computers and smart phones. A similar study by Hess, Küstermann, and Pipek (2008) also report favorable experiences and a high degree of user acceptance. Anoto AB has developed demonstrator solutions with streaming communication from a digital pen for controlling a TV set, and also an application where a computer slide presentation is controlled with digital pen and paper technology.

Another interesting issue regarding using the TV for information access is that traditional computers are designed for single usage, which is not appropriate for homes with more than one member (Frohlich, Dray, & Silverman, 2001). Since TV is designed for social activities, it can function as a family computer rather than a personal computer.

Television is familiar, is understandable to virtually all people, and has the potential to reach a diverse population. According to this view, it has been suggested that television, rather than the personal computer, may be the information appliance of the future (Kaufman & Lane, 1997).

FUTURE RESEARCH DIRECTIONS

In order to realize the full potential of effortless data capture and appliance control with digital pen technology, we need to combine capture of input data with other techniques providing ambient feedback channels supporting e-services with varying degrees of demand for interactivity. Users in the home should have the opportunity to connect to available e-services through various terminal appliances, which can be regular computing devices, mobile phones, etc., but also specially designed terminal solutions based on, for instance, the use of digital paper and pen technologies for convenient input of data.

Example of feed-back devices can be home computers, mobile phones or an ordinary TV with a set-top box. Such a device can also be a web radio receiver, specially designed for the elderly. Requirements and use experience of providing sound-based information services (for instance newspapers, pod radio and personal messages supporting healthcare and banking information services) for elderly or people with reading difficulties were studied in the Audio4all project (Hult, Lind, & Hägglund, 2008), commissioned by the Swedish Post and Telecom Agency.

For the digital pen and paper technology to offer complete and convenient solutions for accessing e-services in the home, there are a number of possible additional needs and requirements for technical developments to be investigated:

- Integration of the digital pen and paper technology for data entry with appropriate feedback channels, suitable both for interactive dialog and for asynchronous interactions, as discussed above. In addition, inclusion of memory support for the elderly, for instance some kind of printing device or other type of persistent medium for saving feedback data, for instance booking reservations, addresses, etc.

- Mechanisms for extraction and adaption of information from the Web to forms suitable to deliver over the everyday access terminals provided for the intended user group. For instance, by using customized search engines, and by summarizing and re-writing of information before it is presented to the user depending on the band-width of the feedback channel.

- Multi-user support with secure identification of users, e.g. role-based identification for professional care personnel sharing the same communication device, but with access restrictions associated with different service channels.

- Connection and integration of systems monitoring safety and security and/or medical sensors at home, both for easy inspection of data by the home user or for reliable transmission to service centers. Such supervision devices can, for instance, be used for readings of medical status, (lack of) physical activity, security surveillance, reminder of water flood in the bathroom, kitchen stove forgotten, etc.

User-oriented research is also needed for studying the trade-offs between multi-service systems with many available functions and dedicated customized solutions offering simpler user interfaces. Digital pen and paper technology also offers a choice between streaming communication with immediate interpretation of written input and transaction processing, where a completed form is submitted at a time. Streaming offers better interactivity, but for some applications and categories of users the transaction model may be more robust and easy to understand.

CONCLUSION

As a way to manage the digital divide and to enable the society to reach all its citizens with various kinds of e-services, there is a need to develop access methods and terminal technologies suited also for groups with weak access to the Internet, such as elderly and people needing care in their homes. Digital pen and paper technologies offers interesting opportunities for this purpose, by using well-known artifacts (pen and paper) to enter data and control commands into a digital system. Preliminary user studies show promising results in terms of user acceptance and ability to manage the technology, even for elderly and severely ill people being cared in the home.

In order to provide a versatile e-service terminal for the home, the digital pen and paper technology can be combined with suitable feedback channels, such as sound channels (mobile phones or internet-connected radio receivers), a TV-set with Internet or mobile broadband (or at least GSM/GPRS) connection, or even physical alerts such as vibration of the pen. Research has shown that the digital pen and paper technology can easily be understood by the users, and that there are numerous useful applications ahead, which can contribute to create a critical size consumer market for home e-service terminals. New access terminals supporting data capture with digital pen and paper technology can fill the gaps left by PCs and mobile phones, terminal technologies which tend to offer too complex functionality and maneuvering skills for many elderly and occasional users. In this way the digital divide in the society can be counteracted and existing, as well as new, e-services can be made conveniently available to more people. More studies are needed, however, in order to find out how an increased number of services offered together with more complex

functionality will affect usability and acceptance, while at the same time contributing to a critical-size market for technology vendors and content providers.

ACKNOWLEDGMENT

The authors thank Petter Ericson at Anoto AB for valuable contributions and points of view and Per Ola Kristensson, University of Cambridge, for background material on Shape Writing.

REFERENCES

Berglund, A., Berglund, E., Larsson, A., & Bang, M. (2006). Paper Remote: an augmented television guide and remote control. *Universal Access in the Information Society*, *4*(4), 300–327. doi:10.1007/s10209-004-0108-8

Berglund, A., & Johansson, P. (2004). Using speech and dialogue for interactive TV navigation. *Universal Access in the Information Society*, *3*(3/4), 224–238. doi:10.1007/s10209-004-0106-x

Boldt, R., & Raasch, J. (2008). Analysis of current technologies and devices for mobile data capture. A qualitative usability study for comparison of data capture via keyboard, tablet PC, personal digital assistant, and digital pen and paper. Report, University of Applied Sciences, Hamburg, Germany.

Daly-Jones, O., & Carey, R. (2000). Interactive TV: a new interaction paradigm? In CHI '00 extended abstracts on Human factors in computer systems, (pp. 306-306). The Hague, The Netherlands: ACM Press.

Dudgeon, D. J., Harlos, M., & Clinch, J. J. (1999). The Edmonton Symptom Assessment Scale (ESAS) as an audit tool. *Journal of Palliative Care*, *15*(3), 14–19.

Ehrmantraut, M., Härder, T., Wittig, H., & Steinmetz, R. (1996). The personal electronic program guide – towards the pre-selection of individual tv programs. In *Proceedings of the fifth international conference on Information and knowledge management,* (pp. 243–250). Rockville, MD: ACM Press.

Fåhraeus, C., Hugosson, O., & Ericson, P. (2006) *Device and Method for Recording Handwritten Information.* US Patent US006985643B1.

Frohlich, D. M., Dray, S., & Silverman, A. (2001). Breaking up is hard to do: family perspectives on the future of the home pc. *International Journal of Human-Computer Studies, 54*(5), 701–724. doi:10.1006/ijhc.2000.0436

Hansen, W. J., & Haas, C. (1988). Reading and writing with computers: a framework for explaining differences in performance. *Communications of the ACM, 31*(9), 1080–1089. doi:10.1145/48529.48532

Herigstad, D., & Wichansky, A. (1998). Designing user interfaces for television. In CHI '98 conference summary on Human factors in computing systems, (pp.165-166). New York: ACM Press.

Hess, J., Küstermann, G., & Pipek, V. (2008) Premote: a user customizable remote control. In CHI'08 extended abstracts on Human factors in computing systems, April 05-10, Florence, Italy.

Hornbæk, K., & Frokjer, E. (2003). Reading patterns and usability in visualizations of electronic documents. *ACM Transactions on Computer-Human Interaction, 10*(2), 119–149. doi:10.1145/772047.772050

Hult, L. Lind, L., & Hägglund, S. (2008) Enabling e-Services for All. A User-Centered Design Approach for Audio-Based Information Services. In Proceedings eChallenges 2008. Amsterdam: IOS Press.

Johnson, W., Jellinek, H., Leigh Klotz, J., Rao, R., & Card, S. K. (1993). Bridging the paper and electronic worlds: the paper user interface. In *Proceedings of the SIGCHI conference on Human factors in computing systems,* (pp 507–512). Amsterdam, The Netherlands: ACM Press.

Kaufman, C. F., & Lane, P. M. (1997). Understanding consumer information needs: The impact of polychromic time use. *Telematics and Informatics, 14*(2), 173–184. doi:10.1016/S0736-5853(96)00032-9

Koike, H., Sato, Y., & Kobayashi, Y. (2001). Integrating paper and digital information on enhanceddesk: a method for realtime finger tracking on an augmented desk system. *ACM Transactions on Computer-Human Interaction, 8*(4), 307–322. doi:10.1145/504704.504706

Kristensson, P. (2007). *Discrete and Continuous Shape Writing for Text Entry and Control.* PhD Thesis, No 1106. Linköping Studies in Science and Technology, Linköping University.

Kristensson, P. O., & Zhai, S. (2004) SHARK2: A Large Vocabulary Shorthand Writing System for Pen-based Computers. In *Proceedings of the 17th Annual ACM Symposium on User Interface Software and Technology (UIST '04),* (pp. 43-52). New York: ACM Press.

Lee, C. F., & Kuo, C. C. (2007) Difficulties on Small-Touch-Screens for Various Ages. In Universal Acess in Human Computer Interaction. Coping with Diversity (Vol. 4554, pp. 968-974). Berlin: Springer.

Liao, C., Guimbretiere, F., & Loeckenhoff, C. E. (2006). Pen-top Feedback for Paper-based Interfaces. In *Proc. of UIST '06,* Montreux, Switzerland.

Lind, L. (2006). *Towards Effortless Use of Information Technology in Home Healthcare with a Networked Digital Pen.* PhD Thesis, No 1039, Linköping Studies in Science and Technology, Linköping University.

Lind, L. (2008b) Evaluation of the Use of Digital Pens for Pain Assessment in Palliative Home Healthcare. In S.K. Andersen et al, (Eds.), eHealth Beyond the Horizon – Get IT There. Amsterdam: IOS Press.

Lind, L., Karlsson, D., & Fridlund, B. (2007). Digital pens and pain diaries in palliative home health care: professional caregivers' experiences. *Medical Informatics and the Internet in Medicine, 32*(4), 287–296. doi:10.1080/14639230701785381

Lind, L., Karlsson, D., & Fridlund, B. (2008a). Patients' use of digital pens for pain assessment in advanced palliative home healthcare. *International Journal of Medical Informatics, 77*(2), 129–136. doi:10.1016/j.ijmedinf.2007.01.013

Luff, P., Heath, C., Norrie, M. C., Signer, B., & Herdman, P. (2004) Only Touching the Surface: Creating Affinities Between Digital Content and Paper. In *Proc. of CSCW 2004*, Chicago, IL.

Rubine, D. (1991) Specifying Gestures by Example. In *Proc. SIGGRAPH 1991 – 18th Annual ACM Conference on Computer Graphics and Interactive Techniques,* (pp. 329–337).

Schreiner, K. (2008). Uniting the Paper and Digital Worlds. *IEEE Computer Graphics and Applications. 28*(6 November/December), 6-10.

Sellen, A., & Harper, R. (1997). Paper as an analytic resource for the design of new technologies. In *Proceedings of the SIGCHI conference on Human factors in computing systems,* (pp. 319–326). Atlanta, GA. New York: ACM Press.

Sellen, A. J., & Harper, R. H. R. (2001). The Myth of the Paperless Office. Cambridge (MA): MIT Press.

Signer, B. (2008). *Fundamental Concepts for Interactive Paper and Cross-Media Information Spaces.*

Stone, A. A., Shiffman, S., Schwartz, J. E., Broderick, J. E., & Hufford, M. R. (2003, April). Patient compliance with paper and electronic diaries. *Controlled Clinical Trials, 24*(2), 182–199. doi:10.1016/S0197-2456(02)00320-3

Sylverberg, T., Kristensson, P. O., Leifler, O., & Berglund, E. (2007) Drawing on paper maps: reliable on-line symbol recognition of handwritten symbols using a digital pen and a mobile phone. In *Proceedings of the 2nd IEEE International Conference on Pervasive Computing and Applications (ICPCA '07).*

Taylor, A., & Harper, R. (2003). Switching on to switch off. In (H. R., ed.), Inside the smart home, (pp 115 – 126). London: Springer-Verlag Limited.

Venkatesh, A. (1996). Computers and other interactive technologies for the home. *Communications of the ACM, 39*(12), 47–54. doi:10.1145/240483.240491

Venkatesh, V., & Brown, S. A. (2001). Longitudinal investigation of personal computers in homes: Adoption determinants and emerging challenges. *MIS Quarterly, 25*(1), 71–102. doi:10.2307/3250959

Zhai, S., & Kristensson, P. O. (2003). Shorthand Writing on Stylus Keyboard. In *Proceedings of the ACM Conference on Human Factors in Computing Systems (CHI '03),* (pp. 97-104). New York: ACM Press.

Zhai, S., Smith, B. A., & Hunter, M. (2002). Performance Optimization of Virtual Keyboards. *Human-Computer Interaction, 17*(2&3), 89–129.

Chapter 3
Evaluating Voice User Interfaces in Ubiquitous Applications

Valéria Farinazzo Martins Salvador
Universidade Presbiteriana Mackenzie, Brasil

João Soares de Oliveira Neto
Universidade Presbiteriana Mackenzie, Brasil

Marcelo de Paiva Guimarães
Centro Universitário Adventista de São Paulo, Brasil

ABSTRACT

In the current trend of applications going more and more ubiquitous, it is necessary to determine some characteristics, requirements and properties that must be assured in order that the application provides quality service to its users. This chapter describes a study on the evaluation of Voice User Interface (VUI) in Ubiquitous Applications and discusses some of issues which may impact the evaluation process when using the voice as a natural way of interacting with computers. The authors present a set of guidelines and usability principles that should be considered when developing VUIs for Ubiquitous Applications. Finally, they present the results of a case study which was performed in order to test and exemplify the concepts presented here.

INTRODUCTION

Besides recognizing the user voice, Voice User Interface (VUI) systems are able to understand what the user says and to supply responses to these inputs, usually in real time. The state-of-the-art in speech technology already allows the development of automatic systems designed to work in real conditions (San-Segundo et al, 2005). Companies such as Philips, AT&T, and IBM have invested on the development of speech systems for restricted domains. On the other hand, the proliferation of computing into the real world promises the ubiquitous availability of computing infrastructure; it demands new paradigms of interaction that are more natural and inspired by constant access to information and computational capabilities.

The current knowledge on VUI comes from small contributions of research projects. These contributions propose an assessment for sub-systems developed in these projects, and try to generalize and make recommendations for the evaluation of

DOI: 10.4018/978-1-61520-843-2.ch003

VUIs, such as PARADISE (Walker et al, 1997), EAGLES (Gibbon; Moore; Winski, 1997) and DISC (Dybkjaer; Bernsen, 2000). However, the general tendency of using VUI is changing from applications that are built to be used in controlled environments to ubiquitous applications. Hence there is an increasing need to determine the principles of evaluating VUIs in this complex scenario.

So far, the principles of VUI evaluation were focused on specific issues, such as adequacy of the noise degree in the inputs of the system and the spontaneity of the interaction by voice. But, in a more complex environment, it is necessary to address other issues intrinsically related to ubiquitous applications, such as: if the communication through voice is a better choice for situations where one desires freedom for eyes and hands; the relevance of noise product by the environment where the applications is running; and privacy concerns (Abowd; Mynatt, 2000), (Dawkins et al, 2009).

According to Deng and Huang (2004), and Niculescu et al (2008), systems based on voice commands must face some challenges to achieve massive acceptance by the several sectors of the society:

- Reduce the gap between what technology currently offers in terms of interface usability and what users want really need from voice-based interaction system;
- Building robust systems in all possible acoustic environments: the voice recognition systems work well in quiet environments, but when the user is in a noisy environment, generally he/she can not use the system effectively, due to the great decreasing of the recognition error rate. For many years that was the main issue studied by researchers of voice recognition, from both universities and companies;
- Need of putting into action systems for natural language: until now, when users

interact with voice-based systems, they are aware that their partner is a machine. This is a failure in the voice recognition process, because, commonly, the user prefers a more natural style and the casual conversation;
- Deal with language accents, slangs and regionalisms.

The main goals of this chapter are:

- Present the state-of-the-art of the use of VUIs in ubiquitous applications;
- Determine general and specific requirements that must be followed to ensure the quality of VUIs in ubiquitous applications;
- Provide specific guidelines and usability principles for this VUIs used in ubiquitous scenarios;
- Present, as example, the development of an ubiquitous application that uses VUI, as well as the process of evaluation of this interface, according to the principles and guidelines mentioned above.

This chapter is organized as follows. Section Use of VUI in ubiquitous applications covers the use of VUI in ubiquitous applications. Section VUI Evaluation brings the definition of VUI Evaluation. Section Usability principles and guidelines for VUI in ubiquitous applications presents the usability principles and guidelines for VUI in ubiquitous applications. Section *Case Study* shows the case study for evaluating VUI in ubiquitous applications. Finally, Section *Conclusion* has the final considerations of this work.

USE OF VUI IN UBIQUITOUS APPLICATIONS

Since the very beginning of the current century, researches pointed out emerging ways of human-machine interactions and the integration of real-time communications, such as voice, video, and music (Cox *et al.*, 2000). For decades, the telephone had remained the most important way of communication over great distances. Voice was used as a natural mode of conversation and dialog among individuals and between individuals and machines. As speech technologies progressed in the last years, the role of voice and VUIs has increased for a broad range of services besides the telephone. In fact, the new networks provide a wide range of opportunities for VUI to become a major component of the telecommunications environment of the contemporary society. Also, the appearance of new devices and services is another opportunity for VUI, regarding the access of these devices and changing dramatically the user experience in interacting with the available network and associated services.

Thinking about the dialogue strategy between man and machine, Cox at al. (2000), proposes a structure of subdialogues based on human communication. The dialogue flows according to the sequence of tasks that are performed, and the machine, or system, has a pre-defined set of possible actions, as prompting the user, receiving information from the user, accessing a database, and so on. Such dialogue strategy is defined as a Markov decision process and has the following goals:

1. Confirmation: used to ascertain correctness of the recognized utterance or utterances.
2. Error recovery: to get the dialogue back on track after a user indicates that the system has misunderstood something.
3. Reprompting: when the system expected input but did not receive any.
4. Completion: to elicit missing input information from the user.
5. Constraining: to reduce the scope of the request so that a reasonable amount of information is retrieved, presented to the user, or otherwise acted upon.
6. Relaxation: to increase the scope of the request when no information has been retrieved.
7. Disambiguation: to resolve inconsistent input from the user (e.g., "I want to travel at 10 a.m. in the evening").
8. Greeting/Closing: to maintain social protocol at the beginning and end of an interaction.

VUIs are also known as eligible to motivate the adoption of ubiquitous applications. If the user wears a headset or a wireless device his mobility is increased. Hands-free communication can avoid the high concentration and distraction demanded by a hand-held communication while driving, for example (Juang, 2001). Companies also obtain several benefit using VUIs in his systems. In 2003, the average cost of transactions made using systems that implements a VUI was US$ 0.20, instead of US$ 6.17, which is the price of call center handled by a call center (Dettmer, 2003). In addition, 74% of callers prefer automated voice-driven systems comparing to talking with a live agent.

Some technologies, such as VXML and SOAP, have made possible enhancing ubiquitous applications by using VUI over a large variety of devices, such as mobile and sensor networks. A sample solution for the combination of VUI and ubiquitous applications is proposed by (Takami, Yamaguchi, & Unno, 2006). In this proposal, there is a personal Web Service that receives the data from the client, but this data is, in fact, the voice. So the user can select a link even while his/her hands are doing something else. The difference is that the Web site has not only normal Web page information but also a corresponding voice dialog scenario in the form of metadata. The metadata is described in VXML. It is necessary to provide the Web browser with a voice browser function, which interprets and executes VXML instructions, and a function to synchronize information displayed on the screen with the voice dialog. The voice browser function must also include speech recognition and voice generation functions.

The sequence of this application is as follows: first, the Web page 1 is shown; when the browser is opened, it receives the HTML file of Web page 1 using a GET message; if the HTML syntax analyzer of the browser detects a voice-tag, it requests the VXML syntax analyzer of the browser to process it using a POST message; the VXML syntax analyzer gets the VXML metadata associated with Web page 1 using a GET message; it interprets the VXML metadata and starts a voice dialog; in response to the user's spoken command, the syntax analyzer gets information about the link referred to in Web page 1, which is a link to Web page 2; it sends this link information to an HTML syntax analyzer as a way of acknowledgment. Based on this information, the HTML syntax analyzer receives the HTML file corresponding to the Web page 2, and changes the screen displayed.

Multimodal interfaces are a significant source of motivation for using VUI nowadays. Multimodal search of the Web and media, as well as speaker recognition for reducing Internet fraud, interactive question/answering for Web-based self-service, Web mining for knowledge discovery, two-way language translation, and Web page personalization and ranking are areas whose progress will help to generate exciting new business opportunities for mobile Internet, secure voice print, ubiquitous multilingual communication, IPTV (Internet Protocol Television), globalization of customer care, and search of massive amounts of data (Gilbert & Junlan, 2008). The simplicity of the querying interfaces for both voice and document search is an important factor for their wide popularity. Search will continue to drive new applications, especially for mobile small devices where it is cumbersome to type using a keyboard. Voice search will also play an important role in entertainment, such as IPTV, as the need for simpler interfaces to control television contents increases.

A number of natural language processing techniques have been explored in document search including stemming, synonyms, and machine translation. For Gilbert and Junlan (2008), stemming refers to the process of mapping a word to its root form when tokenizing documents and queries. The motivation is that a user searching for a keyword, such as "meetings," is also interested in documents containing the word "meeting." Another advantage of stemming is reducing the language complexity. The number of distinct terms is dramatically reduced after stemming. Synonym search brings the search one level closer to semantic search. For instance, a user can type "~meeting" to find pages containing "meeting," "conference," and "netmeeting." Machine translation translates text in a source language to an equivalent text in a target language. Since the Web is rapidly changing from being English dominated to multilingual, translation is becoming a key technology that offers users the ability to search through multilingual documents.

Multimodal search plays an important role in entertainment. In IPTV, for example, the traditional remote control will get less and less importance in the interaction arena (Hjelm, 2008). Using up/down and left/right keys is insufficient when navigating through a large number of channels, programs, movies, and music, all changing continuously every day. With multimodal search, users will have the ability to apply speech to identify the desired program or narrow down the search into a short menu and then use up/down and left/right keys to select the program of choice. In the future, users will also exercise advanced natural language queries such as "show me all action movies by Bruce Willis." The ease-of-use of multimodal search over standard clicking using a remote control will totally change the way people watch television.

It should be noted that much of the progress made in voice and multimodal search is for vertical industries with application-specific language models. There are numerous technical problems that need to be solved before users are able to break down the application barrier and be able to do mobile search freely for unlimited information access. New research in the areas of personalization and customization will be needed as people become accustomed to their devices and become power users of the technology.

On the other hand, some studies reveal some weakness and challenges for the use of VUI in ubiquitous interfaces. Environmental issues, such as noise and security, are the main points exposed (Juang, 2001). But other questions are found in other researches. It is important to mention an empirical experiment in which observed users employed a voice mail system, a typical asynchronous or non-realtime voice-based system (Kim & Kim, 2007). A primary result of this study was to grasp an overview of usability of voice mail, because few studies were made on asynchronous communication through voice until then, while other studies were already carried out to investigate it through text. Some interesting findings were: people used voice mail differently according to different tasks that they should do, e. g. for cooperative work in some tasks but just for socializing in other tasks; and participants used voice mail for personal and social purposes more than for coordinating their work. They also chose habitually other media but voice mail such as cellular phones and text-chatting systems.

In order to guide proper directions for the design of voice-based interactive systems, and explain fundamental characteristics of voice interaction, we can arrange the problems with voice interaction in ubiquitous applications in the following groups (Hee-Cheol, 2008): linearity, locality, privacy intrusion, and inferiority complex. The notions of linearity and nonlinearity here are associated with navigation of information. When an interaction type is linear, it means that users navigate over information only according to a given order. While GUI is nonlinear, voice is linear. GUI is a visual language with interactive tools. When it comes to voice, however, the user

capability to navigate over information spaces is drastically restricted. When you hear one's speech, you cannot know what one will say in 10 minutes, because you cannot help but follow it only according to temporal order. Vocal space is basically linear, which finally reduces control of navigation. For Hee-Cheol (2008), users visit websites to navigate rather than to read. As a matter of fact, text is a better medium than voice as far as navigation is concerned, because texts or books are typical nonlinear media.

Scanning a newspaper for about 10 minutes, we can capture an overview of today's news. We also grasp global perspectives in home pages on the web. While quick overview is possible in GUI and any other visual spaces, it is difficult to achieve in voice. A problem in voice interaction is locality, which means that information is provided only locally at one time. That is, voice interaction does not offer global perspectives properly. Since provision of global perspectives helps users understand the information, its context, tasks, activities, and communication more properly, lack of global perspectives deteriorates users' tasks and their awareness of various contexts. In many cases, computer users want to get a sense of overview.

Voice communication is quite related to the problem of privacy intrusion, which eventually decreases systems usability. How can we speak loudly in public places? If one listens to other voices without a headset or speaks loudly, it clearly interferes with others' activities, which in fact intrudes their privacy in workplaces with many people. Voice in this respect is a source of privacy intrusion unless one is alone in a single space. Before we design voice-based interactive systems, therefore, we first need to answer the crucial questions of where, when, and for what voice is allowed and possible.

According to the results of the case study presented in (Hee-Cheol, 2008), users tend to feel inferiority complex about their voices. One of the participants said, for instance, "If I had a beautiful voice like an announcer in a TV program, I could use the voice mail system more frequently to boast my voice." People were shy and not so confident of their voices. When users feel inferiority complex about their own voices, they naturally avoid utilizing asynchronous voice communication systems. They are also afraid of their recorded voices being left permanently in the media unless they are deleted. Being permanent is another stressful factor by which the act of using voice for communicating can be badly affected. This is true in case of voice email, particularly when users feel inferiority complex about their voices.

Other issues deal with the wide range of disabilities, or differential capabilities of users. Many systems allow partially sighted users, especially elderly users, to increase the font size or contrast in documents, but they rarely allow users to improve readability in control panels, help messages, or dialogue boxes. Blind users will be more active users of information and communications services if they can receive documents by speech generation or in Braille, and provide input by voice or their customized interfaces. Physically disabled users will eagerly use services if they can connect their customized interfaces to standard graphical user interfaces, even though they may work at a much slower pace. Cognitively impaired users with mild learning disabilities, dyslexia, poor memory, and other special needs could also be accommodated with modest changes to improve layouts, control vocabulary, and limit short-term memory demands. Expert and frequent users also have special needs. Enabling customization that speeds high-volume users, macros to support repeated operations, and inclusion of special-purpose devices could benefit many. Research on high-end users could improve interfaces for all users (Shneiderman, 2000).

Hence, we believe that development of VUIs for ubiquitous applications must consider, besides the natural questions about usability and quality, the environment and the different situations that the user may face. The points shown in this section must be understood as challenges for developers and VUI designers.

VUI EVALUATION

Usability is a set of properties of a user interface. Usually, it is associated with: ability to learn, efficiency, memorability, low error rate and satisfaction (Nielsen, 1993).

Usability is becoming an increasingly important issue in the development and evaluation of spoken language dialogue systems (SLDSs). Many companies have been spending a lot of money to know exactly which features make SLDSs attractive to users and how to evaluate whether these systems have these features. In spite of these important considerations far less resources have been invested in the usability aspect of SLDSs over the years than in SLDS component technologies. The usability aspects have been neglected in SLDS development and evaluation and haven't been mentioned enough in important user-related issues, such as user reaction to SLDSs in the field, linguistic behavior, or the main factors that determine the user satisfaction. However, there seems to be growing recognition that usability is as important as, and partly independent of, the technical quality of any SLDS component and that quality usability constitutes an important competitive parameter (Dybkjaer, Bernsen, 2001).

Although much research has been made on how to evaluate graphical user interfaces, research on how to evaluate speech user interfaces is just beginning. The differences between graphical and speech user interfaces originate, mostly, from the fundamental difference between spoken and visual communication human-to-human and human-to-computer. These basic differences affect the user interface design of speech vs. graphical interfaces, impact the implementation of applications with speech or graphical interfaces, and affect our design of an architecture intended to effectively support both of these activities. Evaluating VUI is different from evaluating GUI, mainly because (Hunt; Walker, 2000):

- Visibility: speech is invisible, which makes it challenging to communicate the functional boundaries of an application to the user;
- Transience: speech input and output are transient, once you hear it or say it, it's gone;
- Bandwidth Asymmetry: speech input is typically much faster than typed input whereas speech output can be much slower than reading graphical output, particularly in circumstances that permit visual scanning;
- Temporality: speech input is neither instantaneous nor discrete since an utterance may take many seconds to be spoken and consists of continuous data that is transformed to a word sequence by the speech recognizer. Although the final speech recognition result is effectively an instantaneous event it may be delayed by a noticeable time from when the user stops speaking.
- Concurrency: Speech-only communication tends to be both single-channel and serial.

It's therefore necessary to treat these peculiarities when developing VUI applications.

USABILITY PRINCIPLES AND GUIDELINES FOR VUI IN UBIQUITOUS APPLICATIONS

Developments in ubiquitous computing have lead to the concept of disappearing computing, with a user being unaware that they are interacting with a collection of computing nodes. The aim of this technology is to add additional capabilities to every day objects, allowing them to sense their environment and interact with the people and objects within it, to enhance their existing functionality. Such devices have been termed context aware applications, smart devices that sense the real world they are operating in and use this information combined with a set of rules to enhance their operation. These objectives require that computing technology is seamlessly integrated into an environment. This has become a reality with the ever decreasing cost, size and power requirements of embedded processors (Schltz; Consolvo, 2004).

Therefore, specific requirements are needed for these kinds of interfaces - VUIs. A subset of requirements based on usability principles for VUI (Dybkjaer; Bernsen, 2001) and on principles for ubiquitous applications (Scholtz; Consolvo, 2004), considered more relevant to evaluate VUIs in Ubiquitous Applications is:

a) **Modality appropriateness**: Nowadays, there is an increasing number of systems that combine spoken input/output with other modalities to support ubiquitous applications. But, it is well-known that speech-only interaction is not appropriate for all tasks and applications (e.g. to say their pin code out loud to the bank teller machine on the street). So, developers should attempt to make sure that spoken input and output, possibly combined with other input/output modalities, is an appropriate modality choice for the planned application.

b) **Attention:** this is likely to be more of an issue for ubiquitous computing, as users are handling other physical or mental tasks in parallel to interacting with VUI devices. They may be using those VUI devices in a variety of environments, with a variety of different people nearby.

c) **Input recognition adequacy:** From the user's point of view, good speech recognition means that the system rarely gets the user's spoken input wrong or fails to recognize what the user just said. However, there are many others factors that interfere in speech recognition, like: noisy or quiet environment; variety of dialects and accents; gender; age; voice quality; a low or a loud voice; etc.

d) **Naturalness of user's speech**: Speaking to an SLDS should feel as easy and natural as possible. The vocabulary and grammar input in the system must accord with the vocabulary and grammar expected from the user. Depending on, e.g., the task and user's experience, what is "natural" input language may vary considerably.

e) **Output voice quality**: From the user's point of view, good output voice quality means that the system speech is clear and intelligible, does not demand an extra listening effort, is not particularly noise sensitive or distorted by clicks and other extraneous sounds, has natural intonation and prosody, uses an appropriate speaking rate, and is pleasant to listen to. There are three main types of output speech: a) recordings of entire system utterances – when the information is not dynamic; b) concatenation of recorded words and phrases; and c) text-to-speech (TTS) – there is a component of the system that synthesizes the voice in real time. Obviously, the first type is more pleasant to listen to.

f) **Output phrasing adequacy**: the contents of the system's output should be correct, relevant and sufficiently informative without being over-informative. The form of system expressions should be clear and unambiguous, and language and, as far as possible, terminology should be consistent and familiar to the user.

g) **Feedback adequacy**: adequate feedback means that the user feels in control during interaction. The user must feel confident that the system has understood the information input in the way it was intended, and the user must be told which actions the system has taken and what the system is currently doing. There are there levels of feedback: hardware level – it means that the system has understood the speaker's input; sequence level – it means that the system has understood the required action by the speaker; and functional level – it indicates that the system is working at the problem (messages like "please, wait a moment").

h) **Adequacy of dialogue initiative**: to support natural interaction, a system needs a reasonable choice of dialogue initiative, an appropriate dialogue structure, complete task and domain coverage, and reasoning capabilities. This is linked with how much the user knows about the system. System directed dialogue can work well for tasks in which the system simply requires a series of specific pieces of information from the user, especially if the user is new to the system. On the other hand, to satisfy experienced users, the system will have to be able to cope with the larger packages of input information that are natural to these users.

i) **Error handling adequacy**: VUIs can be able to handle errors using: mixed initiative dialogue, tell the user what it understood and ask for confirmation or correction or transfer the call to a human attendant (in telephony systems).

In order to measure the usability of interactive systems, performance indicators (metrics) must be appointed according to the usability requirements.

Usability metrics are, generally, divided in objective and subjective metrics. Objective indicators are related to the effectiveness with the system; subjective indicators collect the user's opinion about the system. Both indicators can be used to evaluate VUI applications, but, usually, subjective indicators are collected by a questionnaire.

The most used usability metric in VUI applications is word error rate (WER); it is related to accuracy.

Surveying the literature (Walker; Passnneau; Boland, 2001; Möller, 2005; Larsen, 2003; Scholts; Consolvo, 2004), many works propose objective and subjective metrics to evaluate VUI and ubicomp applications. The objectives metrics are: Task completion time; Dialogue completion time; Mean user time; System response times; System Turns; User (Initiated) Turns; Total Turns; Word Error Rate (WER); Response latency; Response latency variance; Exact Scenario Completion; The number of "help" requests and barge-ins; The number of completed tasks and sub-tasks; The number of mean length of utterances; Time and turns used for confirmations; Degree and usage of different modalities; Time and number of turns used for error corrections.

On the other hand, subjective criteria are: User satisfaction; Cognitive load; User preferences; Task ease; User Expertise; Expected behavior; Social acceptance.

According to Alapetite, Boje and Morten (2009), commercially reported recognition rates are generally above 95%. Several factors contribute to these rates:

- Vocabulary affects speech recognition through its size and domain coverage. This way, large vocabularies with good domain coverage are interesting, because they make possible recognition of more words. On the other hand, small vocabularies increase the possibility of correct recognition. Small vocabularies are, however, mostly relevant for voice navigation;

- Speakers influence speech recognition rates by the clarity and consistency of pronunciation. Speaker-dependent systems have higher recognition rates than speaker-independent systems but require some training sessions and may be more sensitive to the background noise, microphone, voice (e.g., due to a cold) and atypical speakers, including non-natives, children and elderly.

- Noise can affect speech recognition in two ways: (a) It can cause alterations of speech signal, that can make it more difficult to distinguish the spoken words. (b) In noisy environments, people change their voice in an attempt to counter the distortion of the speech signal.

- All speech recognition systems are based on principles of statistical pattern matching. In spite of these similarities, each system can differ in their parameters of the speech signal, the acoustic model of each phoneme, and the language model used in predicting the words which are most likely to follow the preceding words. Thus, different systems can differ in recognition errors, even when they have similar recognition rates.

The set of issues pointed out in this section seems to us the main questions that must be observed by developers when designing VUI to ubiquitous applications. Next section shows the architecture of the application that we developed as a case study for evaluating VUIs in an ubiquitous context.

CASE STUDY

Description of the Application

A VUI electronic dictionary specifically for words that have computing context was made using an engine for voice recognition called Sphinx-4. This engine is a product created via a joint collaboration between the Sphinx group at Carnegie Mellon University, Sun Microsystems Laboratories, Mitsubishi Electric Research Labs (MERL), and Hewlett Packard (HP), with contributions from the University of California at Santa Cruz (UCSC) and the Massachusetts Institute of Technology (MIT) (Sphinx-4, 2008). It uses Hidden Markov models, which are statistical models. With this application, the user says a word, the system recognizes this word and reproduces the corresponding audio file - created by Text-To-Speech - with the correct definition e.g. meaning of the word (Braga, 2008). This application has English inputs and English outputs. The meanings of the technology terms were extracted from Tecnologia (2009).

Problems and Solutions about the Implementation of the Application

The implementation of the application described above could be resolved following two approaches:

1) Using an application running stand-alone in the mobiles;
    a. Advantages: quick access to the application with no charge for Internet access.
    b. Disadvantages: lack of tools and free libraries for developing of VUI applications for mobiles; non-uniformity of operational systems for mobiles.
2) Using a client-server architecture in which the mobile requests the recognition service from a Web Server.
    a. Advantages: it is not necessary to have a powerful mobile; availability of the tools and libraries for development of applications for desktops;
    b. Disadvantages: accesses the Internet for transmission of voice data, for every execution; delay between the service request and feedback.

The client-server architecture was chosen because of the problem with the stand-alone architectures: the lack of tools and free libraries for the development of VUI applications for mobile phone.

We used Java technology to develop the application. On the client side, it was developed a Midlet, and in the server side it was developed a Servlet application running on the Apache Tomcat. A MIDlet is a Java application framework for the Mobile Information Device Profile (MIDP) that is typically implemented on a Java-enabled cell phone or other embedded device or emulator. MIDlets are applications, such as games. Servlets are Java programming objects that dynamically process requests and construct responses. A Servlet is an object that receives a request and generates a response based on that request. The basic servlet package defines Java objects to represent servlet requests and responses, as well as objects to reflect the servlet's configuration parameters and execution environment. The Java Servlet API allows a software developer to add dynamic content to a Web server using the Java platform. The generated content is commonly HTML, but may be other data such as XML. The communication protocol used was GPRS (*General Packet Radio Service*), which is a packet oriented mobile data service available to users of the 2G cellular communication systems Global System for Mobile communications (GSM).

This chosen architecture can be visualized through the Figure 1.

Figure 1 shows an overview of the case study. On the mobile (client) the user says a word (1). The client transforms the voice into a wav file (2). Then, it sends the file to the server (3), which recognizes the speech (4) and sends back the word meaning (5).

Tests were done on a LG mobile, model KB775F SCARLET PHONE with the following set up: Quadri Band 3G (WCDMA Dual_Band), memory of 70MB. GPRS transmission protocol that is supported by this mobile phone is widely used, but was the application bottleneck.

The Figure 2 shows the application screen which shows the meaning of the word "firewall".

Figure 1. Case study overview

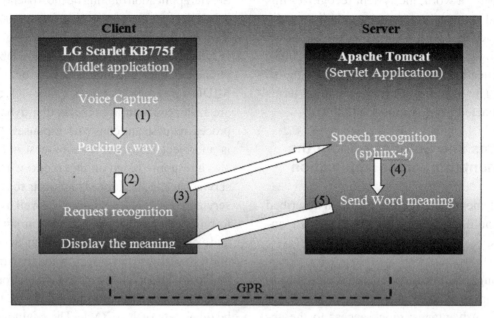

Figure 2. Meaning of "firewall"

Methodology of Evaluation

Two kinds of evaluation were used for this work, each one tested on the four scenarios described below: Heuristic Evaluation – made by three evaluators and Users Observation, with five users. The heuristic evaluation is generally used for detecting and fixing errors, before it is tested by the users.

Four scenarios were created for the test section:

1. user reads the words, but maybe (s)he does not know the right pronunciation. (S)he is in a quiet environment;
2. user is in a quiet environment (probably at home), but (s)he knows now the right pronunciation of each word;
3. user is on the street, (s)he needs to walk, to be aware of the cars and pedestrian;
4. user is driving.

The tests consisted, simply, on trying to find the meaning of ten computing-related words, such as: *cookie, desktop* and *firewall.* Evaluators and users are not native in English language; they have different degree of knowledge in English language and Computers. The words considered for this test were the same for the four scenarios.

The usability tests were carried out using VUI heuristics described in Table 1. This table was based on (Salvador; Oliveira Neto; Kawamoto; 2008).

Table 1. List of VUI Heuristics and severity (Salvador; Oliveira Neto; Kawamoto; 2008)

Heuristics	Severity	Comments
Naturalness of user's speech		
Output voice quality		
Input recognition adequacy		
Feedback adequacy		
Output phrasing adequacy		

The values of the requirements based on Nielsen´s severity degree (1993):

1. Usability catastrophe: it is imperative to fix this before the product can be released;
2. Major usability problem: it is important to fix, so it should be given high priority;
3. Minor usability problem: fixing this should be given low priority;

4. Cosmetic problem only: needs not to be fixed unless extra time is available on the project;
5. I don't agree that this is a usability problem at all.

Some objective and subjective metrics were used in order to analyze the ubiquitous applications using VUI (based on User Observation). Below, these metrics are listed, based on (Dybkjaer; Bernsen, 2001; Scholtz; Consolvo, 2004). The objective metrics were captured through parameters shown below (Table 2), while the subjective metrics were reached through questionnaire applied to users (Table 3).

EVALUATION OF THE RESULTS

The time needed to evaluate the application was about three minutes and fifty seconds for each scenario, because the application is very simple.

Table 2. Objective metrics for usability requirements to UA using VUI

Requirement	Metrics	Score
Input recognition adequacy	Percentage of times that the system could not understand the user input (voice).	
Output voice quality	Percentage of time that the user could not understand the system output	

Table 3. Subjective metrics for usability requirements to UA using VUI

Requirement	Guideline	Severity
Modality appropriateness	The developers should attempt to make sure that spoken input and output, possibly combined with other input/output modalities, are appropriate modal choices for the planned application	
Output phrasing adequacy	The system's answers to the user demands are clear and non-ambiguous	
	It is possible for the user to either use day-to-day vocabulary or adapt himself/herself to system's vocabulary	
Feedback adequacy	The system feedback is correct most of the time.	
Error handling adequacy	The system was able to manage the errors in a suitable way.	
Seamlessness	The system is always accessible when the user needs to access it	
Attention	Overhead	

Grades of severity range from 0 to 10: excellent (9-10), very good (8-9), good (7-8), regular (6-7), Bad (4-6), Very bad (below 4). For the attention requisite, the criteria are: low, medium and high.

Table 4. List of VUI Heuristics and severity

Heuristics	Severity	Comments
Naturalness of user's speech	4	interactions between users and system could be more frequent
Output voice quality	3	Some words were not understood. The TTS was not good enough
Input recognition adequacy	2	Variation in accents can influence the system. The users were non-native-english-speaking, so it is a problem
Feedback adequacy	4	If the system doesn't recognize the word, it displays a message to the user. It could give options to the user (hypothesis).
Output phrasing adequacy	5	The dictionary provides relevant information

Table 5. Score from objective metrics for usability requirements to UA using VUI

	Scenario 1	Scenario 2	Scenario 3	Scenario 4
Requirement	Score			
Input recognition adequacy	2.171	1.371	2.028	1,561
Output voice quality	1	1	1.2	1

Each word must be recognized in five attempts or less. Results are presented below:

- Lists of heuristic problems from the application. These three lists were condensed into one (Table 4).
- The score (average) of objective metrics of the five observed users (Table 5). The range of accepted values for Table 5 is between 0 and 5;
- The condensed results of subjective requirements collected through the questionnaire applied on the five users (Table 6).

Because the tests were made with non native speakers, the major problem was the heuristic (Input recognition adequacy).

The recognition system got better results when the users know how to speak the words perfectly. Furthermore, the results of the test in a silent and in a noisy environment were different. Users have trouble to hear the feedback voice of the system in a noise environment. By observation, we realized that people alter their voice in an attempt to

Table 6. Severity from subjective metrics for usability requirements to UA using VUI

Requirement	Severity
Modality appropriateness	7.6
Output phrasing adequacy	7
Naturalness of user's speech	8.1
Feedback adequacy	7.8
Error handling adequacy	6.5
Seamlessness	9

Attention was classified such as: low (scenario 1), medium (scenario 2), high (scenario 3) and high (scenario 4).

counter the distortion of the speech signal, in the presence of noise.

The system required more user attention when it was used in a noisy environment or when the user was performing other activities (e.g. driving a car). The users agreed that a voice system can return a word meaning faster than a graphical interface. When users are driving, the voice recognition rate decreased and the task completion time increased (about 20%).

The requirement "Error handling adequacy" had the worst classification, because the user just received "Sorry, I can't understand" by the system. As the system is an ubiquitous application, it must work in many different ways, such as by mobile keyboard.

The system didn't fail because the test area was covered by the cell network. But, connection problem of mobile and server could be happen if the users were in places such as the subway.

CONCLUSION

This chapter aimed to present the evaluation of ubiquitous VUIs applications. Ubiquitous applications projects require customized solutions. Consequently, the tests become extremely time and cost consuming. Because of this, it was not possible test these systems with a large number of users.

A specific evaluation plan was used to test the dictionary. It integrated inspection tests with observation of the users and a questionnaire. The literature provided the requirements and metrics to test the application.

The case study presented shows that voice recognition in mobile phone is restricted. Mobiles suffer from hardware and software limitations; and there are few existing software solutions. Java can be used to developed multiplatform applications, but the features have to be customized for each mobile model. Furthermore, the communication protocol (GPRS) used by the mobile used is limited. Developers who have been trying to work with VUI applications for mobiles have been facing these problems. To solve the protocol problem could be used a mobile device which supports Wi-fi. Severin (2005) used the device iPAQ Pocket PC h5500, which supports Wi-Fi, to developed a similar application (interface voice recognition). The mobility becomes restricted to a limited area, but the application performance improves.

The case study results showed that VUI can be used to build ubiquitous applications and that it must be customized to each problem. There are opportunities for future work. We plan to test other mobile devices, voice recognizers and applications.

Future work will involve the evaluation of different modalities, such as gestual, and devices in ubiquitous applications. Other issues in the development of ubiquitous system that should be considered further are: detailing the specification and prototyping phases, as well as, including more real scenarios to the evaluation context.

REFERENCES

Alapetite, A., Boje, A. H., & Morten, H. (2009). Acceptance of speech recognition by physicians: A survey of expectations, experiences, and social influence. *International Journal of Human-Computer Studies, 67*(1), 36–49. doi:10.1016/j.ijhcs.2008.08.004

Braga, D. (2008). *Algoritmos de Processamento da Linguagem Natural para Sistemas de Conversão Texto Fala em Português*. PhD Thesis, University of A Coruña, A Coruña, Spain.

Cox, R. V., Kamm, C. A., Rabiner, L. R., Schroeter, J., & Wilpon, J. G. (2000). Speech and language processing for next-millennium communications services. *Proceedings of the IEEE, 88*(8), 1314–1337. doi:10.1109/5.880086

Dettmer, R. (2003). It's good to talk [speech technology for on-line services access]. *IEE Review, 49*(6), 30–33. doi:10.1049/ir:20030603

Dybkjaer, L., & Bernsen, N. O. (2001). Usability Evaluation in Spoken Language Dialogue Systems. In *Proceedings of the ACL 2001 Workshop on Evaluation Methodologies for Language and Dialogue Systems*.

Gilbert, M., & Junlan, F. (2008). Speech and language processing over the web. *Signal Processing Magazine, IEEE, 25*(3), 18–28. doi:10.1109/MSP.2008.918410

Hee-Cheol, K. (2008). Weaknesses of Voice Interaction. In *Fourth International Conference on Networked Computing and Advanced Information Management, (NCM '08*. Hjelm, J. (2008). *Why IPTV?: interctivity, technologies and services.* Chichester, UK: Wiley.

Hunt, A. & Walker, W. (2000 June). *A fine Grained Component Architecture for Speech Application Development.* SUN Research, Project: SMLI TR-. 2000-86.

Juang, B. H. (2001). Ubiquitous speech communication interface. In *IEEE Workshop on Automatic Speech Recognition and Understanding,* (ASRU '01).

Kim, M. K., & Kim, H. C. (2007). *A Case Study on Usability of Asynchronous Voice Communication Systems.* Paper presented at the HCI International, Beijing, China.

Larsen, L. B. (2003). Issues in the evaluation of spoken dialogue systems using objective and subjective measures. In *Proceedings of IEEE Workshop on Automatic Speech Recognition and Understanding (ASRU'03)*, St. Thomas, U.S. Virgin Islands, USA, (pp. 209-214).

Möller, S. (2005). Quality of Telephone-based Spoken Dialogue Systems. New York: Springer.

Nielsen, J. (1993). Usability Enginnering. Cambridge, MA: Academic Press.

Salvador, V. F. M., Oliveira Neto, J. S., & Kawamoto, A. L. S. (2008). Requirement Engineering Contributions to Voice User Interface. In *Proceedings of First International Conference on Advances in Computer-Human Interaction, ACHI 2008*, (pp. 309-314).

Schltz, J., & Consolvo, S. (2004). *Towards a Discipline for Evaluating Ubiquitous Computing Applications.* Retrieved from http://www.seattle.intel-research.net/pubs/022520041200_232.pdf

Severin, J. (2005). *Speech Interface for a Mobile Audio Application.* Master of Science Thesis, KTH Information and Communication Technology-IMIT/LCN 2005-17, Stockholm, Sweden.

Shneiderman, B. (2000). Universal usability. *Commun. ACM 43*(5, May), 84-91.

Sphinx4. (2008). *Sphinx-4 A speech recognizer written entirely in the JavaTM programming language.* Retrieved July 2009, from http://cmusphinx.sourceforge.net/sphinx4/#what_is_sphinx4

Takami, K., Yamaguchi, T., & Unno, K. (2006). A study on the architecture and voice dialog scheme for a personal Web service in a ubiquitous communication environment. In *First International Conference on Communications and Electronics, ICCE '06.*

Tecnológica. (2009). Retrieved May 2009 from http://www.technologica.inf.br/glossario/exibe.asp

Walker, M. A., & Passnneau, R. (2001). Boland J.E. Quantitative and Qualitative Evaluation of Darpa Communicator Spoken Dialogue Systems. In *Proceedings of the 39rd Annual Meeting on Association for Computational Linguistics*, Toulouse, France.

Chapter 4
A Service for Improving the User Experience in WLANs and WPANs

Ricardo Augusto Rabelo Oliveira
Universidade Federal de Minas Gerais, Brasil

Antonio Alfredo F. Loureiro
Universidade Federal de Minas Gerais, Brasil

ABSTRACT

In this chapter is presented a framework to a service that acts as a middleware to the applications, providing the information about the wireless network context. The increasing use of wireless communications in mobile devices calls for a new level of resource management. Users with mobile devices accessing wireless hot spots are a commonplace, and, thus, their management is becoming more important.

1 INTRODUCTION

Quality of communication in wireless systems is heavily dependent on several factors including interference on the radio signal and mobility of the communicating devices. However, it is very difficult to assess the transmitted signal and predict when a bad quality signal is being caused by interference or mobility. The information about the network context is very important to achieve a better application performance. In a wireless network there is a huge variety of devices and communication protocols that demands a different programming approach than in a wired network. Also, mobile devices with multiple radio interfaces are becoming commonplace,

as a way to provide not only flexibility to select and access different wireless networks, but also to maintain the mobile user connectivity over wider areas of coverage. Currently, the most common radio technologies are Bluetooth, GPRS, UMTS, CDMA2000, IEEE 802.16, for metropolitan area networks, and IEEE 802.11 for local area coverage. A typical case of multiple radio use is a user with a mobile device who initially gets connected to the Internet via a 802.11b access network and, later on, switches the access network to a metropolitan area technology such as CDMA2000. Furthermore, over areas covered with multiple wireless networks, the user may switch, along the time, to the best access network based on different criteria such as connection cost, network state (e.g., channel quality,

DOI: 10.4018/978-1-61520-843-2.ch004

available bandwidth, network load), and application requirements.

The goal of this work is to design a service that communicates directly with the device drivers for monitoring and controlling resources using the information available at the wireless interface. The objective is to have a cross-layer solution for a middleware and applications that use the context information to improve the management and the user experience. The functionality of this service can be separated in two groups. The first one contains the information about the wireless card, such as the basic configuration and statistics about the link. The second one uses the measures done at the energy level of the received signal to describe the events that are happening at the wireless environment. The application uses a communication interface with this service, allowing an adaptation at the current network context.

Given a set of events at the wireless environment, we are interested in identifying mobility and interference, which cause a greater impact at the wireless communications. Over an estimated time interval, a statistical analysis of the energy level of the transmitted signal allows to identify these events associated with both the device mobility and the interference that happen at the communication. The distinction between mobility and interference is possible due to a several types of effects that affect the signal energy level wcp.

The first step in this process is the definition of the metrics to measure the communication quality and what type of impact is caused by these events. These metrics describe the relation between the energy level of the received signal and the integrity of the transmitted data. Considering the communication frame as the basic unit of the data communication, the irradiated frame is identified at the receiver if the energy level of the signal is above a threshold that allows its correct reception at the wireless interface.

Variations of the communication quality have different impacts on the application performance. The wireless interfaces have different strategies to deal with the damaged frames. For example, apply the ARQ mechanism for an automatic retransmission. But when the number of retransmissions increases, the energy consumption and the delay experienced for the upper communication layers also increase, making it prohibitive for some types of devices or applications.

The total loss of communication is an extreme case, but there are effects of the communication quality that affects the application performance. The following metrics identify these effects:

- The maximum speed capacity of the wireless interface, due to the channel conditions. Depending on the environment conditions, the wireless interface changes the rate by selecting another modem;
- The effective throughput seen by the application during the communication. It takes into account the overhead caused by the excessive number of retransmissions and by the control information from the network protocols;
- Measures the impact along the time caused by the successive retransmissions and the changes at the wireless interfaces;
- The variation of the delay, which has the impact maximized when the wireless channel is affected by a great variability of the communication quality.

These metrics are parameterized by the communication quality of the wireless channel, so even they are the same of the wired network, the influence of the wireless channel has a greater impact over them.

To measure the impact of the communication quality, the receiver signal strength indicator (RSSI) is used. This information is collected at the time of the frame reception. The fluctuations of this value are modeled as a stochastic process with a superimposition of the signal fading effects (Suzuki, 1997). In this work, we apply the

Figure 1. Power Transmission Increase under mobility

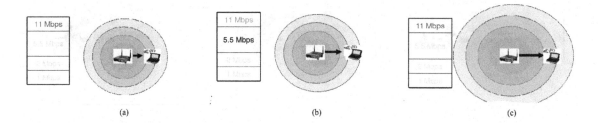

statistical process control theory associated with a multi-resolution analysis with wavelets.

Two of the most popular wireless technologies in mobile computing are used: *Wireless Personal Area Networks* (WPANs) (IEEE 802.15, 2008), and *Wireless Local Area Networks* (WLANs) (IEEE 802.11, 2008). Among all existing protocols for wireless communication we have chosen to work with two of them as they represent the *de facto* standards for WLANs and WPANs: IEEE 802.11 (IEEE 802.11, 2008) and Bluetooth (SIG, 2003), respectively.

1.1 User Experience and Management

Due to the problems of the communication quality, a strategy to mitigate its impact is to provide to the user the information about what is happening. This is a common place in other types of wireless communications. For example, the cell phone has a beep that alerts the user about its low battery. If the cell phone just stops working without any warning, the user will not know if it is because of the battery or any different problem. With the correct information, the user may change the conversation. This type of information is also necessary in the data wireless communication, and even considering the presence of VoIP applications, which are strongly dependent of the communication quality.

Some wireless interfaces have default parameters that reconfigure the interface in presence of different events at the wireless channel. For example, the IEEE 802.11 specification defines several MAC parameters to tune the wireless communication according to the environment conditions. The rate selection changes the speed observing the conditions of the wireless channel. The adjustment is performed with the focus to maintain the connection, selecting lower speed modems, which have a more robust reception. On the other hand, in some cases the user may just want the best speed, without worrying if the connection will be lost. Other interfaces use the automatic roaming strategy, which disconnects the device from the Access Point if the signal level decreases to some value below a threshold and starts to look for another access point. But, some common strategies for interface reconfiguration not works in all the cases. Considering the common sense of increase the power transmission in case of speed decrease. Consider a solution where the mobile client send a feedback about the speed decrease to the access point, allowing it to increase the power transmission. The Figure 1 shows the case where the user is moving away from the access point. The signal strength is showed at the green color pattern, where the more dark colors indicates more power at the transmitted signal. The movement starts at the Figure 1, where the modem speed is working at [11]MBps. Figure 1 shows the speed decreasing due the signal fading. Figure 1 shows the use of the increased power transmission strategy, which allows the receiver use a faster modem. But in another scenario, with

Figure 2. Power Transmission Increase under interference

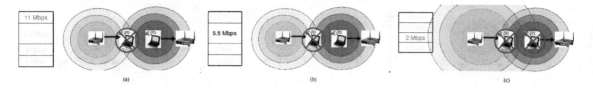

interference, showed at Figure 2, the same strategy maybe not work. Figure 2 shows the impact of the interference over the receiver. In this case the interference do not happens at the access point. The receiver gets a low quality signal, making the speed decrease, as showed at Figure 2. In this case the power increase transmission strategy, not even possibilities an increase at the speed, but also can generate more interference in another nearby networks.

To increase the user experience, the proposed system makes available the information about what is happening at the environment to the user and/or application. This is done by an interface that alerts the user about the behavior of the wireless channel, like message boxes or desktop gadgets alerts at the mobile device interface. With this information, the user and/or applications can deal with the different aspects of the channel.

Consider the following scenario: a user in the office has a VoIP application in a PDA over IEEE802.11g. In that office, there are three different access points (APs), each one available at a different channel (1, 6 and 11). The user is connected to one of the access points using channel 1 and frequency of [2.410]GHz, and starts walking around the office. The power transmission of this access point is good enough to reach the entire area where the user walks. But at the same area, there is another person who uses a cordless phone, which works at the frequency of [2.410]GHz. If the user walks nearby this person, he/she will experience a strong interference, and the VoIP application will get a bad communication quality, with a high jitter. If the user does not know the

problem is due to the interference with the cordless phone, he/she will think that the access point has a weak signal level. But if the user knows that, he/she can walk away from that area, or change the access point, re-connecting to another AP with a different channel.

The importance to deal with the effects of the events is the need to identify when a wireless interface switches between modes, and how to deal with border conditions. When the wireless interface identifies low levels of signal strength, it uses the rate fall-back to select the appropriated modem. So the ideal throughput changes according to the signal level. In the case of interference, these changes occur more intensively, increasing the variation of delay, since the rate changes all the time. In the case of mobility, when the mobile device is moving away from the access point, the rate will change more slowly. This kind of information, when provided to the user, may allow the user to change the configuration of the wireless interface, like increase or decrease the power transmission. This decision can be done according to the device restrictions and the requirements of the application.

The rest of this chapter is organized as followed. Section 2 presents a brief description of the several proposals related to service development and statistical control for event identification. Section 3 describes the wireless channel, identifies its main aspects and proposes a model. Section 4 presents the requirements and the architecture of the proposed service. Section 5 describes the statistical control chart methodology applied to gather the context information. Section 6 shows some applications and tests of this service and, finally, Section 7 presents our conclusions.

2 RELATED WORK

This section shows some relevant work in this type of adaptation and management. Glenn2005 proposes a self-management strategy for dealing with the interference in an outdoor WLAN, considering an unplanned deployment of the access points. This type of deployment is very common, and the proposed management adapts the rate and the power control in order to reduce the overall interference. From the user experience, the users lacks of information about all the process, and all the users are treated equally. There is cases, where the access point is not under interference, but one or more users are. For example, considering an indoor scenario, an user can be under the interference of a cordless phone, bluetooth device or another ad-hoc device which not affect the access point. The system wide solution do not achieve a good result for this user.

(Mhatre, Papagiannaki & Baccelli, 2007) proposes a distributed algorithm for adjust the power control of access points in a high density WLAN to mitigate the interference. The work prove the need to use a cross-layer approach, over the MAC parameters and behavior to adjust a correct power control, without cause starvation in any client. Using the Clear Channel Assessment threshold as metric, the optimization of the transmit power is made, increasing the overall user throughput.

In most cases the strategies to achieve a better performance in wireless communications use the adaptation of communication. The adaptation can be done over the transmitted data, like compression, or over the functionality of the applications, like adjusting the access to the wireless channel. (Chakraborty, Yau & Lui, 2006) study the mobility pattern in a wireless network to allow an efficient use of the battery for the wireless communication, avoiding unnecessary transmissions. (Kim, Hou & Lim, 2006) collect the information about the wireless channel at the physical and link layers in an IEEE 802.11 network card, in order to have a better adaptation. (Narasimhan & Cox, 2000) estimate the mobility speed with an investigation over the wireless channel. The work proposes a technique that analyzes the signal level variation and estimates the mobility speed between a device and a base station. (Calafate & Manzoni, 2003) propose an API for communication that extends some functionalities of the API for Windows and Windows CE. The goal is to have a generic API, allowing a multi-platform programming platform and extract less information from the wireless interfaces.

(BlipNet, n.d.) proposes an integrated API for Bluetooth, where an element defined as BlipServer is connected to an Ethernet network and to several elements BlipNodes (mobile and communicating devices). These devices have Bluetooth interfaces and collect information about other elements that desire to connect to them. BlipServer collects information about these devices and provides a programming API, written in J2ME, for applications to control connections originating at BlipNodes. In this way, it is possible to coordinate the access to the fixed network and to Internet services, according to their characteristics. This API works both in Linux and Windows.

Many studies also address problems such as identifying events and responding accordingly to them. (Sheth & Han, 2003) propose an algorithm to reduce energy consumption in an infrastructured 802.11 WLAN, in which transmission power is controlled to save energy in scenarios with mobility or signal noise. Also the wireless interface is selectively deactivated when there is no established communication. Information about mobility patterns can be obtained through continuous assessment of the signal strength and may help base stations to predict the localization of mobile devices in advance. i (Chen & Kobayashi, 2002) study the behavior of communication patterns in an indoor environment using an 802.11

WLAN as testbed. (Nilsson, Hallberg & Synnes, 2003) perform a similar study but using Bluetooth. (Nordstrom, 2002) develops a system to measure and evaluate the performance of several routing algorithms in ad hoc networks (MANETs). As a result, it is provided information about the signal strength fluctuation of the communication channel in different scenarios.

Interference in wireless environments can happen if at least two different technologies use the same frequency channel at the same time. (Fainberg & Goodman, 2001) and (Jung-Hyuck & Jayant, 2003) present studies about Bluetooth and 802.11 mutual interference. They also propose and evaluate solutions to this problem. Recently, developers of both technologies have proposed their own solutions for mitigating the interference impact on communication.

In most cases the strategies to achieve a better performance in wireless communications uses some sort of adaptation. The adaptation can be done over the transmitted data, like compression, or over the functionality of the applications, like adjusting the access to the wireless channel. (Yu, 2004) applies a cross-layer technique to an ad hoc network to adapt the TCP protocol according to the loss of ACK packets. The mobility is modeled as a connection loss between the devices and the results show an improvement of the performance. (Chakraborty, Yau & Lui, 2006) study the mobility pattern in a wireless network to allow an efficient use of the battery at the wireless communication, avoiding unnecessary transmissions. The application controls the transmission, according to the distance between the transmitter and the receiver. The study evaluates some heuristics for the mobility analysis, estimating an optimal relation between the sending time and the energy consumption. The results show the importance of this adaptation for increasing the battery lifetime. (Kim, Hou & Lim, 2006) collect the information about the wireless channel at the physical and link layers in an IEEE 802.11 network card to have a better adaptation. Using the measures of power transmission and

sensibility levels, they estimate the transmission rate. According to the reconfiguration capacity of the network card, and the noise level, they adjust the transmission power and the sensibility level to achieve a better rate.

At this point, it is possible to identify the importance of the use of the correct information for an efficient adaptation. (Kim & Noble, 2001) estimate the communication quality under the mobility effects using a statistical process control. Assuming that the bandwidth changes according to the device mobility, the study investigates the use of the Exponentially Weighted Moving Average (EWMA) and proposes a new type of EWMA, called FlipFlop-EWMA. (Narasimhan & Cox, 2000) estimate the mobility speed with an investigation over the wireless channel. The work proposes a technique that analyzes the signal level variation and estimates the mobility speed between a device and a base station. When the device is stationary, the signal level variation is described by the lognormal distribution, and under mobility, the signal level is described by the Rayleigh distribution. The mobility causes a doppler spread over the signal, and using a wavelets transform, the speed can be identified. It uses the wavelets daubechies and coiflets, but the latter provides the best results.

(Jeong & Lu, 2003) propose a methodology to allow the control and monitoring of complex data based on the concept of multi-resolution analysis. The methodology was applied to an industrial process of wireless antennas production, verifying if manufactured antennas were functioning properly. The statistical process control was performed using the wavelets coefficients. (Ganesan, Das & Venkataraman, 2004) describe a general vision of the multi-scale statistical process control using wavelets associated with statistical process control to investigate an industrial process. The work explores the main points and features of the data auto-correlation and enumerates the main methods of applying multi-scale statistical process control to this type of data, but none of them could be used in an online system. (Arad-hye, Bakshi, Strauss & Davis, 2003) present a study comparing a multi-scale statistical process control using wavelets to several other classic statistical process controls. Their results show that only MCEWMA control chart outperforms the multi-scale statistical process control, which only happened because the verified process was easily modeled by a temporal series.

3 WIRELESS PROPAGATION MODEL

The model presented here considers a general propagation model and discusses its adequacy for commercial wireless cards. In general wireless communications, the signal propagation can be described by two fading models, namely the *Large Scale Fading* and the *Small Scale Fading*.

Large scale fading model is based on theoretical and experimental analysis that associate the distance between the transmitter and the receiver with the signal fading. It considers that it follows a lognormal distribution wcp, characterized by the density

$$f_{in}(r) = \frac{1}{\sqrt{2\pi}\eta r} \exp\left\{-\frac{(\ln r - v)^2}{2\eta^2}\right\},$$

where $r > 0$ is the distance and $v \in \mathbb{R}$ and $\eta > 0$ are parameters.

Small scale fading is used to describe fast signal amplitude variation over a short time span due to external factors, mainly the multipath effect associated to the scattering of the transmitted signal. The Rayleigh distribution is frequently used for modeling such behavior in the case of no line of sight between the transmitter and the receiver. The Rayleigh distribution is characterized by the density

$$f_R(r) = \frac{r}{\xi} \exp\left\{-\frac{r^2}{2\xi^2}\right\},$$

with $r > 0$ the distance and $\xi > 0$ a scale parameter.

In a joint analysis, the Suzuki distribution, which is a multiplicative model resulting from the above two models, is able to model signal propagation. It is characterized by the density

$$f_s(r) = \int_0^\infty \frac{1}{y} f_R(r/y) f_{LN}(y) dy.$$

The Suzuki distribution becomes the lognormal distribution when describing the long term signal fading, without the scattering effect from the surround objects. When this latter scattering effect is predominant, the Suzuki law becomes the Rayleigh distribution.

PLewma use a propagation model for the prediction of signal trends, by associating trend with the long term variation of the path loss only and thus by ignoring small scale fading. This approach may be unrealistic in real scenarios, since important aspects of the scattering effect are ignored. homenet show that there is no strong correlation between the distance and the received signal quality in home and office wireless networks, which are common indoor scenarios. This is due to the scattering effect that dominate propagation in such environments.

Wireless channel quality is defined by the transmitted frame and its relationship with the effects that actuate on the transmitted signal. The transmitted frame is a sequence of bits that form the data, the header and the preamble of the frame. At the IEEE 802.11b/g interface, the received signal level allows the correct reconstruction of the transmitted frame, but the signal level at the wireless interface, indicated by the receive signal strength indicator, is the level of the last received frame. It can be measured only after the frame reception is complete. The IEEE 802.11 communication protocol defines a mechanism for determining the strength of the received signal directly in the circuit of the wireless communication interface. This parameter, an unsigned integer of size 1 byte

Table 1. Transmission rate and time for Bluetooth

Packet type	Maximal transmission rate (kbps))	Transmission time (μs)
DM1	108.8	625
DH1	172.8	625
DM3	387.2	1875
DH3	585.6	1875
DM5	477.8	3125
DH5	723.2	3125

called RSSI, measured in dBm. Another important measure defined by the IEEE 802.11 protocol is the signal quality, which defines how good the received signal is at the moment of a reception operation. This metric also varies according to each implementation. Some manufacturers use the signal/noise ratio whereas others use the amount of received beacons.

Bluetooth operates in the [2.4]GHz frequency band and utilizes Frequency Hopping Spread Spectrum (FHSS) technology. Devices can communicate up to distances of about 30 feet within the same room. Throughput depends on many factors and depends on which packet type is used. Table 1 relates maximal transmission rate according to each packet type for Bluetooth.

The Bluetooth specification defines its own metric to evaluate signal quality and has a different way to extract information about signal level from the wireless interface. In Bluetooth, the signal quality is proportional to the distance between elements. The provided RSSI is a function of both the received signal level and a predefined table, called *Golden Receiver Power Rank*.

The Bluetooth protocol specification also defines a set of commands, implemented on the *Host Controller Interface* (HCI) layer, that is used by the device driver to access data from the wireless interface. Two commands related to signal quality are:

- *HCI_ReadQualityInfo:* this command returns quality of the communication channel established between the local device and a remote unit. Returned values may range from 0 to 255. The way this metric is calculated depends on each manufacturer implementation and it may be based on throughput or bandwidth.

- *HCI_ReadRSSI:* this command reads the RSSI level. If communication of two elements falls inside the *Golden Range*, this function returns value 0. Otherwise, it returns values from −1 to −127 if the receiver is very far from its communicating peer or values from 1 to 128 if they are too close or a signal overload is detected in the reception.

At the investigation of the communication quality, other factor must be considered. For instance, at the MAC level of the IEEE 802.11 protocol, (Bianchi, Di Stefano, Giaconia, Scalia,, Terrazzino & Tinnirello, 2007) already identified the differences of the implementation over the backoff process. Here we add that the proprietary implementation of each wireless interface chipset vendor generates a specific received signal strength indicator range and granularity of values; this lack of uniformity makes the identification of the correct fading distribution difficult. Nevertheless, due to the temporal correlation between the sampled measures, the impact of the events is preserved.

Considering indoor scenarios and the IEEE 802.11b/g wireless interface, the mobility and interference effects as a specific profile can be described as follows:

- **Mobility:** While moving, the user receives different signal levels at the wireless interface. These signal variations are associated to the speed and to the multipath fading caused by the environment. From the application point of view, this will yield different levels of frame reception that affect the overall performance. (Narasimhan & Cox, 1999) use this signal variation to estimate the mobile speed. In our work we consider the indoor environment due to the limited mobile speed, with the objective to achieve a better description and distinguish from the signal variation caused by interference.

- **Interference:** Common types of indoor interference are, for instance:

  (a) **Cordless phone interference:** Cordless phones use a single channel to send the voice, and it is constantly busy when the phone is being used. High levels of energy are used to achieve good quality, and some cordless phones are able to change the channel in order to avoid interference.

  (b) **Bluetooth interference:** Bluetooth uses frequency hopping to minimize the use of interfering channels. It was created with focus in preserving battery life, therefore it does not send high energy signals. The degrading effect of Bluetooth interference over IEEE 802.11b/g communication is well known.

  (c) **IEEE 802.11 interference:** Interference from IEEE 802.11b/g can be classified in co-channel interference, where the access points uses overlapped channels, and direct interference, when the access points use the same channel.

3.1 Channel Model

Considering as events the presence of mobility and interference, the first step to model the wireless channel is the definition of the time correlation. Assuming a sequence of events or measures that are dependent when observed in a short time interval, it is possible to establish a temporal dependence among them. The duration of this interval is defined by the capacity to sample the measures of the events features, as the signal fading. The measures we consider here are the receiver signal strength, collected at an Intel 2200BG card. Considering that Beacon frames are sent in an interval of [100]ms, and the data frames in a small interval, these measures occur at a time interval of [10]ms. This is small enough to indicate the presence of mobility or interference without affecting the performance of the system, since smaller intervals generate an intensive use of the wireless interface. Also, even if the interference is high enough to destroy the packets, the method deals with quality degradation before total loss of communication. In the case of an interference strong enough to cause a connection loss, this is easily detected with an error code generated by the wireless card at the RSSI (Receiver Signal Strength Indicator) measure, causing a sharp measure transition. It is then possible to assume that the measures are autocorrelated, as discussed in (Graziosi & Santucci, 2002).

Considering I as a indication of the interference event, the RSSI can be described as:

$$RSSI = \begin{cases} SNR + Noise & if I = 0, \\ SNR + SINR & if I = 1 \end{cases}$$

where SNR follows the fading models described in the previous Section and SNIR is the interference component, which depends on the type of interference.

3.2 Wireless Environment and Communication Quality

In order to validate the variation at the RSSI measures over the communication quality, we performed experiments investigating the impact of the presence of mobility and interference. We defined two set of experiments. The first set was used to show the effects of mobility and interference over the signal variation. The second set

Figure 3. Access point distribution

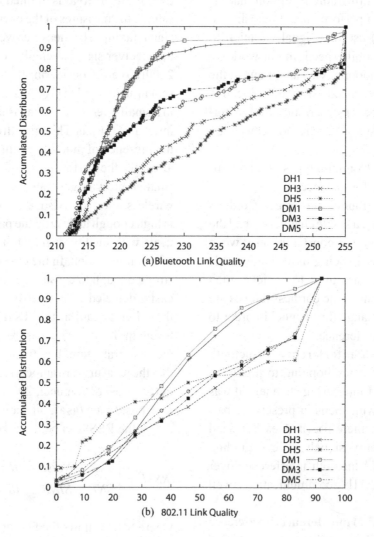

(a) Bluetooth Link Quality

(b) 802.11 Link Quality

we investigated the presence of mobility and interference over the modem speed of the IEEE 802.11 interfaces. All the tests were conducted in an area with Cisco Aironet 1242 and Aironet 1131 access points, located as shown in Figure 3. The color pattern shows the signal strength, from the higher levels, showed at the yellow color regions, to the absence of signal, showed at the blue color regions. We used a Vaio Notebook with Intel Pentium IV processor ([1500]MHz clock and [512] Mb memory), running both Suse Linux (kernel 2.6.14) and Windows XP SP2, and a desktop with Pentium IV processor ([1500]MHz clock and

[512]Mb memory). The 802.11 wireless interfaces used a PCMCIA card from Interlink, with chipset Prism I and a IPW2200 chipset at the notebook. Bluetooth was provided by an Ericsson development kit: interface cards with chipsets ROK 101 007 and ROK 101 008 and a USB-Bluetooth interface from TDK, with chipset Bluecore from Cambridge Silicon Systems. Two access points were used, one from Widcomm for Bluetooth (Bluegate 2100), and the other for 802.11 which used a PCMCIA card from Wavelan.

Considering that the Beacon frames are sent with at intervals of [100]ms, and the data frames in a small interval, these measures occur at [10] ms intervals. This is small enough to indicate the presence of mobility or of interference without affecting the performance of the system; smaller intervals make intensive use of the wireless interface. Also, even if the interference is strong enough to destroy the packets, the method deals with quality degradation before the total loss of communication.

In our first set of experiment, we investigate the presence of mobility and interference over the signal level, measured at the wireless interfaces.

In the first experiment, we started an FTP application on 802.11 and then a CBR traffic on Bluetooth. When both traffics are active, it is possible to observe a decrease on signal quality values of Bluetooth and 802.11 related to the mutual interference.

Figures 3 and 3 demonstrate the effect of using these different packet types on the signal quality observed on both channels when submitted to the same traffic before. These figures represent the accumulated distribution of values in each experiment. In Figure 3, packet types DH1 and DM1 are the ones for which more low values are generated: 90% of all observed values are below 231 for DH1 and 227 for DM1. Packet type DH5 is the one with better distribution of acceptable values for communication (between 200 and 255). This behavior also impacts 802.11 channel. In Figure 3, packet types DM1 and DH1 are the ones that most degrade 802.11 signal quality and DH5 is the one that least impact the other channel. This is a good result because, besides being the one with the highest transmission rate, packet type DH5 is the one that least degrades performance of both Bluetooth and 802.11 channels. It is extremely important to understand the effect of different types of traffic and configuration on several scenarios of communication so we can define politics to access a shared medium. In our case, we could demand a fast change to DH5 packet type on Bluetooth if we observe a traffic like the one used in our experiment.

The next experiment, we analyzed the effects of some results obtained during assessment of 802.11 and Bluetooth channels under the presence of mobility. All displacements were done at approximately [0.5]m/s, an acceptable speed for a user walking and using his mobile device at the same time (human mobility still is a research topic; see, for instance, (González, Hidalgo & Barabási, 2008)).

Figure 6 represents the signal quality and RSSI measures of Bluetooth when the mobile device moves towards the communication point. Figure 5 shows the signal quality measures and Figure 5 shows the RSSI measures during this experiment. For Bluetooth, is showed that signal strength jumps to a high value suddenly, indicating the moment when the mobile device enter the zone known as *Golden Range*. It is clear that the behavior of signal quality and signal strength for mobility is completely different from those presented by interference, which is a good start to define politics that need to distinguish these two kinds of events.

Figure 5 shows the RSSI measured at an IEEE 802.11g interface. Until the moment 90 seconds, the user is nearby the access point. From the time 90 to 110, he walks away from the access point and stops, turning back at the moment 260. From the time interval 110 to 140 seconds, the signal level achieves the lower level, due to multipath effects. Even when walking in a constant speed, the multipath turns difficult to establish the correct distance. But the impact over the communication can be seen, since when achieves the signal level of [−91]dBM, the interface can change its max rate, due to the frame loss. From the application point of view, the interval from 110 to 140 seconds is a worst case of connection, even that point the movimentation is over.

We stated that performance and quality of 802.11 and Bluetooth channels are minimized when we use packet types DM1 and DH1 in Bluetooth, if both channels are communication at the same time. This result could lead to a in-

Figure 4. Accumulated distribution of signal quality on both channels (802.11 with transmission rate of 1Mbps)

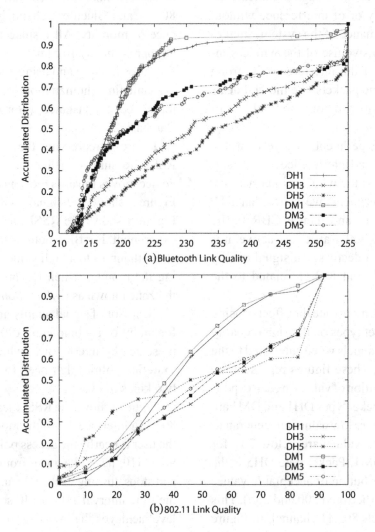

Figure 5. RSSI measures: User walking

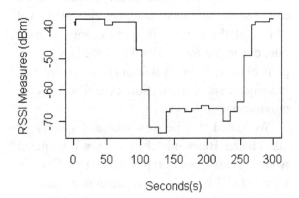

discriminately use of packet type DH5 or other close to that for data transference. However, using packet types DH1 and DM1 is indicated when we wish to sustain the connection longer because they are more robust to losses of connection than other types. Figure 7 represents Bluetooth signal quality when the mobile device moves away from the communication point. It is possible to notice that packet types DM1 and DH1 have a better support for lower levels of signal quality, maintaining the connection alive longer. In this experiment, for packet types DH5 and DM5 the connection was

Figure 6. RSSI and signal quality measures for Bluetooth interface when the mobile device moves towards the communication point

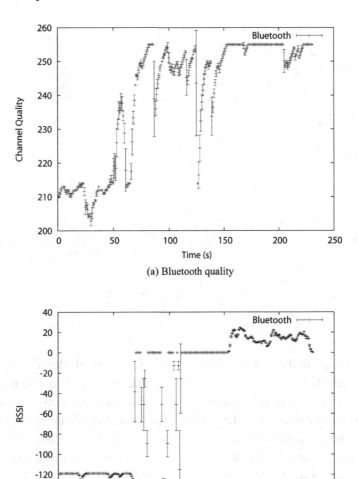

(a) Bluetooth quality

(b) Bluetooth RSSL

lost between 10 to 15 meters of distance from the communication point; for DH1 and DM1 the connection was lost after 20m.

At the second set of experiments, we investigated the impact of the presence of mobility and interference over the modem speed of the IEEE 802.11 interfaces.

The first scenario was done with mobility in a region without interference. Figure 7 shows

the RSSI measures, with variations proportional to the displacement that exhibit an increase at instant 1000. Figure 7 shows the percentage use of the wireless cards velocity. For each velocity a modem is chosen according to the implementation of the auto-rate fallback algorithm of the wireless card. Even though the auto-rate fallback algorithm does not depend only on the RSSI variation, is

Figure 7. Signal quality for Bluetooth when the mobile device moves away from the communication point for all 6 packet types

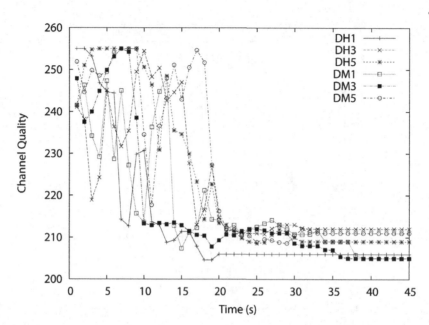

possible to infer the change in the distance and how it affects modem selection.

The second scenario includes direct interference produced by an access point. The device was connected to the access point channel 11, in room 3027 (see Figure 3), and another access point using the same channel was started shortly after. Figure 8 shows the signal variation under this effect, while Figure 8 shows the modem usage at the wireless interface. Notice the oscillation of the auto-rate fallback algorithm, which chooses different modems in a small time interval.

The third scenario shows a common situation of user mobility under interference. The mobile device was connected to the access point at channel 11 and moves near another access point with the same channel but in a different network. Figure 9 shows the signal variation, while Figure 9 shows intensive modem change at the wireless card.

Considering the time dependence at the sample rate, the wireless channel is described as a non-linear, non-Gaussian non-stationary time series, denoted here by $X(t)$. The events presented at the wireless channel affect this time series changing its regime, with shifts on the mean and variance.

The presence of mobility alters the mean as a function of the distance variation, and during the time when this happens it also shifts the variance. This causes a localized transition effect and, according to (Narasimhan & Cox, 2000), it can also be used to describe mobility speed. Both events cause very specific transition effects, which constitute the most salient feature of this model.

A proper description of these events should consider that the time series of measures has varying parameters, such as correlation structure, mean, variance and even probability distribution. Each set of parameters is usually called a 'mode' or a 'regime'.

Usual statistical tests require lots of data in order to achieve certain significance levels, which may introduce delays in the detection of events. In order to achieve an acceptable time for the user centric management, the proposed technique uses sequential data processing, which associates the wavelet multi-resolution analysis, for decom-

Figure 8. RSSI variation and wireless card speed - mobility

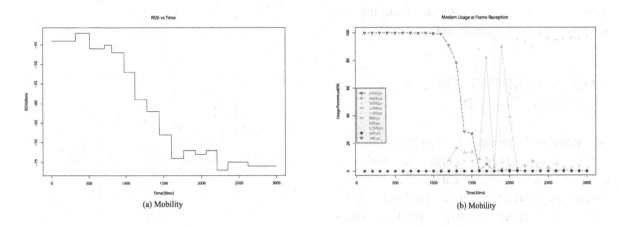

(a) Mobility   (b) Mobility

Figure 9. RSSI variation and wireless card speed - interference

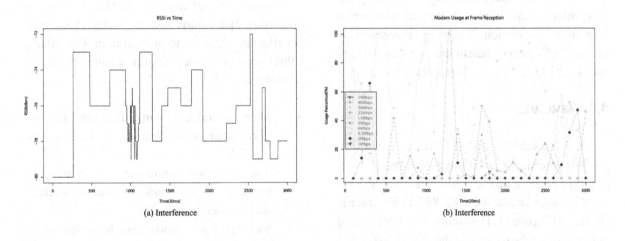

(a) Interference   (b) Interference

Figure 10. RSSI variation and wireless card speed - mobility and interference

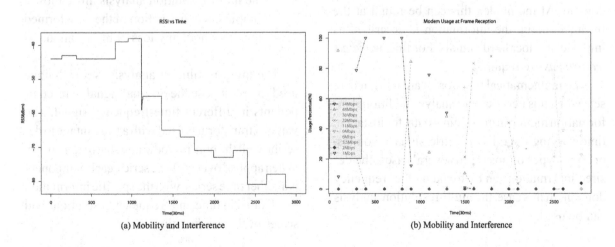

(a) Mobility and Interference   (b) Mobility and Interference

posing the series into time and frequency, with a control chart, which is a statistical tool used to identify regime changes in time series.

4 MULTI SCALE STATISTICAL PROCESS CONTROL

According to the model described in Section 3.1, the detection of a regime change in the nonlinear time series is a strong indication of a change in the events that affect the wireless environment. As pointed by (Tzagkarakis, Papadopouli & Tsaka-lides, 2007), the use of the well-know solution of the exponential weighted moving average is not adequate for identifying high order frequen-cies, since its smoothing effect tends to suppress important information. To perform this detection in an effective and efficient manner, our strategy uses multi scale statistical process control.

4.1 Wavelets

The multi-resolution analysis is necessary in situ-ations where higher variability achieves high level of auto-correlation. The auto-correlation level at the RSSI measures at the IEEE 802.11 interface is showed at Figure 11. The control chart developed here can describe the data at the time domain, but the high level of correlation with non-stationary features needs to be investigated at the frequency domain. At the model, this can be found at the In this domain, the information is described as impulse and localized signals. For this, *wavelets transforms* are required.

The mathematical transforms are used in data sets when it is necessary to analyze additional in-formation hidden in the original data, for instance, time varying data, like electric signals, sounds, or some types of noises. In several cases, the de-sired information can be found on the frequency domain. In this case, the multi-resolution analysis can be used.

Figure 11. Auto-correlation of the RSSI measures, mobility scenario

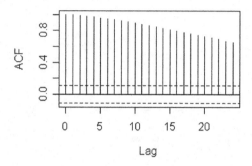

The concept of multi-resolution analysis is based on the possibility to study the data at different levels of resolution and precision. In (Ganeshan, 2002), some properties of multi-resolution analysis are enumerated:

- Data description in different resolu-tions must contain as less redundancy as possible;
- The filter used in multi-resolution analysis has to allow a complete coverage in time and frequency domains;
- Relevant information must be better repre-sented at multi-resolution analysis than in the original data;
- The multi-resolution analysis must allow a complete reconstruction of the transformed signal, without any loss of information.

The multi-resolution analysis is a technique used to decompose the original signal in its com-ponents in different time-frequency signal. The wavelet transform is used with an advantage to de-scribe well the non-periodic and sharp transitions. When applied over the time series, each component is another time series, with the specific information localized in time and frequency resolutions and scales of the original time series.

Figure 12. Wavelet transform

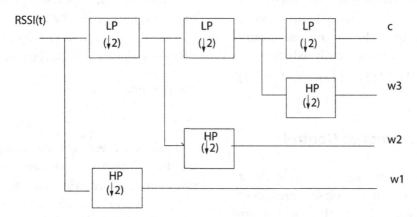

Wavelets are used to characterize the events at the measured time series by the impact of these events on the signal energy. This spectral feature of the wavelets associated with the statistical process control promotes the identification of such events.

Wavelet transforms are apt to describe non-periodic and sharp transitions. When applied to the time series, each component becomes a new time series, with the specific information localized in time and frequency resolutions of the original time series. (Long & Sikdar, 2007) suggest that the scale invariant property of the fast fading can be described by the wavelet decomposition into appropriate sub-bands, but due to the stochastic nature of the wireless channel and the effects of the interference the precision of this analysis needs a large amount of data becoming, thus, prohibitive for our application. The choice of a correct wavelet basis may allow a multi-resolution analysis that describes better these data; it also needs to be associated to a temporal framework for identifying these fluctuations.

Our work is not concentrated in identifying the changes of the fading, since its original behavior is directly related to the commercial wireless card, but on the events that generate such changes.

The orthonormal basis that define the wavelet transform produce a multi-resolution analysis decomposing the original time series in its com-

ponents. The wavelet transform of a time series $X(t)$ is the result of applying a sequence of filtering process applied on the data, as described in Figure 12. Each LP block is a low pass filter form a wavelet base, while HP blocks are high pass filters. Low frequencies components are also called 'approximation coefficients', and high frequency components are termed 'detail coefficients' or 'wavelet coefficients'. More details can be seen, among other references, in the book by (Mallat, 1986).

The final result is stored in the vector $w = \left(c_{0,0}, w_{0,0}, \ldots, w_{n-1,2^{n-1}-1} \right)$, which contains the all the wavelets coefficients w and the approximation coefficients c, where n is the number of levels of the wavelet transform. The coefficients are denoted $w_{k,2^{i-1}}$, where $k,i \in \mathbb{N}$, $1 < i < n$, $1 < k < 2^{i-1}$ and each level i contains 2^i elements. The last item is $w_{0,0}$ and it contains one element, while $c_{0,0}$ is the last scale version. The first order statistic of each item is $E(i) = \sum_{k=0}^{2^i - 1} w_{i,k}^2$. We adopt morettin's (Chiann & Morettin, 1998) definition of scalogram as the vector of energies of size n given by $E = \left[c_{0,0}^2; E(1); E(2); E(3); \ldots; E(n-1) \right]$.

The shifts in the mean and the variance can be identified at the energy levels of the scalogram, according to the intensity and moment of the transitions. Another important issue is that the nature of the transitions can also be identified by the modulus of the coefficients, according to the increase or decrease of the sharp transitions over the time series values. The positive and negative values of each sub-space are analyzed using vector $M = \left[c_{0,0}; M\left(1\right); M\left(2\right); M\left(3\right); \ldots; M\left(n-1\right)\right]$ with $M\left(i\right) = \sum_{k=0}^{2^{i}-1} w_{i,k}$.

4.2 Statistical Process Control

Statistical process control aims at detecting events that might lead to loss of control; such procedures mostly use sequential data analysis and control charts, *Moving Centerline Exponential Weighted Moving Average -- MCEWMA* among them.

Weighted Moving Average techniques for wireless channel information analysis are commented by (Mhatre & Papagiannaki, 2006) and (Wu, Tan, Zhang & Zhang, 2007). This is a well-know and flexible solution since it requires a small amount of information, but our focus is a Moving Centerline that acts as an one-step ahead predictor.

The center line *CL* at instant *t* is defined as $z_t = \lambda x_t + \left(1 - \lambda\right)z_{t-1}$, where x_t is the new measure, λ is the smoothing constant and the upper and lower control limits are $UCL_t = z_{t-1} + 3\sigma\sqrt{\dfrac{\lambda}{2-\lambda}}$ and $LCL_t = z_{t-1} - 3\sigma\sqrt{\dfrac{\lambda}{2-\lambda}}$, respectively.

The analysis consists of comparing the center line to reference limits of previous sampling. At each new sampling, *UCL* (Upper Control Limit) and *LCL* (Lower Control Limit) are recalculated. The estimated value for λ is obtained as the square of the sum of the predicted errors. (Montgomery, 1996) conducts several experiments that indicate that values of λ close to 0.8 are adequate for detection using MCEWMA control charts.

The time series *X(t)* analyzed here requires smoothing, but to a limited extent in order not to eliminate the variability of the measures that will lead to the detection of events (Montgomery, 1996). We achieve this computing the mean and variance over a small window of 10 samples

which, in our case, is of about [100]ms. Over the smoothed time series, the center line z_ε is initialized as $z_{\varepsilon_0} = \hat{x}_0$, where $\hat{x}_0$ is the mean and $\sigma_\varepsilon = \sigma_t$, where σ_t is the standard deviation of the first window. The limits are $UCL_\varepsilon = z_\varepsilon + 3\sigma_\varepsilon\sqrt{\dfrac{\lambda}{2-\lambda}}$ and $LCL_\varepsilon = z_\varepsilon + 3\sigma_\varepsilon\sqrt{\dfrac{\lambda}{2-\lambda}}$, where $\lambda = 0.8$.

Each new event detected changes the centerline. In such case, z_ε is considered a detected event at instant *t*. For deal with this detected event, was created a vector x_ε, where are stored the values of z_ε, when is considered out of control, and the respective time *t*. For simplify, this step of saving the detected event will be writen as $x_\varepsilon[t]=z_\varepsilon$, where $x_\varepsilon[t]$ is the detected event at time *t*. In this vector, the value *t* refers the last detected event, and *t*−1 is the previous. Each new detected event will refered as *t* and the previous last one will be *t*−1. The new z_ε is $z_\varepsilon = \lambda x_\varepsilon\left[t-1\right] + \left(1-\lambda\right)z_{\varepsilon-1}$, where $x_\varepsilon[t-1]$ is the last detected event and $z_{\varepsilon-1}=z_\varepsilon$, the previous z_ε. After that, the new limits UCL_ε and LCL_ε are recalculated.

The standard deviation σ_ε is recalculated whenever z_ε lies outside the current interval. A new σ_ε is calculated according to the smoothed version of the prior standard deviation. Considering that σ_t is the standard deviation of the last measured window and $\sigma_{\varepsilon-1}$ is the prior standard deviation, $\sigma_{\varepsilon-1}=\sigma_\varepsilon$, the new σ_ε is $\sigma_\varepsilon = \lambda\sigma_t + (1-\lambda)\sigma_{\varepsilon-1}$.

We propose a specific control chart, the so-called *Moving Centerline Exponential Weighted Moving Variance -- MCEWMV* to monitor variance. The center line is defined as $S_i^2 = \lambda\left(\hat{x}_i - z_\varepsilon\right)^2 + \left(1-\lambda\right)S_{i-1}^2$ where z_ε and λ are the same at the adaptive MCEWMA, $\hat{x}_i$ is the mean of the current *i* measured data, and S_i^2 is the estimated variance. Control lower and upper limits are $LCL = S_{i-1}^2 - \sigma_\varepsilon$ and $UCL = S_{i-1}^2 + \sigma_\varepsilon$, respectively, which are also updated when an out of control event is detected. For this out of control situation, two vectors were defined, sl_ε and su_ε, with the same principle of the vector x_ε. When this occurs, the value S_i^2 and the time t are stored in $sl_\varepsilon[t]$ if the measure lies below *LCL* and at $su_\varepsilon[t]$ if it trespasses *UCL*. This distinction is because the increase of variability is detected at *UCL* while the decrease is detected at *LCL*.

The control chart outputs three vectors, namely x_ε, su_ε and sl_ε, which identify the values and the time when out of control measures were detected. The sequence of out of control measures can be associated to a patterns that help identifying relevant temporal events. For example, the succession of five or more events su_ε without any sl_ε overlapped and events at x_ε indicates mobility. The same sequence for sl_ε without any su_ε overlapped indicates decreasing variability, i.e., the moment when the user is stopping.

This type of identification helped developing "action maps", a commonplace in statistical process control, indicating what is expected at each out of control detection. The definition and common use of the "action maps" can be seen at (Montgomery, 1996). A specific "action map" developed for this methodology is showed in Section 4.

4.3 Statistical Process Control and Multi resolution Analysis

At this point, the investigated data is the RSSI measures at the indoor environment, described in Section 3, and the time series $X(t)$ as the sampled RSSI measures. Those sampled RSSI measures are a small window of ten consecutive RSSI measures, spaced with the time interval of [10]ms. As described in Section 3, the wireless channel is described as a non-linear, non-Gaussian non-stationary time series. These features are incorporated into the model in order to make it able to describe strongly asymmetry samples and variations of the mean and dispersion. The complexity of the series prevents the use of simple models, justifying the use of a exponentially moving average strategy at the control chart (classical control charts use classical, less expressive models). Also, variability and asymmetry are better characterized by the multi-resolution analysis. With this, the joint use of the both methods is justified for the following points:

- Time analysis: The MCEWMA control chart identifies out of control events over the mean of the sampled RSSI measures and the MCEWMV control chart identifies out of control over the variance. With those control charts, the statistical process control process allows the identification of the out of control tendencies at the signal amplitude. But the information about the variability between the sampled RSSI measures is not totally identified, and a spectral analysis between consecutive sampled RSSI measures is needed;

- Spectral Analysis: The wavelet transform allows to identify the variability of a set of consecutive sampled RSSI measures. Applied over the outcome of the MCEWMA, it is used to describe the variability between the sampled RSSI measures. The wavelet transform is applied over the smoothed measures and not over the RSSI measures in order to avoid the noise information. The result of the wavelet transform is a set of wavelets coefficients which describe the frequency of set of sampled RSSI measures. The noise information and the amplitude of the signal variation is verified by the control charts.

With the vectors generated by the control charts, x_ε, su_ε and sl_ε, associated to vectors E and M, from the wavelet analysis, it is possible to identify the behavior of the time series, and associate it to the events at the wireless environment.

A flowchart of the overall process can be viewed in Figure 13 and Table 2. The received signal strength values are collected in $\hat{x}_0$, and the

Figure 13. Overview of the overall process

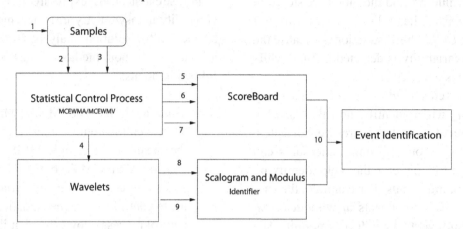

Table 2. Description of the statistical control process and multiresolution analysis, Figure 13

Number	Description
1	Collect the RSSI Measures, creating a samplewindow $\hat{x}_0$ of 10 measures
2	Calculates the μ of the sampled RSSI measures and apply the MCEWMA
3	Calculates the σ of the sampled RSSI measures and apply the MCEWMV
4	Apply the Wavelet Transform over the MCEWMA Output
5	Detected out of control events at the MCEWMA. Information saved at vector x_ε
6	Detected out of control events at the MCEWMV. Information saved at vector su_ε
7	Detected out of control events at the MCEWMV. Information saved at vector sl_ε
8	Scalogram applied over the waveletcoefficients, vector E
9	Modulus of the wavelet coefficients, vector M
10	Distinguish Mobility from Interference using the information from both analysis

sample mean and variance are calculated. Temporal events are identified by vectors x_ε, su_ε and sl_ε. Over the smoothed data, the spectral analysis generates the spectral events, identified by the scalogram and the modulus. The final step is the classification of these events. Two aspects are explored in the next sessions in order to provide an user centric response.

Next section presents the parameter estimation and the computational complexity of the algorithm.

5 ALGORITHM AND PARAMETER ESTIMATION

One of the requisites of this process is the need of a fast response to the user. This response time depends on the computational complexity of the method summarized in Figure 13 and the size of measure data. The overall complexity is dependent on the computation of the scalogram and modulus since they are applied over each wavelet coefficient level. The response time of the identification process is, therefore, limited by the interval between the measures and the size of the window where the wavelet transform will be applied. Those features will be discussed in the following.

5.1 Response Time Estimation

Considering that the receiver signal strength measures were done at the time of the frame reception, it is mandatory to establish the sample rate, the wavelet basis and the size of sampled measures for an efficient description of the time series. A sliding window version of the wavelet transform was applied in order to provide fast response to the user centric management and to attend to the computational restrictions of the mobile device.

The size of the sampled measures is determined by the response time required for correct event detection. Considering that, we define the response time as $\Delta t = \delta t + O\left(mN\log_2\left(N\right)\right)$, where the second term is the order of operations required to compute a discrete wavelet transform with an orthogonal basis applied m levels on a vector of size N. The measures are sampled at $\delta t = 2\kappa\left|H_0\right|m$ intervals, where $\left|H_0\right|$ is the size of the wavelet basis and κ is the interval rate for each sampled measure. With this, the frequency components are identifiable at each δt interval. Increasing the size of this set, increases the quantity of collected data and allows a more precise detection, but also increases the lag before the detection of an event. The response time estimation is the smallest value of δt for which multi resolution analysis is feasible.

As described in Section 3.1, [κ=10]ms is the size of the sampled window to be filtered, corresponding to ten sampled measures. The next step is the choice of the wavelet basis. Due to the size of $\left|H_0\right|$, the first choice is the Haar wavelet, since its size is $\left|H_0\right|$=2 and memory efficient implementations are available. This basis, however, is prone to losing high frequency information. Next choices are Daubechies 4 and Coiflets 6 wavelets, which have basis of sizes 4 and 6, respectively. Both algorithms use overlapping windows (Daubechies,

1992) and their high frequency coefficients map all the changes in the time series. Overlapping windows are also used in order to avoid loss of information.

The minimum level to describe the high frequencies is m=2, leading to [δt =1600]ms. Considering an indoor environment, this δt is small enough to identify the effects from mobility and interference. For comparing the description of each basis, we applied over several collected RSSI, under different hours and situations at the map showed in Figure 3, the slotted version of this wavelet transform, with the size of this defined δt.

The following figures show the log of one of these runs. Considering the mobility effect, Figure 14 shows the windows with [δt =1600]ms, while Table 3 shows the scalogram for this scenario with the three wavelet basis, in the six intervals between 640 and 1600, covering the moment when the device moves away from the access point. Intervals [800-960] and [960-1120] can be seen in Figure 14 as those with the steepest variation, since displacement in these intervals is more intense. This leads to values more representative at the scalogram, as shown in Table 3.

Figure 15 shows the slotted intervals with [δt =1600]mswhere the wavelet transform was applied, and Table 3 shows the scalogram at the intervals between 160 and 1600, both corresponding to the interference scenario. The most intense effect from interference can be seen at the intervals [320-480], [480,640] and [640,800].

With this in mind, it is possible to show that the scalogram describes the frequency components at each time interval. In the presence of mobility, the sharp variation at the event duration is proportional with the size of δt. The proposed size is small enough to cover a movement of a human walk speed and its effects over the signal variation. Daubechies 4 performs better the estimation of low frequency content, with less cost than Coiflets 6.

Figure 14. RSSI Measures in mobility scenario, intervals of [δt =1600]ms

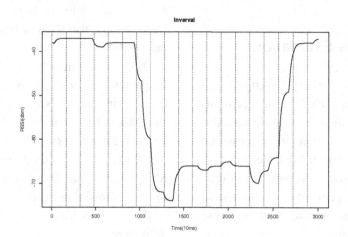

Table 3. Scalogram of 6 intervals with [δt =1600]ms under mobility, Figure 14. Haar, Daubechies 4 and Coiflets 6 basis

Interval (x10ms)	Coef. level	Haar	Daubechies 4	Coiflets 6
640-800	level 1	0.0003071422	0.0005402112	0.0006140733
	level 2	0.0009659273	0.0031429860	0.0022252466
800-960	level 1	2.011387	2.454246	11.762057
	level 2	17.611338	17.959009	4.514971
960-1120	level 1	6.535511	4.397457	43.05892
	level 2	38.854471	21.611537	65.28121
1120-1280	level 1	6.519683	4.947122	17.27091
	level 2	19.954933	16.730719	44.33578
1280-1440	level 1	1.486736	0.893582	7.131191
	level 2	11.453277	7.261554	9.858909
1440-1600	level 1	0.06990697	0.05194556	0.1399066
	level 2	0.21982986	0.18365111	0.5062098

Alone, the use of scalogram and modulus describe only the frequency components at each interval, and does not correlate the sequence of intervals. In this aspect, control charts complements the information, due to the cumulative analysis of the scoreboard. Also, the control chart deals with the absolute signal amplitude and its temporal variation, information which is lost by the wavelet transform.

5.2 Parameter Estimation

As described in Section 4, the vectors x_ε, su_ε and sl_ε, contains the measures and the time that identifies the out of control situations identified by the MCEWMA and MCEWMV control charts. The vectors E and M are the scalogram and modulus analysis from the wavelet transform.

Figures 16 and 17 show the control charts applied to the signal presented in Figure 15. Figure

Figure 15. RSSI Measures in interference scenario, Bluetooth over WiFi intervals of [δt =1600]ms

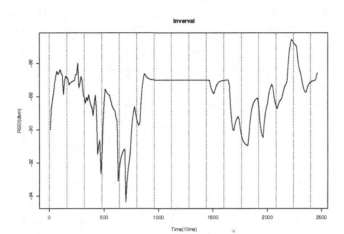

Table 4. Scalogram of 6 intervals with [δt =1600]ms under interference, Figure 15. Haar, Daubechies 4 and Coiflets 6 basis

Interval (x10ms)	Coef. level	Haar	Daubechies 4	Coiflets 6
160-320	level 1	0.4755393	0.9682648	1.220826
	level 2	2.1430760	1.4760479	0.983032
320-480	level 1	4.530454	4.520238	5.310228
	level 2	6.009768	7.127532	4.167756
480-640	level 1	1.177743	1.823898	2.975289
	level 2	13.098290	20.340663	2.443299
640-800	level 1	6.018306	5.14352	4.853243
	level 2	3.737651	5.55892	4.181238
800-960	level 1	0.9226010	1.041698	1.350974
	level 2	0.8779065	2.380095	2.851256
1450-1600	level 1	3.042824e-06	4.118298e-06	6.264931e-06
	level 2	9.544750e-06	5.887381e-06	2.172833e-05

16a shows the RSSI measures, and Figures 16 b--c show the output from the MCEWMA and MCEWMV. Figure 16b presents three events detected, associated with changes at the expected value from the EWMA and changes at the variance. Figure 17a shows the MCEWMA events, x_ε, while Figures 17 b--c show the MCEWMV events, su_ε and sl_ε.

To model an autonomic response to the detected events, we created a scoreboard. This scoreboard

gives a temporal description of a sequence of the MCEWMA and MCEWMV out of control situations. The scoreboard definition is based on the following description. Assuming the time interval $[t_{k-i}, t_k]$ between the time of the last out of control detection at the MCEWMA and MCEWMV, t_k, and a previous out of control identification t_{k-i}, i is the size of this time interval, where $i=1,2,...,n$, and n is the number of out of control situations. The values of the vector su_ε, that fits in this interval

Figure 16. RSSI Measures and the output from MCEWMA and MCEWMV

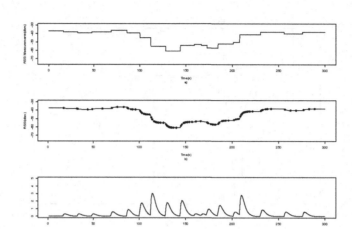

Figure 17. Out of control measures at MCEWMA and MCEWMV over the smoothed signal

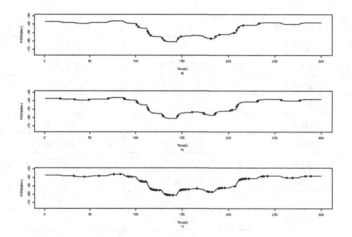

$[t_{k-i}, t_k]$, without any concomitant event at sl_ε at the same interval, indicate a variance increase. The size of this interval, i, indicates that variability increases. The opposite holds for decreasing variability, described by a sequence of out of control detections stored at sl_ε without any at su_ε at the same interval. Associated to that, the out of control stored at the vector x_ε, indicates that variability is not merely due to change, but also the mean of the measures. All these situations can be scored and used to identify the cause of the out of control sequence in this interval.

The scoreboard values were defined using an estimate of the expected occurrence of events and calibrated using over a hundred controlled tests in the proposed scenarios showed here, with 95% confidence intervals. The final information of the scoreboard is used in a joint analysis with the wavelet description. The ``action maps'' developed for our process are shown in Table 5.

Table 5. Rules for the control charts MCEWMA and MCEWMV

Number	Name	Description
-1	No Event	No pattern detected
1	Three-Sigma	CL_{av} out of control limits
2	Three-Sigma	3 CL_{av} successively
	Successively	out of control limits
3	5 Points Successively	5 samples
		in MCEWMA at Zone A
4	6 Points Successively	6 samples in MCEWMA
		between Zone A e B
5	8 Points Sucessively	8 samples in MCEWMA between Zone B e C
6	Mobility Pattern	3 a 4 LSC_{vt} followed by LIC_{vt}
7	Mobility Pattern II	4 LSC_{vt} followed by 7 LIC_{vt}
8	Interference Pattern	2 LSC_{vt} followed by 10 LIC_{vt}
9	Interference Pattern II	3 LSC_{vt} followed by 10 LIC_{vt}
10	Disconnection by Interference Pattern	6 LSC_{vt} and plus
		more than 5 CL_{av} consecutively

These maps are defined according to the environment and features of the investigated event in several empirical tests. For the classification, at each detected situation at the control chart, the possible combinations of the three vectors are identified and a scoreboard is used.

The choice of the values for Table 6 was done according to the chance of a event detection in an interval of 10 to 15 samples, the minimum to cover a variability of the RSSI measures due to the mobility. The effects of the interference can be detected in small intervals. As the control charts MCEWMA and MCEWMV are applied at the same time, rules 1, 2, 3 and 4, associated to the MCEWMA, are triggered at the same time than rules 5, 6, 7, 8 and 9, which are applied over the MCEWMV.

The sequence of events is relevant. After five detections in Table 6, the scoreboard for mobility is increased by five points. With that, at each moment, the impact of the event is accounted for. When one of the values in the scoreboard achieves fifty points, it is compared with the spectral

Table 6. Points for the scoreboard, associated to event identification

Rule	Mobility Event	Interference Event
-1	-1	-1
1	+10	+10
2	+25	+5
3	+5	+5
4	+5	+10
5	+5	+10
6	+25	-5
7	+30	-5
8	-5	+15
9	-5	+20
10	0	+50

analysis of the scalogram E and the modulus M. The mobility is mapped as a sharp transient at the scalogram, with high values at the high frequency components. Also, with the modulus information, is possible to identify if this transient is positive

Table 7. Events classification

Detected Event	Description
1	Connection loss
2	Conn. loss due interference
3	Approaching AP
4	Weak Interference
5	Moving away from AP
6	Medium Interference
7	Moving
8	Strong Interference

or negative. Positive values can be interpreted as the mobile approaching the access point, while negative values the other way around. These values increase during the displacement.

Figure 17 shows the three vectors over the MCEWMA filtered information. Figure 17a shows that x_ε detects a change in the mean during the interval between 80 and [100]seconds. Figure 17c indicates that the variability of the data diminishes with respect to previous points shown in Figure 17b, at the interval between 90 and 100.

With that, at each moment, the impact of the event is accounted for. When one of the values in the scoreboard achieves fifty points, it is compared with the spectral analysis of the scalogram E and the modulus M. The mobility is mapped as a sharp transient at the scalogram, with high values at the high frequency components. Also, with the modulus information, is possible to identify if this transient is positive or negative. Positive values can be interpreted as the mobile is approaching the access point, while negative values the other way around. During the mobile dislocation these values will increase.

In the case of interference the scalogram indicates small values, due to concentrated fluctuations, or in the case of the Bluetooth, an increase at the value with small fluctuations. This type of fluctuation is larger than the one due to white noise coming from the wireless environment.

With this information, and after hundreds of tests in indoor wireless environments, the information of what is taking place was used to create Table 7. This table enumerate the events, associated to interference and mobility and presents their interpretation. The user is presented with the description at the moment of the identification of each event.

Next section presents the validation of these results.

5.3 Event Identification

For this experiment, we used the same environment described in Section 3. The tests were conducted in a home indoor environment, considering a low density of users and a unplanned distribution of access points from the neighborhood. Also, cordless phones and Bluetooth devices were the sources of interference.

All the mobility took place at approximately [0.5]m/s. In all charts, each experiment was done in [300]seconds, and the time resolution at the x axis is associated to the sample rate of [10]ms. To each detected event, our mechanism alerts the user with the description shown in Table 7.

Figure 18 shows the first case, where there is not either user mobility or interference. All the signal fluctuations were due to noise caused by multi-path fading, which is ignored and no event was detected.

Figure 19 shows the detection of a Bluetooth communication. For this type of interference, a Bluetooth external interface at the notebook was activated and started to use the LAN Profile with the Bluetooth Access Point. The events were identified at the highlighted points. The box above shows the exact time when the event was detected and indicated the number of the event, as shown in Table 7.

A mobility scenario is shown in Figure 20. In this test, the user moves away from the access point from [10000]ms to [15000]ms, and event 5 is detected, as shown at the box. When return-

Figure 18. The identification of a stationary device, without interference. No event is addressed

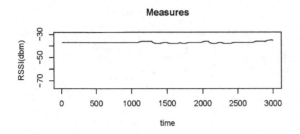

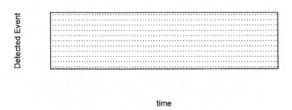

Figure 19. The identification of a stationary device in an ambient with interference

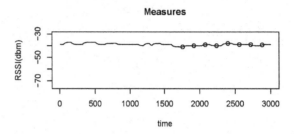

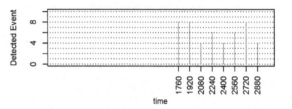

ing to the access point, until time [24400]ms, other events associated to mobility are detected. In this case, two other identifications of interference took place due to interference caused by other nearby access points. With this, the final scenario is shown in Figure 21, where mobility and interference take place: the user walks in a place wheres there is interference from different access points, causing co-channel interference. In this case, this information warns the user about the region he/she is entering. The importance of this result is giving the user the option to walk away from the interference zone or to take any other applicable measure.

6 MANAGEMENT SERVICE ARCHITECTURE

Our service for wireless interface control was developed for both Linux and Windows platforms using WiFi and Bluetooth device drivers, using the C++ language. The service accesses the main features of each system. The focus of

the work was over the Intel interface cards, using the wireless driver for Linux and the Intel Mobile Development SDK in conjunction with the WMI (Microsoft, 2008) for Windows. The service acts as a middleware between drivers and user applications. The service uses these access strategies to monitor events in wireless networks. It is a simple matter of collecting information of radio signals and performing the techniques described below. An application is provided with the information of events along the time and may use this information in their applications to perform whatever adaptation is needed. The basic operations of our service are divided and grouped into several functional blocks, according to their characteristics. Figure 22 shows these blocks.

- **Device Information**: defines operations for identifying wireless interface drivers and controls all functions related to this topic. On IEEE 802.11 interface, it identifies which control characteristics are available, version and chipset manufacturer and which parameters may be configurable

Figure 20. The identification of a moving device

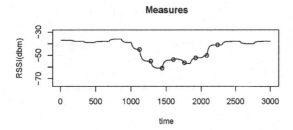

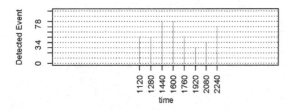

Figure 21. The identification of a device moving into an ambient subjected to interference

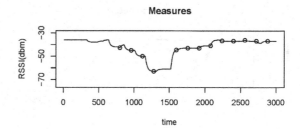

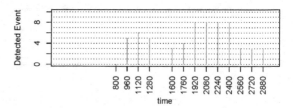

Figure 22. Service architecture

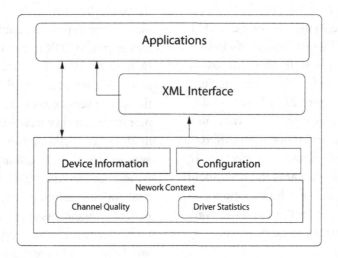

by users. On Bluetooth interface, identifies Bluetooth version used, manufacturer, which operation of the HCI layer are accessible and configuration of the radio modem;

- **Configuration**: this block access information of interface configuration from basic functions to more advanced ones, such as functions for performance enhancement.

Some of these functions can be accessed remotely using some of the XML block functions. Obviously, this has security implications, as for instance, if one tries to adjust packets properties and signal power level remotely on IEEE 802.11 or Bluetooth.

- **Network Context**: this block of function access information related to context of wireless communication and it is the first step to infer behavior on the environment. It is divided in two sub-blocks:

- ○ **Quality of the channel**: collects information of quality of communication channels, by taking sequential measures of RSSI, quality, and transmission power parameters of each interface. From these values it determines connectivity level and mobility of the devices creating an historic of these parameters and allowing future inferences of the network behavior.
- ○ **Local Statistics**: Usage of each interface, such as amount of retransmitted packets and transmission errors.
- **XML Interface**: XML block is responsible to collect information of others modules and convert them according to pre-determined DTDs. Information about network context is generated at each new request while information about other blocks are generated at the starting moment or at each new parameter modification. Using XML in mobile environments allows a more flexible and easy data manipulation, as all information becomes independent of the technology used in the environment.

The communication between the service and the application can be done by the socket interface or by an XML file.

7 ADAPTATION AND USER IMPROVEMENTS

At this point the multi-scale control chart is capable to distinguish the presence of these two main types of events. Implemented as a service, it can act integrated to the desktop or user applications. For example, the user can be alerted of the interference, avoiding an erroneous and common thinking, which always associates a bad communication to the lower power level.

Solutions as change the communication channel can be adopted. But if it is necessary maintain the communication without change the access point or the channel, the user can move away from the interference source.

7.1 Performance Impact

For test this, some adaptive applications were developed. Considering the SOHO environment showed at Figure 23, a simple application that adapts Bluetooth packet type according to the presence of events in the wireless channel was developed. The Bluetooth packet type has great influence on channel quality of both technologies, 802.11 and Bluetooth, in the presence of mutual interference. It was shown that DH1 degrades quality more than any other packet type but it has the advantage of keeping connections alive longer when the device moves away from the communication point. DM5 and DH5 are better choices when interference is identified and DM3 and DH3 are neutral choices when it is not known which type of events is going to be detected on the network. The test consists of a simple FTP transfer sustained on 802.11 channel and an adaptable ping application on Bluetooth. The ping application was started with packet type DH1 and an interference with FTP transmission was then introduced. With no adaptation it is possible to notice a strong decrease on FTP total throughput observed by the FTP client. This is the result of lower channel quality and consequently more collision, packet losses and retransmissions. When using adaptation, the application detects the event of interference and notify the application which responds with an order to modify Bluetooth packet type to DH5 (if only interference is detected) or DH3 (if interference and mobility are detected), which is a guarantee of always having the best system configuration. Table 7 shows FTP total throughput and variance observed in this experiment. Data were transmitted on 802.11 at [11]Mbps. All results were calculated with a confidence interval of 95%. Figure 24

Figure 23. SOHO environment

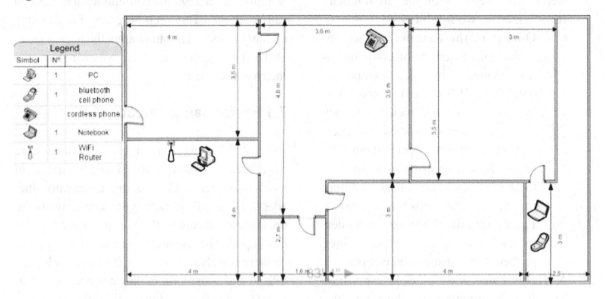

Figure 24. Example of throughput for one run of each system configuration

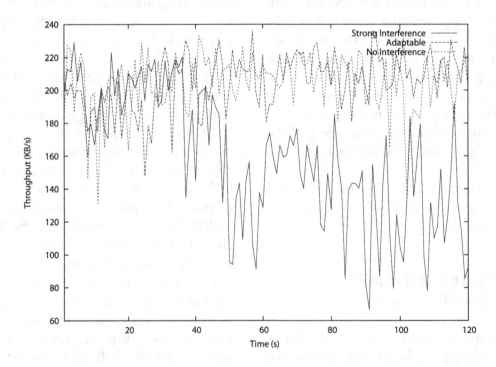

shows an example of one run of the experiment for each one of the following configurations: no interference, strong interference and adaptable. These adaptable applications manage to overcome interference and to sustain a throughput close to the one measured for no interference at all. If no adaptation is applied, throughput decreases substantially.

Table 8. Mean and variance of FTP throughput for the experiment

Experiment	Mean (KB/s)	Variance
No interference	201,3246	0,7878
Strong interference	185,5409	6,8474
Adaptable	196,9777	3,408

For test another applications, the tool Iperf ? was used. Configuring the Iperf for generate VoIP and video streaming traffics, the scenarios were created to test the effects of interference. The IEEE 802.11 interfaces were configured to use the IEEE 802.11b, at [11]Mbps and the IEEE 802.11g, at 54Mbps. The configuration of Iperf was set to generate a 3 minute traffic, with the buffer size set to 768 Kbytes for the streaming scenario. All the tests were repeated 40 times and the results calculated with a confidence interval of 95%. For the IEEE802.11b scenarios, Figure 25, it is possible to see the influence of the adaptation, which switches the Bluetooth packet that causes less interference.

The impact of the interference at the jitter over the VoIP traffic can be viewed in Figure 27. The traffic was over the IEEE802.11b and the interference was caused by a cordless phone. The jitter achieves [300]ms, a prohibitive level at the VoIP traffic. The adaptation detected the interference pattern and changes the power transmission, to a level where the signal fluctuation is less intensive. The direct impact was a better level of jitter. For the IEEE 802.11g scenario, Figure 26, the impact is less intensive, due to OFDM modem.

7.2 IEEE 802.21 Smart Triggers and Events

Mobile devices with multiple radio interfaces are becoming commonplace, as a way to provide not only flexibility to select and access different wireless networks, but also to maintain the mobile user connectivity over wider areas of coverage.

Currently, the most common radio technologies are GPRS, UMTS, CDMA2000, IEEE 802.16, for metropolitan area networks, and IEEE 802.11 for local area coverage. A typical case of multiple radio use is a user with a mobile device who initially gets connected to the Internet via a 802.11b access network and, later on, switches the access network to a metropolitan area technology such as CDMA2000. Furthermore, over areas covered with multiple wireless networks, the user may switch, along the time, to the best access network based on different criteria such as connection cost, network state (e.g., channel quality, available bandwidth, network load), and application requirements.

An important point to enable a smart selection among various radio technologies is the definition of the metrics to use, and how they can be compared. For instance, the signal level of some radio technologies cannot be directly compared (Ali-Yahiya, Sethom & Pujolle, 2007). (Gelabert, Pérez-Romero, Sallent & Agustí, 2008) state that application requirements, such as delay, jitter, and packet loss should be taken into account during radio access selection. Moreover, the available technologies must support the applications requirements.

(Perez-Romero, Salient & Agusti, 2007) identify the following main aspects of a radio selection mechanism:

- **Availability**: the sensing of the radio access infrastructure, such as the antenna;
- **Accessibility**: the adequate access of user applications to the available radio technologies. Application requirements involve estimation of the communication quality, including location, mobility, interference and transmission power. Network level requirements include connection cost, available bandwidth, conection/handover latency, coverage area, among others.

Figure 25. UDP Streaming over IEEE802.11b and Bluetooth interference

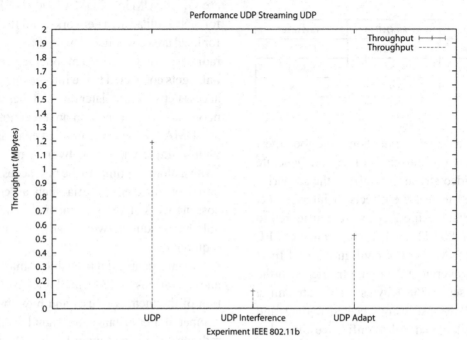

Figure 26. UDP Streaming over IEEE802.11g

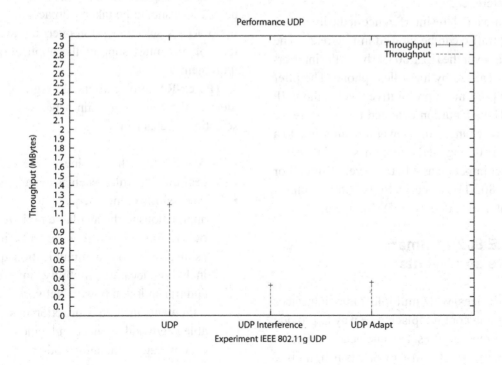

Figure 27. Jitter at Bluetooth interference over IEEE 80211

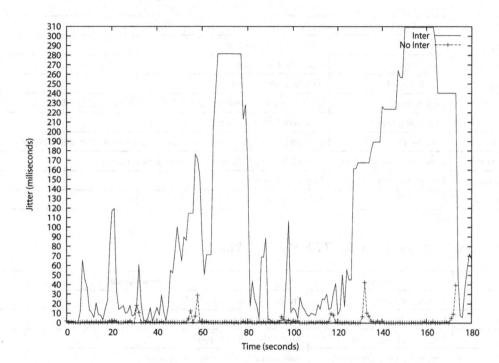

In 2006, a standardization initiative called IEEE 802.21 ? was created to define an integration layer under which the various cellular systems, packet radio and wired packet network technologies could interface. The IEEE 802.21 standard, also called Media Independent Handover Services, aims at allowing the integration of radio and packet network technologies, using a transparent selection among various technologies of choice. Its scope includes the identification and selection among radio access networks, and the connection process at the data link layer. Part of the standard is to be implemented as software components, between the data link and network layers. Therefore, the standard shall provide data link level information to the network layer to assist handover procedures.

Figure 28 depicts the main IEEE 802.21 components:

- *Smart Triggers*: a service that verifies the link layer and detects the behavior of the

Figure 28. IEEE 802.21 main components

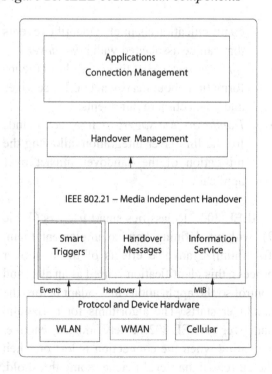

Table 9. Smart triggers over the link layer

Event	Event name	Description
State Change	Link Up	Connection established
State Change	Link Down	Connection is broken
State Change	Link Detected	New link has been found
State Change	Link Parameters	Change in specific link parameters has crossed pre-specified thresholds
Predictive	Link Going Down	Connection breakdown imminent
Administrative	Operator Preferences	Connection change due to wireless network infra-structure requirements
Link Synchronous	Link Handover Imminent	Intra-technology handover imminent (subnet change)
Link Synchronous	Link Handover Complete	Notify handover state
Link Synchronous	Link SDU Transmit	Information exchange about the channel quality

Table 10. Proposed triggers over the IEEE 802.11 link layer

Events	Trigger	Description
Predictive	Link under interference	Presence of interference at link layer
Predictive	Link mobility away	Away from the access point
Predictive	Link mobility approach	Approach the access point
Predictive	Link going down (mobility)	Imminent disconnection due mobility
Predictive	Link going down (interference)	Imminent disconnection due interference

communication channel. It identifies events that can be associated with a *handover*;

- *Info Service*: a MIB that controls all the information about nearby networks, services and connection requirements;
- *Handover Messages*: define commands for the link layer integration, allowing the mitigation of the handover impact over applications.

IEEE 802.21 classifies smart triggers (Table 9), without defining how to implement them. To minimize adverse effects of the handover process, this identification is used as an alert and control so the applications may adapt before the handover starts. The algorithms for horizontal handover at IEEE 802.11 networks are reactive, activating when the connection is lost or when the current signal level reaches some threshold, which generates a delay over the communication

(Mhatre & Papagiannaki, 2006). The objective of this identification framework is to use the service primitives of the link layer to mitigate delay effects by preparing the application to upcoming events. IEEE 802.21 also proposes some extensions for link layer primitives to achieve this goal.

Among the set of triggers, one type needs special attention: the predictive link behavior. This aspect can be technologically dependent, since each wireless network has a specific response to the environment. In our work, we propose an extension for this trigger, identifying the events that influence the link state.

Using Table 7, which identifies the events at the wireless channel, and Table 9, defined at the IEEE 802.21, we propose an extension to IEEE 802.21 standard, as shown in Table 10. The objective of this extension for the predictive events is to equip applications with quality indicators and prepare them for the handover procedure.

As mentioned earlier, the identification of the mobility can be used to determine when a device is moving in or out of an access point. The triggers related to interference avoid an incorrect identification of mobility from signal variations due to interference.

The soft-realtime characteristic of this method allows the use of prediction as a key point to adapt application and improve user experience. An example is a VoIP application, which uses jitter buffer strategy to mitigate the impact of jittering over the communication quality. Predictive events allow a better dimensioning of the jitter buffer.

8 CONCLUSION

This work presented a service that collects important data from the wireless interface. Static information, about the interface configuration and dynamic, about the behavior of the wireless channel. The last one use a multi-scale control chart approach with some modifications specific for wireless channels. Our approach consists in analyzing and classifying the signal variations and their causes in an acceptable time scale. A tool using this result improves the user experience, providing information about the network context and by allowing adaptive application behavior in a timely manner. The proposed extension for IEEE 802.21 and the identification of the sources of degradation is important for adaptive applications. Results were shown, were applications adapt the wireless configuration according to the identification of the environment behavior. For future works, the adaptive content will be to improve the user experience and resource management at another mobile devices, like smartphones.

ACKNOWLEDGMENT

The authors would like to thank Intel Corporation and CNPq/CAPES for supporting this work.

REFERENCES

Ali-Yahiya, T., Sethom, K., & Pujolle, G. (2007, July). A case study: Ieee 802.21 framework design for service continuity across wlan and wman. In *IFIP International Conference on Wireless and Optical Communications Networks*, WOCN '07, (pp. 1-5).

Aradhye, H., Bakshi, B. R., Strauss, R. A., & Davis, J. F. (2003). Multiscale Statistical Process Control Using Wavelets - Theoretical Analysis and Properties. *AIChE Journal. American Institute of Chemical Engineers*, *49*(4), 939–958. doi:10.1002/aic.690490412

Bianchi, G., Stefano, A. D., Giaconia, C., Scalia, L., Terrazzino, G., & Tinnirello, I. (2007, May). Experimental Assessment of the Backoff Behavior of Commercial IEEE 802.11b Network Cards. In Ieee 26th ieee international conference on computer communications infocom 2007 (pp. 1181-1189).

BlipNet. (n. d.). Retrieved from http://www. blipsystems.com/

Calafate, C. M. T., & Manzoni, P. (2003). A multi-platform programming interface for protocol development. In 11th euromicro conference on parallel distributed and network based processing, Genoa, Italy.

Chakraborty, S., D. Yau, & Lui, J. (2006, February). On the E_ectiveness of Movement Prediction to Reduce Energy Consumption in Wireless Communication. *IEEE Transactions on Mobile Computing, 5*(2), 157-169. Retrieved from citeseer.ist. psu.edu/chakraborty04effectiveness.html

Chen, Y., & Kobayashi, H. (2002, May). Signal strength based indoor geolocation. In Ieee international conference on communications (pp. 436-439).

Chiann, C., Chiann, C., Morettin, P.A., & Morettin, P. A. (1998). A wavelet analysis for time series. *Journal of Nonparametric Statistics, 10*, 1–46. doi:10.1080/10485259808832752

Daubechies, I. (1992). Ten lectures in wavelets. SIAM: Society for Industrial and Applied Mathematics.

Fainberg, M., & Goodman, D. (2001, October). Analysis of the interference between ieee 802.11b and bluetooth systems. In Ieee vehicular technology conference (Vol. 2, pp. 967-971).

Ganesan, R. (2002). *Wavelet based multiresolution monitoring of a nanomachining process in semicondutor manufacturing*. Master thesis, Departament of Industrial and Management Systems Engineering University South Florida.

Ganesan, R., Das, T. K., & Venkataraman, V. (2004, September). Wavelet based multiscale statistical process monithoring: a literature review. *IIE Transactions on Quality and Reability, 36*(9), 787–806. doi:10.1080/07408170490473060

Gelabert, X., Prez-Romero, J., Sallent, O., & Agust, R. (2008). A markovian approach to radio access technology selection in heterogeneous multiaccess/multiservice wireless networks. *IEEE Transactions on Mobile Computing, 7*(10), 1257–1270. doi:10.1109/TMC.2008.50

Gonz_alez, M. C., Hidalgo, C. A., & Barab_asi, A.-L. (2008). Understanding individual human mobility patterns. *Nature, 453* (7196), 779-782.

Graziosi, F., & Santucci, F. (2002). A general correlation model for shadow fading in mobile radio systems. *IEEE Communications Letters, 6*(3), 102–104. doi:10.1109/4234.991146

IEEE. (2008a). *Ieee 802.11*. Retrieved from http://grouper.ieee.org/groups/802/11/

IEEE. (2008b). Ieee 802.15. Retrieved from http://grouper.ieee.org/groups/802/15/

Ihmig, M., & Steenkiste, P. (2007, April). Distributed Dynamic Channel Selection in Chaotic Wireless Networks. In 13th european wireless conference.

Jeong, M. K., & Lu, J. (2003). Wavelet-Based SPC Procedure for Complicated Functional Data. In 2003 informs annual conference.

Judd, G., Akella, A., Seshan, S., & Steenkiste, P. (2005, September). Self-Management in Chaotic Wireless Deployments. In *Mobicom '05: Proceedings of the 11th annual international conference on mobile computing and networking* (pp. 185-199), Cologne, Germany.

Jung-Hyuck, J., & Jayant, N. (2003, May). Performance Evaluation of Multiple IEEE 802.11b Wlan Stations in the Presence of Bluetooth Radio Interference. In Ieee international conference on communications (Vol. 2, pp. 1163-1168).

Kim, M., & Noble, B. (2001). Mobile Network Estimation. In *Mobicom '01: Proceedings of the 7th annual international conference on mobile computing and networking* (pp. 298-309).

Kim, T., Hou, J. C., & Lim, H. (2006, September). Improving Spatial Reuse Through Tuning Transmit Power, Carrier Sense Threshold, and Data Rate in Multihop Wireless Networks. In Proceedings of mobicom (pp. 366-377).

Long, X., & Sikdar, B. (2007). Wavelet based detection of shadow fading in wireless networks. In Ieee global telecommunications conference, globecom '07, (pp. 305-309).

Long, X., & Sikdar, B. (2008). A Real-Time Algorithm for Long Range Signal Strength Prediction in Wireless Networks. In Ieee wireless communications and networking conference, Wcnc 2008, (pp. 1120 - 1125).

Mallat, S. G. (1989, December). Multifrequency Channel Decompositions of Images and Wavelet Models. *IEEE Transactions on Acoustics, Speech, and Signal Processing*, *37*(12), 2091–2110. doi:10.1109/29.45554

Mhatre, V., & Papagiannaki, K. (2006). Using Smart Triggers for Improved User Performance in 802.11 Wireless Networks. In *Mobisys '06: Proceedings of the 4th international conference on mobile systems, applications and services* (pp. 246-259). New York, NY, USA: ACM.

Mhatre, V. P., Papagiannaki, K., & Baccelli, F. (2007, May). Interference Mitigation Through Power Control in High Density 802.11 WLANs. In Infocom 2007: 26th ieee international conference on computer communications, (pp. 535-543), Anchorage, AK.

Microsoft. (2008, September). *Wmi - windows management instrumentation*. Retrieved from http://msdn.microsoft.com/en-us/library/aa394582.aspx

Montgomery, D. (1996). Introduction to Statistical Quality Control. Chichester, UK: John Wiley and Sons.

Narasimhan, R., & Cox, D. C. (1999, September). Speed Estimation in Wireless Systems Using Wavelets. *IEEE Transactions on Communications*, *47*, 1357–1364. doi:10.1109/26.789671

Narasimhan, R., & Cox, D. C. (2000, November). Speed Estimation in Wireless Systems Using Wavelets. *IEEE Journal on Selected Areas in Communications*, *18*, 2220–2227. doi:10.1109/49.895027

Nilsson, M., Hallberg, J., & Synnes, K. (2003). Positioning with bluetooth. In 10th international conference on telecommunications ict'2003.

Nordstrom, E. (2002). APE: a Large Scale Ad Hoc Network Testbed for Reproducible Performance Tests. Memoire de Master non publie, Information Technology Department of Computer Systems Uppsala University, Uppsala, Sweden.

Papagiannaki, K., Yarvis, M., & Conner, W. S. (2006). Experimental Characterization of Home Wireless Networks and Design Implications. In Ieee infocom 2006. 25th ieee international conference on computer communications, (pp. 1-13).

Perez-Romero, J., Salient, O., & Agusti, R. (2007, April). A generalized framework for multi-rat scenarios characterisation. In *IEEE 65th Vehicular Technology Conference*, VTC2007-Spring, (pp. 980-984).

Rappaport, T. (2002). Wireless Communication Systems. Upper Saddle River, NJ: Prentice Hall PTR.

Sheth, A., & Han, R. (2003). Adaptive power control and selective radio activation for low-power infrastructure-mode 802.11 lans. In *Icdcsw '03: Proceedings of the 23rd international conference on distributed computing systems* (pp. 812). Washington, DC: IEEE Computer Society.

SIG. (2003). *Bluetooth specifcation version 1.2.*

Suzuki, H. (1997, July). A Statistical Model for Urban Radio Propagation. *IEEE Transactions on Communications*, *7*, 673–680.

Tzagkarakis, G., Papadopouli, M., & Tsakalides, P. (2007). Singular Spectrum Analysis of Traffic Workload in a Large-scale Wireless Lan. In *Mswim '07: Proceedings of the 10th acm symposium on modeling, analysis, and simulation of wireless and mobile systems,* (pp. 99-108). New York: ACM.

Wu, H., Tan, K., Zhang, Y., & Zhang, Q. (2007, May). Proactive Scan: Fast Handoff with Smart Triggers for 802.11 Wireless LAN. In Ieee infocom 2007. 26th ieee international conference on computer communications, (pp. 749-757).

Yu, X. (2004). Improving TCP Performance over Mobile Ad Hoc Networks by Exploiting Cross-layer Information Awareness. In Proceedings of mobicom, (pp. 231-244).

ADDITIONAL READING

For additional reading we recommend the following articles:

(Judd, Akella, Seshan & Steenkiste, 2005), which argue that end-client experience could be significantly improved by making chaotic wireless networks self-managing. We design and evaluate automated power control and rate adaptation algorithms to minimize interference among neighboring APs, while ensuring robust end-client performance.

(Ihmig & Steenkiste, 2007), which work focus on the interference mitigation method, which is a fundamental issue for applying DSA to real wireless systems. The simulation results reveal that the proposed DSA scheme not only improves the spectrum utilization and the profit of operators, but also effectively restrains the inter-system interference between wireless networks under an acceptable level.

Chapter 5
Experiences in Developing Ubiquitous Applications

José Cano
Universidad Politécnica de Valencia, Spain

Juan-Carlos Cano
Universidad Politécnica de Valencia, Spain

Carlos T. Calafate
Universidad Politécnica de Valencia, Spain

Pietro Manzoni
Universidad Politécnica de Valencia, Spain

ABSTRACT

Ubiquitous computing aims at making our lives easier by creating smart environments that are able to adequately react according to the context, the user, and the available devices. This chapter describes a set of prototype applications developed for a wide set of ubiquitous computing environments. These applications provide solutions to improve different kinds of environments, such as academic, business, museum and hospital environments. Since wireless networks are a key component in pervasive applications, a careful selection must take place to find which one suits better the characteristics required, depending on the objective of each case. In the authors' case studies they have mainly concentrated on IEEE 802.11 and Bluetooth technologies. The work has enabled them to translate theoretical concepts to real scenarios, while identifying specific needs in different types of ubiquitous computing applications.

INTRODUCTION

Nowadays our lives increasingly depend on information and communication technologies. People want to be connected anytime, anywhere, and so the use of the Internet through the wide range of mobile devices available in the market is becoming more and more common in our societies, being even indispensable in some cases. Also notice that electronic devices are becoming smaller, and can be integrated into nearly all everyday objects. This leads to the conclusion that pervasive computing and ubiquitous scenarios are becoming a reality.

The concept of ubiquitous computing deals with a world where computational technology and

DOI: 10.4018/978-1-61520-843-2.ch005

services embrace almost everything around us, making many computing devices so naturalized within the environment that people do not even realize that they are using computers (*Weiser, 1991*). The central concept is to harmonize with users through a digital environment that is aware of their presence and context, being able to provide personalized services according to their needs, besides being capable of anticipating their behavior and responding to their movements. Applications may change or adapt their functions, information and user interface depending on the context and the client's profile (*Weiser, 1993*).

For this ubiquitous vision to become a reality we must rely on small, hand-held, wireless computing devices that enable the interaction between users and their environments. These devices should offer functionalities that can be described, advertised and discovered by others. Moreover, they are able to inter-operate even though they have not been specifically designed to perform joint tasks. Therefore, thanks to the advanced technology in devices and low power wireless communication systems, consolidating the ubiquitous computing is more evident every day, being a major motivation to research and develop new systems.

Currently there are many companies and research centers actively working on the issue of context-awareness or, more generally, on ubiquitous computing (Baldauf, 2007). In particular, several proposals focus on smart spaces and intelligent environments (Shafer, 1998; Harter, 1999; Kindberg, 2002; *Fitton, 2005; Oliver, 2006;* Smart-its, 2007), where it is expected that smart devices all around us maintain updated information about their locations, the contexts in which they are being used, along with relevant data about the users. There is no doubt that pervasive computing systems will provide flexible services and unsuspected benefits. However, there are still only a few examples of pervasive computing environments moving out from academic laboratories into our everyday lives. This occurs because their design

is still a difficult task, requiring much theoretical and practical work. Moreover, it is complex to define what a real pervasive system should be like. The OneWorld (Grimm, 2004) project builds an architecture that provides an integrated and comprehensive framework for developing pervasive applications. It includes a set of services that help to structure applications and directly simplify the task of coping with constant change.

This chapter describes the research work we have done in the area of pervasive computing to define ubiquitous systems that fit into different types of environments. These systems are prototypes from which more sophisticated versions can be developed when targeting real ubiquitous scenarios. Selected environments include museums where visitors can get personalized and context-aware computing information, spontaneous networks in academic and business scenarios that allow P2P connections to exchange any type of resources, MANETs (Mobile Ad Hoc Networks) that allow an organized team to communicate independently in different situations, and also intelligent hospitals where it is possible to monitor patients automatically. We provided a detailed description of each prototype, including the system architecture as well as application and implementation details.

BACKGROUND

Pervasive computing has been receiving attention from the research community for more than fifteen years. Although new technologies are emerging and the target scenarios are heterogeneous (museums, schools, malls, official departments, hospitals, military), a great number of leading technological organizations are exploring pervasive computing. The most crucial objective is not necessarily to develop new technologies, but finding ways to integrate existing technologies with a wireless infrastructure in real settings.

Tourism was one of the pioneer areas in the adoption of ubiquitous applications, mainly due to the high number of potential users, and also because in case of a system failure, the consequences were not as dangerous as in other environments, such as hospitals. Other development areas began to emerge gradually, and so we can now find a multitude of applications designed for a wide variety of sectors and fields. In this section we will review some of the most important contributions in recent years.

The Cyberguide project (Abowd, 1997) consists of a series of prototypes of a mobile, hand-held context-aware tour guide that uses the user's current location and a history of past locations to provide services concerning location and information. The project was developed for indoor and outdoor applications. In both cases, Cyberguide uses as a positioning solution based on infra-red (indoor) and GPS technologies (outdoor). Cyberguide was influenced by earlier location-aware works such as the PARCTab at Xerox PARC (Want, 1995), the InfoPad project at Berkeley (Long, 1996), the Olivetti Active Badge system (Want, 1992) and the Personal Shopping Assistant at AT&T (Asthana, 1994). Similar systems to Cyberguide have also been proposed by other researchers, including the GUIDE (Davies, 1998) project proposed at Lancaster University, the HIPS (Broadbent, 1997) project from the University of Siena, and the ILEX (Cox, 1999) project developed at the University of Sussex that talks about intelligent labels.

The CoolTown project (*Kindberg, 2002*) developed at HP Laboratories focuses on building ubiquitous computing systems by integrating web services to enhance communication with mobile users, to provide location-specific services in visited areas, and to provide interaction with the objects that they encounter. The goal is to extend the Web technology together with wireless networks and mobile devices to create a virtual link between the physical entities, including users, and services provided by the environment. The

Websign project (*Pradhan, 2004*) is a component of the CoolTown research program which allows users to visualize services related to physical objects of interest. Although Websign can be adapted to provide tourist guide services, its use generally addresses the interaction between users and services associated with physical objects. The Rememberer system (*Fleck, 2002*), also part of the Cooltown project, is a tool for capturing personal experiences during a museum visit that helps users to build a record of their experiences, which they can use during or after their visit. The record consists of web pages on the statement of the visit, including notes and photos. It is aimed primarily for visitors overwhelmed by the enormous amount of information presented in the museum. Location is identified using infra-red technology and RFID sensors. Other works related to the Cooltown project include (*Spasojevic, 2001*) and (*Semper, 2002*).

At the Tokyo University, the digital museum project (*Sakamura, 1998*) uses smart cards to detect the proximity of visitors and then provide information about the exhibited objects. The information provided can be based on a static profile stored previously in a smart card. Similar work has also been done in (*Davin, 1999*) where an infra-red infrastructure and wireless LAN connections were used for connectivity and location awareness, respectively.

Another environment that has been studied lately is the ubiquitous hospital, where clinical parameters can be monitored automatically. This idea is very important since it can improve the reliability and speed of some hospital procedures, which are extremely important when human lives are at stake. In iHospital (*Thomas, 2006*) the authors create an interactive and pervasive system to be used in hospitals, showing that issues that seem trivial in the laboratory become major obstacles in the real world. The system aims to efficiently coordinate the operations of a large hospital. The system can also monitor the position of users through some mobile devices.

Finally, the Massachusetts Institute of Technology (MIT) has a project called Oxygen (*Rudolph, 2001*) that envisions a future where the goal is to have a very large number of ubiquitous computing devices in the environment, enabling people to interact with them in a very simple way, i.e. through natural perceptual interfaces of speech and vision, to perform the tasks they want. In other words, devices will be freely available and easily accessible as oxygen is today.

AN OVERVIEW OF THE UBIQUITOUS COMPUTING APPLICATIONS DEVELOPED

Our experiences over previous years developing context-aware applications prototypes on different platforms provided us with a significant knowledge into the important issues in developing pervasive applications for context-aware environments. In this section, we summarize some of those prototypes that were developed iteratively by modifying both hardware and software components to improve their functionality.

It is important to note that two main lessons were confirmed when developing applications for pervasive computing systems. Firstly, offering computation and communication capabilities to an ordinary object requires low-cost solutions; otherwise, the construction of a prototype may become too expensive, or even impossible. Secondly, minimizing power consumption and size is mandatory to make more apparent the realization of ubiquitous computing. Therefore, to assess the impact of ubiquitous computing, rapid and inexpensive prototypes based on commercial off-the-shelf components are required.

BluePeer

One of our first experiences in developing a pervasive computing system was BluePeer (*JC. Cano, 2006*), an application framework to deploy an easy,

spontaneous, and infrastructureless network. We combined the Bluetooth technology (*Bluetooth SIG, 2001*) with the concept of peer-to-peer (P2P) networking to develop an experimental application which enables peers to exchange their resources. A P2P approach for spontaneous networks depends on the existence of a mechanism that allows any node in the network to transparently locate close-by devices and discover the type of services they offer. Bluetooth is a versatile and flexible short-range wireless networking technology with low power consumption which features that ability.

The application provides context services to interchange any kind of resources between Bluetooth devices or peers within one-hop wireless distance (the small area covered by the Bluetooth RF range). In the case that two devices are not reachable in one wireless hop, BluePeer allows clients to obtain the information from in-between devices. It is an ideal application for co-workers to synchronize their work. It can also be used in conferences and meetings, allowing the organization to share information with the attendees and also attendees to share their resources (e.g., snaps of the city, presentations, etc) with one another in a peer-to-peer manner. BluePeer can be considered as a proof of concept for other future applications.

The overall network architecture adopts a core peer-to-peer wireless network based on the Bluetooth technology used by mobile devices such as mobile phones and PDAs. The basic philosophy behind pure peer-to-peer applications is serverless communication. Therefore, there must not be a single entity that coordinates, controls and informs about the existence of the services available in the network in a centralized manner. Bluetooth discovery and role-switching functionalities allow low-level search, finding, and communication of remote devices and resources. Figure 1 illustrates our architecture, in a setting where all nodes are able to communicate with each other.

Each participating node or device in the application can assume either server or client roles.

Figure 1. *A pictorial representation of the peer-to-peer application*

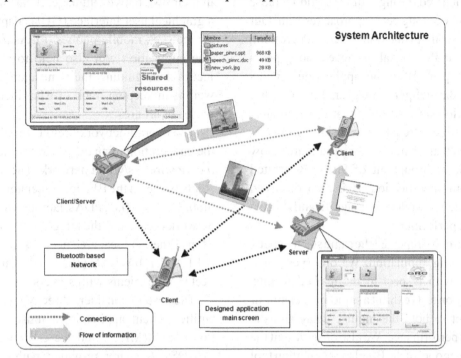

This also means that a node can be in both states at the same time, retrieving information from a server and offering information to one or more clients. When the application starts up, each node starts its server side code and automatically listens for possible clients or peers that may want to interact with that particular node. Moreover, when a node wants to communicate or locate a piece of information or file, it starts looking for nearby nodes that offer that required service, inquiring for the information available.

Therefore, the server side code basically deals with the administration of incoming connections for supplying clients with the files that have been chosen. The server keeps a registry of all connections made and the sent files. Once a client has made a request for a certain file, the server searches for the file and sends it on the L2CAP connection previously created. On the other hand, the client side code has a little more work involved to setup connections. This is mainly due to the necessity for using inquiry/discovery of remote nodes, and then starting a connection to the remote peer. The inquiry function will find available remote devices in the locality of the RF range. Remote nodes will be shown to the user with their device address and name for simplicity. Once a remote device has been discovered, the client side can connect to it and search for a file or download the shared file list. Likewise, the client can connect to other nodes and repeat the operation. The connection uses the same L2CAP connections to transfer data.

Using the developed prototype, we evaluated some of its characteristics through detailed experiments in a small testbed, as well as by using simulation. The performance evaluation of the application with our testbed was made focusing on inquiry delay and throughput performance. In our real-world testbed, we observed that after 3 seconds (on average), users can discover the desired information almost 50% of the times. This waiting time is normally acceptable to a user without causing annoyance. Our experiments also showed that the delay incurred during inquiry could increase as the distance among peers approaches 10m. Our findings show that Bluetooth offers a decreasing throughput as the spatial distance among peers increases. Up to 10m, the application obtains acceptable throughput. However, beyond 10m, the application suffers from a sharp performance degradation due to frequent packet losses. Finally, we observed that all the obtained results are below the maximum throughput of 90.40kB/s stated in Bluetooth specification. It is also observed that the node speed does not significantly affect throughput performance.

Afterward, we repeated the same set of experiments by using simulation. We observed some differences with respect to the testbed results. The simulation tests exhibit a smoother behaviour with respect to both the inquiry delay and the throughput performance. We also observe that the propagation model of the BlueHoc simulation tool used provides less penalty than the one imposed in the real world. Moreover, the simulated inquiry delay does not seem to be sensible to distance. These differences could be affected because of the implementation of the BlueHoc simulator that could slightly fail to produce realistic results.

Overall, our experiments demonstrate the feasibility of Bluetooth technology as an outstanding contender among providers of network support systems for the deployment of applications and communications for spontaneous networks. We proved that low-level features of Bluetooth can be effectively used to support peer-to-peer content exchange in a wireless communications context, and therefore to develop pervasive applications.

UbiqMuseum

In second place we describe an experimental context-aware application called UbiqMuseum (*Cano, 2006*), which provides context-aware information to museum visitors. The system gives precise information to visitors about what they are viewing according to their level of knowledge and in their own native language. It can also provide a graphical user interface (GUI) adapted to their device (i.e., mobile phones, PDAs, or laptops). The application will also help to reduce costs incurred in guiding their museum visitors, as well as in keeping track of what their favourite pieces of art are.

The overall network architecture is based on the cooperation of an *edge* wireless network and *a core* wireless/wired network. The edge side is solely based on the Bluetooth technology used by mobile devices (i.e., PDAs, laptops, etc.). The core network is based on the integration of a fixed 100 Mbps Ethernet local area network and a wireless IEEE 802.11b WLAN (*IEEE, 1999*) used to connect mobile clients with servers.

The system considers three types of software entities: client applications, museum information points (MIPs), and the central data server (MCDS). A visitor provided with a Bluetooth enabled PDA is the basic example of a mobile client. There is a MIP associated to one or more pieces of art or objects. MIPs are connected to the central server using any suitable combination of Bluetooth, Ethernet, or IEEE 802.11 permanent connections. The adequacy of the combination of devices depends on the physical layout of the facility. Figure 2 shows a pictorial representation of the UbiqMuseum architecture.

The first step for each Museum Information Client is initialization: users have to state their preferences as a basic set of input parameters, that is: (a) the type of device, (b) the preferred language and (c) the level of details when receiving information. Although this step requires minimal user interaction, the application also has a predefined profile for those mobile clients that do not consider going through this step. The predefined profile uses the following parameters: (a) laptop, (b) English, and (c) intermediate. Once all the data is filled in, the application will continuously search for new MIPs through Bluetooth inquiry process. When a MIP is found, it is checked to assess whether it can offer any new information of interest by

Figure 2. The UbiqMuseum system architecture

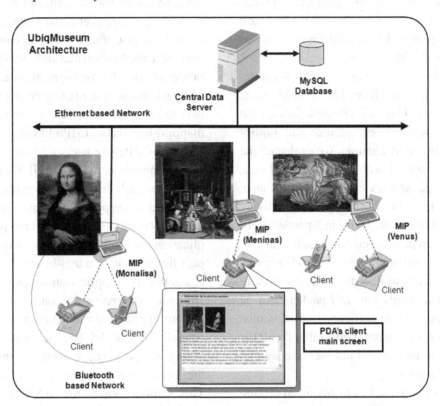

using the Service Discovery Protocol (SDP). If the user wants to receive this new information, he must send the user profile that was entered in the initial configuration process. Knowing the user's profile, the information point can process the request. It will then combine the user profile with an identifier of the object the user is viewing, and it will send it to the central server. There, the request is logged and processed, and a reply is returned to the information point which relays it to the client. The search for a MIP can take place automatically, which is the default option, or upon user request. The user can change his profile at any time - for example, whenever he considers the obtained information to be too advanced or too basic. This allows future accesses to be more in line with user expectations.

The museum central data server (MCDS) has two main functions: (a) to attend to connections for MIP requests, and (b) to manage the SQL database,

i.e., to handle all the information related to the pieces of art in the museum. The SQL database is based on two different tables: (a) the information table, and (b) the description table. The information table consists of three different fields that store, for each art object: its identifier, the title and the author; the identifier field is used as the primary key. The description table has a total of seven fields, and is used to store detailed information related to every art object. SQL-based databases were adopted since they provide a high level of security and a more efficient storage support and maintenance.

The application was developed using the standard Java APIs for Bluetooth wireless technology (JABWT) (Kumar, 2002) proposed by the Java Experts Group JSR-82. The JABWT standard provides the socket API to L2CAP. L2CAP provides a reliable channel and uses segmentation and reassembly on "Asynchronous Connection-Less"

(ACL) packets (*Bluetooth SIG, 2001*). L2CAP also multiplexes communications through the Protocol/ Service Multiplexor (PSM) field abstraction that works as a TCP port.

Performance evaluation of UbiqMuseum was made using a small testbed to confirm its correct behavior. Our experiments focused on evaluating throughput performance and inquiry delay of the Bluetooth channel. We evaluated the impact on throughput with varying packet size, FEC coding types and device separation distance. We observed that Bluetooth offered a relatively steady throughput up to 10 m, independently of the data packet type selected. The results had also confirmed that, although the use of *DM* packets improved efficiency while reducing the probability of successful transmission, *DH* packets can be good candidates for more efficient transmissions. Our experiments had also showed that the delay incurred during inquiry did not increase significantly with distance.

Key issues related to future advanced mobile context-aware systems include optimizations to obtain higher throughput and faster service discovery, while offering the user a fast information download and a simplified entry of user profiles. Therefore, our prototype system allows us not only to confirm the correct behavior of the designed application, but also to acquire experimental data to evaluate the adequacy of Bluetooth for context-aware systems.

VisualDNS

In the next prototype we apply the concept of ubiquitous applications to address the problems of autoconfiguration and communication in MANETs (Manet, 1999). Mobile Ad Hoc Networks, or MANETs, are autonomous systems that do not require any fixed infrastructure of support nor centralized administration. MANETs are composed of independent mobile terminals which communicate among themselves using any sort of wireless technology. Each terminal operates not only as an end-system, but also cooperates on routing and packet forwarding tasks.

We present Visual DNS (*J.Cano, 2007*), a pervasive application that embraces peer collaboration to solve the problem of host discovery in MANETs environments. Our proposal is an extension to the traditional DNS service that, besides mapping host names to IP addresses, goes one step further by offering users a visual identification of other members in the MANET. In particular it offers, for each discovered member, their photo, name and corresponding IP identifier. When the user selects any of the discovered peers, the application allows to start communication with that peer through either a text-based chat application or a multimedia application, supporting both VoIP and videoconference sessions.

Our application runs upon a previously configured Mobile Ad hoc network. In (*J.Cano, 2006*) we proposed a solution that addresses the interface configuration of MANET nodes. This solution makes the MANET initialization process fully automatic by relying on Bluetooth technology, providing a fast and reliable method to auto-configure MANET terminals. To carry out the autoconfiguration task, the system offers a Bluetooth service specifically designed for that purpose called MANET_Autoconf.

Visual DNS relies on a distributed discovery protocol based on a combination of UDP and TCP functionality. Each node will periodically broadcast to its neighbors an UDP packet including a list with the IP addresses of all the known peers in the MANET. Upon receiving this message, all the neighbors will compare the list of advertised members with their own to find out if new members are listed. If new members are detected, the node will open a TCP connection to the neighbor advertising this new information, and then it will proceed to download the data set associated with new members. Figure 3 shows a small scenario which illustrates how the discovery protocol behaves.

Figure 3. Information dissemination with VisualDNS

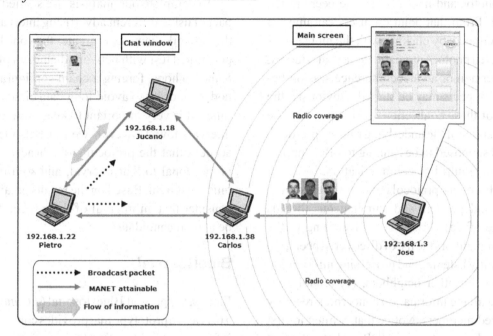

The main goal of the discovery protocol is to disseminate information about all MANET members to all the nodes in the network, independently of whether peers are directly reachable. In our example scenario, although node identified by 192.168.1.3 does not receive the UDP packets disseminated by nodes 192.168.1.18 and 192.168.1.22, it will eventually receive an UDP packet from node 192.168.1.38 advertising information about those two previous nodes. Upon receiving this UDP packet, node 192.168.1.3 will request information about these new nodes to node 192.168.1.38 using a reliable TCP connection. Figure 3 shows that, although a node cannot directly communicate with all the other nodes in the network, it will eventually receive information about all members, and so it will be able to maintain a complete list of MANET peers.

The period of time between consecutive UDP broadcast messages is a configurable parameter which could impact the efficiency and effectiveness of the protocol. However, since our approach limits broadcast communication to direct neighbors, we can guarantee that our discovery

protocol does not exhibit the so called broadcast storm problem (*Ni, 1999*), typical of MANETs scenarios, caused by multiple re-propagations of broadcasted messages.

We implemented our application for both Windows and Linux operating systems using a Java like programming language (J2SE), under the NetBeans IDE platform, which offers a robust object-oriented multiplatform solution. Before the application starts running the proposed discovery protocol, it is assumed that one of the wireless interfaces is already configured adequately for MANET communication to take place, which includes all the information required to configure the Wi-Fi interface (SSID, channel, etc.), setting the station's IP address and mask, and starting the appropriate MANET routing protocol (e.g. DSR, AODV, OLSR).

Each MANET member must fill-in their personal information, including the user's name and photo, which will be used by other peers to visually recognize the user. Once the discovery protocol completes the information dissemination process, Visual DNS' graphical interface will show all the photos and names of all the peers in the MANET. From that point on, users can interact with other peers by clicking with the mouse over any selected photo. Automatically, a chat window, a VoIP session or a videoconference session between both peers may be started. Obviously, the success of these connections will depend on the right behavior of the underlying routing protocol, which is supposed to be running to offer support for mobile, multi-hop communication.

The discovery protocol requires the execution of three independent and simultaneous threads in charge of: (a) periodically advertising to the one-hop neighbors the list of discovered peers, (b) permanently listening and processing information advertised by other neighbors, (c) reliably exchanging all the information concerning recently discovered members. Notice that, while the first two threads operate over UDP sockets, the last one makes use of TCP sockets instead.

We now present some performance results for Visual DNS. Our purpose was to assess the overhead imposed by the proposed data dissemination strategy. We firstly focus on the transference of user data. With Visual DNS, the set of descriptive information for each user occupies between 2.5 and 3.5 kilobytes. As a result of this test we observe that, when transferring information about many new users, the total transference time is usually below 300ms, a very low value, approaching 2 seconds under worst case conditions. Notice, however, that massive data transfers are infrequent, only applying to nodes that have recently joined the MANET.

The second experiment considers that four nodes within radio range of each other conform a simple ad hoc network. We wish to measure the time it takes for completing data dissemination to all nodes using different message advertising intervals. We observed that full configuration times increase almost linearly with the advertisement interval and that, to achieve reasonable setup times, advertisement intervals above five seconds should be avoided.

To complete our analysis, we studied the impact of using different advertising intervals when the network diameter is greater than one hop. We performed test with network diameters of 1, 2, 4, 8 and 16 hops, forcing a chain configuration for nodes. In order to avoid long data dissemination times, it is very important to keep advertisement intervals low. However, we must also take into account that the protocol's overhead is directly proportional to that interval, and so a trade-off must be sought. Based on the results obtained, we consider that an interval of three seconds could be a good candidate.

BlueHospital

Finally, we present BlueHospital (*J.Cano, 2008*), a pervasive prototype that provides context-aware information and location based services to clinicians on hospitals' recovery wards. BlueHospital leverages Bluetooth technologies and Java services to offer patient information to clinical personnel based on the patient's profile and the clinicians' preferences and requirements.

The overall network architecture is based on the cooperation of an edge wireless network and a core wired network. The edge part is based on Bluetooth technology alone. The core network is based on a fixed 100 Mbps Ethernet local area network used to connect the edge infrastructure with the central database. The system considers four network entities: hospital patients, room managers, clinical personnel, and the central database server. Figure 4 shows a pictorial representation of the BlueHospital architecture.

A doctor provided with a Bluetooth enabled PDA/smartphone is the basic example of mobile clinical personnel. Doctors are connected to the central database through the room manager to receive information about patients, including their case history as well as comparable cases. Doctors can make diagnoses faster using all the information available at the central database, choosing the best therapy or medicine for each particular

Figure 4. The BlueHospital System Architecture

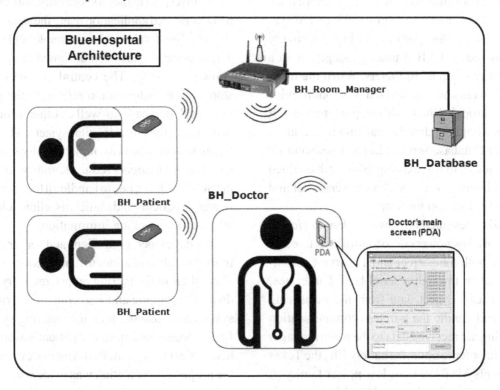

patient. There is a *Patient device* associated to each patient who has been admitted and allocated in a recovery ward. The *Patient device* connects to the *Room manager* to register data in the central database. The data being monitored consists of frequent measurement of body temperature and heart rate. There is a *Room manager* associated to every recovery ward acting as a bridge between doctors and patients' sensors to the central database, and vice versa. Finally, the central database is able to generate precise patient profiles based on clinicians' requests and preferences.

Being BlueHospital a context-aware system, it is able to provide valuable information to clinical personnel without any user interaction. When a clinician is visiting patients at recovery wards, the application will automatically search for the room manager device, which will offer any new information of interest about the patient. If a user wants to look up new information or introduce information in the system he must send the request

together with the user profile that was entered in the initial configuration process to the manager, i.e., the user is a doctor, a nurse, etc. Knowing the user profile, the *Room manager* can process the request combining the user profile with some additional information, and it will send it to the central data server. There the request is logged and processed, and a reply is returned to the room manager which relays it to the clinician. The entire process takes place automatically, and clinicians can change their profile at any time to receive more details about the patients in their own language and adapted to their device, i.e., mobile phone, PDA, or laptop.

The BlueHospital system is also able to track clinical personnel and patients by relying on its location and context aware infrastructure. Instead of using some commercial system which is perhaps more precise and certainly more expensive, we delegate to Bluetooth the location functionality. Since we only require location tracking of patient and clinicians within a room level granularity, we developed our own coarse-grained location system. All *Room Manager* devices in the recovery wards include a USB Bluetooth adapter with a reachability of up to 10 meters. When the manager discovers a new authorized Bluetooth device enabled through Bluetooth's inquiry process, it will accordingly update the tracking information within the Database Server. The proposed solution also allows us to use existing Bluetooth enabled mobile phones owned by clinical personnel and patients for location tracking.

We also designed our own *Patient device*. It consists of a low power microcontroller connected to a Bluetooth transceiver and a heart rate monitoring system through a serial UART interface, so that it can collect data from the measuring system and handle the wireless communication by sending the received data to the room manager device. In order to optimize battery life, the Texas Instruments MSP430 ultra-low power family of microcontrollers has been selected because it is particularly well suited for power constrained applications. A class 1 Bluetooth module has been used for wireless communication.

Concerning the *Room Manager* we adopt a low cost solution based on Wi-Fi routers which accommodate Bluetooth connectivity through an USB port, as well as a Fast Ethernet interface to connect to the central database. Each operating ward is equipped with a *Room Manager* based on the ASUS WL-500g Premium wireless router which contains, at a very reasonable price, almost every feature you may require to deploy a small computer network. When a connection comes in, the *Room Manager* will spawn a child process to deal with the mobile client's request. The child process will receive the client's profile, which is forwarded to the central Server. There, it will be logged and processed according to the client's profile. Eventually the required information will be sent back and passed on to the client. The parent process will carry on waiting for further client connections.

With respect to the Doctor entity, we developed a PDA oriented application using the standard Java APIs for Bluetooth wireless technology (JABWT). The application has been designed to be used by clinicians' PDAs. The central Database Server stores all the information related to the patients in an SQL database, as well as other information concerning the BlueHospital system. The central database server has two main functions: (a) to attend *Room Managers* requests, and (b) to manage the SQL database, i.e., to handle all the information related to patients and clinicians, clinic schedules, and location tracking information.

We developed both client and server applications, providing routines to handle doctor requests about their patients, find empty recovery wards, do profile logging and also content filtering. The system may use the location tracking system to find a doctor and notify a patient's ward about his medical treatment. Performance evaluation of the proposed application was made with focus on energy consumption, throughput and inquiry delay. We found that Bluetooth modules implementing low-power modes could significantly alleviate the power consumption of Bluetooth nodes. Our experiments also showed that Bluetooth also offers a relatively steady throughput up to 10m. Concerning latency, we find that it is completely acceptable for clinical personnel without causing annoyance.

FUTURE RESEARCH DIRECTIONS

We are moving gradually towards the final vision of ubiquitous computing, where almost all everyday objects may communicate and cooperate with each other. However, this vision requires a close cooperation between three converging areas of Information and Communications Technology: computing devices, communications, and user interfaces. Future smart devices will have various shapes and sizes and will be designed for different task-specific purposes. These devices will rely on some kind of wireless communication system (such as WLAN, Bluetooth, or ZigBee) to act intelligently, being able to create the most effective form of connectivity in a given scenario. Finally, the user interface represents the union point between technology and human users. Natural interfaces, based on both speech and gesture recognition, will facilitate a richer variety of communication capabilities.

Envisioning concrete applications is not easy. However, the appropriate combination of these three areas yield up to a wide range of applications not only in traditional areas (e.g., healthcare, education, transport, monitoring, tourism information, and smart networking), but also in those where the Internet already plays an important role, such as mobile commerce, telematics, and entertainment. Emerging technologies supporting those applications include wearable computing, smart homes, smart toys, intelligent environments, and augmented reality, among the many other imaginable. The 21st century will be characterized by the applicability of near-invisible technology that is easy to spread through the environment.

CONCLUSION

The key idea behind pervasive computing is to deploy a wide variety of computing devices throughout our living and working spaces. These devices cooperate with each other to offer network services, with the ultimate goal of seamlessly assisting people in completing their tasks. Pervasive computing marks a major shift in computing, moving away from the current computing paradigm to become more human-centric.

Research about pervasive computing has been around for more than ten years. People are fascinated by the possibilities of pervasive computing due to the proliferation of inexpensive mobile computing devices, wireless communication and sensing technologies, setting up a new kind of intelligent environment where applications can

transparently search and use services without the users' intervention. Despite few real-world applications have been developed and deployed up to now, the constant pace of innovation will definitely contribute to achieving Weiser's vision of an ubiquitous computing world.

REFERENCES

Abowd, G., Atkeson, C., Hong, J., Long, S., Kooper, R., & Pinkerton, M. (1997). Cyberguide: A mobile context-aware tour guide. *ACM wireless. Networks, 3*(5), 421–433.

Asthana, A., Cravatts, M., & Krzyzanouski, P. (1994). An indoor wireless system for personalized shopping assistance. In *Workshop on Mobile Computing Systems and Applications*.

Baldauf, M., Dustdar, S., & Rosenberg, F. (2007). A survey on context-aware systems. *International Journal of Ad Hoc and Ubiquitous Computing, 2*(4). doi:10.1504/IJAHUC.2007.014070

Bluetooth SIG, Promoter Members. (2001). Specification of the Bluetooth System – Core. Version 1.1. *Bluetooth SIG, Inc.*

Broadbent, J., & Marti, P. (1997). Location Aware Mobile Interactive Guides: usability issues. In *Proceedings of the Fourth International Conference on Hypermedia and Interactivity in Museums (ICHIM97)*.

Cano, J., Burgoa, E., Calafate, C., Cano, J. C., & Manzoni, P. (2006). A MANET autoconfiguration system based on Bluetooth technology. In *3rd IEEE International Symposium on Wireless Communication Systems (ISWCS)*, Valencia, Spain.

Cano, J., Cano, J. C., Calafate, C., & Manzoni, P. (2007). Solving the user-to-host binding problem in ad hoc networks through the dissemination of photographic identifiers. In *Fourth ACM International Workshop on Performance Evaluation of Wireless Ad Hoc, Sensor, and Ubiquitous Networks - PE-WASUN'07, co-located with MSWIM'07*, Chania, Crete Island, Greece.

Cano, J., Cano, J. C., Calafate, C., & Manzoni, P. (2008). Deploying Pervasive Technologies. In Encyclopedia of Information Science and Technology, (2nd Ed.). Hershey, PA: Information Science Reference.

Cano, J. C. Manzoni, p., & Toh, CK., (2006). UbiqMuseum: A Bluetooth and Java Based Context Aware System for Ubiquitous Computing. In Wireless Personal Communications Springer Science+Business Media B.V.

Cano, J. C., Cano, J., Manzoni, P., & Kim, D. (2006). On the design of pervasive computing applications based on Bluetooth and a P2P concept. In *1st International IEEE Symposium on Wireless Pervasive Computing*, 16 - 18 January 2006, Phuket, Thailand.

Cox, R., O'Donnell, M., & Oberlander, J. (1999). Dynamic versus static hypermedia in museum education: an evaluation of ILEX, the intelligent labelling explorer. In *Proceedings of the Artificial Intelligence in Education conference*.

Davies, N., Mitchell, K., Cheverst, K., & Blair, G. (1998). Developing a context sensitive tourist guide. Technical Report Computing Department, Lancaster University, Lancaster, UK.

Davin, S., & Ing, L. (1999). Innovations in a technology museum. *IEEE Micro, 19*(6).

Fitton, D. (2005). Rapid Prototyping and User-Centered Design of Interactive Display-Based Systems. *IEEE Pervasive Computing / IEEE Computer Society [and] IEEE Communications Society, 4*(5).

Fleck, M., Frid, M., Kindberg, T., O'Brien-Strain, E., Rajani, R., & Spasojevic, M. (2002). Rememberer: a tool for capturing museum visits. In *Proceedings of the Ubiquitous Computing International Conference*.

Grimm, R., Davis, J., Lemar, E., MacBeth, A., Swanson, S., & Anderson, T. (2004). System support for pervasive applications. *ACM Transactions on Computer Systems, 22*(4), 421–486. doi:10.1145/1035582.1035584

Harter, A., Hopper, A., & Steggeles, P. Ward. A. & Webster, P. (1999). The anatomy of a context-aware application. In *Proceedings of the Fifth Annual ACM/IEEE International Conference on Mobile Computing and Networking (MOBICOM)*.

IEEE/IEC Std 802.11. (1999). *Wireless LAN Medium Access Control (MAC) and Physical Layer (PHY) specifications - High Speed Physical Layer in the 5 GHz Band*. Washington, DC: The Institute of Electrical and Electronics Engineers, Inc.

Kindberg, T. et.al. (2002). People, places, things: web presence for the Real World. *MONET, 7*(5).

Kumar, B. (2002). *JSR-82: Java APIs for Bluetooth*. Retrieved from http://www.jcp.org/en/jsr/detail?id=82

Long, S., Kooper, R., Abowd, G., & Atkeson, C. (1996). Rapid prototyping of mobile context-aware applications: The cyberguide case study. In *Proceedings of the 2nd Annual International Conference on Mobile Computing and Networking*.

Manet Working Group. (1999). *Internet Engineering Task Force*. Retrieved from http://www.ietf.org/html.charters/manet-charter.html

Ni, S.-Y., Tseng, Y.-C., Chen, Y.-S., & Sheu, J.-P. (1999). The broadcast storm problem in a mobile ad hoc network. In *MobiCom: Proceedings of the 5th annual ACM/IEEE international conference on Mobile computing and networking*, (pp. 151–162). New York: ACM Press.

Oliver, S., Adrian, F., Nigel, D., Joe, F., Corina, S., & Jennifer, S. (2006). Public Ubiquitous Computing Systems: Lessons from the e-Campus Display Deployments. *IEEE Pervasive Computing / IEEE Computer Society [and] IEEE Communications Society, 5*(3).

Pradhan, S., Brignone, C., Cui, J., McReynolds, A., & Smith, M. (2004). Websign: hyperlinks from a physical location to the web. Technical Report HP Laboratories.

Rudolph, L. (2001). Project Oxygen: pervasive, human-centric computing-an initial experience. In *13th International Conference on Advanced Information Systems Engineering, CAiSE*.

Sakamura, K. (1998). Digital museum. *Journal of Information Processing Society of Japan, 39*(5).

Semper, R., & Spasojevic, M. (2002). The electronic guidebook: using portable devices and a wireless web-based network to extend the museum experience. In *Proceedings of the museums and the Web*.

Shafer, S., Krumm, J., Brumitt, B., Meyers, B., Czerwinski, M., & Robbins, D. (1998). The New EasyLiving Project at Microsoft Research. In *Proceedings of the 1998 DARPA / NIST Smart Spaces Workshop*, (pp.127-130).

Smart-its. (2007). Interconnected embedded technology for smart artifacts with collective awareness. Lancaster University, ETH Zurich.

Spasojevic, M., Mirjana, A., & Kindberg, T. (2001). A study of an augmented museum experience. Technical Report HP Laboratories.

Thomas, H., Jakob, B., & Mads, S. (2006). Moving Out of the Lab: Deploying Pervasive Technologies in a Hospital. *IEEE Pervasive Computing / IEEE Computer Society [and] IEEE Communications Society, 5*(3).

Want, R., Hopper, A., Falcao, V., & Gibbons, J. (1992). The active badge location system. *ACM Transactions on Information Systems, 10*(1). doi:10.1145/128756.128759

Want, R., Schilit, B., Adams, N., Gold, R., Petersen, K., Ellis, J., et al. (1995). The PARCTAB Ubiquitous Computing Experiment. Palo Alto, CA: Xerox Palo Alto Research Center, CSL-95-1.

Weiser, M. (1991). The computer for the 21st century. *Scientific American, 265*, 94–104. doi:10.1038/scientificamerican0991-94

Weiser, M. (1993). Some computer science problems in ubiquitous computing. In Communications of the ACM.

KEY TERMS AND DEFINITIONS

Pervasive Computing: The next computing paradigm based on environments with information and communication technology everywhere, for everyone, at all times.

Ubiquitous System: A system from which the personal computer has disappeared and it has been replaced by a multitude of wireless computing devices embodied in everyday object.

Context-Aware Application: Applications which may change or adapt their functionality depending on the context, the client profile, and the user interface.

P2P (Peer-to-Peer): A network without any kind of centralized administration. Any node in the network has the same role that any other and can act as a client, as a server or even both at the same time.

Spontaneous Network: A small infrastructureless network formed when a group of people come together to participate in some collaborative activity.

MANET: Or Mobile Ad hoc Network, is an autonomous system composed of independent mobile terminals which communicate among themselves using any sort of wireless technology.

WiFi: Or Wireless-Fidelity, a logo from the Wi-Fi Alliance that certifies network devices comply with the IEEE 802.11 wireless Ethernet standards.

Bluetooth: A short range low power radio technology which allows multiple compatible devices to connect to each other to transmit voice and data.

Zigbee: A low-cost, low-power radio technology used for wireless control and monitoring applications. Its low-power characteristics allow improving battery lifetime, while offering high reliability and larger range to mesh networks.

Chapter 6

Wireless Sensor Network Based Data Fusion and Control Model for an Oil Production Platform

Mitun Bhattacharyya
R. V. College of Engineering, India

Ashok Kumar
University of Louisiana at Lafayette, USA

Magdy Bayoumi
University of Louisiana at Lafayette, USA

ABSTRACT

In this chapter the authors propose methodologies for improving the efficiency of a control system in an industrial environment, specifically an oil production platform. They propose a data fusion model that consists of four steps – preprocessing, classification and association, data association and correlation association, and composite decision. The first two steps are executed at the sensor network level and the last two steps are done at the network manager or controller level. Their second proposal is a distributed hierarchical control system and network management system. Here the central idea is that the network manager and controller coordinate in order to make delays in feedback loops as well as for increasing the lifetime of the sensor network. The authors finally conclude the control system proposal by giving a controlling model using sensor networks to control the flow of hydrocarbons in an oil production platform.

INTRODUCTION

WirelessHART is a standard that has been developed by four major companies in control systems. They mainly deal with field devices and their monitoring and controlling aspects. In this chapter, components

are any process devices. Sensor nodes are referred to as nodes or sensor nodes. The sensor nodes can be connected to a component to make it wireless. The sensor nodes are deployed in uniform distribution. Network related decisions that cover a large area are made by the network manager. Localized network decisions are taken by the sensor nodes themselves.

DOI: 10.4018/978-1-61520-843-2.ch006

According to (Baillieul & Antsaklis, 2007), research is needed for networked control systems that are distributed, fault tolerant, that gracefully degrade under adverse conditions, and can operate in distributed independence. In this chapter we explore a system that incorporates a sensor network system on an oil field platform. The advantages of using sensor networks are the following. They are cost effective, they can have distributed operations, and their deployment and replacement is very easy in most cases. In this work, we have a case study on aspects of monitoring safety of pipelines. From an oil company's proprietary data sheet, we see that not only pipeline flow control is required but options for emergency shut down of several pipelines by the use of valves in different locations is also required. We address both these requirements using sensor networks. The scenario is monitoring of pressure with consideration of important factors like flow rate, corrosion amount and flow regime with options of emergency shut down. This scenario is explored by employing sensor network control systems in the feedback loop.

RELATED WORK

There are a few related works in this field from the control system point of view. These works define the sensor network as a component of the system with varying delays. The work in (Eriksson & Koivo, 2005) gives a model for tuning of a PID controller assuming a Gaussian varying time delays. The work in (Sinopoli, Schenato, Franceschetti, Poolla, & Sastry, 2005) analyzes a control system with time varying delays between sensor and controller and controller and actuator. The work in (Colandairaj, Irwin, Scanlon, & William, 2007) explores a combination of data rate scaling and sample rate adaptation for control systems to handle time varying network conditions. The other works include (Kawka & Alleyne, 2005), (Adam, Brady, & Kosc, 2001), (Peng, Huijin,

Lei, Zhi, & Anke, 2006). In (Nikolakopoulos, Panousopoulou, Tzes, & Lygeros, 2005) a LPQ controller is designed whose parameters are changed depending on number of hops taken in network. Having a system based on complete path knowledge from source to destination is expensive and not implementable in sensor networks. Moreover, the Zigbee and 802.15.4 standards are used in sensor networks. According to (Nixon, Deji, Blevins, & Mok, 2008), control loop should execute 4 to 10 times faster than the processing time plus dead time. In addition to delays in the control loop, there is also a presence of jitter (i.e., variation in inputs, outputs, control execution). In terms of communication, the variation in delay to deliver a measurement from source to destination is referred to as jitter. By synchronizing network related processes with control execution, the need for over-sampling and communicating excessive measurements can be minimized. The work in (Dei, Snickars, Landernas, & Isaksson, 2008) proposes a methodology to counteract controller clock drift. It is seen that the performance improves if a Predictive PI (PPI) controller is used. The work also discusses a simulator tool in Simulink called TrueTime. The work in (Lennvall, Svensson, & Hekland, 2008) gives more details of the TrueTime Simulator.

PROPOSED WORK

The organization of this section is as follows. We begin with a discussion of our proposed system model. Next, we discuss the interaction between the controller and network manager and describe the advantages of our proposed system setup over existing work. This is followed by a discussion of our proposed data fusion model. Finally, we conclude by deriving a dynamic state model of a control system with a feedback loop, using sensor network, and propose a methodology for monitoring the health of the wireless sensor network.

GENERAL SETUP OF SYSTEM

Sensor nodes are connected to a controller through multi hops. In addition we have the Supervisory Control And Data Acquisition (SCADA) system for data gathering purposes. The sensors perform three primary jobs namely, sending data either or both to the SCADA system and the master controller, taking controlling action depending on readings of sensor meters, and determining any emergency situation and taking appropriate action.

DISTRIBUTED CONTROL

Appropriate sensor nodes have the following information in our system

$$
\begin{bmatrix} C_0 \\ C_1 \\ \vdots \\ \\ C_n \end{bmatrix} = \begin{bmatrix} H_{11} & H_{12} & & H_{1n} \\ H_{21} & H_{22} & \cdots & \\ \vdots & \cdot & \ddots & \vdots \\ \\ H_{n1} & \cdots & & H_{nn} \end{bmatrix} \begin{bmatrix} P_1 \\ F_1 \\ \vdots \\ \vdots \\ F_n \\ T_n \end{bmatrix} + \begin{bmatrix} R_1 \\ R_2 \\ \vdots \\ \\ R_n \end{bmatrix} \quad (1)
$$

Equation 1 gives the controlling action details. P_x, F_x are pressure and flow sensors. C_x is the controlling action required for a combination of sensor readings. Such sensors could sense or record pressure, temperature, level etc. The set of actions that could be taken for a combination of sensor meter reading can be, for example, sending error reading to controllers for further action or shutting down one or several valves. H_{xx} is defined as the "Knowledge" factor. It can take the value of 0 or 1 only. It ties a relevant sensor reading to a suitable controlling action. R_x is the risk factor associated with each controlling action. The control action table, as given in Equation 1, is present at appropriate sensor nodes decided by the controller and the network manager.

We have two types of controlling actions, as follows.

- Step wise control to regulate any specific valve to change flow rate when required.
- Shut down operations that include completely shutting down certain parts of pipeline system. This typically involves routing shut down control action anywhere between 1 to 10 destinations.

Shutting down of a set of valves and single variable feedback control is done by the sensor nodes themselves. Multi variable control, cascade, ratio, feed forward control that require interaction between control loops is taken care of by the concerned controller. We assume that routing nodes know the various destination locations, though they may or may not have a path to the destinations. The nodes implement component based routing with end-to-end delay as the priority factor. Most valves work on a self-detection mechanism. For this reason, we expect the functionally related sensors and controlling components, which need to be connected through a set of sensor nodes, to be less within a specified region. The sensor network comes into action when the meter and valve are located at a distance from each other and if any of the instruments self-detecting mechanism fails.

Our proposed system setup is as follows. At the top level, we have a centralized controller and network manager that is responsible for system wide changes. At the next level we have the concerned controllers and network managers. Each set of concerned controller and network manager coordinate with one another to monitor and maintain a set of control loop. A set of functionally connected sensor nodes and process components form the lowest level of our setup. Each element of a lower level is managed by the higher levels.

The following operations need to take place in coordination between network manager and controller.

- Mapping components according to process for localization.

- Functional zone based routing. Easier on obtaining application level information.
- Mapping Electro Magnetic (EM) disturbance and routing. Also using Frequency Hopping Spread Spectrum (FHSS) or Direct Sequence Spread Spectrum (DSSS), depending on process schedule.
- Mapping sensor node energy level and control tables.
- Location of the control table depending on both network and control loop conditions.
- Mapping hot spots and high traffic load with industrial process schedule.
- Sector based monitoring of both health and process status depending on process flow schedule.
- Setting up of proactive routes.
- Scheduling network maintenance operations with respect to the process schedule operation.
- Updating sensor nodes with updated control tables.
- Updating sensor nodes with process schedule in case of process maintenance or some component shutdown during normal operations.
- Time Division Multiple Access (TDMA) scheduling in Medium Access Control (MAC) layer.
- Setting up priority levels in messages.
- Setting of confidence factors in data fusion.

CONTROLLER OPERATIONS

We assume a hierarchical distributed control system for our setup. The system has a centralized controller that takes global level control decisions, and distributed controllers that monitor a set of control loops.

A centralized controller breaks up all process control loops into groups. Each group is assigned to an appropriate controller depending on its proximity and relevance to the components of the control loop. Any query, or major process change information, is passed by the centralized controller to concerned controller. How these processes are grouped together is beyond the scope of this book chapter.

A distributed controller is responsible for a predefined set of control loops and such sets form a module. Since the set of control loops do not change much, we can assume that this set, more or less, remains the same for a long duration. The module consists of a set of control loops that have the most interactions between them. There may be some necessary interaction between modules present in two different controllers. The module has sub modules that are individual control loops. Each sub module has a list of components that are utilized within that loop. Each component has a timing metric associated with it along with a functional metric. The timing metric specifies the monitoring period as well as the activation time for that component. The functional metric gives the associated components of the component and maximum allowable delays permitted between the components. These metrics (functional and timing) can be changed based on two inputs:

- Any system wide process changes that affects the particular controller and initiated by the centralized controller.
- Any change due to observed parameters in the control loops.

The variation of the following factors affect the system wide changes in inputs: raw material quantity and quality; physical condition of the plant processes; control system conditions; production amount requirement; and operator skills and safety requirements. Figure 1 shows the setup of the control system.

Table 1 gives the timing and function metric for a sub module.

Figure 1. Hierarchical distributed control system

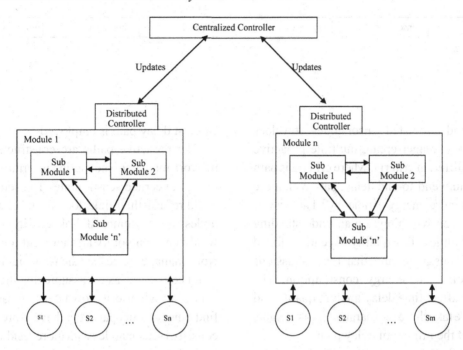

Table 1. Information that is kept at the concerned controller and interchanged with corresponding concerned network manager

Timing Information for Sub Module 1				Function Information	
Component	Monitoring interval	Activation time or interval	Deactivation time or interval	Associated Components	Maximum allowable time delay between them

NETWORK MANAGER

Our proposed system setup has a distributed, hierarchical structure for the network management. The centralized network manager takes system-wide decisions such as functional zone change, if any, as well as actions in case a distributed network manager fails, or for handling queries etc. The distributed network manager keeps track of the components and sensor nodes associated with the control loops monitored by the corresponding controller. The network manager monitors the status of the sensor nodes in terms of residual energy, link delays, link quality etc. During the initial phase of network setup, each

major component (unlimited power supply) keeps a list of nearby sensor nodes present. This list is sent to the network manager. The network manager uses this information to get a mapping of the components along with the associated sensor nodes. Table 2 shows the type of information stored in network manager.

We next discuss some of the design decisions taken by the network manager.

PROBLEM STATEMENT

A key question arises that can be phrased as follows. Given a mapping of components, its activa-

Table 2. Information kept at the Network Manager about sensor nodes connected to it

Component	Sensor Node	Distance	Link Quality	Link Delay	Energy spent

tion times and associated sensor nodes, how does the network manager create multiple proactive paths with different criteria, where criteria is path with minimum end-to-end delay; path with more latency but more energy efficiency? The answer to this question will hinge on an understanding that links with low link quality have more failed number of messages, and that retransmissions increase delay and energy consumption. The factors that affect time delay are link quality and distance. We take these two parameters as weights to construct the minimum delay path.

Suppose that we are given a set of sensor nodes G1(v, e) where v denotes the vertices or sensor nodes and e denotes the edges. Given a transmission range T_r for each sensor node, a minimum delay path is constructed between source and destination (between component and controller, sensor and controlling valves, between different components, between component and SCADA system). A simple greedy method could be used at each step.

$$Proactive_{Path} = \sum_{i=S}^{i=D} \left(d_{ij} \right) \qquad (2)$$

Where d_{ij} is limited by the transmission range of the sensor node; S is the source and D the destination. The link chosen is in the region towards destination. The set of links from which the link is chosen has to have the link quality and residual energy levels above a certain threshold. The threshold for the residual energy could be lower if there is pulsed operation in the sensor node where the sensor node can recover charge. Several such combinations of paths are constructed and the shortest delay path is employed.

The proactive paths are constructed by the network manager. The routing information is sent to the concerned sensor nodes The sensor nodes could refresh their links locally and choose other nodes as substitutes if link quality fails. This would be a temporary arrangement until the network manager refreshes the route again. Energy is not considered as we assume that there will be very few high priority low latency messages. We find other distinct paths that have more delay but consist of sensor nodes with more residual energy. In this proactive route, we take energy (E_i), link quality (LQ_{ij}) and distance (d_{ij}) as the parameters for obtaining the minimum path. We consider a weighted metric for each step to select a suitable neighbor.

$$W_{ij} = w_1 \max\left(E_i \right) + w_2 \max\left(LQ_{ij} \right) + w_3 \max\left(d_{ij} \right) \qquad (3)$$

Depending on controller signal requirements, more proactive routes with consideration for different percentile of energy could be constructed.

$$Proactive_{Path} = \sum_{i=S}^{i=D} \left(W_{ij} \right) \qquad (4)$$

The sensor node with maximum W_{ij} is chosen amongst all eligible next hop neighbors at each step (or loop).

We now consider the interaction between the concerned network manager and controller for the required operations, as described in the following points.

- Mapping components according to process for localization. Component location information is stored in the controller during installation of the particular component. Each ID of component is mapped according to the location and given to the network manager. Since the sensor nodes localize themselves based on component Id, their relative locations are known to the network manager.

- Functional zone based network process. Given the initiating times, schedule of process sequences in the industrial production line and proactive path set up, TDMA schedules for inter nodal communications are assigned. Action is taken to distribute the traffic load in the network.

- Mapping EM disturbance and routing paths. Also using FSSS or DSSS depending on process schedule. Process components that emit high amounts of EM waves are identified and that information is kept at the controller. Initiating times of these processes are given to the network manager if known before hand. Routing paths could be changed proactively, if required by the network manager.

- Mapping control tables onto appropriate sensor nodes (Location, RE levels etc.). First the network sets up the proactive routes required. Next a region is identified where the number of messages (traffic rate) * number of hops from each of the sources are equivalent. The region will be close to sources with high number of messages. Figure 2 shows the location of the sensor node with control tables.

- Mapping hot spots and high traffic load with industrial process schedule. From Table 1, Table 2 we can find the components, their activation and deactivation time schedules and their monitoring time requirements. Given the priority levels for each type of action and proactive path

maps, the network manager can determine the traffic load in a region at different time interval. If the components activation and deactivation schedule is not predetermined then once an event is detected and a component is activated, the Id of the component is passed on to the network manager. Route refresh messages could then be sent depending on the corresponding network requirements.

- Sector based monitoring of both health of sensor nodes and process status of components depending on process flow schedule. Refer to (Bhattacharyya, Kumar, Bayoumi, 2009).

- Scheduling network maintenance operations with respect to the process schedule operation. Sometimes due to maintenance, schedule checks, calibration etc. certain parts of the system are shutdown and process schedule is changed. The network manager needs to be notified of these changes. The network manager informs the sensor nodes and sensor nodes could either go to a sleep state for that period of time or elect to do other operations that are required by other processes.

- Sending sensor nodes with updated control tables. The control table changes depend on the process schedule change. The network manager is updated. Since the network manager knows the region where the control tables are stored, it forwards the information to the concerned region.

- Time Division Multiple Access (TDMA) scheduling in the Medium Access Control (MAC) layer (See Table 3).

In WirelessHART, TDMA based scheduling is used to have contention free transmission. Each network device maintains an identical link list that specifies which channels are used. A black list of frequencies also exists. There can concurrently be several superframes. However the link

Figure 2. Shows the location of the sensor nodes with the control tables

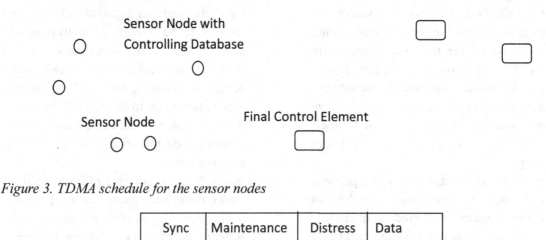

Figure 3. TDMA schedule for the sensor nodes

Sync	Maintenance	Distress	Data

between two devices can exist only in 1 of the superframes. Each link has a set of channels for frequency hopping. In the work (Pouria, Mohsen, 2008) a four-slotted superframe was defined. The first slot was reserved for beacons. The second slot was for MAC commands using CSMA/CA. The third slot was used to send cyclically generated data of sensor nodes and the fourth slot was for data generated by events.

We follow a similar superframe format. Maintenance slot is kept for proactive updates and system updates like process component shut down for maintenance and check for requests from certain special function sensor nodes. Different frequencies could be employed for each sensor node. In case of reactive routing, maintenance is to determine a suitable neighbor to route through. Distress time slot is used to check for distress signals from reactively routed and to take appropriate action. Distress slot is arranged so that there is at least one node in the localized region that will be alerted for distress signal during the superframe schedule. Sync is used to synchronize communication between nodes. Data communication between nodes is done during the data slot. This slot is further divided into frames for the different links that the node is connected to. For further efficiency, we propose and define two frequencies for each link, one for upstream and one for downstream. When a link is scheduled between two devices, both upstream and downstream data can be transmitted simultaneously during assigned time slot. In the data slot we also have a slot for CSMA/CA transmission that is utilized for reactive routing data transmissions.

Setting up of priority levels in messages is done as follows. Codes are defined for setting priority levels for different categories of data. The data is identified and tagged with appropriate priority and the information is sent to the appropriate sensor nodes that receive data.

Setting of confidence factors for data fusion is done as follows. If any error is detected in the observations made by sensor nodes, then these sensor node readings are given a low confidence factor. Due to known high interference environment, if a poor link quality is identified, then the confidence factor can be suitably lowered. This confidence factor is used during the data fusion process.

Figure 4. Shows the interactions between the various major components of our system

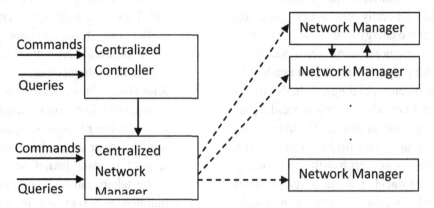

INTER FUNCTIONAL ZONE COMMUNICATION

In our proposed system we deploy a hierarchical distributed network management system as shown in Figure 4. The centralized network manager observes inter functional zone, process changes or end user commands or queries. It then determines the actions that need to be taken at each network manager under it as shown in Figure 4. There are several aspects where network managers need to coordinate with one another, as follows.

- Proactive routes set up by two network managers should not clash creating hot spot regions.
- Identifying sensor nodes with control tables should not be in any proactive zones.
- If more than 50% of two functional zones overlap with one another, then information between the concerned network managers should be shared. It will help in reducing sensor node health monitoring messages.
- Any commands that effect more than one network manager's regions.
- Any queries that effect more than one network manager's region.

DATA FUSION

This section deals with the data fusion aspects of our system. Data fusion of our system takes care of two things, as follows.

- Estimating the difference between set point and measure value (error) in the presence of faulty measurements.
- Taking distributed controlling actions dependent on observed set of parameters.

Any system failure should have a guaranteed detection in oil production platforms. System failures can result in human and economical losses. For fault tolerant data fusion, redundancy of meter readings becomes an important aspect. We assume that all sensor meter instruments are employed redundantly. Even if one fails the others can make observations.

RELATED WORK

The works of (Cetin et al, 2006) and (Hall & Llinas, 1997) give a good introduction to data fusion technologies. Data fusion is addressed at various levels. The works that address information fusion are (Dasarathy, 1997), (Steinberg, 2005), and (Steinberg, Franklin, 1998). Data fusion is also addressed at the microscopic level. All events detected could be directly sent to an aggregation point. However the energy cost for such a system would be very high, not scalable. (Niu, Varshney, & Cheng, 2006) proposes data fusion as a binary decision that is taken depending on whether a data is sensed or not. Once a hypothesis is decided, the hypothesis is sent out instead of the actual data itself. Intermediate nodes fuse data along with link channel errors and probability of a wrong hypothesis being decided at the lower levels of data fusion. Other works in the decision making process are (Hall & Llinas, 1997), (Thomopoulos, Viswanathan, & Bougoulias, 1989), (Wuyan; Liming & Yangwanhai, 2001), (D'Costa & Sayeed, 2003). There are several works proposed in the aggregation process of the observed data. These works include (Xiao, Boyd, & Lall, 2005), (Kumar, Garg, & Zachery, 2006).

PROPOSED WORK

A commonly available method for fusing data of heterogeneous sensor meter readings is based on existing correlation between the observed parameters. Our work is primarily based on it and tuned to our systems requirements and infrastructure. Unlike the previous works, we propose to fuse data and take distributed controlling decisions based on fused data. We address a petroleum platform control system application that has redundancy requirements and time constraints.

The main advantage in using sensor networks is that actions can be taken in a decentralized manner. After deployment, depending on which components the sensor nodes are functionally connected to, sensor nodes are given relevant information from the concerned controller. Three types of data fusion are required in this system

- Shut off control action (slow changing) – In this fusion process if a certain set of conditions are satisfied (certain combination of meter readings), a set of valves are shut off. Tables are sent out by concerned controller and stored in appropriate nodes. Appropriate action is then initiated by the sensor node themselves.

- Knowledge based data fusion (very slow changing) – Corrosion and seasonal changes make the production system time variant. However these changes are slow with respect to data fusion action that needs to be taken and any updates in model is handled and sent out by the Controller. Regression models created from prior data of the pipeline under consideration is used in the fusion process. Based on observed parameters, for example corrosion status are observed through pigs), mathematical models are updated by centralized controller. These updates are also sent to appropriate sensor node. Appropriate action is then taken by the sensor node itself.

- Error Readings (slow or fast changing) – Data fusion is required to get a good estimate of the difference between the required set point and the sensor meter reading. These reading are sent to the concerned controller if the control loop is multivariable or a cascade. Single variable control loops are handled by appropriate sensor nodes themselves. This reduces the time delay for control action.

Figure 5 shows the model proposed in our work.

To illustrate our proposed data fusion system, we take a case study of monitoring oil pipelines. First we start with a brief discussion on some requirements according to codes and regulations for the offshore pipelines in the Gulf of Mexico. We then map the monitoring and controlling requirements of the oil platform industries to our sensor-network-platform based data fusion system.

Figure 5. Proposed data fusion model

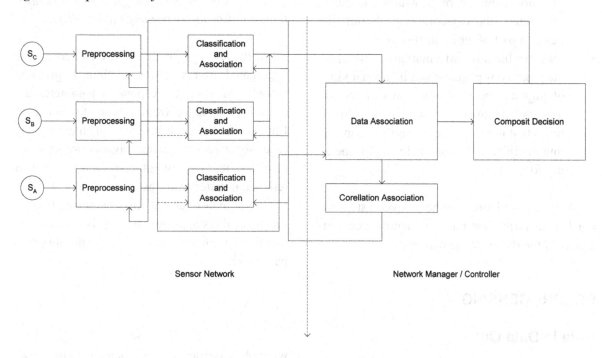

There are two types of pipelines –inline and transmission. In-line pipelines are narrower (6" diameter or less), have higher pressure requirements(43% operate above 2000 psig) and are mostly used for transfering processing fluid, gases and multiphase materials in the process plant. Transmission lines have larger diameter (36" diameter), lower pressure requirements (70% operate between 1000 psig to 2000 psig) and are mostly used for transfering materials over large distances. Usually, corrosion is the biggest factor for leakage. Corrosion led to production shut-in in 67% cases and pipeline shutdown in 100% of the cases. All the pipeline information in this section and consecutive section are taken from (Matos, Powell, Davies, Zhang, Moore, 2006).

In order to detect corrosion, it is recommended to have the following information.

- **History:** Includes pipelines installation year, method, leak history, soil movement and service history

- **Conditions:** Presence of dents or other deformations, repairs, significant inspection reports, grade of steel used, type of coating used, burial conditions, if any, crossing or nearby adjacent pipelines, type of connections, valves used, contaminants or corrosive materials expected and location where it could collect in the pipeline, material composition, any anchors or weights attached to pipeline and elevation changes (near shore).

- **Monitoring / Inspection:** Includes inspection history, leak detection system used, corrosion monitoring through coupons (a coupon is attached to the inside of a pipeline. Over time if there is corrosion or deposition it would affect the coupon and by removing and investigating the coupon, relevant information can be acquired) and probes, set point limits, results from any testing done on materials flowing through pipeline and regular monitoring of pressure, temperature, flowrates and other parameters and detecting any abnormalities as a part of the control system.

- **Others:** Includes information on whether the pipeline is piggable and if so what kind of pigs can be used, shutdown or reducing flow operations possible or not, down times that is acceptable and ability to make line modification through closing or opening some valves.

As given in Figure 5 we have several steps in our data fusion process. Each step handles a certain aspect of the data management process.

PREPROCESSING

Data in Data Out

The functions of this step take place at the sensor node itself. The set of functions performed are

- Data fusion to get a good estimate of the error detected, if any.
- Any conversion (flow to pressure or vice versa) to get better estimate of meter readings for valves shut down operation if required for verifying the error readings.

The nodes sense a reading change if the readings go above a certain threshold. We assume redundant placement of sensor meters to continue normal operation even in case of a failure of a sensor meter.

To counteract out of sequence data, the network manager and controller decide on how much time to wait to fuse data to make decision locally for valves shutdown process. If all data is not received by the time period, an alert is sent to the controller along with data collected.

Total Time to Wait = Time for Sensor Meter reading fusion (network manager) + Time for

the process to occur that might result in variation of sensor meter readings (controller). (5)

At the aggregation node the data needs to be aggregated after a scheduled time. Regression model estimates of corresponding parameters are filled in (conversion from pressure to equivalent flow or vice versa), if possible. In an emergency case, separate verification signals are sent out to obtain readings of interest from original or redundant meter readings.

An estimate of an unknown parameter (sensor meter readings sent out) $\theta_i \in R$ is given by y_i. Reading y_i is a noisy measurement of the unknown parameter.

$$y_i = A_i \theta_i + v \qquad (6)$$

where A_i is the transforming factor and v the noise. We assume the noise to be Gaussian with mean 0 and variance 1.

A_i refers to the transformation parameter. If it is a reading from the same meter it is 1 else it is set to K, where K is the constant for converting from one parameter to the parameter under observation. We consider three algorithms in order to figure out the correct reading in the presence of noise and make a correction before sending out the reading to the next node.

Investigated Algorithms

We fuse data only after a certain time period as determined by Equation 1. The first algorithm is a simple average of data points. In the second method, the weights are given based on confidence level obtained for the data fused at intermediate nodes. The third algorithm is based on a related work in (Xiao, Boyd, & Lall 2005). Data points here are direct readings from sensor meters for the observed parameter or correlated data obtained from sensor meter readings obtained from other sensor meters or error readings.

If more than 50% of the readings are less than 900 or greater than 1440 psi (these values are obtained from discussions with design engineers of Oil Production Platform) Send 'alert' message to concerned controller along with averages of the readings below or above the threshold.

If more than 50% of the readings are between 900 psi and 1440 psi, then the following algorithms are deployed:

Algorithm 1

```
n =1
while (Yt <900 && Yt <1440)
    if  75% of readings lie be-
tween Y_t = Y_t ± 2%
```

$$newY_t = \frac{r1 + r2 + ... + rn}{n}$$

```
(another version is with median
instead of average)
    else
        n+=1
        Y_t = Y_t ± (2%*n)
    end
end
```

Algorithm 2

Errors in detecting the sensor meter readings can occur in two possible ways. One due to corruption due to wireless transmission and the other due to errors occurring in the actual sensor meters themselves.

The first problem can be handled by error check, avoiding regions of high electromagnetic disturbance and robust fault data fusion. The second problem of errors occurring in the sensor meter itself is addressed as follows. Sensor meter failures can be permanent, short term (spike) or slowly changing failure. Spikes are avoided by proper data fusion. Slowly changing faults can be detected by the concerned controller by monitor-

ing all interrelated processes. If a particular meter reading does not match the expected values then further investigation is required. Any readings obtained from the sensor meter during this period are given a low confidence factor. Slow changing failures are taken care of by the confidence factor variation. Permanent failure can be detected by self diagnostic commands given to sensor meters.

The function of confidence factor variation $C_i(t)$ for slow changing failures is decided by the concerned controller and given to the appropriate sensor nodes.

$C(t) = F(t)$ (given by controller)

$$Y_i(t) = \sum C_i(t)A_i(t) \qquad (7)$$

The confidence factor is also influenced by the known presence of electromagnetic disturbance. For example, due to any process change a sub process system is turned on at particular times that generate high amounts of EM disturbances then confidence factor of the surrounding sensor nodes is reduced for that time interval.

$$Y_i(t) = \begin{cases} C_1(t) * A_i(t) & \text{if } t = t_1, t_2, ... \\ C_2(t) * A_i(t) & \text{otherwise} \end{cases} \qquad (8)$$

Where t_1, t_2 are the times when the component that generates high amounts of EM waves is switched on.

Confidence is also based on past performance of the sensor node.

Algorithm 3

In a related work in (Xiao, Boyd, & Lal, 2005), the least mean square error is used to get the maximum likelihood estimate of the parameter. Data fusion is achieved by taking the maximum incident degree and Manhattan weights to give appropriate weight to incident data on a node.

Case Study of monitoring pipelines, this is the point where flow, temperature, pressure are monitored to detect any abnormalities in the pipeline flow.

CLASSIFICATION AND ASSOCIATION

Most of the complex computations are done at the controller and the computed models and tables are sent to the nodes in the region of interest. These actions take place during setup phase and they are updated when required. Functions that are done by the sensor node are the following.

- Receiving and storing the correlations and regression models.
- Receiving and storing controlling action database.

Henceforth the sensor nodes take care of two operations: single variable control loop, and closing of valves on observing a set of thresholds of the various parameters monitored.

Case Study of Monitoring Pipelines – Depending on regression models given to the sensor nodes, appropriate valves can be controlled to regulate the pressure, flowrate or temperature to the set point required. In addition, if a dangerous situation arises where there is leak due to corrosion or any other factor, the monitored parameters start varying and the sensor node can immediately shut off valves to isolate the give section of the pipeline or the entire pipeline.

DATA ASSOCIATION / CORRELATION ASSOCIATION

This step takes place between the concerned controller, network manager and centralized controller and network manager. Given the set of process parameter (set by user) and set of readings obtained

from the monitoring sensor nodes, heterogeneous data association are set up at two levels.

Correlation models are also set up in a similar way. Since the controller has a view of the entire control loop, appropriate correlation and data association models can be setup. At a higher level of fusion, the centralized controller and network manager take input from all lower level controllers and network manager and take system wide decisions. Feature could be some pre-decided controlling action or some network model based on changed parameters.

Functions that are done by the controllers are the following.

- Computing the regression model dependencies of the various parameters (P, F) and sending it to appropriate nodes.
- Updating the models on nodes incorporating any seasonal changes.
- Updating the nodes on any parameter that changes with (e.g. corrosion).
- Updating the nodes in case of a shut down due to normal maintenance and inspections or due to an emergency.
- Sending out appropriate controlling action database to appropriate nodes.

COMPOSITE DECISIONS

Given a set of data models and correlation models, and a set of data obtained by monitoring sensor nodes, decisions are taken. Inputs at this point could also be economical, financial or production based. If more data is required to take a decision, requests could be made to the sensor network for appropriate data to the appropriate component. These set of actions are done at the Centralized center.

Decision-in, Data-out or Decision-in, Decision-out, Data-in, Decision-out.

Case Study of Monitoring Pipelines – To obtain the various factors we need to study the conditions of the pipeline and the environment. The integriy of the pipeline is conventionally monitored in three ways.

- **In line inspection:** There are several methods used for inline inspections – electromanetic, ultrasound and mechanical. In line inspection tools are put into the pipeline through a component called launcher. The tools then move in the pipeline. There are special valves and components that retrieve these tools. The data is then sent to the control point. In line inspection is used to detect corrosion, dents, cracks, bends, shape changes, increase or decrease in pipeline diameter.
- **Hydrostatic pressure test:** In this the pipeline under test needs to be taken off-line. Then water is pumped into pipeline under pressure. This test is done to see how much the pipeline specification matches with current condition to with stand required pressure.
- **Direct Assessment Methodology:** The guidelines, recommendation and Federal rules for this inspection depends on the type of material, characteristics of the pipeline and the environment in which the pipeline is setup, over land, buried, sub sea, shore region etc.

The inspection results are given to the centralized controller. In addition, once a leak is detected it needs to be classified according to its causes so that appropriate remedial operations and avoidance measures can be put into place. Causes are:

- **Internal Corrosion:** find area, depth, type like entire pipeline slowly corroding or spot corrosion.
- **External Corrosion:** dimension of corrosion

- **Time dependent natural hazard** – movement due to currents, area getting inhabited, expose of pipeline in time.
- **Outside forces:** Expansion due to thermal condition of inside or outside environment.
- **Impacts:** Something hitting the pipeline unexpectedly like pipeline anchors.
- **Material:** Faulty seams, inferior pipeline material, defective pipeline, improper welds.
- **Structural:** Movement of platform, losing anodes, support failure.
- **Equipment failure:** seals, valves failing to operate properly.

In order to make this classification, additional data is requested from the sensor nodes. The centralized network manager send the required queries to the appropriate network manager. After inspection of the replies sent back by the sensor nodes, the causes are identified and appropriate actions can be initiated. Additional measures could to be taken in other pipelines that are in similar conditions. The centralized controller and network manager coordinate with one another and identify the components that need to be monitored or changed. Reactive and preventive measure are incorporated by updating the corresponding sensor nodes.

DATA FUSION STATE MODELING OF THE SYSTEM

In this section, we build a sensor network time delay model. Sensor networks are beneficial for the fact there they are wireless and can be easily deployed without laying out any infrastructure. They are built to be fault tolerant and self-healing. They are built to adapt to topological and system (in this case pipeline system) changes. For this work, our target system is a pipeline system. The

Figure 6. Physical system

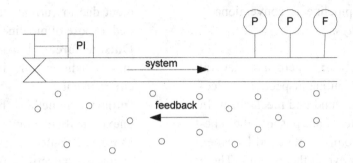

Figure 7. State space system

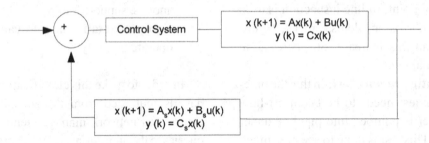

sensor network system is employed in the feedback loop as shown in Figure 6, Figure 7.

A short note on pipelines – Gas pipelines have the highest pressure. Next is oil and then water. The upper pressure limit that the contents of the pipeline can reach before triggering a relief valve and or an alarm system is 80% of its limit. The lowest pressure limit is 50% of its normal operating pressure. Redundant pipelines may be incorporated into the pipeline design for redundancy. As seen from Figure 8, corrosion is highest factor for pipeline leaks.

The state space model of the pipeline system is discussed in (Gong, Cai, Li, Song, 2007) and (Rougier & Goldstein, 2001). We assume that the control system takes appropriate action taking into consideration the time lag between valve position change and corresponding flow rate observations. There is a delay also introduced by the sensor network. From (Rougier & Goldstein, 2001) it is seen that there is a square root relation between valve position change and flow rate, i.e.,

Figure 8. Model of entire system

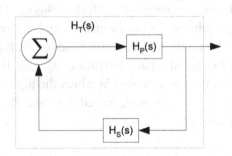

$$H_{CV}(s) = \sqrt{Q(s)} \, / \, Valve(s) \qquad (9)$$

Where Q(t) is the flow rate change in time given a valve position change in time.

We employ a state space model to model the sensor network. There are two parameters that get included by using WSN in the feedback loop. These two parameters are errors made in observation and time delay in transmitting messages. We assume here that errors are corrected by data fusion and error correcting codes. Now, we model the sensor network in terms of the remaining parameter, the time delay, at each node. The dynamic state equations are given by

$$x(k+1) = A_s x(k) + B_s u(k) + w_s(k) \qquad (10)$$

$$y(k) = C_s x(k) \qquad (11)$$

Where $w_s(k)$ is the process noise. We assume process noise is zero. Measurement noise is corrected by data fusion.

$$A_s = \begin{bmatrix} 1 & 0 & \cdots & & 0 \\ 0 & 1 & & & \\ \vdots & & \ddots & & \\ & & & 1 & 0 \\ 0 & & & 0 & 1 \end{bmatrix} \qquad (12)$$

Or can be taken as weighted average or probability instead of identity.

- B_s: 1 for states that the traffic effects
- C_s: 1 for measurable states by sensor nodes.
- Conversion from state space model to transfer function

$$\frac{Y(s)}{U(s)} = C[sI - A]^{-1} B \qquad (13)$$

The other way around is not feasible, as there can exist several combinations of A, B, C for the same transfer function.

In the worst case delay the message is sent forward by complete reactive routing. The best case delay is proactive routes being employed. In our system hybrid routes can also be employed in which case the delay will be between proactive and reactive routing.

PROACTIVE ROUTES

Proactive routes are setup functionally as well as locally depending on component position and control loops. The proactive routes are set up and refreshed by the network manager after obtaining the health status reports of the sensor nodes.

The general equation for the time delay per section is given by $T_{proactive}$. It has two parts: a) The feedback part gives the delay due to the MAC and routing operations; and b) The computation part gives the delay due to data fusion process. The computation delay component is related to any data fusion means employed. The $T_{computation}$ time delay is independent of whether we employ proactive or reactive routing.

$$T_{proactive} = T_{feedbackP} + T_{computationP} \qquad (14)$$

- $T_{computationP}$ is given by the Equation.
- Total Time to Wait ($T_{computationP}$) = Time of Sensor Meter reading fusion (network manager) + Time for the process to occur that might result in variation of sensor meter readings (controller).
- T_{queue} formulation

From priority based preemptive queuing formulation we have

$$Tqueue(i) \frac{\sum_{j=1}^{i} \rho_j E(R_j)}{(1 - (\rho_1 + \ldots + \rho_i))(1 - (\rho_1 + \ldots + \rho_{i-1}))} \qquad (15)$$

Where $T_{queue}(i)$ is the wait time for the ith priority message, ρ_i is the occupation rate or service utilization and $E(Rj)$ is the residual service time. $E(Bi)$ is the service time and we assume a M/G/1 queue model.

MAC

The superframe for the MAC layer is shown in Figure 4. The slots with fixed time schedules have no time delays. This is implemented for proactive routes.

$$T_{proactive} = T_{feedbackP} + T_{computationP} \qquad (16)$$

Where

$$T_{feedbackP} = (T_{next\_neighbor} + T_{queue}) \qquad (17)$$

- $T_{next\_neighbor}$ is the time taken to find the next hop neighbor to send messages to given a destination.
- **Worst case delay:** Finding alternative next level parent. Assuming that there are $N_{next\_level\_parent} < Nei_x$. The total delay is $Req(N_{next\_level\_parent} - 1) + Ack(N_{next\_level\_parent} - 1)$. The minus 1 is to eliminate the parent where a channel failure has been detected.
- **Best case delay:** 0.
- T_{queue} is the time taken to wait in a queue at a node to be processed. Since we assume priority based queuing, T_{queue} is given by Equation 15. We assume a Poisson traffic rate in this section.
- **Worst case delay** is if queue is full with all high priority messages.
- **Best case delay** is when queue is empty.

Considering all the above factors of the dynamic system for proactive routing, we have the state vector $x_A(k)$ as

$$x_A(k) = [Nei_x, T_{queue}, T_{req}, T_{ack}, T_{computationP}, I_x]^T$$
$$(18)$$

Where

- **Nei_x:** Number of neighbors that a node has
- **T_{queue}:** Is the time delay in a node that is dependent on the number of messages at that node.
- **T_{req}:** Is the time required to send out request to neighboring nodes (that can qualify as the next level parent).
- **T_{ack}:** Time delay in receiving acknowledgements.
- **$T_{computationP}$:** Maximum time spent to aggregate data.
- **I_x:** Interference with neighbor 'x' message is sent through.

$$U_A = \lambda_{Poisson} \qquad (19)$$

$$B_A = [0,1,0,0,0,1]^T \qquad (20)$$

Where 1 gives the factors of the state vector that gets effected by the Poisson traffic input U_A.

- **C_A:** All the above state variable can be estimated by the node itself or is set by the system and is known by the node. So we assume the C matrix with a row of all 1s.

REACTIVE ROUTES

In our superframe we have a time slot that transmits CSMA/CA for reactive data. The messages transmitted in this slot might have some time delay due to collisions.

The formulas for T_{sense}, T_{Tx}, T_{wait}, T_{Rx} are obtained from reference (Nordman & Kozlowski, 2001). We also make an assumption that there will be no retransmission if there is no

1) Collision
2) Bit errors in received data.

We define P_{busy} as the probability for the channel to be busy and P_{idle} as the probability for the channel to be idle.

The main time delay is due to transmission and receiving of messages. MAC layer also handles backup strategies and retransmissions at appropriate time in case of a collision.

$$P_{busy} = \frac{\gamma}{1 / (2Nei_x (\lambda + \Delta)) + \gamma} \qquad (21)$$

$$P_{idle} = 1 - P_{busy} \qquad (22)$$

Where γ is the service time, i.e. the service time to transmit and receive messages, Nei_x is the number of neighbors, λ is the traffic arrival rate for each region and Δ is the extra term required to consider additional operations that take place in case of collisions. The value of how many collisions will be acceptable before searching for alternative routes is set by the system and specified by the value of Δ. Refer to equations of (Nordman & Kozlowski, 2001) for additional details of the CSMA/CA transmission.

$$\mathrm{T}_{reactive} = \mathrm{T}_{feedbackR} + \mathrm{T}_{computationR} \qquad (23)$$

$$\mathrm{T}_{feedbackR} = \mathrm{T}_{next\_neighborR} + \mathrm{T}_{queue} + \mathrm{T}_{wait} \qquad (24)$$

$$\mathrm{T}_{computationR} = \mathrm{T}_{computationP} \qquad (25)$$

- $\mathrm{T}_{next\_neighborR}$ worst case delay is if reactive routing is employed.
- $Req(Nei_x) + Status(Nei_x) + \mathrm{T}_{decision}$. Where Req is the requests sent out by node to enquire about neighbor nodes status. Status is the information received from these neighbors and $\mathrm{T}_{decision}$ is the time delay occurred to make a decision about the next hop neighbor.

- T_{queue} – the traffic in this section is considered to be uniform.
- T_{wait} is $\mathrm{T}_{sense} + \mathrm{T}_{Wait} + \mathrm{T}_{Tx} + \mathrm{T}_{Rx}$ of (Nordman & Kozlowski, 2001). Unlike in (Nordman & Kozlowski, 2001), Δ attempts are made to transmit a signal and receive and acknowledgement from next hop neighbor. If unsuccessful, alternative routes are found. T_{sense} is the time delay occurred in sensing whether channel is occupied or not. T_{Wait} is the time delay occurred while waiting for an acknowledge from selected next hop neighbor. T_{Tx} is the time required to transmit the message and T_{Rx} is the time required to receive the acknowledgement.
- The worst case delay is when collision occurs and alternative neighbor needs to be found. We assume here the nest neighbor found will successfully transmit the message. The best case delay is when there is no collision.

Considering all the above factors of the dynamic system at section B, we have the state vector $x_B(k)$ as

$$x_B(k) = [Nei_x, T_{queue}, T_{req}, T_{status}, T_{decision}, I_x, t_{rem}, T_x, D_x, RD_x, P_{length}, Tr, P_c, T_{busy}, P_{busy}, T_{idle}, P_{ok}, t_{suc}, t_{unsuc}, t_{timeout}]^T$$

$$(26)$$

Where

- T_{status}: Time delay in receiving health status information from neighboring nodes.
- $\mathrm{T}_{decision}$: Time delay occurred to make a decision about the next hop neighbor.
- T_{rem}: Time remaining to complete route
- T_x: Time taken to reach destination if 'x' neighbor is taken.
- D_x: Distance to destination if 'x' neighbor is taken.

- **Nei$_x$**: Number of neighbors that a node has
- **T$_{queue}$**: Is the time delay in a node that is dependent on the number of messages at that node.
- **T$_{req}$**: Is the time required to send out request to neighboring nodes (that can qualify as the next level parent).
- **T$_{ack}$**: Time delay in receiving acknowledgements.
- **T$_{computationR}$**: Maximum time spent to aggregate data.
- **I$_x$**: Interference with neighbor 'x' message is sent through.
- **P$_{length}$**: Packet length
- **P$_c$**: Probability that a collision occurs.
- **T$_{busy}$**: Time delay incurred due to a busy channel
- **P$_{busy}$**: Probability that a channel will be busy.
- **T$_{idle}$**: Time delay incurred due to an idle channel.
- **Tr:** Transmission range
- **P$_{ok}$**: Probability for a successful transmission
- **t$_{suc}$**: The times the transceiver is used to perform a sense, transmit, receive and Wait event in case of a success.
- **t$_{unsuc}$**: The times the transceiver is used to perform a sense, transmit, receive and Wait event in case of a unsuccessful transmission.
- **t$_{timeout}$**: is the time that a node wait for a acknowledgement before doing a timeout and stopping the wait.

$$U_B = \lambda_{uniform} \tag{27}$$

$$B_B = [0,1,0,1,0,1,0,1,1,0,1,0,1,1,1,1]^T \tag{28}$$

Where 1 gives the factors of the state vector that gets effected by the Uniform traffic input U$_B$.

- **C$_B$**: All the above state variable can be estimated by the node itself or is set by the system and is known by the node. So we assume the C matrix with a row of all 1s.

TOTAL SYSTEM MODEL

In (6), the tuning of a PID controller is discussed in the presence of delays. In that paper the delay is assumed to be random with a Gaussian distribution. In this work we derive the delay model of the sensor network instead of assuming it as Gaussian. Assuming that the PID controller is tuned and works correctly by employing the theoretical model developed in (Eriksson & Koivo, 2005), we indicate the transfer function of the PID controller as H$_{PID}$(s). From (Rougier & Goldstein, 2001) it is seen that a change in valve position the flow change is in square root as given in Equation (18). We get the pipeline transfer function from either (Gong, Cai, Li, Song, 2007) or (Rougier & Goldstein, 2001) and indicate here as H$_{pipeline}$(s). Therefore the transfer function model for the pipeline system is given by

$$H_P(s) = H_{PID}(s)H_{CV}(s)H_{pipeline}(s) \tag{29}$$

$$H_A(s) = \frac{Y_A(s)}{U_A(s)} = C_A(sI - A_A)^{-1}B_A \tag{30}$$

Similarly we can get the transfer function for H$_B$(s) and H$_C$(s). If H$_S$(s) and H$_P$(s) is the transfer function for the entire sensor network system in the feedback loop and the transfer function of the pipeline system respectively then, the transfer function of the total system is given by H$_T$(s).

$$H_S(s) = H_A(s)\ H_B(s)\ H_C(s) \tag{31}$$

Figure 9. Average energy level obtained for Region 2

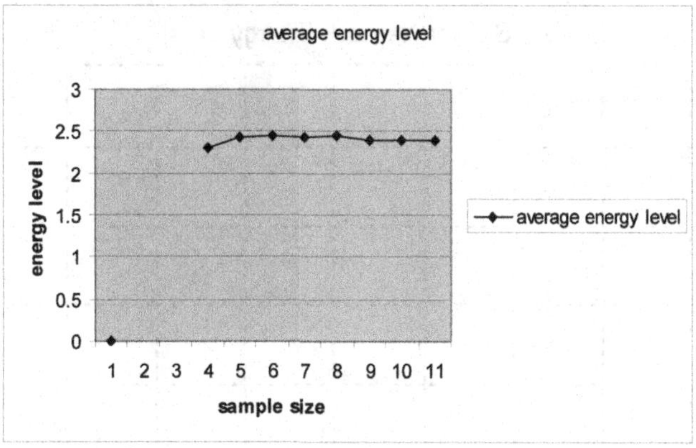

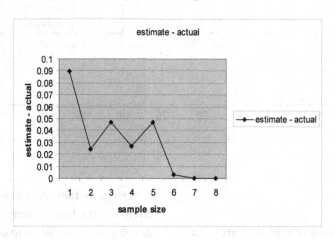

Figure 10. Accuracy for corresponding sample size (Region 2)

$$H_T(s) = \frac{H_P(s)}{1 + H_P(s)H_S(s)} \quad (32)$$

HEALTH MONITORING SYSTEM

For the network manager to make real time decisions about the proactive paths or be aware of the status of the sensor nodes, health monitoring system is required. This system should be able to effectively monitor the status of the sensor nodes in terms of its residual energy, neighborhood interference, effective neighbors etc. We have designed algorithms

that implement the sensor health monitoring system. Our proposed algorithm is based on sector based sampling. Further details can be obtained in (Bhattacharyya, Kumar, Bayoumi, 2009). We obtained SCADA data that gave temporally varying pressure meter reading in gas pipeline. Given this data we could model the sensor meter reading variations. We also obtained a commercial (proprietary) oil platform layout. Our simulation results shows that for a cluster size of 30 sensor nodes (Region 2) we require about 6 samples to get a tolerable error of the status of the sensor nodes (Figure 9, Figure 10). This is mainly due to the inherent quality of sensor networks of load balancing. The error can be corrected using Kalman Filter (Figure 11).

Figure 11. Kalman filter output based on noise variance obtained from Region 2

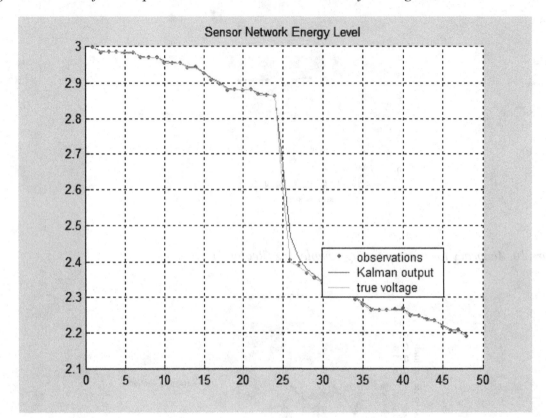

FUTURE WORK

The possibilities for research in this area are endless. There are several areas where sensor network could be harnessed to increase efficiency, reduce cost of deployment and maintenance and require minimum worker training for any technical updates.

An area of research in WSN is the development of material science to withstand extreme conditions. In an industrial environment there can be extreme environments such as high temperature, motion, humidity, dust content etc. Previously wired sensor could not be deployed in certain region due to inaccessibility. However due to wireless technologies sensor nodes can presently be deployed in these regions. However these sensor nodes need to withstand extreme conditions. They cannot be completely enclosed in protective covering, as they also need to interact with the environment being monitored. Another area of development would be to develop biodegradable material for sensor nodes. Sensor nodes are to be deployed in high density. They should not pollute the very environment they are trying to monitor. The material that the sensor node is composed of should degrade after a predefined period of time and the sensor nodes need to be replaced before that time period. The predefined time period should logically be comparable to the battery of the sensor nodes, even with energy harvestation and recharging considerations. Energy harvestation is another area where there is a potential for research. This area also would involve development of new types of battery material that could produce and store charge from other sources for extended periods of time. Biodegradable batteries are another area of research.

Different modulation schemes for reliable communicate in very high interference environment is another area of research. These algorithms should have low hardware complexity, low energy consumption requirements and spend least number of bits to transmit the messages. The methodologies should be able to counteract both narrow band and wide band interference. Antennae technologies to support these requirements would be another area of research.

CONCLUSION

In this book chapter we have a detailed discussion of the proposed hierarchical distributed network management system in oil production platforms. Our proposals have used the existing infrastructure to the maximum extent to increase the efficiency of both the control system and the sensor network. In our knowledge there is very few works that go into details of the system to be employed in an oil production site.

ACKNOWLEDGMENT

Support from Louisiana Board of Regents under research award number LEQSF(2009-12)-RD-A-22 is acknowledged.

REFERENCES

Adam, J., Brady, G., & Kosc, D. (2001). EHT control systems and wireless communications: the wave of the future. In *Petroleum and Chemical Industry Conference, 2001. IEEE Industry Applications Society 48th Annual* Sept. 24-26, (pp. 169 – 178).

Baillieul, J., & Antsaklis, P. J. (2007). Control and Communication Challenges in Networked Real-Time Systems. *Proceedings of the IEEE, 95*(1), 9–28. doi:10.1109/JPROC.2006.887290

Bhattacharyya, M., Kumar, A., & Bayoumi, M. (2009). Residual Energy Monitoring Using Statistical Analysis. In *International Symposium on Digital Life Technologies,* (ISDLT2009), May 28-29.

Bill, L. (n.d.). *Oil Field Safety*. Retrieved from http://www.txoga.org/attachments/OilFieldSafetyNEO1.ppt#256

2Cetin, M., Lei Chen, Fisher III, J.W., Ihler, A.T., Moses, R.L., Wainwright, M.J., & Willsky, A.S. (2006). Distributed fusion in sensor networks. *Signal Processing Magazine, 23*(4), 42–55. doi:10.1109/MSP.2006.1657816

Colandairaj, J., Irwin, G. W., & Scanlon, W. G. (2007). A Co-Design Solution for Wireless Feedback Control. In *IEEE International Conference on Networking, Sensing and Control,* April 15-17, (pp. 404 – 409).

D'Costa, A., & Sayeed, A. M. (2003). Data versus decision fusion for distributed classification in sensor networks. *Military Communications Conference, MILCOM 2003,* (Vol. 1, pp. 585 - 590). Washington, DC: IEEE.

Dasarathy, B. V. (1997). Sensor fusion potential exploitation-innovative architectures and illustrative applications. *Proceedings of the IEEE, 85*(1), 24–38. doi:10.1109/5.554206

De Biasi, M., Snickars, C., Landernas, K., & Isaksson, A. (2008). Simulation of Process Control with WirelessHART Networks Subject to Clock Drift. In *32nd Annual IEEE International Computer Software and Applications, (COMPSAC '08),* (pp. 1355 – 1360).

Eriksson, L., & Koivo, H. N. (2005). Tuning of discrete-time PID controllers in sensor network based control systems. In *Proceedings IEEE International Symposium on Computational Intelligence in Robotics and Automation,* CIRA 2005, (pp. 359 – 364).

Gong, J. Cai, J. Li, X. Song, S., (2007). Research on State Estimation of Oil Pipeline Considering Adaptive Extended Kalman Filtering. In *International Conference on Mechatronics and Automation, ICMA 2007.*

Hall, D. L., & Llinas, J. (1997). An introduction to multisensor data fusion. *Proceedings of the IEEE, 85*(1), 6–23. doi:10.1109/5.554205

HART Communication protocol. (n.d.). Retrieved from http://www.hartcomm2.org/hart_protocol/protocol/hart_data.html

Helson. (2007). *WirelessHART fits into ISA-SP100 standards effort.* Retrieved from http://www.isa.org/ InTechTemplate.cfm?Section=Executive_Corner2&template=/ContentManagement/ContentDisplay.cfm&ContentID=61420

Horiuchi, L., & Stokes, A. (2006), *CISCO Press release.* Retrieved from http://newsroom.cisco.com/dlls/partners/news/2006/pr_prod_09-11.html

Howie, C. L. (1984). *Remote Corrosion Monitoring of Off-Shore Pipelines.* Retrieved from http://www.mms.gov/tarprojects/075/075AA.PDF

IBM WebSphere. (n.d.). Retrieved from http://www.ibm.com/developerworks/websphere/

Intel Research – Sensor Network Research (n.d.). Retrieved from http://techresearch.intel.com/articles/Exploratory/1501.htm

Jiang, P., Ren, H., Zhang, L., Wang, Z., & Xue, A. (2006). Reliable Application of Wireless Sensor Networks in Industrial Process Control. In *The Sixth World Congress on Intelligent Control and Automation, WCICA 2006,* (Vol. 1, pp. 99 – 103).

Kawka, P. A., & Alleyne, A. G. (2005). Stability and feedback control of wireless networked systems. In *Proceedings of the 2005 American Control Conference,* (vol. 4, pp. 2953 - 2959).

Kumar, M., Garg, D. P., & Zachery, R. A. (2006). A generalized approach for inconsistency detection in data fusion from multiple sensors. In *American Control Conference.*

Lennvall, T., Svensson, S., & Hekland, F. (2008). A comparison of WirelessHART and ZigBee for industrial applications. In IEEE International Workshop on Factory Communication Systems, (pp. 85 – 88).

Manning, F., & Thompson, R. (1995). Oil Field Processing (Vol. 2, Crude Oil). Tulsa, OK: Pennwell Books.

Matos, S., Powell, D., Davies, R., Zhang, X., & Moore, P. (2006). *A Guideline Framework for the Integrity Assessment of Offshore Pipelines.* Retrieved from http://www.mms.gov/tarprojects/565/565AA.pdf

Nikolakopoulos, G., Panousopoulou, A., Tzes, A., & Lygeros, J. (2005). Multi-hopping Induced Gain Scheduling for Wireless Networked Controlled Systems. In *44th IEEE Conference on European Control Conference Decision and Control,* (pp. 470 – 475).

Niu, R., Varshney, P. K., & Cheng, Q. (2006). Distributed detection in a large wireless sensor network. *Special Issue on the Seventh International Conference on Information Fusion-Part I, 7*(4), 380-394.

Nixon, M. Deji Chen, Blevins, T., & Mok, A.K., (2008, Aug. 23-26). Meeting control performance over a wireless mesh network. In *IEEE International Conference on Automation Science and Engineering,* CASE 2008, (pp. 540 – 547).

Nordman, M. M., & Kozlowski, W. E. (2001). Modeling data transactions with standard protocols for low power wireless sensor links. In *Proceedings of the First ISA/IEEE Conference on Sensor for Industry*, (pp. 51 – 56).

Rougier, J., & Goldstein, M. (2001). A Bayesian Analysis of Fluid Flow in Pipe-Lines. *Applied Statistics, 50*(1), 77–93. doi:10.1111/1467-9876.00221

Sinopoli, B., Schenato, L., Franceschetti, M., Poolla, K., & Sastry, S. (2005). An LQG Optimal Linear Controller for Control Systems with Packet Losses. In *44th IEEE Conference on Decision and Control & 2005 European Control Conference*, (pp. 458 - 463).

Steinberg, A., & White, F. (1998). *Community Status Report and Proposed Revisions to the JDL Data Fusion Model*. Retrieved from http://stinet.dtic.mil/cgi-bin/GetTRDoc?AD=ADA399488&Location=U2& doc=GetTRDoc.pdf

Steinberg, A. N. (2005). An approach to threat assessment. In *8th, International Conference on Information Fusion* (Vol. 2, pp. 8).

Thomopoulos, S. C. A., Viswanathan, R., & Bougoulias, D. K. (1989). Optimal distributed decision fusion. *IEEE Transactions on Aerospace and Electronic Systems, 25*(5), 761–765. doi:10.1109/7.42092

Wireless, H. A. R. T. (2007). Retrieved from http://www.hartcomm2.org/hart_protocol/wireless_hart/wireless_hart_main.html

Wuyan, L. & Yangwanhai. (2001). Optimal distributed decision fusion in the sense of the Neyman-Pearson test. In *Proceedings CIE International Conference on Radar*, (pp. 708 - 712).

Xiao, L., Boyd, S., & Lall, S. (2005). A scheme for robust distributed sensor fusion based on average consensus. In *Fourth International Symposium on Information Processing in Sensor Networks*, IPSN 2005, (pp. 63 – 70).

Yuan, W., Krishnamurthy, S. V., & Tripathi, S. K. (2003). Synchronization of Multiple Levels of Data Fusion in Wireless Sensor Networks. In *Proceedings of GLOBECOM*.

Zand, P. & Shiva, M. (2008). *Defining a New Frame Based on IEEE 802.15.4 for having the Synchronized Mesh Networks with Channel Hopping Capability.*

Chapter 7
System Framework and Protocols for Ubiquitous Computing Based Monitoring of an Oil Platform

Mitun Bhattacharyya
R.V. College of Engineering, India

Ashok Kumar
University of Louisiana at Lafayette, USA

Magdy Bayoumi
University of Louisiana at Lafayette, USA

ABSTRACT

This book chapter proposes a system based on the WirelessHART standard for monitoring and controlling oil platforms using sensor networks. The authors propose a hierarchical distributed system where sensor nodes and process components are grouped both functionally and in terms of proximity (i.e., spatially). They harness the existing electrical powering supplies to some of the process components to enhance our network routing protocol. They also propose a component based addressing scheme. Then propose a hybrid routing protocol having proactive paths for high priority data and reactive paths for low priority that can help in load balancing and thus improving the lifetime of the sensor network. Finally, the authors discuss about methodologies for assessing the health (residual energy) of the sensor network system. Related research is discussed at appropriate points.

INTRODUCTION

Presently many cross-disciplinary areas are being explored for application of Wireless Sensor Network (WSN). In this book chapter we explore the area of

using WSN for a control system of an oil production platform. It has been suggested that in the near future sensor nodes will be used to measure the flow of petrol consumption at stations. This measured consumption amount along with other economic inputs, will be given to a decision-making system. The system will decide, depending on requirements

DOI: 10.4018/978-1-61520-843-2.ch007

Figure 1. Model of an oil production platform and control system room

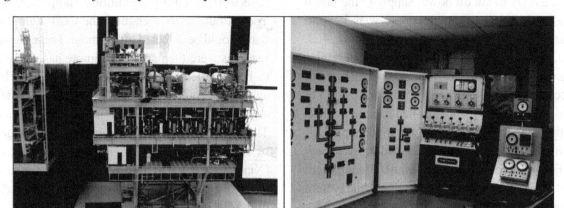

in real time, the amount of oil to be produced. The control system will automatically control all parameters to regulate the oil production flow with maximum provisions in place for worker's safety. Part of this system already exists in the literature (IBM WebSphere).

A key motivation for designing such control system is human safety. From the safety procedure report in (Luther), it is seen that 78% of all injuries come from unsafe acts. The safety procedure report also suggests ways of controlling hazards through the means of removing workers from regions of potential danger; detecting and monitoring new hazards and controlling them automatically; and through isolation of source, lockout procedure, design, process or procedural changes, monitoring and warning equipment. These requirements open up a huge potential where the sensor networks could be employed. In addition WSN could be used to enhance the setup of existing control system infrastructures.

Figure 1 gives a picture of a model of an oil production platform. As seen from the figure, there are several processes that take place. In several industrial environments the interrelation between processes are designed in several tiers, in terms of placement and functionality. The control station has the final display but there is a complex distributed hierarchical control system

in the background that monitors and performs all the controlling actions. According to (Dalbro et al, 2008), oil and gas sensor networks need to be heterogeneous in nature. Heterogeneity arises due to the following factors – different data formats, semantics, communication media (both wireless and wired) and different priorities for different data. In addition, distributed data fusion and decision-making mechanisms may be employed that treat all components, instrumentation sensors and wireless sensor network components, as one coordinated system.

OVERVIEW OF PROPOSED SYSTEM SETUP AND EXISTING STANDARDS

Literature Survey

This section gives summaries of works done in the area of oil production platform. The work in (Meijuan, Jin & Jingwen, 2008) proposed a system of remote monitoring of a pumping unit using wireless sensor networks. In a pump station, the following parameters were monitored: three-phase power, flow rate and temperature. Data collection was done periodically or in response to a query given by the control station. In addition to monitoring, the Micro Controller Unit (MCU) also used a relay to cut off power supply to the pump automatically in case temperature went beyond a set threshold. The work in (Peng, Huijin, Lei, Zhi, & Anke, 2006) gives an overview of applying wireless sensor networks in a control system. According to this work, difficulty occurs due to two reasons. One is uncontrolled communication in the same frequency as the system communication frequency. The second is Radio Frequency (RF) harmonics produced by industrial equipment that are in the same frequency range as the system communication frequencies. The work in (Mohamed & Jawhar, 2008) describes a system that uses wired topology as the main communication medium and wireless as the secondary communication medium in case the wired connection fails. Wired lines are not only used for communication of sensed data and control signals but are also used to power different components. External powers can be provided by solar panels, rotating turbines that are made to rotate by the liquid flow through the pipeline, gas powered generators and other sources. The problem with the wired pipeline is that it is very difficult to detect faults. If there is a fault, all the components connected to the wire fails. The work in (Abdelgawad, et al) discusses the remote measurement of flow meter and associated problems. It gives an in-sight of the modifications required to go from a HART to a WirelessHART standard. It uses the NuFlo Measurement System Model MC-II Flow Analyzer. A mote is connected to the MC-II and this mote sends the pulse signal, generated by MC-II and which is proportional to the flow rate, to the base station. The MC-II generates a signal output that is 200mV peak-to-peak. At the first attempt the signal reading was taken directly from the circuitry that obtained it. This was rejected as it put additional load on the existing circuit. The second idea was to read the signal after the MC-II microprocessor had processed it to some extent. The microprocessor of the flow-meter could be used to aggregate the flow-meter readings. In this case the volume of flow used for each pulse was scaled from 1.001

units to 100.0 units. In addition an amplifier was also introduced to strengthen the weak signal so that it could be detected by the mote. These signal readings were then sent to a remote base station to be recorded in a PostgreSQL database. The aggregator could also be used to obtain flow rates and volumetric unit every sec, minute, hour or day. This could be harnessed to send fewer messages by the mote and thus save energy. The work in (Xiaojuan, Dargie, & Guan, 2008) gives the case study of H_2S monitoring using WSN. The alarm threshold is set to a time-interval that workers can get exposed to without any ill effects. These thresholds are specified in safety codes that vary from country to country. According to (Xiaojuan, Dargie, & Guan, 2008) the short-term exposure limit is 10 parts per million. Also the response time to any leakage detection is typically 20-30 seconds, at most 60 seconds. Deployment of sensor nodes can be done in three ways: *spot*, *area* and *fence*. In spot monitoring, the places where leakage is possible is known and a few sensors are employed in those places. In area coverage, depending on where the sources are, the sensors are deployed but it cannot guarantee blind spot elimination. In fence detection, sensors are deployed in high density to guarantee detection. The paper uses spot monitoring for H_2S detection.

The work in (Bonivento, Carloni, & Sangio-vanni-Vincentelli, 2006) describes a methodology that gives a set of inputs (controlling parameters and underlying hardware of sensor nodes) and gives an output of mapping the controlling system onto a system of WSN, while meeting constraints of power consumption and other system requirements. This project was setup to bridge the gap between control and network system designers. There are specifically two inputs that are very relevant to the network design namely, end-to-end latency, and packet error rate tolerance. This work also proposes having a set of Medium Access Control (MAC) and routing protocols with associated time delay, energy consumption and details of other classification parameters. Depending on the requirements, a particular set of MAC and routing protocols is selected. The work in (Low, Win, & Er, 2005) analyzes the aspects of using WSN in industrial environments. According to this work the disadvantages of wired lines are as follows. We cannot run wires through regions of high humidity, electromagnetic, high vibration and moving machinery parts. Wiring also takes large time for deployment and has higher cost. Redundant lines need to be kept in case a line fails. It is very difficult to locate the position of damage in faulty wires. On the other hand, the main problems of wireless communication are interference, error prone links and end-to-end latency. Interferences can be of two types namely, narrowband and broadband. The mechanisms that can be employed to counteract interferences are Frequency Hopping Spread Spectrum (FHSS) and Direct Sequence Spread Spectrum (DSSS). FHSS is good for small packet transmission in high interference environment. DSSS, on the other hand, is good for large size packet transmission in low to medium interference environments.

Based on the literature survey, we obtained the following information and requirements for our system. Monitoring and control loops have predefined upper limits for time delays that cannot be violated. There are different priorities in the handled data. The industrial infrastructure has components such as actuators, certain valves and process components that require electrical powering. The entire monitoring process of the industrial setup can be digitized. The best infrastructure is a combination of wired and wireless lines. Due to this, sometimes wired and wireless systems need to communicate with one another to harness the advantage that each system has. Delays, allowable limits of hazards, alert generation and other parameters are defined in control and safety codes that vary from one country to another. Usually the control infrastructure consists of a hierarchical control system. According to (Helson, 2007), there are several digital commands and data features in the HART standard that were not being exploited

to its fullest potential due to wired nature of communication. However, now with the development of WirelessHART standard, which enables wireless communications in control systems, all these existing features could be exploited to their fullest potential.

Existing Standard: WirelessHART / HART 7 Standard

This standard supports wireless communications in an industrial control system environment. It operates at 2.4 GHz radio frequency and has an option to incorporate the 802.15.4 standard. Additionally the radio also supports frequency hopping. HART 7 follows the Time Division Medium Access (TDMA) type scheduling. All network-controlling operations are done by a centralized network manager. There are different devices that could be employed in WirelessHART standard. These include field, router and gateway devices as shown in Figure 2. At the lowest level, communications are done in 10ms time slots. Since 16 channels are supported by 802.15.4 standard, there can be 16, 10ms time slots active at the same time. However synchronized time scheduling is required for communication between nodes. Time slots can be dedicated or shared such as with Carrier Sense Medium Access with Collision Avoidance (CSMA/CA) with random back off in case of collision. According to (Lennvall, Svensson, & Hekland, 2008) a WirelessHART device keeps two counters for each of its neighbors – Backoff Exponent and Backoff Counter to determine the backoff time. In case of a retransmission, the default value for the maximum number of retransmissions that are permitted is set to 5. The duration of time slot (10ms) is enough to send and receive 1 package per channel, an acknowledgment and guard band time to execute network wide synchronization.

Functions that the Network Manager performs according to the Wireless HART standard are given in (Kim, Hekland, Petersen, & Doyle, 2008),

Figure 2. General set up of WirelessHART

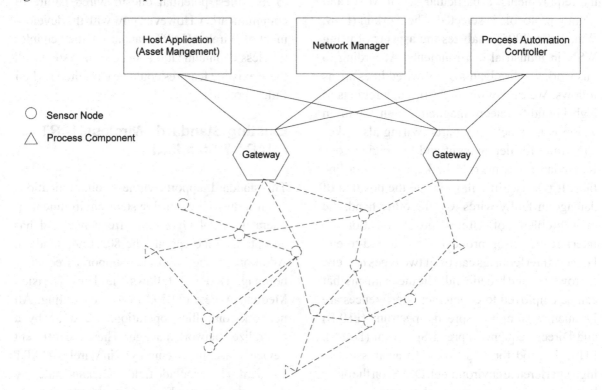

and (Lennvall, Svensson, & Hekland, 2008), as described next.

- Once the network is initially setup, the security manager gives the network manager a unique network Id along with the security keys.
- When a new node wants to join the network, the network manager first verifies if the node can be trusted or not. If verified to be trusted, the network manager provides the node with appropriate network ID, session key and a unique 16-bit address.
- The network manager has record of all devices and network related conditions. Any query regarding network conditions can be directly answered by the network manager.
- Each node keeps a list of neighbors that it would need to route the data through. The network manager can request information

from these lists or tables, as well as it can get information on residual energies of the nodes and the network conditions. From this information, the network manger constructs optimal graphs to take controlling action. Multiple overlapping graphs could be created and each graph is given a unique number. This information is passed onto the nodes. The route to be taken can then be identified by the graph Id placed in the packet header. At least two such routes are stored in each node for fault tolerance. This is called *graph routing*. Another routing called *source routing* can also be deployed. In this routing protocol the route is determined in an ad hoc manner. There are no fault tolerant routes and this routing is mostly used to communicate network health (i.e., residual energy) monitoring signals.

- The network manager centrally decides the time slots for communication between nodes depending on network and application requirements and assigns them to the sensor nodes. This process is updated in real time. It also keeps track of blacklisted channels (channels that should not be used).

There are several data that HART enabled devices support. These include device data, measurement data, supplier data, calibration data, asset management data, safety data, and controlling data. In addition, in HART 7 standard one can specify whether to send the data periodically or as a result of an event. Event can be a query or some threshold violation. The rate at which data is sent can also be varied depending on which thresholds are crossed. The standard supports block transfer of data.

Comparison of the WirelessHART Standard with the Zigbee Standard

According to (Kim, Hekland, Petersen, & Doyle, 2008) HART has been in existence since the 80's and there are presently more than 24 million HART enabled devices deployed. It is also seen that the market for HART device is growing rapidly. WirelessHART builds up on this HART standard to take full advantage of digital signal that these devices generate, through wireless communications. According to (Li, 2006) Zigbee can be used for monitoring purposes where latencies of 100ms could be tolerated. Zigbee is the standard for the network and application layer, for WSN. In control systems the whole control cycle (sensing, deciding what control action to take and sending control signal to actuator) has to have a time delay of 1 sec. To convert the existing wired HART devices into wirelessHART devices, Zigbee adapters could be used. These adapters

have power conditioning cycles that convert the existing 4-20mA line (HART) to 30mA required by the Zigbee adapter.

We next list some important features of the WirelessHART and Zigbee standard in order to make comparison between these two standards.

Features of WirelessHART

- Deploys DSSS and FHSS modulation.
- Interference resistant.
- TDMA scheduling and CSMA/CA if any time slot has shared channel requirement.
- All devices take part in routing, if necessary. There are no Reduced Function Devices (RFD).
- The application layer can handle HART commands.
- Endorsed by ABB, Emerson, Endress+Hauser - Frank Hils, Siemens.
- Has an option to adapt 802.15.4 and Zigbee standard.

Features of Zigbee

- Deploys DSSS modulation.
- Wireless communications have no resistant for narrow band interference. ZigbeePro has been suggested for industrial environment. But this involves in making changes in the MAC layer of the 802.15.4 standard.
- CSMA/CA is preferred in this standard.
- Can have reduced function devices (RFD) that do not take part in any routing.
- Application layer needs to be programmed to handle HART or any other standard commands.
- The standard has been endorsed by large number of companies but is mostly aimed towards home related applications and not industrial type environments.

Figure 3. Proposed system setup (C is a Controller; NM is a Network Manager)

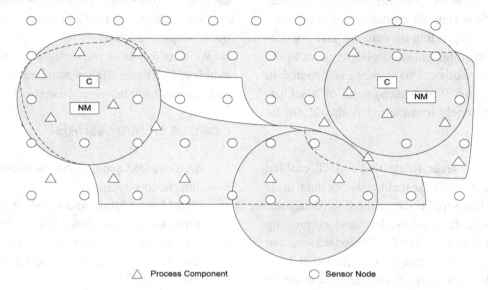

△ Process Component   ○ Sensor Node

Existing Standard: ISA Standard

ISA is a standard that is being developed by almost 250 companies involving more than 400 automation professionals representing end users, government agencies, experts and suppliers. The focus of the forum is to define a set of standards to implement wireless communications for any industrial automation and control systems. This standard is predicted to have a much bigger scope than WirelessHART. In fact, WirelessHART could be considered as one of the standards within the set of standards being developed for ISA. WirelessHART has been specifically designed for interconnectivity between field devices.

PROPOSED SYSTEM

It is seen that the underlying wired automation control system (in existing systems) is hierarchical, decentralized and tiered. There are microprocessors at the lower level that take care of a few control loops. At a higher level, higher capacity microprocessors take care of the interaction between the various control loop sets and define

global requirements. Given this existing infrastructure the network management, which will be required for incorporating WSN to automate the control system, should also be hierarchical and distributed.

Based on these observations, we propose the following topology for our network system setup. We group sensor nodes logically into zones based on their geographical location as well as their membership in functional zones (a sensor is connected with a set of control loops known as its functional zone). We also propose a decentralized network management system corresponding to the existing decentralized control system. Each functional zone has a network manager and a controller. The network manager and controller interact with each other to better manage both the control and network associated industrial components (actuators, valves, sensor etc.) and sensor nodes within a functional zone. The network and controller at the next hierarchy are responsible for the network and control aspects of the entire system (all functional zones). Any system wide changes or reaction to deviations in monitored system, or changes in input parameters, are incorporated at this level. Figure 3 gives a diagrammatic view of our system. The grey areas are functional zones. The yellow areas are zones based on proximity to major components. The two zones overlap in some regions.

We next propose our addressing scheme for our proposed setup. Our aim is to build sensor network algorithms that harness and take advantage of the underlying existing control system infrastructure and build up on the WirelessHART standard.

Proposed Mapping of Geographical Location to Component Mapping Location

In the proposed setup, subsets of components (major components) identify themselves by their geographical coordinates. Sensor nodes and other components map their locations relative to the subset of components. The major components are chosen due to their configuration of continuous power supply, unlike the other components (minor components) and sensor nodes that are battery powered.

Let us define some terms as follows.

- Fine grain routing – Routing executed between major components and minor components / sensor nodes. Short distance routing is implemented.
- Coarse grain routing – Routing executed between sensor nodes / minor components to major components. Long distance routing is implemented.
- Sensor Nodes – Refers to the wireless sensor nodes.
- Components – Refers to industrial process components.

This proposal has the following advantages:

- Unlike environmental monitoring where geographical location is important, in industrial environment it is more important to route messages in the vicinity of processing components. These components can be anything such as a tank, or a major pipeline actuator (something that any worker can identify immediately). The controllers and network managers are also considered as components. Major components are assumed to have unlimited amount of energy. This is a reasonable assumption as major process components and actuators are bulky and many times need electrical power sources. We harness the existing infrastructure to help our routing and other network functions.
- The number of routing messages sent out has a direct correlation with the status of components and associated control loops. Our addressing scheme helps in increasing the efficiency of the routing process.

The major components have unique Id based on their geographical coordinates. The major components act like localizing beacons and continuously send out signals to indicate their Ids and the corresponding controller they are connected to. Minor components localize and address themselves with respect to the major components. Through periodic broadcasts, the major components send out update messages to get the Ids of minor components and sensor nodes that are associated with them. Since the minor components cannot remain switched on for the entire time for receiving routed messages, long distance course grain routing is done to the major components. The messages are then forwarded to the relevant minor components and sensor nodes by the associated major component. A list of component Ids and their location with relation to the process being monitored is kept by the corresponding network manager. The component based system setup is shown in Figure 4.

Sensor nodes or minor components address themselves based on two factors: which major component they are functionally connected to,

Figure 4. Components act as localizing beacons

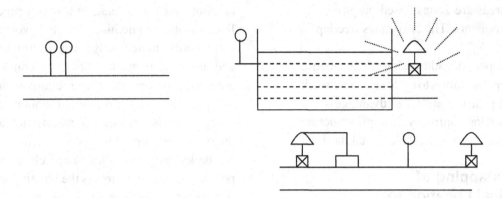

Figure 5. Node 'X' has an address of A, B, C for proximity and D, B for functionality

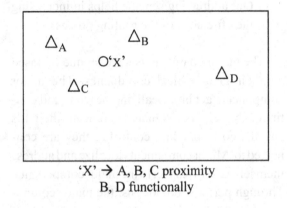

'X' → A, B, C proximity
B, D functionally

and which major component they are close to in terms of distance.

From Figure 5 it can be shown that the address of sensor node 'X' is given by two sets of values containing associated major component Ids. The major component associations help in coarse grain routing. Each major component has a list of all nodes that are in close proximity whether functionally connected or not. This list assists in fine grain routing. In the next section we discuss the further details of our system setup and the proposed routing algorithm.

ROUTING

General setup of system

Our system (Figure 3) consists of a network of sensors set up in a grid pattern. This is done for redundancy and fault tolerance. Sensor nodes are all connected to a master controller through a hierarchical structure. In addition we have the Supervisory Control And Data Acquisition (SCADA) system for data gathering purposes. The sensors perform three primary jobs: sending monitoring data to the SCADA system and controller; taking controlling action depending on sensor meter readings; and determining any emergency situation and taking appropriate action.

Releated Work on Routing

The work in (Tao, Fan, & Biswas, 2007) proposes a system where some routing decisions are off-loaded to a server that is not connected directly to the sensor network (Off-Network Control Processing – ONCP). It has a WirelessHART like topology – flat with a centralized base station where most processing takes place. The network is divided into clusters or zones. The course level routes (base station to a zone or zones) are decided at the server with two input information namely, the sum of residual energy in a zone, and the sum of residual energy of border sensor nodes that connect in between zones. Fine routing, inter zone routing or cluster head to neighbor cluster head routing is done reactively by local nodes. Course grain routing is done by choosing the path with minimum end-to-end energy consumption and avoiding links that can create hot spot regions. Metric used for comparison is packet delivery ratio, end-to-end latency, average energy expenditure and number of packets transmitted. In (Jing, Quesada, & Yuming, 2007), a switch from proactive to reactive and vice versa is done depending on node velocity and network situation. This work deals more with node velocity than network situation. The work in (Venugopalan, Zygmunt & Emin, 2003) proposed SHARP which is a hybrid routing algorithm that creates proactive zone around nodes that have large incoming data. The zone radius is determined by the node. All nodes within that zone create proactive routes to the centralized node. Nodes that are not within any zone execute reactive routing. In the proactive zone, DAG (directed acyclic graph) is created periodically (*reconstruction_interval*) by the nodes with high levels of incoming data. The zone radius or height of the zone is decided by a node independently based on the mobility rate, node degree, and number of sources and distance of the sources from the destination. The routing algorithm proposed in (Junyoung, Jiman, & Yookun, 2009) considers energy cost, delay and reliability of paths. Only paths that satisfy the time delay constraint are chosen and amongst those paths, the least energy path is selected. To ensure reliability, multi path routing is done. The work in (Ganesan, Govindan, Shenker, & Estrin, 2001) discusses the creation and advantages of braided multipath routing as compared to disjoint multipath routing. The work in (Bush, Carothers, & Szymanski, 2005) gives an algorithm that further improves on the work given in (Ganesan, Govindan, Shenker, & Estrin, 2001) by sending data packets across the braided paths to keep the path 'alive' instead of sending 'keep

alive messages'. This technique saves energy in path maintenance.

Proposed Routing

From the literature survey we observe that we need to have path with known end-to-end delay. Therefore there is a need for proactive paths. In our proposed system, we have network managers that are responsible for predefined functional zones dependent on network health status received from sensor nodes periodically. Also proactive paths or frequency of transmitting messages or DSSS instead of FHSS will be changed if the network manger gets to know from the controller the turning on of a component that emits EM disturbances of known range of frequencies. The network manager by setting up proactive paths, helps in reducing messages that would have been needed to be exchanged amongst concerned sensor nodes. However proactive routing is energy expensive and does not achieve load balancing. To counteract this disadvantage, we use reactive routing wherever there are messages that do not have time delay constraints.

In addition, our protocol takes into consideration battery characteristics and proposes setting up of very high priority message paths and transmission of *distress* signal. If the estimate of the time required to reach a destination becomes more that allowable time during reactive routing, then appropriate routing action is taken that is initiated by a distress signal.

Our proposed hybrid routing algorithm builds on the routing algorithm proposed in WirelessHART. Our routing algorithm improves in the following areas.

- It considers battery model
- It proposes reactive routing when there is sufficient time left to convey messages in order to do load balancing.
- It proposes a highway type routing alongside the hybrid routing for high priority

messages that do not happen often but when it does happen immediate action needs to take place.

- It propose component based two tier routing.

We make the following assumption of our system with related to routing.

- The sensor nodes know their location (as discussed in the previous section).
- The sensor nodes can be woken up out of schedule by neighbor nodes. But this is avoided as much as possible.
- The Sensor nodes have FHSS and DSSS capabilities (required by WirelessHART)

For our routing algorithm we have define a metric 'N' as

$$N = \begin{bmatrix} D_1 & D_2 & D_3 & \dots & D_n \\ t_1 & t_2 & & \dots & t_n \\ l_1 & l_2 & & \dots & l_n \\ RD_1 & RD_2 & & \dots & RD_n \\ R_1 & & & \dots & R_n \end{bmatrix} \begin{bmatrix} Ne_1 \\ Ne_2 \\ \vdots \\ Ne_n \end{bmatrix}$$

(1)

where

- D_x: Distance to controller taking Ne_x as the next hop
- T_x: Time taken to controller taking Ne_x as next hop
- I_x: Interference level with neighbor Ne_x.
- RD_x: identifies a neighbor as belongs to proactive path set of nodes, or nodes with specialized function set.
- R_x: Residual energy left before battery capacity hits sharp downward trend; refer to (Bhattacharyya, Kumar, Bayoumi, 2007 – Figure 8a).

The information of Equation 1 is present in all nodes. Next we give details of the various components of our routing algorithm and discuss the algorithms used for the initial setup and continuous running phase of our proposed routing algorithm.

Proactive Routing

All components are connected to the Network Manager through proactive routes. In addition, proactive route connections are set up between major components that may be far apart but connected functionally. Our routing algorithm varies from other zone based routing algorithms in this respect. Localized proactive zones are created to collect sensor node data and either take decision for some action or route it to some distance towards concerned controller. The proactive routes are setup by the network manager instead of the sensor nodes themselves. The reason for this is that the network manager and the controller coordinate with one another, share system wide information to set up the proactive paths. This level of information is not available to the sensor nodes and not energy efficient to be given to the sensor nodes. Locally the nodes can refresh the proactive paths by local sensor node substitution (sensor node with same latency to destination but with more RE levels could be, alternatively, included in the proactive path). In all other regions, reactive routing is done (component to major components etc.). Figure 6 gives an illustrative diagram of the proactive and reactive routes setup.

Reactive Routing

The sensor nodes need to know the location of the major components they need to route messages to, the concerned controller and the concerned network manager. This information should include which neighbor to route through to reach a particular major component and end-to-end time requirement. An initial list of major component

Figure 6. Proactive routes and reactive route setup

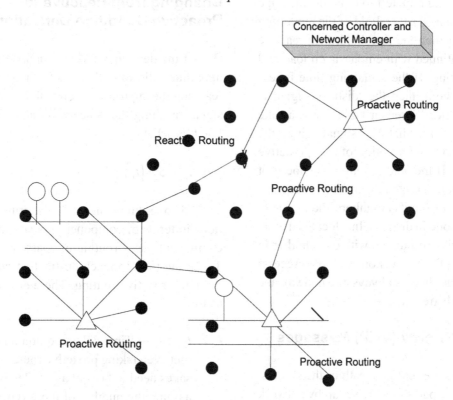

details required by a sensor node is given by the network manager. We assume that this list will not change as components are stationary and the set of controlling functions do not vary much with time with respect to a particular sensor node.

Messages are routed to the component nodes with a major component and destination node address attached to each of them. All messages are routed to major components (coarse grain routing). At each in between sensor node, the routing node address is checked against destination node address in case the routing node itself is the destination. It can use any geographical based routing such as GEAR, GPSR etc. Once the message reaches the vicinity of the major component, the individual node could be located easily as each major component has a list of surrounding sensor nodes and components.

For example, if a node needs to send a message to node 'X'. Depending on message priority and

consequential latency requirements the node first checks which destination major component(s) (A, B, or C) satisfy the latency requirements. If the time that could be used to route the message is more than the latency required for any of the paths to the major components, reactive routing is employed. During the reactive routing load balancing and energy considerations are considered to make decisions on the path(s) to be selected. The metric given in Equation 1 is used to select a next hop neighbor. In addition, functional dependency check is made given the functionally connected components of 'X' to see if any messages need to be routed to associated components, with comparative latencies.

Nodes with normal traffic loads and messages with low priority, route messages reactively. During reactive routing time remaining to route message to destination is checked against time required to send message to destination. At each hop the remaining time left to route the message is compared against a threshold. If the remaining time is greater than the threshold, then reactive routing is continued with emphasis on load and energy balancing. If the remaining time is less than the threshold, then the 'distress' signal is sent out. Any nearby sensor node that is awake and that hears the 'distress' signal, gives the "distressed" node information of any proactive routes nearby. If the neighboring node does not have any proactive route information, it requests the information from its neighbors and the same is sent to the node in distress. In a localized area, the sensor nodes coordinate with one another in their TDMA (Time Division multiple Access) schedule so that there is always one node awake to check for 'distress' messages.

Very High Priority (VHP) Messages

VHP messages are sent by a path of the shortest delay. Proactive paths that are set up by network managers, balance out time delay and resource consumption to some extent. Any localized refreshes done take into consideration energy and time delay balancing. We propose having a sub set of nodes called 'nice' nodes. These nodes are in constant lookout for the best possible way to transmit messages to certain destinations. To be effective, the number of destinations needs to be low in number. This is a reasonable assumption as the destination is usually the central controller or a major valve. The 'nice' nodes also keep track of neighboring 'nice' nodes, and proactive routes with associated time delays. These 'nice' nodes are only a few in number and are exclusively reserved to route VHP messages. They do not route any other messages, however they can give information of proactive routes, in case a distress signal is received. The 'nice' nodes have synchronized sleep schedules with other 'nice' nodes, proactive routes. Sleep schedule can be changed if 'best path' changes. Ultimately the aim is to have minimum time delays in transmitting the messages.

Changing from Reactive to Proactive Condition Derivation

We set the deadlines t_h (hard) dependent on the maximum allowable latency in the error signal reaching the appropriate controller or shut down signal reaching the concerned valve. Soft dead line t_c is set at

$$t_c = t_h - 5\%\left(t_h\right) \qquad (2)$$

The nodes know the various destination locations in terms of component Ids and implement component based routing or coarse routing. Let T_{set} be the time to reach destination component through proactive routing. There are two cases, as follows.

- $t_{set} \geq t_c \rightarrow$ Time delay requirements are not met even taking proactive routes. The messages need to be sent as VHP message. We assume the number of these types of messages is low.
- $t_{set} < t_c \rightarrow$ A combination of reactive and proactive (hybrid) routing is executed.

Proactive paths are set up by the network manager. An in between node can also update the time remaining depending on any information it has of the destination components. We model the communication links as a graph $G = (V, E)$ where V denotes the node set and E the edge set representing communication links between node pairs. For a node u ∈ V, we have an edge e ∈ E denoted by e = (u, v), u is the start node and v is the end node. A weight w(e) is assigned based on 'I' values (Equation 1). Higher the w(e) value, higher the expected retransmissions required. We assume that the message packet size is constant and is denoted by Pc. Let tr(e) be the transmission cost per link or hop. We abstract the unit cost of the link for transmitting data from u to v as c(e). Thus transmission cost tr(e) is given by Equation 3.

$$tr\left(e\right) = P_c c\left(e\right) w\left(e\right) \qquad (3)$$

c(e) is edge dependent and varies with distance 'D' between the node and its neighbors. Longer the distance the more power required to transmit the message.

For reactive routing to be possible – Let $c_{reactive}(e)$ be the unit time delay in making a reactive route decision. If the number of neighbors is Nei_x then

$$t_{temp} = t_c - c_{reactive}\left(e\right) * Nei_x \qquad (4)$$

Let t_{hop} be the time required to transmit the message from the node to its selected neighbor. Then initially t_{rem} becomes

$$t_{rem} = t_c - \left(t_{hop} + t_{temp}\right)$$

t_{rem} is set to the value of estimate time required to reach destination component.

$$t_{rem} = t_{rem} - \left(t_{hop} + t_{temp}\right) \qquad (5)$$

In proactive routing, depending on how old the proactive path information is, the time required to reach destination component could vary from the known time requirement. This variation is scaled to the number of hops (H) away from destination component the message decides to take a proactive route.

$$t_x = \left(t_i * p * H\right) + t_{set} \qquad (6)$$

Where

$$p = \frac{t_{update}}{t_{epoch}\left(set\ by\ system\right)} \qquad (7)$$

t_{epoch} is the time interval after which a proactive route is updated, t_{update} is the time interval that elapses after such a path update is made. t_i is the time taken to destination proactively by the sensor node.

Hybrid Scheme

If $t_x > t_{rem}$ use reactive else proactive Equation (8)

In the reactive phase, amongst the neighbors selected as possible candidates for the next hop to reach destination component, the neighbor with the highest energy level and lowest tr(e) metric cost is selected.

Battery consideration

From the literature survey in (Bhattacharyya, Kumar, Bayoumi, 2007), we see that pulsed energy consumption is the best for utilizing the full extent of capacity of the battery. Also there is a threshold below which it is very difficult to recover charge from a battery.

Proposed Routing Algorithm

After the sensor nodes are deployed we have two more phases. The two phases and the actions taken in them are described next.

Figure 7. Average energy level obtained for Region 1

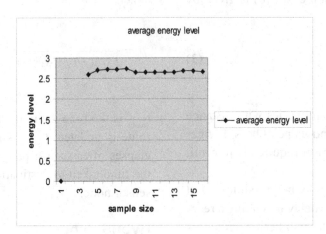

Figure 8. Accuracy for corresponding sample size

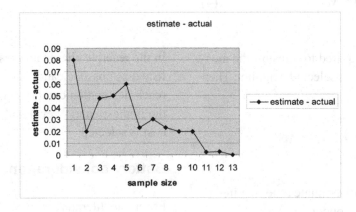

Initial Setup Phase

- Detect major components nearby, note Id of major component and the controller the major components are connect to.
- Major components that have localizing beacons detect and keep a list of components that are in close proximity to it. Give this list to network manager.
- The network manger functionally connects the various components and sensor nodes.
- Addressing is done for all components and sensor nodes.
- Network manager broadcasts estimates of the end-to-end time required to route

a message to the region of the associated components. Interested components store this information.

- The metric information in Equation 1 is gathered by sensor nodes. For reactive routing this information helps in next hop neighbor selection. In proactive routing, this helps in selecting a neighbor with same end-to-end time delay.
- At this step wired links are also identified by network manager. Conversion from wireless to wired communication and vice versa has some time delays. However wired communication is almost instantaneous and is not susceptible to EM disturbances.

Figure 9. Kalman filter output based on noise variance obtained from Region 1

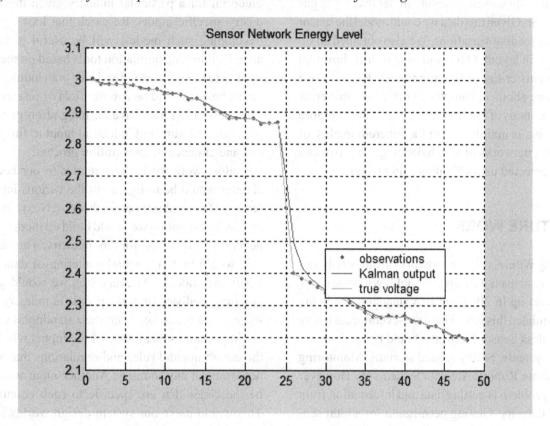

So wired communications is useful to have in few areas of high interference. The time delay is considered and included in proactive path's end-to-end delay.

Running Phase (Normal)

- Repair routes – In case of proactive routing, routes are checked and updated periodically. In reactive routing the 'best' neighbor is selected as next hop based on matrix information (Equation1) present at a node.
- All components send periodic reports to the network manager.
- The priorities of the messages are varied by assigning an appropriate t_c value to each message. For example, monitoring messages that have high t_c values are mostly

reactively routed. Control messages have lower t_c values and could be proactively or reactively routed.

PROPOSED HEALTH MONITORING SYSTEM

For the network manager to make real time decisions about the proactive paths or be aware of the status of the sensor nodes, health monitoring system is required. This system should be able to effectively monitor the status of the sensor nodes in terms of its residual energy, neighborhood interference, effective neighbors etc. We have designed algorithms that implement the sensor health monitoring system. Our proposed algorithm is based on sector based sampling. Further details can be obtained in (Bhattacharyya, Kumar, Bayoumi, 2009). We obtained SCADA data that gave temporally varying pressure meter reading in gas pipeline. Given this data we could model the sensor meter reading variations. We also obtained an oil platform layout. Our simulation results show that for a cluster size of 80 sensor nodes (Region 1) we require about 11 samples to get a tolerable error of the status of the sensor nodes (Figure 7, Figure 8). This is mainly due to the inherent quality of sensor networks of load balancing. The error can be corrected using Kalman Filter (Figure 9).

FUTURE WORK

Using Wireless Sensor Networks in Industrial Control Systems is an emerging field. WirelessHART was set up in 2007 and ISA standards are being formulated this year. There are several areas where Wireless Sensor Networks could be used – Control systems, Safety related systems, Monitoring Systems, Robotic Actuator Systems etc. However one problem is getting data and information from any industry. Getting permission for a total sensor system implementation in an industry is also another problem.

Another emerging field of research is seamless integration of the factory automation system with the outside world. Several issues come up during this integration like security, transferring data between different protocols, automating the whole process of gas consumption input to production output having provisions for human input in between.

Each industry has its unique set of constraints, controlling parameters and environments. Designing a system that uniquely works for that industry is one way to go. This makes it most efficient for that particular industry. However implementation time does go up. Another research area would be to look at all the various parameter of an industry through abstract models. The models are defined in such a way so that any industry specification could be mapped onto the models. Then solving these models could result in an implementation

blueprint for a particular industry given the industry specific inputs. Research that looks into developing such models will be useful in this area. Building of simulation tools based on these models to test out a design and idea in an industrial environment would be another field of research. The tools could also have an integration of application software and industrial input to further test and enhance the integration process.

Future work particularly related to our book chapter would be to figure out the various input required for a wide range of industries. Next based on this investigation we would build up models to generalize the design for any industry. The next step would be to do actual gathering of data to verify our models. At every step we would get practical feedback from the people in industry to incorporate the issues from their standpoint that are important to them. One of the inputs will be the environmental rules and regulations that are necessary in any industry. Another input would be the codes that are specific to each country. This would make our system design worldwide acceptable.

CONCLUSION

In this book chapter we have a detailed discussion of the proposed hierarchical distributed network management system in oil production platforms. Our proposals have used the existing infrastructure to the maximum extent to increase the efficiency of both the control system and the sensor network. In our knowledge there are very few works that go into details of the system to be employed in an oil production site.

ACKNOWLEDGMENT

Support from Louisiana Board of Regents under research award number LEQSF(2009-12)-RD-A-22 is acknowledged.

REFERENCES

Abdelgawad, A., Lewis, A., Elgamel, M., Issa, F., Tzeng, N.-F., & Bayoumi, M. (2006, Aug. 18-20). Remote Measuring of Flow Meters for Petroleum Engineering and Other Industrial Applications. *International Workshop on Computer Architecture for Machine Perception and Sensing, CAMP 2006*, (pp. 99 – 103).

Bhattacharyya, M., Kumar, A. & Bayoumi, M. (2007). A Framework for Assessing Residual Energy in Wireless Sensor Network. *Special Issue on International Journal of Sensor Networks 2*(¾).

Bhattacharyya, M., Kumar, A., & Bayoumi, M. (2009). Residual Energy Monitoring Using Statistical Analysis. *International Symposium on Digital Life Technologies*, ISDLT2009, May 28-29.

Bonivento, A., Carloni, L. P., & Sangiovanni-Vincentelli, A. (2006). Platform-Based Design of Wireless Sensor Networks for Industrial Applications. In *Proceedings Design, Automation and Test in Europe*, DATE '06, (Vol. 1, pp. 1 – 6).

Bush, L. A., Carothers, C. D., & Szymanski, B. K. (2005). Algorithm for optimizing energy use and path resilience in sensor networks. In *Proceedings of the Second European Workshop on Wireless Sensor Networks*, (pp. 391 – 396).

Chao, X., Dargie, W., & Guan Lin (2008) "Energy Model for H2S Monitoring Wireless Sensor Network. In *11th IEEE International Conference on Computational Science and Engineering*, CSE '08, (pp. 402 – 409).

Dalbro, M., & Eikeland, E. in't Veld, A.J., Gjessing, S., Lande, T.S., Riis, H.K., & Sorasen, O. (2008). Wireless Sensor Networks for Off-shore Oil and Gas Installations. In *Second International Conference on Sensor Technologies and Applications, SENSORCOMM '08*, (pp. 258 – 263).

Di Tian, G. N. D. (2003). Energy efficient routing with guaranteed delivery in wireless sensor networks. Wireless Communications and Networking, WCNC 2003, (Vol. 3, pp. 1923 – 1929).

Ganesan, D., Govindan, R., Shenker, S., & Estrin, D. (2001). Highly-resilient, energy-efficient multipath routing in wireless sensor networks. *ACM SIGMOBILE Mobile Computing and Communications Review, 5*(4), 11–25. doi:10.1145/509506.509514

Gao, M., Xu, J., & Tian, J. (2008). Remote monitoring system of pumping unit based on wireless sensor networks. In *IEEE International Conference on Industrial Technology, ICIT 2008*, (pp. 1 – 4).

HART Communication protocol. (n.d.). Retrieved from http://www.hartcomm2.org/hart_protocol/protocol/hart_data.html

Helson. (2007). *Wireless HART fits into ISA-SP100 standards effort*. Retrieved from http://www.isa.org/InTechTemplate.cfm?Section=Executive_Corner2&template=/ContentManagement/ContentDisplay.cfm&ContentID=61420

Heo, J., Hong, J., & Cho, Y. (2009). EARQ: Energy Aware Routing for Real-Time and Reliable Communication in Wireless Industrial Sensor Networks. *IEEE Transactions on Industrial Informatics, 5*(1), 3–11. doi:10.1109/TII.2008.2011052

Horiuchi, L., & Stokes, A. (2006). CISCO Press release. Retrieved from http://newsroom.cisco.com/dlls/partners/news/2006/pr_prod_09-11.html

Howie, C. L. (1984). *Remote Corrosion Monitoring of Off-Shore Pipelines*. Retrieved from http://www.mms.gov/tarprojects/075/075AA.PDF

IBM WebSphere. (n.d.). Retrieved from http://www.ibm.com/developerworks/websphere/

Intel Research – Sensor Network Research. (n.d.). Retrieved from http://techresearch.intel.com/articles/Exploratory/1501.htm

Ishibashi, K., & Yano, M. (2005). A Proposal of Forwarding Method for Urgent Messages on an Ubiquitous Wireless Sensor Network. In *Proceedings 6th Asia-Pacific Symposium on Information and Telecommunication Technologies, APSITT 2005*, (pp. 293 – 298).

Jawhar, I., Mohamed, N., Mohamed, M. M., & Aziz, J. (2008). A Routing protocol and addressing scheme for oil, gas, and water pipeline monitoring using wireless sensor networks. In *5th IFIP International Conference on Wireless and Optical Communications Networks, WOCN '08*, (pp. 1 – 5).

Jiang, P., Ren, H., Zhang, L., Wang, Z., & Xue, A. (2006). Reliable Application of Wireless Sensor Networks in Industrial Process Control. In *Sixth World Congress on Intelligent Control and Automation, WCICA 2006*, (Vol. 1, pp. 99 – 103).

Kim, A. N., Hekland, F., Petersen, S., & Doyle, P. (2008). When HART goes wireless: Understanding and implementing the WirelessHART standard. *IEEE International Conference on Emerging Technologies and Factory Automation, ETFA 2008*, Sept. 15-18, (pp. 899 – 907).

Lennvall, T., Svensson, S., & Hekland, F. (2008). A comparison of WirelessHART and ZigBee for industrial applications. In *IEEE International Workshop on Factory Communication Systems, WFCS*, (pp. 85 – 88).

Low, K. S., Win, W. N. N., & Er, M. J. (2005). Wireless Sensor Networks for Industrial Environments. In *International Conference on Computational Intelligence for Modelling, Control and Automation, 2005 and International Conference on Intelligent Agents, Web Technologies and Internet Commerce*, (Vol. 2, pp. 271 – 276).

Luther, B. (n.d.). *Oil Field Safety*. Retrieved from http://www.txoga.org/attachments/OilFieldSafetyNEO1.ppt#256,1,Oil Field Safety

Manning, F., & Thompson, R. (1995). Oil Field Processing (Vol. 2, Crude Oil). Tulsa, OK: Pennwell.

Matos, S., Powell, D., Davies, R., Zhang, X., & Moore, P. (2006). *A Guideline Framework for the Integrity Assessment of Offshore Pipelines*. Retrieved from http://www.mms.gov/tarprojects/565/565AA.pdf

Mohamed, N., & Jawhar, I. (2008). A Fault Tolerant Wired/Wireless Sensor Network Architecture for Monitoring Pipeline Infrastructures. In *Second International Conference on Sensor Technologies and Applications*, SENSORCOMM '08, (pp. 179 – 184).

Ramasubramanian, V., Haas, Z. J., & Sirer, E. G. (2003). SHARP: a hybrid adaptive routing protocol for mobile ad hoc networks. In *Proceedings of the 4th ACM international symposium on Mobile ad hoc networking*, (pp. 303 - 314).

Steinberg, A., & White, F. (1998). *Community Status Report and Proposed Revisions to the JDL Data Fusion Model*. Retrieved from http://stinet.dtic.mil/cgi-bin/GetTRDoc?AD=ADA399488&Location=U2& doc=GetTRDoc.pdf

WirelessHART. (2007). Retrieved from http://www.hartcomm2.org/hart_protocol/wireless_hart/wireless_hart_main.html

Wu, T., Yu, F., & Biswas, S. (2007). Scalable Hybrid Routing in Very Large Sensor Networks. In *International Conference on Mobile Data Management*, (pp. 366 – 370).

Xie, J., Quesada, L. G., & Jiang, Y. (2007). A Threshold-based Hybrid Routing Protocol for MANET. In *4th International Symposium on Wireless Communication Systems, ISWCS 2007*, (pp. 622 – 626).

Zheng, L. (2006). ZigBee Wireless Sensor Network in Industrial Applications. In *SICE-ICASE, International Joint Conference,* (pp. 1067 – 1070).

Chapter 8
Low Power Considerations in Ubiquitous Computing

Robert Tesch
University of Louisiana at Lafayette, USA

Ashok Kumar
University of Louisiana at Lafayette, USA

Jamie Mason
University of Louisiana at Lafayette, USA

Dania Alvarez
University of Louisiana at Lafayette, USA

Mario Di'Mattia
University of Louisiana at Lafayette, USA

Shawn Luce
University of Louisiana at Lafayette, USA

ABSTRACT

Majority of the devices that are used in ubiquitous computing are expected to be as small as possible, be able to perform as many computations as possible, and transmit the results to another device or computer. Such expectations in performance put a pressure on the power budget of such devices. It is a well-known fact that the advances in battery technology are much slower and cannot keep up with the performance demands of tiny gadgets unless new methods of designing and managing hardware and software are developed and used. This chapter will introduce the motivation for low power design considerations by discussing the power limitations of ubiquitous computing devices. Then the chapter will discuss the research directions that are being pursued in literature for reducing power consumption and increasing efficiency of ubiquitous computing systems.

DOI: 10.4018/978-1-61520-843-2.ch008

Figure 1. Example of ubiquitous computing in a cruise control system of a car

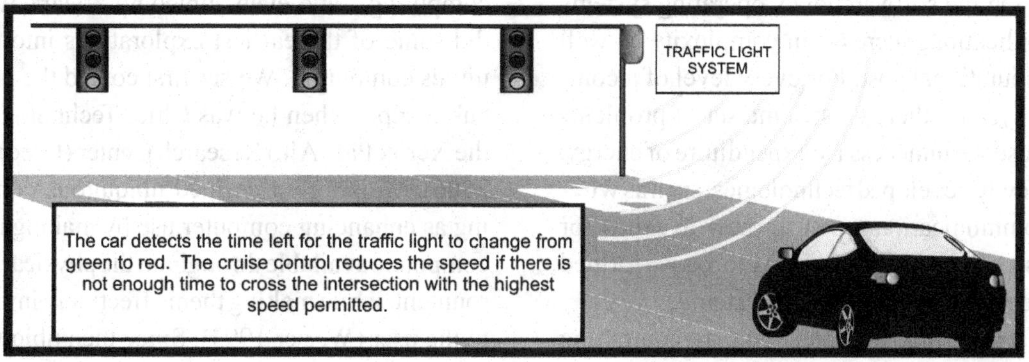

INTRODUCTION

Ubiquitous computing is emerging as one of the biggest applications for computing systems and carries with it a huge potential for use in every walk of life. There are many ubiquitous systems in use right now that have the potential to develop into complex systems that are more context aware. For example, most commercial cars have cruise control. Cruise control detects the current condition of the car, its speed, and quietly makes adjustments to the throttle to match a preset speed (Figure 1). This is similar to how ubiquitous systems should work. Though a simple concept on the surface, the idea of cruise control opens up a whole new field of possibilities regarding context awareness. With the widespread use of global positioning systems, a simple cruise control system can be enhanced with context awareness by contacting a global database to retrieve local traffic information. With the use of a GPS system, the preset speed then becomes dynamic, and can adjust itself automatically to fit the local speed limit. This system can also be used to detect reduced speed zones like school zones and construction areas. With an even more involved database, there exist a possibility of the cruise control system being able to synchronize with traffic lights to advise the driver when to come to a stop in order to avoid potential traffic accidents or tickets.

This example describes a high-end application of ubiquitous computing that is very power-hungry in design. However, this application can rely on the car's battery to act as a big power source, satisfying its power needs. There are a myriad of other possible applications of ubiquitous computing, such as sensors and embedded computers, which do not share such resources. These devices do not have access to large power supplies and instead must operate within the power budget set by small portable batteries.

Thus, power consumption imposes one of the biggest restrictions on the development of ubiquitous computing. The reason for this is that ubiquitous computing systems must be designed to be compact and self-sufficient, which will restrict the amount of resources that can be utilized by the system. Ideally, maintenance levels have to be kept at a minimum and energy costs reduced greatly. If the system is designed to be mobile, then it is expected that the only available power source will be a battery. Subsequently, size restrictions will limit the performance of the battery and the amount of power consumption in the system. Unfortunately, there are also large sources of energy waste present in modern day computing systems, which hinder the application of ubiquitous computing for every walk of life.

The sources that cause this energy waste are at both the hardware and software level. On the hardware level, circuits generate heat and dissipate power. On the software level, operating systems and applications increase in complexity as well as computational cost. For every level of a computing system, there exist some set of problems that cause the unnecessary expenditure of energy. Even newly developed technologies, such as wireless communication, open up new avenues for expensive operations that need to be performed on embedded and distributed systems.

It is generally accepted that as computing systems become more powerful, energy demands will rise. Whereas the traditional mainframe and desktop approaches focus heavily on performance, the ubiquitous computing paradigm must look to balance performance with cost. There are many techniques that can be employed to achieve energy efficiency. For example, circuits can be redesigned to operate at a lower voltage supply. Software systems can be designed to run more efficiently by scheduling for active and inactive periods of time. These systems can even be scaled back in most of its design aspects to accomplish the same task with less overhead costs.

This chapter will approach these problems by first taking an overview of the many sources of energy waste in ubiquitous computing systems, and will cover many power issues in ubiquitous computing ranging from transistor design to the user application layer. Then, there will be a look at the field of low power design that presents a large array of solutions that are being explored to reduce power consumption on a range of computing devices. Then, operating system aspects of low power designs will be explored in greater depth. Lastly, there will be a look at the latest research developments.

BACKGROUND

Ubiquitous computing is a quickly developing area of the computing world and a hot topic in recent research. Ubiquitous computing is also widely recognized as "calm technology," "pervasive computing," and even "ubicomp". Mark Weiser did some of the earliest explorations into ubiquitous computing. Weiser first coined the phrase "ubicomp," when he was Chief Technologist of the Xerox Palo Alto Research Center (Greenfield 2006). Weiser first defined ubiquitous computing as enhancing computer use by making many computers available throughout the physical environment, while making them effectively invisible to the user (Weiser 1993). Since then ubiquitous computing has been extensively developed by many different sources to expand upon the potential behind distributed and embedded systems.

Embedded systems are a key constituent of ubiquitous systems, and are found in many areas of everyday life, from cell phones to automobiles. These embedded systems are growing exponentially in use and complexity, and are an integral part of ubiquitous computing. As ubiquitous computing grows, so does its energy consumption. However, ubiquitous computing has its own set of challenges that separate it from the traditional mainframe and desktop models. Most desktops and laptops have the luxury of enhancing computing performance by utilizing large memory blocks and high power sources. However, for ubiquitous computing systems, the emphasis is placed on being invisible, both in size and in energy consumption. This places a new level of constraints on traditional computing dynamics. Embedded and distributed systems cannot afford the space for large battery blocks or larger hard disks for memory. Without the larger battery blocks, these smaller systems have an increased dependency on power, making low power designs a critical component to its development. As a result, power consumption has become a huge hindrance to developing better embedded systems. To resolve this problem, one must address the issue of energy waste in today's computing technology.

LOW POWER CONSIDERATIONS

Problems That Cause Power Waste

There are many sources of energy waste in today's commonplace computing technology. It is these sources of energy waste that prevent ubiquitous computing from being widely used. Circuits suffer from power dissipation in their design and generate huge amounts of heat that has to be cooled to keep the system functioning normally. Even the at the software level, large amounts of redundant or pointless computation can occur. In this section, the various causes of energy waste are examined and some solutions are presented from both hardware and software perspectives.

Heat Dissipation

Transistors have been a space saving technology, and a key component in the advancement of modern computers. As a result of the increasing density of transistors and thus dense circuit activity, large amounts of power consumption lead to greater concentrations of heat. In order for a system to function properly and avoid severe heat damage, it needs to operate below a safe temperature threshold. This makes heat dissipation a primary concern of circuit designers. In complex circuits, expensive heat removal systems such as heat sinks and CPU fans have to be implemented to remove heat from the circuit board. Not only does this incur extra overhead costs, but also it takes up space within the system, limiting its already restricted size requirements.

Sources of Power Dissipation

Most computational devices for ubiquitous computing are designed in the Complementary Metal Oxide Semiconductor (CMOS) technology. In CMOS circuits, there are three major sources of power dissipation, namely short circuit power, leakage power, and dynamic power (Figure 2).

When the input signal of a circuit causes the transistors inside the circuit to flip, there is a brief moment while switching where the gates are still connected enough to conduct a current. At this moment, a path leading straight from the power sources to the ground is formed, causing a small amount of power to be siphoned off and wasted. The second source for power loss is through leakage power. Leakage power accounts for power lost through transistors that are not conducting or leaking out of diodes (Poppen 2000). Transistors can still leak power from the output node to the ground even if the gate is open and no direct current is established. This happens frequently with extremely small transistors as in the case of nanometer design. A third type of power loss here is dynamic power. Dynamic circuits consume larger amounts of power than static circuits in general. When the clock signal is in its evaluation phase, where the signal from the clock reads high, the external input could evaluate in such a way that the capacitor is discharged. Dynamic circuits will discharge energy from their capacitors frequently as the clock signal cycles.

Wireless Communication

One of the biggest consumers of energy in a ubiquitous system is wireless transmission using a wireless radio (Estrin 2002). For example, 802.11 wireless consumes significant energy and can quickly degrade a battery's life span (Estrin 2002). Most mobile devices today support some form of wireless communication. Other forms of wireless communication include satellite and Bluetooth, which is very common in cell phones and smartphones. All of these wireless technologies offer great communication solutions but present a large problem because of the amount of energy they require to operate.

Figure 2. Sources of power dissipation

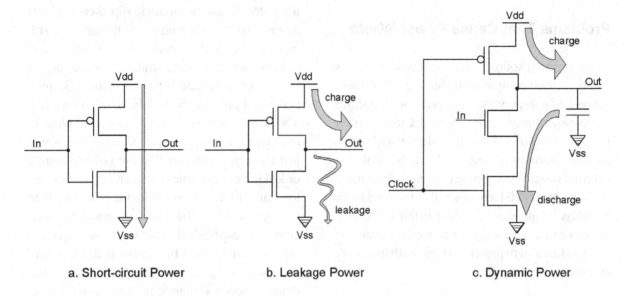

a. Short-circuit Power b. Leakage Power c. Dynamic Power

Solutions for Reducing Power Consumption

Since there are many potential sources for power waste in modern computing systems, several solutions have been proposed in the literature. Wasteful systems can be optimized in several ways, from the hardware level to the software level. Even very complex systems that need an operating system to function can be optimized in selection, design, and execution.

Hardware Design Techniques

The most fundamental source of energy waste occurs at the hardware level. Fortunately, there are plenty of hardware techniques being applied to increase hardware efficiency. Hardware architecture can be optimized in many interesting ways to achieve lower operation costs.

Multi Supply Voltage
Circuitry running at a higher voltage executes processes very quickly but consumes a greater amount of power, while circuits running at a

lower voltage are slower in execution but save on power consumption. The multi-supply voltage technique can be applied to optimize circuit power consumption by taking advantage of this principle. This method works by distributing circuitry throughout a system so that specific circuit blocks can operate at low or high voltage levels. If a circuit block happens to lie along time critical pathways, then that circuit can be assigned to high voltage levels, thus devoting the highest amount of power only to circuit blocks that would otherwise hinder performance. Other, non-crucial circuit blocks can then be assigned to low voltage levels, to prevent power waste. Supply voltage has the maximum impact on reducing power consumption in a circuit. For this reason, multi supply voltage could be an attractive option.

Clock Gating
Clock gating is another popular method of reducing power within a system. Basically, it allows the system to disable the clock input to blocks of dynamic circuitry that are not in use and are absorbing power unnecessarily, and then enable the circuit block when it is needed again for process execution. The

Figure 3. Non-clock gated system vs. clock gated system. In a clock-gated system, the clock signal can be disabled to unused hardware components to reduce power waste

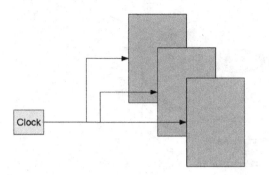
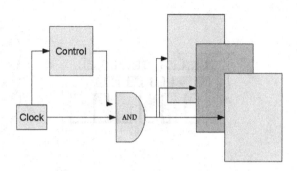

prevention of running unnecessary logic results in extended battery life and a significant decrease in heat production. Furthermore, these improvements greatly enhance the system's reliability. Despite the obvious advantages, this raises the issue of clock gating being extremely area-expensive. This is because every circuit that intends to use a gated clock input must have a logic unit implemented to determine whether or not the circuit needs to be in use (Figure 3). Another dilemma is that since clock gating relies heavily on switching voltage levels to circuit blocks on and off, the process must be done in such a way that will minimize power consumption while maximizing performance. If this process is erroneously implemented, the system could expend more power to turn circuits on and off than it is saving.

Synchronous Vs. Asynchronous Design

Traditionally, every component of a computing system will operate off of a global clock signal. In the past, this design has proven to be efficient and reliable, but as the system complexity increased, several issues have arisen. One major issue is clock skew, which is when the clock signal is received by different components of the hardware at different rates. This causes a loss in efficiency as components have to wait on clock transitions to enable other circuitry. Asynchronous systems

are designed to alleviate this by removing the global clock from the system. Also, by decoupling circuits from a global clock, dynamic circuitry no long dissipates power during operation since its capacitance only needs charging when necessary. Short circuit power is reduced as well for the same reasons. On the other hand, a purely asynchronous system has its downsides. Since each component would have the potential to operate at different rates, there is some extra overhead to support communication between components. A better design philosophy is to use a Globally Asynchronous Locally Synchronous (GALS) design. In this design, a system's components are broken down into multiple, synchronous hardware modules that communicate with each other asynchronously (Iyer 2002). This methodology supports localized module clock signals instead of the addition of a global clock signal, making concepts like clock-gating and multi supply voltage much easier to implement.

Dynamic Process Temperature Compensation (DPTC)

The basic idea behind this method is to dynamically control the temperature of a System-on-a-Chip (SoC) based on comparisons between the minimum normal operating temperature of a system and the change in temperature necessary

Figure 4. Illustration of two commonly used memory storage devices. Flash memory can be implemented in small storage spaces directly on circuit boards to reduce both space and power consumption

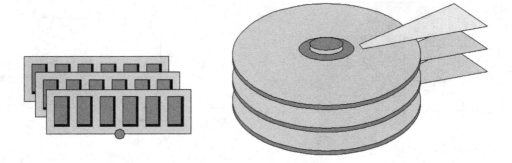

to accomplish a given process. Ring oscillators are typically used to measure the effects of voltage and temperature on a chip and are employed in this technique to observe the available performance of the system (Shearer 2008). There are logic units built into a DPTC system that are used to analyze the data gathered by the ring oscillators and produce temperature increase/reduction results based on system comparisons. Using the results from the logic units, the DPTC system's control unit dynamically allocates the necessary power for the process to operate correctly on the SoC. The principle behind this process is to keep the power supply hovering right above the minimum possible level that is needed to support the required operation.

Environmental Energy Sources

Operating systems for ubiquitous computing should be able to handle cases where the device receives power, fully or partially, from the environment. For example, solar energy could boost the lifetime of an outdoor device indefinitely if the device is able to store energy in rechargeable batteries (Estrin 2002). However, it is up to the designer's discretion on the pros and cons of the implementation of rechargeable batteries. While these additional features create advantages, they also comes with a cost, which may result in undesirable operating system overhead.

Memory and Storage

Since size is limited, the amount of memory and non-volatile storage can be limited too. However, in recent years, flash memory has seen steady decrease in price (Want 2002). The use of solid state drives instead of rotating disks also decreases the use of electricity in a computing system (Figure 4). Even if some flash memory designs are not more efficient in power consumption, they are still much smaller in size. Size reduction allows for larger data storage on local drives, which reduces the need to use wireless communication to transfer data to external storage systems.

Static vs. Dynamic Circuit Logic

In a static circuit design, the output depends exclusively on the inputs. On the other hand, a dynamic circuit design makes use of a clock signal. The use of dynamic and static circuit designs can help or hinder the power conservation. In dynamic logic, a circuit goes through precharge and evaluation phases in every clock cycle. This is the main cause of power dissipation in a dynamic circuit. Certain techniques such as clock gating can be used to reduce power. Dynamic circuits, in general, are much faster than static circuits. On the other hand, a static circuit is devoid of clocks, hence slower in comparisons and do not dissipate dynamic power. However, in static circuits, there are nearly twice as many transistors as in dynamic circuits. In static circuits, leakage is the main source of power dissipation. Also, static logic can take advantage of its independence from the clock signal by suspending operations for indefinitely long periods, which makes putting the system to sleep more practical.

Adiabatic Circuitry

An adiabatic or energy-recovering process is one that attempts to reduce or eliminate heat or energy dissipation within a closed system. Research into low power technology utilizing CMOS circuits is attempting to use this idea to create systems that utilize adiabatic circuitry. Presently, with size reduction in CMOS circuits, power loss through dynamic capacitance and short circuiting when gate switching has become a very pressing issue in the quest for feasible low power techniques. Adiabatic circuits aim to reduce these problems by following two primary rules at design time (Younis 1994). The first is to never switch on a transistor if the voltage is different between the drain and source. To reduce power loss incurred during capacitance charging, adiabatic circuits attempt to maintain a slower, constant charging time across an entire clock cycle. The second rule is to never turn off a transistor if a current is flowing through it. To reduce the power dissipation caused by short circuiting, adiabatic circuits wait until there is no power present to switch gates.

Processor Scaling

The type of hardware chosen in a system makes a large impact on its efficiency. The level of complexity in a system is typically matched by what is expected of it (Figure 5). For systems with a very limited functionality, a circuit can be designed for specific tasks without great production costs, such as RFID chips. However, larger systems, especially those that are applied in research fields, will depend on more sophisticated computing technology. When building a robot or a network of sensors for research interests, microcontrollers will be widely used, due to their reducible but flexible

nature. Microcontrollers are programmable and run much more cost effectively than processors or even microprocessors. Nonetheless, microcontrollers are very limited in computing power, which is why microprocessors are commonly developed for even larger applications, such as smartphones. Smartphones are constantly growing in computing power and are continually pushing the limits of power design. With microprocessors, microcontrollers and even some smaller systems, flexibility is important so that these systems can be used widely for an unpredictable range of applications. However, it is that level of flexibility that generates a lot of energy waste with issues such as non-essential computations, excessive overhead, and inefficient program execution.

Software Design Techniques

Many sources of energy waste can be found in the software architecture, mainly caused by inefficiencies found in many modern day operating systems and programs. However, smart techniques such as powering down at non-crucial times and more efficient implementations can lead to a great boost of power efficiency. Ubiquitous systems are deployed in systems that range from simple radio-frequency identification (RFID) chips to complex smartphones. However, unlike smaller embedded systems, which rely on simplicity for efficiency, smartphones are designed to behave as highly mobile desktops and laptops. The amount of computational power needed to run modern day software places a high demand for power-constrained microcontrollers. Another growing concern of ubiquitous computing is security. Unfortunately, security issues can also cause a number of power problems. This happens for two main reasons. Firstly, ubiquitous systems introduce new mediums for virus to spread, making these systems vulnerable. When a virus infects a system, it can cause meaningless operations to be executed by the processor. Such excessive and purposeless activity quickly becomes expensive.

Figure 5. Illustration of processor complexities. On the left is a small scale integrated circuit for use in extremely simple systems like a RFID chip. In the middle is a microcontroller, like the PIC, which is frequently used for distributed wireless sensor systems. On the right is a microprocessor for use in complex yet portable mutli-use systems such as smartphones

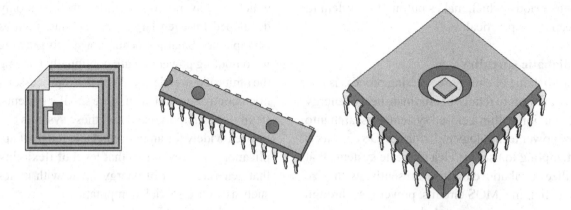

Secondly, to combat security issues, extra software has to exist and special protocols maintained, adding even more overhead. With these concerns in mind, there are approaches a designer can take to minimize the impact of applications in a ubiquitous system.

Scheduling the CPU

Processors are not always efficiently used. Even desktop model processors typically execute in bursts, not continuously. For ubiquitous systems, the processors may only need to process jobs at set intervals or for specific events. There is plenty of potential down time for which the processor is consuming power but not actually executing any instructions. In such cases, a useful technique is to schedule the processor to sleep when it is not in use. Such a strategy can reduce power consumption dramatically. Scheduling, however, can be tricky, and may not always be handled by the kernel. At times, a better technique may be to have the scheduling handled at the application layer for more sophisticated systems.

Network Changes

Many distributed ubiquitous systems are designed with sensors that pick up data then relay the data over a network back to the some other devices for processing. This makes communication crucial to the functions of ubiquitous computing systems. For these systems, wireless communication is the most widely used form of communication. To reduce the expensive cost associated with wireless communication, two things can be evaluated. Firstly, the type of wireless communication can be chosen to reduce cost. Bluetooth for example is generally cheaper to operate than the traditional 802.11 wireless technologies, thus short range communication may be better handled with Bluetooth instead. The second thing to be considered is the network protocols. Choosing the right network protocol model for a ubiquitous system can greatly reduce the expensive overhead costs. In the same manner, the number of bits that are transmitted and the distance to which they are transmitted greatly impact power dissipation.

Task Scheduling

Since a device in a ubiquitous computing system may be forced to work with minimal resources, scheduling approaches for non-ubiquitous applications do not always work optimally in this new environment. In an application such as an embedded system, the priority of scheduled tasks

Figure 6. Concept of a task scheduler implementing a simple FIFO priority queue to execute processes in the CPU

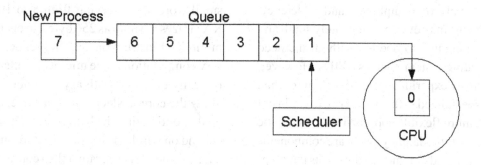

becomes increasingly important. Certain processes may require real time responses, requiring real time priority processing. Though FIFO (First In, First Out) non-preemptive scheduling is simple and easy to implement, it is not the best solution for all cases (Figure 6). Scheduling schemes involving preemption and priority scheduling can be implemented in limited memory systems as well, and should be preferred. There are many algorithms that can be used to assign priority to processes waiting to be executed based on resource limitations.

One method involves using two-level scheduling, which works with a two-level architecture, as in the LIMOS micro-kernel. The two-level architecture is divided into events and threads. Events can be generated by the hardware or software, and generally cannot be preempted by another event or thread, but can be interrupted. Threads are the components of an event and are interruptible. In this two-level scheduling system, events and threads are scheduling by priority. Priority is assigned based on the thread's priority along with the time slice necessary to execute the thread. When the scheduler is invoked, it selects the highest priority thread. When the scheduler runs out of tasks, LIMOS puts some system clocks, peripherals, and wireless access to sleep for reduced electricity consumption (Zhou 2006).

Another method involves selecting a scheduler based on the availability of resources. For example,

tasks can be divided into groups based on the resource needed. A FIFO scheduling algorithm may be best suited for real time tasks, since each task should be quickly processed and not interrupted as it enters the FIFO queue. Round Robin may be used for tasks requesting the network medium, so each task can transmit some data and no one task holds onto the medium for too long (Tianzhou 2006). Ultimately, little research has been done to assess the impact of task scheduling on power consumption in single core, real-time systems.

Operating System Scaling

Like the hardware counterpart, the software can also be scaled appropriately to reduce on power costs. Microcontrollers and microprocessors now have optimized operating systems that are designed specifically for that system. These operating systems typically are designed with reduced instruction sets and have reduced operation costs. However, some of these operating systems will sacrifice more computing capability for more power efficiency. Large amounts of energy can be saved by careful evaluation of what operating system to use, and for which microcontroller or microprocessors.

Operating System Design Techniques

The operating system design of a ubiquitous system has a large impact on its performance.

Fortunately, there are many highly developed operating systems on the market that support different levels of complexity and efficiency. Some systems may even be adequately small and specialized enough to operate without the need of an operating system, such as RFIDs. However, if a system is experimental or developing, then having a specialized software interface would not suffice. A more flexible approach will need to be taken, to accommodate any hardware components that may be added or removed during its development process. Additionally, its applications will be subject to radical changes over time.

Operating systems are being developed specifically to operate for processors of varying sizes. Thus, if a microcontroller is needed, a super small operating system like TinyOS can be used very efficiently. Likewise, with a microprocessor, a more powerful operating system such as Symbian OS, which is the most widely used operating system on the smartphone market today, can be readily applied. Therefore, even if the processor size is predetermined, the choice of which operating system to use can still vary greatly.

Microcontrollers vs. Microprocessors

For today's high end consumer products, such as smartphones, the ARM, or Advanced RISC Machine, architecture has become the most widely used 32 bit architecture. The ARM architecture was started in 1983 and quickly became a popular microprocessor design for embedded systems, due largely in part to its low power design. The features of ARM architecture offer increased computing power over the standard RISC design while still supporting a very low transistor count. The ARM also allows for other power saving techniques such as conditional execution of instructions and the ability to execute instructions in a 16 bit mode. However, for smaller embedded systems, the ARM is still much too large and requires excessive power. For wireless sensing networks in particular, the very popular TinyOS has been developed to run as a minimal operating system

on microcontrollers such as the AVR, MSP, and PIC series. These architectures are designed with small word sizes varying from 8 to 16 bits and RAM sizes as small as 256 bytes, to operate under minimized instruction sets and reduce unnecessary computations. The microcontrollers are also typically designed with asynchronous clocks to allow the core to sleep when inactive, all for the goal of optimizing the battery life. These sensors depend on wireless networks to store and process data on other devices, rather than consuming huge amounts of power to perform this task.

Standard Microcontroller Operating Systems

There are several choices when trying to pick an operating system for ubiquitous computing. Some of these choices include LiteOS, TinyOS, Mantis, Contiki, and SOS. Each operating system has its strengths and weaknesses, and the best operating system can be chosen based on the needs of the users and the hardware of the system. In systems with the most limited hardware, a file system, thread support, and event-based programming may not be desirable. For such limited systems, the Mantis and SOS operating systems may be the best fit. Mantis offers thread support, but lacks dynamic memory, event-based programming, and a file system. SOS offers thread support and dynamic memory, but has no event-based programming or file system. For less limited systems, TinyOS or Contiki may be the best choices. Both offer a single level file system, and some support for threads along with event based programming and dynamic memory. Additionally, neither one of these operating systems offer a remote scriptable wireless shell, or a remote file system interface. While TinyOS has support for remote debugging, Contiki does not. For systems with the least limited resources (and users demanding the most feature support) the LiteOS operating system can best meet those needs. It offers a hierarchical Unix-like file system, thread support, event-based programming, remote debugging, and dynamic memory.

Figure 7. Concept of the interaction between the software components of TinyOS. Pieces of software interact externally by interfaces but execute processes internally by tasks

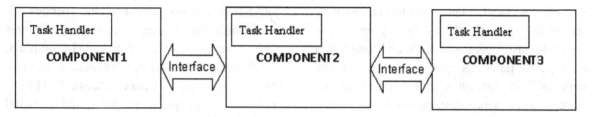

As researches develop, additional features will likely become available for the currently more limited operating systems. However, operating systems for extremely limited hardware will still be needed. The user must prioritize the features that are really necessary in a limited hardware situation in order to determine the best operating system. The limited range of choices available should ease the process of finding an operating system to meet the demands of each situation.

TinyOS

Wireless sensor networks are a common example of a ubiquitous computing system that operates on strict power constraints. The wireless sensor nodes in this kind of network must maintain a small size and low-running cost, greatly limiting the complexity of the system. These sensor devices are usually implemented with 8-bit microcontrollers carrying only a few kilobytes of RAM, which then leaves little room for an operating system. To overcome these constraints, starting in 1999, U. C. Berkley began developing TinyOS specifically to target wireless sensor networks as part of the DARPA NEST program. Today, TinyOS is a widely used open source, event-driven operating system for microcontroller devices. This is mainly due to its efficiency and ease of use. TinyOS is designed around a static allocation model which minimizes the memory overhead. This static binding also helps find and fix hard to find bugs in a dynamic-allocation model. TinyOS is also easy to use because it is coded in nesC, which is very similar to C.

TinyOS deviates from standard operating systems in several ways to allow advanced operations on microcontrollers. Firstly, TinyOS forgoes the implementation of a user interface. TinyOS also does not make use of multithreading, since multithreading is a generally expensive process that forces the operating system to create stack spaces in memory and implement locking mechanisms for shared resources. However, TinyOS still maintains a concurrency model to allow for multiple applications to operate simultaneously. The TinyOS concurrency model uses "Interfaces" and "Tasks" (Figure 7). Interfaces are a set of tightly coupled bi-directional functions, which allows the user to call the provider, but also allows the provider to call the user. Interfaces are used to connect "Components" of the TinyOS application. A component in TinyOS is a unit of code representing a piece of software stored in a separate file. This allows TinyOS to implement bi-directionality without using function pointers, which in turn allows the call backs to be static. Such condition permits the compiler to statically optimize across the reverse path. Furthermore, by knowing exactly what functions are called, the compiler can then be intensely optimized. The other mechanism TinyOS employs is "Tasks", which are the equivalent to deferred procedure calls in traditional operating systems whose purpose is to provide internal concurrency inside components. Components can post tasks to be executed later, which will go onto a task queue to be processed in FIFO order, enabling general purpose background processing within an application when timing requirements are not strict.

To support the concurrency model, the ability to optimize across component boundaries is very important in TinyOS because it has no blocking operations. Instead, all long-latency operations are split-phase: operation request and completion are separate functions. Commands are typically requests to execute an operation. In a blocking system, when a program calls a long-running operation, the call does not return until the operation is complete. In a split-phase system, when a program calls a long-running operation, the call returns immediately, and the called abstraction issues a callback, by signaling an event, when it completes. Split-phase interfaces enable a TinyOS component to easily start several operations at once and have them execute in parallel.

The concurrency model in conjunction with static binding permits lots of optimizations that are normally not done. For example, traditional C languages allow optimization within object files, but not across object files. However, the compiler for TinyOS takes all the source code and puts it into a single C-file, where it topologically sorts the functions so the C compiler can understand them better. This results in a reduction in CPU cycles and stack size in the compiled application. This model is also energy efficient. To conserve energy, a TinyOS application typically has a low duty cycle where it sleeps most of the time. As a result, applications are interrupt driven and follow a restrictive two level concurrency model. The task scheduler is a simple FIFO scheduler, utilizing a bounded size scheduling data structure. It puts the mote to sleep when the task queue is empty, thus ensuring efficient battery usage. Once the queue is empty, another task can be scheduled only as a result of an event, thus there is no need for the mote to wake up until a hardware event triggers activity.

Symbian OS

Symbian is an operating system for handheld smartphones and it is implemented on a microprocessor. It supports computational flexibility, not-as-much but similar to the operating systems on a desktop computer, while maintaining very low power. Because a smartphone operates primarily on battery power, it cuts on many features and resources to save on power consumption. Symbian OS began its development in 1980 by Psion. At the time, Symbian OS was called EPOC and was design primarily for portable digital assistants, PDAs. Symbian OS is a proprietary operating system design for mobile devices that runs primarily on ARM processors.

Symbian supports some of the more powerful features of a desktop operating system, like pre-emptive multitasking and memory protection. However, Symbian OS was designed with specific features to effectively enable operation in a system with scarce resources. For example, Symbian OS does not use exception handlers to handle unexpected errors, because they require a lot of resources. Instead Symbian OS uses a cleanup stack that keeps track of data that can be lost by exceptions. Any object that may need to be deallocated later by the operating system can be placed on the cleanup stack, so that in the event of an error in the code, those objects will be deallocated when no process needs them. This solves the problem of having memory leaks, but it must be implemented by the programmer at the application level to be effective. Strings are another inefficient and memory consuming issue. To handle strings, Symbian OS makes us of descriptors instead. Descriptors differ from traditional strings in that they strictly define the data type and length of the string. This makes descriptors more efficient to use and avoids the problem of accessing data past the end of the string. To support flexibility, Symbian OS supports 8 bit descriptors for ASCII characters and 16 bit descriptors for Unicode characters.

Smartphones typically operate in active and deactive states. A smartphone is active whenever the user is calling someone, using the GPS features, browsing the Internet, or any other installable application. The smartphone then goes into an inactive state where it maintains a minimum set of ubiquitous computing systems, such as watching the battery power, searching for signals, and keeping track of alarms or calendar events. To take advantage of this, Symbian OS is event-based and the CPU can be switched off when intensive applications are not running. Symbian OS achieves this through active objects. In the active objects model, objects will make requests to the operating system to make use of asynchronous services, like wireless or Bluetooth services. These objects operate on threads and will be woken up by the operating system when these services become available. With this scheme, when no applications are making requests or running, then the CPU can be put to sleep. The active objects model also reduces on overhead costs.

These changes enable the Symbian OS to maintain a strong and flexible system while still executing application level software in real time. Symbian OS's design principles allow it to be optimized for many low power systems.

FUTURE RESEARCH DIRECTIONS

The field of power conservation is still a big issue, not only in ubiquitous computing but also in every electronics system. The industry has been taking a more power conscious approach to processor design in recent years. The table below (Figure 8) provides a sample of some commonly used processors and their level of power consumption in the industry today. However, these levels of power consumption are still too high to be considered efficient for most ubiquitous computing solutions. Therefore, there still is a need to further develop cost saving technologies. Fortunately, there are many proposed directions that could potentially save huge amounts of energy when compared to today's systems.

New Transistors and Circuits

Currently, there is extensive research in the development of new transistors to handle power more efficiently. For example, Rice University is doing research into a new type of CMOS circuitry called Probabilistic CMOS (PCMOS). Typically, in order for CMOS circuits to overcome inherent background noise during operation, a high voltage is fed to the circuit. This strong current insures that the probability of accuracy in the circuit's calculations is extremely high. PCMOS is interesting in the respect that the idea behind it is to induce a greater margin of error in calculations by reducing the operating voltage. Due to the voltage reduction, the circuit may calculate an acceptable amount of incorrect answers for particular applications such as audio or video processing. By relaxing the chances of correctness slightly, significant power reduction can be achieved.

Semiconductor Innovations

An emerging power-friendly technology being heavily researched by large corporations like IBM is new semiconductor technology. IBM has been and is continuing development on a semiconductor production technique that uses pure crystal silicon and silicon oxide for integrated circuits and microchips. The chip resulting from this process is called Silicon-on-Insulator (SOI). The biggest difference between these chips and normal silicon-based devices is that there is an electrical insulator layer between silicon layers, which provides multiple benefits. This technology is currently in use within IBM's iSeries servers.

Load Balancing on Multiprocessor Systems

Multi-core processors and multiprocessor systems offer new avenues for computational power, but they also open up more possibilities for power reduction. Processor cores can be alternated during

Figure 8. Table providing commonly implemented industry level processors and their power consumption level for various devices and applications of various sizes

Processor	Power Usage	Manufacturer
ARC 700 • Primarily used in SoC(System on Chip) due to its user customization properties.	0.15 mW/MHz	ARC International
Intel Atom Series (45nm) • Intel's smallest processor used in MIDs (mobile internet devices) such as netbooks, nettops and other portable computing devices.	0.537 – 1.344 mW/MHz	Intel
Intel Pentium III (with Intel SpeedStep Technology) • Used in mobile PCs and sub 3 lb notebooks	1.6667 mW/MHz	Intel
Intel Core 2 Extreme Mobile quad core (average of all models) • Intel's most commonly used mobile processors used in netbooks and pda's	41.2-55 mW/MHz	Intel
Intel Core 2 Duo Mobile (average of all models) • Used in mini PC's, cellphones, and pda's	10.72 mW/MHz	Intel
Mobile AMD Sempron • Used in ultra thin notebooks and MIDs	15.55 mW/MHz	AMD
Mobile AMD Turion • Used in networking and telecommunication equiptment, servers and embeded systems	13.58 mW/MHz	AMD

execution to reduce heat dissipation. Processors of different sizes can also be integrated into the same system, so that operations that are crucial can be diverted to the high power processor while the non-essential operations can be diverted to the cheaper and slower processor. Algorithms for load balancing are also an important research direction for load balancing. Making decisions to run operations concurrently as opposed to sequentially may have huge impacts on power efficiency.

CONCLUSION

Power consumption imposes huge restrictions on the development of ubiquitous computing. That is good motivation for addressing the issue for low power designs in ubiquitous computing. These systems are designed to be lightweight and invisible. However, to achieve this, they have to also be very cost effective to operate. It has been shown that sources for energy waste originate at both the hardware and software level. Circuits will generate heat and dissipate power, while operating systems will mismanage the processors and waste execution time. On every layer, there is some issue that needs addressing, and this drives the research in ubiquitous computing today that will make a difference in people's lives tomorrow.

ACKNOWLEDGMENT

Helpful assistance from K. Srivastava, S. Luce, and M. Jakub-Wood is acknowledged. The authors acknowledge support from Louisiana Board of Regents under research award number LEQSF(2009-12)-RD-A-22.

REFERENCES

Chen, T., Wei, H., Bin, X., & Like, Y. (2006). A Real-Time Scheduling Algorithm for Embedded Systems with Various Resource Requirements. *International Workshop on Networking, Architecture, and Storage.*

Estrin, D., Culler, D., Pister, K. & Sukhatme, G. (2002). Connecting the Physical World with Pervasive Networks. *Pervasive Computing, IEEE, 1*(1, January-March), 59-69.

Greenfield, A. (2006). Everyware: the dawning age of ubiquitous computing, (pp. 11–12). Indianapolis, IN: New Riders.

Iyer, A., & Marculescu, D. (2002, May). Power-Performance Evaluation of Globally Asynchronous, Locally Synchronous Processors. In *Intl. Symposium on Computer Architecture (ISCA).*

Morris, B., Davies, C., Day, W., De Jode, M., & McNabb, S. (2007). The Symbian OS Architecture Sourcebook: Design and Evolution of a Mobile Phone OS. Chichester, UK: John Wiley & Sons, Inc.

Poppen, F. (2000). Low Power Design Guide, (Version 30.06.00). Oldenburger Forschungs-Und Entwicklingsintitut Fur Informatik-Werkzeuge Und-Systeme.

Shearer, F. (2008). Low Power Design Techniques. In Power management in mobile devices, (pp. 77-78). New York: Elsevier Inc.

Want, R., Pering, T., Borriello, G. & Farkas, K. I. (2002). Disappearing Hardware. *IEEE Pervasive Computing, 1* (1, January-March), 36 – 47.

Weiser, M. (1993, July). Some Computer Science Issues in Ubiquitous Computing. *Communications of the ACM, 36*(7). doi:10.1145/159544.159617

Younis, S., & Knight, T. (1994). *Asymptotically zero energy computing using split-level charge recovery logic.* Technical Report AITR-1500, MIT AI Laboratory.

Zhou, H.-Y., Hou, K.-M., Chanet, J. P., de Vaulx, C., & de Sousa, G. (2006, Sept. 22-24). LIMOS: a Tiny Real-Time Micro-Kernel for Wireless Objects. *International Conference on Wireless Communications, Networking and Mobile Computing,* (pp. 1 – 4)

ADDITIONAL READING

Banavar, G., Beck, J., Gluzberg, E., Munson, J., Sussman, J., & Zukowski, D. "Challenges: an application model for pervasive computing." In Proceedings of the 6th annual international conference on Mobile computing and networking, pages 266-274, ACM Press, 2000.

Cao, Q., Abdelzaher, T., Stankovic, J., & He, T. "The LiteOS Operating System: Towards Unix-like Abstractions for Wireless Sensor Networks". 2008 International Conference on Information Processing in Sensor Networks.

A. Chandrakasan, S. Sheng and R. Brodersen, " Low-Power CMOS Digital Design", *IEEE Journal Of Solid-State Circuits* Vol. 27. No. 4. April 1992.

Cooprider, N., Archer, W., Eide, E., Gay, D., & Regehr, J. "Efficient memory safety for TinyOS", SenSys '07: Proceedings of the 5th international conference on Embedded networked sensor systems (2007), pp. 205-218

Dunkels, A., Gronvall, B., & Voigt, T. "Contiki - a Lightweight and Flexible Operating System for Tiny Networked Sensors". 29th Annual IEEE International Conference on Local Computer Networks, 2004. 16-18 Nov. 2004 Page(s):455 - 462

Dunkels, A., Grönvall, B., & Voigt, T. "Contiki – a Lightweight and Flexible Operating System for Tiny Networked Sensors", IEEE Emnets 2004.

Hai-ying, Z., & Kun-mean, H. "LIMOS: a Lightweight Multi-threading Operating System dedicated to Wireless Sensor Networks", IEEE Emnets 2007

Healy, M., Newe, T., & Lewis, E. "Power Management in Operating Systems for Wireless Sensor Nodes". *Sensors Applications Symposium*, 2007. 6-8 Feb. 2007 Page(s):1 - 6

Hoang, N., Belloir, N., Pham, C.-D., & Sentilles, S. "Valentine: a dynamic and adaptive operating system for wireless sensor networks". Annual IEEE International Computer Software and Applications Conference 2008.

Hobbs, J. S., & Williams, T. W. "Reaching the Limits of Low Power Design", IEEE Journal 2008.

Jonietz, E. "TR10: Probabilistic Chips", http://technologyreview.com/read_article.aspx?ch=specialsections&sc=emerging08&id=20246

Mark Weiser, John Seely Brown. "The Coming Age of Calm Technology". XEROX PARC. October 5, 1996.

Park, S., Won Kim, J., Shin, K.-Y., & Kim, D. "A Nano Operating System for Wireless Sensor Networks". The 8th International Conference on Advanced Communication Technology, 2006. ICACT 2006. Volume 1, 20-22 Feb. 2006 Page(s):4 pp. - 348

Shearer, F. "Low Power Design Techniques, Design Methodology, and Tools", Power Management DesignLine 2008.

Shearer, F. "Low Power Design Techniques, Design Methodology, and Tools", http://www.powermanagementdesignline.com/showArticle.jhtml?articleID=206905270

Stephen Doheny-Farina. (1994, October 1). Default = Offline Or Why Ubicomp Scares Me. *The Last Link Computer-Mediated Communication Magazine*, *1*(6), 18.

Toshiba, "Power-Saving Clock-Gating Technique is an Inseparable Part of SoC Design", http://www.toshiba.com/taec/adinfo/socworld/images/Pointers_Pitfalls_ClockGating.pdf

Chapter 9
Wireless Sensor Networks Advances for Ubiquitous Computing

João B. Borges Neto
Federal University of Ceará, Brazil

Rossana M. C. Andrade
Federal University of Ceará, Brazil

Pedro Fernandes Ribeiro Neto
State University of Rio Grande do Norte, Brazil

ABSTRACT

Wireless Sensor Networks (WSN) have considerably evolved in recent years. Their main focus has been always restricted to the extraction of information from the environment, but only data collected by the network has been considered. All internal operations and challenges encountered in achieving the requirements assigned to the data have been ignored. However, the advances in the area of WSN, allowing their operation in scenarios under different conditions, make us believe that they are sufficiently mature and optimized to solve problems in other related areas. So, considering the WSN as an ideal laboratory to find solutions to several problems in wireless networks, this Chapter discusses how the advances of these networks may be useful to help the development and creation of smart environments, essential to make ubiquitous computing part of our everyday life.

INTRODUCTION

Wireless Sensor Networks (WSN) are usually defined just as a source of collected data specific to a particular environment, such as temperature, pressure, light, etc. Assuming this statement is not false, the initial research that motivated WSN de-velopment had as the main interest the use of this technology for the support of military operations, which were set up, basically, from simple tasks, such as collection and dissemination of data to a destination. Their goal was usually able to identify the presence of enemies in hostile territories and make explorations of unknown environments.

However, in recent years, WSN have been the focus of various researchers, who have tried to solve

DOI: 10.4018/978-1-65120-843-2.ch009

problems from the energy of sensor nodes to the discovery of new scenarios and applications that can benefit from the use of such network. The research boosted the state of the art in the area of WSN, what makes us conclude that the improvements achieved during the search for solutions to these problems are sufficiently mature and optimized that can be useful to solve problems in other related areas.

So, if we consider the innovations achieved in the area of WSN and identify its operation scenarios as case studies to assess the main challenges of wireless communication networks, we can say that WSN is an ideal laboratory to find solutions to several problems in wireless networks. Some of these problems are only emerging in the new network architectures, as in the paradigm of ubiquitous computing, also known as Internet of Things. Factors such as high mobility of nodes, high level of congestion and dynamism of the nodes, severe restrictions imposed to the computing devices and the need to operate according to the requirements of Quality of Service (QoS) are some examples of the various problems encountered during the design and operation of the WSN as these new wireless networks paradigm.

This chapter describes how the experience gained through studies and research in the area of WSN may be useful in helping the development of this new computing paradigm known as ubiquitous computing. We discuss the Mark Weiser's vision of ubiquitous computing and the main challenges encountered so that it can become a reality. Then, we present WSN and the main components that make the intelligent sensors. In the following section, we discuss the main features in the design of WSN and how the experiences in developing these networks can be useful for the creation of ubiquitous computing systems. Finally, we present our observations on what remains to be done for WSN may be, not just a tool for data collection to feed the ubiquitous systems, but an active component that can contribute to all

potential these new systems promise to improve in our everyday life.

UBIQUITOUS COMPUTING

Since its idealization in 1991, we would like to reach the level of technological development necessary to make the Mark Weiser's vision a reality. His vision is known as the ubiquitous computing, which can be characterized by the total immersion of computational capacity in people's lives. However, according to Davies and Gellersen (2002), only when we reach the level of pervasiveness enough for the ubiquitous computing be an integral part of our everyday life, is that we have made this vision a reality.

The main feature of this new computational paradigm is the change in the way of interactions between human and computers. For ubiquitous computing, computational intelligence can be found not only in computers as we know today, but also embedded in a variety of common objects we use in our everyday life. This immersion will allow the creation of smart environments, providing us services and computational intelligence at anytime and anywhere (Weiser, 1991).

Based on the theoretical foundation derived from this new computing paradigm, there is the need that research had driven to find for new technologies capable of ensuring the correct deployment of the devices in the environment, which can be transparent to users, and can operate together, in a coordinated and distributed way.

This subject has required that researchers find in other existing technologies, solutions capable of supplying the needs of the new applications to be implemented in these new ubiquitous environments. This need has resulted, in addition to the advantages and benefits of these technologies, in problems from every new concept that was incorporated in this paradigm. Some examples of the technologies ubiquitous computing have sustained is the distributed, embedded and real time systems, and mobile and pervasive computing (il Hwang et al., 2005).

Challenges in Deploying Ubiquitous Computing Systems

For ubiquitous computing becomes real and present in our everyday life, it is necessary the creation of the so-called ubiquitous, or smart, environments. The smart environments are those scenarios where computational components are integrated to common objects of these environments. Lamps, refrigerators, televisions, microwave devices, doors and windows, as many others, are examples of common objects that can embedded a component to itself that aggregates computational capabilities for their operations.

Nowadays, to create these smart environments, there are still several challenges that must be solved. Besides the need for integration of computing in our everyday life, through the integration of devices embedded in common objects, it is necessary that all such devices operate in a coordinated and collaborative way.

Only with the integration of all computational devices in the environment and their operation in a coordinated and collaborative way, the ubiquitous computing systems can be effectively useful in helping our tasks. Then, with the deployment of this kind of ubiquitous computing systems, the vision of Mark Weiser of a world fulfilled of ubiquitous computing devices can become a reality (Weiser, 1991).

According to Davies and Gellersen (2002), the main challenges for the deployment of ubiquitous computing systems are identified from two perspectives. The technical perspective deals with problems closer to the physical world, and the scientific perspective takes into account the needs of users and high level applications.

Under the technical perspective, we identify the following challenges that must be considered in the creation of environments capable of supporting these applications and ubiquitous scenarios:

1. **Limitations:** For requiring a high degree of pervasiveness, computing devices embedded in the objects of an environment needs to have reduced size, so that your functionality is not compromised. This affects the capacity of the computational device, specially its power supply. For these devices, this problem is usually solved by the use of batteries, with limited capacity, as the main source of energy for these devices and that affects other functionalities of the devices, adding other limitations to it.

2. **Mobility:** The presence or absence of a device in the environment in a given moment may result in loss of connectivity and operation of other devices. To ubiquitous applications, this may affect the loss of transparency of their operation.

3. **Communication:** The reduced capacity for communication of computational devices is directly related to the limitations of power and miniaturization of them. It is necessary to save resources by optimizing the number of transmissions and receptions made by the devices, which also interferes with the maintenance of their connectivity.

4. **Collaboration:** The need for the devices operating together is essential for applications to extract the full potential that can be provided by a ubiquitous environment, then, these applications will be increasingly relevant to the tasks of our everyday life.

For the scientific perspective, Davies and Gellersen (2002) define the following major challenges that should be considered during the design and development of ubiquitous computing systems:

1. **Component interaction:** A ubiquitous system should operate like any other distributed system, allowing communication among multiple heterogeneous devices. This will extract the full potential of smart

environments, enabling the development of applications more dynamic and useful to the users.

2. **Adaptation and contextual sensitivity:** A ubiquitous system should allow the mobility of applications, ensuring its adaptability for each different context in which the user is inserted. It should also be able to inform which services the ubiquitous environment provides, and the way applications can retrieve information on these services, so that the context needed to its adaptation to be satisfied.

3. **Appropriate management mechanisms and policies:** Besides the problems of coordination in the operation of a variable number of communicating devices, the increase in the number of these devices requires efficient mechanisms and policies to ensure the scalability of the system on increasing the network size, and the correct treatment of the whole amount of data generated and of the traffic on the network.

4. **Component association and task analysis:** It is necessary that the system can detect the presence of users in the environment, identify their actions and determine the association between the components necessary to satisfy these actions.

5. **Viable economic models and supporting infrastructure:** How should users pay for the ubiquitous services and the cost needed for the creation of the smart environments are open problems that must be considered, in addition to technical problems, for the deployment of ubiquitous systems.

6. **User interface integration:** Many applications can benefit from the capacity allowed with the ubiquitous environments, however, the form of interaction between users and these applications should be reconsidered. How this will be done, especially in an integrated and coordinated way between all

devices of the environment is still an open problem.

7. **Social, legal, and technical solutions to privacy and security concerns:** All possibilities of applications allowed by ubiquitous computing systems must also consider the integration of computing in our life to deal with numerous personal and restricted information of their users. Concerns about privacy and security in dealing with such information should be considered, both in social and legal scope.

We can identify these challenges have unique characteristics that require specific solutions, which differ from other computer systems that already have more consolidated and well-defined causes and consequences for their problems. However, we can take some characteristic points in ubiquitous systems, and according to their needs, observe their relation with other computer systems, which may serve as a basis for finding the most appropriate solutions for this new paradigm.

The need for creation of these ubiquitous environments, composed of various embedded devices, with computational restrictions, limited resources and that must operate transparently to users, can be supported through the use of new technologies that have emerged since Weiser has idealized them. New technologies such as Global Positioning System (GPS), Radio-frequency identification (RFID), Smart Cards, the proliferation of Internet, mobile phones and mobile telephony are examples that may be useful for creating ubiquitous environments (Davies and Gellersen, 2002).

Moreover, if we look at the needs in this new computational paradigm, we can identify relationships between a ubiquitous system and another computer system, which emerged in order to solve a very specific problem and optimize the interaction between its users with the physical environment. This computer system is a wireless sensor network.

In the following section, we describe Wireless Sensor Networks - WSN, their main characteristics and challenges encountered in the development and operation of these types of networks. Having defined and explained the main points of this system in particular, we return to the problems in ubiquitous systems, building upon the experiences already gained with WSN, in order to help creating ubiquitous environments, and making them more real and possible to be deployed.

WIRELESS SENSOR NETWORKS

Wireless Sensor Networks have been the focus of the research in computer networks in recent years, ranging from solutions for energy saving and better utilization of limited resources of sensor nodes, to the discovery of new proposals for their use for monitoring environments that are hostile and inaccessible to humans.

The initial research in WSN was motivated by the interest that the governments had in the use of this technology to support military operations. The U.S. Defense Advanced Research Projects Agency (DARPA) was one of the entities funding research for developing sensors to become smaller and more efficient (Römer and Mattern, 2004).

The more accepted definition until then, which became the *de facto* definition, was motivated by military applications, and was that

WSN are large-scale networks (thousands of nodes, covering large geographical areas), not partitioned, using wireless communication, ad hoc and multi-hop, consisting of homogeneous sensor nodes, tiny, usually statics that are randomly arranged for monitoring of a particular area of interest (Römer and Mattern, 2004).

However, due to WSN popularity and increase in the amount of research in this area, this definition can not be applied to a large number of other WSN applications anymore, such as applications for civil use, agriculture, health, environmental monitoring, and others (Römer and Mattern, 2004).

For some applications, only a small number of sensors satisfies their requirements, others allow the sensors to communicate using the conventional infrastructure of the Internet, for other applications, the sensors nodes were heterogeneous, each one having different components to perform different tasks, according to the needs of the environment.

Thus, to consider all these new concepts, the definition of WSN that will be used in the rest of this chapter, based on the concepts defined by (Ruiz et al., 2004) and (Ribeiro Neto, 2006), is that

WSN are networks composed of devices equipped with computing limitations, also called smart sensors, capable of monitoring and, in some cases, control the environment where they are inserted. These sensors communicate with each other in an ad hoc fashion for, collaboratively, realize tasks and increasing its operation time.

Components of a Smart Sensor

It is impossible to study WSN and have no mention of their main components, the smart sensors, or sensor nodes or, simply, sensors. As stated earlier, WSN are composed of limited computing devices. There is no definition of a quantity of sensors needed to be characterized the existence of a WSN. According to the need of the application, this amount may vary from units and tens to hundreds and thousands.

The term smart sensor refers to the micro embedded computer systems that have the capacity, in addition to sensing the physical conditions of an environment, to perform other scheduled tasks. They are able to perform processing on the collected data, perform tasks in cooperation with other sensors and meet the diverse needs that their applications may require (Shorey et al., 2006).

There is not a common standard to define the hardware of a sensor node, some standards have been proposed, as seen in Chen and Helal (2008). Generally, the model of a sensor node to WSN is composed of the following basic components (Sohraby et al., 2007):

1. **Processor:** Responsible for the control of the other components of the sensor, it is the component that allows the computational intelligence assigned to sensor node.
2. **Memory:** Necessary for handling and storage of collected data.
3. **Battery:** Source of energy to feed the sensor during its operation.
4. **Transceptor:** Formed by the integration of transmitter and receptor, it is responsible for communicating the sensor node with other network sensors.
5. **Sensor:** It is the component responsible for the source of the data collected by WSN. It is able to respond to physical stimuli of the environment and produce events, which will be responsible for generating predetermined actions, when these events are of interest of the network (Tilak et al., 2002). There are several types of sensors, including:
   a) Acoustic
   b) Seismic
   c) Optical
   d) Temperature
   e) Movement
   f) Pressure
   g) Infrared.

A smart sensor may also have other components, according to the needs of its application. When the sensor must act more actively in the network, changing the conditions of the environment it is inserted, in order to correct faults and control monitored equipments, it will need another component, called actuator. A sensor that has the function of sensor and actuator is called

transducer (Ribeiro Neto, 2006). Moreover, the sensors may also have other components, such as GPS, alternative power supplies (solar energy or electromagnetic waves), accelerometers to measure their displacement, etc (Akyildiz et al., 2002).

The definition and development of smart sensors used by WSN serve as a basis for understanding how to deal with computational limitations, allowing various operations on the environment in which it is inserted. Since operations are optimized for this scenario, the current advances in the capacity of processing, memory and other features of these devices is sufficient for us to create computer systems whose components can perform many tasks, including the coordination between all components, with different features, shapes and abilities.

WSN AND UBIQUITOUS COMPUTING

For the scenarios of ubiquitous computing, WSN are responsible for capturing, abstract and collecting context information of environmental conditions (Hong et al., 2009). For the ubiquitous applications, which use WSN, only the collected data is of interest, ignoring the operation of sensor nodes, tasks and challenges that WSN needs to meet the requirements assigned to these data.

Looking at the internal operations of WSN, we identified that in order to operate correctly and according to their requirements, the challenges that sensors must deal with go beyond a simple collection and dissemination of data. Mobility and continuous change in the number of active sensor nodes in the communication, the need for the sensor nodes to operate in a coordinated and collaborative way, and able to meet the requirements allocated to the data delivery, in a optimized way, and still save their limited resources, are some examples of these challenges.

The WSN Advances for Ubiquitous Computing

WSN have very peculiar characteristics that make them different networks of all other existing computer networks. Many of these characteristics are derived from the needs of their applications, other from the technologies that have originated them and other characteristics are inherent in the very possibilities that these networks can provide to their users. The following is the main features and experiences in the development of WSN that can help in the development of ubiquitous computing systems.

Viable Economic Models and Supporting Infrastructure

Even for WSN, which are computer systems generally applied to solve problems of industrial scope where no other technology is capable of being used, the definition of an economic model that meets the needs of both developers and users is not an easy task. To solve the problem of the cost in the development of WSN, enabling their popularization in a large scale and where their use was not constrained by financial limitations, the first designers of the sensors networks were concerned with various computational restrictions. In order to reduce the costs of their production, the need for the operation of these sensors in an optimized way and aware of all these limitations was taken in consideration.

For the ubiquitous computing systems, we can also identify these needs for restrictions on the operation of some of their devices, being the impact of the deployment as minimum as possible. The main concern for the deployment of the ubiquitous systems is the ability to insert computational capabilities into objects without harming their conventional operation.

These limitations refer basically to the need for wireless communication and miniaturization of devices in the environment. This factor limits the ability of these computational devices, because they are now limited to smaller sizes, for maintaining the transparency to their users.

Limitations

This is the main feature when WSN are remembered. As already discussed in this chapter, the existing computational limitations for sensor nodes are factors that guided the need for several other changes in the hardware of these devices.

As legacy of computing systems that forms the basis of the architecture of a sensor, the need to build cheap and disposable sensor nodes has geared researchers to find new ways of miniaturization of the architectures, without affecting the efficient operation of the device. So sensor sizes have increasingly been reduced as well as the capacity of power supply. Then, other aspects such as processing power, storage capacity and transmission ranges have also been reduced. Therefore, all components of the sensor need to share the same small and limited power supply.

We can also identify this characteristic in the embedded devices that allow the creation of ubiquitous environments. Like WSN, energy is the main limitation these devices have. For the sensors, generally, their lifetime corresponds to your battery lifetime, making them inactive for the network when their energy is gone. Several studies on this theme of energy saving can be found in the literature. The highlight of this research is described in the IEEE 802.15.4 (IEEE, 2006) specification, where they describe it is possible to turn off some of the components of the sensors during a certain time and return to turn it on only when they will be used.

Whereas the components of sensing and transmission can be disabled without interfering in the functioning of the device, the main operation modes of a sensor are as follows (Mini et al., 2004):

1. **Mode 1:** Sensor off and radio off
2. **Mode 2:** Sensor on and radio off
3. **Mode 3:** Sensor on and radio receiving
4. **Mode 4:** Sensor on and radio sending

While some devices can be embedded on objects where the energy is no longer a problem, as in cars or offices, for example, the energy factor should still be considered crucial for most other applications, being conventional sensors or embedded in other devices that have also limited power such as PDAs or cell phones (Riva and Borcea, 2007).

Mobility

Regarding mobility for WSN, it is necessary to consider changes in the network topology, due to the movement of the devices. The presence or absence of a device in the environment in a given moment and position can cause loss of routes and, consequently, failure during the communication between the sensors nodes.

For ubiquitous computing, the mobility of both applications and devices should be considered. The mobility of applications needs to deal with, mainly, adaptation and Quality of Service (QoS) assurance according to the context in which applications are inserted. The mobility of devices must handle the discovery and management of devices in the environment, dealing with the possibility of their absence in a given moment.

The treatment of the mobility of the nodes is essential for the maintenance of two important factors in a WSN:

1. **Energy saving:** The process of discovery and recovery of routes is mainly composed of transmissions of control packets between the nodes and their neighbors. The tasks with higher consumption of power in a sensor are the transmission and reception of packets. Therefore, a simple and efficient

maintenance of the routes due to mobility of nodes is essential to their energy saving.

2. **Quality of service:** Maintaining QoS for some applications of WSN, as the response time and latency in the delivery of the collected data, for example, depends on the reliability on routes defined for data transmission. Constant changes in the communication routes and losses should be crucial when the QoS factor is important for these WSN applications. Failures from mobility directly affect the maintenance on the QoS of the tasks performed by the network.

Both for WSN and for ubiquitous computing, the number of active nodes in the communication should be considered variable. New devices can be added to the communication as well as active devices may change to an inactive state. The number of devices in the environment is a factor arising from both their mobility and the possibility of the end of their energy, mainly for WSN, which brings the end of their lifetime.

The variation on the quantity of devices is directly dependent of the mobility and can lead to various problems for the correct operation of the system. It may affect with changes in congestion during transmissions, where multiple devices ranges have overlapping coverage, and periods of total inaccessibility, when a device moves far away from other devices.

Communication

The communication process in an environment over wireless communication, such as the cases of WSN and ubiquitous computing, consists, basically, of the task of transmitting and receiving data. As stated earlier, these tasks are responsible for increasing the power consumption of a device.

Considering this fact, all operations that require communication between the devices must be optimized and simplified to the maximum. The smaller the number of transmissions and receptions made, the higher the level of energy savings achieved.

Because the topology of WSN is characterized by being decentralized, they are identified as a kind of ad hoc networks. This type of network is characterized by networks that are regularly distributed and the only communication the node has is with its neighbors. Despite being connected to a wireless channel, typically in broadcast, the limitations in transmission power of radios reduce the possibility of communication of nodes only with those that are closer to them, in the radius of their transmission range (Lewis, 2004, Tilak et al., 2002).

One of the main factors, which acts as a responsible for the power saving of nodes, is the routing process. The task of routing is the act of choosing the best path (route) through which data will be transmitted. The definition of a route in WSN is given by the set of sensor nodes that participate in the process of transmission of collected data, from its origin to its destination. For the most of WSN, there is the existence of special nodes within the network, called sink nodes, which have specific tasks of leadership within the network and is usually the destination of the data collected by other nodes (Ruiz et al., 2004).

As any ad hoc network, the nodes of these networks have an important role in the contribution of the communication network. They operate collaboratively by directly communicating with each other and acting as routers and repeaters that receive and transmit the packets (Römer and Mattern, 2004).

The routing of data in WSN occurs through multi-hop transmissions. A node that originated a packet, after the collection of a data, is the first to send it to their neighbors. Each neighbor is now responsible for the routing of this packet to its own neighbors, excluding those from whom he received the packet. This process is repeated until the packet is delivered to its destination. Various algorithms and routing protocols have been proposed (Akkaya and Younis, 2005). Each

one is concerned with the solution to a problem or willing to meet a particular need for their applications. Protocols that support communication through redundant routes between the nodes of origin and destination, to prevent the problem of failures due to loss of routes, and protocols that create virtual topologies in the logic organization of nodes as hierarchical structures and trees, are examples of some of these protocols.

The communication in WSN can be considered one of their main challenges, with very particular characteristics that are not identified in the most of other computer systems. Their challenges require highly optimized and efficient solutions that, also for ubiquitous computing systems, may be considered essential to achieve all the autonomy and transparency necessary for the correct operation. Even if in some cases of ubiquitous environments do not have many restrictions and needs of operation, the finding for efficiency and optimization is always necessary to improve the quality produced by their applications.

Collaboration

WSN are provided with many opportunities, many are the applications that can benefit from their capabilities. However, an individual sensor node is not able to realize the full potential that is attributed to the set of sensors, working collaboratively. The cooperation between the sensor nodes is the main factor to achieve all the potential of WSN. Various tasks assigned to the network are executed in a distributed way, where each node performs a specific and individual action, and associated with the actions of other nodes enable the entire network to perform more complex and robust activities.

The basic function of a sensor node in a WSN is the data collection, performed individually and according to the capabilities of its components. However, the task of transmitting the collected data to the destination is a task that should run collaboratively, routing the data until they are delivered to their destination (Tilak et al., 2002). Other tasks such as network aggregation of data, location and tracking of moving objects and time synchronization, are examples of tasks that also need to be implemented collaboratively.

This need for collaboration can also be identified in ubiquitous computing systems, which should provide to their users not only a single feature, but a set of capabilities to the applications that can be useful to a higher number of tasks of our everyday life.

Components Interaction

Most WSN, unlike the other types of ad hoc network, are essentially composed by homogeneous sensors, composed of components with similar operations and capable of performing the same tasks. This factor helps WSN to be tolerant to failures that may occur in the sensors, through the redundancy of similar operations. However, when applications require specific functionalities, it is necessary the insertion of new components to the sensor nodes. This allows the creation of an environment composed of heterogeneous components, performing different tasks but still requiring the integrated operation, always trying to reduce the power consumption of the entire network.

Some solutions have been proposed to define a unified way of communication among the various types of embedded devices. For example, the Gridkit project (Hughes et al., 2008) allows the communication between these heterogeneous devices through the creation of a network abstraction. This virtual network is used to solve the problem of the communication between the different components, both in WSN and in the diversity of devices present in the ubiquitous computing environments.

Adaptation and Contextual Sensitivity

According to Khedr and Karmouch (2005), contextual sensitivity means that people, services

and artifacts in an environment are integrated in a homogeneous manner in order to provide seamless services while still preserving privacy. WSN are usually responsible for extracting context information of the elements in the environment to ensure that applications can adapt to different conditions encountered in these scenarios.

The incorporation of the experiences with the current development of WSN for ubiquitous computing corresponds to the possibility of identifying the various types of information from the sensors that we can extract from the environment (Dimakis et al. 2008). However, when the aspect of adaptation and contextual sensitivity of ubiquitous applications is extended to more autonomous mechanisms, they can make more use from WSN, benefiting from the ability of sensing and actuation of sensor nodes, controlling and modifying the conditions of environments, and directly affecting in their context.

Currently, there are several kinds of context information that sensor nodes can collect from the environment, in order to provide personalized services to different users (Park et al. 2009). From unique data, identified to each node that collected it, to global contextualized data, related to several obtained samples, many are the context information an application can obtain. According to some applications, the sensor nodes that constitute the network need not to be identified, i.e., according to their needs, it is not necessary that collected data are individually identified by the node that collected it. Information such as geographic positions or the area where the data has been collected, are essential for the application that uses these data.

For example, sensors that monitor a specific external area, such as forests or oceans, only need to know the data with respect to changes in the conditions of this region and not specific to each sensor (Ruiz et al., 2004). Otherwise, there are cases when each sensor represents a certain position that is necessarily important to be known, as the sensors that control an industrial equipment, for example. To that node is given a unique address that allows the network to identify it from other devices and send messages directly to it. Thus, this justifies the nodes that, depending on your application, have specific components, such as GPS, capable of calculating the geographic position of the sensor and insert this information in their collected data.

Component Association and Task Analysis

Resulting from the capacity of interaction between the various components of both WSN and ubiquitous systems, and the ability to extract various information from the environment, the possibility that the devices can detect the presence or absence of a user in the environment and the identification of changes in their context becomes an easier task to be executed.

Along with these possibilities is the ability of these devices to operate collaboratively and, through the analysis of the needs of their users and the system itself, make the more appropriate tasks to the observed context. An example of a collaborative task performed by WSN, to meet the needs of optimizations and reduction on the costs of the network is the task of handling the collected data by the nodes. Generally, the amount of collected data in a WSN can be huge, depending on your application. It is estimated that over 70% of the collected data from systems that help in the decision-making are never used (Koronios, 2006). This factor can be considered relevant to the systems that deal with collecting context information, as the case applied to WSN, which collects temperature, pressure and lightness, for example.

Some applications of WSN implement collaborative techniques of aggregation and summarization of the collected data by sensors and ways to restrict the data collection only according

to preconditions for them, as a maximum interval which the data is valid, in the case of real time communication systems. These techniques reduce the data traffic on the network and optimize the process of its analysis (Nakamura et al., 2006).

For those applications whose each collected data of WSN are unique and can not be aggregated, summarized or manipulated in any way, these manipulation techniques can not be used, requiring that other ways for optimizing the processes of communication be applied, by using another routing techniques or by reducing the amount of collected data.

User Interface Integration

How ubiquitous applications should interact with their users is still an open problem, but what can we say until now is that the conventional human-machine interaction can not be applied to this new paradigm. The need for transparency between applications and their users is a factor that should be considered fundamental to the success on the creation of ubiquitous environments.

The current status for WSN already allows ubiquitous applications to be able to interact with their users with autonomy and distribution, as seen in Cardenas-Tamayo et al. (2009). By using sensors contextual data from the environment and its users, applications can obtain information that serve as input parameters for their operation. For the reverse process, the return of the processing system through actions and services for users, the WSN actuators may be useful as modifiers of the environment's conditions.

However, as previously discussed, it is still necessary to achieve major advances in the use of WSN. Not only using them as mere sources of collected data, but also as a network of smart and pervasive devices in the environment, with capability to perform various tasks with transparency and optimization.

Appropriate Management Mechanisms and Policies

Among all of the already mentioned characteristics of WSN, we present another one that is essential for their correct operation, it is the need for autonomy of sensor nodes. A new approach in the management of the nodes is necessary to ensure that the network does not stop running its tasks due to the lack of human intervention, as is common in most cases of nodes use. Also motivated by applications for inaccessible environments to humans and for applications where no man should realize that there is a computational device interacting with it, similar to the case identified by applications for ubiquitous computing, the concepts from autonomic computing become necessary to be integrated to sensor nodes.

For the sensor nodes can be able to perform their tasks with autonomy, it is necessary the ability to self-management. Self-management is the act when the nodes themselves are able to manage their operations without requiring human intervention. The autonomic computing defines the following four aspects to achievement of self-management (Kephart and Chess, 2003):

1. **Self-Configuration:** Automatic configuration of components and systems, according to rules and high-level policies.
2. **Self-Optimization:** The components and systems must continually search for opportunities to improve their performance and efficiency.
3. **Self-Healing:** Components should automatically detect, diagnose and repair problems found.
4. **Self-Protection:** The system should automatically defend itself against malicious attacks, usually using a knowledge database of prior events to anticipate and prevent such failures.

In the context of WSN, the nodes should be reorganized automatically and regularly, ensuring that even with new nodes being added or removed from the network, they can be identified, organized and managed. This is necessary to the nodes can provide resources and also ensure that they can work collaboratively, running their specific tasks together in order to perform the task set for the entire network (Ruiz et al., 2004).

Social, Legal, and Technical Solutions to Privacy and Security Concerns

The ubiquitous computing, by being a new type of system that deals directly with information from its users, more personal, and private than other systems, requires very specific and appropriate solutions to their problems of social and legal context. However, technical factors on the safety and privacy of information collected by these systems can benefit from experiences gained in developing WSN.

Pathan et al. (2006) presents some of the key issues and challenges about security for WSN. Factors ranging from the need for encryption of collected data by nodes to the risks involving various types of attacks in the environment and operation of WSN are discussed in this research.

Although the ubiquitous applications require even more complex factors of security and privacy than WSN, given the similar characteristics between the devices that make the environments of ubiquitous computing and WSN, the identified needs during the development and deployment of both systems are also similar. Allowing developers of ubiquitous applications to be based on the challenges already encountered by the WSN experiences.

THE FUTURE OF WSN FOR UBIQUITOUS COMPUTING

Experiences with the development of WSN and with the need to overcome the limited capabilities of sensor nodes are always a factor that motivates the researchers to a continuous search for improvements and more efficient solutions. Combining this thought with the need for creation of smart environments, capable to provide the autonomy and support to the applications of ubiquitous systems, we identified that WSN can assume a new role in this context, under a new operation perspective, making it more useful and essential to ubiquitous systems.

WSN can no longer be restricted to only a source of data for ubiquitous applications, in addition, they can be an essential tool in optimizing the process of interaction between users and ubiquitous systems. The main required change in the paradigm for this is related to the type of communication between the external world and WSN inside nodes. When the use of a gateway between sensor nodes and the outside world is no longer necessary, the restriction of access to information and capacity of WSN will be eliminated, allowing the sensor nodes to be an integral part of the ubiquitous systems and not only a tool to help them.

Thus, besides the possibility of creating new services and features, it is possible the creation and deployment of ubiquitous computing systems that can be supported by the experience gained with the development of WSN, reusing the progress already achieved in this area, from the use of hardware optimizations to apply concepts and developments in the optimization of communication and collaboration of sensor nodes.

CONCLUSION

Although WSN have already had their moment of peak, being the focus of many research and development, ubiquitous computing systems are still in full development moment. The needs and challenges researchers had identified in this new computational paradigm bring back to light all challenges other systems had. This makes it possible that the experiences of these systems can be used to help in solving the current ubiquitous computing problems, which is the case of the WSN advances.

This chapter has discussed the current advances on the WSN development world, including their main characteristics, challenges and potentialities that can serve as experience basis in the deployment of the ubiquitous computing systems. According to the already known challenges these systems face, we had identified which aspects of WSN can help to solve each challenge. Also, we discussed about what is necessary to evolve in the WSN paradigm to help ubiquitous computing to become a reality.

REFERENCES

Akkaya, K., & Younis, M. (2005). A survey on routing protocols for wireless sensor networks. *Elsevier Ad Hoc Network Journal*, *3*(3), 325–349. doi:10.1016/j.adhoc.2003.09.010

Akyildiz, I. F., Su, W., Sankarasubramaniam, Y., & Cayirci, E. (2002). Wireless sensor networks: a survey. *Computer Networks*, *38*(4), 393–422. doi:10.1016/S1389-1286(01)00302-4

Cardenas-Tamayo, R. A., García-Macías, J. A., Miller, T. M., Rich, P., Davis, J., & Albesa, J. (2009). Pervasive Computing Approaches to Environmental Sustainability. *IEEE Pervasive Computing / IEEE Computer Society [and] IEEE Communications Society*, *8*(1), 54–57. doi:10.1109/MPRV.2009.14

Chen, C., & Helal, S. (2008). Sifting through the jungle of sensor standards. *IEEE Pervasive Computing / IEEE Computer Society [and] IEEE Communications Society, 7*(4), 84–88. doi:10.1109/MPRV.2008.81

Davies, N., & Gellersen, H. (2002). Beyond Prototypes: Challenges in Deploying Ubiquitous Systems. *IEEE Pervasive Computing / IEEE Computer Society [and] IEEE Communications Society, 1*(1), 26–35. doi:10.1109/MPRV.2002.993142

Dimakis, N., Soldatos, J. K., Polymenakos, L., Fleury, P., Curín, J., & Kleindienst, J. (2008). Integrated development of context-aware applications in smart spaces. *IEEE Pervasive Computing / IEEE Computer Society [and] IEEE Communications Society, 7*(4), 71–79. doi:10.1109/MPRV.2008.75

Hong, J., Suh, E., & Kim, S. (2009). Context-aware systems: A literature review and classification. *Expert Systems with Applications, 36*(4), 8509–8522. doi:10.1016/j.eswa.2008.10.071

Hughes, D., Bencomo, N., Blair, G., Coulson, G., Grace, P., & Porter, B. (2008). Exploiting extreme heterogeneity in a flood warning scenario using the Gridkit middleware. In *Proceedings of the ACM/IFIP/USENIX, Middleware Conference*, (pp. 54-57).

IEEE. (2006). IEEE specific requirements part 15.4: Wireless medium access control (mac) and physical layer (phy) specifications for low-rate wireless personal area networks (wpans). *IEEE Std 802.15.4-2006 (Revision of IEEE Std 802.15.4-2003)*.

il Hwang. K., Kim, J. W., In, J., & Eom, D. S. (2005). Lightweight real-time embedded systems for scalable ubiquitous networks. In *Proceedings of the Second ICESS, International Conference on Embedded Software and Systems* (pp. 135-143). Washington, DC: IEEE Computer Society.

Kephart, J. O., & Chess, D. M. (2003). The vision of autonomic computing. *Computer, 36*(1), 41–50. doi:10.1109/MC.2003.1160055

Khedr, M., & Karmouch, A. (2005). ACAI: agent-based context-aware infrastructure for spontaneous applications. *Journal of Network and Computer Applications, 28*(1), 19–44. doi:10.1016/j.jnca.2004.04.002

Koronios, A. (2006). Challenges of managing information quality in service organizations. Hershey, PA: Idea Group Inc.

Lewis, F. L. (2004). Wireles Sensor Networks. In D. Cook & S. Das, (eds.), Smart Environments: Technology, Protocols and Applications. Chichester, UK: Wiley-Interscience.

Mini, R. A. F., Loureiro, A. A. F., & Nath, B. (2004). A more realistic energy dissipation model for sensor nodes. In *Proceedings of the 22nd SBRC, Brazilian Symposium on Computer Networks* (pp. 365-378), Gramado, Brazil.

Nakamura, E. F., Figueiredo, C. M. S., & Loureiro, A. A. F. (2006). Information fusion algorithms for wireless sensor networks. In A. Boukerche, (Ed.), Handbook of Algorithms for Wireless Networking and Mobile Computing. Boca Raton, FL: Chapman & Hall/CRC.

Park, K., Yoon, U. H., & Kim, S. (2009). Personalized service discovery in ubiquitous computing environments. *IEEE Pervasive Computing / IEEE Computer Society [and] IEEE Communications Society, 8*(1), 58–65. doi:10.1109/MPRV.2009.12

Pathan, A. S. K., Lee, H. W., & Hong, C. S. (2006). Security in wireless sensor networks: issues and challenges. In *ICACT, International Conference on Advanced Communication Technology, 2*, 1043-1048.

Ribeiro Neto, P. F., Perkusich, A., Perkusich, M. L. B., & Almeida, H. O. (2006). A formal verification and validation approach for real-time database. In A. Dasso & A. Funes, (Eds.), Verification, Validation and Testing in Software Engineering. Hershey, PA: IGI Publishing.

Riva, O., & Borcea, C. (2007). The urbanet revolution: Sensor power to the people! *IEEE Pervasive Computing / IEEE Computer Society [and] IEEE Communications Society*, 6(2), 41–49. doi:10.1109/MPRV.2007.46

Römer, K., & Mattern, F. (2004). The design space of wireless sensor networks. *IEEE Wireless Communications*, *11*(6), 54–61. doi:10.1109/MWC.2004.1368897

Ruiz, L. B., Nogueira, J. M. S., & Loureiro, A. A. F. (2004). Sensor Network Management. In M. Ilyas & I. Mahgoub. (Eds.). Handbook of Sensor Networks: Compact Wireless and Wired Sensing Systems. Boca Raton, FL: CRC Press.

Shorey, R., Ananda, A. L., Chan, M. C., & Ooi, W. T. (2006). Mobile, Wireless and Sensor Networks: Technology, Applications and Future Directions. New York: John Wiley & Sons.

Sohraby, K. Minoli, and D., Znati, T. (2007). Wireless Sensor Networks: Technology, Protocols, and Applications. New York: John Wiley & Sons, Inc.

Tilak, S., Abu-Ghazaleh, N. B., & Heinzelman, W. (2002). A taxonomy of wireless microsensor network models. *SIGMOBILE Mobile Computing and Communications*, *6*(2), 28–36. doi:10.1145/565702.565708

Weiser, M. (1991). The computer for the 21st century. *Scientific American, 265*(3), 94–104. doi:10.1038/scientificamerican0991-94

Chapter 10
Disability vs. Smart Environments

Rachid Kadouche
Université de Sherbrooke, Canada

Bessam Abdulrazak
Université de Sherbrooke, Canada

ABSTRACT

This chapter discusses a novel approach to manage the human environment interaction in case of disability. It provides accessible services to the user in smart environment. This approach is based on the user limitation capabilities ("handicap situations") in smart environment. It is built upon formalisms based on ΣΗΟΘ(Δ) Description logic (DL) named Semantic Matching Framework (SMF). The architecture of SMF is designed in a way that Human-Environment Interaction (HEI) is generated online to identify and compensate the handicap situation occurring in the course of daily life activities. The SMF architecture is based on modules and implemented using semantic web technologies and integrated into a demonstrator, which has been used to validate the concept in laboratory conditions. The chapter includes the time response and the scalability analysis of SMF.

INTRODUCTION

The quality of life would benefit from smart homes and pervasive computing designed under the "assistive environment" paradigm and can experience significant enhancements due to the increased support received from the environment. This support includes facilities for environmental control, information access, communication, monitoring, etc., and built over various existing and emerging technologies. Nevertheless, people with special needs are usually confronted to accessibility barriers due to the user's disability. These problems include both, physical difficulties to handle devices and objects, and cognitive barriers to understand and reach suitable functionalities. Actually the main objective of researchers is focused on the human deficiency study that allows identifying the user's limit capabilities according to each environment, and then personalizing the environment access. We mean by environment, the infrastructure and the devices that are around the users. We believe that novelty

DOI: 10.4018/978-1-61520-843-2.ch010

is not located at an engineering level, where most of technological problems could be solved, but mainly on the usability issue where human behavior should interfere with available functionalities of any system. This multidisciplinary approach focused on user modeling, which should guide future research work on context awareness in the pervasive computing community. The challenge is to understand the interaction between the human and his environment to design an ubiquitous assistive environment dedicated to people with special needs.

Handicap Situation

Disability refers to the social effects of physical or cognitive impairment. This definition makes a clear distinction between the impairment itself (such as a medical condition that prevents a person to sit or to walk) and the interaction between the environment and that impairment. The real issue is that the living environment infrastructure is creating physical barriers, in term of accessibility, mobility and so on, which limits the autonomy of people with special needs, this situation is called "Handicap situation". Proper use of information and communication technologies could minimize the impact of those barriers on daily living activities. It could thus help improve the quality of life and facilitate social and professional integration of people with disabilities. Our research work is centered on the human-environment interaction that identifies the relationship between the environment and the impairment. We are working on how to identify the differences between a person with severe disabilities and a person with no known disabilities in terms of daily activities. This difference is related, on one hand, to the user's physical disability (ies) causing the handicap situation and, on the other hand, to the environmental elements becoming an obstacle for the user. To achieve that, we focus on the interaction between the human body and its environment which we have defined as Human Environment

Interaction (HEI), to compensate human limitations (Kadouche, Abdulrazak, Mokhtari, Giroux, & Pigot, 2009), (Kadouche, Mokhtari, & Maier, 2005), (Kadouche, Abdulrazak, & Mokhtari, 2004) (Kadouche, 2004). Our work belongs to the assistive pervasive computing community.

RELATED WORK

Many system architectures have greatly contributed to facilitate the development and deployment of context-aware applications and aimed at supporting rapid prototyping of ubicomp applications. ParcTab system (Want, Schilit,, Adams, Gold, Petersen, Goldberg, Ellis, & Weiser, 1996) was the first context-aware infrastructure; it was developed at Xerox PARC to explore the capabilities and impact of mobile computers in an office setting. Context Toolkit (Dey, & Abowd, 2000) is a toolkit aimed at handling component distribution and provides frameworks for acquiring and managing sensed context. Microsoft's Easyliving (Brumitt, Meyers, Krumm, Kern, & Shafer, 2000) provides context-aware spaces, with a particular focus on the home and office. HP's CoolTown project (Krishnan, 2000) is an infrastructure for bridging people, places, and things in the physical world with web resources that are used to store information about them. Context aware applications integrates several technologies; particularly the mobile computing paradigm in which applications, using mobile platforms, can discover and take advantage of contextual information (such as user location, and user activity, time of day) (Aleksy, Butter, & Schader, 2008), (Sadeh, Chan, & Van, 2002).

Actually, in this domain, researchers focus mainly on usability of context-aware applications, focusing on the user implication, issues of control, feedback, (Gulliver, Ghinea, Patel, & Serif, 2007), (Weikum, 2008) to guide designers to a user-centred standpoint.

Recent projects carried out by leading universities and companies are specifically addressing support for monitoring of people with special needs in providing both effective and economical care in the home and in long-term care facilities. Each project explores the problem from different angles. Some of them (exp: (LaMarca, Chawathe, Consolvo, Hightower, Smith, Scott, Sohn, Howard, Hughes, & Potter, 2005), (Ferguson, Allen, Blaylock, Byron, Chambers, Dzikovska, Galescu, Shen, Swier, & Swift, 2002),(MARC),(Kidd, Orr, Abowd, Atkeson, Essa, MacIntyre, Mynatt, Starner, & Newstetter, 1999), (Abowd, Mynatt, & Rodden, 2002b), (Abowd, Bobick, Essa, Mynatt, & Rogers, 2002a)) have built an infrastructure equipped with sensors, panels, cameras,.. etc. integrating an observation rooms for monitoring the interaction and activities of the elderly within the environment. Other research groups are focusing on more specific aspects of the use of technologies to improve living conditions, such as DOMUS LAB under the Archipel project (Pigot, Lussier-Desrochers, Bauchet, Lachapelle, & Giroux, 2007) focus on helping peoples with dementia to carry out a daily activity task; Harvard University's CodeBlue (Fulford-Jones, Malan, Welsh, & Moulton, 2004) developed an emergency system for tracking and observing solution for Assisted Living Facilities; the Assisted Cognition Project (Kautz, Arnstein, Borriello, Etzioni, & Fox, 2002), provides techniques to enhance the quality of life of people having cognitive disorders particularly people suffering from Alzheimer disease. Microsoft's EasyLiving Project (Brumitt, Meyers, Krumm, Kern, & Shafer, 2000), using video tracking technologies, the system provide the user location; and Intel's Proactive Health Research (Dishman, 2004), explores the different ways to support the daily health and wellness living.

All these projects focus on monitoring and usually cater to a specific application and sensor suite. Furthermore, none provides generic system that dynamically explores the environment to identify the different barriers which prevent the user to access some environment services and deliver the user limitation capabilities or handicap situations in each environment. In addition, most of these systems have progressed in various aspects of pervasive computing, but are weak in supporting knowledge sharing and context reasoning due to their lack on common ontology with explicit semantic representation.

Then, there is the ICIDH model (Gray, & Hendershot, 2000) which is a conceptual framework based on a cause-and-effect relationship between impairment and handicap, and the PPH model (Fougeyrollas, 2000) who treated also the interaction problem between the environment and the human and defined the handicap as an inadequacy between the environment factor and the human factor. Both projects are conceptual models, they are based on sociological parameters related to the users and the environment; they are limited to a specific applications (social and professional integration, etc.) and used by particular community such as sociologist, ergonomist. Our work is similar to those last two projects they are also based on defining the handicap situation in an environment. But they are different from our task of presenting a technical model, which could be handled by any technological system, based on clinical, sociological, and usage analysis studies in the field of assistive technologies. We also quantified the users and environment characteristics and formalized the relationship between the user's physical parameters and the technical parameters of the environment under a semantic framework which brings out the handicap situation for each user in a given environment and allow him to identify the accessible services in this environment. We chose Description Logic to represent the contextual information which is adequate for knowledge sharing, machine processing and reasoning.

Figure 1. SMF structure

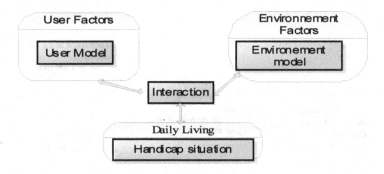

SEMANTIC MATCHING FRAMEWORK (SMF)

In order to explicit the problematic and the related scientific issues, let's consider the following **motivational** scenario:

Mr., Alain, who is living on his own in a small apartment, suffers from muscular dystrophy which involves four limbs impairments. Alain is using an electrical wheelchair to move and has a hand force of 5 Newton (N) as well as a hand workspace of 3 cm³ (in the rest of the chapter we consider the **hand force** *as the user's pushing hand force and* **hand workspace** *as the volume space required by the hand posture). Alain, enjoys Western movies, so his hobby is playing DVDs. He usually gets in touch with his friends mainly by telephone. He has the control of two main windows in his living room, but, the reflexion of sun light from one of them prevents Alain from watching TV in daylight and he does not like to open it.*

Alain wants to know, in all sub environments (Kitchen, bathroom, bedroom, and living room) of his home, the accessible services to him.

In this chapter, for clarity reasons, we will focus mainly on environmental home control services based on this scenario.

This scenario shows that the user should be able to perform daily activities in a complex environment with a limited number of degrees of freedom as input. This is usually the case in any ubiquitous environment where the services provided are much more important than what is really accessible and needed. Thus, we present our approach (SMF) which provides a formal solution to study the usage of each available service by the user in the environment.

Semantic Matching Framework (SMF) is built upon two models: the user model, characterizing the user factors and the environment model, describing the environment factors as illustrated in Figure 1.

The relationship between both models is defined as **matching** relation which has a particularity that generates the handicap situation.

User Model

This model defines the user characteristics. It is built upon categories (features, behaviors). Any category can contain several subcategories (Figure 2). In order to support the user's characteristics to allow system matching, the user-model is extensible and is designed to capture two main aspects: user features and user behaviors. The features are the quirks and distinctive aspects that differentiate one user from another while the behaviors are the actions or reactions of the user in response to external or internal stimuli.

Figure 2. Profile of Pierre

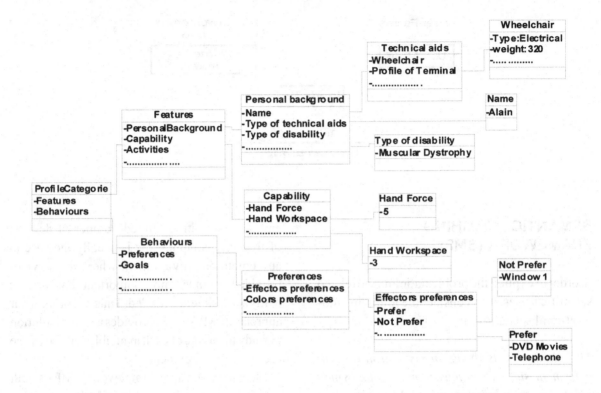

User profile defines user model instances with particular sets of instance attributes. Each user characteristic is represented by an attribute. To explicit the concept, let us consider the illustration based on the motivational scenario shown in the Figure 2: The user profile is defined as a tree structure, where the root defines the main user profile category, the nodes represent sub-categories, and the leaves represent the instance's attributes (values). For instance, in Figure 2, we can see the attributes with their values: type of disability= "*Muscular Dystrophy*", hand force="*5*", hand workspace="*3*",.. etc.

Environment Model

This model describes environment profiles (EP). It specifies devices (e.g., doors, windows, sensors, etc.), defined as "*effectors*", or services (Internet access, Video on Demand, remote alarm, etc.), that compose the ubiquitous environment. Each EP is structured into several categories; the category represents an environment domain, classified into effectors or into other subcategories. We have defined two main categories pertaining to the Indoor and the Outdoor environments. Figure 3 represents the home environment profile (the outdoor environment could be represented similarly).

Similarly to the user profile, the EP is defined as a tree structure, the root represents the main environment category, the leaves define the effectors and the nodes define the sub-categories. Figure 3 underlines the different categories and effectors that constitute the Indoor environment. It contains the subcategories bathroom, living room, toilet... The subcategory "bathroom" contains the

Figure 3. Indoor environment profile

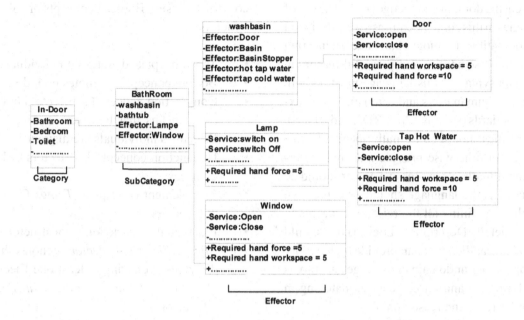

subcategories washbasin, bathtub, etc., with effectors such as mirror, lamp, window, door...

In order to perform the matching, we defined two types of effector's attributes:

1- Attributes that define the physical characteristic of effectors, such as the weight of the effector, its dimension, size, etc. These also contain special attributes, which define the elements that are required in order to allow these effectors to be usable. For example, required hand force, in Newton (N), required hand workspace (in cm^3), whose values are mainly provided by the effector manufacturers or can be measured in vitro. In this chapter, we only consider two attributes, namely, required hand force and required hand workspace. These attributes are chosen because of their ability to lead the user to a handicap situation.

2- Attributes that define the related services of effectors, which are numbered according to each effector. For instance, in Figure 3, the services related to the effector "door" are "open" and "close". However the physical characteristics of door are: required hand workspace (which is about 5 cm^3) and the required hand force (10 N).

Matching Between User Model and Environment Model

The matching is a virtual relationship based on the semantic interpretation of the user and environment attributes leading to the handicap situation; it allows us to identify the limit of the user's abilities in the environment. In order to define this matching we should find how an attributes can lead to a handicap situation. For instance, the user Alain having muscular dystrophy with a hand force of 5 N, all effectors that require a force greater than 5 N become obstacles, and lead to the handicap situation. We formalized the matching relation by the "*HandicapSituation*" property which will be discussed on details in the next section.

KNOWLEDGE REPRESENTATION IN SMF

In order to provide a uniform way to make the different entities understanding each other and to describe the semantics of the attributes (which we name as Meta-Data), we used ontology to represent the domain knowledge (DO). The use of ontologies in this context requires a well-designed and compatible ontology language supporting well-defined semantics and powerful reasoning tools. The syntax of this language must be both intuitive to human users and compatible with existing standards (such as XML, RDF, and RDFS). Its semantics should be formally specified since it could not otherwise provide a shared understanding. Finally, its expressive power should be adequate i.e. the language should be expressive enough for defining all the relevant concepts in enough detail. Description Logic (DL) should be an ideal candidate. It can provide high quality ontologies for our domain knowledge and allows us to formalize and implement the matching in first order rules and reason on it.

Before presenting our DL approach for modelling an assistive environment, let us provide a brief introduction to description logic.

Description Logic

Description logic (Baader, Calvanese, McGuinness, Nardi, & Patel-Schneider, 2007) is a family of class-based knowledge representation formalisms, equipped with well-defined model-theoretic semantics (Griss, Letsinger, Cowan, Sayers, VanHilst, & Kessler, 2002), and was first developed to provide formal declarative meaning to semantic networks (Quillian, 1965), and frames (Minsky, 1981). DLs differ from their predecessors, such as semantic networks and frames, in that they are equipped with a formal logic-based semantics.

A DL knowledge base is comprised by two components: a "TBox" (terminological box) and an "ABox" (assertional box) (Baader, Calvanese, McGuinness, Nardi, & Patel-Schneider, 2007). The TBox contains assertions about concepts (e.g., User, Effectors) and roles (e.g., Prefer, HandicapSituation). The ABox contains assertions about individuals (e.g., "Alain", Lamp, Prefer(Alain, DVD)).

Concepts and roles can be either atomic or constructed using Boolean concepts or role constructors:

- Top concept T: denotes all individuals
- Bottom concept $\perp$: denotes no individuals.
- Conjunction concept $\cap$: Effectors $\cap$ Users $\subseteq \perp$: means that both sets of User's and Effector's individuals are disjoint
- Disjunction concept $\cup$: Effectors $\cup$ Users $\subseteq$ *Things*
- Complement concept $\neg$: *Things* $\cap \neg$ Users $\subseteq$ Effectors
- Existential restriction constructor $\exists R.C$: $\exists Prefer.ElectricalEffectors$ denotes the individuals Preferring at least one Electrical effectors where *ElectricalEffectors* $\subseteq$ Effectors

The value restriction constructor $\forall R.C$: $\forall HandicapSituation.Effectors$ denotes the effectors who can lead to a handicap situation.

Semantics of Description Logic

The semantics of Description Logic is given in terms of an interpretation, consisting of a non empty set Δ^I, which define the set of all individuals in DO, and an interpretation function $\cdot^I$, symbolically defined as $I = (\Delta^I, \cdot^I)$. An individual i is an instance of a class C just in case i is interpreted as an element of the class interpretation C (i.e., $i^I \in C^I$), and a class C is a subclass of a class D just in case the interpretation of C is a subset of the interpretation of D (i.e., $C^I \subseteq D^I$).

The interpretation function gives the extension of the concepts and roles, and it assigns to every atomic concept a subset of Δ^I and to every atomic role a binary relation in $\Delta^I \times \Delta^I$.

The semantic interpretation of the operators described above is defined as in Table 1:

For example the semantic interpretation of the concept *Users* is Users^I={ *"Alain", "Pierre",...*}, for the role *Prefer* the semantic interpretation

Table 1. Semantics of DL

Syntax	Semantics
C	$C^I \subseteq \Delta^I$
R	$R^I \subseteq \Delta^I \times \Delta^I$
$\top$	Δ^I
$\perp$	$\varnothing$
$C \cap D$	$C^I \cap D^I$
$C \cup D$	$C^I \cup D^I$
$\neg C$	$\Delta^I \setminus C^I$
$\exists R.C$	$\{x \mid \exists y : (x,y) \in R^I \rightarrow y \in C^I\}$
$\forall R.C$	$\{x \mid \forall y : (x,y) \in R^I \rightarrow y \in C^I\}$

is:Prefer$^I \subseteq$ Users$^I \times$ Effectors^I Prefer^I={*Prefer ("Alain",DVD),Prefer("Alain","Telephone"), Prefer ("Pierre", TV)......*}

DL Approach for Modelling an Assistive Environment:

DL, as described above, is not suitable to define some attributes and individuals of our domain knowledge. For example, to define the roles *Age* and *HandForce,* which are user properties, there are no DL descriptions available to represent data types (integers and strings) and values such as "10".

Many extensions have been introduced to DL in order to be more expressive and supporting more properties and data. ΣH is one of the families of extended Description Logics (Horrocks, Sattler, & Tobies, 2000) which adds properties such as inverse properties and generalised cardinality restrictions properties and adds the ability to define a class by enumerating its instances (e.g., the class week:{Monday, Tuesday, Wednesday, Thursday, Friday, Saturday, Sunday }). The ΣH family members define different DL extensions; one of these members is ΣHOΘ(Δ) Description logic (Horrocks, & Sattler, 2001). In our project, we used ΣHOΘ(Δ) as the basis for the description of our ontology.

In the ΣHOΘ(Δ) Description Logic (Horrocks, & Sattler, 2001), the data type interpretations of values are separated from that of classes and individuals:ΣHOΘ(Δ) interpretations include an additional interpretation domain for data values Δ^I_D which is disjoint from the domain of individuals Δ^I. Data types, such as integer, are interpreted as a subset of Δ^I_D, and values such as the integer "10" are interpreted as elements of Δ^I_D. The interpretation of roles is also divided into two disjoint sets of abstract and data type interpretations. Abstract interpretations such as *Prefer* are interpreted as binary relations on the subsets of $\Delta^I \times \Delta^I$, data type interpretations such as *HandForce* are interpreted as binary relations on the subset $\Delta^I \times \Delta^I_D$.

User Model and Environment Model in ΣHOΘ(Δ)

We are interested in defining a group of individuals that have a homogenous concept structure (have similar properties and data types). For example, we define the *Users group*, which includes specific values for properties such as "Age", "TypeOfDisability", "Prefer", etc, and we define the *Effectors group*, which includes a value for properties such as "RequiredHandForce" and "RequiredHandWorkspace". We named such groups of individuals a *ClassModel*. In our framework, the ClassModel represents the **User** and **Environment Model** By the following definitions we will present our approach to define the different entities of our domain knowledge (DO).

ClassModel can be defined in the context of ΣHOΘ(Δ) as follow:

Definition 1
Let Δ be the set of all concepts in Domain Knowledge (DO) and R the set of roles.

A *ClassModel* is defined as a set of concepts C where:

- $C \subseteq \Delta$
- $\exists R \mid R \subseteq R \; \forall r \in R, D_Y = \{v_2 \mid (v_1, v_2) \in r\}$, and $C \subseteq \forall R.D_Y$

Attributes in ΣHOΘ(Δ)

We define *attributes* as the set of roles that characterize the ClassModel C. These attributes represent the relationships with other concepts in C. We denote the domain values of the attribute r as D_r. On the other hand, a ClassModel C is characterized by a finite set of attributes A_C, where each attribute $a \in A_C$ is defined as follows.

Definition 2
Let C be a ClassModel in the domain ontology.

An *attribute* $a \in A_C$ is a 2-tuple, $a = \langle T_a, D_a \rangle$ where:

- T_a is the *type* values of the attribute a.
- D_a is the *domain* values of the attribute a;

T_a, D_a are different, T_a defines the concrete data type of the attribute a and $D_a \in dom(T_a)$.

For example *Integer* defines the type of the attribute *Age*, whereas $D_{Age} = [0,100]$.

We named the *Users* ClassModel C_{Users} and the *Effectors* ClassModel $C_{Effectors}$

HandicapSituation Property

We define the *HandicapSituation* as a role belonging to C_{Users} ClassModel representing a property between the Users and Effecteurs ClassModels where:

- $HandicapSituation^I \subseteq \Delta^I_U \times \Delta^I_E$
- $HandicapSituation(x, y) \mid (x \in \Delta^I_U, y \in \Delta^I_E)$, means that the Effector y leads the user x to a handicap situation

Attributes Prefer and NotPrefer

Simillary to the *HandicapSituation* role, both attributes, *Prefer* and *NotPrefer*, belongs to C_{Users} ClassModel. They are interpreted as follow:

- $Prefer^I \subseteq \Delta^I_U \times \Delta^I_E$ and $NotPrefer^I \subseteq \Delta^I_U \times \Delta^I_E$
- $Prefer(x,y)$, $NotPrefer(x,y) \mid (x \in \Delta^I_U, y \in \Delta^I_E)$ respectively mean that the user x prefer(resp, dos not prefer) the effector y.

Services Attribute

The services provided by an effector are defined by the Effectors attribute *Services;*

Definition 3
A_{Users} represents the user ClassModel attributes
$A_{Users} \in A_C$
$A_{Users} = \{$Name, TypeOfDisability, TypeOfTechnicalAid, HandForce, HandWorkSpace, Prefer, NotPrefer, HandicapSituation, ...$\}$
$A_{Effectors}$ represents the Effectors ClassModel attributes $A_{Effectors} \in A_C$
$A_{Effectors} = \{$Name, RequiredHandWorkSpace, RequiredHandForce, Services.....$\}$

Category of Attributes

Definition 4
A category of attributes is a subset of attributes $A_{Category}$ such as:

$$A_{Categorie} \subseteq A_{Users} \; Or \; A_{Category} \subseteq A_{Effecteurs}$$

Profile in ΣHOΘ(Δ)

Definition 5
Given a, b two attributes such $b = \langle T_b, D_b \rangle$ and $a = \langle T_a, D_a \rangle$

b is an *instance of* $a \leftrightarrow D_b \in D_a$, and $T_b = T_a$

Table 2. HandicapSituation program rules (P_HandicapSituation)

- *HandicapSituation (x,y)← Users(x), HandForce(x,a), Effector(y), RequiredHandForce(y,b), ¬ less_than(b,a)*
- *HandicapSituation (x,y) ← Users(x),HandWorkspace(x,a),* Effecteur(y), *RequiredHandWorkspace(y,b), ¬ less_than(b,a)*
- *HandicapSituation (x," Lamp") ← Users(x), TypeOfDisability(x,a), equal(a,"Blind")*
- *HandicapSituation (x," Radio") ← Users(x), TypeOfDisability(x,a), equal(a,"Deaf")*
- *HandicapSituation (x," Stairs") ← Users(x), TypeOfTechnicalAids(x,a), equal(a,"Wheelchair")*

Given a ClassModel C with attribute set $A_C = \{ a_1^C, a_2^C, \ldots a_n^C \}$, P is an *instance of* ClassModel C, iff

- P has attributes $A_P = \{ a_1^P, a_2^P, \ldots a_n^P \}$
- $\forall a_i^P$, a_i^P is an instance of a_i^C, for $1 \leq i \leq n$.

P is called the **Profile** of the *ClassModel C*, for instance profile of *Alain* is {Alain, Muscular dystrophy, Wheelchair, 5, 3, Prefer(Alain, DVD), … } which is an instance of the *ClassModel* C_{Users}

Definition 6

Δ^I_{All} defines the set of all ClassModel instances of the DO

We call a *viewof* Δ^I_{All}, a subset V of Δ^I_{All} ($V \subset \Delta^I_{All}$)

Definition 7:

- Δ^I_U: Is the interpretation domain of C_{Users}, it represents the set of all Users ClassModel instances in DO

  $\forall P \in \Delta^I_U \Leftrightarrow P$ is *instance of* C_{Users}

- Δ^I_E: Is the interpretation domain of $C_{Effectors}$, it represents the set of all Effectors ClassModel instances in DO

  $\forall P \in \Delta^I_E \Leftrightarrow P$ is *instance of* $C_{Effectors}$

Formal Description of the Matching Using First Order Logic Rules

The matching represents the relationship between the user and effectors attributes. We implement the matching as a set of first order logic rules. The rules involve the different *ClassModel* attributes defined above.

Let C_P be a set of predicates symbols (unary and binary predicate of the TBox). A *term* is either a constant to define the individuals (denoted by *a, b, c*) or a variable (denoted by *x, y, z*). An *atom* has the form $P(s_1, \ldots, s_n)$, where P is a predicate symbol and S_i are terms. A rule has the form

$$H \leftarrow B_1, \ldots, B_n$$

Where H and B_i are atoms; H is called the *rule head*, and the set of all B_i is called the *rule body*. A *program P* defines a finite set of rules (Horrocks, & Patel-Schneider, 2004).

The matching defines a relation between ClassModel attributes. The attribute *HandicapSituation*, for instance, involves the attributes *HandForce, HandWorkspace, …etc.* This relationship is formalized by a *program* rules that defines the links between attributes.

Table 2 represents $P_{HandicapSituation}$, the program that defines the rules involving the *HandicapSituation* attribute; the predicate *less_than* defines the Boolean function *lessThan(x,y)* which returns true if $x \geq y$ and false else. The predicate *equal* defines the Boolean function *equal(x,y)* returns true if $x = y$ and false if not.

Example

The following rule defines the matching between the attribute "Stairs" and the technical aid "Wheelchair" of the user x

Figure 4.

Algorithm 1 Reasoning Algorithm

Require: $(\Delta^I_{C_1}, \Delta^I_{C_2}, ... \Delta^I_{C_n})(t), (P_1, P_2 ... P_m)$
Ensure: $(V_1, V_2 ... V_n)$
1: $(\Delta'^I_1, \Delta'^I_2, ... \Delta'^I_n)$ a **null** vector
2: **repeat**
3:    $(V_1, V_2 ... V_n) = \phi((P_1, P_2 ... P_m), (\Delta^I_{C_1}, \Delta^I_{C_2}, ... \Delta^I_{C_n})(t))$
4:    $(\Delta'^I_{C_1}, \Delta'^I_{C_2}, ... \Delta'^I_{C_n}) = (\Delta^I_1, \Delta^I_2, ... \Delta^I_n)(t)$
5:    $t = t + 1$
6: **until** $(\Delta'^I_{C_1}, \Delta'^I_{C_2}, ... \Delta'^I_{C_n}) = (\Delta^I_{C_1}, \Delta^I_{C_2}, ... \Delta^I_{C_n})(t)$

HandicapSituation (x, "Stairs") ← Users(x), TypeOfTechnicalAids(x,a), equal(a, "Wheelchair")

It means, when we have an environment containing a stairs and a user is having a wheelchair, this context provides a handicap situation.

Reasoning

One of the reasons we use DL to define our domain knowledge is the power and the efficiency of reasoning provided by DL systems. The *Inference Reasoning* process is summarized in Figure 4.

The Algorithm has 2 inputs: the set $(\Delta^I_{C1}, ..., \Delta^I_{Cn})$ at time t where Δ^I_{Ci} define the instances set of the ClassModel C_i and the set of the program rules $(P_1, ..., P_m)$. The algorithm output is the set $(V_1, ..., V_n)$ where V_i represents a view of Δ^I_{Ci}. The function Φ, implements a DL reasoner, processes iteratively the set $(\Delta^I_{C1}, ..., \Delta^I_{Cn})(t)$ and the programs $(P_1, ..., P_m)$. The algorithm stops when there are no changes in the DO instances.

Assistive Service Delivery

Assistive services delivered to the user are the set of accessible services provided by effectors that do not lead to the handicap situation. It is defined as a view V_E *(user(i))* of Δ^I_E representing the effectors that lead the *user(i)* to handicap situation in the environment E. It is computed by the reasoning

algorithm over the set of views $(\Delta^I_{\text{User}(i)}, \Delta^I_E)$ and the program rules $P_{HandicapSituation}$.

Formerly we define V_E *(user(i))* by the following tuple:

$$V_E \text{ (user(i))}: < (\Delta^I_{\text{User}(i)}, \Delta^I_E), P_{HandicapSituation}, IR >,$$

where $P_{HandicapSituation}$ is the *HandicapSituation* program rule, $\Delta^I_{\text{User}(i)}$ the profile of *Users(i)* and *IR* the reasoning algorithm.

Implementation of SMF

In order to implement the semantic matching framework and to process the scenario defined above as well as to adequately provide assistive services we need an architecture that will:

1. Operate with external data, such as the user's location in the environment and the user's identification.
2. Dynamically deliver accessible services according to each user's profile.
3. Enable rapid prototyping of accessible assistive services in the environment.

These will imply the implementation of the framework based on modules and components which are depicted in Figure 5 and consists of a knowledge base, an instantiation manager, inference reasoner, and a query engine.

Figure 5. SMF architecture

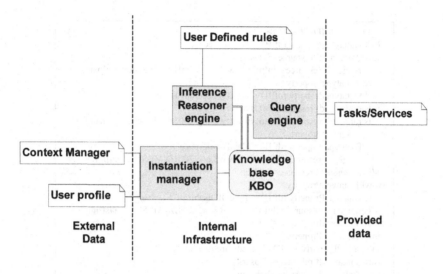

The Knowledge Base Ontology

The knowledge base ontology (KBO) implements the C_{Users} and $C_{Effectors}$ using OWL-DL (McGuinness, & van Harmelen, 2004) languages. The following tables (Table 3 and Table 4) define respectively the Effectors and the Users ClassModels described using the OWL-DL *class* structure.

KBO defines also the set of User instances (Δ^I_U) and Effectors instances (Δ^I_E) which are represented by the object generated by the Users and Effectors Classes. It links the different instances and provides interfaces for the query engine and the inference reasoner in order to enable them to manipulate correlated instances.

Instantiation Manager

The instantiation manager (IM) obtains raw data from the following two components: the context manager module, that provides Δ^I_E defining the environment effectors and the contextual information such as the user location in the environment and the User profile module that generates the user's characteristics. IM instantiate the Users and Effectors classes to generate the instances of Δ^I_U

and Δ^I_E. It has a direct access to attribute values of each instance in KBO.

Inference Reasoner Engine and Program Rules

This component implements the Inference Reasoner algorithm (*IR*). We used JENA 2 API Reasoner (McBride, 2001) and do the inference reasoning through the program rules P. It provides dynamically views according to $\Delta^I_{User(i)}$ (user) and Δ^I_E (environment effectors) and performs hybrid reasoning over the KBO. The algorithm extracts the environment context from the ontology as OWL-DL classes (Figure 6). And formats the matching rules as a Jena rules standard (McBride, 2001). Then the inference engine is started using the reasoner API of JENA (Φ). The result (output) is checked with the Inputs (Ontology new instances checking). If they are different, the reasoner runs again, otherwise it stops. This result is then used to update the ontology.

Context Query Engine

The context query engine (CQE) provides views "on demand", by sending sets of queries to KBO.

Table 3. Users ClassModels in OWL-DL

```
<owl:Class rdf:ID="Users"/>
<owl:DatatypeProperty rdf:ID="HandForce">
<rdfs:domain rdf:resource="#Users"/>
<rdfs:range rdf:resource="http://www.w3.org/2001/XMLSchema#float"/>
</owl:DatatypeProperty>
<owl:DatatypeProperty rdf:ID="TypeOfThechnicalAids">
<rdfs:domain rdf:resource="#Users"/>
<rdfs:range rdf:resource="http://www.w3.org/2001/XMLSchema#string"/>
</owl:DatatypeProperty>
<owl:DatatypeProperty rdf:ID="HandWorkSpace">
<rdfs:range rdf:resource="http://www.w3.org/2001/XMLSchema#float"/>
<rdfs:domain rdf:resource="#Users"/>
</owl:DatatypeProperty>
<owl:DatatypeProperty rdf:ID="TypeOfDisability">
<rdfs:range rdf:resource="http://www.w3.org/2001/XMLSchema#string"/>
<rdfs:domain rdf:resource="#Users"/>
</owl:DatatypeProperty>
<owl:ObjectProperty rdf:ID=" HandicapSituation ">
<rdfs:domain rdf:resource="#Users"/>
<rdfs:range rdf:resource="#Effectors"/>
</owl:ObjectProperty>
<owl:ObjectProperty rdf:ID="Prefer">
<rdfs:range rdf:resource="#Effectors"/>
<rdfs:domain rdf:resource="#Users"/>
</owl:ObjectProperty>
<owl:ObjectProperty rdf:ID="NotPrefer">
<rdfs:range rdf:resource="#Effectors"/>
<rdfs:domain rdf:resource="#Users"/>
</owl:ObjectProperty>
```

Table 4. Effectors ClassModels in OWL-DL

```
<owl:Class rdf:ID="Effectors"/>
<owl:DatatypeProperty rdf:ID=" RequiredHandForce ">
<rdfs:domain rdf:resource="#Effectors"/>
<rdfs:range rdf:resource="http://www.w3.org/2001/XMLSchema#float"/>
</owl:DatatypeProperty>
<owl:DatatypeProperty rdf:ID=" RequiredHandWorkspace ">
<rdfs:range rdf:resource="http://www.w3.org/2001/XMLSchema#float"/>
<rdfs:domain rdf:resource="#Effectors"/>
<owl:DatatypeProperty rdf:ID="Service">
```

Figure 6. Architecture of the inference engine module

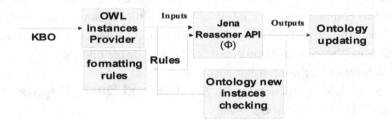

Table 5. Query example of supplying views from KBO

```
SELECT Effectors(i) WHERE (Users = "Alain")
    AND (Environment="Env(i)")
    AND Effector(i) belongs into "Env(i)"
    AND (HandicapSituation ("Alain", Effectors(i))
```

The queries are formatted regarding $\Delta^I_{User(i)}$ and $\Delta^I_{E.}$ The following example (table 5) shows the query that supplies views of the environment effectors that lead *Alain* to a handicap situation in the environment Env(i)

We implemented the framework using Java2 platform. The class diagram in Figure 7 shows in details the cohabitation and implementation of SMF modules.

The different modules are developed as classes, the knowledgeBaseManager() class is the heart of the framework. It invokes the different modules on three successive phases:

1. The initiation manager does the initiation phase. It receives external data through the Ivy event-based bus [16]. It is composed on three classes:

    ○   The servicesInitiator() class initiates the environment services; received from the ServicesProvider() class which provides events regarding the environment's effectors and their services and characteristics.

    ○   The ContextInitiator() class updates the contextual information which are received from the ContextProvider() class which integrates all information related to the user's context such as,

Figure 7. SMF Class diagram

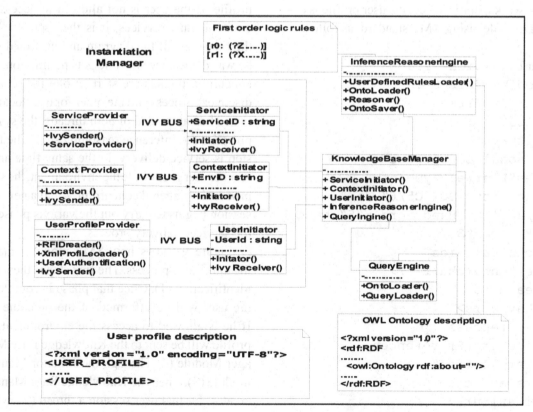

time, user's location, sensors states, etc.

- ◦ The UserInitiator() class makes the user identification through the UserProfileProvider() class which contains the user profile.

2. The inference reasoning phase, managed by inferenceReasoerIngine() class, process iteratively the OWL-DL ontology description base and makes the inference reasoning through the semantic matching rules.

3. The extracting of relevant services from the OWL-DL ontology description base, using declarative queries via the queryEngine() class.

SMF is designed to be integrated in general smart home demonstrator operating with other frameworks to ensure a context aware application. SMF receives, by the Instantiation manager, events from these Frameworks. Thus we adopted a standard way to exchanges data between these Frameworks. For instance, the user profile is defined in a file, using XML standard, as follow:

```
<?xml version="1.0"
encoding="UTF-8"?>
<USER_PROFILE>
<CLASS>
<Features>
<Personal_Background
Name="Pierre" Type_of_
disability="SCI_C5/6" />
<Capability Hand_Force="5" hand_
workspace="3"/>
<Technical_Aids
Type="Wheelchair" />
</Features>
<Bihaviours>
<Preferences>
<Effectors_Preferences
Prefer="Coffee" />
</Preferences>
</Bihaviours>
```

```
</CLASS>
</USER_PROFILE>
```

The UserProfileProvider() class receives the XML file and, throw initiator() function, update or creates a new user instance in KBO. By the same way ServicesProvider() and ContextProvider() classes update the KBO with the new initiated values, coming from other frameworks.

Multi-User Management

SMF is designed to support multi users; each user is processed separately by a session and delivered by adapted services. First we highlight the different steps regarding one session, and then we define, in details, how SMF modules mange the multi users process.

Steps of one user session are shown in the activity diagram of Figure 8. At the first we have the user authentication step. An environment access decision is taken according to the user profile. If the user is not allowed to access the environment's services, it is then sent back to the final state of the diagram and informed why he was denied access. If he gets permission, two concurrent threads are started: one for services discovery process and the other for user localization. Then at the end of both threads, the system precedes the Inference reasoning step. The final step is service delivery. In the same time and if another user goes inside the environment, the same process is triggered concurrently, and a new user session begins to carry out the various phases of the services delivery process.

Figure 9 shows how SMF modules mange the multi-user process. The first step is the user's identification (1). Once that phase is completed, the user will be informed of the outcome (2): If he is allowed to access the environment, his profile will be sent to the Knowledge Base Manager Module (4) Through the Initiator Manager module (3). Then the Knowledge Base Manager creates, for that user session a thread (5), which

Figure 8. Activity diagram

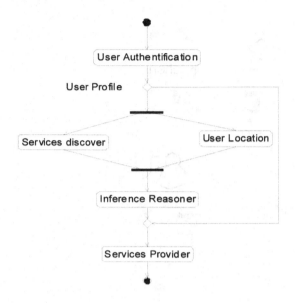

Figure 9. Multi-user management

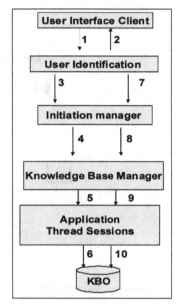

loads and sets up the profile in the KBO (6). As soon as the user leaves the environment, the User Identification module inform the initiation manager by the state of the user (7) which forwards it to the Knowledge Base Manager (7) in order to stop the thread from that session (9) and updates the KBO (10)

EXPERIMENTATION

Using our laboratory, we first built a prototype of a smart environment. This prototype integrates two other frameworks developed by colleagues in Handicom Lab which are: context aware Framework (CAE) (Feki, & Mokhtari, 2006) and the Service Discovery and Management Framework (SDMF) (Ghorbel, Mokhtari, & Renouard, 2006), (Mokhtari, Ghorbel, Kadouche, & Feki, 2007) based on OSGi technology (Alliance, 2007). In this chapter we will focus on SMF operation and will not cover the details functionalities of both frameworks (CAE and SDMF).

We considered the indoor environment as a home with two sub environments, the kitchen

(Env1) and the living room (Env2) together with necessary accessories (Figure 10). The *HandicapSituation* program rules was implemented in order to provide, as *views*, the effectors that lead the user to a handicap situation, then the accessible and preferred services of each user in both environments (Env1 and Env2).

Table 6 defines the different effectors in each sub environment and their characteristics. The *Required Hand Force* value is expressed in Newton and the *required hand workspace* is in cm³.

Three users, unknown from the environment, are involved in this experimentation, two of them having a disability (Alain & Francoise) and another with no disability (Pierre). Table 7 and Table 8 define the users' diagnostics.

Infrared motion detectors are deployed in both environments to ensure user localization. We used the RFID technology to implement the user's profile under XML Format (see (Ghorbel, Kadouche, & Mokhtari, 2007) for more details). An RFID reader is deployed on the outside of both environments in order to ensure the identification process. We used a tablet PC as a mobile handheld for the user terminal. It contains a JAVA

Figure 10. Experimentation demonstrator

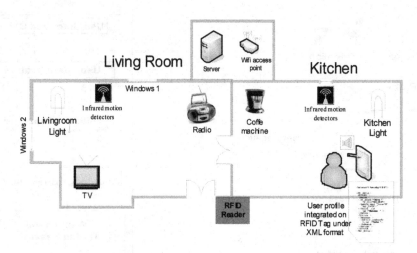

Table 6. Environment description

Environment name	Environment effectors	Required Hand Force (Newton)	Required hand workspace (cm³)
Kitchen environment (Env1)	KitchenLight	5	0
	Coffee-machine	2	3
Living-room environment (Env2)	LivingRoomLight	5	0
	Radio	5	1
	Television	5	2
	Window1	25	10
	Window2	25	10

Table 7. Users diagnostics (part 1)

User name	Hand force (Newton)	Hand work space (cm³)	Type of disability
Alain	5	3	Muscular dystrophy
Francoise	20	1	SCI C5/6
Pierre	75	10	-

Table 8. Users diagnostics (part 2)

User name	Type of technical aids	Prefer	Not Prefer
Alain	Wheelchair	DVD player, Telephone	Window
Francoise	Wheelchair	-	
Pierre	-	Telephone	

Figure 11. Identification Message for the user "François"

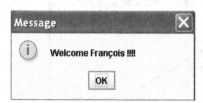

Figure 12. Service Discovery Message for Env2

client application that allows the user environment interaction and communication with the server. Our framework runs on a server machine, located outside the home (Figure 10), which contains the demonstrator of our platform. The communication between the server and the user terminal is ensured by the WIFI communication protocol.

Each user was invited to fellow next scenario:

The users have to badge before coming inside the house. The RFID reader transmits the user profile to the server by the Ivy event-based bus (Chatty, 2002), which allows the system to identify the user and display a personalized welcome message (Figure 11).

Within the house, infrared motion sensors track user's position. According to each location (Env1&Env2) the server discovers the effectors belonging to this environment and provides a service discovery message to the user (Figure 12).

After that, the server runs the SMF Framework which extracts the effectors that lead the user to the handicap situation and then provides the accessible services according to his/her profile (Figure 13).

In the case of Françoise, when she is in Env2, the system discovers the effectors inside this environment (LivingRoomLight, Radio, Television, Window1, and Window2) (Figure 12). Because of the required hand force of windows 1 and 2 (25 N) is superior to the user's hand force (5 N), SMF, using the filtering process, hides both effectors (windows 1 and 2) from the user interface and

delivers her just the accessible effectors (LivingRoomLight, Radio and Television) (Figure 13). Then the Service Discovery and Management Framework deliver the services related to these effectors, for instance, switch on/off the Living Room Light as shown in Figure 13.

The user interface is automatically updated in the mobile handheld according to the user environment interaction.

Sequence Process

Once user is detected (identification phase) and the location of the user is identified (see Figure 14), the context aware Framework (CAE) exchanges information with the SMF instantiation manager module in order to instantiate the KBO (instantiation phase).

The *Inference Reasoner Engine* module, using the *HandicapSituation* program rules, iteratively processes the KBO instances and performs the matching between the user and the environment (reasoning phase). The *Context Query Engine* module, using declarative queries (querying phase), extracts the view from the updated KBO and provides accessible Efectors to the Service Discovery and Management Framework (SDMF) which adapts the application on the terminal side to the user. The exchange events between the client's applications and frameworks are done by an Ivy event-based bus (Chatty, 2002).

Figure 13. Assistive Services clients

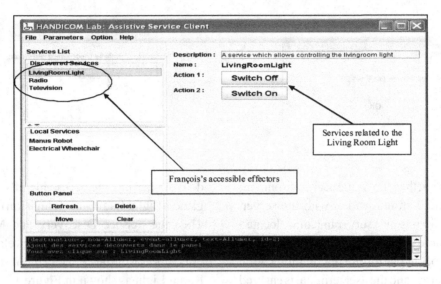

Figure 14. Sequence process

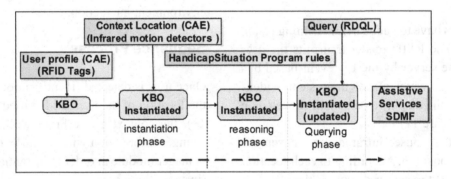

PERFORMANCE

We evaluated the scalability of the system by measuring the reasoning response time (RT), in milliseconds (ms), of the Inference Reasoner Engine module (IRE). The system was implemented with Java runtime platform on a 2.4 GHZ processor with 1.0 Gbyte of RAM running on Windows.

First, as shown in graph *a* of Figure 15, we varied the number of ClassModel instances from 10 to 60 and fixed the number of rules to 10, then by the same way, we fixed the number of ClassModel instances to 60 and varied the number of rules from 10 to 60 (see graph *b* in Figure 15).

Finally, in graph *c* of Figure 15, both the number of rules and the number of ClassModel instances are varied from 10 to 60. For the first two graphs (*a* and *b*) we have also drawn the smooth straight lines to compare their grades.

The grade of graph *a* (11.4) is superior to the grade of graph *b* (4.28); which imply that, for the same abscissa interval, the reasoning time response grows quickly for the graph *a* then the graph *b*, i.e. for both graphs (*a* and *b*) varying the number of ClassModel instances and the number of rules from 10 to 60 gives a gap of 800 ms (RT increases from 400 ms to 1200 ms) ms for graph *a* and a gap of 200ms (RT increases from 1050 ms

Figure 15. SMF reasoning response time

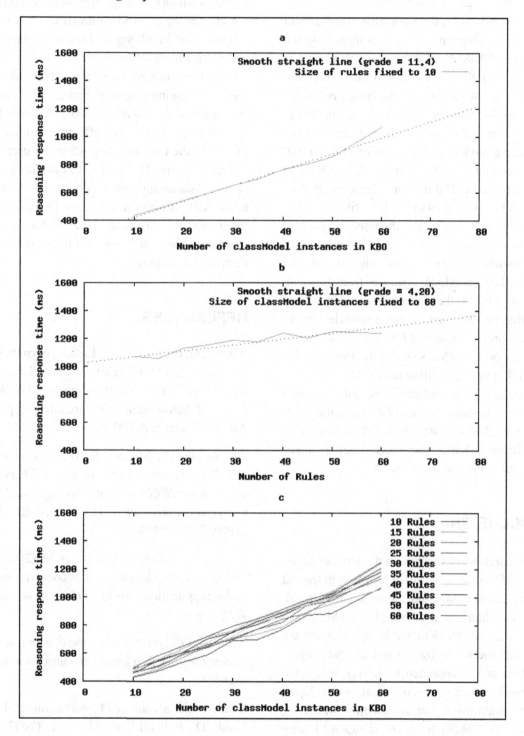

to 1250ms) for graph *b*. We remark that increasing the number of rules, does not have much impact on the reasoning time as much as increasing the number of ClassModel instances. This remark is confirmed by the graph *c* which shows the time response when varying, in the same time, from 10 to 60 the number of ClassModel instances and the number of rules. The ten curves have the same bihaviors as the curve of graph *a*, but are concentrated on one thin band. The RT gap does not exceed 200 ms for a large interval of rule numbers (form 10 to 60) for a fixed number of ClassModel instances in the interval [10, 60]. Contrariwise the RT gap exceeds 700 ms for any fixed number of rules in the interval [10, 60] varying the ClassModel instances from 10 to 60. We conclude that the reasoning response time of the inference Reasoner Engine module largely depends on the number of ClassModel instances in KBO, on the other side the number of rules does not have much influence on RT.

Consequently, in order to improve the response time of our system, we should decrease the number of ClassModel instances which are unused or unavailable in KBO. The ClassModel instances gather effectors and users profiles.

CONCLUSION

Our research work focuses on the Human-Environment Interaction in case of people with special needs (Ghorbel, Mokhtari, & Renouard, 2006), (Feki, Mokhtari, & Ibrahim, 2006), (Mokhtari, & Feki, 2007). Particularly in this chapter we presented the formalization and the data representation of our approach to deliver accessible services in smart environment. It is developed under a framework named Semantic Matching Framework (SMF) based on $\Sigma HO\Theta(\Delta)$ (one members of DLs family). SMF was implemented and experimented in a general smart homes dem-

onstrator which was tested in laboratory condition; we are aiming at validating this concept in real environment involving end-users by deploying this platform within pilot sites.

The reasoning response time of the Inference Reasoner Engine module depends on the number of ClassModel instances in KBO. Actually SMF does not detect defective effectors and does not eliminate the user instance when the user is no longer at home. The idea is to develop a smart refiner instance module which will be connected to the KBO in order to eliminate the unused and the unavailable instances in KBO. For instance, as soon as the user leaves the house the system destroys his instance.

REFERENCES

Abowd, G. D., Bobick, A., Essa, I., Mynatt, E., & Rogers, W. (2002a). The aware home: developing technologies for successful aging. In AAAI Workshop and Automation as a Care Giver, (pp.1–7). Alberta, Canada: AAAI Press.

Abowd, G. D., Mynatt, E. D., & Rodden, T. (2002b). The human experience. *IEEE Pervasive Computing / IEEE Computer Society [and] IEEE Communications Society, 1*1),48–57. doi:10.1109/MPRV.2002.993144

Aleksy, M., Butter, T., & Schader, M. (2008). Architecture for the development of context-sensitive mobile applications. *Mobile Information Systems, 4*(2), 105–117.

Alliance, O. (2007). *Osgi – the dynamic module system for java*. Retrieved from http://www.osgi.org/

Baader, F., Calvanese, D., McGuinness, D. L., Nardi, D., & Patel-Schneider, P. F. (2007). The Description Logic Handbook. New York: Cambridge University Press.

Brumitt, B., Meyers, B., Krumm, J., Kern, A., & Shafer, S. A. (2000). Easyliving: technologies for intelligent environments. In *HUC '00: Proceedings of the 2nd International Symposium on Handheld and Ubiquitous Computing*, (pp.12–29). London: Springer-Verlag.

Chatty, S. (2002). *The ivy software bus-a white paper*. CENA Technical Note NT02-816. Retrieved from http://www.tls.cena.fr/products/ivy

Dey, A. K., & Abowd, G. D. (2000). The context toolkit: aiding the development of context-aware applications. In *Proceedings of the 2nd International Symposium on Handheld and Ubiquitous Computing*, (pp.172–186). London: Springer-Verlag.

Dishman, E. (2004). Inventing wellness systems for aging in place. *Computer, 37*(5), 34–41. doi:10.1109/MC.2004.1297237

Feki, M. A., & Mokhtari, M. (2006). Context awareness for pervasive assistive environment. In I.K. Ibrahim, (Ed.), Handbook of Research on Mobile Multimedia. Hershey, PA: Idea Group Publisher.

Feki, M.A., Mokhtari, M., & Ibrahim, I. K. (2006). A novel approach for ontology distribution in ubiquitous environments. *International Journal of Web Systems, 2*(3–4).

Ferguson, G., Allen, J., Blaylock, N., Byron, D., Chambers, N., Dzikovska, M., Galescu, L., Shen, X., Swier, R. & Swift, M. (2002). *The medication advisor project: preliminary report*. Technical report.

Fougeyrollas, P. (2000). *Classification qubcoise: Processus de production du handicap*. Technical report, RIPPH, SCCIDIH; Réseau international du processus de production du handicap.

Fulford-Jones, T., Malan, D., Welsh, M., & Moulton, S. (2004). Codeblue: an ad hoc sensor network infrastructure for emergency medical care. In *International Workshop on Wearable and Implantable Body Sensor Networks*, (pp.12–14).

Ghorbel, M., Kadouche, R., & Mokhtari, M. (2007, April). User and service modeling in assistive environment to enhance accessibility of dependent people. In ICTA.

Ghorbel, M., Mokhtari, M., & Renouard, S. (2006). A distributed approach for assistive service provision in pervasive environment. In *Proceedings of the 4th International Workshop on Wireless Mobile Applications and Services on WLAN Hotspots*, (pp. 91–100). New York: ACM.

Gray, D. B., & Hendershot, G. E. (2000). The icidh-2: developments for a new era of outcomes research. *Archives of Physical Medicine and Rehabilitation, 81*(12PB), 10–14. doi:10.1053/apmr.2000.20616

Griss, M., Letsinger, R., Cowan, D., Sayers, C., VanHilst, M., & Kessler, R. (2002). *Coolagent: intelligent digital assistants for mobile professionals-phase 1 retrospective*. HP Laboratories Report HPL-2002-55 (R), July.

Gulliver, S., Ghinea, G., Patel, M., & Serif, T. (2007). A context-aware tour guide: user implications. *Mobile Information Systems, 3*(2), 71–88.

Horrocks, I., & Patel-Schneider, P. F. (2004) A proposal for an owl rules language. In *Proceedings of the 13th International Conference on World Wide Web*, (pp.723–731). New York: ACM.

Horrocks, I., & Sattler, U. (2001). Ontology reasoning in the shoq (d) description logic. *International Joint Conference on Artificial Intelegence*, (Vol. 17, pp.199–204). Mahwah, NJ: Lawrence Erlbaum Associates, Ltd.

Horrocks, I., Sattler, U., & Tobies, S. (2000). Practical reasoning for very expressive description logics. *Logic Journal of IGPL, 8*(3), 239–263. doi:10.1093/jigpal/8.3.239

Kadouche, R. (2004) Towards strategies and methods for disabled users profile. In *Workshop on Personalisation of ICT Products and Services*, ETSI, October 2004.

Kadouche, R., Abdulrazak, B., & Mokhtari, M. (2004) Designing an evaluation method for computer accessibility for people with severe disabilities. In ICCHP, (pp. 845–848). Paris: Springer.

Kadouche, R., Abdulrazak, B., Mokhtari, M., Giroux, S., & Pigot, H. (2009). Personalization and multi-user management in smart homes for disabled people. *Journal of Smart Home, 3*(1), 39–48.

Kadouche, R., Mokhtari, M., & Maier, M. (2005, July 24–29). Modeling of the residual capability for people with severe motor disabilities: analysis of hand posture. In *Proceedings of User Modeling 2005: 10th International Conference, UM 2005*, Edinburgh, UK. Berlin: Springer.

Kautz, H., Arnstein, L., Borriello, G., Etzioni, O., & Fox, D. (2002) An overview of the assisted cognition project. In *AAAI-2002 Workshop on Automation as Caregiver: The Role of Intelligent Technology in Elder Care*, Edmonton, Alberta, (pp.60–65).

Kidd, C. D., Orr, R., Abowd, G. D., Atkeson, C. G., Essa, I. A., MacIntyre, B., et al. (1999). The aware home: a living laboratory for ubiquitous computing research. In Lecture Note In Computer Science, (pp.191–198).

Krishnan, V. (2000). Location awareness in hp's cooltown, Position paper. In *W3C/WAP Workshop on Position Dependent Information*, (pp.15–16), Sophia Antipolis, France.

LaMarca, A., Chawathe, Y., Consolvo, S., Hightower, J., Smith, I., Scott, J., et al. (2005) Place lab: device positioning using radio beacons in the wild. In Proceedings of Pervasive, (pp.116–133). Berlin: Springer.

MARC. (n.d.). Retrieved from http://marc.med.virginia.edu/.

McBride, B. (2001). Jena: implementing the rdf model and syntax specification. In *Proceedings of the Second International Workshop on the Semantic Web SemWeb*, Hong Kong.

McGuinness, D. L., & van Harmelen, F. (2004). *Owl web ontology language overview*. Retrieved from http://www.w3.org/TR/owl-features/

Minsky, M. (1981). Framework for representing knowledge. In Mind Design, (pp.95–128). Cambridge, MA: MIT Press.

Mokhtari, M. & Feki, M.A. (2007). User needs and usage analysis in a smart environment for people requiring assistance. *Topics in Geriatric Rehabilitation, 23*(1).

Mokhtari, M., Ghorbel, M., Kadouche, R., & Feki, M. A. (2007). From smart home to smart space in independent living: a framework for multiple contexts management. In Wireless and Mobile Computing, Networking and Communications, 2007, WiMOB.

Pigot, H., Lussier-Desrochers, D., Bauchet, J., Lachapelle, Y., & Giroux, S. (2007). A smart home to assist recipes completion. *Festival of International Conferences on Caregiving, Disability, Aging and Technology (FICCDAT), 2nd International Conference on Technology and Aging (ICTA)*, Toronto, Canada.

Quillian, R. (1965). Word concepts: a theory & simulation of some basic semantic capabilities. *Behavioral Science, 12*(5), 410–430. doi:10.1002/bs.3830120511

Sadeh, N. M., Chan, E., & Van, L. (2002). Mycampus: an agent-based environment for context-aware mobile services. In *Proceedings of Workshop on Ubiquitous Agents on Embedded, Wearable and Mobile Devices.(ubiagents 2002)*, Bologna.

Want, R., Schilit, B. N., Adams, N. I., Gold, R., Petersen, K., Goldberg, D., et al. (1996). The parctab ubiquitous computing experiment. In Kluwer International Series In Engineering and Computer Science, (pp.45–97). Amsterdam: Kluwer.

Weikum, G. (2008). *Context and social network speci_cation (deliverable d7.1)*. Technical report.

Chapter 11
XAC Project:
Towards a Middleware for Open Wireless Sensor Networks

Kenji Tei
Waseda University, Japan & National Institute of Informatics, Japan

Shunichiro Suenaga
Nihon Unisys Ltd., Japan

Yoshiyuki Nakamura
Waseda University, Japan

Yuichi Sei
Mitsubishi Research Institute, Inc., Japan

Hikotoshi Nakazato
Waseda University, Japan

Yoichi Kaneki
The University of Tokyo, Japan

Nobukazu Yoshioka
National Institute of Informatics, Japan

Yoshiaki Fukazawa
Waseda University, Japan

Shinichi Honiden
National Institute of Informatics, Japan & The University of Tokyo, Japan

ABSTRACT

In pervasive computing environment (Satyanarayanan, 2001), common context management system, that make context of the real world be shared among the context-aware applications, is required to reduce development cost of each context-aware applications. A wireless sensor network (WSN) will be a key infrastructure for the context management system. Towards pervasive computing, a WSN integrated into context management system should be open infrastructure. In an open WSN should (1)handle various kinds of tasks, (2)manage tasks at runtime, (3)save resource consumption, and (4)adapt to changes of environments. To develop such an open WSN, middleware supports are needed, and our XAC project tries to develop a middleware for the open WSN. The XAC project is a research project to develop a middleware for open WSN. In this chapter, the auhors show research issues related to open WSN from the viewpoints of task description language, runtime task management, self-adaptability, and security.

DOI: 10.4018/978-1-61520-843-2.ch011

INTRODUCTION

In pervasive computing environments, many context-aware applications controlling various devices embedded in environments, support human activity more proactively and effectively. A context-aware application captures current context of the real world and affects the real world to reach expected context. Common context management system, that makes context of the real world be shared among context-aware applications, is effective to reduce development cost of such context-aware applications.

Context management system should be able to capture various kinds of context required by context-aware applications, and should be able to be deployed easily to various environments. A wireless sensor network (WSN) will be a key infrastructure for the context management system. The WSN is a wireless ad-hoc network consisting of tiny computers equipped with sensors and wireless communication devices. A WSN can produce data about environments, measured by some nodes in WSN using equipped sensors. The WSN can change data to produce according to requirements of applications, since each node can be programmed to use an adequate sensor among equipped sensors. Moreover, the WSN can be deployed easily on environments, since it does not require any communication cables. Nodes in a WSN communicate with each other via wireless links and transmit measured data via multi-hop communications. Therefore, the WSN is useful to develop the context management system.

Towards pervasive computing, a WSN integrated into context management system should be open infrastructure. An open WSN should

- handle various kinds of measuring tasks,
- manage tasks at runtime,
- save resource consumption, and
- adapt to changes of environments.

It is used by many context-aware applications that require different kinds of data to a different level of accuracy, at the same time. Therefore, the WSN should be able to handle various kinds of task, to produce multiple data required by these applications to a required accuracy. Additionally, applications using a WSN appear and disappear dynamically. Therefore, the open WSN should add or remove tasks without stopping itself. Moreover a WSN has severe resource limitations, since each node in a WSN has only poor CPU, memory, bandwidth, and battery. Therefore, the WSN should reduce needless resource consumptions to increase the number of tasks that it can handle, and to prolong its lifetime. Finally, adequate behavior of an open WSN depends on state of environments. Therefore, an open WSN should adapt its behavior to changes of environments without human's instructions.

To develop such an open WSN, middleware supports are needed, and our XAC project (*XAC project*, 2009) tries to develop a middleware for the open WSN. The XAC project is tackling research issues related to open WSN, is developing a middleware for WSN integrating these research results, and will publicize the middleware as open source. In this chapter, we show research issues related to the open WSN, and introduce research and development activities of XAC project related to these issues.

BACKGROUND

WSN programming is complicated, since it requires programmers to have deep knowledge about various fields, such as data analysis, distributed programming upon wireless ad-hoc networks, and optimization of embedded system. In this section we will present concrete examples of typical wireless sensor network tasks to identify the issues that need to be tackled when operating open wireless sensor networks.

Figure 1. An environment in office building

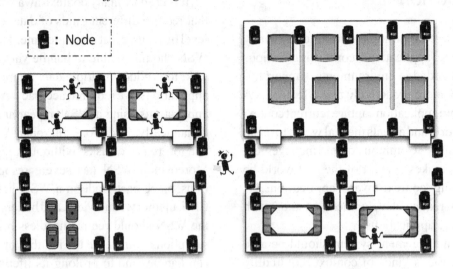

Figure 2. Examples of context-aware application scenarios

Number	Application name	Operational tasks	Environmental information	Accuracy requirement
S1	Temperature management	Adjust room temperature to present people's preferences	Room temperature	Within 2 degree of actual value
S2	Meeting room management	Maintain usage information of conference rooms based on their occupancy and reservations	Presence of people in conference rooms	Determine correct room occupancy with 99% accuracy
S3	Staff presence management	Determine if and in which room staff members are present	Location of specific staff members	Within 1m range in open plan office rooms, or by room otherwise
S4	Intruder detection	Determines suspicious intruders for instance by raising an alarm if people remain near an access lock for long periods without authenticating	Presence and position of people in certain locations	Localization accuracy in a 2m range

Let us first define a setting in which a pervasive computing environment has been set up in an office building and context-aware applications are introduced to optimize everyday business tasks (Figure 1). Sensor nodes are deployed throughout the building's floors in rooms, corridors and stairwells to enable monitoring and extracting information on the environmental conditions inside the building. Data sensed by the nodes of the network are transferred via multi-hop communication between the nodes and collected at a central server (which will be called base station from here on) to maintain that information.

Based on the environmental data collected throughout the office building, we envision context-aware applications to operate as specified in scenarios S1, S2, S3 and S4 of Figure 2. Scenario S1 consists of an application that maintains temperature levels in conference rooms according to the preferences of users present in a given room. The application in S2 determines the occupancy of conference rooms based on the presence of people in the room and the room's reservation data. Scenario S3 is concerned with tracking the whereabouts of staff inside the building, and the application in S4 is responsible for detecting suspicious intruders.

Each of the context-aware applications requires certain environmental context information related to its own operational tasks. S1 needs temperature readings, S2 data on the presence of people in conference rooms, S3 the location information of each staff member, and S4 the location information of people in specific areas.

As we can see, each scenario poses different requirements in regard to the accuracy of context information. Generally speaking, data readings from sensors can be expected to exhibit a certain level of error or noise. To improve the accuracy of environmental information extracted, a common approach is to use multiple sensor readings and aggregate the data. For instance, in S3 we may only need to acquire the rough whereabouts of a staff member - like in which room a person is currently located - so the low accuracy requirements in regard to the location information can probably be satisfied with a very low number of sensor readings. In S4 on the other hand it becomes necessary to determine very specific positions of people in the building up to accuracy levels to track them in 2m ranges, translating into the necessity to acquire far more sensor readings than in the scenario before.

On the other hand, from the viewpoint of the network operation in general, it is desirable to limit executing sensing tasks and resource usage as much as possible so that network lifetime can be prolonged. We have to take into account that nodes of a wireless sensor network are resource constrained in terms of CPU, memory and com-

munication capabilities. Each node is powered by battery, making load concentrations on specific nodes drain their battery and render them useless. For example, the commonly used Crossbow Mica2 node will deplete its battery on an average of 7 days when reading its temperature sensor value and transmitting it every second (Shnayder, Hempstead, Chen, Allen, & Welsh, 2004).

So, to extend the network lifetime, it becomes necessary to employ various optimization methods to improve each node's operational time, for instance by aggregating sensor readings before transmitting, by adjusting the sensing frequency to meet certain accuracy requirements, or by duty-cycling the node operation. These methods at the same time need to be coordinated with the requirements coming from the multiple applications to yield optimal results.

RESEARCH ISSUES FOR OPEN WSN MIDDLEWARE

XAC project tackles research issues related to middleware for open WSN. In this section, we show the research issues, existing works, and contributions of XAC project from the viewpoint of

- task description language
- runtime task management
- self-adaptability
- and security.

Task Description Language

Middleware provides a task description language, which is a domain specific language to define the behavior of a WSN for capturing the current context of target phenomena. The task description language provides an abstract view of the WSN to programmers, and thus constitutes different levels of programmability.

Figure 3. Model-driven development for task descriptions

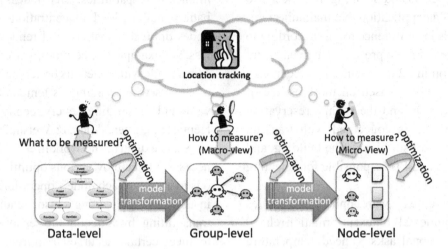

Existing Solutions

Existing task description languages can be classified into data-level, group-level, and node-level languages according to their level of abstraction.

Data-Level Languages

Data-level languages such as languages provided by *TinyDB* (Madden, Franklin, Hellerstein, & Hong, 2005), *Cougar* (Yao & Gehrke, 2002), *TinyLIME*(Curino et al., 2005), and *TeenyLIME*(Costa, Mottola, Murphy, & Picco, 2007), allow programmers to describe what kind of data they require and how this data is supposed to be processed to produce a context. These languages each take different approaches to abstraction. For example, *TinyDB* and Cougar abstract the WSN as a relational database and provide SQL-like languages, whereas *TinyLIME* and *TeeneyLIME* abstract the WSN as a tuple space and provide tuple-query languages. Figure 3 shows a sample task description written in the language provided by *TinyDB*. The description produces an average of temperature value measured by all sensors on the 4th floor.

The data-level languages focus not on how to measure data, but on what to measure. Therefore

the concrete behaviors of nodes in the WSN are managed by the middleware and remain transparent to programmers. There are many ways to derive the required data processing functionality. The middleware may support a set of behaviors selected from potentially adequate functionality. An example of task description in TinyDB is shown below.

SELECT AVG(temp)
FROM sensors
WHERE roomId=5
SAMPLE PERIOD 10S

To handle the task, TinyDB manages a tree-based network topology to route the measured data (i.e. the temperature) and aggregates (i.e. the average) the data along the routing tree. However, the programmer cannot change this concrete routing behavior to alternate ones for the purpose of optimization.

Group-Level Languages

Group-level languages such as languages provided by *EnviroTrack*(Abdelzaher et al., 2004), *Hood*(Whitehouse, Sharp, Brewer, & Culler, 2004), *Abstract Region*(Welsh & Mainland, 2004), and *DFuse*(Kumar et al., 2003) allow the programmer to describe macro level behaviors for a group of nodes to achieve the desired data processing functionality in a WSN. A programmer usually defines conditions of nodes to form a group. The condition is defined by the number of hops from the node closest to the target in the case of *EnviroTrack*, physical distances in the case of *Hood* and *Abstract Region*, or the battery level, equipped sensor types, or bandwidth in the case of *DFuse*.

Moreover, a programmer can define macro-behaviors of a group by assigning roles to the nodes in a group. For example, EnviroTrack provides two roles: *member role* to measure data and *leader role* to aggregate or fuse data retrieved from member nodes through a cluster-based network topology. Some language allows a programmer to describe the network topology between the roles. For example, *Hood*, *Abstract Region*, and *Dfuse* allow the programmer to specify a topology such as geographic, planar mesh, spanning tree, or more complex topology.

The group-level languages provide a more concrete view of the WSN to the programmer compared to the data-level languages. Therefore, a task written in a group-level language can be optimized more effectively but that in turn requires knowledge about more detailed node behaviors in the WSN.

Node-Level Languages

Middleware such as *Squawk*(Simon & Cifuentes, 2005), *Agilla*(Fok, Roman, & Lu, 2005), *ActorNet*(Kwon, Sundresh, Mechitov, & Agha, 2006) provide node-level languages. The node-level languages allow a programmer to describe the behavior of a task running on a single node.

Squawk provides the Java programming language to define the behavior of a node. *Agilla* and *ActorNet* provide mobile agent-based languages to describe a task that can migrate from one node to another.

Node-level languages provide a more concrete view of the WSN to the programmer than group-level languages. Since they program behaviors of each node directly, a task written in a node-level language can be optimized more than one written in a group-level language. However, the burden of the programmer increases.

The Solution of the XAC Project

Existing language have different levels of abstraction. The data-level languages provide the most abstract, and the node-level languages provide the most concrete view of a WSN. The level of abstraction constitutes a tradeoff between description cost and room for optimization. A higher abstraction reduces description cost, but reduces room for optimization at the same time. An adequate level of optimization also depends on non-functional requirements of the tasks.

Existing solutions each provide only one language with a fixed level of abstraction. For example, TinyDB only supports spanning tree-based network topologies, and does not allow a programmer to use other network topologies such as planar mesh based topologies or cluster-based topologies. From the point of view of resource consumption, an adequate topology depends on characteristics of a task to be implemented, such as the geographical space to be covered by the task, type of data the task measures, etc. Therefore, the programmer has to carefully adopt an adequate network topology to optimize resource consumption. Group-level or data-level languages allow this, but the data-level languages hide network topology from the programmer.

The XAC project provides languages with multi-level abstractions. We provide data-level, group-level, and node-level languages so that a programmer can choose an adequate level of abstraction. An adequate level of abstraction may depend on the knowledge level of the programmer and on non-functional requirements of his tasks, such as resource consumption, response time, or the accuracy of their results. Moreover we are trying to find a proper model transformation for task development (Figure 3). A task described at an abstract level should be transformable into a concrete one. A task at the data-level may be transformed into a corresponding task at the group-level that achieves the data processing functionality described in the data-level task with basic protocols necessary for group management, and a task at the group-level may be transformed into a corresponding task at the node-level that achieves macro-behaviors described in the group-level task.

A transformed model should have enough information to be executed in the WSN. If needed, a programmer should be able to optimize behaviors at arbitrary levels to fulfill non-functional requirements. We can apply suitable optimization patterns regarding data processing at the data-level, that of topology, routing, and in-network aggregation in a group at the group-level, and that of duty-cycling or network device management at the node-level, to achieve desirable accuracy levels of the results, and to decrease the resource consumption. For example, consider the scenarios S2 and S4 specified in Figure 2. Both S2 and S4 require locations of people near a target location, but S4 requires higher accuracy for its result than S2. From the viewpoint of data processing, simple localization in which sensors detect a radio signal from beacons people carry is enough for S2, but sophisticated localization such as one based on RSSI (Radio Signal Strength Indication) that sensors measure to determine locations are required for S4. If such an RSSI based method is applied at the data processing level, the accuracy and resource consumption depend on group-level behavior such as the number of nodes that measure the RSSI, the routing topology in a group, and on in-network aggregation techniques.

The XAC project has been tackling these research issues regarding model-driven development of tasks in WSN. We analyzed descriptive capabilities of existing languages, and constructed a reference model for each level of abstraction. Moreover, we aggregated optimiza-

tion patterns at each level, and transformation patterns from abstract levels to more concrete levels to support optimization and manual model transformation(Tei, Fukazawa, & Honiden, 2007). In the near future we will construct transformation rules and development processes according to model transformation and optimization patterns. Moreover, we will propose verification methods to ensure the consistency between models at each level in order to guarantee that behaviors written in higher-level descriptions hold after optimizations are made at lower-levels.

Runtime Task Management

Sensing tasks have to be assigned to specific nodes for execution, resulting in the necessity to manage such resource allocations. A very general approach taken in early days of wireless sensor networks was to assign tasks to certain nodes by physically connecting each node to a base station and deploying specific tasks in form of installing code modules to the nodes. This made changing tasks or assigning new tasks after deploying the sensor nodes a tedious task requiring the physical retrieval of the nodes in question. Nowadays nodes are being reprogrammed by deploying tasks dynamically over the wireless communication channel.

Existing Solutions

Reprogramming techniques can be divided into two distinct approaches.

- Managed by the base station
- Managed by the tasks

Task Deployment Management by Base Station
In case the base station centrally manages tasks deployment, it becomes necessary to decide whether tasks are disseminated to the whole network or only sent to specific nodes. For instance,

in scenario S1 of Figure 2, the tasks need only be deployed to nodes inside rooms that need their temperature managed, while in S3 the sensing tasks must be deployed on all sensor nodes throughout the building. Assuming that changes for instance in the sensing conditions and task settings make updating the tasks of S1 and S3 necessary, we need to consider which range of nodes are affected, namely only specific nodes as in the case of S1, or all nodes as in S3.

One representative existing solution for managing tasks at the base station by specifying a certain range of nodes for updates is Deluge(Hui & Culler, 2004). Deluge allows the user to optionally define specific node IDs to limit the dissemination of tasks throughout the network. To cope with the energy and communication restraints of wireless sensor nodes, Deluge proposes the below approaches to improve efficiency.

- by adjusting transmission intervals dynamically, congestion in areas of high node density is avoided.
- asymmetric links are handled by selectively using stable nodes.
- by introducing the concept of communication rounds, broadcast storms between nodes are avoided.

Deluge sends the complete code necessary to execute a task from the base station to the nodes. This method is inefficient in so far as it induces high transfer costs that drain the node batteries. To address this issue, other solutions deploy code bases shared among different tasks preliminary, so that only task specific updates need to be transferred in case task changes become necessary. A representative example of this approach is Mate(Levis & Culler, 2002). Mate provides a virtual machine (VM) on each node that can execute task specific lightweight code. Its VM is based on a byte code interpreter that uses 1 byte per byte code. As such, a script consisting of 100 lines amounts only to 100 bytes to be transferred.

Mate doesn't allow to specify certain deployment ranges, but the recent revision of Trickle(Levis, Patel, Culler, & Shenker, 2004) provides exactly that functionality.

Self-Adaptive Task Deployment Management

In case tasks manage themselves autonomously but are deployed from the base station, the base station is always responsible for distributing tasks to the nodes. In this approach – if it is impossible to preliminarily deploy all tasks to all nodes - changes in the locations to execute certain tasks make it necessary to redeploy the tasks from the base station. For example in the previously described scenario S4 in Figure 2, if the goods to be monitored are moved, the tasks have to be redeployed to the nodes in the vicinity of the goods' new location every time. This results in a heavy traffic load especially on nodes around the base station. If the tasks can manage and also redeploy themselves by moving autonomously, that burden can be alleviated. [1]

In face of this aspect the research community has come up with a number of solutions. Representative examples are Agilla(Fok et al., 2005), ActorNet(Kwon et al., 2006). Agilla extends Mate VM and gives tasks the ability to move throughout the network. Tasks in Agilla are based on a 1–2 byte ISA(Instruction Set Architecture) and thus provide lightweight task codes similar to Mate. Agilla can also conduct intra-task communication based on a distributed tuple space(Gelernter, 1985).

ActorNet introduces the actor model to wireless sensor networks and executes each actor on its scheme interpreter. It further provides a virtual memory space, scheduling of I/O to the scheme interpreter and garbage collection functionality.

The Solution of the XAC Project

The XAC project assumes a wireless sensor network to be an open networking environment that can be utilized by multiple and arbitrary us-

Figure 4. Example scenario based on GDD

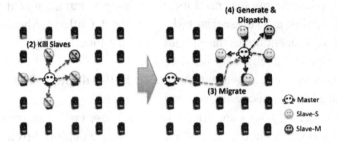

ers. Under this assumption, it becomes unlike in traditional wireless sensor networks commonplace for users to add/change/delete tasks. [2]

Furthermore, as described in scenario S4 of Figure 2, tasks may change their execution location. As a consequence, we focused on task-based autonomous deployment management as discussed in the previous section. The existing solutions allow tasks to be comprised of multiple components running on different nodes. For instance, in case of scenario S1 of Figure 2 (temperature management), the task of measuring temperature can be assigned to a certain number of components running on specific nodes inside a room. However, the relocation and dynamic reconstruction of multiple components is not possible in existing solutions and remained a problem to be addressed. We focused on that case of managing tasks comprised of multiple components.

Multiple Components Relocation

Our relocation mechanism called GDD (Generative Dynamic Deployment) of multiple components (Suenaga et al., 2009) provides its functionality as a middleware. GDD consists of an architecture to relocate multiple components and a novel relocation method. Past solutions did not offer any architecture for deployable components and thus the reliability of the relocation process itself was not given. GDD proposes an architecture comprised of three component types (Master, Slave-S, Slave-M) that ensure the reliability of component relocation. Generally speaking, if com-

ponents are to execute a relocation task and need to communicate among each other to coordinate that task, the reliability of relocation declines. To address this problem, GDD proposes making Master components reconstruct other component types (Slave-S, Slave-M) on demand and only Master components actually relocate, thus resulting in better reliability of relocation. The Master component is also responsible for deleting Slave-S and Slave-M components before relocation.

Figure 4 shows a relocation example scenario based on GDD.

1. Master, Slave-S and Slave-M components are deployed.
2. The Master component deletes Slave-S and Slave-M components if relocation becomes necessary.
3. The Master component moves to the new target location.
4. The Master component, upon relocating, reconstructs Slave-S and Slave- M components and deploys them on nearby nodes.

By repeating this process, task execution can be continued at arbitrary locations inside the network. By using GDD, the applicability of tasks comprised of multiple components is increased.

Dynamic Components Reconstruction

Dynamic component reconstruction as proposed by Platon et al. (Platon, Suenaga, Yoshioka, & Honiden, 2008) also deploys tasks as multiple

Figure 5. Example scenario based on Ragillat

(1) Fail   (2) Leader Election   (3) Recovery

components and adapts the redeployment to the state of nodes through their proposed Ragilla middleware. In existing solutions, the depletion of node batteries or malfunctions of nodes in general caused tasks comprised of components running on such nodes to fail fulfilling their requirements. Ragilla on the other hand allows defining relocation conditions for components (by number of components, geographical areas, battery level) that control the relocation and reconstruction process of each component by maintaining the operational conditions required by the component.

For instance, as illustrated in Figure 5, if a hardware failure occurs, the following steps make it possible to reconstruct the component dynamically at a node within a specified geographical range and continue its sensing task.

1. Due to hardware failure, the node hosting a leader component ceases operation.
2. The middleware detects the hardware failure and selects the next leader out of a number of candidate nodes.
3. The middleware also maintains a copy of the leader component and deploys it to the selected new node.

By using this method, it becomes possible to improve task execution by reconstructing tasks while maintaining the user's requirements.

Current efforts of the XAC project are not limited to GDD and Ragilla, but aim to provide relocation functionality that adapts dynamically to network conditions, for instance by modeling the role distribution of tasks comprised of multiple components in more detail and making proper deployment decisions based on such component roles.

Self-Adaptability

In a WSN, situation inside a node, such as the calculation resource and the amount of the battery, may change at time. Moreover, situation outside a node, such as movement of target and change in communication environment, may change too. In response to these changes of situation, behavior of a task can be optimized using programmer's intention. However, if the programmer's instruction is required every time the situation changes, the programmer's load grows. Then, the part where the middleware can be judged self-adapts on the middleware side, and can reduce the programmer's load.

Existing Solutions

An existing research researches the self-adaptability of the following points.

Self-Adaptability for the Change Inside the Node

When some tasks are executed at the same time on the same node, the processing performance is insufficient because the processing resource of the node is scarce. If each task uses nodes at its choice, the resource competition is generated on the node and the task cannot be executed. As described in the section about runtime task management, it is important that one task use some nodes to improve the quality of the observation. Therefore, the resource competition in the node is frequently occurred in open WSN.

To avoid the resource competition, the research on the decision of the node that task uses and the decision of scheduling of the sensor becomes important. In these researches, it is necessary to decide the node that the task uses and the schedule of the sensor in consideration of the demand of the task. Literatures (Heinzelman, Murphy, Carvalho, & Perillo, 2004; Dunkels, Finne, Eriksson, & Voigt, 2006) are the research on the arrangement decision of the task.

Self-Adaptability for the Change Outside the Node

In the pervasive environment, the task should change the node used according to the situation. In such environment, the situation in surroundings of the node that operates the task changes like the density of node and the communication link between nodes. Moreover, the situation in the node surroundings changes by moving the object and the obstacle also on the same node. To obtain the quality demanded from the task, it is necessary to change the algorithm and the parameter used by the task responding to the situation.

For such a problem, an existing research adjusts the parameter of the communication algorithm responding to the situation(Sohrabi, Gao, Ailawadhi, & Pottie, 2000; W. Ye, Heidemann, & Estrin, 2002; Rajendran, Obraczka, & Garcia-Luna-Aceves, 2006). For instance, when each node cannot communicate with the node on the routing tree, it is possible to adjust to the situation by restructuring the tree with other node that can communicate.

The Solutions of the XAC Project

The XAC project tackles the following research issues related to the self-adaptability.

Self-adaptability for the Change Inside the Node

The XAC project researches composition of minimum node group that meets demand of task(Nakamura, Tei, Fukazawa, & Honiden, 2008), and the middleware of task evacuation management for resource competition(Ishiguro, Tei, Fukazawa, & Honiden, 2006).

In WSN, the task with different required accuracy and priority exist together like the scenario described in Figure 2. Moreover, these tasks have the requirement. For instance, (S2) should be disposed to all rooms, (S1, S3) should be disposed to the room where the person exists. In the middleware of task evacuation management, tasks are disposed based on such a requirement, and the one with lower priority of each task is moved to another node when the competition is not avoided. By using this middleware, the resource competition of the task can be suppressed. When the resource competition was happened, the middleware judge whether the task can execute processing on another node or not, and evacuate the task.

Self-Adaptability for the Change Outside the Node

As self-adaptability to changes in the environment, the XAC project does the research to which the communication algorithm is changed responding to the environment. When the environment around the node changes depending on the factor like the movement of the object, the reliability and the communication traffic can be improved by selecting the appropriate algorithm for the environment. For instance, in the task of reporting on employee's present place, the report comes from the node of various rooms when the employee is in a separate place. Oppositely, the report comes frequently from the same node when most employees are in a meeting in the same room. When the report frequency is different like this, the middleware can switch network protocol, such as routing or MAC protocol, to suitable one, in order to reduce communication cost.

Moreover, the XAC project researches concerning the parameter adjustment in the algorithm. The communication traffic can be suppressed by aggregating data in the group when the report is received from the node group. Then, an appropriate node and the method in the data aggregating are researched to communicate efficiently. By this research, we can do the data aggregation and communication efficiently when routing algorithm is changed.

When the environment around the node changes, these researches can change the algorithm to the appropriate one for the environment, and the quality of the task can be improved.

Security

For the practical operation of WSN security issues need to be addressed as well. In case of intrusion detection applications for instance, it can be assumed that an attacker will also try to compromise the WSN itself to make it unable to detect suspicious activities. In this section, security issues that are specific to WSN are presented, as well as related work and future issues being discussed.

Security Issues in WSN

In WSN, third parties with malicious intent can physically access sensor nodes. In many cases however, nodes don't have tamper-resistant hardware due to cost limitations. Thus, an attacker can attain data from a compromised sensor node including its secret keys. This *Node Compromis-*

ing Attack makes it difficult to solve security problems in WSN.

Furthermore, since nodes are battery powered, it is necessary to reduce the amount of message traffic and computation as much as possible. To reduce computational costs of security mechanisms, a number of open issues exist. Although public key systems are widely used in conventional networks, their overhead in computation compared to common key systems make them unsuitable to be used in WSN. Another problem is that WSN nodes tend to break easily, making it a necessity for security methods to be fault-tolerant and operate despite such cases of node failures.

Attacks in WSN

The following kinds of attacks can be carried out against each of the three aspects of security: confidentiality, integrity, and availability,

- Confidentiality: Eavesdropping on intra-node communications
- Integrity: Falsification of messages (Marti, Giuli, Lai, & Baker, 2000), or injection of false messages (Yu & Guan, 2006)
- Availability: DoS attacks by making up a large number of messages, dropping messages (Ganesan, Govindan, Shenker, & Estrin, 2001), or inserting incorrect routing information (Khalil, Bagchi, & Shroff, 2007)

Moreover, node replicating attacks (compromising one node and then replicating it by using data extracted from the compromised node (Conti, Di Pietro, Mancini, & Mei, 2007; Parno, Perrig, & Gligor, 2005)) or attacks by giving false location information to nodes when multiple node cooperate to determine location information (Ekici, McNair, & Al-Abri, 2008) can also be used as a base for the above attacks.

Existing Solutions

Confidentiality

Confidentiality against eavesdropping can be kept by encrypted communication using a key that is shared among certain neighbor nodes as long as none of the nodes has been compromised. A lot of work on distributing keys to nodes has been presented in (Chan, Perrig, & Song, 2003; Du, Deng, Han, Chen, & Varshney, 2004; Du, Deng, Han, & Varshney, 2003). If intermediate nodes do not need to read messages, the sending node may encrypt the message with a key it shares with the base station.

Integrity

Sending multiple messages on different routes can be effective to some extent against interpolation (Deb, Bhatnagar, & Nath, 2003; Ganesan et al., 2001). It is necessary to reduce the number of messages as much as possible while keeping the rate of messages arriving at the base station. By adding message authentication codes to messages using the key shared with the base station, falsified messages can be detected. Since it can be assumed that nodes close to each other retrieve similar environmental information in WSN, the base station can to some extent verify messages that have been send by a group of nodes reporting a certain event.

Availability

To protect networks from DoS attacks made of a large number of false messages, it is necessary to detect false messages on intermediate nodes. Multiple methods to distribute keys have been presented in (F. Ye, Luo, Lu, & Zhang, 2005; Yu & Guan, 2006). To detect dropped messages, which is the same as detecting falsified messages, sending multiple messages on multiple routes is an effective mean. Against the insertion of false routing information, existing techniques can be used for wireless networks, such as the cost effective one presented in (Khalil et al., 2007).

The Solutions of the XAC Project

Most of past security methods in WSN are limited in their applicability only to the respective issues they address. For example to detect suspicious individuals, it is necessary to deliver a message created by the node that detected the suspicious person to the base station as fast as possible. Sending multiple messages on multiple routes is necessary for detecting message falsification or message drops as mentioned in the last section. However, such an approach makes it easy for an adversary to conduct DoS attacks.

The XAC project proposed a method for detecting nodes that initiated DoS attacks with less amount of traffic than existing research has proposed (Sei & Honiden, 2007, 2008). However, since this method only works after a certain number of false messages have reached the base station, it is unable to detect DoS attacks immediately.

The following problems exist in past methods for detecting false messages at intermediary nodes. When more than a certain threshold number of nodes are compromised, it is impossible to detect (F. Ye et al., 2005; Yu & Guan, 2006). Furthermore, it is necessary to restrict the route from the node that sent a message to the base station (Yang, Ye, Yuan, Lu, & Arbaugh, 2005). In the latter case, if one of the intermediary nodes fails or is compromised, messages cannot reach the base station. Moreover, the efficiency of sending messages is limited due to the restrictions of the multiple routes. The XAC project proposed a method to solve these problems (Sei & Honiden, 2009), one that can detect false messages in earlier stages.

As discussed above, the main goal of the XAC project regarding security is that valid messages reach the base station fast and unfailingly. We are currently investigating the problem of how to protect the WSN from DoS attacks while making it possible to send messages on multiple arbitrary routes.

Figure 6. Architecture of prototype implementation

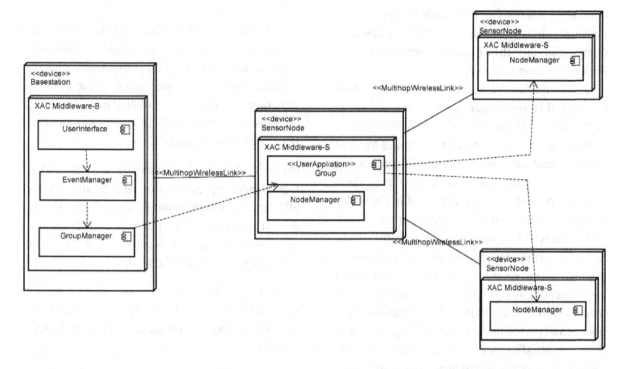

INTRODUCTION OF XAC MIDDLEWARE

In XAC project, we are developing a middleware for wireless sensor network adopting the results of research that we introduced in the section about research issues for open WSN middleware. We release a prototype version implemented on the SunSPOT (the sensor node Sun Microsystems developed) in September, 2009, at our site(*XAC project*, 2009). In the prototype version, it possesses the group-level task description language and the task placement function at the time of use. We are going to add the task description language of plural levels, the task replacement function at the time of use, self-adaptability, and security function, step by step.

A Summary of Prototype Implementation

In Figure 6, it shows the constitution of XAC middleware for prototype version. The XAC Middleware consists of middleware working on the basestation (XACMiddleware-B) and middleware working on the sensor nodes (XAC-Middleware-S).

A task is injected through, and managed by XACMiddleware-B. XACMiddleware-B consists of three components: UserInterface, EventManager and GroupManager. UserInterface component is responsible for performing the registration and deletion of task, and that of handler for event, the results of task measured. Event handler is managed by EventManager component, and task is managed by GroupManager component. GroupManager component generates Group components corresponding to the task and posts them on sensor nodes and start measurement processing. Group component is responsible for producing an event when measurement data satisfies the appointed condition, and notify it to EventManager component through GroupManager. Then EventManager component starts the handler corresponding to the kind of the event.

XACMiddleware-S consists of components of Group and NodeManager component. In Group, both the condition of nodes to place Group component, nodes to measure data and kind of measurement data, and data unification processing are described. Group is generated by GroupManager component, and then deployed in the nodes that satisfy the condition programmer appointed. Group finds and selects nodes to satisfy the condition of measurement, and gives the measurement requests of necessary data to the NodeManager component of nodes to fall under. Group collects the measurement results from NodeManager component and performs data unification processing. If the data satisfies the appointed condition, Group regards it as occurrence of event and notifies it to GroupManager component.

CONCLUSION

A WSN is a key technology to pervasive computing. Middleware approach is quite effective to reduce cost to develop measurement tasks for a WSN. Our XAC project aims to develop a middleware, in order to enable a WSN to be shared among multiple context-aware applications. In this chapter, we overview research issues related to a middleware for such an open WSN, from the viewpoint of task description language, runtime task management, self-adaptability, and security. Moreover, we show unsolved problems and our research to clarify contributions of XAC project to these problems.

We are developing a middleware adopting research results of XAC project. Current middleware is just a prototype, but adopts research results step-by-step. The middleware is going to be released at our site (*XAC project*, 2009).

REFERENCES

Abdelzaher, T., Blum, B., Cao, Q., Chen, Y., Evans, D., George, J., et al. (2004). Envirotrack: Towards an environmental computing paradigm for distributed sensor networks. In the 24th international conference on distributed computing systems (ICDCS) (p. 582-589). Washington, DC: IEEE Computer Society.

Boulis, A., Han, C.-C., & Srivastava, M. B. (2003). Design and implementation of a framework for efficient and programmable sensor networks. In the 1st international conference on mobile systems, applications and services (MobiSys) (pp. 187–200). New York: ACM Press.

Chan, H., Perrig, A., & Song, D. (2003). Random key predistribution schemes for sensor networks. In IEEE symposium on security and privacy (pp. 197–213).

Conti, M., Di Pietro, R., Mancini, L., & Mei, A. (2007). A randomized, efficient, and distributed protocol for the detection of node replication attacks in wireless sensor networks. In the eight ACM international symposium on mobile ad hoc networking and computing (MobiHoc), (pp. 80–89).

Costa, P., Mottola, L., Murphy, A. L., & Picco, G. P. (2007). Programming wireless sensor networks with the teenylime middleware. In the ACM/IFIP/USENIX 2007 international conference on middleware (Middleware) (pp. 429–449). New York: Springer-Verlag, Inc.

Curino, C., Giani, M., Giorgetta, M., Giusti, A., Murphy, A. L., & Picco, G. P. (2005, mar). TinyLime: Bridging mobile and sensor networks through middleware. In *the 3rd IEEE international conference on pervasive computing and communications (PerCom)* (pp. 61–72). Washington, DC: IEEE Computer Society. Available from http://www.inf.unisi.ch/murphy/Papers/percom05.pdf

Deb, B., Bhatnagar, S., & Nath, B. (2003). Reinform: Reliable information forwarding using multiple paths in sensor networks. In 28th annual IEEE international conference on local computer networks (LCN) (pp. 406–415).

Du, W., Deng, J., Han, Y. S., Chen, S., & Varshney, P. K. (2004). A key management scheme for wireless sensor networks using deployment knowledge. In the 23rd conference on computer communications (INFOCOM).

Du, W., Deng, J., Han, Y. S., & Varshney, P. K. (2003). A pairwise key pre-distribution scheme for wireless sensor networks. In the 10th ACM conference on computer and communications security (pp. 42–51).

Dunkels, A., Finne, N., Eriksson, J., & Voigt, T. (2006). Run-time dynamic linking for reprogramming wireless sensor networks. In the 4th international conference on embedded networked sensor systems (SenSys) (pp. 15–28). New York: ACM Press.

Ekici, E., McNair, J., & Al-Abri, D. (2008). Secure probabilistic location verification in randomly deployed wireless sensor networks. *Ad Hoc Networks*, 6(2), 195–209. doi:10.1016/j.adhoc.2006.11.006

Fok, C.-L., Roman, G.-C., & Lu, C. (2005). Rapid development and flexible deployment of adaptive wireless sensor network applications. In the 25th IEEE international conference on distributed computing systems (ICDCS) (pp. 653–662). Washington, DC: IEEE Computer Society.

Ganesan, D., Govindan, R., Shenker, S., & Estrin, D. (2001). Highly-resilient, energy-efficient multipath routing in wireless sensor networks. *SIGMOBILE Mobile Computing and Communications Review*, 5(4), 11–25. doi:10.1145/509506.509514

Gelernter, D. (1985). Generative communication in linda. *ACM Transaction on Programming Language and Systems*, 7(1), 80–112. doi:10.1145/2363.2433

Heinzelman, W. B., Murphy, A. L., Carvalho, H. S., & Perillo, M. A. (2004). Middleware to support sensor network applications. *IEEE Network*, 18(1), 6–14. doi:10.1109/MNET.2004.1265828

Hui, J. W., & Culler, D. (2004). The dynamic behavior of a data dissemination protocol for network programming at scale. In the 2nd international conference on embedded networked sensor systems (SenSys) (pp. 81–94). New York: ACM Press.

Ishiguro, M., Tei, K., Fukazawa, Y., & Honiden, S. (2006). A sensor middleware for lightweight relocatable sensing programs. In International conference on computational intelligence for modelling, control and automation (CIMCA) (p. 195). Washington, DC: IEEE Computer Society.

Khalil, I., Bagchi, S., & Shroff, N. B. (2007). Liteworp: Detection and isolation of the wormhole attack in static multihop wireless networks. *Computer Networks*, 51(13), 3750–3772. doi:10.1016/j.comnet.2007.04.001

Kumar, R., Wolenetz, M., Agarwalla, B., Shin, J., Hutto, P., Paul, A., et al. (2003). Dfuse: a framework for distributed data fusion. In the 1st international conference on embedded networked sensor systems (SenSys), (pp. 114–125). New York: ACM Press.

Kwon, Y., Sundresh, S., Mechitov, K., & Agha, G. (2006). Actornet: an actor platform for wireless sensor networks. In the fifth international joint conference on autonomous agents and multiagent systems (AAMAS), (pp. 1297–1300). New York: ACM Press.

Levis, P., & Culler, D. (2002). MatÅLe: a tiny virtual machine for sensor networks. In the 10th international conference on architectural support for programming languages and operating systems (ASPLOS) (pp. 85–95). New York: ACM Press.

Levis, P., Patel, N., Culler, D., & Shenker, S. (2004). Trickle: a self-regulating algorithm for code propagation and maintenance in wireless sensor networks. In the 1st conference on symposium on networked systems design and implementation (NSDI) (pp. 15–28). Berkeley, CA: USENIX Association.

Madden, S. R., Franklin, M. J., Hellerstein, J. M., & Hong, W. (2005). Tinydb: an acquisitional query processing system for sensor networks. *ACM Transactions on Database Systems, 30*(1), 122–173. doi:10.1145/1061318.1061322

Marti, S., Giuli, T. J., Lai, K., & Baker, M. (2000). Mitigating routing misbehavior in mobile ad hoc networks. In the seventh annual international conference on mobile computing and networking (MobiCom) (pp. 255–265).

Nakamura, Y., Tei, K., Fukazawa, Y., & Honiden, S. (2008). Region-based sensor selection for wireless sensor networks. In the 2008 IEEE international conference on sensor networks, ubiquitous, and trustworthy computing (SUTC) (pp. 326–331). Washington, DC: IEEE Computer Society.

Parno, B., Perrig, A., & Gligor, V. (2005). Distributed detection of node replication attacks in sensor networks. In IEEE symposium on security and privacy (pp. 49–63).

Platon, E., Suenaga, S., Yoshioka, N., & Honiden, S. (2008). Transparent application lifetime management in wireless sensor networks. In Demo track of the 10th international conference on ubiquitous computing (Ubicomp).

Rajendran, V., Obraczka, K., & Garcia-Luna-Aceves, J. J. (2006). Energyefficient, collisionfree medium access control for wireless sensor networks. *Wireless Networks, 12*(1), 63–78. doi:10.1007/s11276-006-6151-z

Satyanarayanan, M. (2001). Pervasive computing: Vision and challenges. *IEEE Personal Communications, 8*(4), 10–17. doi:10.1109/98.943998

Sei, Y., & Honiden, S. (2007). Resilient security for false event detection without loss of legitimate events in wireless sensor networks. In the 9th international symposium on distributed objects, middleware, and applications (DOA) (pp. 454–470). Berlin: Springer.

Sei, Y., & Honiden, S. (2008). Distributed detection of node replication attacks resilient to many compromised nodes in wireless sensor networks. In the 4th international wireless internet conference (WICON).

Sei, Y., & Honiden, S. (2009). Reporter node determination of replicated node detection in wireless sensor networks. In the 3rd international conference on ubiquitous information management and communication (ICUIMC) (pp. 566–573). New York: ACM.

Shnayder, V., Hempstead, M., Chen, B.-r., Allen, G. W., & Welsh, M. (2004). Simulating the power consumption of large-scale sensor network applications. In the 2nd international conference on embedded networked sensor systems (pp. 188–200). New York: ACM Press.

Simon, D., & Cifuentes, C. (2005). The squawk virtual machine: Java on the bare metal. In Companion to the 20th annual ACM sigplan conference on object-oriented programming, systems, languages, and applications (OOPSLA) (pp. 150–151). New York: ACM Press.

Sohrabi, K., Gao, J., Ailawadhi, V., & Pottie, G. J. (2000). Protocols for self-organization of a wireless sensor network. [see also IEEE Wireless Communications]. *Personal Communications, IEEE, 7*(5), 16–27. doi:10.1109/98.878532

Suenaga, S., Yoshioka, N., & Honiden, S. (2009). Generative dynamic deployment of multiple components in wireless sensor networks. In the sixth international conference on wireless on-demand network systems and services (WONS) (p. 197-204).

Tei, K., Fukazawa, Y., & Honiden, S. (2007). Applying design patterns to wireless sensor network programming. In the first international workshop on wireless mesh and ad hoc networks (WiMAN) in conjunction with ICCCN (pp. 1099–1104). Washington, DC: IEEE.

Welsh, M., & Mainland, G. (2004). Programming sensor networks using abstract regions. In the 1st conference on symposium on networked systems design and implementation (NSDI) (p. 29-42).

Whitehouse, K., Sharp, C., Brewer, E., & Culler, D. (2004). Hood: a neighborhood abstraction for sensor networks. In the 2nd international conference on mobile systems, applications, and services (MobiSys) (pp. 99–110). New York: ACM Press.

Xac project. (2009). Retrieved from http://xac-project.jp/index_e.html

Yang, H., Ye, F., Yuan, Y., Lu, S., & Arbaugh, W. (2005). Toward resilient security in wireless sensor networks. In the 6th acm international symposium on mobile ad hoc networking and computing (MobiHoc) (pp. 34–45).

Yao, Y., & Gehrke, J. (2002). The cougar approach to in-network query processing in sensor networks. *SIGMOD Record, 31*(3), 9–18. doi:10.1145/601858.601861

Ye, F., Luo, H., Lu, S., & Zhang, L. (2005, April). Statistical en-route filtering of injected false data in sensor networks. *IEEE Journal on Selected Areas in Communications, 23*(4), 839–850. doi:10.1109/JSAC.2005.843561

Ye, W., Heidemann, J., & Estrin, D. (2002). An energy-efficient mac protocol for wireless sensor networks. In the 21st conference on computer communications (INFOCOM), (pp. 1567–1576). Washington, DC: IEEE.

Yu, Z., & Guan, Y. (2006). A dynamic en-route scheme for filtering false data injection in wireless sensor networks. In the 25th conference on computer communications (INFOCOM), (pp. 1–12).

ENDNOTES

[1] In case the distance between base station and the node where a task is supposed to be redeployed is longer than the distance between the current deployment node and the new deployment location, the cost of moving a task from the current node to the new node is less on average than redeploying the task from the base station.

[2] Wireless sensor networks not capable of deploying all tasks of all users preliminary are also known to commonly suffer from packet loss (Suenaga, Yoshioka, & Honiden, 2009)

Chapter 12
Pervasive Computing Applications, Technologies, and Challenges for E-Health

Thienne Johnson
University of Sao Paulo, Brazil

Eleri Cardozo
State University of Campinas, Brazil

Eliane Gomes Guimarães
Information Technology Center Renato Archer, Brazil

ABSTRACT

The pervasive computing paradigm offers many tools to facilitate health care applications. It allows more robust local and remote monitoring applications, because of many personal acquired contexts that can be used to provide better specialized health services, such as emergency, elderly care, etc. This chapter provides an overview of pervasive environments for eHealth applications. The most common applications and some technologies used to provide pervasive computing environment to collect information for the eHealth applications will be described. Some challenge issues that need research and discussion will be presented, such as security, use of context, user acceptance and performance requirements.

INTRODUCTION

The vision of a pervasive environment is characterized by the use of tiny sensors and other computational devices embedded into everyday objects, working invisibly in the background, collecting information about the environment and the users, and reacting to provide full integration of the user and the environment. Most healthcare applications do not yet behave that way, so there are almost no genuine pervasive computing applications in healthcare today.

Healthcare applications allow the monitoring of people's health through the use of diverse medical sensors in and on the body and the interconnection of these sensors with a monitoring system. In a hospital environment, the patients, nowadays, are still connected to the monitoring systems using sensors installed over the body and are connected to machines by cables, causing much discomfort.

DOI: 10.4018/978-1-61520-843-2.ch012

The pervasive computing paradigm offers many ways to facilitate the monitoring of people, allowing them to move freely while they are monitored by health professionals. Remote monitoring (an aspect of telemedicine) can verify vital signs such as heart rate and pressure, cerebral functioning, etc. This remote monitoring, together with the technologies of pervasive computing, allows the interaction of the environment and its computational resources with the monitored people, supplying means of local interaction in cases of emergency and situations where there are no other people around. So, doctors and medical staff can interact with patients' medical devices to provide help within a shorter timeframe, which can save lives and avoid more damages.

Amongst the new used technologies inside a pervasive computing environment are Wireless Sensors Networks (WSN) (Akyildiz et al, 2002), Body Area Networks (BAN) (Li et al, 2007), and Network Robotics (Moraes et al, 2009; Coelho et al, 2009) that consists of a multitude of networked robots and other devices capable of interacting with the environment through the use of perception and action for the performance of tasks. These technologies offer ways to detect patient's situation contexts (through the acquisition of vital signs, movement, localization, etc). Beyond collecting data, these technologies allow the interaction with medical equipment located in the BAN, through remote access systems, for example, insulin injectors.

The objective of this chapter is to provide an overview of new technologies that can be used to provide better services for eHealth applications in a pervasive environment.

This chapter is divided into more four sections. The second section presents some eHealth applications, and discusses how those applications can be applied to pervasive environments. In the third section, some technologies used to allow pervasive computing environments to collect information for eHealth applications are reviewed, such as sensor networks (and its applications for

BAN), network robotics and remote access. The fourth section is devoted to discussing challenges related to pervasive environments in the context of eHealth applications, such as security and privacy, context and activity awareness, user acceptance, applications performance requirements and network performance requirements. Finally, the fifth section concludes this chapter.

E HEALTH APPLICATIONS

Accordingly to Bednarcikova et al (2008), eHealth stands for "medical informatics, public health and business, referring to health services and information delivered or enhanced through the Internet and related technologies" (p. 283).

Health informatics (eHealth) applications encompass a range of services, such as Electronic Medical Records, Telemedicine, Telepresence and m-Health (mobile Health). Many of them use Electronic Health Records (EHR), which refers to an individual patient's medical record in digital format. EHR may be composed of Electronic Medical Records (EMRs) from many sources, e.g., hospitals and doctors' offices.

In this section we present some eHealth applications and how they can be integrated into pervasive environments.

Telemedicine and Remote Patient Monitoring

Medical telemetry systems, also known as Telemedicine (Liszka et al, 2004) is the use of communications and information technology to deliver clinical care. It can be more cost-effective and convenient for patients, and it is especially attractive for healthcare delivery to remote or underserved populations (Jurik & Weaver, 2008). It has the purpose of consulting, and sometimes remote medical procedures or examinations.

In a pervasive environment, the remote examination could be integrated with many local

Figure 1. Example of patients monitoring application

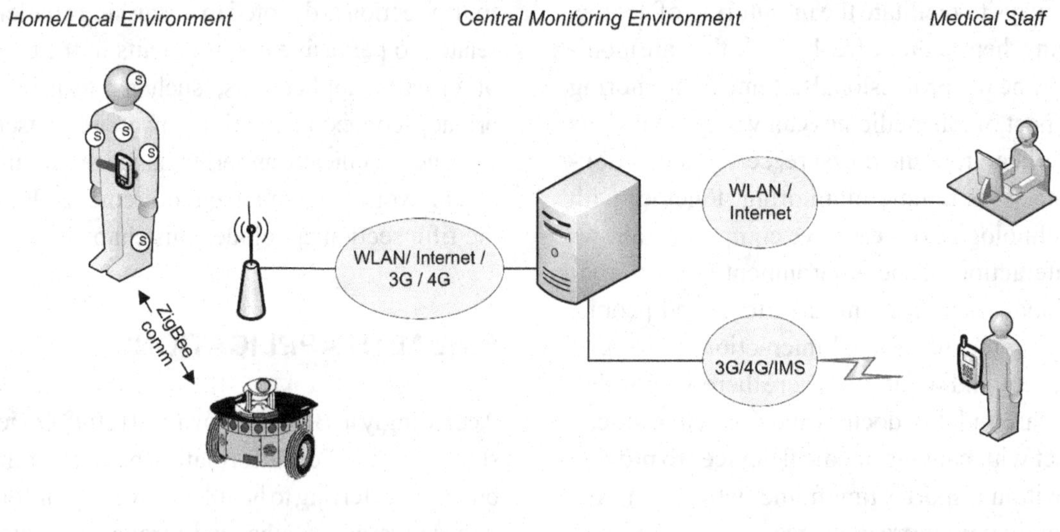

devices, such as cameras, audio, and sensors, to provide more information on the current health status of the patient, as well as information on the physical environment, such as room temperature, that could be relevant. Basic remote patient monitoring applications are the ambulatory (Jovanov et al, 2005) and home (Otto et al, 2006) monitoring, where a patient is continuously monitorated by machines (such as heart beat and arterial pressure), but new technologies such as sensors and wireless communications are now used to allow patient mobility.

Figure 1 shows an example of a pervasive environment for an eHealth application for remote monitoring, using a BAN for the body monitoring, which connects to a central monitoring server (located, for example, in a hospital) by Internet through a WLAN (Wireless Local Area Network) connection or by a robot collecting the sensor's data. Physicians can access the patient's data via Internet (or directly via WLAN if inside the hospital) or via cellular telephony, using 3G/4G (Zahariadis, & Doshi, 2004) or IMS (IP Multimedia Subsystem) (Mosmondor et al, 2006) communications. Contextual information can be also collected, by using sensors in the environment, plus some positioning information obtained from

technologies such as CellID (Meneses & Moreira, 2006), GPS (Bajaj et al, 2002) or WLAN SSIDs (Chen et al, 2005).

In this example environment, besides receiving information on the patients current status, the physicians may setup alerts on patient's conditions, act through actuators (e.g., using a Remote Intelligent Drug Delivery System) and also using the robot to execute some action (for example, if the patient data are not being received, use the robot to look at the patient and starting sending his/hers sensors data, or alerting the Emergency Service if the patient's signals are critical).

There are many examples of remote monitoring applications, such as in-bed monitoring, elderly care, and physical security. An example of remote monitoring was presented by Bustamante et al (2008). In this system, all the movements of an in-bed patient were registered in order to study habitual movements (getting in and out of bed, lying down, leaving the bed, etc.) and unusual actions like the movements preceding a fall, or the fall itself.

The patient's behavior patterns obtained in this study lead to a possible system capable of recognizing the different situations, movements or positions that usually take place, and detect when the in-bed person is in a position that indicates a risk of falling or when the system must sound an alarm in time so that the fall can be avoided. The patient's contexts are obtained by using many kinds of sensors, such as shock, punctual pressure, infrared; also height scales under the bed legs, horizontal vibration detector and a video camera with motion detection.

As people grow older, they experience a steady decline in their cognitive, sensory and motor control functions. Because of these functional declines, elderly people steadily become less able to look after themselves safely (Steele et al, 2006). Pervasive environments allow elder people to maintain their independence by offering assistance as necessary and using pervasive sensors to monitor vital signs and health indicators (Stanford, 2002).

Besides health monitoring, pervasive systems allow movement detection, for example, to prevent the elder to leave some area (such as the family home area or the retirement home area), sending alarms when they are about to leave, or when the elderly keep walking in circles, being disoriented at times and beginning to wander, as in a person with Alzheimer. Being able to identifying each person in an environment, the same technology may improve physical security in hospitals, preventing non-authorized patients from leaving, or preventing baby theft.

Telepresence

Telemedicine may use a robot to let videoconferencing go mobile, allowing a specialist working from a remote location to consult his/her patients (Greenemeier, 2008). The robot may carry a screen to project the doctor's face and voice from speakers, while using digital cameras, microphones, and sensors to receive patients data (video, voice, and vital signals), enabling a telepresence application. The physician may also move the robot through a hospital, to "visit" more patients. The use of an Internet-connected robot lets the doctor communicate with patients in remote areas without specialized physicians, giving patients there access to experts' scores of miles away (Nellis, 2009).

Telepresence technologies and the use of robots by caregivers also enable other telecare practices including tele-rehabilitation, tele-nursing, tele-medicine and tele-psychotherapy (Helal & Abdulrazak, 2006).

Remote Intelligent Drug Delivery System

Drug delivery research looks for more efficient ways to deliver therapies, such as the usage of "pharmacy on a chip". This technology allows microchips, implanted under the skin, to deliver drugs on demand or by remote commands (Cui et al, 2008).

Micro fabricated systems for the drug delivery have become a promising but challenging field in BioMEMS (Micro-Electro-Mechanical Systems for biological applications) due to the commercial and research interest in health care (Qi-feng et al, 2008). A Remote Intelligent Drug Delivery System (RIDDS) focused on the safer and more effective use of drugs by the patients, being the dosages prescribed remotely by physicians and the drugs usage automatically injected by dedicated actuators.

A drug delivery system using BioMEMS contains, on the device, a drug supply (reservoir), micro pumps, valves and sensors (Amer & Badawy, 2005). The sensors will detect the patient's context (vital signals, PH, pressure of tissues, blood, etc.) and it can deliver a dose or some drug amount using the pump or valve.

As an example, Qi-feng et al (2008) developed a delivery system for diabetics, which combines many MEMS devices and components such as micro pumps, micro needle arrays and micro sensors. The advantage of this small system is its ability to automatically inject the right dosages based on patient's physiological information, which can efficiently avoid the heart and neural complications resulting from superfluous injections.

This kind of system is very powerful if combined with some remote monitoring application, which can send alarms if there is any problem on the drug dosage and the patient's sensors data (or behavior) do not follow their expected pattern.

Pervasive Devices

Portable devices, such as cell phones and personal digital assistants (PDAs) play an important role in providing interaction on eHealth applications. For example, smart phones and PDAs may be used as a service gateway for BAN (Morón et al, 2007), collecting sensors data, and sending them to telemonitoring services. Besides acting as information service end points for an information service, portable devices may be used as remote controllers for particular devices in the wireless range and can be also used as ID tokens, when they act as a secure personal device that stores information used to verify user identity and determines when to disclose this information (Roussos et al, 2005).

As the new devices have wireless local area network capabilities, they can roam between a WLAN to a 3G network, thus supporting mobility for the eHealth application (maintaining end-to-end transport connections (Prado et al, 2008)). On the local area, the support for Personal Area Networks (Bluetooth and Zigbee, for example), allows them to interact with another devices in a pervasive environment, such as RF location badges and mobile robots.

Assistive Robot is a technology that plays an increasingly important role in the life of people with special needs. Some examples are smart wheelchairs for smooth navigation, walker assistances that aid users in their movement and tele-manipulator robots that allow users to manipulate objects. These devices are helping people to maintain a higher quality of life by improving work productivity and social activities (Helal & Abdulrazak, 2006).

Devices for eHealth applications also include systems that can even perform surgery, such as a robotic surgical system capable of working with more accuracy than a human surgeon. Accordingly to Geer (2006), "in most cases, patients have recovered more quickly from robotic than conventional surgery. Patient expenses were lower because they left the hospital sooner" (p. 85).

Some Proposals on eHealth Monitoring Systems

Many systems have been considered recently for telemedicine. Generally speaking, MobiHealth (Konstantas & Herzog, 2007), Human++ (Gyselinckx et al, 2005), m-Health (Jovanov et al, 2005), and the systems proposed by Otto et al (2006) and Morón et al (2007), propose remote monitoring systems based on Body Area Networks and their connections to remote servers, using Wi-Fi or cellular networks. They are not integrated into pervasive environments nor do they use contextual information to provide services.

An example of a more complete eHealth system is the iHospital System (Hansen et al, 2006), which supports intense coordination of operations in a large hospital and possesses several pervasive computing characteristics, such as location tracking, a context-awareness system, large interactive displays, and mobile phones.

The Elite Care's Oatfield Estates Cluster (Geer, 2006), created to assist the elderly, uses a pervasive computing infrastructure to help staff identify when seniors actually need assistance using pervasive, but not obtrusive, sensors to monitor vital signs and health indicators. Thus, staff assists residents in maintaining their independence, offering assistance as necessary.

TECHNOLOGIES

There are many technologies which enable pervasive computing environments, such as wireless local area networks, context-aware analyzers, middlewares, etc. This section will review some of the technologies used to collect information for the eHealth applications, such as sensor networks (and its applications to BAN) and network robotics.

Sensors and BAN Networks

Wireless Sensor Networks (WSNs) have gained worldwide popularity, particularly with the proliferation in MEMS technology which has facilitated the development of smart sensors (Yick et al, 2008). The smart sensors, called motes, are small devices generally consisting of a processor, memory, low-power radio, antenna, and power supply. The motes incorporate sensing, computing, and radio capabilities in small form factors with low power requirements (Geer, 2006).

A WSN is composed of a large number of sensor nodes that are deployed either inside the phenomenon or very close to it (Akyildiz et al, 2002). The mass-production of intelligent sensors and the use of pervasive networking technology give WSNs a new kind of scope that can be applied to a wide range of uses, from environmental and habitat monitoring to disaster management (Culler at al, 2004).

Sensor nodes can sense, measure, and gather information from the environment and, based on some local decision process, they can transmit the sensed data to the user, via a node called a sink, which is responsible for interacting with external networks, such as the Internet or 3G. There are static and mobile WSNs, which demonstrate enhanced performance over static wireless sensor networks. Because of the mobility of the sink node, much work can be shared by the mobile sink (Munir et al, 2007).

A subtype of WSNs is a BAN, which are very small-scale communication network, with the range of 2 meters, less than a PAN (Personal Area Network) (Li et al, 2007). Figure 2 shows a comparison of communication ranges among wireless local area networks.

A BAN is a network of several wireless sensors located in the human body or in nearby locations, such as clothing. Due to the low power transmission of wireless devices, the human body can be used as a communications channel between the devices to form a wireless network (Domenicali & Benedetto, 2007).

For eHealth applications, in a hospital environment, patients today are still connected to monitoring equipment by sensors installed on the body, which in turn are connected via cables to the machinery, possibly causing discomfort. With the use of BAN networks, the cables are replaced by wireless communications. The monitor next to the bed should be replaced by a device for collecting data from the sensors, and it can act as a gateway to a central monitoring system. Small devices such as PDAs and cell phones are also considered as gateways for the BAN, and also can be used as the person's vital signals verification unit, so that the mobility of the monitored person is not affected (Drude, 2007) (Figure 3).

Another option to the last scenario is the use of the BAN network in scenarios of WLANs interconnected by a common backbone connected to a network like the Internet, thus providing network coverage throughout the local area where the patient can be monitored, as in a residence or a medical center without the additional cost of using the telephone network.

The current systems are based on BAN and its integration with other communication systems. The technologies of 3G and WLAN (for communication with Internet) are generally considered to communicate with the BAN for remote monitoring point (hospital, doctor, etc.). The use of a cellular telephone network has high costs due to the fact

Figure 2. Wireless networks communication range

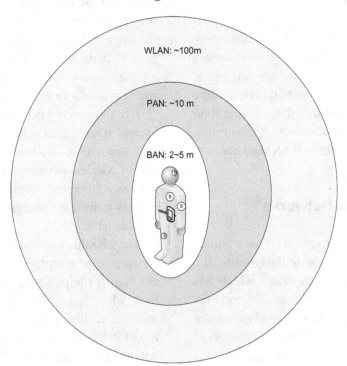

Figure 3. Example of a BAN

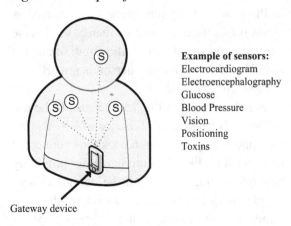

Example of sensors:
Electrocardiogram
Electroencephalography
Glucose
Blood Pressure
Vision
Positioning
Toxins

Gateway device

that applications often require periodic data, but does allow for high mobility of its users.

Commercially available technologies for BAN include Bluetooth, ZigBee and UWB (Ultra Wideband). Bluetooth is a mature technology, which is already integrated in mobile phones and PDAs, enabling communications up to 720kbps, which

is more than enough for eHealth applications. However, the power consumption and complexity of the protocol stack are limiting factors for BAN applications (Jovanov, 2005). ZigBee is an emerging standard for low data rates, low power applications, with data-rates up to 250kbps, sufficient for eHealth monitoring systems. Testing (Sukor et al, 2008) with the ZigBee technology shows that the technology can be successfully used for applications with low data rates. In 2007, IEEE created the standard 802.15 for wireless communication technology within a BAN, which may be deployed in high density in/on a person's body and in the vicinity (Zhen, 2007).

Network Robotics in eHealth

The miniaturization of robotics building blocks makes possible the construction of small and precise mobile robots at a reduced price. At the same time, networking products are becoming cheaper, more powerful, and energy efficient.

By adding to the small mobile robots an efficient communication system we achieve a device that combines the ability to monitor the environment, act on it, and communicate with other networked devices. Network robotics is a recent research field that combines robotics and communication technologies in order to increase the spectrum of applications envolving mobile and stationary robots. A networked robot has the ability to communicate with a human operator (e.g., via a cell phone), with a supervisory system, or with another networked robots in order to perform a cooperative task. Networked robots also increase the coverage of pervasive environments by adding to the sensors the ability to dislocate.

In the area of eHealth, networked robots can help in applications described previously by adding to them the ability to monitor and assist persons at home or hospitals. A mobile robot can perform monitoring tasks close to the patient and to assist him/her in many tasks difficult for a person debilitated by age or disease. A mobile robot can monitor a patient and alarm abnormal situation such as falls and agitation. Once detected, the robot can call emergency services or relatives. A robot can also assist debilitated persons in tasks such as seeking help, delivering drugs, and communication in general (e.g., place phone calls or send short messages with voice commands). Another interesting application is when the robot is inserted in an already automated environment. For instance, the robot can adjust room temperature, turn lights and appliances on and off, and open/close doors and windows. In all of these cases, the robot employs its mobile and communication capabilities in order to perform some action on the environment and/or to communicate with remote entities such as physicians, paramedic services, relatives, or medical recording systems.

Although possibilities of networked robotics in eHealth are endless, challenges exist. Autonomy is one of them. No matter expensive robots employing laser-based navigation systems are able to move autonomously to a dock station and charge their batteries, less equipped robots do not have this capacity yet. Small robots demand conventional battery charging like cell phones and laptop computers. Another challenge is autonomous navigation and its related issues such as pattern recognition (obstacles, aisles, doors, etc.), location (find precisely where the robot is in the environment), and path planning (how to drive the robot to a target point). These activities are computationally intensive and usually exceed the processing power of the robot. Navigation in dynamic environments such as hospitals and homes is another challenging subject for eHealth applications.

Another challenge is human-robot interaction. The robot must be able to interpret simple voice commands (as most modern cell phones do), or to identify hand gestures such as "come here". The robot must be trained to interpret such interactions correctly which requires sophisticated algorithms of speech and image processing. Again, processing power is a major issue for these algorithms. Finally, secure remote access is a key point for networked robotics. As the robot acquires images and other data from patients, privacy must be assured in order to avoid unauthorized access to patient data, both in transit and after storage.

At home, the following scheme for remote access is possible. Most home internet connections employ a wireless access point with a WAN (Wide Area Network) port, four or more Ethernet ports, and a wireless port. Except for the WAN port, the remaining ports are configured with private addresses preventing direct access from external to the devices connected to these ports. Such devices are always clients, that is, they initiate a communication session, never responds to a session initiated from external. Home robots usually employ short range protocols such as Bluetooth or ZigBee, connecting the robot to a more powerful computer (Bluetooth comes with most laptop computers). As these communications are short range, interception is very unlikely to occur. The computer may be permanently connected to a monitoring central employing a secure protocol and authentication. It permanently checks for calls, commands, or messages placed on the central (popular conferencing systems work in this way). This computer also sends videos, messages, and call requests to the central that, in its turn, routes to the callee (physician, relatives, etc.). The robot informs the home computer the information it processes and this computer decides if the central station must be contacted or not. The home computer also communicates with the robot, for instance, when a physician wants to see/listen to the patient.

CHALLENGES

In this section we discuss the following requirements for eHealth applications: standardization, security and privacy, reliability, context and activity-awareness, user acceptance and performance.

Standardization

eHealth applications may need to interact with services offered by multiple organizations, for instance, diagnostic, care, communication, transportation, and health insurance services. In such cases, standardization is of prime importance. Service-oriented architecture (SOA) is a trend for multi-organizational applications. SOA can be implemented with a multitude of technologies, being Web services the most common one. Web services, a comprehensive set of standards from the OASIS (Organization for the Advancement of Structured Information Standards) and W3C (World Wide Web Consortium), are strongly supported by the major industry and open software consortia. On the server side, Web services can be deployed on a wide range of modern and extensible application servers. Such application servers support virtualization, load balancing, programming of new core functions, and a comprehensive set of

functions enabled via configuration. On the client side, Web services are supported by applications running on the desktop or on the Web browser.

Security and Privacy

The protection of the patient and his/her data demands the integration of diverse services to verify the identity of the patients, to protect the confidentiality of the carrier, to guarantee the integrity of sensor data from the initial acquisition to the final storage, and to protect the access to stored or in-transit data (Warren et al, 2005). The trustworthiness of a telemedicine system depends on preventing misoperations/malfunctioning in order to provide continuous and correct service. Equally important are data privacy and integrity. The system must have robust procedures in place to guarantee the ownership of the data that is being recorded and who will have access to those data.

Security attacks on any eHealth system could have serious consequences not only to the patient's privacy but quite possibly also to their survival prospects (MacDonald, 2008). As a consequence, security for eHealth applications, including patients' data privacy, remote access technologies, which systems have access to sensors worn by patients among other potential attack points, are huge security concerns.

eHealth Security and Privacy

An Electronic Healthcare Record (EHR) is the lifelong documentation of a patient's medical history (Slamanig, 2008). This medical data can only be accessed by the patient herself and persons who are directly involved in the treatment of the patient, such as his/her doctors and family. Considering pervasive eHealth applications, which can allow remote access via Internet or other networks to the patient's current status and medical records, it is crucial to prevent attacks on the patient's privacy.

A list of the most common security attacks on eHealth pervasive systems was compiled by Kargl et al (2008), and it includes eavesdropping on medical data, modification of medical data, forging of alarms on medical data, denial of service (overloading the system to make it unusable), non-authorized location tracking of users (privacy infringement that needs to be prevented) and non-authorized activity tracking of users.

As medical information can be in one of three states: storage, transmission, or processing, there are some aspects which should be considered regarding it. These aspects include to identify vulnerabilities and to perform a complete asset/threat/risk analysis; use of strong encryption/decryption algorithm for all data, including names, prescriptions, medications, procedures; user authenticity to reduce the chance of a successful attack; a strong digital signature scheme has to be present to accompany every individual communication taking place; use of secure transmission and secure storage (Adibi & Agnew, 2008); verifying physical security of the server infrastructure; conducting password audits to assure that all default passwords have been changed; auditing the system software to guarantee libraries are up to date; verifying administration of database management systems or other server software, closing any default accounts; recommending regular monitoring of system logs; verifying that no unauthorized software has been installed from outside; closing primitive services such as telnet and FTP; auditing server security from the outside using port scans; and encrypting backups before they leave the medical servers for off-site storage (Stanford, 2002-b).

Security in Remote Access Applications

Security consists basically of procedures related to authentication and authorization. Securing identity is fundamental for e-health applications (MacDonald, 2008). Typical authentication processes rely on username and passwords transferred over a secure protocol such as HTTPS (Hypertext Transfer Protocol Secure).

More elaborate schemes may demand the user to present a certificate issued by the organization to which the user belongs. A certificate is a text identifying the user and digitally signed by the user's organization. Once the user is authenticated, the organization issues a set of credentials with assertions about the user. Credentials are also signed by the organization and inspected on subsequent interactions with the application. Authorization is the process of verifying if an authenticated user is allowed to perform a given action. Authorizations are commonly based on ACLs (Access Control Lists), or policies. A policy can be expressed as a set of condition/action statements (rules).

A policy condition checks many access parameters such as user's identity, credentials, location, resource being accessed, etc. A policy action allows or denies the access to the resource, or lets other policies to decide. For instance, a policy can state that administrative services must be invoked only by users with a credential of administrator. Another example is a policy stating that medical records can be read or modified only by users with credential of health professional.

Security in Networking

Additional security issues arise because almost all pervasive systems use wireless networking in some form (Stanford, 2002) as they are open to several types of attack specific to wireless connectivity. As there are many wireless technologies used in pervasive systems, such as 3G (Elmufti et al, 2007), Bluetooth, cellular phones (Jasemian, 2006), Zigbee, security standards of mobile technology must satisfy the application's security and privacy requirements in order to be adopted as the basis for securing a mobile e-health service (MacDonald, 2008) or a pervasive eHealth system.

Local devices, such as sensors and actuators (e.g., implantable devices), are also a target of these kinds of attacks (Halperin, 2008). As access to the sensors and actuator is quite straightforward via BAN, attackers might modify actuators values (Kargl et al, 2008), thus incurring very high security risks for the patient's life.

Protecting the patient's data requires integration of various services to verify the identity of the holder of the BAN (i.e. user authentication), protecting the confidentiality of the BAN user to establish and maintain secure links between the BAN and the pervasive environment, and also between each individual sensor and the BAN gateway device, maintaining the integrity of data from the sensor's initial acquisition to final storage, and protect access to stored or in-transit data (Warren, 2005).

Authentication is essential. The sensors need to know who they detected so that the information collected is allocated to the correct patient. For a BAN, it is difficult for remote computers to ensure that the sensors are on the correct person without human intervention (Jurik, 2008).

The low computational capacity (Chong et al, 2005) of network nodes (sensors) can be obstacle for data encryption, because of its high processor consumption (and therefore, energy consumption). But there are studies (Wander et al, 2005; Großschädl et al, 2007) which show that for sensors networks, depending on the configuration of the sensor node, some techniques such as authentication and encryption key exchange using optimized software implementations of public key encryption, are viable for devices with low computational power, depending on the frequency of calculations to generate keys.

Reliability

Reliability is a non functional requirement of the application that is difficult to assess. The reliability of a pervasive eHealth system depends on preventing failures so that the system can provide correct and continuous service.

Reliability in eHealth applications can be enhanced by adopting best practices in the design, implementation, and testing phases of the software development process. In the design phase, the adoption of proven architectural patterns strongly favors reliability. Service oriented architectures offer high level of decoupling among the modules (services) and favor evolution (by adding new services) and testing. Implementation of eHealth applications must adopt well established technologies and software infrastructures. Web protocols, application servers, and access from Web browsers are a trend. Finally, testing and quality assurance procedures employing modern methodologies, standards and software tools are of prime importance in eHealth developments.

Context and Activity Awareness

Pervasive eHealth applications must deal with large amounts of information, including patient medical records. There is much contextual information that can be used to guide a pervasive application, such as location, patients' health status, and considering the medical staff, role in the medical center, time of day, and current activity. Patients' health contexts may be obtained by BAN or wearable systems (Kang et al, 2006; Gatzoulis & Iakovidis, 2007), and can include location information, using GPS or wireless networks point of connection.

Activity information could be relevant for many eHealth applications, such as deciding whom to call for help or facilitating access to relevant patient information (Favela et al, 2006). eHealth activity-aware applications can also manipulate resources in a more efficient way and select the one most relevant to the current task (Tentori & Favela, 2008), depending on the activities scheduled for a given room or a physician, for example.

User Acceptance

Another important issue for pervasive eHealth is user acceptance. Users must accept the technology deployed all around him/her, maybe sensors on the body or inside the clothes, and his/her personal information (location, activities, vital signs, etc.) being monitored by other people 24 hours a day. There are some studies on user acceptance, and they obtained some interesting conclusions.

The research by Steel et al (2007) with elderly people found that the elderly see embedded sensor technology as such as preferable to ambient or wearable monitoring. They also expressed a strong desire for some level of control over the system and strongly rejected the use of any camera, video or still. But the elderly did not perceive privacy to be a significant concern because they believed their medical data to contain no value to any third party.

Scheermesser et al (2008) conducted a research on users and medical staff on the use of pervasive technologies. They found that "usefulness, usability, data privacy and accordance with social norms do influence the acceptance of pervasive technologies in healthcare" (p. 212). It was true for patients, physicians, nurses and physiotherapists. Usefulness was the main factor of acceptance. Security was another factor investigated, and they found that in case of emergencies, data privacy is no issue, but in normal cases (non-emergency applications) respecting data privacy is a necessary acceptance factor.

Interestingly, even though we tend to believe pervasive systems technology will be well accepted by medical staff, in the iHospital system (Hansen, 2006), even though the system was well accepted by the staff, the system's developers had some problems with the location tracking system use, because staff tended not to pick up the location chip, and the developers did not find an easy solution to this problem.

Performance Requirements

Finally, eHealth applications must attend performance requirements. With steadily increasing hardware performance, the quality of service

(QoS) offered by the network becomes a bottleneck. QoS consists of a set of control and management functions that allows the network to guarantee some end-to-end metrics such as delay and jitter for the traffic flows generated by the applications. QoS is not assured on large internet backbones as the management in a per flow basis does not scale. A more scalable approach to QoS is traffic priorization where the network establishes relative priorities (classes of services - CoS) for the flows, without reserving resources for each particular flow.

Today's public internet services do not support QoS or CoS. eHealth applications accessed from home or with components installed at home (e.g., robots) must adopt some strategies where QoS and CoS are not supported. In this scenario, a good strategy is to adjust (adapt) part or all the application for working properly with the internet connection available. For example, consider the scenario of a teleoperated mobile robot at home or in the hospital. The delay imposed by the network can be estimated by exchanging probing packets between the robot and the operating station. The application can set the maximum speed of the robot according to this delay in order to favor a stable navigation. It is important to notice that adaptation compensates not only the end-to-end internet connection delay but also the processing power of the communicating devices.

High speed dedicated networks for eHealth are already deployed around the world. Such networks link hospitals, universities, and public health services. As such networks serve few users and applications, QoS and CoS management strategies can be deployed without concerns regarding to scalability. In such networks, applications can exchange high volumes of data (e.g., high quality video and audio) as well as can perform remote actions with real time constraints (e.g., to operate a home robot from a navigation program running on a monitoring center).

FUTURE TRENDS

Pervasive systems for eHealth applications need to meet many requirements, such as colleting patients' local information, storing, and transmitting data to the pervasive environments and/or to a monitoring system. They also need to provide services to the users, thus allowing them to experience the facilities of a pervasive environment, which will be responsible for a better health care, from the patients and the medical staff perspective.

Much research must be carried out on new technologies on medical devices, including sensors and actuators, so many physical parameters can be detected and limitations (communication, battery life, miniaturization, etc.) can be overcome. New medical devices have potential for improved healthcare and long-term cost savings (Geer, 2006). The integration of these devices with pervasive environments must be well defined, so wireless connectivity will not be a limitation to BAN networks integrated with monitoring systems. It includes very strong security mechanisms, privacy concerns, and performance; also standards and regulations are necessary to apply to such devices to be so designed as to optimize both the efficient use of the radio spectrum, and the usefulness of the wireless link in the context of eHealth (Chadwick, 2007).

Future pervasive environments will also include mobile robots, which will interact with patients and devices, to offer new services, such as patient's localization and sensors data collection. They also allow new applications such as medical telepresence. Networked robot technologies need development on robot hardware, so they can have adequate size to be used in home or can walk around a hospital, conducted by a remote doctor. They need integration with sensors networks and multimedia devices, such as cameras and screens to allow a bidirectional conversation between the doctor and the patient. Remote access to BANs and mobile robots must deal with network performance

and restrictions, so network standardization may lead to better applications performance.

The system security is a very demanding topic of research, which includes the local devices, local area network, local pervasive environment and its integration to an external system. Much research must be carried out to provide secure, but also lightweight mechanisms to be implemented in the new devices on a pervasive environment for eHealth.

CONCLUSION

Pervasive eHealth is a very promising area of research and will become very popular in a few years, because of the great importance of health care systems.

This chapter provided an overview of pervasive environments for eHealth applications. In the applications section, the most common proposed applications were described, such as elderly care, in-bed monitoring, telemedicine, and telepresence. In the Technologies section, some technologies used to provide pervasive computing environment to collect information for the eHealth applications were reviewed, such as sensor networks (and its applications for BAN) and network robotics. In the Challenges section, some issues were discussed, such as security and privacy, context and activity awareness, user acceptance, and network performance requirements. Future work on these topics was proposed in the Future Trends section.

REFERENCES

Adibi, S., & Agnew, G. B. (2008). On the diversity of eHealth security systems and mechanisms. In *Engineering in Medicine and Biology Society* (pp. 1478-1481). Vancouver, Canada.

Akyildiz, L. F., Su, W., Sankarasubramaniam, Y., & Cayirci, E. (2002). A Survey on Sensor Networks. *Communications Magazine, 40*(8), 102–114. doi:10.1109/MCOM.2002.1024422

Amer, S., & Badawy, W. (2005). An Integrated Plataform for Bio-Analysis and Drug Delivery. *Pharmaceutical Biotechnology, 6*, 57–64.

Bajaj, R., Ranaweera, S. L., & Agrawal, D. P. (2002). GPS: location-tracking technology. *Computer, 35*(4), 92–94. doi:10.1109/MC.2002.993780

Bednarcikova, L., Petrik, M., Toth, T., Michalikova, M., Krajnak, S., & Zivcak, J. (2008). Informatics in Health Care. In *IEEE International Conference on Computational Cybernetics* (pp. 283-284), Stara Lesna, Slovenia.

Bustamante, P., Guarretxena, N., Solas, G., & Bilbao, U. (2008). In-bed Patients Behaviour Monitoring System. In *International Conference on Biocomputation, Bioinformatics, and Biomedical Technologies* (pp. 1-6), Bucharest, Romania.

Chadwick, P. E. (2007). Regulations and Standards for Wireless applications in eHealth. In *International Conference of Engineering in Medicine and Biology Society*, (pp.6170-6173), Lyon, France.

Chen, K. Y., Refai, J., & H.H. (2005). WLAN-based, indoor medical residents positioning system. In *International Conference on Wireless and Optical Communications Networks* (pp.556-560), Dubai, United Arab Emirates.

Coelho, P., Moraes, D., Cardozo, E., Guimarães, E., Johnson, T., & Atizani, F. (2009). A Network Architecture for Mobile Robotics. In *XXVII Brazilian Symposium on Computer Networks* (pp. 1-14), Recife, Brazil.

Cui, Q., Liu, C., & Zha, X. F. (2008). Intelligent Drug Delivery System Using UML Diagrams Analysis. *Journal of Shanghai Jiaotong University (Science.), 13*(3), 312–317. doi:10.1007/s12204-008-0312-4

Culler, D., Estrin, D., & Srivastava, M. (2004). Overview of Sensor Networks. *Computer, 37*(8), 41–49. doi:10.1109/MC.2004.93

Elmufti, K., Weerasinghe, D., Rajarajan, M., Rakocevic, V., & Khan, S. (2006). Privacy in Mobile Web Services for eHealth. In *Pervasive Health Conference and Workshops* (pp. 1-6), Innsbruck, Austria.

Favela, J., Tentori, M., Castro, L. A., Gonzalez, V. M., Moran, E. B., & Martinez-Garcia, A. I. (2006). Estimating Hospital Work Activities in Context-Aware Healthcare Applications. In *Pervasive Health Conference and Workshops* (pp. 1-10), Innsbruck, Austria.

Gatzoulis, L., & Iakovidis, I. (2007). Wearable and Portable eHealth Systems. *Engineering in Medicine and Biology Magazine, 26*(5), 51–56. doi:10.1109/EMB.2007.901787

Geer, D. (2006). Pervasive Medical Devices: Less Invasive, More Productive. *Pervasive Computing, 5*(2), 85–87. doi:10.1109/MPRV.2006.37

Greenemeier, L. (2008). Who Needs a Doctor When There's a Robot in the House, er, Hospital? *Scientific American*. Retrieved May 1, 2009, from http://www.scientificamerican.com/article.cfm?id=robot-telemedicine

Gyselinckx, B., Hoof, C. V., Ryckaert, J., Yazicioglu, R. F., Fiorini, P., & Leonov, V. (2005). Human++: Autonomous Wireless Sensors for Body Area Networks. In *IEEE Custom Integrated Circuits Conference* (pp. 13-19), San Jose, CA.

Halperin, D., Kohno, T., Heydt-Benjamin, T. S., Fu, K., & Maisel, W. H. (2008). Security and Privacy for Implantable Medical Devices. *Pervasive Computing, 7*(1), 30–39. doi:10.1109/MPRV.2008.16

Hansen, T. R., Bardram, J. E., & Soegaard, M. (2006). Moving Out of the Lab: Deploying Pervasive Technologies in a Hospital. *Pervasive Computing, 5*(3), 24–31. doi:10.1109/MPRV.2006.53

Helal, A., & Abdulrazak, B. (2006). TeCaRob: Tele-Care using Telepresence and Robotic Technology for Assisting People with Special Needs. *International Journal of Human-friendly Welfare Robotic Systems, 7*(3), 46–53.

Jasemian, Y. (2006). Security and privacy in a wireless remote medical system for home healthcare purpose. In *Pervasive Health Conference and Workshops* (pp. 1-7), Innsbruck, Austria.

Jovanov, E. (2005). Wireless Technology and System Integration in Body Area Networks for m-Health Applications. In *IEEE Engineering in Medicine and Biology Conference* (pp. 7158-7160), Shanghai, China.

Jovanov, E., Milenkovic, A., Otto, C., Groen, P. D., Johnson, B., Warren, S., & Taibi, G. (2005). A WBAN System for Ambulatory Monitoring of Physical Activity and Health Status: Applications and Challenges. In *IEEE Engineering in Medicine and Biology Annual Conference* (pp. 3810-3813), Shanghai, China.

Jurik, A. D., & Weaver, A. C. (2008). Remote Medical Monitoring. *Computer, 41*(4), 96–99. doi:10.1109/MC.2008.133

Kang, D., Lee, H., Ko, E., Kang, K., & Lee, J. (2006). A Wearable Context Aware System for Ubiquitous Healthcare. In *IEEE Annual International Conference on the Engineering in Medicine and Biology Society* (pp. 5192-5195), New York.

Kargl, F., Lawrence, E., Fischer, M., & Lim, Y. Y. (2008). Security, Privacy and Legal Issues in Pervasive eHealth Monitoring Systems. In *International Conference on Mobile Business,* (pp. 296-304), Barcelona, Spain.

Konstantas, D., & Herzog, R. (2003). Continuous monitoring of vital constants for mobile users: the MobiHealth' approach. In *IEEE Annual International Conference on the Engineering in Medicine and Biology Society,* 4 (pp. 3728-3731), Cancun, México.

Li, H.-B. Takizawa, K., Zhen, B., & Kohno, R. (2007). Body Area Network and Its Standardization at IEEE 802.15.MBAN. In Mobile and Wireless Communications Summit, (pp. 1-5), Budapest, Hungary.

Liszka, K. J., Mackin, M. A., Lichter, M. J., York, D. W., Pillai, P., & Rosenbaum, D. S. (2004). Keeping a beat on the heart. *Pervasive Computing, 3*(4), 42–49. doi:10.1109/MPRV.2004.10

MacDonald, J. A. (2008). Authentication considerations for mobile e-health applications. In *International Conference on Pervasive Computing Technologies for Healthcare* (pp. 64 – 67), Tampere, Finland.

Meneses, F., & Moreira, A. (2006). Using GSM CellID Positioning for Place Discovering. In *Pervasive Health Conference and Workshops,* (pp. 1-8), Innsbruck, Austria.

Moraes, D. H., Coelho, P. R. S. L., Cardozo, E., Guimarães, E., Johnson, T., & Atizani, F. (2009). A Network Architecture for Large Mobile Robotics Environments. In *IEEE International Conference on Robot Communication and Coordination,* (pp. 1-6), Odense, Denmark.

Morón, J., et al. (2007). J2ME and smart phones as platform for a Bluetooth Body Area Network for Patient-telemonitoring. In *International Conference of the IEEE Engineering in Medicine and Biology Society* (pp. 2791-2794), Lyon, France.

Mosmondor, M., Skorin-Kapov, L., & Kovacic, M. (2006). Bringing location based services to IP multimedia subsystem. In *IEEE Mediterranean Electrotechnical Conference,* (pp. 746-749), Malaga, Spain.

Munir, S. A., Ren, B., Jiao, W., Wang, B., Xie, D., & Ma, J. (2007). Mobile Wireless Sensor Network: Architecture and Enabling Technologies for Ubiquitous Computing. In *International Conference on Advanced Information Networking and Applications Workshops,* (pp. 113-120), Niagara Falls, Canada.

Nellis, S. (2009). Long-distance medicine - InTouch robots can help rural patients get treatment. *Pacific Coast Business Times.* Retrieved May, 01, 2009, from http://pacbiztimes.com/index.php?option=com_ content&task= view&id=756& Itemid=29

Otto, C. A., Jovanov, E., & Milenkovi, A. (2006). A WBAN-based System for Health Monitoring at Home. In *International Summer School and Symposium on Medical Devices and Biosensors* (pp. 20-23), Cambridge, MA.

Prado, R., Zagari, E., Cardozo, E., & Johnson, T. (2008). A reference architecture for micro-mobility support in IP networks. In *The Thirteenth IEEE Symposium on Computers and Communications* (pp. 624-630). Marrakech, Morocco.

Roussos, G., Marsh, A. J., & Maglavera, S. (2005). Enabling Pervasive Computing with Smart Phones. *Pervasive Computing, 4*(2), 20–27. doi:10.1109/MPRV.2005.30

Scheermesser, M., Kosow, H., Rashid, A., & Holtmann, C. (2008). User acceptance of pervasive computing in healthcare: Main findings of two case studies. In *International Conference on Pervasive Computing Technologies for Healthcare,* (pp. 205-213), Tampere, Finland.

Slamanig, D., & Stingl, C. (2008). Privacy Aspects of eHealth. In *International Conference on Availability, Reliability and Security* (pp.1226-1233), Barcelona, Spain.

Stanford, V. (2002). Using pervasive computing to deliver elder care. *Pervasive Computing, 1*(1), 10–13. doi:10.1109/MPRV.2002.993139

Stanford, V. (2002). Pervasive health care applications face tough security challenges. *Pervasive Computing, 1*(2), 8–12. doi:10.1109/MPRV.2002.1012332

Steele, R., Secombe, C., & Brookes, W. (2006). Using Wireless Sensor Networks for Aged Care: The Patient's Perspective. In *Pervasive Health Conference and Workshops* (pp. 1-10), Innsbruck, Austria.

Tentori, M., & Favela, J. (2008). Activity-Aware Computing for Healthcare. *Pervasive Computing, 7*(2), 51–57. doi:10.1109/MPRV.2008.24

Warren, S., Lebak, J., Yao, J., Creekmore, J., Milenkovic, A., & Jovanov, E. (2005). Interoperability and Security in Wireless Body Area Network Infrastructures. In *International Conference on the Engineering in Medicine and Biology* (pp. 3837-3840), Shanghai, China.

Yick, J., Mukherjee, B., & Ghosal, D. (2008). Wireless sensor network survey. *Computer Networks, 52*(12), 2292–2330. doi:10.1016/j.comnet.2008.04.002

Zahariadis, T., & Doshi, B. (2004). Applications and services for the B3G/4G era. *Wireless Communications, 11*(5), 3–5. doi:10.1109/MWC.2004.1351675

Zhen, B., Li, H., & Kohno, R. (2007). IEEE Body Area Networks for Medical Applications. In *International Symposium on Wireless Communication Systems* (pp. 327-331), Trondheim, Norway.

Chapter 13
On the Design of Self-Organizing Ad Hoc Networks

Carlos M. S. Figueiredo
FUCAPI – Research and Innovation Foundation, Brazil

Antonio A. F. Loureiro
Federal University of Minas Gerais, Brazil

ABSTRACT

Self-organization concept has become very important to the vision of pervasive and ubiquitous systems because such systems are expected to be composed by lots of interconnected computing devices immersed in the environments. In particular, general Mobile Ad hoc networks, and their specializations such as Sensor and Vehicular networks can be seen as the main technologies for pervasive infra-structures. These networks were conceived under the self-organization paradigm due to many characteristics such as a high number of devices, dynamic network topology and the need of autonomous operation. Although several mechanism and techniques for achieving self-organizing behavior are already applied, there is still the lack of general methodologies for the design of new self-organizing functions. Thus, this chapter will present an overview of self-organizing networks introducing important functions and techniques, and it will focus on important design aspects that can be useful to new designs.

INTRODUCTION

Mobile Ad hoc Networks (MANETs) (Haas et al., 1999) are an important subject for research as mobile devices (laptops, PDAs, cell phones), wireless networks and applications became widespread during the last decade. For instance, specialized ad hoc networks such as the Wireless Sensor Networks (WSNs) (Pottie & Kaiser, 2000; Akyildiz et al., 2002) and the Vehicular Ad hoc Networks (VANETs) (Kosch et al., 2006) are very active research areas.

A WSN consists of sensor nodes connected among themselves by a wireless medium to perform distributed sensing tasks, and these networks are expected to be used in different applications (Arampatzis et al., 2005) such as environmental and health monitoring, surveillance, and security. A VANET is composed by wireless devices to allow communications among nearby vehicles, or among

DOI: 10.4018/978-1-61520-843-2.ch013

them with the roadside infra-structure, to provide an information system regarding traffic, roads and contextualized events.

Following the vision of Pervasive Computing (Satyanarayanan, 2001), we are starting to interact with computing devices around us, many time in an invisible way, and in many contexts such as intelligent homes, factories or transport systems. All these devices are expected to be interconnected to provide a common communication system to access information anywhere, anytime. Thus, it is very clear that mobile ad hoc networks and its specializations are the main technologies to achieve a ubiquitous and pervasive world.

The scenarios where MANETs are applied may be very dynamic. In these networks, topological changes are very frequent. For example, sensor nodes can be destroyed by the environment, nodes can have their energy depleted, vehicles are frequently moving, new nodes can be added or leave the network, or the wireless communication can be intermittent due to interferences or obstacles. Thus, the algorithms and protocols for this kind of network must be able to enable network operation during its initialization, and both normal and exception situations. Besides, many applications require the adoption of a totally autonomous behavior. This is due to the necessity of creating infra-structure in remote places, which can be inhospitable or of hard access, or in consequence of the network scale, which increases the network complexity due to the exponential number of possible interactions among nodes and can make massive or even impossible the execution of management actions by administrators or centralized entities.

In this context, self-organization has become an important concept that has been applied in such large-scale and autonomous network systems. Its main idea is the *"achievement of a global behavior through local interactions"* (Heylighen, 2002, pp. 1), which leads to networks less dependent of central control and that tend to be scalable, adaptable and,consequently, robust.

In the development of MANETs, several studies have applied the self-organization concept (sometimes implicitly) in specific functions, such as communication and clustering. However, they did not cover a more general and practical view of the concept application that can be used for new designs and developments. Thus, this chapter will present a general view of the concept application to these networks, it will present important functions and techniques applied in the development of these networks, and it will focus on important design aspects that can be useful to new designs.

The rest of this chapter is organized as follows. In the next section, we introduce the self-organization concept and present some fundamental work in literature. Next, we present our main contributions on the design aspects of self-organizing functions by organizing important design ideas in a methodological view. Finally, we present some conclusions and future trend in this promising research area.

FUNDAMENTALS AND RELATED WORK

Self-organization is a well known concept in the literature and it has been employed in different areas such as Physics, Chemistry and Biology (e.g., see Haken, 1983). Its idea is the creation of a coherent global behavior only from local interactions among the system elements (Heylighen, 2002), and its consequent decentralized aspect leads to systems that are more adaptable, scalable and robust. These characteristics have led to the application of the self-organization concept in several computer systems, which are becoming more distributed and composed of many elements. In particular, many examples of self-organization in the computer network are already studied (Zambonelli et al., 2005), varying the scale from microsensor networks to the entire internet, and particular mechanisms achieving self-organization are also known (Prehofer & Bettstetter, 2005) and applied to specific organization functions.

In particular, as initially discussed in this work, the MANETs have many characteristics that demand self-organizing features, such as the scale, their deployment in dynamic scenarios, the need of unattended operation, the independence of the elements and their cooperative requirement to perform global network functions. Thus, self-organization has been considered in these networks since their first studies, as in Blazevic et al., 2001 for MANETs and in Clare et al., 1999 for WSNs. Some works like Collier & Taylor, 2004, evolved the concept application through general initial aspects for the application of self-organization concept.

Under a practical view, in the following, we exemplify some fundamental network functions that have been applied under the self-organization concept.

Communication

It is a basic functionality in any data communication network and contains the first class of algorithms developed considering the self-organizing approach (e.g. Sohrabi et al., 2000). The problem is the creation of a communication infrastructure in a distributed manner and the maintenance of this infrastructure in the presence of topological changes. Basically, the fundamental communication functions deal with the establishment of links (link layer), mainly the channel access organization (MAC sublayer) (Ye et al., 2002; Naik & Sivalingam, 2004), and routes between nodes (network layer) (Al-Karaki & Kamal, 2004).

In the MAC layer, several proposals consist in organizing the channel access in collision-free links, mainly based on TDMA schemes, such as in S-MAC (Ye et al., 2002) and in many other examples that can be found in Naik & Sivalingam, 2004. The network layer also concentrates several proposals treating routing infrastructure creation and maintenance (Al-Karaki & Kamal, 2004).

Basically, source and destination nodes interact with their neighbors and these interactions are propagated in a multi-hop way in the network for route discovery and maintenance. Some examples are the Diffusion solutions (Heidemann et al., 2003), the adaptive hybrid Multi solution (Figueiredo et al., 2004) and bio-inspired solutions such as in Câmara & Loureiro, 2001 and Caro et al., 2005.

Density Control

Some solutions treat the redundancy of the network (radio connectivity and/or sensing coverage) in order to deactivate instantaneous unnecessary nodes to save their resources. In the self-organization context, the nodes themselves interact to establish their roles as active or inactive according to their local vision of the network. Some examples are ASCENT (Cerpa & Estrin, 2002), CCP (Wang et al., 2003) and OGDC (Zhang & Hou, 2005).

Clustering

Network clustering is the process of dividing it into node groups which are coordinated by a node with a special role called cluster-head. The organization of networks in clusters divides their complexity in subdomains and can give support to higher level organizational functions. A classic clustering example in WSNs is LEACH (Heinzelman et al., 2000), and many other proposals exist such as Krishnan & Starobinski, 2003 and Kochhal et al., 2003.

Others

Many other functions are also treated under the self-organization paradigm, such as localization (Capkun et al., 2001), security (Walters et al., 2005), and synchronization (Ganeriwal et al., 2003).

As we can see, particular mechanisms achieving self-organization are known and have been applied to specific organization functions of MANETs. However, there is still the lack of general methodologies for guiding the design of new self-organizing functions.

DESIGNING SELF-ORGANIZING MANETS

For the design of self-organizing MANETs, local interaction rules must be devised to achieve a desired global goal for the whole network. In practice, this top-down translation is not easy because of the lack of formal models and the complexity of the interactions, mainly if efficiency is required due to network constraints. However, some general aspects and insights can be helpful in this intent, and this work represents a step forward in the design of self-organizing networks.

This work presents a design methodology composed by some general aspects, a design framework that unites important insights and practical characteristics of the application of self-organization in MANETs, and a design guideline that directs the search of self-organizing solutions in a more objective way. They are presented as follows.

General Aspects

In the self-organizing MANET design, we need to devise simple local interaction rules, codified in distributed algorithms, to achieve a desired global goal. We can extract general features of these algorithms as follows:

Decentralized Control. There is no centralized entity that controls the participation of the system elements, and the global behavior must be mapped to local goals at each system element.

Common Goal. The entire system must have a common goal to be achieved through the cooperation of the individuals. This common goal can be seen as the global behavior to be achieved from local interactions among the system elements,

and can represent a particular arrangement or configuration of these elements, or a desired global performance.

Dynamic. The system must be dynamic. The state of a system element must change based on its inputs (perceptions) and the local interactions with the other elements. Two important aspects related to obtaining dynamics are adaptation and exploration. Adaptation refers to the design of algorithms that adapt to changes in its environment. Basically, adaptation occurs when an element reacts to a perceived situation, such as a failure or an event, by changing its internal behavior or the way in which it interacts with the other system elements. A simple example of adaptation is multihop routing recovery in ad hoc and sensor networks. After a failure in an element of a path, the other nodes that use it have to react to discover an alternative route. Such an example was proposed by Nakamura et al., 2005, and an example regarding event adaptation was proposed by Figueiredo et al., 2007. With the exploration aspect, the network elements must constantly try to increase its individual and consequently the whole system performance. Thus, the elements should explore different alternatives to perform their functions efficiently. A clear example of this aspect is found in the ant-foraging behavior, which is also applied to ad hoc routing (e.g., Caro et al., 2005). Here, elements sometimes search for better paths towards the destiny.

Resource Preservation. The nodes must preserve their limited resources and the self-organization cannot sacrifice the goal of the application running on the network. Thus, the dynamics of the system from local interactions must be objective and precise through simple established rules.

A Design Framework

In the following, we present a framework which joins common characteristics found in practical self-organization functions and that can become

Figure 1. Framework overview

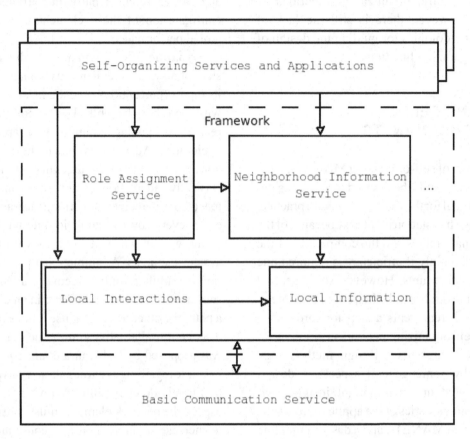

easier and more comprehensive the design process of new self-organizing functions and applications. This framework is proposed by surveying the existing related work, and it can be improved according to the experience acquisition.

Figure 1 shows a general view of the framework. In the lowest level, we have the core of the framework that deals with local interactions and local information, which is also the core of the self-organization concept. This core uses the basic communication service for interacting with network elements. On top of the core, we introduce two basic services: Role-Assignment service and Neighborhood information abstraction. These services are present in the development of practical self-organizing functions in network systems, and can create an abstraction level for the development of new services or applications.

Framework Core

The goal of self-organizing systems is to obtain a global behavior from local interactions. So, based on these interactions and on the information acquired through them, an element can establish its form of participation in the system and how it contributes with the global behavior.

Local Information. In self-organizing systems, local decisions to actions (or reactions) may depend on the availability of information at a network element. Basically, we divided the local information set in two main classes:

- **Self-dependent information.** Many functions consider internal information of a node for the decision of its role or how it will respond to local interactions. It can be an internal state information, for example, the current role, or local information, such as node energy measurement, positional coordinates and sensed data. LEACH (Heinzelman et al., 2000) is an example in which the role (cluster-head or common node) to be assumed by a node depends only on a probability function over its residual energy.

- **Neighborhood acquired information.** This type of information is dynamic and depends on message exchanges among neighbors and their carried data. Depending on the information acquired in a neighborhood, a node can take some reaction or change its state. For example, in the density control function (e.g., OGDC by Zhang & Hou, 2005), a node can receive the positional information and state of its neighbors, it can verify if they cover its sensing area, and depending on this result, it can decide to assume an active or inactive state.

Local Interactions. In a communication network, local interactions occur among nodes in a neighborhood, i.e., among nodes which are reached directly, through message exchanges. In a wireless network, the neighbors of a node are the nodes that are in its radio communication range. Generally, these interaction messages inform the neighborhood about a node state and/or its local information in order to let them take their own decisions. Additionally, these interactions can be propagated iteratively in a hop-by-hop way through the network elements, like chain reactions. The same behavior is also seen in natural systems, such as chemical gradient reactions secreted by biological cells or propagating neural synapses in brain.

In the MANET context, messages carrying local and/or propagated information can be exchanged through mechanisms such as: Flooding, in which information is propagated for all con-nected nodes in an n-hop neighborhood without modification, for example, to inform neighbors of a node presence and its local information; Gradient, which is similar to flooding but information being propagated can be modified (e.g., accumulated) in every hop, and that can be used to establish cost functions in the network, for example; Direct interaction, in which a direct neighborhood that must receive the message is specified.

Besides specific mechanisms, other approaches are found in the literature for local interaction activities, such as Tuple-based programming (Cabri et al., 2002) or Smart Messages (Borcea et al., 2002) for autonomous agent cooperation, including models considering mobile application programming, as in TOTA Middleware (Mamei & Zambonelli, 2004).

Service Abstraction Level

The goal of the framework abstraction level is to provide a set of common services that can be used to compose the design of higher level self-organizing activities or applications. Services in this level use the set of core primitives of the framework to abstract design particularities from higher levels. We envisioned this level to be totally extensible as experience and new implementation occurs, but we focus in two considered basic services:

Neighborhood Information Service. As described before, many local decisions taken by network nodes depend on acquired neighborhood information. Thus, a basic service that creates a list of neighbors and their acquired information through the interaction primitives can help in the design of several self-organizing functions. In fact, some proposals deal specifically with these services by implementing particular mechanisms and providing an API function set for easier sensor network programming. Some of them are Hood (Whitehouse et al., 2004) and Abstract Regions (Welsh & Mainland, 2004), which abstract neighborhood information exchange. Thus, the

Figure 2. Design guideline

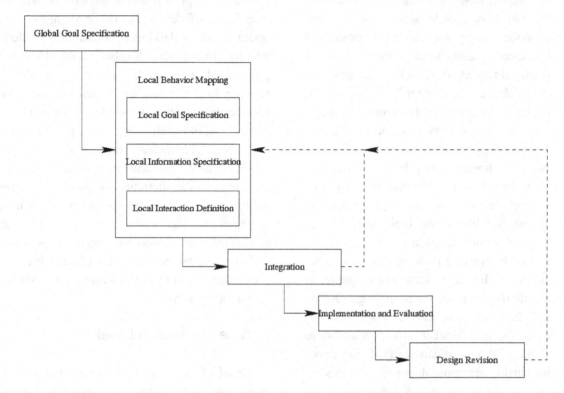

implemented services or their applied mechanism can be used for new designs.

Role Assignment Service. Many self-organizing activities are associated with special roles which are assigned to network elements in order to establish a specific behavior. For example, the clustering function can be seen as a role assignment problem where the roles can be cluster-head or common node. In a general way, the role assignment service is composed by methods for role specification, by defining the different roles that can be assumed by a node; and role conditions, by describing the conditions (local or acquired neighborhood information) in which a role is established. The Generic Role-Assignment proposal (Frank & Römer, 2005) is a very clear example in the WSN domain following these characteristics.

A Design Guideline

In order to assist system designers in the development of self-organizing functions for WSNs, we propose a guideline which directs the search of these self-organizing solutions by exploring the framework insights described before. The guideline starts from the definition of the desired global system behavior, and it goes through several steps to produce the local behavior of the network elements to fulfill the system requirements. These steps are shown in Figure 2 and they are detailed in the following.

It is important to note that this guideline will not generate solutions to be directly applied in the MANETs, and the experience and knowledge of the designer is fundamental for the generation of correct and efficient solutions.

Global Goal Specification

The first step is the description of the global behavior or pattern to be obtained by the network. As much details can be provided in this phase better the specification and characteristics to be considered in the subsequent steps.

As global behavior examples we can cite the formation of a tree structure connecting the network nodes from the sink, which is a very common applied infra-structure in WSNs, or a density control function, in which the network nodes form a subset of active nodes to perform the sensing task and maintain the network coverage by considering sensing ranges for the nodes.

Important details that can be surveyed for these examples could be: if their organization must be maintained pro-actively or only on-demand, in case of adaptation due to some specified situation as failures; or still if their organization must change along the network lifetime to share the resource consumption among all network nodes, in this case by requiring the introduction of a random factor in the organization process or the usage of memory and historical behavior.

Local Behavior Mapping

The main problem in the self-organizing design is the process of translating a desired global behavior in local interaction rules among its elements. And once they are established, not necessarily the global goal is achieved with its all performance requirements.

An important aspect in this intend is the use of nature-inspired solutions, in which a desired self-organizing behavior found in natural systems can be mapped in the design of computational systems. This nature-inspired engineering process is a promising technique to achieve intelligent autonomic systems and some examples are under the term *Swarm Intelligence* (Bonabeau et al., 1999).

By considering a design "from scratch", the common characteristics found in the proposed framework of the last subsection may be very helpful. For example, if possible, the developer can think the self-organizing function under treatment as a role assignment problem, and then follow the described ideas to guide the design process, or even use some service already implemented. If the function can not be dealt this way, the developer can still try to use some known or available information mechanisms. In summary, the existing knowledge implicit in these services can help the design task.

Anyway, in order to better guide the design process or turn it more comprehensive, we divide this *"local behavior mapping step"* in the following sub-steps.

Local Goal Specification

The first step on the attempt for global to local behavior mapping is the specification of the local goals, i.e., the goals for each network element. Basically, a local goal relates the decision to be taken by an element with the conditions observed by it (from itself and/or from neighborhood). Besides, this decision can result in adjusting a parameter set, the definition of a state or the roles to be played by an element.

Following the examples cited in the first step, we can describe the local goal of an element as: in the tree organization case, setting a neighbor node as parent; or in case of the density control function, deciding for the inactive role if it is covered by active neighbors or active if otherwise. Again, some details can be important to generate solutions in compliance with the global system requirements. For example, if the distribution of energy among the nodes is important, the local goal in the tree organization could be to choose a neighbor node with the highest residual energy as parent, and in the density control case, to decrease the chance to be active according to the decrease of the energy level.

Local Information Specification

To support local decision and accomplish the local goal, all local information necessary must be specified. As described in the conceptual framework, these data can be self-dependent (internal information of a network element) or acquired from the neighborhood. The specification of the needed information will help in the definition of the interaction mechanisms (next step) to accomplish the local goals (previous step).

As an example, in the tree organization case, a node must know about the existence of neighbors and some metric about them (such as residual energy, position or number of hops to sink) for the choice of a parent. In the density control example, a node must acquire the position, state (if active or not) and the sensing range of the neighbors, and its own residual energy to check if its area is covered and choose its own state.

Local Interaction Definition

An interaction mechanism must be defined when neighborhood information is needed in a self-organizing function in order to a node take a decision and accomplish its local goal. This mechanism will establish the information which must be exchanged and how it is done. Due to restrict resources of some networks, as in WSNs, this interaction must be very objective and efficient, and its definition consists of a critical phase in the design task. Besides, it is the moment in which the designer's experience is most important.

Basically, local interaction mechanisms are comprised of: The definition of the messages and the information carried by them; How these messages are exchanged among the neighborhood – in this case, the temporal aspect of the interactions and/or their conditions are important (e.g. interact periodically, or only as a response to other interactions or detected condition); The establishment of the relation between the local interactions and local decisions, i.e., it is necessary to determine the moment of the interaction process the local decisions are taken.

All these sub-steps comprise an information service, as described in the conceptual framework. Thus, at this moment, the definition of a generic mechanism which will benefit other self-organizing functions or the consideration of an existing one can be useful.

As an example, in the tree infrastructure case of the last step, a common interaction mechanism found in literature (Zhou & Krishnamachari, 2003) defines a local interaction mechanism as a flooding started from the sink node in which each node broadcasts the building message with its own id, position, residual energy, and the number of hops obtained from the received messages incremented by one. Regarding the parent decision, it can be done during the flooding process after receiving some neighbor broadcasts (controlled by a random timer, for example) and before sending its own broadcast and continuing the process. By this way, the parent choice can be restricted, but this process permits the construction of the tree structure at once and avoids the formation of loops.

Following the density control example, local interactions are necessary to inform a node about the neighbor states. This could be done through broadcasts by the nodes in rounds. However, the nodes need information from each other to take a local decision, and so this decision can not be performed independently at the same time. Thus, a scheme such as choosing some random nodes to start local interactions in the active state, and proceeding with these interactions in a similar way but using the already propagated information for local decision must be introduced. This exactly idea is present in the OGDC (Wang et al., 2003) solution.

From these two examples, we can see that the relation between local interactions and local decisions is very important to obtain correct and efficient self-organizing functions.

Consideration of Integration Possibilities

As described in Section 2, many self-organizing functions are expected to be applied in MANETs. This is very clear in several communication protocol layers such as MAC and routing, but other functions must also be considered for efficient WSNs, such as density control and clustering. As a consequence, integration aspects of different functions must be considered in order to achieve a correct as well as an efficient operation of these networks.

As a clear example of the need of integration, we can consider the routing and density control functions. With a density control algorithm running independently, additional dynamics are introduced to the network topology alternating redundant nodes to active or inactive states to save energy. Thus, some previously established routes by a routing algorithm can be destroyed by the density control algorithm, and this will lead to data packet losses until the route recovery.

In this guideline, we present two general approaches that can guide the design of integrated self-organizing functions in WSNs, and they are described as follows.

Synchronization Approach

A very simple solution consists of a simple synchronization of the considered functions. In this case, the functions must execute in a given order satisfying their dependencies for a proper operation of the network. The advantage of this approach is that the self-organizing functions are considered with the minimum of modification, i.e., their deployment can be done as they were independently proposed.

For the previous routing and density control integration example, the routing infrastructure formation could be scheduled to execute just after the density control organization, so routes are reestablished after the topology alteration by the density control.

Obviously, such synchronization approach is only possible when the functions occur in well-defined periods and have a well-defined duration of execution. However, many organizational aspects of WSNs are treated in rounds, as the examples of LEACH (Heinzelman et al., 2000) in clustering and OGDC (Zhang & Hou, 2005) in density control.

Even with the execution in rounds, this synchronization can be hard to be implemented. Due to distributed character of the self-organizing functions, their execution duration may be variable and cannot be determined without having a global view of the network. An alternative is the use of extra mechanisms for providing this support, which can increase the solution complexity, or a synchronization point can be estimated (or super-estimated to avoid problems), but in this case the network performance can be impacted with longer organization intervals. As a solution, a more aggressive approach for integration of self-organizing functions is discussed as follows.

Integrated Design Approach

The second approach consists of an attempt of integrating the design of several self-organizing functions. Generically, this approach optimizes different functions by unifying their goals and utilizing common information and interaction mechanisms. Ideally, when all these unifications can be done, we obtain a fully integrated solution in which several self-organizing functions can be considered as a single one.

The advantage of this approach is that it can lead to more efficient solutions which meet the design requirements of constrained WSNs, for instance. By unifying the local interaction mechanisms and the exchanged information among the network nodes for different functions we have a great reduction of resource consumption with less message exchange. Besides, in opposition to the last described approach, it also allows a more efficient interaction among the self-organizing functions, since they can be designed to work concurrently in perfect synchronization and without extra costs.

Regarding the same routing and density control example described before, the negotiation messages to inform node states (active or inactive) and position for coverage verification can flow from the sink to the network edges and be used directly to define a routing tree for data forwarding by considering only the active nodes. This example is better explored by Siqueira et al., 2006.

Of course, this approach turns the design process more complex by requiring from the designer the identification of integration opportunities. Besides, it is not possible to be used in all the cases. For example, in some localization functions some special negotiations using special elements (such as beacons) are necessary for the establishment of a global coordinate system, and these elements do not participate of others self-organizing functions. Thus, this function cannot be considered to be fully integrated with others and the synchronization approach would be complementary applied.

The issue of integrated design is already applied to MANETs under the term *"cross-layer design"*. Many proposals exist but mainly regarding aspects of communication protocols (e.g., MAC and routing) (Sichitiu, 2004). Additionally, not necessarily the functions are fully integrated as one solution, but they can only consider a knowledge between layers. In our approach we discuss the need of such integration in a wider view considering self-organizing functions not only related to the network stack, and a fully integration is possible and can bring benefits.

In fact, integration aspects can be considered not only after the previous steps of the methodology, but also during the design of a new function, diluted in the previous steps. This can be done by considering previously designed functions and their characteristics that can be used by the new one, and so, requesting experience from the designer.

Implementation and Evaluation

After the design of the local behavior of the network elements, it is necessary to verify if the global behavior is achieved, and of course, the network must be put in operation. Thus, the system must me implemented to be evaluated.

A faster way to verify if the design will perform properly is through simulations. Simulations permit the test of specific and different conditions and its results can be used for design revision (as described in the next step) without the costs of a real implementation and experimentation, which can be performed only when the design is considered mature. Recent work like Niazi & Hussain, 2009, discusses the importance of modeling and simulating self-organized networks.

Design Revision

Due to the difficulties of mapping globals to local behaviors, many attempts can be necessary until a global goal is achieved considering a desired performance. Thus, the result of the last step can be used in a possible redesign in order to improve or correct the system performance.

This consequent cycle in the design task can be specially useful in the design of nature-inspired solutions or in the integration of different self-organizing functions. In the former case, nature and computer needs and requirements may not match very well, so repetitive design cycles may be necessary to adequate the nature-inspired solution. A similar idea is introduced by Zambonelli et al., 2005. In the latter case, previously designed functions can be reviewed to accommodate the integration of a new one.

FUTURE RESEARCH DIRECTIONS

As Pervasive and Ubiquitous System become popular, general MANETs and specializations like WSNs and VANETs will be more applied in practice. As we discussed through this chapter, self-organization is an important and active research concept in these networks. Thus, it is a must-know concept for Pervasive and Ubiquitous infra-structure developers.

Besides the concept application and general design aspects surveyed in this chapter, it would be very useful to explore some self-organizing mechanisms with illustrated practical examples. For instance, a survey with some common and important self-organizing algorithms can be presented and have their applicability showed in real or simulated applications. A better discussion of some methodologies like approaches based in game theory and exploration, common in natural systems, can also be interesting to create new self-organizing models.

Based on the present ideas, a possible evolution of this work can consider the implementation of a middleware or API set for the development of self-organizing functions. In this case, some discussed implementation aspects could be available as primitives in a given platform (e.g., in TinyOS for WSNs) to be directly used by developers. As described through this chapter, some works already exist treating some specific aspects, such as Generic Role Assignment (Frank & Römer, 2005) and Hood (Whitehouse et al., 2004). Other general design models can be envisioned to help the design task.

Finally, it is know in literature that there is no formal methods to devise local interactions rules from desired global behaviors in the self-organization design. Much of the work is obtained from developers experience with distributed algorithms and implementations. Thus, in order to help the exploration of self-organizing techniques, it is an important issue to study modeling and simulation techniques and tools to be applied in the design task of such networks. As complementary, formal languages or models to the specification of self-organizing functions can bring the advantage of formal verification, simulation and automatic code generation by considering an uniform way to specify the designed functions.

FINAL CONSIDERATIONS

Self-organization is an important and challenging concept to be applied in the current large-scale computer systems, especially in MANETs and their instances like WSNs and VANETs. This concept is based on the achievement of a desired global behavior from local interactions among the system elements, and it can be used to achieve autonomic operation of these systems, i.e., an unattended operation without a central control.

In this chapter, we presented important insights and practical characteristics of self-organization concept application in MANETs focused on the design process. Besides some general aspects, we organized a general framework that unites common characteristics found in self-organizing functions, and a design guideline that can guide the design process of new ones. These contributions can be considered as a step-forward in the methodologies of self-organizing MANETs and a complement to the exiting proposals in literature.

REFERENCES

Akyildiz, I. F., Su, W., Sankarasubramaniam, Y., & Cyirci, E. (2002). Wireless sensor networks: A survey. *Computer Networks*, *38*(4), 393–422. doi:10.1016/S1389-1286(01)00302-4

Al-Karaki, J. N., & Kamal, A. E. (2004). Routing techniques in wireless sensor networks: a survey. *IEEE Wireless Communications*, *11*, 6–28. doi:10.1109/MWC.2004.1368893

Arampatzis, T., Lygeros, J., & Manesis, S. (2005). A survey of applications of wireless sensors and wireless sensor networks. In *Proceedings of Mediterranean Control Conference (Med05)*, Limassol Cyprus.

Blazevic, L., Butty, L., Capkun, S., Giordano, S., Hubaux, J.-P., & Boudec, J.-Y. L. (2001). Self-organization in mobile ad-hoc networks: the approach of terminodes. IEEE Communications Magazine.

Bonabeau, E., Dorigo, M., & Theraulaz, G. (1999). Swarm Intelligence: From Natural to Artificial Systems, (Santa Fe Institute Studies in the Sciences of Complexity). New York: Oxford University Press.

Borcea, C., Iyer, D., Kang, P., Saxena, A., & Iftode, L. (2002). Cooperative computing for distributed embedded systems. In *Proceedings of IEEE International Conference on Distributed Computing Systems (ICDCS 2002)*.

Cabri, G., Leonardi, L., & Zambonelli, F. (2002). Engineering mobile agent applications via context-dependent coordination. *IEEE Transactions on Software Engineering*, *28*(11), 1039–1055. doi:10.1109/TSE.2002.1049403

Câmara, D., & Loureiro, A. (2001). Gps/ant-like routing in ad hoc networks. *Telecommunication Systems*, *18*(1/3), 85–100. doi:10.1023/A:1016739402641

Capkun, S., Hamdi, M., & Hubaux, J. (2001). Gps-free positioning in mobile ad-hoc networks. In *Proceedings of the 34th IEEE Annual Hawaii International Conference on System Sciences (HICSS-34)*, (Vol. 9, pp. 9008).

Caro, G. D., Ducatelle, F., & Gambardella, L. (2005). Anthocnet: An adaptive nature-inspired algorithm for routing in mobile ad hoc networks. *European Transactions on Telecommunications (ETT), Special Issue on Self Organization in Mobile Networking, 16*(2).

Cerpa, A., & Estrin, D. (2002). Ascent: Adaptive self-configuring sensor networks topologies. In *Proceedings of the 21st International Annual Joint Conference of the IEEE Computer and Communications Societies (INFOCOM'02)*, (Vol. 3, pp. 1278–1287).

Clare, L. P., Pottie, G. J., & Agre, J. R. (1999). Self-organizing distributed sensor networks. In *Proceedings of the SPIE Conf. on Unattended Ground Sensor Technologies and Applications.*

Collier, T. C., & Taylor, C. E. (2004). Self-organization in sensor network. *Journal of Parallel and Distributed Computing*, *64*(7), 866–873. doi:10.1016/j.jpdc.2003.12.004

Figueiredo, C., Nakamura, E., & Loureiro, A. (2004). Multi: A hybrid adaptive dissemination protocol for wireless sensor networks. In *Proceedings of the 1st International Workshop on Algorithmic Aspects of Wireless Sensor Networks (Algosensors 2004)*, (LNCS Vol. 3121, pp. 171–186). Berlin: Springer.

Figueiredo, C. M., Nakamura, E. F., & Loureiro, A. A. (2007). An event-detection estimation model for hybrid adaptive routing in wireless sensor networks. In *Proceedings of the IEEE International Conference on Communications (ICC'07)*.

Frank, C., & Römer, K. (2005). Algorithms for generic role assignment in wireless sensor networks. In *Proceedings of the 3rd ACM Conference on Embedded Networked Sensor Systems (SenSys'05)*.

Ganeriwal, S., Kumar, R., & Srivastava, M. B. (2003). Timing-sync protocol for sensor networks. In *Proceedings of the 1st ACM International Conference on Embedded Networked Sensor Systems, (SenSys '03)*.

Haas, Z. J., Gerla, M., Johnson, D. B., Perkins, C. E., Pursley, M. B., Steenstrup, M. E., & Toh, C.-K. (1999). Special issue on wireless ad hoc networks. *IEEE Journal on Selected Areas in Communications, 17*.

Haken, H. (1983). Synergetics: An Introduction. Nonequilibrium Phase Transition and Self-Organization in Physics, Chemistry, and Biology, (3rd Rev. & Enlarged Ed.).

Heidemann, J., Silva, F., & Estrin, D. (2003). Matching data dissemination algorithms to application requirements. In *Proceedings of the 1st ACM International Conference on Embedded Networked Sensor Systems (SenSys'03)*.

Heinzelman, W. R., Chandrakasan, A., & Balakrishnan, H. (2000). Energy-efficient communication protocol for wireless microsensor networks. In *Proceedings of the IEEE Hawaii International Conference on System Sciences*, (pp. 4–13).

Heylighen, F. (2002). The science of self-organization and adaptivity. The Encyclopedia of Life Support Systems. Oxford, UK: EOLSS Publishers.

Kochhal, M., Schwiebert, L., & Gupta, S. (2003). Role-based hierarchical self-organization for wireless ad hoc sensor networks. In *Proceedings of the 2nd ACM International Conference on Wireless Sensor Networks and Applications*, (pp. 98–107).

Kosch, T., Adler, C., Eichler, S., Schroth, C., & Strassberger, M. (2006). The scalability problem of vehicular ad hoc networks and how to solve it. *IEEE Wireless Communications Magazine, 13*(5), 22–28. doi:10.1109/WC-M.2006.250354

Krishnan, R., & Starobinski, D. (2003). Message-efficient self-organization of wireless sensor networks. In *Proceedings of the IEEE Wireless Communications & Networking Conference (WCNC'03)*, (pp. 1603–1608).

Mamei, M., & Zambonelli, F. (2004). Programming pervasive and mobile computing applications with the tota middleware. In *Proceedings of the Second IEEE International Conference on Pervasive Computing and Communications (PerCom 2004)*, (pp. 263–276).

Naik, P., & Sivalingam, K. M. (2004). A survey of MAC protocols for sensor networks. In Wireless sensor networks, (pp. 93–107). Norwell, MA: Kluwer Academic Publishers.

Nakamura, E. F., Nakamura, F. G., Figueiredo, C. M., & Loureiro, A. A. (2005). Using information fusion to assist data dissemination in wireless sensor networks. *Telecommunication Systems, 30*(1-3), 237–254. doi:10.1007/s11235-005-4327-y

Niazi, M., & Hussain, A. (2009). Agent-based tools for modeling and simulation of self-organization in peer-to-peer, ad hoc, and other complex networks. *IEEE Communications Magazine, 47*(3), 166–173. doi:10.1109/MCOM.2009.4804403

Pottie, G. J., & Kaiser, W. J. (2000). Wireless integrated network sensors. *Communications of the ACM, 43*(5), 51–58. doi:10.1145/332833.332838

Prehofer, C., & Bettstetter, C. (2005). Self-organization in communication networks: Principles and design paradigms. *IEEE Communications Magazine, 43*(7), 78–85. doi:10.1109/MCOM.2005.1470824

Satyanarayanan, M. (2001). Pervasive computing: vision and challenges. *IEEE Personal Communications, 8*(4), 10–17. doi:10.1109/98.943998

Sichitiu, M. L. (2004). Cross-layer scheduling for power efficiency in wireless sensor networks. In *Proceedings of the 23rd Annual Joint Conference of the IEEE Computer and Communications Societies (INFOCOM'04)*.

Siqueira, I., Figueiredo, C. M., Loureiro, A., Nogueira, J., & Ruiz, L. (2006). An integrated approach for density control and routing in wireless sensor networks. In *Proceedings of the 20th IEEE International Parallel and Distributed Processing Symposium (IPDPS 2006)*.

Sohrabi, K., Gao, J., Ailawadhi, V., & Pottie, G. (2000). Protocols for self-organization of a wireless sensor network. *IEEE Personal Communications*, 7(5), 16–27. doi:10.1109/98.878532

Walters, J. P., Liang, Z., Shi, W., & Chaudhary, V. (2005). Wireless sensor networks security: A survey. Technical report, Wayne State University, USA.

Wang, X., Xing, G., Zhang, Y., Lu, C., Pless, R., & Gill, C. (2003). Integrated coverage and connectivity configuration in wireless sensor networks. In *Proceedings of the 1st ACM Internation Conference on Embedded Networked Sensor Systems (SenSys'03)*, (pp. 28–39).

Welsh, M., & Mainland, G. (2004). Programming sensor networks using abstract regions. In *Proceedings of the First USENIX/ACM Symposium on Networked Systems Design and Implementation (NSDI 2004)*.

Whitehouse, K., Sharp, C., Brewer, E., & Culler, D. (2004). Hood: A neighborhood abstraction for sensor networks. In *Proceedings of the International Conference on Mobile Systems, Applications, and Services (MOBYSYS 2004)*.

Ye, W., Heidemann, J., & Estrin, D. (2002). An energy-efficient mac protocol for wireless sensor networks. In *Proceedings of the 21rd Annual Joint Conference of the IEEE Computer and Communications Societies (Infocom'02)*, (pp. 1567–1576).

Zambonelli, F., Gleizes, M., Mamei, M., & Tolksdorf, R. (2005). Spray computers: Explorations in self-organization. *Journal of Pervasive and Mobile Computing*, 1(1), 1–20. doi:10.1016/j.pmcj.2005.01.001

Zhang, H., & Hou, J. C. (2005). Maintaining sensing coverage and connectivity in large sensor networks. *International Journal of Wireless Ad Hoc and Sensor Networks*, 1(1–2), 89–124.

Zhou, C., & Krishnamachari, B. (2003). Localized topology generation mechanisms for self-configuring sensor networks. In *Proceedings of the IEEE Wireless Communication Symposium (Globecom 2003)*.

Chapter 14
Hybrid Intelligent Systems in Ubiquitous Computing

Andrey V. Gavrilov
Novosibirsk State Technical University, Russia

ABSTRACT

In this chapter hybrid approach to development of intelligent systems is applied to ubiquitous computing systems, in particular, to smart environment. Different classifications of Hybrid Intelligent Systems (HIS) are looking and two examples of hybrid approach for smart environment are suggested: framework based on expert system and neural network for programming of behavior of smart objects and paradigm of context-based programming-learning of behavior of intelligent agent. Besides this chapter offers an attempt to systematize concepts for development of HIS as any introduction to methodology for development of HIS is suggested. The author hopes that this chapter will be useful for researchers and developers to better understand challenges in development of ambient intelligence and possible ways to overcome them.

INTRODUCTION

Now ubiquitous computing, ambient intelligence and smart cooperative objects are viewed as a major paradigms shift from conventional desktop application development. This view is enabled through the use of diverse hardware (sensors, user devices, computing infrastructure etc.) and software, anticipating user needs and acting on their behalf in a proactive manner (Weiser, 1991; Satyanarayanan, 2001). This

diversity of hardware and software information increases the degree of heterogeneity.

In order to realize such ubiquitous computing environment, three technology areas are required:

1. Sensing technology where information on user and surrounding environment are perceived and collected,
2. Context aware computing (Schilit, Adams & Want, 1994; Baldauf & Dustdar, 2004) technology where such information are processed and properly presented to users as different

DOI: 10.4018/978-1-61520-843-2.ch014

services,

3. Wireless network technologies (Mahalik, 2007) where information are collected from sensors and distributed to customers – services and users.

One of most perspective technologies for sensing and perception is neural networks.

We may pick out following main features of ubiquitous computing systems (UCS):

1. distribution of obtaining and processing of sensor information,
2. variety of information needed processing,
3. necessity of learning during interaction with environment, in particular, in respect to existing of unexpected events and objects needed for including into processing,
4. key role of different kinds of human-machine interaction,
5. high requirements to security,
6. data processing in real time,
7. wide usage of embedded processing units.

There are following tasks for neural networks in development of ubiquitous computing systems:

1. perception, i.e. recognition of objects and changes in environment, in particular, invariant recognition of moving objects, e.g. recognition of gesture, position and emotions of human beings,
2. clustering and recognition of events and scenarios (sequence of events in time),
3. prediction of future events and situations,
4. indoor localization of mobile devices and continues mapping,
5. reactive behavior based managing of actions,
6. speech recognition.

From above we can formulate following requirements to neural networks for UCS:

1. Relatively fast processing of information in both learning and recalling,
2. Incremental learning, i.e. availability to perceive new information without loss of old knowledge,
3. Availability of easy extraction of structure from learnt neural network for building of symbolic knowledge for usage in machine-human interaction and planning.

On the other hand context awareness usually is implemented by symbolic based reasoning and knowledge-based techniques (Hung, Shehzad, Kiani, Riaz, Ngoc & Lee, 2004). Besides rules based approach is appropriate for human-machine interface for programming of behavior of smart objects (Tarik, Sarcar, Hasn, Huq, Gavrilov, Lee & Lee, 2008) and for any explanation for user.

The following tasks are more relevant to rule based and other symbolic techniques:

1. A prior description of behavior of smart object with respect to perceived objects/situations and context, including managing of dialog with user;
2. Reflex to perceived important situation starting determined behavior;
3. Diagnostics of sensor network;
4. Specific tasks in ubiquitous computing system, for example, dealing with medical diagnostics of patient in healthcare system, or decision making in recommendation systems;
5. Human-computer interaction based on natural language.

Therefore, obviously that hybrid intelligent system (HIS) approach based on combination of neural networks and formalized knowledge is most perspective for implementation of ambient intelligence in ubiquitous computing systems (Gavrilov, 2008, 3).

There are some challenges to be solved for usage of Hybrid Intelligent Systems in UCS:

1. Cooperation between sensing neural networks and reasoning knowledge structures, consisting of forward and feedback connections between them, transformation from one to another,
2. Knowledge acquisition from learnt neural networks,
3. Architecture of distributed hybrid intelligent system in heterogeneous wireless network.

In this chapter author are focusing on first of them, looking different kinds of HIS and suggesting two cases of hybrid intelligent systems in UCS: architecture of hybrid embedded expert system for control of smart objects (Gavrilov, 2008, 2) and context-based programming-learning of smart objects, in particular, mobile robots, using natural language (Gavrilov, 2008, 1; Gavrilov, 2009). Besides, in this chapter author try to introduce systematic view on methodology for development of hybrid intelligent systems.

HYBRID APPROACH TO DEVELOPMENT OF INTELLIGENT SYSTEMS

Hybrid approach in wide sense is combination of different paradigms of knowledge representation and reasoning such as rules, semantic nets, frames, fuzzy logics, neural networks, genetic algorithms, swarm intelligence and so on. Alternate and narrower view on one is combination or fusion in one system symbolic knowledge based and associative neural based (connectionist) techniques. Last opinion is more interesting for us and more perspective because is more constructive and is attempting to simulate processes in natural mind. So in this paper we will talk about this paradigm of hybrid intelligent systems.

Before appearance of hybrid intelligent system paradigm these techniques were investigating separately in classical Artificial Intelligence and neurocybernetics (later Computational Intelligence) and it is continued. Thus in these areas researches obtained many efficient and suitable techniques. To combine these one it is needed to think about interfaces between them. According to features of interfaces different classifications of hybrid intelligent systems are known.

In (Medsker & Bailey, 1992) first classification of HIS was proposed. Note that in this paper authors say about classification of hybrid expert systems but one is possible to extend on other kinds of intelligent systems. They suggested following kinds of hybrid expert systems: stand-alone, transformational, loosely-coupled, tightly-coupled and fully-integrated models. This classification focuses on features of system structure and interaction between different paradigms.

Stand-alone model of HIS consists of independent software components. In this case interaction between them to solve any task is possible only by human.

Transformational model is similar to stand-alone model but in this case we have any automated mechanism of transformation of knowledge base to neural network and vice versa. Usually this mechanism is executed sometimes during development and/or exploitation of system.

Loosely-coupled models comprise the first true form of integrated intelligent systems. In this model components interact between them but this interaction is enough brief and one is executed through file. That allows implementing these components independently providing any simple interface by this file.

Tightly-coupled model is oriented on more close cooperation between components. However, tightly-coupled systems pass information via memory resident data structures rather than external data files.

Fully-integrated model shares data structures and knowledge representations between different paradigms. Communication between them is accomplished via the dual nature (symbolic and neural) of the structures.

Figure 1. Classification of HIS architectures in (Funabashi, Maeda, Morooka, Mori, 1995): a) – combination, b) integration, c) fusion, d) association

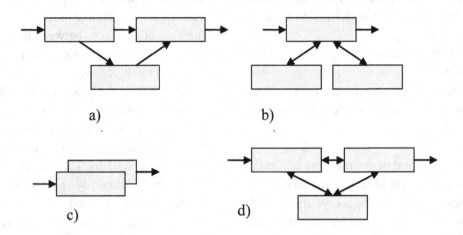

a)   b)

c)   d)

In (Goonatilake & Khebbal, 1995) was suggested another classification of hybrid intelligent systems. This classification focuses on connection between functionality and different paradigms and consists of three kinds of HIS: functional-replacing, intercommunicating and polymorphic hybrids.

Function-replacing hybrids address the functional composition of a single intelligent technique. In this hybrid class, a principal function of the given technique is replaced by another intelligent processing technique.

Inter-communicating hybrids are independent, self-contained, intelligent processing modules that exchange information and perform separate functions to generate solutions. These independent modules, which collectively solve the given task, are coordinated by a control mechanism.

Polymorphic hybrids are systems that use a single processing architecture to achieve the functionality of different intelligent processing techniques. The broad motivation for these hybrid systems is realizing multi-functionality within particular computational architectures. These systems can functionally mimic, or emulate, different processing techniques.

Another classification of hybrid architectures was proposed in (Funabashi, Maeda, Morooka, Mori, 1995) focusing on features of process structure for solving any task. In this classification authors describe follow kinds of HIS (Figure 1): combination, integration, fusion and association.

Very similar classification was proposed in (Jacobsen, 1998).

At last, in (McGarry, Wermter, & MacIntyre, 1999) was proposed newest classification consisting of three types of HIS: unified, transformational and modular hybrid systems.

The first group, "unified hybrid systems", consists of those systems that have all processing activities implemented by neural network elements. Such systems may be classified under the unified approach. So far these systems have only limited impact upon real world applications, due to the complexity of implementation, issues of model scalability and rather limited knowledge representation capability. This kind of HIS is basically similar to fully-integrated model in (Medsker & Bailey, 1992), polymorphic HIS in (Goonatilake & Khebbal, 1995) and fusion in (Funabashi, Maeda, Morooka, Mori, 1995).

The second group of systems can transfer a symbolic representation into a neural one and vice versa. It is with the second category, "transformational hybrid systems", that hybrid system begin to demonstrate some unique properties. The most interesting feature is the ability to insert, extract and refine symbolic knowledge within the framework of a neural network system. This kind of HIS is mostly similar to transformational model in (Medsker & Bailey, 1992).

The third category of "modular hybrid systems" covers those hybrid systems that are modular in nature, i.e. they are comprised of several neural networks and rule-based modules which can have different degrees of coupling and integration. An important aspect is that they do not involve any changes regarding the conceptual operation of either the neural network or rule-based components. The vast majority of hybrid systems fall into this category. The main reason is that they are powerful processors of information and are relatively easy to implement. This model is similar to loosely-coupled and tightly-coupled models in (Medsker & Bailey, 1992), inter-communicating HIS in (Goonatilake & Khebbal, 1995) and almost all models in (Funabashi, Maeda, Morooka, Mori, 1995) except fusion model.

At last twenty years hybrid intelligent systems are wide application, in particular, expert systems in different areas (Medsker & Bailey, 1992; Funabashi, Maeda, Morooka, Mori, 1995), control systems for mobile robots (Wermter & Ron Sun 2000; Gavrilov, Gubarev, Jo & Lee, 2004), core technology for development of artificial general intelligence and model of mind (Goertzel, Pennachin, 2007).

Besides structure and protocols features of interfaces between neural based and symbolic components of HIS covered by above classifications, it is needed to overcome challenges dealing with different nature of information processing in these components. These problems are more sophisticated and deep because descend from nature of our mind. For example, how to extract formalizing knowledge from pattern stored in neural network without loss of sufficient information, how to use formalized knowledge to control of flexible distributed actuator such as hand-like manipulator. This problem is close to such questions as: "What is consciousness and subconsciousness?", "What roles of them in thinking?", "What is sufficient information deserving of formalization as knowledge?" and at last "What are basic principles of mind oriented to interaction with unknown and uncertain environment?" (Gavrilov, 2003, 2007). These problems are investigated in different theories of mind and exceed the bounds of this paper.

Below author propose two examples of employment of hybrid approach to ubiquitous computing systems.

HYBRID EMBEDDED EXPERT SYSTEM FOR CONTROL OF SMART OBJECTS

In (Gavrilov, 2008, 2) author have proposed for development of hybrid intelligent systems for smart environment employment of framework implemented in hybrid expert shell ES Win (Gavrilov & Novickaja, 2001; Gavrilov & Chistyakov, 2005) combining with neural networks (ES Win 2.1 is free downloadable from http://www.insycom.ru). Previously this shell was oriented to development of dialog hybrid expert systems for solving of tasks for diagnostics and recommendations in well structured areas. But now ES Win is improving and expending for building of embedded systems in smart environment and robotics.

Proposed architecture of hybrid intelligent system may be classified as both loosely-coupled and modular with accordance to above classifications.

Figure 2. Architecture of ESWin

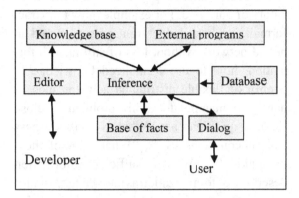

Knowledge Representation and Processing

Knowledge representation in ESWin (Figure 2, Figure 3) is based on frames, fuzzy rules and linguistic variables (Zadeh, 1975). Frames are used for description of structure of world (area) including properties and hierarchies of entities as frames-classes. Besides frames aim to store current facts about entities in frames-instances. Rules are used for description of solving of tasks, e.g. behavior of any smart object. Linguistic variables are determined inside frames and are used for description of fuzzy properties of objects or situations which may have both quantitative and qualitative values at the same time.

Solving of task is a fuzzy rule based backward chaining using data from frames and perception devices (e.g. user interface or perception subsystem based on neural network). Backward chaining provides execution of any behavior or decision making depending on current set of facts and goal. Goal means what we want to get from this behavior. For example, in simplest case it may be name of behavior.

Let take up ubiquitous service helping to find and operate the objects in room for elderly or handicapped people. This task may be executed by mobile robot too. Assume that we have one or more camera for monitoring of location and state

of person. Below you see fragment of knowledge base of this service realized in knowledge representation language of ESWin, modified for smart environment.

```
// This frame describes possible
goals for backward
// inference
Frame = Goal
     Find: (Cornflakes box;
Book; TV control; Medication;
Thermometer)
EndF
// These frames are in knowledge
base (model of world)
Frame = Cornflakes box
     Parent: Cereal box
EndF
Frame = Cereal box
     Parent: Box
     Action: (Pour out; Fill)
EndF
Frame = Box
     Parent: Object
     Fullness: (Full; Empty)
     Openness: (Opened; Closed)
     Action: (Open; Close)
EndF
Frame = Object
     Name: ()
     Action: (Take; Put; Find)
     Location: (Into; Visible;
Anywhere)
     Into: ()
// Here "lv" is a slot's type
"linguistic variable"
// Linguistic variable's member-
ship functions are described in
another special file
     Where (lv): (Near; Far;
Not far; Close by)
     Direction: (Ahead; To
left; To right; To back)
     Path: ()
```

Figure 3. Screenshot of ESWin's shell for developers

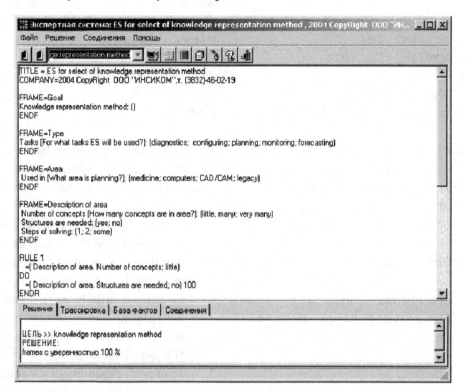

```
Color: (Red; Green; Yel-
low; Blue; White; Black)
    Size (lv): (Huge; Large;
Small; Tiny)
    Form: (Sphere; Cube; Rect-
angle; Complex)
EndF
// This and above frames pro-
vide generation of frame-fact //
from slot Name of Frame-parent
// with Name like value of cor-
responding slot of Object with
inheritance
// of properties of Object
Frame = Name
    Parent: Object
EndF
Frame = Person
    Action: (Turn to right;
Turn to left; Forward; Stop;
Turn back; Go to; Find)
```

```
    State: (Stand; Lie; Sit;
Walk)
    Direction of view: ()
EndF
// These frames are in base of
facts
Frame (instance) = Cornflakes
box
    Color: Green
    Location: Into
    Into: Cupboard
EndF
// Facts about visible (recog-
nized) objects
Frame (instance) = Person
    State: Stay
EndF
// Distances to visible objects
Frame (instance) = Cupboard
    Where: 1, 7
    Direction: Ahead
```

```
EndF
Frame (instance) = Window
     Where: Not far
     Direction: To left
EndF
// Rules for prompting to find
any object being into cupboard
Rule 1
     =(Object.Name; *Object)
     =(*Object.location; Into)
     =(*Object.into; Object_2)
     =(*Object_2.path; Any)
     =(*Object_2.Direction;
Ahead)
     <(*Object_2.Distance; 0,3)
DO
     =(Goal.Find; *Object)
     MS(Action.Ms; Stop, Please
take *Object from *Object_2)
EndR
Rule 2
     =(*Object.Into; Object_2)
     =(*Object_2.Direction;
Ahead)
     <>(*Object 2.Distance;
Close by)
DO
     =(*Object_2.Path; Ahead)
     MS(Action.Ms; Go straight
ahead to cupboard)
EndR
```

Note that term *Object is analog of identifier of variable which replaced by corresponding value from previous steps of interpretation of rules.

In this example some data (values of frame's slots), such as *Direction* and *Distance* to any objects-places (*Cupboard* or *Window*), *Form* of *Object* (*Sphere, Cube,* and so on), *Color* (*Green, Red* and so on), *State* and so on, may be obtained from sensing subsystem based on one or more neural networks. Any of them may be produced by rules, for example, *Cupboard. Direction* may be got from *Person. Direction of view* by executing of rule:

```
Rule 3
     =(Person.Direction of
view; *Object)
DO
     =(*Object.Direction;
Ahead)
EndR
```

To get more appropriate language for smart environment the knowledge representation language of ESWin had modified as follow:

1. To provide more compact knowledge base with description of different behaviors, was introduced a concept of variables-references in rules which may assume value (replaced by value similarly as in macro substitution) during interpretation of rules until task is solved (e.g., reference *Object and *Object_2 in our example).

2. To provide capability of solving of task during long time, were introduced two modes of interpretation (inference) – short time (for decision making in one moment) and long time (decision making during monitoring and control like in our example).

3. To provide capability to control of several processes simultaneously (e.g. our fragment of knowledge and any reaction for recognized important situation), multi-task capability was introduced into the interpreter. It means that start of any task (chaining) causes a process. And we have to support interaction between processes, in particular, interruption, waiting and shut down of processes. In above described example the interpretation of Rule 1 may be stopped and waits until condition <(Cupboard.Distance; 0,3) or "distance between person and cupboard < 0,3 meters" is true. It means that process will wait when person (or mobile robot) would come to cupboard. It is obvious that we have to implement any mechanism for interruption and shut down of this process.

Figure 4. Layers of information processing

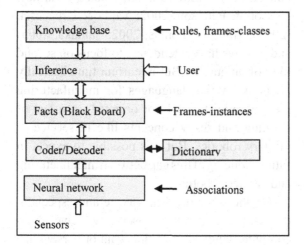

4. To provide reactive capabilities is implementing forward chaining (in ESWin 2.1 it is absent). Although it is possible to simulate reactive capability by backward chaining with multi-task capability and waiting of respect condition. But this simulation of reactive response is not enough suitable, visibility and effective.

Interaction Between Inference and Neural Networks

To support of interaction between rule-frame based inference and neural networks the following mechanism was proposed in (Gavrilov & Chistyakov, 2005) (Figure 4).

Special data structure SOURCE describes necessary parameters for the definition of interaction of expert shell with other program, in particular, neural network based sensing routine. If knowledge base interpreter will find this special frame in the condition of checking rule during process of inference, it realizes a pause of process and sends an inquiry for the reception of fact from other program. After receipt of fact the process of inference continues. If inquired fact does not enter from the external source in specifying gap of time, the fact is taken as empty (it means ab-

sence of the fact) and the inference continues. But if this special frame is used in conclusion rules, the expert system sends a fact to other program. The example of this structure for connection with neural network by socket is:

```
SOURCE = NN1
    Type: Connection
    Port: 1234
    IP: 127.0.0.1
    TimeOut: (10) // time of
waiting of response
    Old: (60) // time for ag-
ing of fact got from NN1
EndF
```

This structure contains all information needed for interface with neural network with name NN1 by socket. Usage of socket allows deploying modules of this hybrid intelligent system in network of smart environment.

Variables values of which are produced by neural network are described in frame with same name like this structure:

```
FRAME = NN1
    Form: (Cube; Sphere; Rect-
angle; Complex)
    Color: (Green; Red; Yel-
low; Blue; White; Black)
ENDF
```

If we use forward inference then the neural network is able to produce fact in arbitrary moment of time when it recognizes any situation or object. In both cases of inference (backward or forward) the result of execution of neural network is fact understandable for inference engine.

A dictionary for interface between neural network and inference engine is used. It is employed for coding of words (phrases) contained in frame for interface as vectors for neural network and for decoding of vectors obtained from neural network as words (phrases) constructing facts.

In our example described above we must have in dictionary following words: *Form, Cube, Sphere, Complex* (using for recognition of form), *State, Stay, Lie, Sit* (for recognition of state of person), *Object, Cupboard, Cornflakes box, Cup, Bottle, Window* (for recognition of objects).

Note that if any fact checked by rule exists already in base of fact (obtained from neural network earlier) then this fact is used without execution of neural network while difference between current time and time from one's appearance less than *Old*.

CONTEXT BASED PROGRAMMING-LEARNING OF SMART OBJECTS

One of most challenges in development of intelligent robots and other intelligent agents in ubiquitous computing systems is human-computer interface. Two kinds of such interfaces are known, oriented on programming and learning respectively. Concern to robotics a programming is used usually for industrial robots and other technological equipment; learning is more oriented for service and toy robotics. Here author will talk basically about robots but all lower statements can be applied to other kinds of smart objects.

There are many various programming languages for different kinds of intelligent equipment, for industrial robots-manipulators, mobile robots, technological equipment (Wan (Ed.), 2001), (Pembeci & Hager, 2002). The re-programming of robotic systems is still a difficult, costly, and time consuming operation. In order to increase flexibility, a common approach is to consider the work-cell programming at a high level of abstraction, which enables a description of the sequence of actions at a task-level. A task-level programming environment provides mechanisms to automatically convert high-level task specification into low level code. Task-level programming languages may be procedure oriented (Meynard, 2000) and declarative oriented (Williams, Ing-

ham, Chung & Elliott, 2003; Hudak, Courtney, Nilsson & Peterson, 2002; Vajda & Urbancsek (2003); Wahl & Thomas, 2002; Samaka, 2005) and now we have a tendency to focus on second kind of languages. But in current time basically all programming languages for manufacturing are deterministic and not oriented on usage of learning and fuzzy concepts like in service or military robotics. But it is possible to expect in future reducing of this gap between manufacturing and service robotics.

On the other hand in service and especially domestic robotics most users are naive about computer language and thus cannot personalize robots using standard programming methods. So at last time robot-human interface tends to usage of natural language (Gavrilov, 1988; Lauria, Bugmann, Kyriacou, Bos & Klein, 2001) and, in particular, spoken language (Spiliotopoulos, Androutsopoulos & Spyropoulos, 2001); Seabra Lopes, Teixeira, Rodrigues, Gomes, Teixeira, Ferreira, Soares, Girão & Sénica, 2003). Such mobile robot for example must understand such phrases as "Bring me cup a of tea", "Close the door", "Switch on the light", "Where is my favorite book? Give it to me", "When must I take my medication?".

Using natural language dialog with mobile robot we need to connect words and phrases with process and results of perception of robot by neural networks. In (Beetz, Kirsch, & Muller, 2004) to solve this problem the extension of robot programming language by introducing of corresponding operators was proposed. But it seems that such approach is not enough perspective.

Here we suggest bio- and psychology-inspired approach to combine programming and learning to perception of robot based on usage of neural networks algorithms and context as results of recognition of concepts obtained by learning during dialog in natural language (Gavrilov, 1988; Gavrilov, 2008; Gavrilov, 2009). In this approach author do not distinguish learning and programming and combine a declarative (description of

Figure 5. Relationships between paradigm "Context based Programming-Learning" and other paradigms

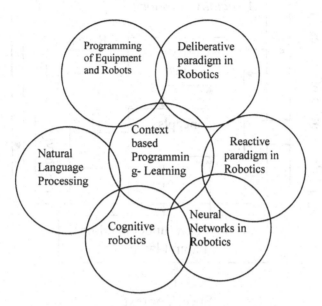

context) and procedural knowledge (routines for processing of context implementing elementary behavior) on the one hand, learning in neural networks and ordering of behavior by dialog in natural language on the other hand.

Proposed Paradigm and Architecture of Intelligent Agent

Our paradigm is based on relationships with other known paradigms and is shown in Figure 5. In Figure 6 you can see architecture of intelligent agent based on this paradigm.

Concepts are associations between images (visual and others) and phrases (words) of natural language. In simple case we will name as concept just name of them (phrases). These phrases are using for determination of context in which the robot is perceiving environment (in particular, natural language during dialog) and planning actions. We will name them as *context variables.*

Context is a tree of concepts (context variables) and is recognizing by sensor information and determining by dialog with user. Feedbacks

between concepts/context and recognition of images/phrases mean that recognition is controlled by already recognized things.

Dialog with user aims to describe elementary behaviors and conditions for its starting. To start any behavior it is needed recognize corresponding concept-releaser as in reactive paradigm of control system of robot (Murphy, 2000).

Behavior is not influence on just actions but also on context. Moreover, behavior may be not connecting directly with actions in environment. In this case we have just thinking under context variables. And even when behavior is oriented on execution of actions it is possible to block this connection and in this case we have any simulation in mind sequence of actions (e.g., it may be mean as planning).

The associative memory must satisfy to follow requirements:

1. To allow usage of both analog and binary inputs/outputs,
2. To provide incremental learning,

Figure 6. Intelligent agent functional structure oriented on context based programming-learning

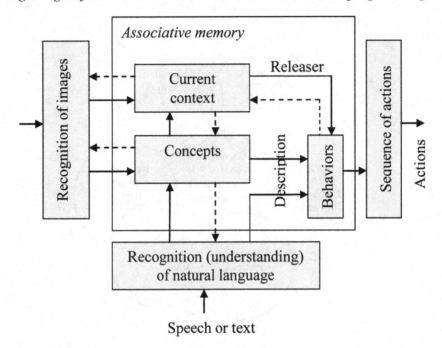

3. To provide storing of chain of concepts (as behavior or scenarios).

The elementary behavior is similar to subroutine and contains sequence of actions adaptable to context variables which may be viewed as parameters of subroutine. Of cause, we need to use some primitives directly connecting with elementary actions and describing parameters of these actions or basic context variables. Connections between these primitives and words of natural language must be a prior knowledge of robot obtaining at development of robot or during a preliminary teaching by specialist. It may be simple language similar to CBLR, proposed by author for context based programming of industrial robots in (Gavrilov, 1988; Gavrilov, 2008). Feature of this language is absence of different motion primitives. There we have just one motion primitive. All other primitives aim to represent of context variables needed for execution of this motion primitive. To distinguish these primitives

and usually using motions or geometric primitives we will call ones below as *output primitives*.

This hybrid architecture may be classified as fully-integrated model or tightly-coupled model in Medsker's classification and fusion or association in taxonomy of Funabashi et al. More concrete kind depends on details of implementation.

Cross-Modal Incremental Learning and Associative Memory

Associative memory satisfied to above requirements may be based on hybrid approach and similar to Long-Short Term Memory (LSTM) (Hochreiter & Schmidhuber, 1997) or table based memory proposed in (Gavrilov, Gubarev, Jo & Lee, 2004).

Note that *Concept* in Figure 6 is more common thing as *context*. Concepts are introducing by dialog subsystem for determination of objects, events, properties and abstraction. But *context* consists of several concepts separated by three rules: 1) preliminary defined concepts (names) are using as names of "parameters" to utilize in elementary behavior; 2) some concepts are using as values of these "parameters"; 3) some concepts (releasers) are using as names of any events causing any behavior.

Dialog subsystem must provide robustness to faults in sentences. For one's implementation may be used approach as proposed in (Gavrilov, 2003) and based on semantic networks combining with neural networks algorithms. This approach is oriented on fuzzy recognition of semantics. Dialog subsystem must provide attend visual recognition subsystem when it is needed to connect word (phrase) with recognizing image. In this case the recognition subsystem create new cluster with center as current feature vector. And couple of this feature vector and word (phrase) is storing in associative memory for concepts. It may be like result of processing of follow sentence "This is table". In contrast to this case when system processes sentence "Table is place for dinner" the new cluster is not created and associative memory is used for storing of association between just words (phrases).

Thus associative memory must be able to store associations between both couple of symbolic information and couple word (phrase) and feature vector. Besides concept storing in associative memory must have some tags: basic concept (preliminary defined) or no, name or value, current context or no. And every concept in associative memory must be able to connect in chain with other ones. The order of concepts in chain can be defined by dialog subsystem.

Output Primitives for Mobile Robot

Set of output primitives may be selected by different way. One approach to that is determination of enough complex behaviors, such as "Find determined object", "Go to determined place" and so on. These actions may be named as *motion primitives*. Determined *object* and *place* must be

obtained from context as value of corresponding context variable. And these variables may be viewed as another kind of output primitives: *context primitives*. In this case such actions must include inside any enough strong intelligence and ones limit capabilities of mobile robot to learn. Another approach may be based on very simple *motion primitives* such as "act", which may be just one. If the robot has any manipulator we may use also similar primitive for action of it. In this case may be primitive "act" for manipulator and "move" for mobile platform. If we want to make capability to say anything by robot not only during dialog inside dialog subsystem, we need introduce also at least one motion primitive "say". All another *output primitives* are *context primitives* and ones define features of execution of primitives "act" and "say". In other words ones are parameters of subroutine "act". Examples of robot's context variables are shown in Table 1.

INTRODUCTION TO METHODOLOGY FOR DEVELOPMENT OF HYBRID INTELLIGENT SYSTEMS

When we need to build any Hybrid Intelligent System, in particular, for ubiquitous computing system, we must answer follow questions:

- How to select different paradigms of AI,
- How to combine these paradigms,
- How to select interfaces (user and/or others),
- How to connect developed architecture for solving of the tasks with interfaces.

To answer these questions for any concrete task (application) we need:

1. to determine the methods of representation and solving of the task,
2. to perform the forms of input and output data,

Table 1. Examples of context primitives for mobile robot

Name of context primitive	Possible value	How this parameter influence on execution of motion primitive
Object	Name of object	May be used in action "say"
Internal state	Good, Bad, Normal	May cause motion to or from *Object*
Direction	Left, Right, Forward, Back	May cause corresponding turn depending on *Internal state*
Person	Name of person	May be used in action "say"
Obstacle distance	Far, Middle, Close	May be used in "act"
Obstacle type	Static, Dynamic	May be used in "act"
Speed	Low, Normal, High	May be used in "act"

3. to select the methods of hybridization.

Process of solving of task may be decomposed by follow ways:

1. Sequence of subtasks,
2. Set of concurrent subtasks, decision is a decision of subtask-winner,
3. Tree of subtasks,
4. Network of subtasks, described by oriented graph.

Real application may use input data of three kinds: Boolean vector, analog vector and symbolic data (in particular, words of natural language). Forms of presentation of these input data may be performed by follow taxonomy:

1. Visual stream;
2. Visual picture;
3. Sound;
4. Voice;
5. Signals from special equipment;
6. Formatted text;
7. Non-structured text.

The output data may be distinguished as:

1. Symbolic data;
2. Numeric data;
3. Signals;

4. Pictures;
5. Animation;
6. Diagrams.

Forms of present of output data may be wrote as:

1. Words of natural language;
2. Sentences of natural language;
3. Tables;
4. Graphics;
5. Sound;
6. Speech;
7. Control signals for equipment.

Particular kind of output data is data for explanation of solution.

Separated task or subtasks may be performed by follow taxonomy:

- Recognition or classification. In this task the result is usually symbolic data, and this task usually can not viewed as sequence of similar subtasks, but may be viewed as a tree of classification subtasks;
- Acquisition of knowledge. This task basically is similar to recognition, but one may be composed from subtasks of different kinds;
- Reasoning or decision making. The result of solving of this task is symbolic data and

this task can viewed as consecutive solving of different subtasks or tree of different subtasks;

- Calculation. In this task the result is value of any known function;
- Approximation. In this task the result is value of any unknown function;
- Prediction In this task the result is value of any unknown function from time;
- Planning. In this task the result is sequence of symbolic or numeric data in time;
- Explanation.

Every of above tasks has special performing and solving methods. And to select one of them we need respect to kind of input-output data and requirements to implementation (e.g., limits of resources, requirements to interfaces and so on). Then we must select kind of hybrid architecture with respect to system's requirements.

This description of taxonomy of different components for HIS development obviously is not full. One is oriented on local system, e.g. for development of intelligent system for any smart object (e.g., smart bed, intelligent agent based on mobile phone, mobile robot and so on). But for development of smart environment most important issue is to take account of distribution of smart objects and necessity to communicate among them. Therefore we need to introduce into methodology also parameters of communications, such as, parameters of signals, traffic, features of protocols. Besides, it is essential to understand and to describe somehow the relationship between distributed tasks (and its implementation) and features of communication. For example, is it possible and how to communicate between two neural networks in ubiquitous computing system? This problem is close to communication between human beings and evolution of natural language. These problems overstep the limits of this paper and show that this "introduction" is just start in a long way.

CONCLUSION

Usage of hybrid approach to development of ambient intelligence in ubiquitous computing systems is obviously perspective way. This approach is bio-inspired and final goal of researchers is development of human-like mind implementing advantages of artificial intelligent system (may be phantom), such as, high speed and capacity of memory, easiness of communication with equipment, without loss of flexible and learnable of natural mind.

Future of ubiquitous computing with ambient intelligence may be viewed as appearance of thinking and speaking home or office (or shop) building consisting of thinking and speaking (may be not all) smart objects including assistive robots. Thus human person will deal with artificial characters being able help him to access different capabilities of building to improve comfort of life and efficacy of job. May be two ways to implement such ambient intelligence: to make separated intelligent agents (artificial persons) collaborating by communication or to centralize artificial person. In last case all smart objects may be viewed as parts of this person for perception, communication and action.

REFERENCES

Baldauf, M., Dustdar, S., & Rosenberg, F. (2007). A Survey on Context-Aware Systems. *Int. J. Ad Hoc and Ubiquitous Computing, 2*(4), 263–277. doi:10.1504/IJAHUC.2007.014070

Beetz, M., Kirsch, A., & Muller, A. (2004). RPL_{LEARN}: Extending an Autonomous Robot Control Language to Perform Experience-based Learning. In *Proceedings of the Third International Joint Conference on Autonomous Agents and Multiagent Systems AAMAS 2004* (pp. 1022 – 1029). New York: ACM.

Bishop, C. (1995). Neural Networks for pattern recognition. Oxford, UK: Clarendon Press.

Chen, G., & Kotz, D. (2000). *A survey of context-aware mobile computing research.* Tech. Rep. TR2000-381, Dept. of Computer Science, Dartmouth College.

Funabashi, M., Maeda, A., Morooka, Y., & Mori, K. (1995). Fuzzy and Neural Hybrid Expert Systems: Synergetic AI. *IEEE Expert, 10*(4), 32–40. doi:10.1109/64.403949

Gavrilov, A. V. (1988). Dialog system for preparing of programs for robot. Automatyka, 99, Glivice, Poland, 173-180 (in Russian).

Gavrilov, A. V. (2003). A combination of Neural and Semantic Networks in Natural Language Processing. In H-H. Lee, (Ed.), *Proceedings of the 7th Korea-Russia International Symposium KORUS-2003,* (Vol. 2, pp. 143-147). Republic of Korea: University of Ulsan.

Gavrilov, A. V. (2003). The principles of action of intelligent systems. In *Proceedings of International Conference on Information Systems and Technologies IST-2003,* (Vol.3, pp. 91-94), Novosibirsk State Technical University, Novosibirsk, Russia.

Gavrilov, A. V. (2007). The principles of action of intelligent systems. In G. Marchetti (Ed.) *Mind, Consciousness and Language.* Retrieved from http://www.mind-consciousness-language.com/articles.htm

Gavrilov, A. V. (2008). Context and Learning based Approach to Programming of Intelligent Equipment. In J.-S. Pan & P. Kellenberger (Eds.), *The 8th International Conference on Intelligent Systems Design and Applications ISDA-2008* (pp. 578-582). Washington, DC: IEEE Computer Society.

Gavrilov, A. V. (2008). Hybrid Rule and Neural Network based Framework for Ubiquitous Computing. In J. Kim, D. Delen, Park, F. Ko, Y. J. Na, (Eds.), *The 4th International Conference on Networked Computing and Advanced Information Management:* (Vol. 2, pp. 488-492). Washington, DC: IEEE Computer Society.

Gavrilov, A. V. (2008). Usage of Neural Networks in Ubiquitous Computing Systems. In N.V. Pustovoy (Ed.), *Proceedings. of the 3rd International Forum on Strategic Technologies IFOST-2008.* Novosibirsk, Russia: Novosibirsk State Technical University.

Gavrilov, A. V. (2009). New Paradigm of Context based Programming-Learning of Intelligent Agent. In A. Pascoal & V. Ufranovsky (Eds.), *Proceedings of 1st Workshop on Networked embedded and control system technologies. In conjunction with 6th International Conference on Informatics in Control, Automation and Robotics ICINCO-2009* (pp. 94-99). Portugal: INSTICC Press.

Gavrilov, A. V., & Chistyakov, N. A. (2005). An architecture of the toolkit for development of Hybrid Expert Systems. In Yu, I. Shokin, O.I. Potaturkin, (Eds.), *Proceedings of The Second IASTED International Multi-Conference Automation, Control and Information Technology ACIT-2005.* Novosibirsk, Russia: ACTA Press.

Gavrilov, A. V., Gubarev, V. V., Jo, K.-H., & Lee, H.-H. (2004). An architecture of hybrid control system of mobile robot. *Mechatronics, Automation. Control, 8,* 30–37.

Gavrilov, A. V., Gubarev, V. V., Jo, K.-H., & Lee, H.-H. (2004). Hybrid Neural-based Control System for Mobile Robot. In Y.P. Pokholkov (Ed.), *Proceedings of the 8th Korea-Russia International Symposium KORUS-2004,* (Vol. 1, pp. 31-35). Tomsk, Russia: Tomsk Polytechnic University.

Gavrilov, A. V., & Lee, S.-Y. (2007). Usage of Hybrid Neural Network Model MLP-ART for Navigation of Mobile Robot. In de-Shuang Huang, Luonan Chen (Eds.) *International Conference on Intelligent Computing* ICIC-2007, (LNAI 4682, pp. 182-191). Berlin: Springer-Verlag.

Gavrilov, A. V., & Novickaja, J. V. (2001). The Toolkit for development of Hybrid Expert Systems. In Y.P. Pokholkov (Ed.) *Proceedings of the 5th Korea-Russia International Symposium KORUS-2001,* (Vol. 1, pp. 73-75). Tomsk, Russia: Tomsk Polytechnic University.

Goertzel, B., & Pennachin, C. (Eds.). (2007). Artificial General Intelligence. Berlin, Germany: Springer-Verlag.

Goonatilake, S., & Khebbal, S. (Eds.). (1995). Intelligent Hybrid Systems. San Francisco, CA: Wiley.

Hochreiter, S., & Schmidhuber, J. (1997). Long Short-Term Memory. *Neural Computation, 9*(8), 1735–1780. doi:10.1162/neco.1997.9.8.1735

Hudak, P., Courtney, A., Nilsson, H., & Peterson, J. (2002). Arrows, Robots, and Functional Reactive Programming. *LNCS, 2638,* 159–187.

Hung, N. Q., Shehzad, A., Kiani, S. L., Riaz, M., Ngoc, K. A., & Lee, S.-L. (2004). Developing Context-Aware Ubiquitous Computing Systems with a Unified Middleware Framework. In L.T. Yang (Ed.), *The 2004 International Conference on Embedded & Ubiquitous Computing* (pp. 672-681). Berlin: Springer-Verlag.

Jacobsen, H.-A. (1998). A generic architecture for hybrid intelligent systems. In *Fuzzy Systems Proceedings, IEEE World Congress on Computational Intelligence,* (Vol. 1, pp. 709-714).

Lauria, S., Bugmann, G., Kyriacou, T., Bos, J., & Klein, E. (2001). Training Personal Robots Using Natural Language Instruction. *IEEE Intelligent Systems, 16,* 38–45.

Mahalik, N. P. (Ed.). (2007). Sensor Networks and Configuration. Berlin, Germany: Springer-Verlag

McGarry, K., Wermter, S., & MacIntyre, J. (1999). Hybrid Neural Systems: From Simple Coupling to Fully Integrated Neural Networks. *Neural Computing Surveys, 2,* 62–94.

Medsker, L. R., & Bailey, D. L. (1992). Models and Guidelines for Integrating Expert Systems and Neural Networks. In A. Kandel & G. Langholz (Eds.), Hybrid Architectures for Intelligent Systems (pp. 154-171). Boca Raton, FL: CRC Press.

Meynard, J.-P. (2000). *Control of industrial robots through high-level task programming.* Thesis, Linkopings University, Sweden.

Murphy, R. (2000). Introduction to AI Robotics. Cambridge, MAL: MIT Press.

Pembeci, I., & Hager, G. (2002). A comparative review of robot programming language. Technical report, CIRL Lab.

Rabunal, J. R., & Dorado, J. (2006). *Artificial Neural Networks in Real Life Applications.* Hershey, PA: IDEA Group Publishing. Kiani, S. L., Riaz, M., Zhung, Y., Lee. S & Lee, Y-K. (2005). A Distributed Middleware Solution for Context Awareness in Ubiquitous Systems. In *Proceedings of 11th IEEE International Conference on Embedded and Real-time Computing Systems and Applications* (pp. 451-454). Washington, DC: IEEE Computer Society.

Samaka, M. (2005). Robot Task-Level Programming Language and Simulation. In Proc. of World Academy of Science, Engineering and Technology, (Vol. 9).

Satyanarayanan, M. (2001 August). Pervasive Computing: Vision and Challenges. *IEEE Personal Communications,* (pp. 10-17).

Schilit, B., Adams, N., & Want, R. (1994). Context-aware computing applications. In *IEEE Workshop on Mobile Computing Systems and Applications*. Santa Cruz, CA: IEEE Computer Society.

Seabra Lopes, L., Teixeira, A., Rodrigues, M., Gomes, D., Teixeira, C., Ferreira, L., et al. (2003). Towards a Personal Robot with Language Interface. In *Proceedings of 8th European Conference on Speech Communication and Technology EUROSPEECH'2003* (pp. 2205—2208), Geneva.

Spiliotopoulos, D., Androutsopoulos, I., & Spyropoulos, C. D. (2001). Human-Robot Interaction based on Spoken Natural Language Dialogue. In *Proceedings of the European Workshop on Service and Humanoid Robots (ServiceRob '2001)* (pp. 123-128), Santorini, Greece.

Tarik-Ul Islam, K., Jehad, S., Kamrul, H., Rezwanul, H. M., Gavrilov, A. V., Lee, Y.-K., & Lee, S.-Y. (2008). A Framework of Smart Objects and their Collaboration in Smart Environment. In H. H. Lee (Ed.), *The 10th International Conference on Advanced Communication Technology*, (Vol. 1, pp. 852-855). Washington, DC: IEEE Computer Society.

Vajda, F., & Urbancsek, T. (2003). High-Level Object-Oriented Program Language for Mobile Microrobot Control. In *IEEE Proceedings of the conference INES 2003*, Assiut - Luxor, Egypt. Washington, DC: IEEE Computer Society.

Wahl, F. M., & Thomas, U. (2002). Robot Programming - From Simple Moves to Complex Robot Tasks. In *Proceedings of First Interntional Colloquium "Collaborative Research Center 562 – Robotic Systems for Modelling and Assembly"* (pp. 249-259), Braunschweig, Germany.

Wan, J. (Ed.). (2001). Computational Intelligence in Manufacturing Handbook. Boca Raton, FL: CRC Press LLC.

Weiser, M. (1991). The Computer for the 21st Century. *Scientific American*, (September): 94–104. doi:10.1038/scientificamerican0991-94

Wermter, S., & Sun, R. (2000). Hybrid Neural Systems. Heidelberg, Germany: Springer.

Williams, B. C., Ingham, M. D., Chung, S. H., & Elliott, P. H. (2003). Model-based programming of intelligent embedded systems and robotic space explorers. In. *Proceedings of IEEE: Special Issue on Modeling and Design of Embedded Software*, *91*(1), 212–237.

Zadeh, L. A. (1975). The concept of a linguistic variable and its application to approximate reasoning. *Inform. Sci.*, *9*, 43–80. doi:10.1016/0020-0255(75)90017-1

ADDITIONAL READING

Amit, K. (2000). Artificial intelligence and soft computing. London, New-York: CRC Press.

Basten, T., Geilen, M., & de Groot, H. (Eds.). (2003). Ambient intelligence: impact on embedded system design. New York, Boston, Dordrecht, London, Moscow: Kluwe Academic Publishers.

Bunke, H., & Kandel, A. (Eds.). (2002). Hybrid methods in pattern recognition. Singapore: World Scientific Publishing Company.

Gavrilov A.V. Hybrid intelligent systems. Novosibirsk, Russia: Novosibirsk State Technical University (in Russian).

Jang, J.-S. R., Sun, C.-T., & Mizutani, E. (1996). Neuro-fuzzy and soft computing. Upper Saddle River, NJ: Prentice Hall.

Melin, P., & Castillo, O. (2005). Hybrid intelligent systems for pattern recognition using soft computing. Berlin, Heidelberg, Germany: Springer-Verlag.

Minsky, M. (2006). The emotional machine. New-York, NY: Simon & Shuster.

Negnevitsky, M. (2002). Artificial intelligence: a guide to intelligent systems. Harlow, UK: Addison-Wesley.

Ovaska Seppo, J. (Ed.). (2004). Computationally Intelligent Hybrid Systems: The Fusion of Soft Computing and Hard Computing. Wiley-IEEE Press.

Remagnino, P., Foresti, G. L., & Ellis, T. (Eds.). (2005). Ambient intelligence: a novel paradigm. Boston, MA: Springer.

Tetsuya, H. (2005). Artificial mind system. Berlin, Heidelberg, Germany: Springer-Verlag.

Tim, J. M. (2008). Artificial intelligence: a systems approach. Hingham, MA: Infinity Science Press LLC

Toshiniri, M. (2008). Fundamentals of the new artificial intelligence. London, UK: Springer-Verlag.

Weber, W., Rabaey, J. M., & Aarts, E. (Eds.). (2005) Ambient intelligence. Berlin, Heidelberg: Springer.

Zhang, Z., & Zhang, C. (2005). Agent-based hybrid intelligent systems. LNAI, 2938, Berlin, Heidelberg, Germany: Springer-Verlag.

Zomaya Albert, Y. (Ed.). (2006). Handbook of nature-inspired and innovative computing. Berlin, Heidelberg: Springer.

Chapter 15
A Primer of Ubiquitous Computing Challenges and Trends

Cristiano André da Costa
Universidade do Vale do Rio dos Sinos, Brazil

Jorge Luis Victoria Barbosa
Universidade do Vale do Rio dos Sinos, Brazil

Luciano Cavalheiro da Silva
Universidade Federal do Rio Grande do Sul, Brazil

Adenauer Corrêa Yamin
Universidade Católica de Pelotas, Brazil

Cláudio Fernando Resin Geyer
Universidade Federal do Rio Grande do Sul, Brazil

ABSTRACT

The growing availability of wireless networks and the proliferation of portable devices have made mobile computing a reality. Furthermore, the widespread use of location systems stimulates the creation of context-aware and adaptive systems. Ubiquitous computing integrates and extends these approaches through a new proposal where users' applications are available in a suitable adapted form, wherever they go and however they move. In this scenario, issues related to development of software need to be tackled. This chapter reviews essential concepts of the ubiquitous computing area, its evolution, and challenges that must be managed. To deal with these issues, the authors describe the main requirements for the development of ubiquitous software. This analysis starts with the discussion of limitations in the use of traditional programming models, and then goes on to the proposition of techniques to address these limitations. The authors trust that this discussion can help the future development of ubiquitous applications.

DOI: 10.4018/978-1-61520-843-2.ch015

INTRODUCTION

Nowadays, studies about mobility in distributed systems are being stimulated by the proliferation of portable electronic devices (for example, cell phones, handheld computers, tablet PCs, and notebooks) and the use of new interconnection technologies based on wireless communication (such as WiFi, Bluetooth, and WiMAX). This new mobile and distributed paradigm is called mobile computing (Satyanarayanan, 1996). What is more, the dissemination of location systems (Hightower, LaMarca & Smith, 2006) is enabling the use of mobile computing tailored to the physical location of the user. This scenario fosters the development of context-aware applications (Dey, 2001). The idea consists in the perception of characteristics related to the users and their surroundings. These characteristics are normally referred to as context, i.e. any information that can be used to describe the circumstances concerning an entity. Based on perceived context, the application can modify its behavior. This process, in which software modifies itself according to sensed data, is named adaptation (Satyanarayanan, 1996). In this scenario ubiquitous computing is emerging (Weiser, 1991).

Current practical approaches to the ubiquitous computing usually rely upon traditional computing paradigms envisioned when mobile applications where not a reality. Ubiquity aspects bring many new concerns, such as coping with the limited processing power of mobile devices, frequent disconnections, the migration of code between heterogeneous devices, context management, among others. These aspects demand a discussion of the issues involved in creating ubiquitous software.

In this chapter we review essential concepts of ubiquitous computer area, its evolution, and challenges that must be addressed. To address these issues, we describe the main requirements for the development of ubiquitous computing software. This analysis starts with the discussion of limitations in the use of traditional programming models, and then goes on to the proposition of characteristics and techniques to deal with these limitations.

The chapter is organized in six sections. In section two we present background, mainly discussing definitions and ubiquitous computing evolution. The following section focuses on the ubiquitous computing challenges. The fourth section discusses why traditional programming models alone are insufficient to develop ubiquitous applications. In the fifth section we describe the requirements that should be tackled in ubiquitous software. Section six presents future trends for the area. Finally, in the last section, we draw some conclusions.

BACKGROUND

We should begin by defining ubiquitous computing (also called ubicomp). Mark Weiser created this term, so he is considered one of the area's fathers. He presents computer ubiquity as the idea of integrating computers seamlessly, invisibly enhancing the real world. Weiser (1991) formulates a "new way of thinking about computers in the world, one that takes into account the natural human environment and allows the computers themselves to vanish into the background" (p. 94). Computers will vanish as a consequence of human psychology: when people use things without consciously thinking about them, they focus beyond. This is a phenomenon defined by some philosophers and psychologists (Weiser, 1991): people cease to be aware of something when they use it sufficiently well and frequently. Philosopher Heidegger calls this phenomenon ready-to-hand[1] and Edmund Husserl calls it the horizon.[2]

Heidegger makes a phenomenological analysis of the way people deal with the world. According to him, our first behavior toward entities such as tools, devices, and systems within the world is one of use. These entities, viewed from their aspect of use, are called ready-to-hand. In "Being and Time"[3], Heidegger (1996) affirms that

The peculiarity of what is proximally ready-to-hand is that, in its readiness-to-hand, it must, as it were, withdraw in order to be ready-to-hand quite authentically. That with which our everyday dealings proximally dwell is not the tools themselves. On the contrary, that with which we concern ourselves primarily is the work. (p. 99)

Edmund Husserl was the first to propose the horizon concept (Keen, 1975). Husserl was a philosopher, one of the founders of phenomenology, and a mathematician. The concept refers to human experience as a background that turns experiences possible. Horizon points to a network of known meanings focusing not much on physical things, but on an ordered pattern which we formulate implicitly in our act of being (Keen, 1975).

To achieve the physical integration of computers into the world, as a background, we must apply some conceptual changes. In this perspective, Weiser also defines embodied virtuality in opposition to virtual reality, as computers cannot be limited to their devices and software installed. Moreover, it is inadequate to consider the Internet or distributed file systems access as an example of seamless integration. Weiser points out that the power of ubiquitous computing does not stem from the capacity of a particular device, but rather from the interaction of all devices.

Besides computer interaction, scale and location are two important topics highlighted by Weiser. There will be many computers per room, in different sizes, with different user's interfaces, and suitable for specific jobs. Computers must also know where they are and use this information to adapt to the environment. Adaptation is then currently one of the crucial concerns in ubicomp.

Analyzing Weiser's vision, Saha and Mukherjee (2003) state that, in spite of significant hardware developments, computers are still machines that run programs in virtual environments and

not yet a "portal into an application-data space." Want et al. (2002) agree that many hardware components are now ready for ubiquitous computing, as a consequence of many improvements since Weiser's seminal article, including wireless networks, high-performance low-powered processors, enhancements in displays, high-capacity, and low-powered storage devices.

To achieve ubiquitous computing, we need advances in physical integration and in spontaneous interoperation as defined by Kindberg and Fox (2002). Integration between devices and the physical world is crucial. There should be system boundaries and specifications for the scope of the environment, but these should not be a constraint to interoperation. As components move among devices and environments, they must change both identity and functionality in order to interoperate.

We must understand and support everyday practices of people to reach Weiser's vision, offering different forms of interactive experiences through heterogeneous devices connected via integrated network components (Abowd et al., 2000).

Defining Pervasive Computing

The origin of the term pervasive computing is frequently associated with IBM. This is perhaps because it was used as the main subject of a whole issue of the IBM System Journal (vol. 38, no. 4, 1999). This issue defines pervasive computing as a change in the way we view computers and their use. Computers are everywhere and are used not as distinct machines but rather as "sophisticated, computerized, networked machines" (Hoffnagle, 1999), i.e. parts of larger devices.

A group of IBM researchers (Banavar et al., 2000) defined three characteristics associated to pervasive computing:

First, it concerns the way people view mobile computing devices, and use them within their en-

vironments to perform tasks. Second, it concerns the way applications are created and deployed to enable such tasks to be performed. Third, it concerns the environment and how it enhanced by the emergence and ubiquity of new information and functionality. (p. 266)

As a consequence of these characteristics, authors maintain that a new application model is needed in pervasive computing. Devices must be a portal into application and data space; applications are means for performing tasks; and the environment is the physical world with the user's information (Banavar et al., 2000).

Grimm et al. (2004) affirms that pervasive computing suggests a "computing infrastructure that seamlessly and ubiquitously aids users in accomplishing their tasks and that renders the actual computing devices and technology largely invisible." This vision creates the need for smart devices in the real world. Devices must coordinate with each other, in order to accomplish user's tasks. The difficulty lies in designing, building, and deploying applications in these circumstances (Grimm et al., 2004).

Another definition (Satyanarayanan, 2001) suggests that the essence of pervasive computing is "the creation of environments saturated with computing and communication capability, yet gracefully integrated with human users". Satyanarayanan also asserts that pervasive computing and ubiquitous computing are basically different terms used to describe the same concept. The main difference between both concepts is that pervasive computing is a bottom-up vision that emerged from the widespread exploitation of computing services, while ubiquitous computing is a top-down approach were these services are used in a transparent manner and integrated with the environment (Robinson et al., 2005). We adhere to this vision, although many authors nowadays treat both terms as synonyms.

Evolution

The advent of Personal Computers (PCs) in the mid 1970s, besides making computers popular, brought them closer to people and represented a first step in the direction of ubiquitous computing (Saha & Mukherjee, 2003). However, making the computer personal is a technological misplacement in Weiser's vision. The computer remains the focus of attention, and is thus isolated from the overall situation (Weiser, 1993).

Distributed computing is generally considered a major step in ubicomp evolution. The need to exchange information and communication stimulated the development of computer networks. Distributed systems benefited from this already existing infrastructure, acting as a set of interconnected computers using communications links in different media and topology. In such systems, processing entities exchange information using message passing through a variety of protocols to perform an execution of distributed tasks. To accomplish this distributed computing, more research was and is still needed in many areas.

Satyanarayanan (2001) emphasizes some areas important to pervasive computing foundation in the spectrum of distributed systems:

- *Remote communication*: techniques such as message passing, remote procedure call (RPC) and group communications are common possibilities for interaction in distributed systems. More recently, with the wide dissemination of object-oriented programming, approaches like remote method invocation (RMI) and code mobility are being widely used. RMI integrates RPC with the object-oriented paradigm. Code Mobility is a different method that makes it possible to create a dynamic change of location in which objects are executed (Fuggetta et al., 1998). This is an interesting concept to apply to ubiquitous computing;

- *Fault Tolerance*: the aim is to make computing systems more reliable in handling faults. Faults are defects at the lowest level and may cause errors. An error, in effect may lead to a failure deviating the system from its correct specification (Gärtner, 1999). An important measure in this field is the dependability of a system, which is the ability to avoid service failures that are more frequent and more severe than acceptable (Avižienis et al., 2004);
- *High availability*: availability is concerned with the readiness for correct services (Avižienis et al., 2004). High availability requires mechanisms such as data replication and recovery. By data replication we mean maintaining multiple copies of data in different machines. This increases availability by allowing access to data even when some computers are unavailable. Optimistic replication increases availability and is better suited for mobile computing (Saito & Shapiro, 2005);
- *Remote information access*: distributed file system (DFS) and databases are a common information repository. They allow users of distributed computers to share data across the network in a transparent manner (Levy & Silberschatz, 1990). An important aspect of DFS is user mobility. In the system users can log and use their files from any machine. It is up to the system to locate the data and to transport them to the client machine;
- *Security*: an important issue in distributed systems is how to ensure authenticity, authority, integrity, confidentiality, and non-repudiation. Security mechanisms such as cryptography and secure protocols are used. Privacy and trust are major concerns and these increase with ubiquitous computing. Another concern is that users must trust infrastructure and the exchange of information. It is important to define how

much information or how many resources should be disclosed to others (Robinson et al., 2005). The application of trust management systems and models is necessary.

Another important step in evolution is the World Wide Web (hereafter referred to simply as the Web). With the Web, information and communication have become nearly ubiquitous. The simple mechanism used for linking resources is a good way of integrating distributed information and a potential starting point for ubiquitous computing, even though the Web does not integrate the physical world (Saha & Mukherjee, 2003).

The final step in evolution is mobile computing. This arises from advances in two areas: wireless networking and portable devices. With these devices the user can access information anywhere, regardless of their physical location or mobility (Jing et al., 1999). The difference from traditional computing is that computing services go with people and become more present, providing expanded capabilities. Combined with network access, those services transform computing "into an activity that can be carried" (Lyytine & Yoo 2002).

Limited resources such as wireless bandwidth, battery life, computational power, screen size, etc. are typical mobile constrains. On the other hand, software does not change significantly as we move. To address these problems, adaptation is needed. This consists in reacting to changes and creating a dynamic balance between available resources and applications needs.

Moreover, Jing et al (1999) discusses two other major research aspects of mobile computing, apart from adaptation: extended client-server model[4] and mobile data access. The former consists of dynamically partitioning responsibilities between client and server, while the latter covers issues related to remote data access, cache consistency, and ways of structuring data.

An additional contribution from mobile computing in this evolution, emphasized by

Table 1. Ubiquitous computing challenges

Issue	Alias	Focus Area	Motive
Heterogeneity		Distributed systems	- Variety and difference - Different types of devices, networks, systems, and environments
Scalability	Localized Scalability[5]	Distributed systems	- Large scale - Increase in the number of resources and users
Dependability and Security	Fault Tolerance[6]	Mission-critical and Distributed Systems	- Avoiding failures that are more frequent and more severe than acceptable - Providing availability, confidentiality, reliability, safety, integrity, and maintainability
Privacy and Trust		Internet and Mobile computing	- Protecting against bad use of personal data - Defining the trustworthiness of interacting components
Spontaneous Interoperation	Volatility	Mobile computing	- Allowing interaction with a set of components that can change both identity and functionality - Permitting association and interaction
Mobility	Follow-me applications	Mobile computing	- Application and data access anywhere and any time - The user environment goes along
Context awareness	Perception	Mobile and Ubiquitous computing	- Perceiving user's state and surroundings - Inferring context information
Context management[7]	Smartness, Masking uneven condition, Adaptability	Mobile and Ubiquitous computing	- Modifying the behavior of the system based on the perceived context information - Adapting
Transparent User Interaction	Human-computer interaction[8]	Ubiquitous computing	- Merging user interface with the real world - Allowing user focus on tasks with minimal distraction
Invisibility	Ubiquity, Pervasively	Ubiquitous computing	- Allowing users focus on task, not tools - Making computers disappear in the background

Satyanarayanan (2001), is location sensitivity. Research in this field proposes algorithms and techniques for sensing physical location. Certain systems also provide location-aware behavior.

The integrated possibilities brought about by the development of PC, distributed systems, the Web, as well as mobile computing, set the stage for ubiquitous computing to evolve. The main issues involved in achieving ubiquity will be described in the next section.

UBIQUITOUS COMPUTING CHALLENGES

To achieve ubiquitous computing, as proposed by Weiser, some challenges must be addressed. A number of previous studies enumerate issues unique or still open in the field (Banavar et al., 2000; Costa et al., 2008; Kindberg & Fox, 2002; Saha & Mukherjee, 2003;). In this section the key challenges are presented and discussed. Table 1 summarizes the main challenges and presents their aliases, areas in which they gain focus and central motivations to address these in the scope of ubicomp.

Heterogeneity is a concern derived from distributed systems. Applications must be able to run in different kinds of devices, with assorted operating systems, and user's interfaces. Software must mask differences in infrastructure to the user and manage the required conversions from one environment to another. As a result, we must address protocol mismatches. In this scenario, it is impossible to recreate device-specific software.

Consequently, application logic must be created only once with a device-independent approach.

Another related issue inherited from distributed systems is scalability. In pervasive computing, a large number of users, devices, applications, and communications are expected on a scale never established before. Furthermore, it would be impractical to explicitly distribute and install applications. We must avoid centralized solutions for better scalability and bottleneck prevention. Moreover, distant interactions must be reduced to a minimum.

Sometimes, the system cannot execute according to functional specifications. Additionally, there might arise problems related to misspecifications. These situations lead to failures. A failure is defined as a transition from a correct service to an incorrect service (Avižienis et al., 2004). A correct service is obtained when the system implements the desired function. Incorrect service should be detected and execution restored to a correct state. Avoiding failures that are more frequent and more severe than acceptable leads to dependability, a concept that integrates the attributes of availability, reliability, safety, integrity, and maintainability. The term pervasive dependability has been used to refer to these needs in the scope of ubicomp (Fetzer & Högstedt, 2002).

Security is a concept strictly related to the dependability of a system. A system is considered secure if there are measures to assure availability, integrity, and confidentiality. There are many mechanisms to provide security in distributed systems that could also be used in ubicomp. However, these actions must be lightweight, to preserve both the spontaneity of interactions and the limitations of some devices, in the provision of security for resources and user data (Coulouris et al., 2005).

The privacy of that user data is a noteworthy matter. As ubicomp becomes more a part of everyday life, almost invisible devices will collect user information, including personal data, without even being noticed. Guarantee the ways in which

such information could be used or passed on will be extremely difficult. Another associated challenge is trust. In a very heterogeneous and dynamic scenario, the trustiness of interacting components should be evaluated. Since there is no fixed infrastructure and neither a specific domain, we must use a trust management system to measure what should be disclosed to other components (Robinson et al., 2005).

Bringing together varied components available in several devices, as well as making communication and understanding among these possible, is a challenge identified as spontaneous interoperation. A component interoperates spontaneously if it "interacts with a set of communication components that can change both identity and functionality over time as its circumstances change" (Kindberg & Fox, 2002). We need this spontaneity because of the volatile nature of ubicomp. The components are in movement and interacting with a constantly changing set of services.

Another challenge named mobility provides access to applications and data wherever users go and however they move (Augustin et al., 2002). This is because, in portable devices, such as PDAs and notebooks, the environment goes along with the user. However, physical mobility (of equipments or the users) is not the only option. Moving components such as applications, data and services (logical mobility) is also desirable. Nowadays, many of these components are attached to a specific device, so that the user cannot carry them along. Applications should move from one device to another, and data access should be maintained (follow-me applications) (Augustin et al., 2002).

Mobile computing has also introduced the idea of context awareness, i.e., inferring context to supply information or services to the user when the availability of services is limited or intermittent (Dey, 2001). The concept is broader in ubicomp than in mobile computing, as devices must sense changes and software should act proactively. Context is defined as any information that can be used to describe the situation of entities (persons, places, or objects) (Dey, 2001). It is generally acquired using embedded computers or sensors. However, most devices today cannot sense their environment, and neither can the software react to these changes.

Since it is possible to perceive context, it is necessary to use this information and act proactively. Context management is action in response to sensing. Based on sensed data, the system makes decisions such as configuring services according to environmental change or keeping memory of past environments to restart services when users reenter in those (Lyytinen & Yoo, 2002). Management can also expand the capacity of devices by using available resources in the current context.

Human-computer interaction (HCI) design is also a significant subject. With ubicomp there will be many ways of interacting with users. On top of that, as computers become 'smarter', the intensity and quality of human-computer interaction is bound to increase (Saha & Mukherjee, 2003). Focus on user interface evolved from software design, but it acquired a different meaning since the emergence of mobile computing and new modes of interaction. Merging user data with the real environment is another condition for HCI development in ubicomp. This redirects the attention to transparent user interaction. The idea is to preserve human attention, avoiding information saturation (Siewiorek, 2002). Users must be able to focus on the task without distractions from the system.

The last issue is directly related to ubicomp itself. Invisibility is about keeping user focus on the task, not on the tool (Weiser, 1994). To fulfill this vision, software must satisfy user intent, by helping, not obstructing it. Software should learn with users and, in some cases, let they change their preferences, interacting "almost at a subconscious level" (Satyanarayanan, 2001).

In the development of ubiquitous computing software we should consider these challenges. The next section starts with a discussion on why tradi-tional models do not fit ubiquitous computing. The requirements for the development of ubiquitous computing software are then presented.

IMPLEMENTING UBIQUITOUS APPLICATIONS

A great effort is dedicated today to the development of distributed systems. Many languages and frameworks have been in use to implement such systems. The Object Oriented Paradigm (OOP) is the dominant programming model utilized. Distributed objects are accordingly becoming more common. Despite the use and dissemination of this model, some authors affirm that this is not sufficient to ubiquitous computing and a new programming framework is required. Some of the major reasons for that are the challenges presented in the previous section: the traditional programming models does not usually address all topics discussed.

In this text, traditional programming models are considered the techniques currently used when implementing software. In general, these models are applied for the development of distributed software and based in OOP. In the core of these models are programming languages such as Java, C++, and C#.

There are three central limitations, in the traditional programming models presently in use, to implement distributed systems that affect pervasive computing (Grimm et al., 2004):

- *Distribution is transparent*: communications mechanisms employed such as distributed objects, RMI, and DFS hide physical location to developers. This transparency simplifies programming, since both local and remote resources can be used practically in the same manner, but that makes context awareness and management more difficult;

- *Components integration via interfaces*: All objects export an interface of methods to be used by other components. This facilitates composition among objects but presupposes a tight coupling, complicating the addition of new behaviors. Usually the interface is considered quite stable;
- *Object abstraction*: objects encapsulate code and data. Keeping data inside objects makes data sharing more difficult. Also, data is usually stored without proper format definition.

In addition to these limitations, traditional computing development models usually are based on static assumptions: architectures, applications, data, operating systems, etc. Moreover, in general, all resources that are used must be known a priori. To make matters more complicated application interfaces are commonly developed integrated with the program logic. As a result, it is not easy to create pervasive and seamlessly integrated applications using only traditional models and OOP.

An important shortcoming of traditional models is the lack of support for changes in the system. Frequently, manual intervention is required to address these changes. Saha and Mukherjee (2003) defend that adaptation to the environment is one of the chief characteristics that differentiate ubiquitous computing from traditional computing.

Although there is need to address many features in traditional computing to conceive ubiquitous applications, we must consider support for legacy applications, popular operating systems, use of existing data, and users' knowledge on how to use current software and systems (Kindberg & Fox, 2002). Because of that, it is normal that architectures for the development and execution of ubiquitous applications be based on traditional models with extended functionalities. Typically, a software infrastructure is built, creating layers of abstraction for ordinary hardware, operating systems, and traditional programming models, adding a set of new services to address general limitations.

Ubiquitous applications need a middleware to interface between many different devices (desktops, notebooks, PDAs, wireless equipment, etc.) and end-user applications (Costa, 2008; Saha & Mukherjee, 2003). The aim is to hide environment complexity isolating applications from explicit management of protocols, distributed memory access, data replication, communications faults, etc. A middleware can also solve heterogeneity problems related to architectures, operating systems, network technologies, and even programming languages, promoting the interoperation of them. On the other hand, a framework is an environment, composed of APIs (Application Program Interfaces), user interfaces and tools, that simplifies software development and management in a specific domain (Bernstein, 1996). A framework is used to build software that runs on a middleware. The middleware itself can be developed using existing frameworks.

REQUIREMENTS OF UBIQUITOUS SOFTWARE

In this section we show an overview of characteristics proposed to address each one of the challenges presented before. The focus is on highlighting numerous requirements that should be covered by ubiquitous software. In presenting these requirements, we emphasize techniques and tools that widen the spectrum of commonly used languages and systems.

The next subsections show a more detailed discussion of requirements for each challenge. Since the challenges were described before, the focus will be on the characteristics proposed to address each one of those.

Heterogeneity

There are several levels of heterogeneity both in hardware (networks, devices, screen sizes, power capability, etc.) and in software (languages, component models, structures, etc.). To facilitate the bridging between heterogeneous systems, we should use open standards, with published interfaces and standardized communications mechanisms, allowing easier system extension or re-implementation.

Also, frameworks for device-independent projects can make it possible for different hardware, even from diverse vendors, to use the same source-code, sometimes with little alteration. Thus, we can keep the developed application almost unmodified, limiting change to device-drivers or to the framework itself.

The current solution to heterogeneity is to use middleware with a common and integrated Application Programming Interface (API), and a unified binary format. This binary file should run on a virtual machine, like Java, which would be available on all platforms. However, depending on device capability, we cannot always employ the same virtual machine, run the same binary code, or expect that the set of available features remain unchanged. For instance, Java has different virtual machines for mobile devices and PCs. Nevertheless, the use of virtual machine reduces the cost of heterogeneity because fewer changes are needed compared to languages that generate specific machine codes.

Finally, we need to focus on the interoperability of components, the "ability to understand the exchanged information and to provide something new originating from the exchanged information" (Niemelä & Latvakoski, 2004, p.72). Interoperability languages, such as XML, are commonly used, making it possible to represent data in a standard and structured form, more portable between applications. In other cases, software converts source data into an expected format. This conversion is transparent to the user, but differences may occur between the source and destination versions. Besides, protocols that can negotiate services and resources between applications and devices must be available, allowing integration during load and execution.

Scalability

To address the problem of scalability, we need to develop software that considers the abundance of users, interactions, components and devices, avoiding centralized solutions and bottlenecks. The management and loading of applications should be automatically done at load time. Besides, whenever a new application is available, it should be automatically deployed and installed, since manual distribution and installation of software for each device would be impractical.

During execution time, interaction with distant resources should be reduced. This idea, localized scalability (Satyanarayanan, 2001) should be a goal of ubicomp, even if it disagrees with the current guideline of network transparency, in which local and remote resources are accessed with identical operations, their physical location notwithstanding. We should consider the location of resources and give priority to local interactions over distant ones.

Dependability and Security

Among the attributes encompassed by dependability, in the scope of ubicomp, we need to maximize reliability, availability, and safety. It is also vital to minimize the cost of maintainability and the effort to preserve integrity. In terms of security, we have to deal directly with the attribute of confidentiality, but also with availability and integrity.

During the development of applications, verification could diagnosis and remove faults. Verification is the process of checking if the system adheres to certain characteristics. Causing faults should otherwise be diagnosed, corrected, and the verification process should be repeated

(Avižienis et al., 2004). Testing is a widely used type of dynamic verification.

Failure detection and recovery strategies used today (such as checkpointing, compensation, isolation, or reconfiguration) could be applied to ubicomp as well. However, there are some concerns to address in ubicomp, because requirements are different from those of traditional computing, since applications execute in environments, and there is always a context involved. Also, devices are means of access to applications, but some failures in devices may not be specified in application or middleware. Besides devices and applications failure, we should also consider network and services failure (Chetan et al., 2005).

We ought to differentiate failures from changes in the system, i.e., situations requiring detection and recovery mechanisms from those where adaptation takes place. In order to have an adaptable system, we need to specify which types of changes will cause adjustments, even though we cannot predict all kinds of possible situations. Sometimes, some unpredicted changes occur. The system may also generate unspecified results. These are examples of failures, in which no adaptation mechanism is possible. In these cases, we must detect and recover the failures. We also should not consider disconnections as failures, but rather as part of the system specifications, treating them with adaptation mechanisms.

There are some approaches that can be used in ubiquitous system to increase dependability (Chetan et al., 2005):

- *Using a surrogate*: when a failure of an application is detected, one common technique is to restart this application with the last state saved in a stable store. Sometimes however, the application has failed because of a device problem. In this case, a surrogate device can be used to run the restarted application. Other possibility is that this device could not run the same application, and in that case an equivalent one can be used;

- *Alternate notification mechanisms*: if the system detects that a communication with the user has failed, other communication interfaces can be used. Various ways of interacting with the user provide redundancy;

- *Handling Errors in sensing and inferring context*: to avoid errors in the perception of context, multiple sensors and/or algorithms to infer context can be used. A complementary approach is to permit users to indicate errors observed by the system;

- *N-versions approach*: the idea is to use redundant modules with different implementations to execute the same task. A software arbitrator is then used to determines the correct answer and provide the result.

The security design of a ubiquitous system must consider some aspects (Dourish et al., 2004). First, it should be user-centered, i.e., consider usability. Users can circumvent security mechanisms that are discordant to common practices (Bardram, 2005). Second, security depends on the context and because of that mechanisms should be near the activity in which it makes sense. Third, the design must be made in a way that users understand and manage the employed solutions. Only thus can the user choose the suitable mechanism according to the security needed in each action and context.

The mechanisms to deal with security in the perspective of ubicomp must also consider three characteristics. They should be scalable to devices with limited resources, expect lack of knowledge, and allow dynamicity of mobility (Robinson et al., 2005). For instance, user authentication for each and every device through login and password would not be feasible. We need other methods; for example, the system could exploit biometric information, or authenticate based on the location of people.

Privacy and Trust

Directly related with the security concerns are the aspects of privacy and trust. They are treated separately from the previous issue because of their magnitude in ubicomp. Although privacy is typically a subject of legislation, technology should be applied in this new scenario of ubiquity due to the risks of the user exposing too much personal information to an environment, sometimes even unaware of the surveillance. On top of that, an increase is expected in the amount and accuracy of data collected. Furthermore, the protection of privacy is particularly difficult in ubiquitous system because of location-sensitivity. The context-aware mechanism of sensing the exact user location could be exploited for tracking purposes. With this mechanism, it is possible to infer the movement of the users and their activities, associating it with their personal information.

During software design, we can apply privacy standards. These standards are enforced by jurisdiction and market, and consist of a group of procedures that should be observed in the collection of data (Robinson et al., 2005). During the execution phase, we can employ protection mechanisms to realize these standards. For instance, data could be accumulated anonymously or deleted after a period of time.

A trust management can establish the trust in the relationship among components to the exchange of information and resources access. The difficulty lies in precisely defining the trustworthiness of an interacting entity and grant permissions based on that decision. In some cases, there is little or even no evidence available about an entity and, as in our daily trust decisions, it is more of a subjective notion. Apart from being subjective, trust has other characteristics (Cahill et al., 2003): non-symmetry (two interacting components can have different trust in each other), situation-specific (dependent of context), dynamic (increase or decrease in time), and it is inherently associated with risk (no reason to trust if there is no risk involved). Because of

these, there should be trust reasoning support. This reasoning analysis is made based on available information and considering the various aspects of trust. In this case, solutions for uncertainty should also be present.

Spontaneous Interoperation

The first step is the design of spontaneous components, i.e., entities that support a frequent change in the communicating partners and that can easily interact with others. To accomplish this design, we need not a fixed, but a dynamic environment, with assorted infrastructure and partners. The availability of a framework can facilitate the development of spontaneous components and provide a generic interface, which will be combined to specific entities during execution. Ideally, we should employ a uniform description language for the specification of components, and build them independently of context (Niemelä & Latvakoski, 2004).

During execution, components associate with each other. Association is the logical relationship established between components that allow interactions; we call these interactions interoperation (Coulouris et al., 2005). When assessing association, three points are important (Coulouris et al., 2005; Kindberg & Fox, 2002): scale – efficiently choosing components to associate in a scenario with various possible partners; scope – defining the extent to which components must be considered and including all possible partners; boundary principle – considering the physical limits (or other criteria) when defining the scope of association. We can also use discovery services (in these architectures, a context awareness characteristic) as a part of the association solution.

Interoperation depends on the communication models employed. In ubicomp, we tend to use models based on event systems or tuple spaces, due to the asynchronous nature of the former, or the ease of development and inherent persistence of the latter. Occasionally, both models are used in the same middleware. Conversely, we can apply other forms of communication such as message passing, remote invocation, or agent systems.

Composition is a special case of association, in which external components control inner ones, since all interoperation passes through the former, redirecting or modifying the association. Composition facilitates adaptation and mobility. Each device can have a specific component nesting all others and making all the required changes to their specific interfaces and capabilities. When a component migrates from one device to another, it enters in the specific device components and continues to issue the same set of operations. The adaptation process is up to the outer component of each device, as is the redirection of messages or events arriving after an inner component has migrated.

Mobility

In ubicomp, users changes devices frequently, but user applications and data must always be available. This means that the environment should migrate from one device to another. Besides, migration also helps reducing communication costs or preventing disconnection.

To support code migration during load- and runtime, components must be designed with mobile technology. We can obtain this by using languages and systems compatible with code mobility (Fuggetta et al., 1998). During execution, middleware has to deal with the mobile component and manage migration. To achieve this, the middleware should be aware of the network, and not treat it in a transparent manner.

We must also address data mobility. We cannot always employ remote data access, due to the possibility of disconnection or deficiency of resources. In these situations, data could be moved or copied to different locations, provided attention is given to data coherence and synchronization. Also, conversion between different formats, for specific applications, or hardware, may be necessary.

Besides code and data mobility support, also known as logical mobility, we need to consider physical mobility. As people move, the devices in use will change their network addresses. This is because they will be communicating with different access points and being assigned to different IP addresses. The DHCP provides this dynamic acquisition of addresses, allowing devices to maintain service access, regardless of location. However, it might be difficult for other components to interoperate with those devices, because the IP routing mechanism is based on fixed locations, and may lose packets when addresses change. Besides, their updating on the DNS is slow, due to extensive use of cache.

To support physical mobility, we can employ a location management strategy. Conceptually, this strategy consists of two operations (Adelstein et al., 2005): search – operation invoked by a node that needs to communicate with a mobile device; and update or registration – operation performed by the mobile node to inform its current location. Another crucial concern is ensuring that a mobile node remains connected while moving from one scope to another. This is known as handoff, and involves the following steps (Adelstein et al., 2005): deciding when to change to a new scope, selecting it, acquiring resources, and rerouting packets to the new location.

Context Awareness

To be ubiquitous, middleware must use relevant information and services available in the surroundings. Discovery is the component that detects services and devices in the current context, while sensors infer the significant information that can be used by the context manager to reason about actions to take. The addition of context awareness characteristics to middleware increases the usability of devices and allows better user interaction (Loke, 2006).

We need framework support to assist the implementation of context-aware applications.

Two characteristics are fundamental in this (Dey, 2001): a set of abstract services that programmers can employ in the building of their components, and high-level interfaces that hide specific devices or sensors details from the user.

During execution, we must store and share context data generated by sensors. We suggest a uniform data representation to improve data access anywhere and from any application. For a truly ubiquitous system, instead of just representing data, we also need some form of knowledge representation. Ontologies could be used to explicit semantic representation. One possible model, among various ongoing solutions, is SOUPA – Standard Ontology for Ubiquitous and Pervasive Applications (Chen et al., 2004), that is a shared ontology specifically designed for ubicomp.

To manage this contextual information, middleware must provide four categories of contextual services (Adelstein et al., 2005; Dey et al., 2001): context subscription and delivery – a service that can notify a component in the occurrence of some event; context query – a mechanism to find suitable information or service; context transformation – the conversion of low-level data into high-level information; context synthesis – the aggregation of context information to generate a more precise or detailed context. Besides these services, we also need dynamic resource discovery, which are detailed in the next subsection.

Discovery

Dynamic resource discovery is a mechanism to dynamically locate and enumerate resources, available in the environment or matching certain requirements (Zhu et al., 2005). A resource could be a service, application, device or any other component. Requirements are sets of specifications or characteristics to which the needed resource must comply.

Many resource discovery systems exist today with different purposes and design. However, when applied to ubicomp, these existing approaches have some limitations, such as interoperability, integration to user, and scalability (Friday, 2004; Zhu et al., 2005). We desire a system with no need for manual or static configuration, which can find required resources in every environment at any time.

Besides this dynamicity, we must avoid centralized solutions. The solution could be using multiple resource providers, in a distributed fashion, or peer-to-peer (hereafter referred to simply as P2P) approaches. In this last solution, there are direct communications among nodes without the intermediation of centralized servers. An important characteristic of P2P is self-organization, i.e. the capacity of dealing with failures, variable quantities of nodes, and network variations (Androutsellis-theotokis & Spinellis, 2004). Although P2P is suitable for ubiquitous computing, existing systems are limited to file sharing and not general enough for resource discovery (Vanthournout et al., 2005).

Below are some of the most important characteristics of resource discovery in the ubicomp area (Friday et al., 2004):

- *Location-awareness*: pervasive applications execute in the physical world and because of that, the pinpointing of resources is essential to discovery mechanisms. This mechanism should locate resources near to the user, in the same context. A resource that matches many of the requirements but is distant is useless to the system;

- *Temporal elements*: to aid the discovery of services, it is possible to associate usage profile with resources. With the history and preferences of the resources, usability can be improved. This can be achieved by finding the most suitable resource in each context for that specific user;

- *Resources states*: the discovery resource system must deal with the dynamic states of resources. Besides meeting specifications and location, states are central requirements. The representation of states, as well as their dynamic changes, must be covered;

- *Security and control*: Many resources need authentication and controlled use. Resource discovery mechanisms should exploit resources without user intervention, to maintain invisibility, but with certain constraints. Whenever possible, it must prevent malicious actions and automate authentication.

Context Management

By detecting context, we can affect system behavior. This change can be made by adapting the system to the new conditions or augmenting the available resources to compensate for the lack of some feature. Another possibility is changing the context by the use of actuators, i.e., software-controlled devices that affect the real world. An actuator can activate a device; alter a physical condition, such as temperature or luminosity; or execute a logical action (load code, alter parameterization, move components, etc.). To support this management, we need abstract interaction elements in design time. These elements can also be used during execution, according to context.

The two most important characteristics of this issue are adaptation and cyber foraging. They will be described in the next two subsections respectively.

Adaptation

Adaptability is a central concept in pervasive computing. Adaptation consists in adjusting aspects of applications to changes in operating environments

Charles Darwin originally formulated the concept of adaptation in the context of natural selection[9]. It is defined as a process that makes species better at surviving. Piaget, in his developmental theory, states that knowledge development was a biological process, and consists of an adaptation by an organism to an environment, as previous asserted by Darwin. Piaget defined adaptation as a process of assimilation and accommodation (Piaget, 1971).

Based on Piaget's model, Costa and Dimuro (2005) applied the concept of adaptation to describe how machines adjust to environments: "Adaptation is the process of self-regulated adjustment of internal and external operations of the computing machine to the possibilities and constraints determined by the environment."

This adaptation concept involves assimilation and accommodation, as proposed by Piaget. The former is the processes of applying currently available operations to internal and external objects, while the latter is the ability to adjust this set of operations to make them applicable in those objects (Costa & Dimuro, 2005).

Satyanarayanan (1996) defines three strategies for adaptation. In the laissez-faire approach, the individual applications are responsible for adapting. There is no system support. On the other hand, the system could be totally responsible for its own adaptation. This approach, called application-transparent, permits existing applications to continue working in a mobile environment without modifications. The intermediate approach is called application-aware adaptation. This means collaboration between the system and the applications. Applications are free to decide how to best adapt, while maintaining system ability to enforce resource allocation decisions and monitor resources.

Application-aware adaptation is probably the best-suited strategy for pervasive computing. It mixes programming with automatic adaptation from the system. Adaptation at programming level could be more easily achieved with Aspect Oriented Programming (AOP). The idea in AOP is specifying separately the concerns (properties) of a system and leaving its composition to the environment. This facilitates programming, since scattered concerns can be treated together as aspects and not hierarchically as with OOP (Elrad et al., 2001). Different aspects can be attached to or detached from components, facilitating adaptability. In some AOP systems, there are even some constructors for dealing with unexpected changes (Pace & Campo, 2001).

The most common use of adaptation is in resource-aware applications, when there is a significant difference between resources presented in the environment and those needed (Augustin et al., 2002). These resources could be, among others, network bandwidth, energy, storing space, or computing power. There are some approaches to resource adaptation: fidelity reduction, quality of service (QoS) systems, or the suggestion of corrective actions (Satyanarayanan, 2001). The first method consists in changing the application to a minimal use of limited resources. The second keeps a certain resource at a satisfactory level. The last one relies on user intervention to make the desired resources available.

Adaptation is important to other kinds of applications besides resource-aware ones. This gives rise to three other types of applications (Augustin et al., 2002):

- *Location-aware applications* need to consider physical location. This is not only important in resource discovery, but also when adapting. Location-dependent actions could be made. Location is a key point in determining the context of an application. Therefore, this category can be considered as a subset of the next one;
- *Context-aware applications* use sensors or monitors to infer state and better choose an adaptation strategy. These states describe information related to the capabilities and preferences of the user, location, devices, and the environment in general;
- *Situation-aware applications* use the most general form of adaptation. These applications, perceive other near applications and their context of usage. Adaptation takes place depending on usage context and user preferences. Situation-aware applications are different from the previous approach, because adaptation decision is made externally to applications.

Cyber Foraging

A special case of adaptation is cyber foraging. Mobile devices usually have limited capabilities, such as processor power, memory, and battery life. With those constraints, it is sometimes difficult to satisfy the user's computational needs. To minimize this problem, we can use near machines as computing and data-staging servers, thus augmenting capability (Satyanarayanan, 2001). Cyber foraging means sharing or dividing code or data among servers and mobile devices, which middleware can automatically do, during load and execution time. Alternatively, it could be user-initiated – for instance, when anticipating changes in connectivity or exchange of device.

Servers used to augment capabilities of mobile devices are sometime called surrogates (Garlan, 2002). These surrogates may employ encryption algorithms in stored data. Thus, the users of these servers cannot access information saved there.

Transparent User Interaction

We should design device-neutral applications, i.e., we should not start with the presentation and then build up the programming logic from that (Banavar & Berstein, 2002). To accomplish this, during design time we can define abstract user interfaces and predict different types of interaction, so that the decision of which interface to use can be postponed to execution-time. Another option is to dynamically generate the interfaces during execution, based on the abstract definitions, specific devices features, and contextual information. This option requires less effort during design, and tends to consume more processor power and communication latency during execution. However, it facilitates the use of contextual data.

The generation of interfaces suited to each specific device is one of the characteristics towards achieving transparent user interaction. These interfaces must consider the most natural form of interaction for those specific devices, and also contextual information and user behavior (preferences, history needs, etc.) (Canny, 2006; Nylander et al., 2005). For example, speech recognition is one of the best interfaces for cell phones because they have small screens and tiny buttons and are optimized for voice communication (Canny, 2006).

A broader concept would not focus only on the human-computer interface of devices, but rather on designing the physical interaction itself. This idea leads to tangible interaction and its use in the scope of ubicomp (Holmquist et al., 2004). The proposal is to create a richer interaction experience, by coupling digital information with physical artifacts, using the human body as an interface and combining real objects and devices with computers in interactive spaces (Hornecker, 2005). The challenge consists in creating interfaces seamlessly integrated with the real world, and considering social, personal, and emotional human experience (Ross & Keyson, 2007). Finally, to achieve a proper transparency, people should be able to focus on their task intuitively, and to get minimally involved with system issues.

Invisibility

The first step towards an invisible system is to design adaptable applications. We need framework support that eases this development, following the goals of disappearing computing and of keeping the user focus on the task. At runtime, we require uninterrupted use, with minimal user intervention. For instance, disconnection periods could occur in mobile devices. Actually, the system must mask this disconnection, by keeping services uninter-

rupted, and still satisfy the user's needs, maybe with some degradation.

An important characteristic towards invisibility is seamless integration, i.e., the transparent association and cooperation of various components. The idea of components that interoperate with each other seamlessly requires much effort from the middleware and careful development of each system element, considering many aspects presented on the other layers of the architecture proposed. Banavar et al. (2002) propose a task-based model that links the abstract interaction to the application logic. This model facilitates integration, since tasks are highly abstract, and can be used at load- and runtime to compose with other applications, services, and capabilities available in the pervasive environment. This can bring the notion of a *task-aware system* (Sousa et al., 2006).

To be invisible during runtime, a system must act unobtrusively, meeting the user's expectations. It also needs minimal human intervention. Saha and Mukherjee (2003) affirm that "humans can intervene to tune smart environments when they fail to meet user expectations automatically." The system should not only respond to actions initiated by users, but also anticipate users' needs, in a non-intrusive way, by capturing their intent. Preserving user attention is another characteristic that has to be considered. Users are the most important resource in a system, (Garlan et al., 2002) and keeping their focused on the task can foster invisibility.

Invisibility is the most difficult issue to be obtained in a ubiquitous computing system. We are still far from reaching a truly invisible system that fulfils Weiser's vision. Some authors are even skeptical about reaching this feature and propose some solutions near to our reality today, such as engaging computing (Rogers, 2006). In this, instead of making the surroundings proactive and smart, the goal is in engaging people more actively in their actions by consciously acting upon the environment.

FUTURE TRENDS

The next years will be characterized by high levels of mobility, heterogeneity, and transactions among devices connected to global networks. These interconnected networks will use as much wired connections as wireless. The first researches involving wide-area distributed systems answered many questions concerning resource management, even though they fall short in dealing with issues related to heterogeneity and dynamic adaptation in an environment of high scalability and transparent user interaction.

On the other hand, mobility is fast becoming a key aspect in software development. It is only the first step toward what has been called ubiquitous applications. This new class of software presents, as previously detailed in this chapter, a set of new requirements and challenges to software development. The origin of these challenges comes from a dynamic operating environment, initiated by users in using assorted devices, in different locations and contexts, and by the particular nature of mobile environment, in a large scale distributed system.

Another behavior that will be presented in ubiquitous applications is the notion of planned disconnections. A mobile device, for example, would rather operate disconnected to reduce battery consumption, and at specific moments, reconnect to update the state of the global execution. Such disconnection and reconnection procedures should be, whenever possible, transparent to the applications.

Traditional distributed systems are still created based on some system assumptions, such as permanent connection or resources availability, which are not always true in a dynamic environment with the many challenges presented.

The complexity of software development increases according to the functionalities we want to provide to the user. With the advent of ubiquitous computing, we need software that is able to run using innumerous and assorted network-connected devices, seamlessly integrate with the real world, to keep the focus on the users, and to disappear into the environment, as if it was invisible. To these features we should also add the characteristics that a particular software should provide. Imagine trying to solve a real world problem in a specific domain, and also having to include all the features of ubicomp. To draw a parallel in the history of Computing Science, we can compare it to Lotus 1-2-3 in the beginning of the PC era. The spreadsheet was completely written in assembly language, which involved the development of various complex routines, such as floating-pointing and fixed-pointing math (Kapor, 2007). At that time, assembly was chosen because the requirements were small memory usage and the fastest speed possible (Kapor, 2007). This choice introduced an overhead in software development, since many libraries and routines had to be implemented.

We are nowadays living the beginning of the Ubicomp era. Although we have had a huge evolution in languages and tools for software development since the advent of the PC, when we focus on the ubiquitous computing requirements, we are at the first steps. We need middleware and framework to smooth the progress of software implementation in this scenario. It is still difficult to find a software infrastructure that has all the necessary characteristics of ubiquitous computing; besides, the tendency today is providing middleware or frameworks for specific issues. In spite of this tendency, we think that a general infrastructure model for software may help to develop pervasive middleware or frameworks. Our vision is that, in order to fulfill Weiser's vision, future ubiquitous infrastructures should seamlessly integrate many different challenges.

An additional problem in the ubicomp scenario is how the infrastructure can let users access their data and applications wherever they go and however they move. The promise of "at all times, everywhere" that came with the idea of ubicomp is difficult to be obtained. Another related problem is how to use these data and applications in a seamlessly integrated fashion with the real world. These issues involve the addressing of mobility, heterogeneity, and scalability among other concerns.

CONCLUSION

The development of ubiquitous software is still hindered by the lack of a software infrastructure covering all the necessary characteristics for ubiquitous computing. The main reason for this absence is based on the complexity of pondering many different open research topics in one project. However, many projects nowadays provide solutions for specific issues. In spite of this tendency, we think that a general solution to the field can help the development of ubiquitous software.

In this chapter we have summarized the main issues related to the development of ubiquitous software. First, we have defined the main concepts related to the area, focusing on the challenges presented. Secondly, we concentrate on the difficulties in implementing ubiquitous software. Next, we presented the main characteristics and techniques to address each and every challenge showed. Finally, we drew some future trends related to the field.

We trust that this chapter could be useful to the advance of the development of ubiquitous computing. What is more, we consider that to carry out Weiser's seminal vision of ubicomp, future systems should seamlessly integrate with the surroundings, dealing with various issues related to the challenges discussed.

REFERENCES

Abowd, G., Mynatt, E., & Rodden, T. (2002). The Human Experience. *Pervasive Computing, IEEE, 1*(1), 48–57. doi:. doi:10.1109/MPRV.2002.993144

Adelstein, F., Gupta, S. K., Richard, G., III, & Schwiebert, L. (2004). Fundamentals of Mobile and Pervasive Computing (1st ed.). New York: McGraw-Hill Professional.

Androutsellis-Theotokis, S., & Spinellis, D. (2004). A survey of peer-to-peer content distribution technologies. *ACM Computing Surveys, 36*(4), 335–371. doi:. doi:10.1145/1041680.1041681

Augustin, I., Yamin, A. C., Barbosa, J. L. V., & Geyer, C. F. R. (2002). Towards Taxonomy for Mobile Applications with Adaptive Behavior. In *International Symposium on Parallel and Distributed Computing and Networking (PDCN 02)* (Vol. 20). Innsbruck, Austria: ACTA Press.

Avižienis, A., Laprie, J., Randell, B., & Landwehr, C. (2004). Basic concepts and taxonomy of dependable and secure computing. *Dependable and Secure Computing. IEEE Transactions on, 1*(1), 11–33. doi:.doi:10.1109/TDSC.2004.2

Banavar, G., Beck, J., Gluzberg, E., Munson, J., Sussman, J., & Zukowski, D. (2000). Challenges: an application model for pervasive computing. In *Proceedings of the 6th annual international conference on Mobile computing and networking* (pp. 266-274). Boston, MA: ACM. doi: 10.1145/345910.345957

Banavar, G., & Bernstein, A. (2002). Software infrastructure and design challenges for ubiquitous computing applications. *Communications of the ACM, 45*(12), 92–96. doi:. doi:10.1145/585597.585622

Bardram, E. (2005). The trouble with login: on usability and computer security in ubiquitous computing. *Personal and Ubiquitous Computing, 9*(6), 357–367. doi:10.1007/s00779-005-0347-6

Bernstein, P. A. (1996). Middleware: a model for distributed system services. *Communications of the ACM, 39*(2), 86–98. doi:. doi:10.1145/230798.230809

Cahill, V., Gray, E., Seigneur, J., & Jensen, C., Yong Chen, Shand, B., et al. (2003). Using trust for secure collaboration in uncertain environments. *IEEE Pervasive Computing / IEEE Computer Society [and] IEEE Communications Society, 2*(3), 52–61. doi:. doi:10.1109/MPRV.2003.1228527

Canny, J. (2006). The Future of Human-Computer Interaction. *ACM Queue; Tomorrow's Computing Today, 4*(6), 24–32. doi:. doi:10.1145/1147518.1147530

Chen, H., Perich, F., Finin, T., & Joshi, A. (2004). SOUPA: standard ontology for ubiquitous and pervasive applications. In *Mobile and Ubiquitous Systems: Networking and Services, 2004. MOBIQUITOUS 2004. The First Annual International Conference on* (pp. 258-267).

Chetan, S., Ranganathan, A., & Campbell, R. (2005). Towards fault tolerance pervasive computing. *IEEE Technology and Society Magazine, 24*(1), 38-44. doi: 10.1109/MTAS.2005.1407746

Costa, A. C. D. R., & Dimuro, G. P. (2005). Interactive Computation: Stepping Stone in the Pathway From Classical to Developmental Computation. *Electronic Notes in Theoretical Computer Science, 141*(5), 5–31. doi:. doi:10.1016/j.entcs.2005.05.014

Costa, C., Yamin, A., & Geyer, C. (2008). Toward a General Software Infrastructure for Ubiquitous Computing. *IEEE Pervasive Computing / IEEE Computer Society [and] IEEE Communications Society, 7*(1), 64–73. doi:. doi:10.1109/MPRV.2008.21

Coulouris, G., Dollimore, J., & Kindberg, T. (2005). Distributed Systems: Concepts and Design (4th Edition) (4th ed., pp. 927). Reading, MA: Addison Wesley.

Dey, A. K. (2001). Understanding and Using Context. *Personal and Ubiquitous Computing, 4-7*(5). doi:.doi:10.1007/s007790170019

Dey, A. K., Abowd, G. D., & Salber, D. (2001). A conceptual framework and a toolkit for supporting the rapid prototyping of context-aware applications. *Human-Computer Interaction, 16*(2), 97–166. doi:. doi:10.1207/S15327051HCI16234_02

Elrad, T., Filman, R. E., & Bader, A. (2001). Aspect-oriented programming: Introduction. *Communications of the ACM, 44*(10), 29–32. doi:. doi:10.1145/383845.383853

Fetzer, C., & Högstedt, K. (2003). Challenges in Making Pervasive Systems Dependable. In *Future Directions in Distributed Computing*, (LNCS Vol. 2584, pp. 186-190). Berlin: Springer. doi:10.1007/3-540-37795-6_37.

Friday, A., Davies, N., Wallbank, N., Catterall, E., & Pink, S. (2004). Supporting Service Discovery, Querying and Interaction in Ubiquitous Computing Environments. *Wireless Networks, 10*(6), 631–641. doi:. doi:10.1023/B:WINE.0000044024.54833.cb

Fuggetta, A., Picco, G., & Vigna, G. (1998). Understanding code mobility. *IEEE Transactions on Software Engineering, 24*(5), 342–361. doi:. doi:10.1109/32.685258

Garlan, D., Siewiorek, D., Smailagic, A., & Steenkiste, P. (2002). Project Aura: toward distraction-free pervasive computing. *IEEE Pervasive Computing / IEEE Computer Society [and] IEEE Communications Society, 1*(2), 22–31. doi:. doi:10.1109/MPRV.2002.1012334

Gärtner, F. C. (1999). Fundamentals of fault-tolerant distributed computing in asynchronous environments. *ACM Computing Surveys, 31*(1), 1–26. doi:. doi:10.1145/311531.311532

Gene F. Hoffnagle. (1999). Pervasive Computing - Preface. *IBM Systems Journal, Pervasive Computing, 38*(4), 502. doi: DOI: 10.1147/sj.384.0502

Grimm, R., Davis, J., Lemar, E., Macbeth, A., Swanson, S., & Anderson, T. (2004). System support for pervasive applications. *ACM Transactions on Computer Systems, 22*(4), 421–486. doi:. doi:10.1145/1035582.1035584

Heidegger, M. (1996). Being and time: a translation of Sein und Zeit. New York: State University of New York. doi: 10.1109/MPRV.2006.55.

Hightower, J., LaMarca, A., & Smith, I. (2006). Practical Lessons from Place Lab. *IEEE Pervasive Computing / IEEE Computer Society [and] IEEE Communications Society, 5*(3), 32–39. doi:10.1109/MPRV.2006.55

Holmquist, L. E., Schmidt, A., & Ullmer, B. (2004). Tangible interfaces in perspective. *Personal and Ubiquitous Computing, 8*(5), 291–293. doi:. doi:10.1007/s00779-004-0292-9

Hornecker, E. (2005). A Design Theme for Tangible Interaction: Embodied Facilitation. In *9ᵗʰ European Conference on Computer-Supported Cooperative Work* (pp. 23-43). Netherlands: Springer. doi: 10.1007/1-4020-4023-7_2

Jing, J., Helal, A. S., & Elmagarmid, A. (1999). Client-server computing in mobile environments. *ACM Computing Surveys, 31*(2), 117–157. doi:. doi:10.1145/319806.319814

Kapor, M. (2007). Recollections on Lotus 1-2-3: benchmark for spreadsheet software. *IEEE Annals of the History of Computing, 29*(3), 32-40. doi: 10.110910.1109/MAHC.2007.45

Keen, E. (1975). A primer in phenomenological psychology. New York: Holt, Rinehart & Winston.

Kindberg, T., & Fox, A. (2002). System software for ubiquitous computing. *IEEE Pervasive Computing / IEEE Computer Society [and] IEEE Communications Society, 1*(1), 70–81. doi:. doi:10.1109/MPRV.2002.993146

Levy, E., & Silberschatz, A. (1990). Distributed file systems: concepts and examples. *ACM Computing Surveys, 22*(4), 321–374. doi:. doi:10.1145/98163.98169

Loke, S. (2006). Context-aware artifacts: two development approaches. *IEEE Pervasive Computing / IEEE Computer Society [and] IEEE Communications Society, 5*(2), 48–53. doi:. doi:10.1109/MPRV.2006.27

Lyytinen, K., & Yoo, Y. (2002). Issues and challenges in ubiquitous computing - Introduction. *Communications of the ACM, 45*(12), 62–65. doi:. doi:10.1145/585597.585616

Niemelä, E., & Latvakoski, J. (2004). Survey of requirements and solutions for ubiquitous software. In Mobile and Ubiquitous Multimedia: Vol. 83 (pp. 71-78). College Park, MD. New York: ACM. doi: 10.1145/1052380.1052391.

Nylander, S., Bylund, M., & Waern, A. (2005). Ubiquitous service access through adapted user interfaces on multiple devices. *Personal and Ubiquitous Computing, 9*(3), 123–133. doi:. doi:10.1007/s00779-004-0317-4

Pace, J. A. D., & Campo, M. R. (2001). Analyzing the role of aspects in software design. *Communications of the ACM, 44*(10), 66–73. doi:. doi:10.1145/383845.383859

Piaget, J. (1971). Biology and Knowledge: an essay on the relations between organic regulations and cognitive processes. Chicago: The University of Chicago.

Rogers. (2006). Moving on from Weiser's Vision of Calm Computing: Engaging UbiComp Experiences. In *UbiComp 2006: Ubiquitous Computing*, (LNCS (Vol. 4206, pp. 404-421). Berlin Heidelberg: Springer. doi: 10.1007/11853565_24

Ross, P., & Keyson, D. (2007). The case of sculpting atmospheres: towards design principles for expressive tangible interaction in control of ambient systems. *Personal and Ubiquitous Computing, 11*(2), 69–79. doi:. doi:10.1007/s00779-005-0062-3

Saha, D., & Mukherjee, A. (2003). Pervasive computing: a paradigm for the 21st century. *Computer, 36*(3), 25–31. doi:. doi:10.1109/MC.2003.1185214

Saito, Y., & Shapiro, M. (2005). Optimistic replication. *ACM Computing Surveys, 37*(1), 42–81. doi:. doi:10.1145/1057977.1057980

Satyanarayanan, M. (1996). Fundamental challenges in mobile computing. In *ACM Symposium on Principles of Distributed Computing* (pp. 1-7), Philadelphia. New York: ACM. doi:10.1145/248052.248053

Satyanarayanan, M. (2001). Pervasive computing: vision and challenges. *IEEE Personal Communications, 8*(4), 10–17. doi:. doi:10.1109/98.943998

Siewiorek, D. P. (2002). New frontiers of application design. *Communications of the ACM, 45*(12), 79–82. doi:. doi:10.1145/585597.585619

Sousa, J., Poladian, V., Garlan, D., Schmerl, B., & Shaw, M. (2006). Task-based adaptation for ubiquitous computing. *IEEE Transactions on Systems, Man and Cybernetics. Part C, Applications and Reviews, 36*(3), 328–340. doi:. doi:10.1109/TSMCC.2006.871588

Vanthournout, K., Deconinck, G., & Belmans, R. (2005). A taxonomy for resource discovery. *Personal and Ubiquitous Computing, 9*(2), 81–89. doi:. doi:10.1007/s00779-004-0312-9

Want, R., Pering, T., Borriello, G., & Farkas, K. (2002). Disappearing hardware. *IEEE Pervasive Computing / IEEE Computer Society [and] IEEE Communications Society, 1*(1), 36–47. doi:. doi:10.1109/MPRV.2002.993143

Weiser, M. (1991). The computer for the 21st century. *Scientific American, 265*(3), 94–104. doi:10.1038/scientificamerican0991-94

Weiser, M. (1993). Some computer science issues in ubiquitous computing. *Communications of the ACM, 36*(7), 75–84. doi:10.1145/159544.159617

Weiser, M. (1994). The world is not a desktop. *Interactions (New York, N.Y.), 1*(1), 7–8. doi:. doi:10.1145/174800.174801

Zhu, F., Mutka, M., & Ni, L. (2005). Service discovery in pervasive computing environments. *IEEE Pervasive Computing / IEEE Computer Society [and] IEEE Communications Society, 4*(4), 81–90. doi:. doi:10.1109/MPRV.2005.87

ENDNOTES

[1] Vorhandenheit in the original.

[2] *Horizont* in the original.

[3] The book was first published in 1927 with the title *Sein und Zeit*. For this text the translation to English published in 1996 was used.

[4] In the context of ubiquitous computing referred as *cyber foraging*.

[5] This term was used by Satyanarayanan (2001) and means that physical distance is a significant issue in pervasive computing and that we must consider the important role played by local interactions.

[6] Actually this term is more restrictive. Recently the community is converging to use the more general word *dependability*.

[7] Some authors consider context management as a part of context awareness.

[8] This term is used in a more general sense.

[9] A detailed description can be found in The Origin of Species by Charles Darwin available on-line at <http://www.gutenberg.org/etext/2009>.

Compilation of References

Abdelgawad, A., Lewis, A., Elgamel, M., Issa, F., Tzeng, N.-F., & Bayoumi, M. (2006, Aug. 18-20). Remote Measuring of Flow Meters for Petroleum Engineering and Other Industrial Applications. *International Workshop on Computer Architecture for Machine Perception and Sensing, CAMP 2006*, (pp. 99 – 103).

Abdelzaher, T., Blum, B., Cao, Q., Chen, Y., Evans, D., George, J., et al. (2004). Envirotrack: Towards an environmental computing paradigm for distributed sensor networks. In the 24th international conference on distributed computing systems (ICDCS) (p. 582-589). Washington, DC: IEEE Computer Society.

Abowd, G. D., Bobick, A., Essa, I., Mynatt, E., & Rogers, W. (2002). The aware home: developing technologies for successful aging. In AAAI Workshop and Automation as a Care Giver, (pp.1–7). Alberta, Canada: AAAI Press.

Abowd, G., Atkeson, C., Hong, J., Long, S., Kooper, R., & Pinkerton, M. (1997). Cyberguide: A mobile context-aware tour guide. *ACM wireless. Networks*, *3*(5), 421–433.

Abowd, G., Mynatt, E., & Rodden, T. (2002). The Human Experience. *Pervasive Computing, IEEE*, *1*(1), 48–57. doi:. doi:10.1109/MPRV.2002.993144

Adam, J., Brady, G., & Kosc, D. (2001). EHT control systems and wireless communications: the wave of the future. In *Petroleum and Chemical Industry Conference, 2001. IEEE Industry Applications Society 48th Annual* Sept. 24-26, (pp. 169 – 178).

Adelstein, F., Gupta, S. K., Richard, G., III, & Schwiebert, L. (2004). Fundamentals of Mobile and Pervasive Computing (1st ed.). New York: McGraw-Hill Professional.

Adibi, S., & Agnew, G. B. (2008). On the diversity of eHealth security systems and mechanisms. In Engineering in Medicine and Biology Society (pp. 1478-1481). Vancouver, Canada.

Akkaya, K., & Younis, M. (2005). A survey on routing protocols for wireless sensor networks. *Elsevier Ad Hoc Network Journal*, *3*(3), 325–349. doi:10.1016/j.adhoc.2003.09.010

Akyildiz, I. F., Su, W., Sankarasubramaniam, Y., & Cyirci, E. (2002). Wireless sensor networks: A survey. *Computer Networks*, *38*(4), 393–422. doi:10.1016/S1389-1286(01)00302-4

Akyildiz, L. F., Su, W., Sankarasubramaniam, Y., & Cayirci, E. (2002). A Survey on Sensor Networks. *Communications Magazine*, *40*(8), 102–114. doi:10.1109/MCOM.2002.1024422

Alapetite, A., Boje, A. H., & Morten, H. (2009). Acceptance of speech recognition by physicians: A survey of expectations, experiences, and social influence. *International Journal of Human-Computer Studies*, *67*(1), 36–49. doi:10.1016/j.ijhcs.2008.08.004

Aleksy, M., Butter, T., & Schader, M. (2008). Architecture for the development of context-sensitive mobile applications. *Mobile Information Systems*, *4*(2), 105–117.

Ali-Yahiya, T., Sethom, K., & Pujolle, G. (2007, July). A case study: Ieee 802.21 framework design for service continuity across wlan and wman. In *IFIP International Conference on Wireless and Optical Communications Networks*, WOCN '07, (pp. 1-5).

Al-Karaki, J. N., & Kamal, A. E. (2004). Routing techniques in wireless sensor networks: a survey. *IEEE Wireless Communications, 11*, 6–28. doi:10.1109/MWC.2004.1368893

Alliance, O. (2007). *Osgi – the dynamic module system for java*. Retrieved from http://www.osgi.org/

Amer, S., & Badawy, W. (2005). An Integrated Plataform for Bio-Analysis and Drug Delivery. *Pharmaceutical Biotechnology, 6*, 57–64.

Androutsellis-Theotokis, S., & Spinellis, D. (2004). A survey of peer-to-peer content distribution technologies. *ACM Computing Surveys, 36*(4), 335–371. doi:. doi:10.1145/1041680.1041681

Aradhye, H., Bakshi, B. R., Strauss, R. A., & Davis, J. F. (2003). Multiscale Statistical Process Control Using Wavelets - Theoretical Analysis and Properties. *AIChE Journal. American Institute of Chemical Engineers, 49*(4), 939–958. doi:10.1002/aic.690490412

Arampatzis, T., Lygeros, J., & Manesis, S. (2005). A survey of applications of wireless sensors and wireless sensor networks. In *Proceedings of Mediterranean Control Conference (Med05)*, Limassol Cyprus.

Asthana, A., Cravatts, M., & Krzyzanouski, P. (1994). An indoor wireless system for personalized shopping assistance. In *Workshop on Mobile Computing Systems and Applications.*

Augustin, I., Yamin, A. C., Barbosa, J. L. V., & Geyer, C. F. R. (2002). Towards Taxonomy for Mobile Applications with Adaptive Behavior. In *International Symposium on Parallel and Distributed Computing and Networking (PDCN 02)* (Vol. 20). Innsbruck, Austria: ACTA Press.

Avižienis, A., Laprie, J., Randell, B., & Landwehr, C. (2004). Basic concepts and taxonomy of dependable and secure computing. *Dependable and Secure Computing. IEEE Transactions on, 1*(1), 11–33. doi:.doi:10.1109/TDSC.2004.2

Baader, F., Calvanese, D., McGuinness, D. L., Nardi, D., & Patel-Schneider, P. F. (2007). The Description Logic Handbook. New York: Cambridge University Press.

Bahl, P., & Padmanabhan, V. (2000). RADAR: An In-Building RF-based User Location and Tracking System. In *Proc. of IEEE Infocom*, (pp. 775-784). Los Alamitos, CA: IEEE CS Press.

Baillieul, J., & Antsaklis, P. J. (2007). Control and Communication Challenges in Networked Real-Time Systems. *Proceedings of the IEEE, 95*(1), 9–28. doi:10.1109/JPROC.2006.887290

Bajaj, R., Ranaweera, S. L., & Agrawal, D. P. (2002). GPS: location-tracking technology. *Computer, 35*(4), 92–94. doi:10.1109/MC.2002.993780

Baldauf, M., Dustdar, S., & Rosenberg, F. (2007). A survey on context-aware systems. *International Journal of Ad Hoc and Ubiquitous Computing, 2*(4). doi:10.1504/IJAHUC.2007.014070

Banavar, G., & Bernstein, A. (2002). Software infrastructure and design challenges for ubiquitous computing applications. *Communications of the ACM, 45*(12), 92–96. doi:. doi:10.1145/585597.585622

Banavar, G., Beck, J., Gluzberg, E., Munson, J., Sussman, J., & Zukowski, D. (2000). Challenges: an application model for pervasive computing. In *Proceedings of the 6th annual international conference on Mobile computing and networking* (pp. 266-274). Boston, MA: ACM. doi: 10.1145/345910.345957

Bardram, E. (2005). The trouble with login: on usability and computer security in ubiquitous computing. *Personal and Ubiquitous Computing, 9*(6), 357–367. doi:10.1007/s00779-005-0347-6

Bednarcikova, L., Petrik, M., Toth, T., Michalikova, M., Krajnak, S., & Zivcak, J. (2008). Informatics in Health Care. In *IEEE International Conference on Computational Cybernetics* (pp. 283-284), Stara Lesna, Slovenia.

Beetz, M., Kirsch, A., & Muller, A. (2004). RPL$_{LEARN}$: Extending an Autonomous Robot Control Language to Perform Experience-based Learning. In *Proceedings of the Third International Joint Conference on Autonomous Agents and Multiagent Systems AAMAS 2004* (pp. 1022 – 1029). NewYork: ACM.

Berglund, A., & Johansson, P. (2004). Using speech and dialogue for interactive TV navigation. *Universal Access in the Information Society, 3*(3/4), 224–238. doi:10.1007/s10209-004-0106-x

Berglund, A., Berglund, E., Larsson, A., & Bang, M. (2006). Paper Remote: an augmented television guide and remote control. *Universal Access in the Information Society, 4*(4), 300–327. doi:10.1007/s10209-004-0108-8

Bernstein, P. A. (1996). Middleware: a model for distributed system services. *Communications of the ACM, 39*(2), 86–98. doi:. doi:10.1145/230798.230809

Bhattacharya, A., & Das, S. K. (2002). LeZi-update: An information theoretic approach for personal mobility tracking in PCS networks. [WINET]. *ACM Wireless Networks, 8*(2/3), 121–137. doi:10.1023/A:1013759724438

Bhattacharyya, M., Kumar, A. & Bayoumi, M. (2007). A Framework for Assessing Residual Energy in Wireless Sensor Network. *Special Issue on International Journal of Sensor Networks 2*(¾).

Bhattacharyya, M., Kumar, A., & Bayoumi, M. (2009). Residual Energy Monitoring Using Statistical Analysis. In *International Symposium on Digital Life Technologies,* (ISDLT2009), May 28-29.

Bianchi, G., Stefano, A. D., Giaconia, C., Scalia, L., Terrazzino, G., & Tinnirello, I. (2007, May). Experimental Assessment of the Backoff Behavior of Commercial IEEE 802.11b Network Cards. In Ieee 26th ieee international conference on computer communications infocom 2007 (pp. 1181-1189).

Bill, L. (n.d.). *Oil Field Safety.* Retrieved from http://www.txoga.org/attachments/OilFieldSafetyNEO1.ppt#256

Bishop, C. (1995). Neural Networks for pattern recognition. Oxford, UK: Clarendon Press.

Blazevic, L., Butty, L., Capkun, S., Giordano, S., Hubaux, J.-P., & Boudec, J.-Y. L. (2001). Self-organization in mobile ad-hoc networks: the approach of terminodes. IEEE Communications Magazine.

BlipNet. (n. d.). Retrieved from http://www.blipsystems.com/

Bluetooth SIG, Promoter Members. (2001). Specification of the Bluetooth System – Core. Version 1.1. *Bluetooth SIG, Inc.*

Boldt, R., & Raasch, J. (2008). Analysis of current technologies and devices for mobile data capture. A qualitative usability study for comparison of data capture via keyboard, tablet PC, personal digital assistant, and digital pen and paper. Report, University of Applied Sciences, Hamburg, Germany.

Bonabeau, E., Dorigo, M., & Theraulaz, G. (1999). Swarm Intelligence: From Natural to Artificial Systems, (Santa Fe Institute Studies in the Sciences of Complexity). New York: Oxford University Press.

Bonivento, A., Carloni, L. P., & Sangiovanni-Vincentelli, A. (2006). Platform-Based Design of Wireless Sensor Networks for Industrial Applications. In Proceedings Design, Automation and Test in Europe, DATE '06, (Vol. 1, pp. 1 – 6).

Borcea, C., Iyer, D., Kang, P., Saxena, A., & Iftode, L. (2002). Cooperative computing for distributed embedded systems. In *Proceedings of IEEE International Conference on Distributed Computing Systems (ICDCS 2002).*

Boulis, A., Han, C.-C., & Srivastava, M. B. (2003). Design and implementation of a framework for efficient and programmable sensor networks. In the 1st international conference on mobile systems, applications and services (MobiSys) (pp. 187–200). New York: ACM Press.

Bowling, M., & Velso, M. (2001). Rational and Convergent Learning in Stochastic Games, In *Proceedings of the Seventeenth International Joint Conference on Artificial Intelligence,* Seattle, WA.

Braga, D. (2008). *Algoritmos de Processamento da Linguagem Natural para Sistemas de Conversão Texto Fala em Português.* PhD Thesis, University of A Coruña, A Coruña, Spain.

Broadbent, J., & Marti, P. (1997). Location Aware Mobile Interactive Guides: usability issues. In *Proceedings of the Fourth International Conference on Hypermedia and Interactivity in Museums (ICHIM97).*

Brumitt, B., Meyers, B., Krumm, J., Kern, A., & Shafer, S. A. (2000). Easyliving: technologies for intelligent environments. In *HUC '00: Proceedings of the 2nd International Symposium on Handheld and Ubiquitous Computing*, (pp.12–29). London: Springer-Verlag.

Bush, L. A., Carothers, C. D., & Szymanski, B. K. (2005). Algorithm for optimizing energy use and path resilience in sensor networks. In *Proceeedings of the Second European Workshop on Wireless Sensor Networks*, (pp. 391 – 396).

Bustamante, P., Guarretxena, N., Solas, G., & Bilbao, U. (2008). In-bed Patients Behaviour Monitoring System. In *International Conference on Biocomputation, Bioinformatics, and Biomedical Technologies* (pp. 1-6), Bucharest, Romania.

Cabri, G., Leonardi, L., & Zambonelli, F. (2002). Engineering mobile agent applications via context-dependent coordination. *IEEE Transactions on Software Engineering, 28*(11), 1039–1055. doi:10.1109/TSE.2002.1049403

Cahill, V., Gray, E., Seigneur, J., & Jensen, C., Yong Chen, Shand, B., et al. (2003). Using trust for secure collaboration in uncertain environments. *IEEE Pervasive Computing / IEEE Computer Society [and] IEEE Communications Society, 2*(3), 52–61. doi:. doi:10.1109/MPRV.2003.1228527

Calafate, C. M. T., & Manzoni, P. (2003). A multi-platform programming interface for protocol development. In 11th euromicro conference on parallel distributed and network based processing, Genoa, Italy.

Câmara, D., & Loureiro, A. (2001). Gps/ant-like routing in ad hoc networks. *Telecommunication Systems, 18*(1/3), 85–100. doi:10.1023/A:1016739402641

Canny, J. (2006). The Future of Human-Computer Interaction. *ACM Queue; Tomorrow's Computing Today, 4*(6), 24–32. doi:. doi:10.1145/1147518.1147530

Cano, J. C. Manzoni, p., & Toh, CK., (2006). UbiqMuseum: A Bluetooth and Java Based Context Aware System for Ubiquitous Computing. In Wireless Personal Communications Springer Science+Business Media B.V.

Cano, J. C., Cano, J., Manzoni, P., & Kim, D. (2006). On the design of pervasive computing applications based on Bluetooth and a P2P concept. In *1st International IEEE Symposium on Wireless Pervasive Computing,* 16 - 18 January 2006, Phuket, Thailand.

Cano, J., Burgoa, E., Calafate, C., Cano, J. C., & Manzoni, P. (2006). A MANET autoconfiguration system based on Bluetooth technology. In *3rd IEEE International Symposium on Wireless Communication Systems (ISWCS),* Valencia, Spain.

Cano, J., Cano, J. C., Calafate, C., & Manzoni, P. (2007). Solving the user-to-host binding problem in ad hoc networks through the dissemination of photographic identifiers. In *Fourth ACM International Workshop on Performance Evaluation of Wireless Ad Hoc, Sensor, and Ubiquitous Networks - PE-WASUN'07, co-located with MSWIM'07,* Chania, Crete Island, Greece.

Cano, J., Cano, J. C., Calafate, C., & Manzoni, P. (2008). Deploying Pervasive Technologies. In Encyclopedia of Information Science and Technology, (2nd Ed.). Hershey, PA: Information Science Reference.

Capkun, S., Hamdi, M., & Hubaux, J. (2001). Gps-free positioning in mobile ad-hoc networks. In *Proceedings of the 34th IEEE Annual Hawaii International Conference on System Sciences (HICSS-34),* (Vol. 9, pp. 9008).

Cardenas-Tamayo, R. A., García-Macías, J. A., Miller, T. M., Rich, P., Davis, J., & Albesa, J. (2009). Pervasive Computing Approaches to Environmental Sustainability. *IEEE Pervasive Computing / IEEE Computer Society [and] IEEE Communications Society, 8*(1), 54–57. doi:10.1109/MPRV.2009.14

Caro, G. D., Ducatelle, F., & Gambardella, L. (2005). Anthocnet: An adaptive nature-inspired algorithm for routing in mobile ad hoc networks. *European Transactions on Telecommunications (ETT), Special Issue on Self Organization in Mobile Networking, 16*(2).

Cerpa, A., & Estrin, D. (2002). Ascent: Adaptive self-configuring sensor networks topologies. In *Proceedings of the 21st International Annual Joint Conference of the IEEE Computer and Communications Societies (INFOCOM'02),* (Vol. 3, pp. 1278–1287).

Cetin, M., Lei Chen, Fisher III, J.W., Ihler, A.T., Moses, R.L., Wainwright, M.J., & Willsky, A.S. (2006). Distributed fusion in sensor networks. *Signal Processing Magazine, 23*(4), 42–55. doi:10.1109/MSP.2006.1657816

Chadwick, P. E. (2007). Regulations and Standards for Wireless applications in eHealth. In *International Conference of Engineering in Medicine and Biology Society*, (pp.6170-6173), Lyon, France.

Chakraborty, S., D.Yau, & Lui, J. (2006, February). On the E_ectiveness of Movement Prediction to Reduce Energy Consumption in Wireless Communication. *IEEE Transactions on Mobile Computing, 5*(2), 157-169. Retrieved from citeseer.ist.psu.edu/chakraborty04effectiveness.html

Chan, H., Perrig, A., & Song, D. (2003). Random key predistribution schemes for sensor networks. In IEEE symposium on security and privacy (pp. 197–213).

Chao, X., Dargie, W., & Guan Lin (2008) "Energy Model for H2S Monitoring Wireless Sensor Network. In *11th IEEE International Conference on Computational Science and Engineering*, CSE '08, (pp. 402 – 409).

Chatty, S. (2002). *The ivy software bus-a white paper.* CENA Technical Note NT02-816. Retrieved from http://www.tls.cena.fr/products/ivy

Chen, C., & Helal, S. (2008). Sifting through the jungle of sensor standards. *IEEE Pervasive Computing / IEEE Computer Society [and] IEEE Communications Society, 7*(4), 84–88. doi:10.1109/MPRV.2008.81

Chen, G., & Kotz, D. (2000). *A survey of context-aware mobile computing research.* Tech. Rep. TR2000-381, Dept. of Computer Science, Dartmouth College.

Chen, H., Perich, F., Finin, T., & Joshi, A. (2004). SOUPA: standard ontology for ubiquitous and pervasive applications. In *Mobile and Ubiquitous Systems: Networking and Services, 2004. MOBIQUITOUS 2004. The First Annual International Conference on* (pp. 258-267).

Chen, K. Y., Refai, J., & H.H. (2005). WLAN-based, indoor medical residents positioning system. In *International Conference on Wireless and Optical Communications Networks* (pp. 556-560), Dubai, United Arab Emirates.

Chen, T., Wei, H., Bin, X., & Like, Y. (2006). A Real-Time Scheduling Algorithm for Embedded Systems with Various Resource Requirements. *International Workshop on Networking, Architecture, and Storage.*

Chen, Y., & Kobayashi, H. (2002, May). Signal strength based indoor geolocation. In Ieee international conference on communications (pp. 436-439).

Chetan, S., Ranganathan, A., & Campbell, R. (2005). Towards fault tolerance pervasive computing. *IEEE Technology and Society Magazine, 24*(1), 38-44. doi:10.1109/MTAS. 2005.1407746

Chiann, C., Chiann, C., Morettin, P. A., & Morettin, P. A. (1998). A wavelet analysis for time series. *Journal of Nonparametric Statistics, 10*, 1–46. doi:10.1080/10485259808832752

Clare, L. P., Pottie, G. J., & Agre, J. R. (1999). Self-organizing distributed sensor networks. In *Proceedings of the SPIE Conf. on Unattended Ground Sensor Technologies and Applications.*

Coelho, P., Moraes, D., Cardozo, E., Guimarães, E., Johnson, T., & Atizani, F. (2009). A Network Architecture for Mobile Robotics. In *XXVII Brazilian Symposium on Computer Networks* (pp. 1-14), Recife, Brazil.

Colandairaj, J., Irwin, G. W., & Scanlon, W. G. (2007). A Co-Design Solution for Wireless Feedback Control. In *IEEE International Conference on Networking, Sensing and Control*, April 15-17, (pp. 404 – 409).

Collier, T. C., & Taylor, C. E. (2004). Self-organization in sensor network. *Journal of Parallel and Distributed Computing, 64*(7), 866–873. doi:10.1016/j.jpdc.2003.12.004

Conti, M., Di Pietro, R., Mancini, L., & Mei, A. (2007). A randomized, efficient, and distributed protocol for the detection of node replication attacks in wireless sensor networks. In the eight ACM international symposium on mobile ad hoc networking and computing (MobiHoc), (pp. 80–89).

Cook, D. J., & Das, S. K. (2004). Smart Environments: Technology, Protocols and Applications. Chichester, UK: John Wiley & Sons.

Costa, A. C. D. R., & Dimuro, G. P. (2005). Interactive Computation: Stepping Stone in the Pathway From Classical to Developmental Computation. *Electronic Notes in Theoretical Computer Science, 141*(5), 5–31. doi:. doi:10.1016/j.entcs.2005.05.014

Costa, C., Yamin, A., & Geyer, C. (2008). Toward a General Software Infrastructure for Ubiquitous Computing. *IEEE Pervasive Computing / IEEE Computer Society [and] IEEE Communications Society, 7*(1), 64–73. doi:. doi:10.1109/MPRV.2008.21

Costa, P., Mottola, L., Murphy, A. L., & Picco, G. P. (2007). Programming wireless sensor networks with the teenylime middleware. In the ACM/IFIP/USENIX 2007 international conference on middleware (Middleware) (pp. 429–449). New York: Springer-Verlag, Inc.

Coulouris, G., Dollimore, J., & Kindberg, T. (2005). Distributed Systems: Concepts and Design (4th Edition) (4th ed., pp. 927). Reading, MA: Addison Wesley.

Cover, T. M., & Thomas, J. A. (1991). Elements of Information Theory. Chichester, UK: John Wiley.

Cox, R. V., Kamm, C. A., Rabiner, L. R., Schroeter, J., & Wilpon, J. G. (2000). Speech and language processing for next-millennium communications services. *Proceedings of the IEEE, 88*(8), 1314–1337. doi:10.1109/5.880086

Cox, R., O'Donnell, M., & Oberlander, J. (1999). Dynamic versus static hypermedia in museum education: an evaluation of ILEX, the intelligent labelling explorer. In *Proceedings of the Artificial Intelligence in Education conference.*

Cui, Q., Liu, C., & Zha, X. F. (2008). Intelligent Drug Delivery System Using UML Diagrams Analysis. *Journal of Shanghai Jiaotong University (Science.), 13*(3), 312–317. doi:10.1007/s12204-008-0312-4

Culler, D., Estrin, D., & Srivastava, M. (2004). Overview of Sensor Networks. *Computer, 37*(8), 41–49. doi:10.1109/MC.2004.93

Curino, C., Giani, M., Giorgetta, M., Giusti, A., Murphy, A. L., & Picco, G. P. (2005, mar). TinyLime: Bridging mobile and sensor networks through middleware. In *the 3rd IEEE international conference on pervasive computing and communications (PerCom)* (pp. 61–72). Washington, DC: IEEE Computer Society. Available from http://www.inf.unisi.ch/murphy/Papers/percom05.pdf

D'Costa, A., & Sayeed, A. M. (2003). Data versus decision fusion for distributed classification in sensor networks. *Military Communications Conference, MILCOM 2003,* (Vol. 1, pp. 585 - 590). Washington, DC: IEEE.

Dalbro, M., & Eikeland, E. in't Veld, A.J., Gjessing, S., Lande, T.S., Riis, H.K., & Sorasen, O. (2008). Wireless Sensor Networks for Off-shore Oil and Gas Installations. In *Second International Conference on Sensor Technologies and Applications, SENSORCOMM '08,* (pp. 258 – 263).

Daly-Jones, O., & Carey, R. (2000). Interactive TV: a new interaction paradigm? In CHI '00 extended abstracts on Human factors in computer systems, (pp. 306-306). The Hague, The Netherlands: ACM Press.

Das, S. K., Cook, D. J., Bhattacharya, A., Heierman, E., & Lin, T. Y. (2002). The Role of Prediction Algorithms in the MAVHome Smart Home Architecture. [Special Issue on Smart Homes]. *IEEE Wireless Communications, 9*(6), 77–84. doi:10.1109/MWC.2002.1160085

Dasarathy, B. V. (1997). Sensor fusion potential exploitation-innovative architectures and illustrative applications. *Proceedings of the IEEE, 85*(1), 24–38. doi:10.1109/5.554206

Daubechies, I. (1992). Ten lectures in wavelets. SIAM: Society for Industrial and Applied Mathematics.

Davies, N., & Gellersen, H. (2002). Beyond Prototypes: Challenges in Deploying Ubiquitous Systems. *IEEE Pervasive Computing / IEEE Computer Society [and] IEEE Communications Society, 1*(1), 26–35. doi:10.1109/MPRV.2002.993142

Davies, N., Mitchell, K., Cheverst, K., & Blair, G. (1998). Developing a context sensitive tourist guide. Technical Report Computing Department, Lancaster University, Lancaster, UK.

Davin, S., & Ing, L. (1999). Innovations in a technology museum. *IEEE Micro, 19*(6).

De Biasi, M., Snickars, C., Landernas, K., & Isaksson, A. (2008). Simulation of Process Control with WirelessHART Networks Subject to Clock Drift. In *32nd Annual IEEE International Computer Software and Applications,(COMPSAC '08)*, (pp. 1355 – 1360).

Deb, B., Bhatnagar, S., & Nath, B. (2003). Reinform: Reliable information forwarding using multiple paths in sensor networks. In 28th annual IEEE international conference on local computer networks (LCN) (pp. 406–415).

Dettmer, R. (2003). It's good to talk [speech technology for on-line services access]. *IEE Review, 49*(6), 30–33. doi:10.1049/ir:20030603

Dey, A. K. (2001). Understanding and Using Context. *Personal and Ubiquitous Computing, 4-7*(5). doi:. doi:10.1007/s007790170019

Dey, A. K., & Abowd, G. D. (2000). The context toolkit: aiding the development of context-aware applications. In *Proceedings of the 2nd International Symposium on Handheld and Ubiquitous Computing*, (pp.172–186). London: Springer-Verlag.

Dey, A. K., Abowd, G. D., & Salber, D. (2001). A conceptual framework and a toolkit for supporting the rapid prototyping of context-aware applications. *Human-Computer Interaction, 16*(2), 97–166. doi:. doi:10.1207/S15327051HCI16234_02

Di Tian, G. N. D. (2003). Energy efficient routing with guaranteed delivery in wireless sensor networks. Wireless Communications and Networking, WCNC 2003, (Vol. 3, pp. 1923 – 1929).

Dimakis, N., Soldatos, J. K., Polymenakos, L., Fleury, P., Curín, J., & Kleindienst, J. (2008). Integrated development of context-aware applications in smart spaces. *IEEE Pervasive Computing / IEEE Computer Society [and] IEEE Communications Society, 7*(4), 71–79. doi:10.1109/MPRV.2008.75

Dishman, E. (2004). Inventing wellness systems for aging in place. *Computer, 37*(5), 34–41. doi:10.1109/MC.2004.1297237

Du, W., Deng, J., Han, Y. S., & Varshney, P. K. (2003). A pairwise key pre-distribution scheme for wireless sensor networks. In the 10th ACM conference on computer and communications security (pp. 42–51).

Du, W., Deng, J., Han, Y. S., Chen, S., & Varshney, P. K. (2004). A key management scheme for wireless sensor networks using deployment knowledge. In the 23rd conference on computer communications (INFOCOM).

Dudgeon, D. J., Harlos, M., & Clinch, J. J. (1999). The Edmonton Symptom Assessment Scale (ESAS) as an audit tool. *Journal of Palliative Care, 15*(3), 14–19.

Dunkels, A., Finne, N., Eriksson, J., & Voigt, T. (2006). Run-time dynamic linking for reprogramming wireless sensor networks. In the 4th international conference on embedded networked sensor systems (SenSys) (pp. 15–28). New York: ACM Press.

Dybkjaer, L., & Bernsen, N. O. (2001). Usability Evaluation in Spoken Language Dialogue Systems. In *Proceedings of the ACL 2001 Workshop on Evaluation Methodologies for Language and Dialogue Systems.*

Ehrmantraut, M., Härder, T., Wittig, H., & Steinmetz, R. (1996). The personal electronic program guide – towards the pre-selection of individual tv programs. In *Proceedings of the fifth international conference on Information and knowledge management*, (pp. 243–250). Rockville, MD: ACM Press.

Ekici, E., McNair, J., & Al-Abri, D. (2008). Secure probabilistic location verification in randomly deployed wireless sensor networks. *Ad Hoc Networks, 6*(2), 195–209. doi:10.1016/j.adhoc.2006.11.006

Elmufti, K., Weerasinghe, D., Rajarajan, M., Rakocevic, V., & Khan, S. (2006). Privacy in Mobile Web Services for eHealth. In *Pervasive Health Conference and Workshops* (pp. 1-6), Innsbruck, Austria.

Elrad, T., Filman, R. E., & Bader, A. (2001). Aspect-oriented programming: Introduction. *Communications of the ACM, 44*(10), 29–32. doi:. doi:10.1145/383845.383853

Eriksson, L., & Koivo, H. N. (2005). Tuning of discrete-time PID controllers in sensor network based control systems. In *Proceedings IEEE International Symposium on Computational Intelligence in Robotics and Automation,* CIRA 2005, (pp. 359 – 364).

Estop, T. D. (1978). Applied Thermodynamics for Engineering Technologists: S.I. Units. London: Longman Publishers.

Estrin, D., Culler, D., Pister, K. & Sukhatme, G. (2002). Connecting the Physical World with Pervasive Networks. *Pervasive Computing, IEEE, 1*(1, January-March), 59-69.

Fåhraeus, C., Hugosson, O., & Ericson, P. (2006) *Device and Method for Recording Handwritten Information.* US Patent US006985643B1.

Fainberg, M., & Goodman, D. (2001, October). Analysis of the interference between ieee 802.11b and bluetooth systems. In Ieee vehicular technology conference (Vol. 2, pp. 967-971).

Favela, J., Tentori, M., Castro, L. A., Gonzalez, V. M., Moran, E. B., & Martinez-Garcia, A. I. (2006). Estimating Hospital Work Activities in Context-Aware Healthcare Applications. In *Pervasive Health Conference and Workshops* (pp. 1-10), Innsbruck, Austria.

Feki, M. A., & Mokhtari, M. (2006). Context awareness for pervasive assistive environment. In I.K. Ibrahim, (Ed.), Handbook of Research on Mobile Multimedia. Hershey, PA: Idea Group Publisher.

Feki, M. A., Mokhtari, M., & Ibrahim, I. K. (2006). A novel approach for ontology distribution in ubiquitous environments. *International Journal of Web Systems, 2*(3–4).

Ferguson, G., Allen, J., Blaylock, N., Byron, D., Chambers, N., Dzikovska, M., Galescu, L., Shen, X., Swier, R. & Swift, M. (2002). *The medication advisor project: preliminary report.* Technical report.

Fetzer, C., & Högstedt, K. (2003). Challenges in Making Pervasive Systems Dependable. In Future Directions in Distributed Computing, (LNCS Vol. 2584, pp. 186-190).

Berlin: Springer. doi:10.1007/3-540-37795-6_37.

Figueiredo, C. M., Nakamura, E. F., & Loureiro, A. A. (2007). An event-detection estimation model for hybrid adaptive routing in wireless sensor networks. In *Proceedings of the IEEE International Conference on Communications (ICC'07).*

Figueiredo, C., Nakamura, E., & Loureiro, A. (2004). Multi: A hybrid adaptive dissemination protocol for wireless sensor networks. In *Proceedings of the 1st International Workshop on Algorithmic Aspects of Wireless Sensor Networks (Algosensors 2004),* (LNCS Vol. 3121, pp. 171–186). Berlin: Springer.

Fitton, D. (2005). Rapid Prototyping and User-Centered Design of Interactive Display-Based Systems. *IEEE Pervasive Computing / IEEE Computer Society [and] IEEE Communications Society, 4*(5).

Fleck, M., Frid, M., Kindberg, T., O'Brien-Strain, E., Rajani, R., & Spasojevic, M. (2002). Rememberer: a tool for capturing museum visits. In *Proceedings of the Ubiquitous Computing International Conference.*

Fok, C.-L., Roman, G.-C., & Lu, C. (2005). Rapid development and flexible deployment of adaptive wireless sensor network applications. In the 25th IEEE international conference on distributed computing systems (ICDCS) (pp. 653–662). Washington, DC: IEEE Computer Society.

Fougeyrollas, P. (2000). *Classification qubcoise: Processus de production du handicap.* Technical report, RIPPH, SCCIDIH; Réseau international du processus de production du handicap.

Frank, C., & Römer, K. (2005). Algorithms for generic role assignment in wireless sensor networks. In *Proceedings of the 3rd ACM Conference on Embedded Networked Sensor Systems (SenSys'05).*

Friday, A., Davies, N., Wallbank, N., Catterall, E., & Pink, S. (2004). Supporting Service Discovery, Querying and Interaction in Ubiquitous Computing Environments. *Wireless Networks, 10*(6), 631–641. doi:. doi:10.1023/B:WINE.0000044024.54833.cb

Frohlich, D. M., Dray, S., & Silverman, A. (2001). Breaking up is hard to do: family perspectives on the future of the home pc. *International Journal of Human-Computer Studies, 54*(5), 701–724. doi:10.1006/ijhc.2000.0436

Fuggetta, A., Picco, G., & Vigna, G. (1998). Understanding code mobility. *IEEE Transactions on Software Engineering, 24*(5), 342–361. doi:. doi:10.1109/32.685258

Fulford-Jones, T., Malan, D., Welsh, M., & Moulton, S. (2004). Codeblue: an ad hoc sensor network infrastructure for emergency medical care. In *International Workshop on Wearable and Implantable Body Sensor Networks*, (pp.12–14).

Funabashi, M., Maeda, A., Morooka, Y., & Mori, K. (1995). Fuzzy and Neural Hybrid Expert Systems: Synergetic AI. *IEEE Expert, 10*(4), 32–40. doi:10.1109/64.403949

Ganeriwal, S., Kumar, R., & Srivastava, M. B. (2003). Timing-sync protocol for sensor networks. In *Proceedings of the 1st ACM International Conference on Embedded Networked Sensor Systems, (SenSys '03)*.

Ganesan, D., Govindan, R., Shenker, S., & Estrin, D. (2001). Highly-resilient, energy-efficient multipath routing in wireless sensor networks. *SIGMOBILE Mobile Computing and Communications Review, 5*(4), 11–25. doi:10.1145/509506.509514

Ganesan, R. (2002). *Wavelet based multiresolution monitoring of a nanomachining process in semicondutor manufacturing.* Master thesis, Departament of Industrial and Management Systems Engineering University South Florida.

Ganesan, R., Das, T. K., & Venkataraman, V. (2004, September). Wavelet based multiscale statistical process monithoring: a literature review. *IIE Transactions on Quality and Reability, 36*(9), 787–806. doi:10.1080/07408170490473060

Gao, M., Xu, J., & Tian, J. (2008). Remote monitoring system of pumping unit based on wireless sensor networks. In *IEEE International Conference on Industrial Technology, ICIT 2008*, (pp. 1 – 4).

Garey, M. R., & Johnson, D. S. (1979). Computers and Intractability: A Guide to the Theory of NP-Completeness. New York: W. H. Freeman Publishers.

Garlan, D., Siewiorek, D., Smailagic, A., & Steenkiste, P. (2002). Project Aura: toward distraction-free pervasive computing. *IEEE Pervasive Computing / IEEE Computer Society [and] IEEE Communications Society, 1*(2), 22–31. doi:. doi:10.1109/MPRV.2002.1012334

Gärtner, F. C. (1999). Fundamentals of fault-tolerant distributed computing in asynchronous environments. *ACM Computing Surveys, 31*(1), 1–26. doi:. doi:10.1145/311531.311532

Gatzoulis, L., & Iakovidis, I. (2007). Wearable and Portable eHealth Systems. *Engineering in Medicine and Biology Magazine, 26*(5), 51–56. doi:10.1109/EMB.2007.901787

Gavrilov, A. V. (1988). Dialog system for preparing of programs for robot. Automatyka, 99, Glivice, Poland, 173-180 (in Russian).

Gavrilov, A. V. (2003). A combination of Neural and Semantic Networks in Natural Language Processing. In H-H. Lee, (Ed.), *Proceedings of the 7th Korea-Russia International Symposium KORUS-2003,* (Vol. 2, pp. 143-147). Republic of Korea: University of Ulsan.

Gavrilov, A. V. (2003). The principles of action of intelligent systems. In *Proceedings of International Conference on Information Systems and Technologies IST-2003,* (Vol.3, pp. 91-94), Novosibirsk State Technical University, Novosibirsk, Russia.

Gavrilov, A. V. (2007). The principles of action of intelligent systems. In G. Marchetti (Ed.) *Mind, Consciousness and Language*. Retrieved from http://www.mind-consciousness-language.com/articles.htm

Gavrilov, A. V. (2008). Context and Learning based Approach to Programming of Intelligent Equipment. In J.-S. Pan & P. Kellenberger (Eds.), *The 8th International Conference on Intelligent Systems Design and Applications ISDA-2008* (pp. 578-582). Washington, DC: IEEE Computer Society.

Gavrilov, A. V. (2008). Hybrid Rule and Neural Network based Framework for Ubiquitous Computing. In J. Kim, D. Delen, Park, F. Ko, Y. J. Na, (Eds.), *The 4th International Conference on Networked Computing and*

Advanced Information Management: (Vol. 2, pp. 488-492). Washington, DC: IEEE Computer Society.

Gavrilov, A. V. (2008). Usage of Neural Networks in Ubiquitous Computing Systems. In N.V. Pustovoy (Ed.), *Proceedings. of the 3rd International Forum on Strategic Technologies IFOST-2008.* Novosibirsk, Russia: Novosibirsk State Technical University.

Gavrilov, A. V. (2009). New Paradigm of Context based Programming-Learning of Intelligent Agent. In A. Pascoal & V. Ufranovsky (Eds.), *Proceedings of 1st Workshop on Networked embedded and control system technologies. In conjunction with 6th International Conference on Informatics in Control, Automation and Robotics ICINCO-2009 (*pp. 94-99). Portugal: INSTICC Press.

Gavrilov, A. V., & Chistyakov, N. A. (2005). An architecture of the toolkit for development of Hybrid Expert Systems. In Yu, I. Shokin, O.I. Potaturkin, (Eds.), *Proceedings of The Second IASTED International Multi-Conference Automation, Control and Information Technology ACIT-2005.* Novosibirsk, Russia: ACTA Press.

Gavrilov, A. V., & Lee, S.-Y. (2007). Usage of Hybrid Neural Network Model MLP-ART for Navigation of Mobile Robot. In de-Shuang Huang, Luonan Chen (Eds.) *International Conference on Intelligent Computing* ICIC-2007, (LNAI 4682, pp. 182-191). Berlin: Springer-Verlag.

Gavrilov, A. V., & Novickaja, J. V. (2001). The Toolkit for development of Hybrid Expert Systems. In Y.P. Pokholkov (Ed.) *Proceedings of the 5th Korea-Russia International Symposium KORUS-2001,* (Vol. 1, pp. 73-75). Tomsk, Russia: Tomsk Polytechnic University.

Gavrilov, A. V., Gubarev, V. V., Jo, K.-H., & Lee, H.-H. (2004). An architecture of hybrid control system of mobile robot. *Mechatronics, Automation. Control, 8,* 30–37.

Gavrilov, A. V., Gubarev, V. V., Jo, K.-H., & Lee, H.-H. (2004). Hybrid Neural-based Control System for Mobile Robot. In Y.P. Pokholkov (Ed.), *Proceedings of the 8th Korea-Russia International Symposium KORUS-2004,* (Vol. 1, pp. 31-35). Tomsk, Russia: Tomsk Polytechnic University.

Geer, D. (2006). Pervasive Medical Devices: Less Invasive, More Productive. *Pervasive Computing, 5*(2), 85–87. doi:10.1109/MPRV.2006.37

Gelabert, X., Prez-Romero, J., Sallent, O., & Agust, R. (2008). A markovian approach to radio access technology selection in heterogeneous multiaccess/multiservice wireless networks. *IEEE Transactions on Mobile Computing, 7*(10), 1257–1270. doi:10.1109/TMC.2008.50

Gelernter, D. (1985). Generative communication in linda. *ACM Transaction on Programming Language and Systems, 7*(1), 80–112. doi:10.1145/2363.2433

Gene F. Hoffnagle. (1999). Pervasive Computing - Preface. *IBM Systems Journal, Pervasive Computing, 38*(4), 502. doi: DOI: 10.1147/sj.384.0502

Ghorbel, M., Kadouche, R., & Mokhtari, M. (2007, April). User and service modeling in assistive environment to enhance accessibility of dependent people. In ICTA.

Ghorbel, M., Mokhtari, M., & Renouard, S. (2006). A distributed approach for assistive service provision in pervasive environment. In *Proceedings of the 4th International Workshop on Wireless Mobile Applications and Services on WLAN Hotspots,* (pp. 91–100). New York: ACM.

Gilbert, M., & Junlan, F. (2008). Speech and language processing over the web. *Signal Processing Magazine, IEEE, 25*(3), 18–28. doi:10.1109/MSP.2008.918410

Goertzel, B., & Pennachin, C. (Eds.). (2007). Artificial General Intelligence. Berlin, Germany: Springer-Verlag.

Gong, J. Cai, J. Li, X. Song, S., (2007). Research on State Estimation of Oil Pipeline Considering Adaptive Extended Kalman Filtering. In *International Conference on Mechatronics and Automation, ICMA 2007.*

Gonz_alez, M. C., Hidalgo, C. A., & Barab_asi, A.-L. (2008). Understanding individual human mobility patterns. *Nature, 453* (7196), 779-782.

Goonatilake, S., & Khebbal, S. (Eds.). (1995). Intelligent Hybrid Systems. San Francisco, CA: Wiley.

Gray, D. B., & Hendershot, G. E. (2000). The icidh-2: developments for a new era of outcomes research. *Archives of Physical Medicine and Rehabilitation, 81*(12PB), 10–14. doi:10.1053/apmr.2000.20616

Graziosi, F., & Santucci, F. (2002). A general correlation model for shadow fading in mobile radio systems. *IEEE Communications Letters, 6*(3), 102–104. doi:10.1109/4234.991146

Greenemeier, L. (2008). Who Needs a Doctor When There's a Robot in the House, er, Hospital? *Scientific American.* Retrieved May 1, 2009, from http://www.scientificamerican.com/article.cfm?id=robot-telemedicine

Greenfield, A. (2006). Everyware: the dawning age of ubiquitous computing, (pp. 11–12). Indianapolis, IN: New Riders.

Grimm, R., Davis, J., Lemar, E., MacBeth, A., Swanson, S., & Anderson, T. (2004). System support for pervasive applications. *ACM Transactions on Computer Systems, 22*(4), 421–486. doi:10.1145/1035582.1035584

Griss, M., Letsinger, R., Cowan, D., Sayers, C., VanHilst, M., & Kessler, R. (2002). *Coolagent: intelligent digital assistants for mobile professionals-phase 1 retrospective.* HP Laboratories Report HPL-2002-55 (R), July.

Gulliver, S., Ghinea, G., Patel, M., & Serif, T. (2007). A context-aware tour guide: user implications. *Mobile Information Systems, 3*(2), 71–88.

Gyselinckx, B., Hoof, C. V., Ryckaert, J., Yazicioglu, R. F., Fiorini, P., & Leonov, V. (2005). Human++: Autonomous Wireless Sensors for Body Area Networks. In *IEEE Custom Integrated Circuits Conference* (pp. 13-19), San Jose, CA.

Haas, Z. J., Gerla, M., Johnson, D. B., Perkins, C. E., Pursley, M. B., Steenstrup, M. E., & Toh, C.-K. (1999). Special issue on wireless ad hoc networks. *IEEE Journal on Selected Areas in Communications, 17*.

Haken, H. (1983). Synergetics: An Introduction. Nonequilibrium Phase Transition and Self-Organization in Physics, Chemistry, and Biology, (3rd Rev. & Enlarged Ed.).

Hall, D. L., & Llinas, J. (1997). An introduction to multisensor data fusion. *Proceedings of the IEEE, 85*(1), 6–23. doi:10.1109/5.554205

Halperin, D., Kohno, T., Heydt-Benjamin, T. S., Fu, K., & Maisel, W. H. (2008). Security and Privacy for Implantable Medical Devices. *Pervasive Computing, 7*(1), 30–39. doi:10.1109/MPRV.2008.16

Hansen, T. R., Bardram, J. E., & Soegaard, M. (2006). Moving Out of the Lab: Deploying Pervasive Technologies in a Hospital. *Pervasive Computing, 5*(3), 24–31. doi:10.1109/MPRV.2006.53

Hansen, W. J., & Haas, C. (1988). Reading and writing with computers: a framework for explaining differences in performance. *Communications of the ACM, 31*(9), 1080–1089. doi:10.1145/48529.48532

HART Communication protocol. (n.d.). Retrieved from http://www.hartcomm2.org/hart_protocol/protocol/hart_data.html

Harter, A., & Hopper, A. (1994). A distributed location system for the active office. *IEEE Network, 8*(1), 62–70. doi:10.1109/65.260080

Harter, A., Hopper, A., Steggles, P., Ward, A., & Webster, P. (1999). The anatomy of a context-aware application. In *Proc. 5th Annual Int'l Conference on Mobile Computing and Networking*, (pp. 59-68).

Hee-Cheol, K. (2008). Weaknesses of Voice Interaction. In *Fourth International Conference on Networked Computing and Advanced Information Management, (NCM '08.* Hjelm, J. (2008). *Why IPTV?: interctivity, technologies and services.* Chichester, UK: Wiley.

Heidegger, M. (1996). Being and time: a translation of Sein und Zeit. New York: State University of New York. doi: 10.1109/MPRV.2006.55.

Heidemann, J., Silva, F., & Estrin, D. (2003). Matching data dissemination algorithms to application requirements. In *Proceedings of the 1st ACM International Conference on Embedded Networked Sensor Systems (SenSys'03).*

Heinzelman, W. B., Murphy, A. L., Carvalho, H. S., & Perillo, M. A. (2004). Middleware to support sensor network applications. *IEEE Network*, *18*(1), 6–14. doi:10.1109/MNET.2004.1265828

Heinzelman, W. R., Chandrakasan, A., & Balakrishnan, H. (2000). Energy-efficient communication protocol for wireless microsensor networks. In *Proceedings of the IEEE Hawaii International Conference on System Sciences*, (pp. 4–13).

Helal, A., & Abdulrazak, B. (2006). TeCaRob: Tele-Care using Telepresence and Robotic Technology for Assisting People with Special Needs. *International Journal of Human-friendly Welfare Robotic Systems*, *7*(3), 46–53.

Helson. (2007). *WirelessHART fits into ISA-SP100 standards effort*. Retrieved from http://www.isa.org/InTechTemplate.cfm?Section=Executive_Corner2&template=/ContentManagement/ContentDisplay.cfm&ContentID=61420

Heo, J., Hong, J., & Cho, Y. (2009). EARQ: Energy Aware Routing for Real-Time and Reliable Communication in Wireless Industrial Sensor Networks. *IEEE Transactions on Industrial Informatics*, *5*(1), 3–11. doi:10.1109/TII.2008.2011052

Herigstad, D., & Wichansky, A. (1998). Designing user interfaces for television. In CHI '98 conference summary on Human factors in computing systems, (pp.165-166). New York: ACM Press.

Hess, J., Küstermann, G., & Pipek, V. (2008) Premote: a user customizable remote control. In CHI'08 extended abstracts on Human factors in computing systems, April 05-10, Florence, Italy.

Heylighen, F. (2002). The science of self-organization and adaptivity. The Encyclopedia of Life Support Systems. Oxford, UK: EOLSS Publishers.

Hightower, J., LaMarca, A., & Smith, I. (2006). Practical Lessons from Place Lab. *IEEE Pervasive Computing / IEEE Computer Society [and] IEEE Communications Society*, *5*(3), 32–39. doi:10.1109/MPRV.2006.55

Hochreiter, S., & Schmidhuber, J. (1997). Long Short-Term Memory. *Neural Computation*, *9*(8), 1735–1780. doi:10.1162/neco.1997.9.8.1735

Holmquist, L. E., Schmidt, A., & Ullmer, B. (2004). Tangible interfaces in perspective. *Personal and Ubiquitous Computing*, *8*(5), 291–293. doi:. doi:10.1007/s00779-004-0292-9

Hong, J., Suh, E., & Kim, S. (2009). Context-aware systems: A literature review and classification. *Expert Systems with Applications*, *36*(4), 8509–8522. doi:10.1016/j.eswa.2008.10.071

Hopper, A. (1999). *Sentient computing*. The Royal Society Clifford Patterson Lecture. House n Living Laboratory (n.d.). *Introduction*. Web resource available at http://architecture.mit.edu/house n/web/publications

Horiuchi, L., & Stokes, A. (2006), *CISCO Press release*. Retrieved from http://newsroom.cisco.com/dlls/partners/news/2006/pr_prod_09-11.html

Hornbæk, K., & Frokjer, E. (2003). Reading patterns and usability in visualizations of electronic documents. *ACM Transactions on Computer-Human Interaction*, *10*(2), 119–149. doi:10.1145/772047.772050

Hornecker, E. (2005). A Design Theme for Tangible Interaction: Embodied Facilitation. In *9th European Conference on Computer-Supported Cooperative Work* (pp. 23-43). Netherlands: Springer. doi: 10.1007/1-4020-4023-7_2

Horrocks, I., & Patel-Schneider, P. F. (2004) A proposal for an owl rules language. In *Proceedings of the 13th International Conference on World Wide Web*, (pp.723–731). New York: ACM.

Horrocks, I., & Sattler, U. (2001). Ontology reasoning in the shoq (d) description logic. *International Joint Conference on Artificial Intelegence*, (Vol. 17, pp.199–204). Mahwah, NJ: Lawrence Erlbaum Associates, Ltd.

Horrocks, I., Sattler, U., & Tobies, S. (2000). Practical reasoning for very expressive description logics. *Logic Journal of IGPL*, *8*(3), 239–263. doi:10.1093/jigpal/8.3.239

Howie, C. L. (1984). *Remote Corrosion Monitoring of Off-Shore Pipelines.* Retrieved from http://www.mms.gov/tarprojects/075/075AA.PDF

Hu, J., & Wellman, M. P. (2003). Nash Q-Learning for General-Sum Stochastic Games. *Journal of Machine Learning, 4,* 1039–1069. doi:10.1162/jmlr.2003.4.6.1039

Hudak, P., Courtney, A., Nilsson, H., & Peterson, J. (2002). Arrows, Robots, and Functional Reactive Programming. *LNCS, 2638,* 159–187.

Hughes, D., Bencomo, N., Blair, G., Coulson, G., Grace, P., & Porter, B. (2008). Exploiting extreme heterogeneity in a flood warning scenario using the Gridkit middleware. In *Proceedings of the ACM/IFIP/USENIX, Middleware Conference,* (pp. 54-57).

Hui, J. W., & Culler, D. (2004). The dynamic behavior of a data dissemination protocol for network programming at scale. In the 2nd international conference on embedded networked sensor systems (SenSys) (pp. 81–94). New York: ACM Press.

Hult, L. Lind, L., & Hägglund, S. (2008) Enabling e-Services for All. A User-Centered Design Approach for Audio-Based Information Services. In Proceedings eChallenges 2008. Amsterdam: IOS Press.

Hung, N. Q., Shehzad, A., Kiani, S. L., Riaz, M., Ngoc, K. A., & Lee, S.-L. (2004). Developing Context-Aware Ubiquitous Computing Systems with a Unified Middleware Framework. In L.T. Yang (Ed.), *The 2004 International Conference on Embedded & Ubiquitous Computing* (pp. 672-681). Berlin: Springer-Verlag.

Hunt, A. & Walker, W. (2000 June). *A fine Grained Component Architecture for Speech Application Development.* SUN Research, Project: SMLI TR-. 2000-86.

IBM WebSphere. (n.d.). Retrieved from http://www.ibm.com/developerworks/websphere/

IEEE. (2006). IEEE specific requirements part 15.4: Wireless medium access control (mac) and physical layer (phy) specifications for low-rate wireless personal area networks (wpans). *IEEE Std 802.15.4-2006 (Revision of IEEE Std 802.15.4-2003).*

IEEE. (2008). *Ieee 802.11.* Retrieved from http://grouper.ieee.org/groups/802/11/

IEEE. (2008). Ieee 802.15. Retrieved from http://grouper.ieee.org/groups/802/15/

IEEE/IEC Std 802.11. (1999). *Wireless LAN Medium Access Control (MAC) and Physical Layer (PHY) specifications - High Speed Physical Layer in the 5 GHz Band.* Washington, DC: The Institute of Electrical and Electronics Engineers, Inc.

Ihmig, M., & Steenkiste, P. (2007, April). Distributed Dynamic Channel Selection in Chaotic Wireless Networks. In 13th european wireless conference.

il Hwang. K., Kim, J. W., In, J., & Eom, D. S. (2005). Lightweight real-time embedded systems for scalable ubiquitous networks. In *Proceedings of the Second ICESS, International Conference on Embedded Software and Systems* (pp. 135-143). Washington, DC: IEEE Computer Society.

Intel Research – Sensor Network Research (n.d.). Retrieved from http://techresearch.intel.com/articles/Exploratory/1501.htm

Ishibashi, K., & Yano, M. (2005). A Proposal of Forwarding Method for Urgent Messages on an Ubiquitous Wireless Sensor Network. In *Proceedings 6th Asia-Pacific Symposium on Information and Telecommunication Technologies, APSITT 2005,* (pp. 293 – 298).

Ishiguro, M., Tei, K., Fukazawa, Y., & Honiden, S. (2006). A sensor middleware for lightweight relocatable sensing programs. In International conference on computational intelligence for modelling, control and automation (CIMCA) (p. 195). Washington, DC: IEEE Computer Society.

Iyer, A., & Marculescu, D. (2002, May). Power-Performance Evaluation of Globally Asynchronous, Locally Synchronous Processors. In *Intl. Symposium on Computer Architecture (ISCA).*

Jacobsen, H.-A. (1998). A generic architecture for hybrid intelligent systems. In *Fuzzy Systems Proceedings, IEEE World Congress on Computational Intelligence,* (Vol. 1, pp. 709-714).

Jasemian, Y. (2006). Security and privacy in a wireless remote medical system for home healthcare purpose. In *Pervasive Health Conference and Workshops* (pp. 1-7), Innsbruck, Austria.

Jawhar, I., Mohamed, N., Mohamed, M. M., & Aziz, J. (2008). A Routing protocol and addressing scheme for oil, gas, and water pipeline monitoring using wireless sensor networks. In *5th IFIP International Conference on Wireless and Optical Communications Networks, WOCN '08*, (pp. 1 – 5).

Jeong, M. K., & Lu, J. (2003). Wavelet-Based SPC Procedure for Complicated Functional Data. In 2003 informs annual conference.

Jiang, P., Ren, H., Zhang, L., Wang, Z., & Xue, A. (2006). Reliable Application of Wireless Sensor Networks in Industrial Process Control. In *The Sixth World Congress on Intelligent Control and Automation, WCICA 2006*, (Vol. 1, pp. 99 – 103).

Jing, J., Helal, A. S., & Elmagarmid, A. (1999). Client-server computing in mobile environments. *ACM Computing Surveys, 31*(2), 117–157. doi:. doi:10.1145/319806.319814

Johnson, W., Jellinek, H., Leigh Klotz, J., Rao, R., & Card, S. K. (1993). Bridging the paper and electronic worlds: the paper user interface. In *Proceedings of the SIGCHI conference on Human factors in computing systems*, (pp 507–512). Amsterdam, The Netherlands: ACM Press.

Jovanov, E. (2005). Wireless Technology and System Integration in Body Area Networks for m-Health Applications. In *IEEE Engineering in Medicine and Biology Conference* (pp. 7158-7160), Shanghai, China.

Jovanov, E., Milenkovic, A., Otto, C., Groen, P. D., Johnson, B., Warren, S., & Taibi, G. (2005). A WBAN System for Ambulatory Monitoring of Physical Activity and Health Status: Applications and Challenges. In *IEEE Engineering in Medicine and Biology Annual Conference* (pp. 3810-3813), Shanghai, China.

Juang, B. H. (2001). Ubiquitous speech communication interface. In *IEEE Workshop on Automatic Speech Recognition and Understanding*, (ASRU '01).

Judd, G., Akella, A., Seshan, S., & Steenkiste, P. (2005, September). Self-Management in Chaotic Wireless Deployments. In *Mobicom'05: Proceedings of the 11th annual international conference on mobile computing and networking* (pp. 185 -199), Cologne, Germany.

Jung-Hyuck, J., & Jayant, N. (2003, May). Performance Evaluation of Multiple IEEE 802.11b Wlan Stations in the Presence of Bluetooth Radio Interference. In *Ieee international conference on communications* (Vol. 2, pp. 1163-1168).

Jurik, A. D., & Weaver, A. C. (2008). Remote Medical Monitoring. *Computer, 41*(4), 96–99. doi:10.1109/MC.2008.133

Kadouche, R. (2004) Towards strategies and methods for disabled users profile. In *Workshop on Personalisation of ICT Products and Services*, ETSI, October 2004.

Kadouche, R., Abdulrazak, B., & Mokhtari, M. (2004) Designing an evaluation method for computer accessibility for people with severe disabilities. In ICCHP, (pp. 845–848). Paris: Springer.

Kadouche, R., Abdulrazak, B., Mokhtari, M., Giroux, S., & Pigot, H. (2009). Personalization and multi-user management in smart homes for disabled people. *Journal of Smart Home, 3*(1), 39–48.

Kadouche, R., Mokhtari, M., & Maier, M. (2005, July 24–29). Modeling of the residual capability for people with severe motor disabilities: analysis of hand posture. In *Proceedings of User Modeling 2005: 10th International Conference, UM 2005*, Edinburgh, UK. Berlin: Springer.

Kang, D., Lee, H., Ko, E., Kang, K., & Lee, J. (2006). A Wearable Context Aware System for Ubiquitous Healthcare. In *IEEE Annual International Conference on the Engineering in Medicine and Biology Society* (pp. 5192-5195), New York.

Kapor, M. (2007). Recollections on Lotus 1-2-3: benchmark for spreadsheet software. *IEEE Annals of the History of Computing, 29*(3), 32-40. doi: 10.110910.1109/MAHC.2007.45

Kargl, F., Lawrence, E., Fischer, M., & Lim, Y. Y. (2008). Security, Privacy and Legal Issues in Pervasive eHealth Monitoring Systems. In *International Conference on Mobile Business,* (pp. 296-304), Barcelona, Spain.

Kaufman, C. F., & Lane, P. M. (1997). Understanding consumer information needs: The impact of polychromic time use. *Telematics and Informatics, 14*(2), 173–184. doi:10.1016/S0736-5853(96)00032-9

Kautz, H., Arnstein, L., Borriello, G., Etzioni, O., & Fox, D. (2002) An overview of the assisted cognition project. In *AAAI-2002 Workshop on Automation as Caregiver: The Role of Intelligent Technology in Elder Care*, Edmonton, Alberta, (pp.60–65).

Kawka, P. A., & Alleyne, A. G. (2005). Stability and feedback control of wireless networked systems. In *Proceedings of the 2005 American Control Conference*, (vol. 4, pp. 2953 - 2959).

Keen, E. (1975). A primer in phenomenological psychology. New York: Holt, Rinehart & Winston.

Kephart, J. O., & Chess, D. M. (2003). The vision of autonomic computing. *Computer, 36*(1), 41–50. doi:10.1109/MC.2003.1160055

Khalil, I., Bagchi, S., & Shroff, N. B. (2007). Liteworp: Detection and isolation of the wormhole attack in static multihop wireless networks. *Computer Networks, 51*(13), 3750–3772. doi:10.1016/j.comnet.2007.04.001

Khedr, M., & Karmouch, A. (2005). ACAI: agent-based context-aware infrastructure for spontaneous applications. *Journal of Network and Computer Applications, 28*(1), 19–44. doi:10.1016/j.jnca.2004.04.002

Kidd, C. D., Orr, R., Abowd, G. D., Atkeson, C. G., Essa, I. A., MacIntyre, B., et al. (1999). The aware home: a living laboratory for ubiquitous computing research. In Lecture Note In Computer Science, (pp.191–198).

Kim, A. N., Hekland, F., Petersen, S., & Doyle, P. (2008). When HART goes wireless: Understanding and implementing the WirelessHART standard. *IEEE International Conference on Emerging Technologies and Factory Automation, ETFA 2008*, Sept. 15-18, (pp. 899 – 907).

Kim, M. K., & Kim, H. C. (2007). *A Case Study on Usability of Asynchronous Voice Communication Systems.* Paper presented at the HCI International, Beijing, China.

Kim, M., & Noble, B. (2001). Mobile Network Estimation. In *Mobicom'01: Proceedings of the 7th annual international conference on mobile computing and networking* (pp. 298-309).

Kim, T., Hou, J. C., & Lim, H. (2006, September). Improving Spatial Reuse Through Tuning Transmit Power, Carrier Sense Threshold, and Data Rate in Multihop Wireless Networks. In Proceedings of mobicom (pp. 366-377).

Kindberg, T. et.al. (2002). People, places, things: web presence for the Real World. *MONET, 7*(5).

Kindberg, T., & Fox, A. (2002). System software for ubiquitous computing. *IEEE Pervasive Computing / IEEE Computer Society [and] IEEE Communications Society, 1*(1), 70–81. doi:. doi:10.1109/MPRV.2002.993146

Kochhal, M., Schwiebert, L., & Gupta, S. (2003). Role-based hierarchical self-organization for wireless ad hoc sensor networks. In *Proceedings of the 2nd ACM International Conference on Wireless Sensor Networks and Applications*, (pp. 98–107).

Koike, H., Sato, Y., & Kobayashi, Y. (2001). Integrating paper and digital information on enhanceddesk: a method for realtime finger tracking on an augmented desk system. *ACM Transactions on Computer-Human Interaction, 8*(4), 307–322. doi:10.1145/504704.504706

Konstantas, D., & Herzog, R. (2003). Continuous monitoring of vital constants for mobile users: the MobiHealth' approach. In *IEEE Annual International Conference on the Engineering in Medicine and Biology Society*, 4 (pp. 3728 - 3731), Cancun, México.

Koronios, A. (2006). Challenges of managing information quality in service organizations. Hershey, PA: Idea Group Inc.

Kosch, T., Adler, C., Eichler, S., Schroth, C., & Strassberger, M. (2006). The scalability problem of vehicular ad hoc networks and how to solve it. *IEEE Wireless*

Communications Magazine, 13(5), 22–28. doi:10.1109/WC-M.2006.250354

Krishnan, R., & Starobinski, D. (2003). Message-efficient self-organization of wireless sensor networks. In *Proceedings of the IEEE Wireless Communications & Networking Conference (WCNC'03)*, (pp. 1603–1608).

Krishnan, V. (2000). Location awareness in hp's cooltown, Position paper. In *W3C/WAP Workshop on Position Dependent Information*, (pp.15–16), Sophia Antipolis, France.

Kristensson, P. (2007). *Discrete and Continuous Shape Writing for Text Entry and Control*. PhD Thesis, No 1106. Linköping Studies in Science and Technology, Linköping University.

Kristensson, P. O., & Zhai, S. (2004) SHARK2: A Large Vocabulary Shorthand Writing System for Pen-based Computers. In *Proceedings of the 17th Annual ACM Symposium on User Interface Software and Technology (UIST '04)*, (pp. 43-52). New York: ACM Press.

Krumm, J., Harris, S., Meyers, B., Brumitt, B., Hale, M., & Shafer, S. (2000). Multi-Camera Multi-Person Tracking for Easy Living. In *Proceedings of 3rd IEEE International Workshop on Visual Surveillance*, (pp. 3-10). Piscataway, NJ: IEEE Press.

Kumar, B. (2002). *JSR-82: Java APIs for Bluetooth*. Retrieved from http://www.jcp.org/en/jsr/detail?id=82

Kumar, M., Garg, D. P., & Zachery, R. A. (2006). A generalized approach for inconsistency detection in data fusion from multiple sensors. In *American Control Conference*.

Kumar, R., Wolenetz, M., Agarwalla, B., Shin, J., Hutto, P., Paul, A., et al. (2003). Dfuse: a framework for distributed data fusion. In the 1st international conference on embedded networked sensor systems (SenSys), (pp. 114–125). New York: ACM Press.

Kwon, Y., Sundresh, S., Mechitov, K., & Agha, G. (2006). Actornet: an actor platform for wireless sensor networks. In the fifth international joint conference on autonomous agents and multiagent systems (AAMAS), (pp. 1297–1300). New York: ACM Press.

LaMarca, A., Chawathe, Y., Consolvo, S., Hightower, J., Smith, I., Scott, J., et al. (2005) Place lab: device positioning using radio beacons in the wild. In Proceedings of Pervasive, (pp.116–133). Berlin: Springer.

Larsen, L. B. (2003). Issues in the evaluation of spoken dialogue systems using objective and subjective measures. In *Proceedings of IEEE Workshop on Automatic Speech Recognition and Understanding (ASRU'03)*, St. Thomas, U.S. Virgin Islands, USA, (pp. 209-214).

Lauria, S., Bugmann, G., Kyriacou, T., Bos, J., & Klein, E. (2001). Training Personal Robots Using Natural Language Instruction. *IEEE Intelligent Systems, 16*, 38–45.

Lee, C. F., & Kuo, C. C. (2007) Difficulties on Small-Touch-Screens for Various Ages. In Universal Acess in Human Computer Interaction. Coping with Diversity (Vol. 4554, pp. 968-974). Berlin: Springer.

Lennvall, T., Svensson, S., & Hekland, F. (2008). A comparison of WirelessHART and ZigBee for industrial applications. In IEEE International Workshop on Factory Communication Systems, (pp. 85 – 88).

Lesser., et al. (1999). The Intelligent Home Testbed. In Proc. of Autonomy Control Software Workshop.

Levis, P., & Culler, D. (2002). MatÅLe: a tiny virtual machine for sensor networks. In the 10th international conference on architectural support for programming languages and operating systems (ASPLOS) (pp. 85–95). New York: ACM Press.

Levis, P., Patel, N., Culler, D., & Shenker, S. (2004). Trickle: a self-regulating algorithm for code propagation and maintenance in wireless sensor networks. In the 1st conference on symposium on networked systems design and implementation (NSDI) (pp. 15–28). Berkeley, CA: USENIX Association.

Levy, E., & Silberschatz, A. (1990). Distributed file systems: concepts and examples. *ACM Computing Surveys, 22*(4), 321–374. doi:. doi:10.1145/98163.98169

Lewis, F. L. (2004). Wireles Sensor Networks. In D. Cook & S. Das, (eds.), Smart Environments: Technology, Protocols and Applications. Chichester, UK: Wiley-Interscience.

Li, H.-B. Takizawa, K., Zhen, B., & Kohno, R. (2007). Body Area Network and Its Standardization at IEEE 802.15.MBAN. In Mobile and Wireless Communications Summit, (pp. 1-5), Budapest, Hungary.

Liao, C., Guimbretiere, F., & Loeckenhoff, C. E. (2006). Pen-top Feedback for Paper-based Interfaces. In *Proc. of UIST '06*, Montreux, Switzerland.

Lind, L. (2006). *Towards Effortless Use of Information Technology in Home Healthcare with a Networked Digital Pen.* PhD Thesis, No 1039, Linköping Studies in Science and Technology, Linköping University.

Lind, L. (2008) Evaluation of the Use of Digital Pens for Pain Assessment in Palliative Home Healthcare. In S.K. Andersen et al, (Eds.), eHealth Beyond the Horizon – Get IT There. Amsterdam: IOS Press.

Lind, L., Karlsson, D., & Fridlund, B. (2007). Digital pens and pain diaries in palliative home health care: professional caregivers' experiences. *Medical Informatics and the Internet in Medicine, 32*(4), 287–296. doi:10.1080/14639230701785381

Lind, L., Karlsson, D., & Fridlund, B. (2008). Patients' use of digital pens for pain assessment in advanced palliative home healthcare. *International Journal of Medical Informatics, 77*(2), 129–136. doi:10.1016/j.ijmedinf.2007.01.013

Liszka, K. J., Mackin, M. A., Lichter, M. J., York, D. W., Pillai, P., & Rosenbaum, D. S. (2004). Keeping a beat on the heart. *Pervasive Computing, 3*(4), 42–49. doi:10.1109/MPRV.2004.10

Loke, S. (2006). Context-aware artifacts: two development approaches. *IEEE Pervasive Computing / IEEE Computer Society [and] IEEE Communications Society, 5*(2), 48–53. doi:. doi:10.1109/MPRV.2006.27

Long, S., Kooper, R., Abowd, G., & Atkeson, C. (1996). Rapid prototyping of mobile context-aware applications: The cyberguide case study. In *Proceedings of the 2nd Annual International Conference on Mobile Computing and Networking.*

Long, X., & Sikdar, B. (2007). Wavelet based detection of shadow fading in wireless networks. In Ieee global telecommunications conference, globecom '07, (pp. 305-309).

Long, X., & Sikdar, B. (2008). A Real-Time Algorithm for Long Range Signal Strength Prediction in Wireless Networks. In Ieee wireless communications and networking conference, Wcnc 2008, (pp. 1120 - 1125).

Low, K. S., Win, W. N. N., & Er, M. J. (2005). Wireless Sensor Networks for Industrial Environments. In *International Conference on Computational Intelligence for Modelling, Control and Automation, 2005 and International Conference on Intelligent Agents, Web Technologies and Internet Commerce*, (Vol. 2, pp. 271 – 276).

Luff, P., Heath, C., Norrie, M. C., Signer, B., & Herdman, P. (2004) Only Touching the Surface: Creating Affinities Between Digital Content and Paper. In *Proc. of CSCW 2004*, Chicago, IL.

Luther, B. (n.d.). *Oil Field Safety.* Retrieved from http://www.txoga.org/attachments/OilFieldSafetyNEO1.ppt#256,1,Oil Field Safety

Lyytinen, K., & Yoo, Y. (2002). Issues and challenges in ubiquitous computing - Introduction. *Communications of the ACM, 45*(12), 62–65. doi:. doi:10.1145/585597.585616

MacDonald, J. A. (2008). Authentication considerations for mobile e-health applications. In *International Conference on Pervasive Computing Technologies for Healthcare* (pp. 64 – 67), Tampere, Finland.

Madden, S. R., Franklin, M. J., Hellerstein, J. M., & Hong, W. (2005). Tinydb: an acquisitional query processing system for sensor networks. *ACM Transactions on Database Systems, 30*(1), 122–173. doi:10.1145/1061318.1061322

Mahalik, N. P. (Ed.). (2007). Sensor Networks and Configuration. Berlin, Germany: Springer-Verlag

Mallat, S. G. (1989, December). Multifrequency Channel Decompositions of Images and Wavelet Models. *IEEE Transactions on Acoustics, Speech, and Signal Processing, 37*(12), 2091–2110. doi:10.1109/29.45554

Mamei, M., & Zambonelli, F. (2004). Programming pervasive and mobile computing applications with the tota middleware. In *Proceedings of the Second IEEE International Conference on Pervasive Computing and Communications (PerCom 2004)*, (pp. 263–276).

Manet Working Group. (1999). *Internet Engineering Task Force*. Retrieved from http://www.ietf.org/html.charters/manet-charter.html

Manning, F., & Thompson, R. (1995). Oil Field Processing (Vol. 2, Crude Oil). Tulsa, OK: Pennwell Books.

MARC. (n.d.). Retrieved from http://marc.med.virginia.edu/.

Marti, S., Giuli, T. J., Lai, K., & Baker, M. (2000). Mitigating routing misbehavior in mobile ad hoc networks. In the seventh annual international conference on mobile computing and networking (MobiCom) (pp. 255–265).

Matos, S., Powell, D., Davies, R., Zhang, X., & Moore, P. (2006). *A Guideline Framework for the Integrity Assessment of Offshore Pipelines*. Retrieved from http://www.mms.gov/tarprojects/565/565AA.pdf

McBride, B. (2001). Jena: implementing the rdf model and syntax specification. In *Proceedings of the Second International Workshop on the Semantic Web SemWeb*, Hong Kong.

McGarry, K., Wermter, S., & MacIntyre, J. (1999). Hybrid Neural Systems: From Simple Coupling to Fully Integrated Neural Networks. *Neural Computing Surveys, 2*, 62–94.

McGuinness, D. L., & van Harmelen, F. (2004). *Owl web ontology language overview*. Retrieved from http://www.w3.org/TR/owl-features/

Medsker, L. R., & Bailey, D. L. (1992). Models and Guidelines for Integrating Expert Systems and Neural Networks. In A. Kandel & G. Langholz (Eds.), Hybrid Architectures for Intelligent Systems (pp. 154-171). Boca Raton, FL: CRC Press.

Meneses, F., & Moreira, A. (2006). Using GSM CellID Positioning for Place Discovering. In *Pervasive Health Conference and Workshops*, (pp. 1-8), Innsbruck, Austria.

Meynard, J.-P. (2000). *Control of industrial robots through high-level task programming*. Thesis, Linkopings University, Sweden.

Mhatre, V. P., Papagiannaki, K., & Baccelli, F. (2007, May). Interference Mitigation Through Power Control in High Density 802.11 WLANs. In Infocom 2007: 26th ieee international conference on computer communications, (pp. 535-543), Anchorage, AK.

Mhatre, V., & Papagiannaki, K. (2006). Using Smart Triggers for Improved User Performance in 802.11 Wireless Networks. In *Mobisys '06: Proceedings of the 4th international conference on mobile systems, applications and services* (pp. 246-259). New York, NY, USA: ACM.

Microsoft. (2008, September). *Wmi - windows management instrumentation*. Retrieved from http://msdn.microsoft.com/en-us/library/aa394582.aspx

Mini, R. A. F., Loureiro, A. A. F., & Nath, B. (2004). A more realistic energy dissipation model for sensor nodes. In *Proceedings of the 22nd SBRC, Brazilian Symposium on Computer Networks* (pp. 365-378), Gramado, Brazil.

Minsky, M. (1981). Framework for representing knowledge. In Mind Design, (pp.95–128). Cambridge, MA: MIT Press.

Mohamed, N., & Jawhar, I. (2008). A Fault Tolerant Wired/Wireless Sensor Network Architecture for Monitoring Pipeline Infrastructures. In *Second International Conference on Sensor Technologies and Applications*, SENSORCOMM '08, (pp. 179 – 184).

Mokhtari, M. & Feki, M.A. (2007). User needs and usage analysis in a smart environment for people requiring assistance. *Topics in Geriatric Rehabilitation, 23*(1).

Mokhtari, M., Ghorbel, M., Kadouche, R., & Feki, M. A. (2007). From smart home to smart spacein independent living: a framework for multiple contexts management. In Wireless and Mobile Computing, Networking and Communications, 2007, WiMOB.

Möller, S. (2005). Quality of Telephone-based Spoken Dialogue Systems. New York: Springer.

Montgomery, D. (1996). Introduction to Statistical Quality Control. Chichester, UK: John Wiley and Sons.

Moraes, D. H., Coelho, P. R. S. L., Cardozo, E., Guimarães, E., Johnson, T., & Atizani, F. (2009). A Network Architecture for Large Mobile Robotics Environments. In *IEEE International Conference on Robot Communication and Coordination,* (pp. 1-6), Odense, Denmark.

Morón, J., et al. (2007). J2ME and smart phones as platform for a Bluetooth Body Area Network for Patient-telemonitoring. In *International Conference of the IEEE Engineering in Medicine and Biology Society* (pp. 2791-2794), Lyon, France.

Morris, B., Davies, C., Day, W., De Jode, M., & McNabb, S. (2007). The Symbian OS Architecture Sourcebook: Design and Evolution of a Mobile Phone OS. Chichester, UK: John Wiley & Sons, Inc.

Mosmondor, M., Skorin-Kapov, L., & Kovacic, M. (2006). Bringing location based services to IP multimedia subsystem. In *IEEE Mediterranean Electrotechnical Conference,* (pp. 746-749), Malaga, Spain.

Mozer, M. C. (1998). The Neural Network House: An Environment that Adapts to its Inhabitants. In *Proc. of the American Association for Artificial Intelligence Spring Symposium on Intelligent Environments,* (pp. 110-114).

Munir, S. A., Ren, B., Jiao, W., Wang, B., Xie, D., & Ma, J. (2007). Mobile Wireless Sensor Network: Architecture and Enabling Technologies for Ubiquitous Computing. In *International Conference on Advanced Information Networking and Applications Workshops,* (pp. 113-120), Niagara Falls, Canada.

Murphy, R. (2000). Introduction to AI Robotics. Cambridge, MAL: MIT Press.

Naik, P., & Sivalingam, K. M. (2004). A survey of MAC protocols for sensor networks. In Wireless sensor networks, (pp. 93–107). Norwell, MA: Kluwer Academic Publishers.

Nakamura, E. F., Figueiredo, C. M. S., & Loureiro, A. A. F. (2006). Information fusion algorithms for wireless sensor networks. In A. Boukerche, (Ed.), Handbook of Algorithms for Wireless Networking and Mobile Computing. Boca Raton, FL: Chapman & Hall/CRC.

Nakamura, E. F., Nakamura, F. G., Figueiredo, C. M., & Loureiro, A. A. (2005). Using information fusion to assist data dissemination in wireless sensor networks. *Telecommunication Systems, 30*(1-3), 237–254. doi:10.1007/s11235-005-4327-y

Nakamura, Y., Tei, K., Fukazawa, Y., & Honiden, S. (2008). Region-based sensor selection for wireless sensor networks. In the 2008 IEEE international conference on sensor networks, ubiquitous, and trustworthy computing (SUTC) (pp. 326–331). Washington, DC: IEEE Computer Society.

Narasimhan, R., & Cox, D. C. (1999, September). Speed Estimation in Wireless Systems Using Wavelets. *IEEE Transactions on Communications, 47,* 1357–1364. doi:10.1109/26.789671

Narasimhan, R., & Cox, D. C. (2000, November). Speed Estimation in Wireless Systems Using Wavelets. *IEEE Journal on Selected Areas in Communications, 18,* 2220–2227. doi:10.1109/49.895027

Nash, J. F. (1951). Non-cooperative games. *The Annals of Mathematics, 54,* 286–295. doi:10.2307/1969529

Nellis, S. (2009). Long-distance medicine - InTouch robots can help rural patients get treatment. *Pacific Coast Business Times.* Retrieved May, 01, 2009, from http://pacbiztimes.com/index.php?option=com_ content&task=view& id=756& Itemid=29

Ni, S.-Y., Tseng, Y.-C., Chen, Y.-S., & Sheu, J.-P. (1999). The broadcast storm problem in a mobile ad hoc network. In *MobiCom: Proceedings of the 5th annual ACM/IEEE international conference on Mobile computing and networking,* (pp. 151–162). New York: ACM Press.

Niazi, M., & Hussain, A. (2009). Agent-based tools for modeling and simulation of self-organization in peer-to-peer, ad hoc, and other complex networks. *IEEE*

Communications Magazine, 47(3), 166–173. doi:10.1109/MCOM.2009.4804403

Nielsen, J. (1993). Usability Enginnering. Cambridge, MA: Academic Press.

Niemelä, E., & Latvakoski, J. (2004). Survey of requirements and solutions for ubiquitous software. In Mobile and Ubiquitous Multimedia: Vol. 83 (pp. 71-78). College Park, MD. New York: ACM. doi: 10.1145/1052380.1052391.

Nikolakopoulos, G., Panousopoulou, A., Tzes, A., & Lygeros, J. (2005). Multi-hopping Induced Gain Scheduling for Wireless Networked Controlled Systems. In *44th IEEE Conference on European Control Conference Decision and Control*, (pp. 470 – 475).

Nilsson, M., Hallberg, J., & Synnes, K. (2003). Positioning with bluetooth. In 10th international conference on telecommunications ict'2003.

Niu, R., Varshney, P. K., & Cheng, Q. (2006). Distributed detection in a large wireless sensor network. *Special Issue on the Seventh International Conference on Information Fusion-Part I, 7*(4), 380-394.

Nixon, M. Deji Chen, Blevins, T., & Mok, A.K., (2008, Aug. 23-26). Meeting control performance over a wireless mesh network. In *IEEE International Conference on Automation Science and Engineering*, CASE 2008, (pp. 540 – 547).

Nordman, M. M., & Kozlowski, W. E. (2001). Modeling data transactions with standard protocols for low power wireless sensor links. In *Proceedings of the First ISA/IEEE Conference on Sensor for Industry*, (pp. 51 – 56).

Nordstrom, E. (2002). APE: a Large Scale Ad Hoc Network Testbed for Reproducible Performance Tests. Memoire de Master non publie, Information Technology Department of Computer Systems Uppsala University, Uppsala, Sweden.

Nylander, S., Bylund, M., & Waern, A. (2005). Ubiquitous service access through adapted user interfaces on multiple devices. *Personal and Ubiquitous Computing, 9*(3), 123–133. doi:. doi:10.1007/s00779-004-0317-4

Oliver, S., Adrian, F., Nigel, D., Joe, F., Corina, S., & Jennifer, S. (2006). Public Ubiquitous Computing Systems: Lessons from the e-Campus Display Deployments. *IEEE Pervasive Computing / IEEE Computer Society [and] IEEE Communications Society, 5*(3).

Orr, R. J., & Abowd, G. D. (2000). The Smart Floor: A Mechanism for Natural User Identification and Tracking. In *Proceedings of Conference on Human Factors in Computing Systems (CHI 2000)*. New York: ACM Press.

Otto, C. A., Jovanov, E., & Milenkovi, A. (2006). A WBAN-based System for Health Monitoring at Home. In *International Summer School and Symposium on Medical Devices and Biosensors* (pp. 20-23), Cambridge, MA.

Pace, J. A. D., & Campo, M. R. (2001). Analyzing the role of aspects in software design. *Communications of the ACM, 44*(10), 66–73. doi:. doi:10.1145/383845.383859

Papagiannaki, K., Yarvis, M., & Conner, W. S. (2006). Experimental Characterization of Home Wireless Networks and Design Implications. In Ieee infocom 2006. 25th ieee international conference on computer communications, (pp. 1-13).

Park, K., Yoon, U. H., & Kim, S. (2009). Personalized service discovery in ubiquitous computing environments. *IEEE Pervasive Computing / IEEE Computer Society [and] IEEE Communications Society, 8*(1), 58–65. doi:10.1109/MPRV.2009.12

Parno, B., Perrig, A., & Gligor, V. (2005). Distributed detection of node replication attacks in sensor networks. In IEEE symposium on security and privacy (pp. 49–63).

Pathan, A. S. K., Lee, H. W., & Hong, C. S. (2006). Security in wireless sensor networks: issues and challenges. In *ICACT, International Conference on Advanced Communication Technology, 2,* 1043-1048.

Pembeci, I., & Hager, G. (2002). A comparative review of robot programming language. Technical report, CIRL Lab.

Perez-Romero, J., Salient, O., & Agusti, R. (2007, April). A generalized framework for multi-rat scenarios characterisation. In *IEEE 65th Vehicular Technology Conference,* VTC2007-Spring, (pp. 980-984).

Piaget, J. (1971). Biology and Knowledge: an essay on the relations between organic regulations and cognitive processes. Chicago: The University of Chicago.

Pigot, H., Lussier-Desrochers, D., Bauchet, J., Lachapelle, Y., & Giroux, S. (2007). A smart home to assist recipes completion. *Festival of International Conferences on Caregiving, Disability, Aging and Technology (FIC-CDAT), 2nd International Conference on Technology and Aging (ICTA)*, Toronto, Canada.

Platon, E., Suenaga, S., Yoshioka, N., & Honiden, S. (2008). Transparent application lifetime management in wireless sensor networks. In Demo track of the 10th international conference on ubiquitous computing (Ubicomp).

Poppen, F. (2000). Low Power Design Guide, (Version 30.06.00). Oldenburger Forschungs-Und Entwicklungsin-titut Fur Informatik-Werkzeuge Und-Systeme.

Pottie, G. J., & Kaiser, W. J. (2000). Wireless integrated network sensors. *Communications of the ACM, 43*(5), 51–58. doi:10.1145/332833.332838

Pradhan, S., Brignone, C., Cui, J., McReynolds, A., & Smith, M. (2004). Websign: hyperlinks from a physical location to the web. Technical Report HP Laboratories.

Prado, R., Zagari, E., Cardozo, E., & Johnson, T. (2008). A reference architecture for micro-mobility support in IP networks. In *The Thirteenth IEEE Symposium on Computers and Communications* (pp. 624-630). Marrakech, Morocco.

Prehofer, C., & Bettstetter, C. (2005). Self-organization in communication networks: Principles and design paradigms. *IEEE Communications Magazine, 43*(7), 78–85. doi:10.1109/MCOM.2005.1470824

Priyantha, N., Chakraborty, A., & Balakrishnan, H. (2000). The Cricket location support system. In *Proc. 6th Ann. Int'l Conference on Mobile Computing and Networking*, (pp. 32-43).

Quillian, R. (1965). Word concepts: a theory & simulation of some basic semantic capabilities. *Behavioral Science, 12*(5), 410–430. doi:10.1002/bs.3830120511

Rabunal, J. R., & Dorado, J. (2006). *Artificial Neural Networks in Real Life Applications.* Hershey, PA: IDEA Group Publishing. Kiani, S. L., Riaz, M., Zhung, Y., Lee. S & Lee, Y-K. (2005). A Distributed Middleware Solution for Context Awareness in Ubiquitous Systems. In *Proceedings of 11th IEEE International Conference on Embedded and Real-time Computing Systems and Applications* (pp. 451-454). Washington, DC: IEEE Computer Society.

Rajendran, V., Obraczka, K., & Garcia-Luna-Aceves, J. J. (2006). Energyefficient, collision-free medium access control for wireless sensor networks. *Wireless Networks, 12*(1), 63–78. doi:10.1007/s11276-006-6151-z

Ramasubramanian, V., Haas, Z. J., & Sirer, E. G. (2003). SHARP: a hybrid adaptive routing protocol for mobile ad hoc networks. In *Proceedings of the 4th ACM international symposium on Mobile ad hoc networking,* (pp. 303 - 314).

Rappaport, T. (2002). Wireless Communication Systems. Upper Saddle River, NJ: Prentice Hall PTR.

Ribeiro Neto, P. F., Perkusich, A., Perkusich, M. L. B., & Almeida, H. O. (2006). A formal verification and validation approach for real-time database. In A. Dasso & A. Funes, (Eds.), Verification, Validation and Testing in Software Engineering. Hershey, PA: IGI Publishing.

Riva, O., & Borcea, C. (2007). The urbanet revolution: Sensor power to the people! *IEEE Pervasive Computing / IEEE Computer Society [and] IEEE Communications Society, 6*(2), 41–49. doi:10.1109/MPRV.2007.46

Rogers. (2006). Moving on from Weiser's Vision of Calm Computing: Engaging UbiComp Experiences. In *UbiComp 2006: Ubiquitous Computing,* (LNCS (Vol. 4206, pp. 404-421). Berlin Heidelberg: Springer. doi: 10.1007/11853565_24

Römer, K., & Mattern, F. (2004). The design space of wireless sensor networks. *IEEE Wireless Communications, 11*(6), 54–61. doi:10.1109/MWC.2004.1368897

Ross, P., & Keyson, D. (2007). The case of sculpting atmospheres: towards design principles for expressive tangible interaction in control of ambient systems. *Per-*

sonal and Ubiquitous Computing, *11*(2), 69–79. doi:. doi:10.1007/s00779-005-0062-3

Rougier, J., & Goldstein, M. (2001). A Bayesian Analysis of Fluid Flow in Pipe-Lines. *Applied Statistics, 50*(1), 77–93. doi:10.1111/1467-9876.00221

Roussos, G., Marsh, A. J., & Maglavera, S. (2005). Enabling Pervasive Computing with Smart Phones. *Pervasive Computing, 4*(2), 20–27. doi:10.1109/MPRV.2005.30

Roy, A., Das, S. K., & Basu, K. (2007). A Predictive Framework for Location Aware Resource Management in Smart Homes. *IEEE Transactions on Mobile Computing, 6*(11), 1270–1283. doi:10.1109/TMC.2007.1058

Roy, N. (2008) *A Context-aware Learning, Prediction and Mediation Framework for Resource Management in Smart Pervasive Environments.* Ph.D Thesis, University of Texas at Arlington, TX.

Roy, N., Das, S. K., Basu, K., & Kumar, M. (2005). Enhancing Availability of Grid Computational Services to Ubiquitous Computing Application. In *IEEE International Conference on Parallel and Distributed Processing Symposium*, Denver, CO.

Roy, N., Roy, A., & Das, S. K. (2006). Context-Aware Resource Management in Multi-Inhabitant Smart Homes: A Nash H-learning based Approach. In *Proc. of IEEE Int'l Conf. on Pervasive Computing and Communications (PerCom)*, (pp. 148–158).

Roy, N., Roy, A., Basu, K., & Das, S. K. (2005). A Cooperative Learning Framework for Mobility-Aware Resource Management in Multi-Inhabitant Smart Homes. In *Proc. of IEEE International Conference on Mobile and Ubiquitous Systems: Networking and Services (MobiQuitous)*, (pp. 393–403).

Roy, N., Roy, A., Das, S. K., & Basu, K. (2005). A Reinforcement Learning Framework for Location-Aware Resource Management in Multi-Inhabitant Smart Homes. In *Proc. of 3rd International Conference on Smart Homes and Health Telematic(ICOST)*, (pp. 180–187).

Rubine, D. (1991) Specifying Gestures by Example. In *Proc. SIGGRAPH 1991 – 18th Annual ACM Conference on Computer Graphics and Interactive Techniques,* (pp. 329–337).

Rudolph, L. (2001). Project Oxygen: pervasive, human-centric computing-an initial experience. In *13th International Conference on Advanced Information Systems Engineering, CAiSE.*

Ruiz, L. B., Nogueira, J. M. S., & Loureiro, A. A. F. (2004). Sensor Network Management. In M. Ilyas & I. Mahgoub. (Eds.). Handbook of Sensor Networks: Compact Wireless and Wired Sensing Systems. Boca Raton, FL: CRC Press.

Sadeh, N. M., Chan, E., & Van, L. (2002). Mycampus: an agent-based environment for context-aware mobile services. In *Proceedings of Workshop on Ubiquitous Agents on Embedded, Wearable and Mobile Devices. (ubiagents 2002)*, Bologna.

Saha, D., & Mukherjee, A. (2003). Pervasive computing: a paradigm for the 21st century. *Computer, 36*(3), 25–31. doi:. doi:10.1109/MC.2003.1185214

Saito, Y., & Shapiro, M. (2005). Optimistic replication. *ACM Computing Surveys, 37*(1), 42–81. doi:. doi:10.1145/1057977.1057980

Sakamura, K. (1998). Digital museum. *Journal of Information Processing Society of Japan, 39*(5).

Salvador, V. F. M., Oliveira Neto, J. S., & Kawamoto, A. L. S. (2008). Requirement Engineering Contributions to Voice User Interface. In *Proceedings of First International Conference on Advances in Computer-Human Interaction, ACHI 2008*, (pp. 309-314).

Samaka, M. (2005). Robot Task-Level Programming Language and Simulation. In Proc. of World Academy of Science, Engineering and Technology, (Vol. 9).

Satyanarayanan, M. (1996). Fundamental challenges in mobile computing. In *ACM Symposium on Principles of Distributed Computing* (pp. 1-7), Philadelphia. New York: ACM. doi: 10.1145/248052.248053

Satyanarayanan, M. (2001). Pervasive computing: vision and challenges. *IEEE Personal Communications, 8*(4), 10–17. doi:. doi:10.1109/98.943998

Scheermesser, M., Kosow, H., Rashid, A., & Holtmann, C. (2008). User acceptance of pervasive computing in healthcare: Main findings of two case studies. In *International Conference on Pervasive Computing Technologies for Healthcare,* (pp. 205-213), Tampere, Finland.

Schilit, B., Adams, N., & Want, R. (1994). Context-aware computing applications. In *IEEE Workshop on Mobile Computing Systems and Applications.* Santa Cruz, CA: IEEE Computer Society.

Schltz, J., & Consolvo, S. (2004). *Towards a Discipline for Evaluating Ubiquitous Computing Applications.* Retrieved from http://www.seattle.intel-research.net/pubs/022520041200_232.pdf

Schneps-Schneppe, M., & Iverson, V. B. (2003). Service Level Agreement as an issue of Teletraffic. In *Proceedings of the ITC,* Berlin.

Schreiner, K. (2008). Uniting the Paper and Digital Worlds. *IEEE Computer Graphics and Applications. 28*(6 November/December), 6-10.

Seabra Lopes, L., Teixeira, A., Rodrigues, M., Gomes, D., Teixeira, C., Ferreira, L., et al. (2003). Towards a Personal Robot with Language Interface. In *Proceedings of 8th European Conference on Speech Communication and Technology EUROSPEECH'2003* (pp. 2205—2208), Geneva.

Sei, Y., & Honiden, S. (2007). Resilient security for false event detection without loss of legitimate events in wireless sensor networks. In the 9th international symposium on distributed objects, middleware, and applications (DOA) (pp. 454–470). Berlin: Springer.

Sei, Y., & Honiden, S. (2008). Distributed detection of node replication attacks resilient to many compromised nodes in wireless sensor networks. In the 4th international wireless internet conference (WICON).

Sei, Y., & Honiden, S. (2009). Reporter node determination of replicated node detection in wireless sensor networks. In the 3rd international conference on ubiquitous information management and communication (ICUIMC) (pp. 566–573). New York: ACM.

Sellen, A. J., & Harper, R. H. R. (2001). The Myth of the Paperless Office. Cambridge (MA): MIT Press.

Sellen, A., & Harper, R. (1997). Paper as an analytic resource for the design of new technologies. In *Proceedings of the SIGCHI conference on Human factors in computing systems,* (pp. 319–326). Atlanta, GA. New York: ACM Press.

Semper, R., & Spasojevic, M. (2002). The electronic guidebook: using portable devices and a wireless web-based network to extend the museum experience. In *Proceedings of the museums and the Web.*

Severin, J. (2005). *Speech Interface for a Mobile Audio Application.* Master of Science Thesis, KTH Information and Communication TechnologyIMIT/LCN 2005-17, Stockholm, Sweden.

Shafer, S., Krumm, J., Brumitt, B., Meyers, B., Czerwinski, M., & Robbins, D. (1998). The New EasyLiving Project at Microsoft Research. In *Proceedings of the 1998 DARPA / NIST Smart Spaces Workshop,* (pp.127-130).

Shearer, F. (2008). Low Power Design Techniques. In Power management in mobile devices, (pp. 77-78). New York: Elsevier Inc.

Shelton, C. R. (2000). Balancing Multiple Sources of Reward in Reinforcement Learning. *Advances in Neural Information Processing Systems,* 1082–1088.

Sheth, A., & Han, R. (2003). Adaptive power control and selective radio activation for low-power infrastructure-mode 802.11 lans. In *Icdcsw '03: Proceedings of the 23rd international conference on distributed computing systems* (pp. 812). Washington, DC: IEEE Computer Society.

Shnayder, V., Hempstead, M., Chen, B.-r., Allen, G. W., & Welsh, M. (2004). Simulating the power consumption of large-scale sensor network applications. In the 2nd international conference on embedded networked sensor systems (pp. 188–200). New York: ACM Press.

Shneiderman, B. (2000). Universal usability. *Commun. ACM 43*(5, May), 84-91.

Shorey, R., Ananda, A. L., Chan, M. C., & Ooi, W. T. (2006). Mobile, Wireless and Sensor Networks: Technology, Applications and Future Directions. New York: John Wiley & Sons.

Sichitiu, M. L. (2004). Cross-layer scheduling for power efficiency in wireless sensor networks. In *Proceedings of the 23rd Annual Joint Conference of the IEEE Computer and Communications Societies (INFOCOM'04)*.

Siewiorek, D. P. (2002). New frontiers of application design. *Communications of the ACM, 45*(12), 79–82. doi:. doi:10.1145/585597.585619

SIG. (2003). *Bluetooth specifcation version 1.2.*

Signer, B. (2008). *Fundamental Concepts for Interactive Paper and Cross-Media Information Spaces.*

Simon, D., & Cifuentes, C. (2005). The squawk virtual machine: Java on the bare metal. In Companion to the 20th annual ACM sigplan conference on object-oriented programming, systems, languages, and applications (OOPSLA) (pp. 150–151). New York: ACM Press.

Singh, S., Jaakkola, T., Littman, M. L., & Szepesvari, C. (2000). Convergence Results for Single-Step On-Policy Reinforcement-Learning Algorithms. *Machine Learning, 38*(3), 287–290. doi:10.1023/A:1007678930559

Sinopoli, B., Schenato, L., Franceschetti, M., Poolla, K., & Sastry, S. (2005). An LQG Optimal Linear Controller for Control Systems with Packet Losses. In *44th IEEE Conference on Decision and Control & 2005 European Control Conference,* (pp. 458 - 463).

Siqueira, I., Figueiredo, C. M., Loureiro, A., Nogueira, J., & Ruiz, L. (2006). An integrated approach for density control and routing in wireless sensor networks. In *Proceedings of the 20th IEEE International Parallel and Distributed Processing Symposium (IPDPS 2006)*.

Slamanig, D., & Stingl, C. (2008). Privacy Aspects of eHealth. In *International Conference on Availability, Reliability and Security* (pp.1226-1233), Barcelona, Spain.

Smart-its. (2007). Interconnected embedded technology for smart artifacts with collective awareness. Lancaster University, ETH Zurich.

Sohrabi, K., Gao, J., Ailawadhi, V., & Pottie, G. J. (2000). Protocols for self-organization of a wireless sensor network. [see also IEEE Wireless Communications]. *Personal Communications, IEEE, 7*(5), 16–27. doi:10.1109/98.878532

Sohraby, K. Minoli, and D., Znati, T. (2007). Wireless Sensor Networks: Technology, Protocols, and Applications. New York: John Wiley & Sons, Inc.

Sousa, J., Poladian, V., Garlan, D., Schmerl, B., & Shaw, M. (2006). Task-based adaptation for ubiquitous computing. *IEEE Transactions on Systems, Man and Cybernetics. Part C, Applications and Reviews, 36*(3), 328–340. doi:. doi:10.1109/TSMCC.2006.871588

Spasojevic, M., Mirjana, A., & Kindberg, T. (2001). A study of an augmented museum experience. Technical Report HP Laboratories.

Sphinx4. (2008). *Sphinx-4 A speech recognizer written entirely in the JavaTM programming language.* Retrieved July 2009, from http://cmusphinx.sourceforge. net/sphinx4/#what_is_sphinx4

Spiliotopoulos, D., Androutsopoulos, I., & Spyropoulos, C. D. (2001). Human-Robot Interaction based on Spoken Natural Language Dialogue. In *Proceedings of the European Workshop on Service and Humanoid Robots (ServiceRob '2001)* (pp. 123-128), Santorini, Greece.

Stanford, V. (2002). Pervasive health care applications face tough security challenges. *Pervasive Computing, 1*(2), 8–12. doi:10.1109/MPRV.2002.1012332

Stanford, V. (2002). Using pervasive computing to deliver elder care. *Pervasive Computing, 1*(1), 10–13. doi:10.1109/ MPRV.2002.993139

Steele, R., Secombe, C., & Brookes, W. (2006). Using Wireless Sensor Networks for Aged Care: The Patient's Perspective. In *Pervasive Health Conference and Workshops* (pp. 1-10), Innsbruck, Austria.

Steinberg, A. N. (2005). An approach to threat assessment. In *8th, International Conference on Information Fusion* (Vol. 2, pp. 8).

Steinberg, A., & White, F. (1998). *Community Status Report and Proposed Revisions to the JDL Data Fusion Model.* Retrieved from http://stinet.dtic.mil/cgi-bin/GetTRDoc?AD=ADA399488 & Location=U2& doc=GetTRDoc.pdf

Stone, A. A., Shiffman, S., Schwartz, J. E., Broderick, J. E., & Hufford, M. R. (2003, April). Patient compliance with paper and electronic diaries. *Controlled Clinical Trials, 24*(2), 182–199. doi:10.1016/S0197-2456(02)00320-3

Suenaga, S., Yoshioka, N., & Honiden, S. (2009). Generative dynamic deployment of multiple components in wireless sensor networks. In the sixth international conference on wireless on-demand network systems and services (WONS) (p. 197-204).

Suzuki, H. (1997, July). A Statistical Model for Urban Radio Propagation. *IEEE Transactions on Communications, 7,* 673–680.

Sylverberg, T., Kristensson, P. O., Leifler, O., & Berglund, E. (2007) Drawing on paper maps: reliable on-line symbol recognition of handwritten symbols using a digital pen and a mobile phone. In *Proceedings of the 2nd IEEE International Conference on Pervasive Computing and Applications (ICPCA '07).*

Takami, K., Yamaguchi, T., & Unno, K. (2006). A study on the architecture and voice dialog scheme for a personal Web service in a ubiquitous communication environment. In *First International Conference on Communications and Electronics, ICCE '06.*

Tarik-Ul Islam, K., Jehad, S., Kamrul, H., Rezwanul, H. M., Gavrilov, A. V., Lee, Y.-K., & Lee, S.-Y. (2008). A Framework of Smart Objects and their Collaboration in Smart Environment. In H. H. Lee (Ed.), *The 10th International Conference on Advanced Communication Technology,* (Vol. 1, pp. 852-855). Washington, DC: IEEE Computer Society.

Taylor, A., & Harper, R. (2003). Switching on to switch off. In (H. R., ed.), Inside the smart home, (pp 115 – 126). London: Springer-Verlag Limited.

Tecnológica. (2009). Retrieved May 2009 from http://www.technologica.inf.br/glossario/exibe.asp

Tei, K., Fukazawa, Y., & Honiden, S. (2007). Applying design patterns to wireless sensor network programming. In the first international workshop on wireless mesh and ad hoc networks (WiMAN) in conjunction with ICCCN (pp. 1099–1104). Washington, DC: IEEE.

Tentori, M., & Favela, J. (2008). Activity-Aware Computing for Healthcare. *Pervasive Computing, 7*(2), 51–57. doi:10.1109/MPRV.2008.24

Thomas, H., Jakob, B., & Mads, S. (2006). Moving Out of the Lab: Deploying Pervasive Technologies in a Hospital. *IEEE Pervasive Computing / IEEE Computer Society [and] IEEE Communications Society, 5*(3).

Thomopoulos, S. C. A., Viswanathan, R., & Bougoulias, D. K. (1989). Optimal distributed decision fusion. *IEEE Transactions on Aerospace and Electronic Systems, 25*(5), 761–765. doi:10.1109/7.42092

Tilak, S., Abu-Ghazaleh, N. B., & Heinzelman, W. (2002). A taxonomy of wireless micro-sensor network models. *SIGMOBILE Mobile Computing and Communications, 6*(2), 28–36. doi:10.1145/565702.565708

Tzagkarakis, G., Papadopouli, M., & Tsakalides, P. (2007). Singular Spectrum Analysis of Traffic Workload in a Large-scale Wireless Lan. In *Mswim '07: Proceedings of the 10th acm symposium on modeling, analysis, and simulation of wireless and mobile systems,* (pp. 99-108). New York: ACM.

Vajda, F., & Urbancsek, T. (2003). High-Level Object-Oriented Program Language for Mobile Microrobot Control. In *IEEE Proceedings of the conference INES 2003,* Assiut - Luxor, Egypt. Washington, DC: IEEE Computer Society.

Vanthournout, K., Deconinck, G., & Belmans, R. (2005). A taxonomy for resource discovery. *Personal and Ubiquitous Computing, 9*(2), 81–89. doi:. doi:10.1007/s00779-004-0312-9

Venkatesh, A. (1996). Computers and other interactive technologies for the home. *Communications of the ACM, 39*(12), 47–54. doi:10.1145/240483.240491

Venkatesh, V., & Brown, S. A. (2001). Longitudinal investigation of personal computers in homes: Adoption determinants and emerging challenges. *MIS Quarterly, 25*(1), 71–102. doi:10.2307/3250959

Wahl, F. M., & Thomas, U. (2002). Robot Programming - From Simple Moves to Complex Robot Tasks. In *Proceedings of First Interntional Colloquium "Collaborative Research Center 562 – Robotic Systems for Modelling and Assembly"* (pp. 249-259), Braunschweig, Germany.

Walker, M. A., & Passnneau, R. (2001). Boland J.E. Quantitative and Qualitative Evaluation of Darpa Communicator Spoken Dialogue Systems. In *Proceedings of the 39rd Annual Meeting on Association for Computational Linguistics*, Toulouse, France.

Walters, J. P., Liang, Z., Shi, W., & Chaudhary, V. (2005). Wireless sensor networks security: A survey. Technical report, Wayne State University, USA.

Wan, J. (Ed.). (2001). Computational Intelligence in Manufacturing Handbook. Boca Raton, FL: CRC Press LLC.

Wang, X., Xing, G., Zhang, Y., Lu, C., Pless, R., & Gill, C. (2003). Integrated coverage and connectivity configuration in wireless sensor networks. In *Proceedings of the 1st ACM Internation Conference on Embedded Networked Sensor Systems (SenSys'03)*, (pp. 28–39).

Want, R., Hopper, A., Falcao, V., & Gibbons, J. (1992). The active badge location system. *ACM Transactions on Information Systems, 10*(1). doi:10.1145/128756.128759

Want, R., Pering, T., Borriello, G. & Farkas, K. I. (2002). Disappearing Hardware. *IEEE Pervasive Computing, 1* (1, January-March), 36 – 47.

Want, R., Schilit, B., Adams, N., Gold, R., Petersen, K., Ellis, J., et al. (1995). The PARCTAB Ubiquitous Computing Experiment. Palo Alto, CA: Xerox Palo Alto Research Center, CSL-95-1.

Warren, S., Lebak, J., Yao, J., Creekmore, J., Milenkovic, A., & Jovanov, E. (2005). Interoperability and Security in Wireless Body Area Network Infrastructures. In *International Conference on the Engineering in Medicine and Biology* (pp. 3837-3840), Shanghai, China.

Watkins, C. J. C. H. (1989). *Learning from delayed rewards.* PhD thesis, King's College, Cambridge, UK.

Weikum, G. (2008). *Context and social network speci_cation (deliverable d7.1).* Technical report.

Weiser, M. (1991). The computer for the 21st century. *Scientific American, 265*(3), 94–104. doi:10.1038/scientificamerican0991-94

Weiser, M. (1993). Some computer science issues in ubiquitous computing. *Communications of the ACM, 36*(7), 75–84. doi:10.1145/159544.159617

Weiser, M. (1994). The world is not a desktop. *Interactions (New York, N.Y.), 1*(1), 7–8. doi:. doi:10.1145/174800.174801

Welsh, M., & Mainland, G. (2004). Programming sensor networks using abstract regions. In *Proceedings of the First USENIX/ACM Symposium on Networked Systems Design and Implementation (NSDI 2004)*.

Wermter, S., & Sun, R. (2000). Hybrid Neural Systems. Heidelberg, Germany: Springer.

Whitehouse, K., Sharp, C., Brewer, E., & Culler, D. (2004). Hood: A neighborhood abstraction for sensor networks. In *Proceedings of the International Conference on Mobile Systems, Applications, and Services (MOBYSYS 2004)*.

Williams, B. C., Ingham, M. D., Chung, S. H., & Elliott, P. H. (2003). Model-based programming of intelligent embedded systems and robotic space explorers. In. *Proceedings of IEEE: Special Issue on Modeling and Design of Embedded Software, 91*(1), 212–237.

WirelessHART. (2007). Retrieved from http://www.hartcomm2.org/hart_protocol/wireless_hart/wireless_hart_main.html

Wu, H., Tan, K., Zhang, Y., & Zhang, Q. (2007, May). Proactive Scan: Fast Handoff with Smart Triggers for 802.11 Wireless LAN. In Ieee infocom 2007. 26th ieee international conference on computer communications, (pp. 749-757).

Wu, T., Yu, F., & Biswas, S. (2007). Scalable Hybrid Routing in Very Large Sensor Networks. In *International Conference on Mobile Data Management,* (pp. 366 – 370).

Wuyan, L. & Yangwanhai. (2001). Optimal distributed decision fusion in the sense of the Neyman-Pearson test. In *Proceedings CIE International Conference on Radar,* (pp. 708 - 712).

X10 web resources. (n.d.). Retrieved from http://www.x10.com

Xac project. (2009). Retrieved from http://xac-project.jp/index_e.html

Xiao, L., Boyd, S., & Lall, S. (2005). A scheme for robust distributed sensor fusion based on average consensus. In *Fourth International Symposium on Information Processing in Sensor Networks*, IPSN 2005, (pp. 63 – 70).

Xie, J., Quesada, L. G., & Jiang, Y. (2007). A Threshold-based Hybrid Routing Protocol for MANET. In *4th International Symposium on Wireless Communication Systems, ISWCS 2007,* (pp. 622 – 626).

Yang, H., Ye, F., Yuan, Y., Lu, S., & Arbaugh, W. (2005). Toward resilient security in wireless sensor networks. In the 6th acm international symposium on mobile ad hoc networking and computing (MobiHoc) (pp. 34–45).

Yao, Y., & Gehrke, J. (2002). The cougar approach to in-network query processing in sensor networks. *SIGMOD Record, 31*(3), 9–18. doi:10.1145/601858.601861

Ye, F., Luo, H., Lu, S., & Zhang, L. (2005, April). Statistical en-route filtering of injected false data in sensor networks. *IEEE Journal on Selected Areas in Communications, 23*(4), 839–850. doi:10.1109/JSAC.2005.843561

Ye, W., Heidemann, J., & Estrin, D. (2002). An energy-efficient mac protocol for wireless sensor networks. In the 21st conference on computer communications (INFOCOM), (pp. 1567–1576). Washington, DC: IEEE.

Yick, J., Mukherjee, B., & Ghosal, D. (2008). Wireless sensor network survey. *Computer Networks, 52*(12), 2292–2330. doi:10.1016/j.comnet.2008.04.002

Youngblood, M. (2005). *MavPad Inhabitant 2 Trial 2 Data Set, The MavHome Project.* Computer Science and Engineering Department, The University of Texas at Arlington, http://mavhome.uta.edu

Youngblood, M., Cook, D. J., & Holder, L. B. (2005). Managing Adaptive Versatile Environments. In *Proc. of IEEE Int'l Conf. on Pervasive Computing and Communications (PerCom),* (pp. 351-360).

Younis, S., & Knight, T. (1994). *Asymptotically zero energy computing using split-level charge recovery logic.* Technical Report AITR-1500, MIT AI Laboratory.

Yu, X. (2004). Improving TCP Performance over Mobile Ad Hoc Networks by Exploiting Crosslayer Information Awareness. In Proceedings of mobicom, (pp. 231-244).

Yu, Z., & Guan, Y. (2006). A dynamic en-route scheme for filtering false data injection in wireless sensor networks. In the 25th conference on computer communications (INFOCOM), (pp. 1–12).

Yuan, W., Krishnamurthy, S. V., & Tripathi, S. K. (2003). Synchronization of Multiple Levels of Data Fusion in Wireless Sensor Networks. In *Proceedings of GLOBECOM.*

Zadeh, L. A. (1975). The concept of a linguistic variable and its application to approximate reasoning. *Inform. Sci., 9,* 43–80. doi:10.1016/0020-0255(75)90017-1

Zahariadis, T., & Doshi, B. (2004). Applications and services for the B3G/4G era. *Wireless Communications, 11*(5), 3–5. doi:10.1109/MWC.2004.1351675

Zambonelli, F., Gleizes, M., Mamei, M., & Tolksdorf, R. (2005). Spray computers: Explorations in self-organization. *Journal of Pervasive and Mobile Computing, 1*(1), 1–20. doi:10.1016/j.pmcj.2005.01.001

Zand, P. & Shiva, M. (2008). *Defining a New Frame Based on IEEE 802.15.4 for having the Synchronized Mesh Networks with Channel Hopping Capability.*

Zhai, S., & Kristensson, P. O. (2003). Shorthand Writing on Stylus Keyboard. In *Proceedings of the ACM Conference on Human Factors in Computing Systems (CHI '03),* (pp. 97-104). New York: ACM Press.

Zhai, S., Smith, B. A., & Hunter, M. (2002). Performance Optimization of Virtual Keyboards. *Human-Computer Interaction, 17*(2&3), 89–129.

Zhang, H., & Hou, J. C. (2005). Maintaining sensing coverage and connectivity in large sensor networks. *International Journal of Wireless Ad Hoc and Sensor Networks, 1*(1–2), 89–124.

Zhen, B., Li, H., & Kohno, R. (2007). IEEE Body Area Networks for Medical Applications. In *International Symposium on Wireless Communication Systems* (pp. 327-331), Trondheim, Norway.

Zheng, L. (2006). ZigBee Wireless Sensor Network in Industrial Applications. In *SICE-ICASE, International Joint Conference,* (pp. 1067 – 1070).

Zhou, C., & Krishnamachari, B. (2003). Localized topology generation mechanisms for self-configuring sensor networks. In *Proceedings of the IEEE Wireless Communication Symposium (Globecom 2003).*

Zhou, H.-Y., Hou, K.-M., Chanet, J. P., de Vaulx, C., & de Sousa, G. (2006, Sept. 22-24). LIMOS: a Tiny Real-Time Micro-Kernel for Wireless Objects. *International Conference on Wireless Communications, Networking and Mobile Computing,* (pp. 1 – 4)

Zhu, F., Mutka, M., & Ni, L. (2005). Service discovery in pervasive computing environments. *IEEE Pervasive Computing / IEEE Computer Society [and] IEEE Communications Society, 4*(4), 81–90. doi:. doi:10.1109/MPRV.2005.87

About the Contributors

Francisco Milton Mendes Neto received a Ph.D. in Electrical Engineering from Federal University of Campina Grande. He received the MSc degree in Informatics from Federal University of Campina Grande and received the Bachelor's degree in Computer Science from State University of Ceará. He was Software Development Project Manager for Federal Service of Data Processing for several years. In 2006, after an incursion in industry, he joined the Rural Federal University of the Semi-Arid, Brazil, where he is currently an adjunct professor of the Graduate Program in Computer Science and of the Postgraduate Program in Computer Science and coordinator of the Research Group in Software Engineering. His main research areas are in Knowledge Engineering, Software Engineering and Computer-Supported Collaborative Learning. Dr. Mendes Neto is a member of the Brazilian Computing Society, the ACM, and the IEEE Computer Society.

Pedro Fernandes Ribeiro Neto graduated at Computer Science from State University of Ceará (1997), He received his master degree in Electric Engineering from Federal University of Paraíba (2001) and Ph.D. degree in Electric Engineering from Federal University of Campina Grande (2006). He is currently head of Postgraduate Department and Adjunt Professor at State University of Rio Grande do Norte. He is also a permanent member of Mastering in Computer Science MCC/UERN/UFERSA, and contributing member of the Postgraduate Department in Teleinformatics Engineering at UFC. He has experience in Computer Science, focusing on Software Engeneering, acting on the following subjects: Real-Time Databases, Mobile Computing, Ubiquitous and Pervasive Computing, Wireless Sensor Networks, Petri Networks and Software Processes.

* * *

Bessam Abdulrazak is an Assistant Professor of Computer and Science and Engineering at the University of Sherbrooke, Canada. Previously, he was a Post-Doc at the university of Florida (US), and before that at Telecom-SudParis (France). He received his Ph.D. in computer science from Telecom-SudParis and university of Evry, M.S. of Robotics from Paris VI university (France), and B.Sc. Ing, from USTHB (Algeria). His research interests include ubiquitous and pervasive computing, ambient Intelligence, smart spaces, assistive technologies, rehabilitation robotics and health telematics.

Dania Alvarez is currently pursuing BS degree in Computer Science at the University of Louisiana at Lafayette. Her areas of interest for research are software engineering, computer graphics, database design, and web and Internet systems. She plans to continue with a MS degree in Computer Science at the same university.

Rossana Andrade has Ph.D. in Computer Science in the University of Ottawa (2001), Masters in Computer Science from Universidade Federal da Paraíba (1992), and graduate in Computer Science from State University of Ceará (1989). She teaches at the Federal University of Ceará, Department of Computer Science, since 1994. She has experience in computer science, with emphasis on Teleinformática, acting on the following topics: software engineering (software patterns, frameworks and middleware) and computer networks (mobile computing, grid computing and security).

Magnus Bång received a Ph.D. in Informatics in 2004 from Linkoping University, Sweden. He was research leader at the Interactive Institute in Sweden between 2005-2008. Since 2009 he is a lecturer and researcher at the Department of Computer and Information Science at Linkoping University. His main research areas are ubiquitous computing and interaction design for healthcare applications such as the electronic medical record.

Jorge Luis Victoria Barbosa is a full professor at the University of Vale do Rio dos Sinos. His research interests include ubiquitous computing, context awareness, ubiquitous learning, pervasive games, and program languages. He received his PhD in computer science from the Federal University of Rio Grande do Sul. He's a member of the Brazilian Computer Society. Contact him at Programa de Pós-Graduação em Computação Aplicada, Universidade do Vale do Rio dos Sinos (UNISINOS), Av. Unisinos 950, 93022-000, São Leopoldo, RS, Brazil; jbarbosa@unisinos.br.

Magdy Bayoumi is the Director of the Center for Advanced Computer Studies (CACS) and Department Head of Computer Science Department, University of Louisiana at Lafayette. He is also the Edmiston Professor of Computer Engineering and Lamson Professor of Computer Science at the Center for Advanced Computer Studies, University of Louisiana at Lafayette, where he has been a faculty member since 1985. Dr. Bayoumi received the B.Sc. and M.Sc. degrees in Electrical Engineering from Cairo University, Egypt; M.Sc. degree in Computer Engineering from Washington University, St. Louis; and the Ph.D. degree in Electrical Engineering from the University of Windsor, Canada. Dr. Bayoumi's research interests include VLSI Design Methods and Architectures, Low Power Circuits and Systems, Digital Signal Processing Architectures, Parallel Algorithm Design, Computer Arithmetic, Image and Video Signal Processing, Neural Networks and Wideband Network Architectures.

Aseel Berglund received a Ph.D. in Computer Science from Linköping University, Sweden 2004. She received the MSc degree in Computer Technology from Linköping University, Sweden. She works at SAAB Aerosystems Linköping, Sweden, as Project Manager for a European project.

Erik Berglund received a Ph.D. in Computer Science from Linköping University, Sweden. He received the MSc degree in Mechanical Engineering from Linköping University Sweden. Since 2002 he spends his time working as a researcher and teacher at Linköping University in the areas of web technology, software engineering and ubiquitous computing. Also, he runs a spin-off called Omnitus AB, together with colleagues from Linköping University, focused on web-based one-to-one communication. His main research areas are in the applied ubiquitous computing and applied web/mobile computing.

Mitun Bhattacharyya is an Assistant Professor in the department of computer science at the Bangalore University, India. She currently guides a project in the area of applying Wireless Sensor Networks to Oil Production Platforms. Dr. Bhattacharyya obtained her PhD in 2008 from the Center for Advanced Computer Studies, University of Louisiana at Lafayette, LA.

João B. Borges Neto graduated at Computer Science from State University of Rio Grande do Norte (2006) and received his master degree in Teleinformatic Engineering from Federal University of Ceará (2009). He is currently researcher at Federal University of Ceará. He has experience in Computer Science, acting on the following subjects: Wireless Sensor Networks, Mobile Computing, Ubiquitous and Real-Time Systems.

Carlos T. Calafate graduated with honors in Electrical and Computer Engineering at the University of Oporto (Portugal) in 2001. He received his Ph.D. in Computer Engineering from the Technical University of Valencia in 2006, where he has worked as an assistant professor since 2005. He is a member of the Computer Networks research group (GRC). His research interests include mobile and pervasive computing, security and QoS on wireless networks, as well as video coding and streaming.

José Cano received the MSc degree in computer science from the Technical University of Valencia (UPV), Spain, in 2004. He is a member of the Computer Networks Research Group (GRC) at UPV since 2005 and is currently working on his PhD thesis, entitled "Integrated architecture configuration and service management on mobile ad hoc networks". His research efforts focus mainly on ubiquitous applications, wireless technologies and mobile ad hoc networks. You can contact him at jocare@doctor.upv.es.

Juan-Carlos Cano is an assistant professor in the Department of Computer Engineering at the Polytechnic University of Valencia (UPV) in Spain. He earned an MSc and a Ph.D.in computer science from the UPV in 1994 and 2002 respectively. Between 1995-97 he worked as a programming analyst at IBM's manufacturing division in Valencia. His current research interests include power aware routing protocols for mobile ad hoc networks and pervasive computing. You can contact him at jucano@disca.upv.es.

Eleri Cardozo is a professor of Electrical and Computer Engineering at the School of Electrical and Computer Engineering, University of Campinas, Brazil. He holds a B.S. in Electrical Engineering from the University of São Paulo, Brazil (1978), a M.S. in Electronic Engineering from the Technological Institute of Aeronautics, Brazil (1981), and a Ph.D. in Electrical Engineering from Carnegie Mellon University, USA (1987). His research interests include distributed systems, computer networks, and software engineering.

Cristiano André da Costa is an associate professor at the University of Vale do Rio dos Sinos. His research interests include software infrastructure for ubiquitous computing, context awareness, distributed systems, and operating systems. He received his PhD in computer science from the Federal University of Rio Grande do Sul. He's a member of the IEEE, the ACM, and the Brazilian Computer Society. Contact him at Programa de Pós-Graduação em Computação Aplicada, Universidade do Vale do Rio dos Sinos (UNISINOS), Av. Unisinos 950, 93022-000, São Leopoldo, RS, Brazil; cac@unisinos.br.

Sajal K. Das is a University Distinguished Scholar Professor of Computer Science and Engineering and the Founding Director of the Center for Research in Wireless Mobility and Networking (CReW-MaN) at the University of Texas at Arlington (UTA). He is also an E.T.S. Walton Professor of Science Foundation of Ireland; a Visiting Professor at the Indian Institute of Technology (IIT) at Kanpur and IIT Guwahati; an Honorary Professor of Fudan University in Shanghai and International Advisory Professor of Beijing Jiaotong University, China; and a Visiting Scientist at the Institute of Infocomm Research (I2R), Singapore. His current research interests include wireless sensor networks, mobile and pervasive computing, design and modeling of smart environments, pervasive security, smart health care, resource and mobility management in wireless networks, mobile grid computing, biological networking, applied graph theory and game theory. He is the founder of IEEE WoWMoM and co-founder of IEEE PerCom conference. He has served as General or Technical Program Chair as well as TPC member of numerous IEEE and ACM conferences. More information about him can be found at http://crewman. uta.edu/\~das. He is a senior member of the IEEE.

Mario Di'Mattia is a graduating senior at the University of Louisiana at Lafayette pursuing his BS degree in Computer Science. His interests include emerging technologies in hardware and software, large-scale project management, and web design. He plans to pursue graduate studies while working in industry.

Carlos M. S. Figueiredo is a Researcher and Professor at FUCAPI Research and Technological Innovation Center, Brazil. He received his Ph.D. in Computer Science from the Federal University of Minas Gerais, Brazil, in 2007. His research interests include embedded and mobile systems, wireless ad hoc and sensor networks, mobile and pervasive computing. In the last 6 years, he has published regularly in international conferences and journals related to those areas, such as ICC, ACM SAC, ISCC, and DSOM. He has also served as TPC member of LAACs and IADIS WAC.

Yoshiaki Fukazawa received the B.E and D.E degreeds in electrical engineering from Waseda University, Japan, in 1976, and 1986, respectively. He joined Department of Computer Science of Sagami Institute of Technology as a Lecturer in 1983 and Department of Electrical Engineering of Waseda University as an Associate Professor in 1987. He is now a professor of Department of Information and Computer Science, Waseda University. His research interests include software engineering, program optimization, and computer aided design. He is a member of IPSJ, JSST, ACM and IEEE.

Andrey V. Gavrilov finished high education in NETI (Novosibirsk Electrotechnical Institute) (now NSTU - Novosibirsk State Technical University) in 1974. Title of qualification - "System Engineer", title of specialization -"Automatized Control Systems". He finished post-graduate school in 1977. Title of specialization - "Computer Systems and Networks". In 1979, he got the degree of candidate (equivalent to PhD) of technical science (thesis "The Control of flow of tasks in Distributed Computer Systems"). He is professor in Department of Computer Engineering of Kyung Hee University from September, 1, 2005. Duties: courses "Intelligent Systems", "Soft Computing", "Neural Networks and its applications", "Technologies of Expert Systems", "Intelligent Robots", "Artificial Life", "Development of Games" (now), "Machine Learning" (now) (4 lectures per week), supervising of researches of graduate and postgraduate students.

Cláudio Fernando Resin Geyer is an associate professor at the Informatics Institute of the Federal University of Rio Grande do Sul. His research interests include ubiquitous computing, parallel and distributed computing, grid, and distributed objects. He received his PhD in informatics from the Joseph Fourier University. He's a member of the ACM and the Brazilian Computer Society. Contact him at Universidade Federal do Rio Grande do Sul, Av. Bento Gonçalves 9500, Porto Alegre, 91501-970, RS, Brazil; geyer@inf.ufrgs.br.

Eliane Gomes Guimarães is a research scientist at the Robotics and Computer Vision Division, Information Technology Center Renato Archer, Campinas, Brazil. She received the B.S. degree in Computer Science in 1977, and the M.S. and Ph.D. degrees in Electrical Engineering in 1990 and 2004, respectively, all from the University of Campinas. Her research interests include network robotics, WebLabs, and distributed systems.

Marcelo de Paiva Guimarães is professor at Faculdade Campo Limpo Paulista and Centro Universitário Adventista, Brazil. He received a PhD in electrical engineering at University of São Paulo in 2004 and the MSc in computer science at Federal University of São Carlos in 2000. He graduated in technology in data processing in 1994 at Instituto Municipal de Ensino Superior de Assis. He has been working with distributed systems and virtual reality since 2000.

Sture Hägglund received a Ph.D. in Computer Science from Linköping University in Sweden in 1980. He is also since 1999 Scientific Director and CEO at Santa Anna IT Research Institute, which is a subsidiary of SICS, Swedish Institute of Computer Science and part of Swedish ICT Research, owned jointly by industry and the government. His research background is mainly in knowledge-based systems, human-computer interaction, software engineering and database technology. He has for many years been a member of the ACM and the IEEE Computer Society. He was elected member of the Royal Swedish Academy of Engineering Sciences in 1997 and deputy chairman for its Information Technology Division 2006-2009.

Shinichi Honiden received his PhD degree in electrical engineering from Waseda University, Japan, in 1986. From 1978 to 2000 he was with Toshiba Corporation. Since 2000, he has been a professor and a director, Information Systems Architecture Research Division, National Institute of Informatics, Japan. He has also been a professor in the Graduate School of Information Science and Technology,The University of Tokyo since 2001. He is visiting professors at University College London and Waseda University. He was an invited professor at Le Laboratoire d'Informatique de Paris 6, Pierre et Marie Curie in 2006. His research interests include agent technology, ubiquitous computing, and software engineering.

Thienne Johnson is a professor of Information Systems at the School of Arts, Science and Humanities, University of Sao Paulo, Brazil. She holds an Associate Degree on Data Processing Technology from the University of Amazonia, Brazil (1994), a M.S. in Computer Science from the Federal University of Sao Carlos, Brazil (1999), and a Ph.D. in Computer Science from Federal University of Pernambuco, Brazil (2005). Her research interests include pervasive and mobile computing and computer networks.

Rachid Kadouche is holding a postdoctoral research fellowship at the University of Sherbrooke, Canada. He received his Ph.D. in computer science from TelecomSudParis and university of Evry in

2007. In 2003 he obtained his Master degree from University Denis Diderot Paris7, France. His research activity focuses on personalization in smart environment in case of dependent peoples and development for pervasive software applications. He is also interested in human machine interaction.

Yoichi Kaneki is a master course student at Department of Computer Science, the University of Tokyo, Japan. He is also a member of XAC project and worked in the field of wireless sensor networks. He received a degree in information science (Bsc) from the University of Tokyo in 2008.

Ashok Kumar is an Assistant Professor in the department of computer science at the University of Louisiana at Lafayette. He currently leads several projects in the areas of computer architecture and software/hardware design. Dr. Kumar obtained his Ph.D. in 1999 and worked for four years in industry before joining the academia full time. He has over forty publications in refereed journals, conferences, and book chapters. He has served on the program committees of several conferences.

Leili Lind received a Ph.D. in Medical Informatics from Linköping University, in 2006. Before graduating she studied medicine, mathematics, physics and computer science at Linköping University. She has worked both as a reg. nurse within the Swedish Healthcare, and as a software engineer at Ericsson AB. After receiving her Ph.D. she has performed research in medical informatics at Santa Anna IT Research Institute AB and Linköping University with projects in cooperation with industry and the public sector. She pioneered studies of digital pen and paper technology combined with mobile Internet in helping patients in their end-of-life to effortlessly report on symptoms to their caregivers. Her main research interest is in the eHealth area.

Antonio Alfredo F. Loureiro received his B.Sc. and M.Sc. degrees in computer science from the Federal University of Minas Gerais (UFMG), Brazil, and the Ph.D. degree in computer science from the University of British Columbia, Canada. Currently, he is a professor of computer science at UFMG, where he leads the research group in wireless sensor networks. His main research areas are wireless sensor networks, mobile computing, and distributed algorithms. In the last 10 years he has published regularly in international conferences and journals related to those areas, and also presented tutorials at international conferences.

Shawn Luce: "I am a 24 years old native of Destrehan Louisiana. I attended Destrehan High School and graduated in 2004. Afterwards I attended Louisiana State University for a year and then transferred to the University of Louisiana at Lafayette where I graduated with a bachelors degree in Computer Science in December of 2009."

Pietro Manzoni received the MS degree in computer science from the "Universitá degli Studi" of Milan, Italy, in 1989, and the PhD degree in computer science from the Polytechnic University of Milan, Italy, in 1995. He is an associate professor of computer science at the Polytechnic University of Valencia, Spain. His research activity is related to wireless networks protocol design, modeling, and implementation. He is member of the IEEE.

Jamie Mason, a native of Carencro, Louisiana, is currently pursuing a master's degree in computer science from Center for Advanced Computer Studies at the University of Louisiana at Lafayette. Her research interests include data mining, bioinformatics, and artificial intelligence.

Yoshiyuki Nakamura received master's degree in Engineering from Waseda University, Japan in 2009. Currently, he is a Ph.D. student in Waseda University and a research assistant in National Institute of Informatics. He worked in the field of wireless sensor networks.

Hikotoshi Nakazato majors in Engineering and graduated from Waseda University, Japan in 2008. Currently, he is a master student in Waseda University, and a research assistant in National Institute of Informatics. He worked in the field of wireless sensor networks and is a member of XAC project.

João Soares de Oliveira Neto has graduated in Computer Science at Federal University of Maranhão in 2009. His master (2003) research was at Federal University of Santa Catarina. He is doing his doctoral in a programme of cotutelle between the University of São Paulo and the University Paris XI. He has worked as professor and researcher in several projects related to human-computer interaction in communication activities, communications design, multimedia applications, and web-based systems. He actually is professor/researcher at Mackenzie Presbyterian University, in São Paulo. His research interests include user experience design and evaluation, mediated communication, electronic government, and crossmedia.

Ricardo Augusto Rabelo Oliveira has graduate at Computer Science from Federal University of Minas Gerais (2001), master's at Computer Science from Federal University of Minas Gerais (2003) and ph.d. at Computer Science from Federal University of Minas Gerais (2008). He is Professor at the Computer Science Department at Federal University of Ouro Preto. Has experience in Computer Science, acting on the following subjects: wavelets, neural networks, bluetooth, ieee 802.11 and Mobile Computing.

Nirmalya Roy is currently a postdoctoral fellow in Mobile and Pervasive Computing group in Electrical and Computer Engineering Department at the University of Texas at Austin. He received his MS and PhD degree in Computer Science and Engineering from the University of Texas at Arlington in 2004 and 2008, respectively. He received his B.E. degree in 2001 from Jadavpur University, Calcutta. His research interests include resource management in mobile, pervasive and grid computing environment. More information about him can be found at http://crewman.uta.edu/~nirmalya. He is a member of the IEEE.

Valéria Farinazzo Martins Salvador has graduated in Computer Science at the University of the State of São Paulo, Brazil (2005). She was a researcher in Virtual Reality (1996-1998) at the Federal University of São Carlos, Brazil. Her master dissertation was about Virtual Reality and Software Engineering area at the Federal University of São Carlos (2000). Today, she is preparing her doctoral thesis in Electrical Engineering at the University of São Paulo in Voice User Interface area. Also, she is assistant professor/researcher at Mackenzie Presbyterian University, in São Paulo, and assistant professor at the Federal University of São Carlos, in Campus Sorocaba. She has researched about non-conventional interface requirements analysis and evaluation, such as Voice User Interface, Augmented Reality and Virtual Reality.

Yuichi Sei received Ph.D. in Information Science and Technolog from The University of Tokyo, Japan in 2009. His research interests are in wireless networking, distributed algorithms, and security in wireless sensor networks. Currently, he works on the area of software engineering in Mitsubishi Research Institute, Inc.

Luciano Cavalheiro da Silva is PhD student at the Federal University of Rio Grande do Sul (UFRGS) and assistant professor at the University of Vale do Rio dos Sinos (UNISINOS). His research interests include ubiquitous and context-aware computing, large-scale distributed systems, and operating systems. He received his Bachelor and Masters degree from Federal University of Rio Grande do Sul. He is a member of the Brazilian Computer Society. Contact him at Programa de Pós-Graduação em Computação, Instituto de Informática, Universidade Federal do Rio Grande do Sul, Av. Bento Gonçalves 9500, Porto Alegre, 91501-970, RS, Brazil; lucc@inf.ufrgs.br/lcavalheiros@unisinos.br.

Shunichiro Suenaga received Ph.D. in Informatics from The Graduate University for Advanced Stidies (Sokendai), Japan in 2009. Currently, he is working for Nihon Unisys Ltd. and focusing on applying wireless technologies to industrial customers.

Kenji Tei received the B.E and D.E degreeds in information and computer scinece from Waseda University, Japan, in 2003, and 2005, respectively, and he received Ph.D. in Engineering from Waseda University, Japan in 2008. He joined Department of Information and Computer Science in Waseda University, and National Institute of Informatics as an research assistant. Currently, he is an assistant professor in Media Network Center, Waseda University, and a project assistant professor in National Institute of Informatics. He worked in the field of mobile ad-hoc networks, wireless sensor networks, and cyber physical systems, and heads XAC project. He is a member of IPSJ, and IEEE computer society.

Robert Tesch is pursuing a master's degree in computer science from the Center for Advanced Computer Studies at the University of Louisiana at Lafayette. His research interests are bioinformatics and computer architecture. He is currently involved in several research projects in these areas as well as in video game design.

Adenauer Corrêa Yamin is an associate professor in the Computer Science Department at the Catholic University of Pelotas and works in the technical staff of the Informatic Center of Federal University of Pelotas. His research interests include ubiquitous, grid, parallel, and distributed computing. He obtained his PhD in computer science from the Federal University of Rio Grande do Sul. He's a member of the ACM and the Brazilian Computer Society. Contact him at Universidade Católica de Pelotas, Rua Félix da Cunha 412, Pelotas, 96010-000, RS, Brazil; adenauer@ucpel.tche.br.

Nobukazu Yoshioka is a researcher at the National Institute of Informatics, Japan. Dr. Nobukazu Yoshioka received his B.E degree in Electronic and Information Engineering from Toyama University in 1993. He received his M.E. and Ph.D. degrees in School of Information Science from Japan Advanced Institute of Science and Technology in 1995 and 1998, respectively. From 1998 to 2002, he was with Toshiba Corporation, Japan. From 2002 to 2004 he was a researcher, and since August 2004, he has been an associate professor, in National Institute of Informatics, Japan. His research interests include agent technology, object-oriented methodology, software engineering, and software evolution.

340

Index

Symbols

ΣΗΟΘ(Δ) description logic 190, 197, 198, 210

A

Abstract Region language 218, 219
academic environments 97, 98
access methods 24, 41
access methods development 24, 41
acoustic environments 45
Active Badge paradigm 3
Active Bat paradigm 3
ActorNet middleware 219, 221
actuators 180
adaptive systems 282
addressing scheme, component-based 138
ad hoc networks 248, 249, 260, 261
agent technologies 1
Agilla middleware 219, 221
ambient intelligence 263, 264, 277
Anoto technology 26, 27, 29, 30, 31, 32, 34,
    35, 37, 39, 41
application requirements 60, 89
Archipel project 192
artificial intelligence (AI) 265
Assisted Cognition Project 192
assisted living facilities 192
assistive environment paradigm 190, 191, 196,
    211
automatic patient monitoring 98
automatic repeat request (ARQ) mechanism 60
autonomous network systems 249
available bandwidth 60, 89
Aware Home paradigm 3

B

base stations 216, 220, 221, 226, 231
battery technology 158, 159, 160, 161, 163,
    168, 170, 171, 215, 217, 219, 223, 225
Bluetooth 27, 31, 33, 34, 35, 59, 61, 63, 64,
    66, 67, 68, 69, 70, 71, 72, 81, 84, 85, 86,
    87, 89, 90, 91, 94, 95, 97, 100, 102, 103,
    104, 106, 107, 108, 109, 110, 112, 161,
    166, 171, 283
body area networks (BAN) 232, 233, 234, 236,
    237, 238, 242, 244
business environments 97, 98

C

calm technology 160
carrier sense medium access with collision
    avoidance (CSMA/CA) 141, 143
CDMA2000 mobile technology standards 59,
    89
CellID technology 234, 246
channel quality 59, 65, 87, 89, 92
circuit technology 160, 161, 162, 163, 164,
    165, 171
clock gating 162, 163, 164
CodeBlue system 192
code mobility 285, 294, 301
cognitive barriers 190
cognitive impairment 191
common context management systems 214
communication, loss of 60, 67, 69
communication quality 59, 60, 61, 62, 64, 66,
    67, 89, 93
communication quality, problems of 61